C0-ANF-846

A HISTORY OF GLASS IN JAPAN

Kodansha International Ltd. and The Corning Museum of Glass

A HISTORY OF
GLASS IN JAPAN

Dorothy Blair

M. CUDAHY
LOYOLA
UNIVERSITY
MEMORIAL LIBRARY

A Corning Museum of Glass monograph

Cover calligraphy by Kōzō Kagami

NK
5184
A1
B55
1973

WITHDRAWN

Distributed in the British Commonwealth (except Canada and the Far East) by George Allen & Unwin Ltd., London; in Continental Europe by Boxerbooks, Inc., Zurich; in Canada by Fitzhenry & Whiteside Limited, Ontario; and in the Far East by Japan Publications Trading Co., P.O. Box 5030 Tokyo International, Tokyo. Published by Kodansha International/USA, Ltd., Harper & Row Bldg., 10 East 53rd Street, New York, N.Y. 10022 and The Wells Fargo Bldg., Suite 505, 44 Montgomery Street, San Francisco, California 94104. Copyright in Japan, 1973, by Kodansha International Ltd. All rights reserved. Printed in Japan.

LCC 72-94022
ISBN 0-87011-196-5
JBC 0072-783806-2361

First edition, 1973

E. M. CUDAHY
LOYOLA
UNIVERSITY
MEMORIAL LIBRARY

CONTENTS

IN GRATEFUL REMEMBRANCE

Eunice Cole Smith
> *Who made possible the author's
> initial studies in Japan.*

Kōsaku Hamada
> *Who first aroused the author's
> interest in glass.*

FOREWORD

IT IS AN astonishing fact that in the vast literature on the history of glass published during the last one hundred years, there has been a notable lack of concern with developments in the Far East. Archaeology, the reports of early travelers, accounts in classical texts, as well as later mercantile records, attest that over the last two millennia glass has had a role varying in importance but technically and culturally significant. Yet few scholars have shown an interest in it. Bushell's important history of Chinese art was, perhaps, among the first Western works to deal with Chinese glass as a matter worthy of scholarly interest. Some decades later, he was followed by Seligmann and Beck, who revealed in a concise volume the great technical interest of Chinese glass and who proved that, from a compositional point of view, one could segregate part of China's early production as being unique in the annals of glass history. Shortly after, W. B. Honey published an important article in the *Burlington Magazine*—which is still a major reference on the subject.

While the eyes of the West were turned timidly toward China, the possible contribution of Japan was completely ignored, in spite of the fact that archaeological data showed that glass was made in Japan at a very early date and that it continued to be used from at least the third century onward in a most interesting, indeed unique manner. For, to the Japanese, glass was more than a material; it was imbued with spiritual significance. This fact either remained hidden from, or ignored by, Western scholars; and the Japanese themselves, as they eagerly explored the rich intricacy of their earlier culture, either overlooked glass, alluded to in *en passant*, or only singled out those more glamorous remains, mostly of Near Eastern origin, in the treasury of the Shōsō-in.

After the Second World War the situation changed. Japanese scholars, in the aftermath of those crushing years, started a careful reexamination of their earlier culture, and the tremendous industrial expansion that started in the 1950s led to the rapid development of a reborn glass industry, taking advantage of the most advanced Western technologies and, in some cases, improving upon them. Those two factors, among others, led to the gradual realization that in Japan glass had a distinguished past. A number of special exhibitions took place, articles were published, and scientific analyses made, all attempting to single out those aspects that could be considered indigenous Japanese contributions to the medium.

These efforts, however, were few, and only rarely did the catalogue of an exhibition provide a foundation upon which further study could be based. Hence there is yet no comprehensive view of the subject that might compare, for example, with Dillon's brilliant synthesis, *Glass*, of 1907, Schmidt's *Das Glas*, of 1912, or Honey's concise catalogue of the Victoria and Albert Museum, published in 1946. There was simply no one with the interest or necessary technical knowledge to undertake the task, reexamine the literary evidence—the reports of mythographers and early travelers—sift through the vast numbers of archaeological reports (and the even greater amount of materials from later periods), and organize this material into a comprehensive overview.

It is a paradox that this task has now been accomplished in English by a frail, charming but retiring American woman, who has given over a quarter of century of her life to the subject and whose work is presented here. Details concerning Dorothy Blair's biography are found elsewhere in this volume. Suffice it to say that she was for twenty-five years assistant curator at The Toledo Museum of Art, that from 1952 to 1954 and 1956 to 1958 she was associated with the Center for Japanese Studies of the University of Michigan, and that she gained first-hand experience of Japan, its lore, history, and culture during an aggregate of eight years of residence on three occasions, starting in 1927.

She first visited The Corning Museum of Glass in 1957, shortly after a large foundation had declined interest in underwriting the preparation of a history of Japanese glass. During the course of a conversation with Miss Blair, the then Director of the Museum, Thomas S. Buechner, suggested that the Corning Museum would be willing to give her the opportunity to complete her research. None of us had the vision, then, to realize that there was sufficient material to do more than a catalogue, or, at best, a few essays. Perhaps a lesser scholar would have done just that—for compared with the wealth of glass left from classical antiquity or the Renaissance, the quantity of Japanese glass is small, and, more troublesome, much is not particularly appealing in its appearance. Yet Miss Blair, with her deep sympathy and understanding of Japanese culture, has most superbly singled out that quality referred to above, certainly present in the earlier period of Japanese glass, which gives it a unique place in glass history: it is more than a material of practical use or monetary value, it is a substance imbued with a significance, a spiritual or "sacred" quality that goes back to the basic religious sensitivity of the Japanese. There is, I believe, no parallel for such a status in Western cultures, and there seems to be none either in the still scarcely known glass tradition of China.

In presenting this virtually new facet to the literature of glass, Miss Blair has done more than deal with the material, its chemistry, and manufacture; she has given a comprehensive overview of the history of Japan during the last two millennia.

Those who may be less than fascinated with glass history will find in these pages a learned but highly readable account of the political, economic, religious, and cultural growth out of which emerged a cohesive empire, dominated in the early centuries by a powerful emperor, then by ruthless, conniving warlords and barons, whose struggles culminated in the 250-year rule of the Tokugawa shogunate, characterized by a mistrust of foreign intrusion and an intense pride in the nation. Within this highly complex history, Miss Blair has found that glass played a role, and that, indeed, it was the increasing contact with foreign elements that gradually brought glass to the level of an everyday material, whose spiritual importance finally waned under the impact of Western techniques and a mercantile economy.

The writer of this introduction has been associated with Miss Blair since she started assembling the material that led to this volume. He has watched her meticulous concern for accuracy; he has witnessed the affection she has for the people whose culture she investigated; and he has repeatedly received testimony of the high regard by which she is held by her colleagues in Japan. With them, he has found a friend; he has also found a deeper meaning for the word "patience." For in the elaboration of this study, Miss Blair has had *patience*. She had the patience to accumulate the obscure data; she has had the patience to seek out photographs of unknown objects from a great variety of sources throughout Japan and to secure permissions to publish them. Finally, she has had the patience to put up with an editor who, at times, exercised drastic surgery on her manuscript to keep it within the manageable bounds of a single volume. In brief, the writer of this introduction has found in Miss Blair, as dozens had found before him, a dedicated scholar, and a gracious lady. Her volume will be a foundation for further research, one upon which the second phase of scholarship in Japanese glass will rest; a phase that will take advantage of new technologies in archaeology and analytical procedures; a phase that can now look toward the Asian continent in the hope of finding, in the light of recent archaeological discoveries, a new interpretation and further clues that may reveal the origin of the earliest glass and glass technology in Japan, and perhaps throw a brighter light on the sources for the unique role this material has played in the spiritual life of the Japanese people.

Washington, D.C., 1973

Paul N. Perrot

PREFACE

WHETHER GLASS was independently discovered in ancient Japan is still unknown. Some finds excavated from early sites are undoubtedly connected with glassmaking, as we shall see; but where the glass was formed, in Japan or brought in from abroad, is still an unresolved question. Some scholars believe that if the earliest glass beads were not imported, at least the raw glass and the manner of fabrication must have been. In other fields, the early Japanese were quick to adapt certain foreign ideas and, as will be seen, they developed early the technique of manipulating small amounts of glass, which were put to simple and clear uses. Yet these uses suggest overtones of a spiritual response to the environment that we can no longer comprehend.

The study of glass in Japan is such a relatively new field that the trail is none too clearly marked. Fortunately, new archaeological discoveries and the contributions of the physical sciences are adding to the corpus of evidence of man's progress in early Japan. His ability to advance technically and economically, his concern with beauty, his humor, and his moments of religious fervor will be glimpsed in the following chapters.

The reader will quickly discover that there are many gaps and many instances of the inconclusive. A further handicap is our incomplete knowledge of ancient Chinese and Korean glassmaking.

To write an ideal history of glass in Japan one should be a general historian, an art historian, an economic historian, an archaeologist, a glass technician, a chemist, and, not the least, an adept linguist. No one is more fully aware of my inability to meet these standards than I. Nevertheless, the amount and nature of the material at hand and the lack of English reference sources in this field suggest the desirability of offering this exploratory survey. It is hoped that others may carry on the search and present supplementary or corrective data as new evidence or different interpretations emerge.

I have been privileged to experience generous guidance and substantial aid from many quarters.

To the late J. Arthur MacLean (Oka-Katana), disciple of the famous Japanese savant, Kakuzō (Tenshin) Okakura, I owe the original stimulation and growth of my interest in Oriental art. For my studies of glass in Japan I am fundamentally indebted to the two persons to whom this book is dedicated: the late Miss Eunice Cole Smith of Alton, Illinois, whose financial backing made possible an initial year of study in Japan; and the late Dr. Kōsaku Hamada, the author's revered teacher during a remarkable and rewarding year at Kyoto Imperial University in 1927. Dr. Hamada's enthusiasm over glass then coming from Korean and Japanese tombs not only fired my interest but guided my thoughts into channels that were later to further my studies in Japanese glass.

During the years of my association with The Toledo Museum of Art my interests were stimulated by that institution's extensive glass collection and the varied glass activities of the city. But Toledo's concern was entirely with Occidental and West Asian glass; nowhere in America, at that time, was there any appreciable interest in East Asian glass, and no knowledge whatsoever of glass in Japan. This unfortunate hiatus naturally led me to investigations in this field. The late Dr. Donald E. Sharp of the Libbey-Owens-Ford Glass Company and other Toledo "glass men" encouraged and helped my initial studies in glass. When, after retirement, I returned to Japan in 1952 for service at the University of Michigan's Research Center for Japanese Studies in Okayama, my research was focused upon the history of glass in Japan.

To the late Governor Yukihara Miki of Okayama Prefecture in Japan, to members of his staff, and to many local historians and archaeologists, appreciation is expressed for encouragement and aid of various sorts. In particular, thanks are due to Mr. Chikao Ueda, then of the prefectural government, who remained constantly helpful in many ways.

To Dr. Sueji Umehara, successor to Dr. Hamada as chief of the Archaeological Research Institute of Kyoto University (now in retirement), I am especially indebted for continual help.

Dr. Kazuo Yamasaki of the Chemical Institute of the Faculty of Science, Nagoya University, has been of continuous and sympathetic help in technical and other aspects of the study over a number of years, as was Dr. Tei-ichi Asahina, formerly of the National Science Museum in Tokyo. Members of the Tokyo National Museum and of the Nara and Kyoto national museums were gracious and generous in their personal aid and in providing opportunities for study of the valuable collections in their care.

From some officials of the Imperial Household Agency, both of the Board of Chamberlains and the Division of Archives and Mausolea, assistance was forthcoming and is greatly appreciated. Mr. Gun-ichi Wada, former Director, and Mr. Junsei Matsushima, Curator of the Treasures, the Shōsō-in Office, Nara, contributed valuable help.

Mr. Masao Ishizawa, former Curator of Fine Arts of the Tokyo National Museum, later Chief of the Fine Arts Division of the Bunkazai Hogo Iin Kai (Commission for the Protection of Cultural Properties) and now Director of the Museum Yamato Bunkakan in Nara, has been continually of the great assistance as has Mr. Takaaki Matsushita, and other members of the commission gave gracious cooperation.

To the Kokusai Bunka Shinkōkai (Society for International Cultural Relations) in Tokyo, through Mr. Nagatake Okabe, then President, I am indebted for the required "sponsorship" during my last sojourn in Japan.

11

During various trips throughout Japan, widespread indebtedness was incurred to local government officials, university professors, museum personnel, officials of research institutions, librarians, lineal descendants of former feudal lords, private collectors, and many others. Many are referred to in the text, but I wish to mention several in particular: Mr. Nagamasa Kataoka of the Tsūshō Sengyō Shōkōgyō Gijutsu-in (government-sponsored Commercial and Industrial Engineering Institute) and the Osaka Kōgyō Gijutsu-in (Osaka Industrial Research Institute) of Ikeda city, Osaka Prefecture; Dr. Masao Mine and Professor Takeshi Kagamiyama of Kyushu University; Mr. Genkichi Hayashi, then Director of the former Nagasaki Municipal Museum of Science and Art; Mr. Tetsuya Etchu, Curator of the present Nagasaki Municipal Museum; Mr. Tadashige Shimazu, Tokyo, and his son, Mr. Kanehisa Shimazu, of Kagoshima; and Mr. Takejirō Tanabe of Hagi. In the sphere of modern glass, important cooperation was received from officials of glass companies and from their glass technicians. Over many years the author was especially indebted to the late Mr. Kuranosuke Iwaki and to Mr. Tōshichi Iwata. There are also other sources not included herein, which could not be presented for lack of data and illustration, such as the interesting items assembled in the Ginrei Restaurant, Nagasaki, by its proprietor, Mr. Isokichi Hashimoto. I should also take this opportunity to qualify the collection attributions; with the recent increased appreciation and collection of glass in Japan, it is almost certain that some of the objects presented here have changed ownership.

To Dr. Chewon Kim, Director of the National Museums of Korea (now retired), and to his staff, I am indebted for the opportunity of studying in detail the ancient glass of Korea, which, for comparative purposes, has been exceedingly helpful in this study.

That it is impossible to mention individually the many who have collaborated in this work is a matter of deep regret. For it is really all of these friends and colleagues who have brought this study to fruition. Although it is neither intended nor possible to hold any of them in any respect responsible for opinions or remarks expressed herein (sometimes, perhaps, at variance with their own views), or for the nature of presentation and interpretation, I am acutely aware that only through their cooperation could the research have been advanced. To each I am profoundly grateful.

More recently, others have been generous in their help. Dr. John Whitney Hall, the A. Whitney Griswold Professor of History at Yale University, kindly read the manuscript and made several suggestions that have been incorporated in the text. The author has also had the benefit of helpful suggestions from Dr. Richard K. Beardsley, then Director of the Center for Japanese Studies at the University of Michigan, who was also kind enough to read the manuscript.

Indebtedness for the use of illustrations is widespread. Owners, or glassmakers, are indicated in the Plate Notes; in each instance permission was granted. Certain owners also provided photographic prints. Copyrighted photographs are used by permission of Asuka-en, Nara (Pls. 69, 125); Itsukushima Jinja, Hiroshima Prefecture (Pl. 14); Kasuga-taisha, Nara (Pls. 13, 15); Nagano Rokumeisō, Nara (Pls. 77, 122); Ōmi Jingū, Ōtsu, Shiga Prefecture (Pl. 6); Sakamoto Photo Research Laboratory, Tokyo (Pls. 45,

114); Shōsō-in, Nara (Pls. 7–12, 16); Tokyo National Museum, Tokyo (Pls. 1, 2, 4, 5, 23); and Mr. Kidō Ushio, Tokyo (Pls. 17–19, 22, 24, 25). I am also indebted to Hōryū-ji temple for permission to use Plates III, VI, XXIII from *Hōryū-ji Gojū-no-tō Hihō no Chōsa* (Pl. 70).

The author also wishes to thank Mr. Kōzō Kagami for writing the calligraphic Japanese title that appears on the front cover of the book.

Lastly, and vitally, the author is beholden to The Corning Museum of Glass for the opportunity of the final two and one-half years of research in Japan and Korea as a Research Fellow of the Museum, and for encouragement and constant help on all points. Especially to be mentioned are Thomas S. Buechner, first Director and now President; Paul N. Perrot, former Director, under whose guidance this publication has come to completion; Dr. Axel von Saldern, former Curator of the Collections and Kenneth M. Wilson, his successor; and Dr. Robert H. Brill, formerly Administrator of Scientific Research and now Director and Research Scientist. The work is offered in the hope that it may foster, in the West, further inquiry into this hitherto neglected but significant phase of Japan's cultural achievements.

Corning, New York, and Tokyo, 1973

LANGUAGE NOTES

In Japanese, vowels are pronounced approximately as follows:

> *a* as in *ah*
> *e* as in b*e*t
> *i* as in h*e*
> *o* as in h*o*
> *u* as in f*oo*l

Since the Japanese name order system—surname preceding personal name—is often confusing for research and reference work in the West, an arbitrary but often used name order system is adopted in this publication. All names of persons living prior to the Meiji Restoration in 1868 are given in Japanese order, with surname first; all names of persons living after 1868 are given in Western order. This sytem is not wholly satisfactory, but should eliminate confusion, particularly in the case of modern Japanese authors who have published in English.

Macrons have been eliminated from commonly used place names: Tokyo, Osaka, Kyoto, Kobe, Kyushu, Hokkaido, and Honshu. Kyoto-*fū*, Osaka-*fū*, and Tokyo-*tō*, are municipalities, but since they occupy areas considerably larger than the cities themselves, they are herein referred to as prefectures to avoid confusion. There has been considerable difficulty regarding place names in modern Japan because of rapidly changing political divisions, such as the amalgamation of villages and towns, forming larger administrative units. When both old and new names are known, they have been noted.

Japanese nouns in this book are not pluralized.

A HISTORY OF GLASS IN JAPAN

1. Cut glass bowl • Interred, 6th century • tomb of Emperor Ankan, Osaka Pref. • H. ▷
   8.2 cm.
2. Cut glass bowl • Tomb period • Niizawa Senzuka tombs, Nara Pref. • H. 6.8 cm. ▷

3. Cinerary urn · probably 7th century · Miyajidake Shrine, Fukuoka Pref. · H. 9.5 cm.

4. Cinerary urn of Fumi no Nemaro · before 707 · Nara Pref. · H. 17.0 cm.

5. *Kumi-obi* interwoven with *kodama* (fragment) • 8th century • *kodama*, D. 0.2–0.3 cm.

6. *Shari* installation • 8th century • Sūfuku-ji, Shiga Pref. • glass, H. 3.0 cm.

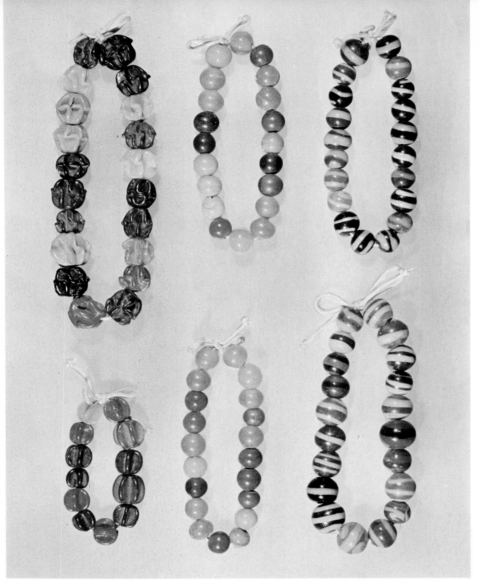

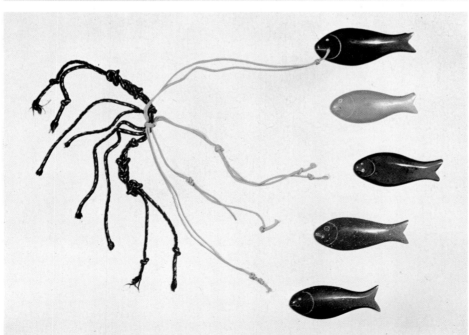

7. *Nejiredama, marudama,* and *tomodama* • 8th century • Shōsō-in • max. D. 2.3 cm.

8. Fish-form tallies • 8th century • Shōsō-in • max. L. 8.2 cm.

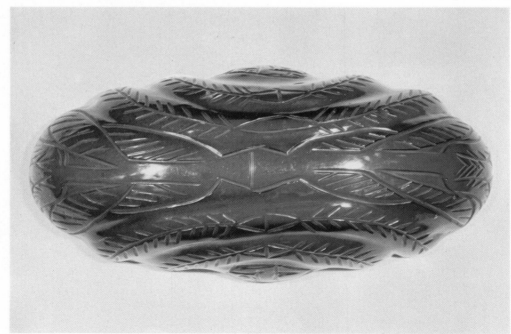

9. Ewer • 8th century
• Shōsō-in • H. 27.0
cm. (see Pl. 103).
10. Twelve-lobed
bowl • 8th century •
Shōsō-in • L. 22.5 cm.
(see Pl. 107).

11. Dark blue cup • probably Korean • *ca.* 700 • Shōsō-in • H. 11.2 cm.

12. Cloisonné-backed mirror · 8th century · Shōsō-in · D. 18.5 cm. (see Pl. 113).

13. Lantern with glass beads · *ca.* 1038 (?) · Kasuga-taisha, Nara.

14. Glass plaque on one of the Heike *Nōkyō* ·
Dedicated, 1163 · Itsukushima Shrine, Hiroshima Pref. · glass, L. 5.495 cm.

15. Sword with tweezer motif (detail) · Late Heian period · Kasuga-taisha, Nara.

16. Dark blue jar · Chinese (?) · Probably Sung dynasty · Shōsō-in · H. 9.0 cm.

17. Enameled *kugikakushi* · Momoyama period · L. 10.2 cm.

18. Nest of boxes with *biidoro-e* · Edo period · H. 22.0 cm.

19. Saké bottles • late Edo period • Nagasaki • av. H. 18.5 cm.
20. Tobacco pipe • late Edo period • Nagasaki • L. 32.0 cm. ▷
21. Wine pot • Edo period • Nagasaki • L. 24.5 cm. ▷

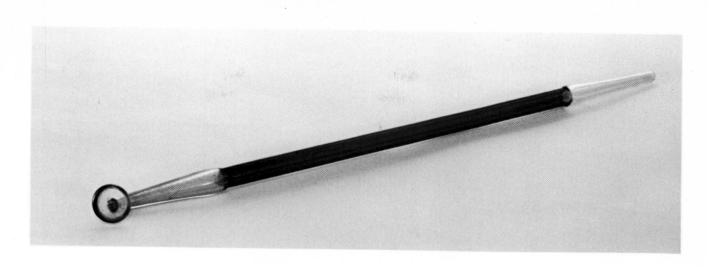

22. Quail cage • Edo period • Nagasaki • H. 33.0 cm.

23. Comb • late Edo period • Edo • L. 9.17 cm. ▷
24. Cut glass bowls • late Edo period • Edo • D. 14.8 cm. ▷

25. Cut glass bottle • 1857–58 • Satsuma.

26. "Raspberry red" wine glass • 1857–58 • Satsuma • H. 20.3 cm.

27. Cut glass wine bottles · 1857–58 · Satsuma · H. 25.4 cm.

LOYOLA UNIVERSITY LIBRARY

28. Cut glass saké cup set · 1857–58 · Satsuma · cups, D. 4.6–5.2 cm.

29. Bead with goldfish insert • Meiji era • D. 0.95 cm.

30. Enameled wine glasses • between 1908 and 1913 • Asahi Joint Stock Company • max. H. 11.5 cm.

31. Agate ware bowl • between 1908 and 1913 • Asahi Joint Stock Company • H. 8.3 cm.
32. Agate ware box • between 1908 and 1913 • Asahi Joint Stock Company • H. 7.8 cm.

33. *Pâte de verre* incense burner
by Sotoichi Koshiba • 1970 • H.
9.2 cm.

34. Vase by Tōshichi Iwata •
1967 • H. 24.0 cm.

◁ 35. Wall panel by Itoko Iwata · 1971 · H. 105.0 cm.

36. Vase by Kōzō Kagami · 1970 · H. 24.0 cm.

37. Haniwa figures by Masakichi Awashima · 1971 · max. H. 48.3 cm.

BEGINNING OF GLASS
IN JAPAN

ACCORDING TO Japanese legendary histories, the islands came into being long ago by volition of the gods in the "Plain of High Heaven." To inhabit and rule the land thus formed, god progeny were sent down to earth. The first "emperor" was assigned such lineage. A profuse mythology evolved, not only formulating a tradition of the creation of the Japanese islands but narrating at great length the exploits of the descendants of the god rulers through generation after generation. This body of myth and tradition was later brought together, as Japanese history, and exists for us in the eighth century compilations known as the *Kojiki* and the *Nihon Shoki* (or *Nihongi*).[1] As the Chinese system of calendar cycles was then employed for this purpose, the date of the accession of the first emperor, Jinmu Tennō, was set at 660 B.C. and thereby some extraordinarily long reigns were by necessity assigned to some of his successors. Modern studies place this date considerably later.

Although year by year more factual data are accumulating, there seems, still, to be much uncertainty and much diversity of opinion among scholars regarding the prehistoric and even early protohistoric centuries in Japan. We shall consider only such aspects as provide the background needed to understand the cultural developments that led to the first appearance of glass.

Recent excavation of paleolithic sites in various parts of Japan reveal the presence of man in Japan prior to the fortieth millennium B.C. Whatever the time of their arrival, the first-comers lived in a nonceramic age from which only stone implements survive.

JŌMON PERIOD (*ca.* 10,000 B.C. to *ca.* 250 B.C.)

The term *jōmon* ("cord-marked") for this period derives from the type of pottery excavated. The pottery, fired at low temperature, was built up from coils of rather coarse clay wound spirally by hand, then decorated by impressing something like cord (perhaps twisted fibers) against the clay walls thus formed, or, as is recognized in many pieces, by indenting with the edge of a shell, a fingernail, a piece of bamboo, or, as time passed, by rolling a carved rod over the surface, and also by hand modeling. In the beginning this pottery was extremely simple, but gradually form and decoration became more elaborate, at times even sculptural, and passed through sundry variations. In its most handsome examples, of which there are many, it expresses a strong sense of proportion and design.

The Jōmon period, aside from its ceramic ware, is further characterized by the gradual appearance of many small decorative objects in stone, shell, fishbone, deerhorn, and clay; and at the very end of the period by items carved from wood, or of wood covered with red or red and black lacquer.

Knowledge of Jōmon man comes from remains found in caves, from pit-dwellings and shellmounds. Where ruins of pit-dwellings exist, the shellmounds are not far away, often actually adjoining, for there Jōmon man discarded the shells and bones left over from his meals, his broken pottery, and other objects no longer useful. Human burials have also been found in shellmounds, with the bones well preserved by the shells.

There is no evidence for glass technology in the Jōmon period, but one curious, very early glass artifact exists (Pl. 38) that may be the result of some of the earliest glass-making efforts in Japan. The archaeological record is still too scant in this area of early technology to allow the student more than conjectures based on whatever small hints the fortunes of the archaeologist (or heavy rains) may unearth.

About the middle of the third century B.C., it is generally estimated, a new development known as the Yayoi culture appeared in northern Kyushu, the southern island, whence it eventually spread northeastward, not immediately replacing the Jōmon culture but to a great extent overlapping or merging with it. In some regions the Jōmon culture held on, contemporaneous with the new Yayoi culture.

YAYOI PERIOD (*ca.* 250 B.C. to *ca.* 250 A.D.)

The term "Yayoi" derives from Yayoi-chō, the neighborhood in Tokyo where remains of this culture were first unearthed. The general time limits of the Yayoi culture can, to a certain extent, be checked by referring to existing continental literature and to known dates for certain Chinese artifacts, as well as to an increasing body of Japanese archaeological evidence.

The main contribution of foreign influences was the transformation of the Japanese into true agriculturists through the introduction of rice cultivation by the flooded, or irrigated, paddy-field method used on the continent, which necessitated a more sedentary life at more permanent sites. Settled life affected many phases of life and introduced architectural changes, tending toward more permanency, although the general nature of the dwelling pits with tamped earth floors remained basically the same.

Concomitant with the more settled life, greater attention was paid to human burials, which, from this time on, provide the best sources of our knowledge. Human burial in northern Kyushu and the western tip of Honshu in the Yayoi period was, generally speaking, either (a) in pottery urns placed about three feet underground, often beneath a huge flat stone, one large jar serving for the body with a second one fitted on as cover and sealed, or one jar alone with a cover of stone, pottery, or wood or (b) in a stone cist in an open pit covered by a single enormous stone—a type considered as slightly later. In other areas, such as Oku-chō in Okayama Prefecture, the shellmounds of the Jōmon period persisted, and no burial jars are found.

Another conspicuous element in the Yayoi period was the introduction of the potter's wheel, making a thinner-walled ware possible through the use of a buff-colored clay of finer body, which replaced the rougher type of the Jōmon period and led to greater surface refinement. This new type, known as *haji* ware, shows some affinity with continental wares of the time, although traces of Jōmon design survived briefly. Dr. Edward Kidder thinks that some of the ceramic changes toward the end of the Jōmon period must have been due to firing in a partial enclosure at a higher temperature than had theretofore been achieved—that is, 600°-700° C. instead of an earlier 400°-500° C.[2] This achievement suggests developing comprehension of the possibilities of fire and heat, which might have prepared the way for the melting of ingredients to form glass.

The appearance of metal, both bronze and iron, was an important innovation. Bronze objects in burials in northern Kyushu include Chinese weapons and mirrors as well as Japanese imitative, but modified, examples. Notable finds are those of burials at Mikumo and Suku in Okamoto in Fukuoka Prefecture, where much of the Yayoi period glass was found (see Pl. N. 39, 40; Sup. N. 1–4). It is largely on the Chinese bronzes found there that Yayoi period dating was first based.

The new methods and new appurtenances introduced in western Japan during this interval were balanced by the continuity of tradition and slow change that runs through the later Jōmon centuries and the succeeding Yayoi period. Although the pit-dwelling, for instance, became somewhat larger with improvements in roofing, it remained basically the same. Items not unlike Jōmon artifacts in wood, bone, deerhorn, and shell continued to be used. Even the change-over to double-urn burials, in northern Kyushu, may have been gradual. Progress seems to have been the result of slow, albeit conspicuous, infiltration of ideas and probably immigrants from a higher cultural level emanating outside the country. There is no evidence of any sudden invasion that could have displaced the native culture.

The adoption of rice cultivation, which inevitably produced a class of settled farmers, the potter's wheel, and the beginning of metal forging and casting—which would not have become a general activity, but the prerogative of a comparatively few skilled metal workers—introduced certain divisions of labor, laying the foundation for the classified society of later centuries. Further, such a situation would have led to other specialized skills, with consequent new developments in the crafts. In such circumstances is not it surprising to come upon the appearance of glass.

Glassmaking was sufficiently developed in China as early as the middle fifth century B.C. to produce stratified beads of superb quality; and during the Han dynasty, items of various sorts were produced. It is Dr. Sueji Umehara's opinion, expressed to the author, that for several centuries after the appearance of glass in Yayoi burials, the Japanese could not have known how to produce the basic glass metal and must either have used imported materials or melted down Chinese glass objects in order to fabricate *magatama* and beads. Light may be thrown upon this by the as yet unpublished joint researches of Dr. Sueji Umehara and Dr. Kazuo Yamasaki.[3]

The two outstanding sites from which much of the knowledge of Yayoi remains derives are Mikumo and Suku at Okamoto, Kasuga-mura, Tsukushi-gun, Fukuoka Prefecture. A jar burial at Mikumo-Okamoto is mentioned in a manuscript record of 1822.[4] The Middle Yayoi period is assigned on the basis of thirty-five Chinese bronze mirrors and two items of Chinese glass found in the burial. This was the first of many burials found at Okamoto. The following glass items from the burial were preserved at the Tokyo Imperial Museum up to the time of the 1923 earthquake.

1) A Chinese ritual disk, *pi*, of a glasslike substance beneath a white coating. This was said to have been about 8.48 centimeters in diameter and less than 0.61 centimeters thick overall, with a center perforation diameter of 2.12 centimeters.
2) Fragment of a Chinese *pi*.
3) A *magatama* ("curved bead").
4) A *kudatama* ("tubular bead").
5) A *kodama* ("small bead").

At Suku-Okamoto, believed to be slightly later than the Mikumo-Okamoto site (i.e., Middle or Late Yayoi), many burials were discovered from 1899 to the present. This area was first excavated by archaeologists of Kyoto Imperial University.[5] The burials at Suku-Okamoto included Chinese bronze mirrors and Japanese pottery, in addition to items that have made this area vital for knowledge of the early appearance of glass in Japan. Dating has been based on the Chinese mirrors, whose chronology is known.[6]

However, there can have been but little foreign influence in the first glass production of Japan. Of the many glass forms used in China at this time, only two or three types, chiefly funerary and exceedingly rare, are at present known to have made their way to Japan and they, unlike the bronze weapons and mirrors, were not imitated by the Japanese, perhaps because their purposes were not understood, or, if comprehended, did not relate to Japanese burial customs. No other strictly Chinese types have come from Yayoi graves. Bracelets were not new in Japan, for many, fashioned from shell, were used in Jōmon times, and stone bracelets were common in Yayoi burials. The *magatama*, of both stone and glass, was definitely and uniquely a Japanese form. Moreover, the discovery of a mold for casting *magatama* (Pl. 41) attests to local manufacture.

The individual sites where glass has been found are few and widely separated, and the forms restricted to small items, but the glass is of good quality. Except for a few opaque items (Pl. 40; Sup. N. 3), all are translucent or semitranslucent. Both lead glass and soda-lime glass were known, the color range being limited to varying tones of green and blue, chiefly a deep yellow green, a turquoise green, turquoise blue, a paler blue, sometimes rather grayed, and, rarely, a dark purplish blue. Some items were manipulated or rolled; others were cast in molds; some seem to have been coiled around a core; and still others formed by cutting short lengths from a tube. Included here is a generous selection of such items as were known at the time of writing.

What symbolic or amuletic significance glass items of the Yayoi period possessed in the minds of the people cannot be known precisely. In Kyushu they have come from graves, but it is impossible to tell whether they were placed there merely as precious objects, worn and treasured by the deceased in life, or whether they accompanied the deceased as dedicatory offerings in a propitiatory sense. From what is known of the reverence for *magatama*, a "curved bead" suggesting the comma shape, *kudatama*, a "tubular bead," *marudama*, a "round bead," and *kodama*, a "small bead," in the immediately following centuries, and from references in the *Kojiki* and the *Nihon Shoki*, it seems logical to assume that these items were used ornamentally yet were venerated for some peculiar, suprahuman protective virtue believed to be inherent in them. When these specific descriptive terms were first used is problematical, but they have long been common nomenclature.

1. *Kojiki* [Record of Ancient Matters]; compilation completed in 712. Basil Hall Chamberlain (tr.), "*Kojiki*, Record of Ancient Matters," *TASJ*, X, Supplement, Yokohama, R. Meiklejohn & Co., 1882; second ed. with annotations by W. G. Aston, Kobe, J. L. Thompson & Co., Ltd., 1932.

   Nihon Shoki [Chronicles of Japan]; compilation completed in 720. W. G. Aston, trans. "*Nihongi*, Chronicles of Japan from the Earliest Times to A.D. 697," *Transactions of the Japan Society*, Supplement, London, Kegan Paul, Trench, Trubner & Co., Ltd., 1896; reprinted, London, George Allen & Unwin, Ltd., 1956.

2. J. Edward Kidder, Jr., *Japan Before Buddhism*, Ancient Peoples and Places, New York, Praeger, 1959, p. 66; *The Jōmon Pottery of Japan*, Artibus Asiae Supplementum, XVII, Ascona, 1957, p. 7.

3. *Yamasaki, "Namari Garasu to Sōda Garasu," p. 20, reported that, among glass objects from Suku in Fukuoka Prefecture, he found barium and that the composition was extremely close to pre-Han glass *pi* of China. This suggests importation of glass metal from China, or the melting-down in Japan of imported objects. The finding of glass *pi* fragments in Japanese sites seems to uphold this theory.

4. Tsunenobu Aoyagi, "Chikuzen-no-kuni Ido-gun Mikumo-mura Koki Zusetsu" [Illustrated Description of Ancient Wares Excavated at Mikumo Village, Ido-gun, Chikuzen]—manuscript in facsimile as an appendix in *KTDKH*, XI, 1930.

5. Sadahiko Shimada, "Chikuzen Suku Shizen Iseki no Kenkyū" [Studies on the Prehistoric Site of Okamoto-Suku in the Province of Chikuzen], *KTDKH*, XI, Kyoto, 1930. (English summary).

6. Sueji Umehara, "Suku Chikuzen Hakkutsu no Kokyō ni tsuite" [Ancient Mirrors Excavated at Suku in Chikuzen Province], *KTDKH*, XI, pp. 24–28; see also p. 13. (English summary).

PERIOD OF THE
GREAT TOMBS

Y AYOI MAN PASSED on to his successors of the Tomb period a worthy heritage on which to base an even more rapid progress. Since this Tomb period is still in a proto-historic age, definite datings cannot be assigned even for the more tangible changes.

Although pit-dwellings and shellmounds remained in certain remote areas throughout the period, homes and other structures in general came above ground, where—rotted, washed away, or ploughed under—they eventually disappeared. But the clay models (*haniwa*) installed in the tumuli, and certain motifs appearing on cast bronze mirrors, in addition to various architectural details surviving today that are reminiscent of those ancient representations, reveal something of the nature of the buildings at that time.

The recorded annals of the Sui dynasty in China, of about 600 A.D., suggest what life was like in Japan toward the end of the Tomb period;[1] and, although there are no native contemporary historical records, the detailed statements in the *Kojiki* and *Nihon Shoki* take on a tone of greater credulity for the latter part of this period.

The main cultural center of the Yayoi period lay in northern Kyushu. However, to the northeast, an area centering in present-day Okayama Prefecture, which came later to be known as the Kibi region, is rich not only in Jōmon but in Yayoi relics. A powerful group from Kyushu seemingly fought its way along the eastern coast of Honshu, through this Kibi region, to the fertile Yamato plain at the eastern end of the Inland Sea. According to the *Kojiki* and the *Nihon Shoki*, it was their leader who settled at Kashiwara in Yamato (present Nara Prefecture) and became the first emperor (known posthumously as Jinmu Tennō), establishing the imperial house of Japan and what was to be the first centralized government. By the fourth century the Yamato rulers seem to have been in control of at least central and western Japan, and the relations between Yamato and Kibi were thereafter always closely knit. Yamato is the outstanding area of great tombs, many of them imperial; but Kibi also has a multitude of tumuli, from some of which important relics have been recovered—among them, glass of good quality.

Tumuli dating from this period exist over most of Honshu and in Shikoku, Kyushu, and some of the smaller islands. The vast dimensions of some tombs and the richness of their contents are evidence that the class distinctions that had their origins in the occupational divisions of the Late Yayoi period had expanded rapidly. One can but infer a wealthy ruling class, which had at its command the services of skilled engineers, craftsmen, and hordes of laborers. The earlier tombs appear to have been chiefly earthen mounds of some prominence and often on a hilltop; in the upper part, one or more trenches were dug, in which were placed hollowed-out log coffins or simple, shallow stone coffins, with some votive offerings placed with the body and outside the coffin. The later stone chambers seem to have evolved from encasing such a burial in layers of stones, flat and more or less cut to shape. At first scarcely larger than the coffin itself, by the latter part of the period roomy dolmenlike burial chambers were constructed, with proportionately larger and more elaborate sarcophagi. Some are of handsome proportions and finish; the earlier examples of these chamber tombs had an opening at the top for exit after burial rites; but those developed toward the end of the period had a passage leading off horizontally. Walls and ceilings were often formed of tremendous stone slabs or large boulders, as much as 2.5 or 3 meters long, 1.3 or 1.7 meters wide and of varying thickness (Pl. 45), held together without mortar. Sometimes these were embellished with painted designs. Over the chamber, earth was piled to form an imposing mound.

The largest of the mounds have not been easily eroded, partly because of their sturdy construction, partly, perhaps, because the trees that have grown on them have held the soil in place, but largely because of the reverence and care accorded them over the centuries. Prominent is a type whose keyholelike mound shape is known only in Japan, the *zenpō-kōen kofun* (literally, "ancient tomb with square front and round back"). The tomb said to be that of the Emperor Nintoku (Pl. 46) is considered the largest tomb known in the world, extending to a length of about five hundred meters. Three moats surround it, adding to the grandeur and prestige of the now wooded tumulus, which rises high above them. Although the Emperor Nintoku's traditional reign extended from 313 to 399, the revised chronology brings the erection of this tomb into the fifth century.

In addition to the artifacts from investigated tombs, the clay *haniwa* tell us much. Many *haniwa*, of *haji* ware, seem to have been plain cylindrical forms, used almost like structural reinforcements; but hundreds of others were surmounted by sculptural forms and were often installed at the top of the tumulus or inside the tomb. Much has been written in recent years regarding the significance of the *haniwa* sculptures, but whatever their original meaning, they have substantiated local traditions and foreign references. They often corroborate or explain disarranged physical remains found in and about the coffins and uphold literary references in the *Kojiki*, the *Nihon Shoki*, and in later poems, concerning the use of beads and *magatama*. For example, the *haniwa* representing a *miko* (a maiden in the service of a Shintō shrine), or a shaman, dressed in festive apparel, illustrates explicitly how beads—seemingly more often than not of glass—were worn on the head, neck, breast, or wrists and ankles (Pl. 47).

This was a period of amazing skill in many materials, including—in addition to glass—

bronze, much iron, deerhorn, stone, and ceramics. Bronze and iron had come to be well handled by the Late Yayoi period. Deerhorn had been in use since early Jōmon days for implements and ornaments; now used in new luxurious ways, it was ingeniously applied to sword handles and other objects. Utilitarian implements of stone all but disappear, replaced chiefly by iron. Some of these items are so like artifacts from Korean tombs that, without other evidence, one could conjecture a large influx of immigrants from the mainland. In this period most of these were Koreans; often they were artisans intentionally invited by the Japanese court, sent by friendly Korean rulers, or brought as prisoners of war from unfriendly areas. Not only did the Japanese admire Korean skills and seek out Korean craftsmen, but the Koreans in turn seem to have respected the accomplishments of the Japanese; hence the flow of influence was by no means all eastward. After 400, with unrest on the continent, Koreans began to arrive in Japan in considerable numbers; amongst them were members of the nobility, officials and scholars, artists and workers skilled in various trades.

Contacts with the Chinese, though more infrequent and less recognizable at this time, also increased, and Chinese artisans and scholars came by invitation; and perhaps others fled to Japan to avoid the confusions of the Six Dynasties.

By this time western Japan was well on the way to cohesion and strength as a national entity. Thenceforward she was able to aid the Korean kingdom of Paekche against the incursions of the neighboring kingdom of Silla and is also said to have fought against Koguryŏ in the north. These contacts unquestionably brought into Japan new cultural elements, which are prominent among the splendid relics of the tombs: beautiful gilt-bronze saddles, stirrups, and other fine trappings testifying to the increased use of the horse in Japan; elaborate crowns, ceremonial shoes, and waist ornaments of gilded bronze; and ornate ear pendants. Since in Korea many of these articles were decorated with additions of glass in various forms, it is not surprising to find glass beads and glass insets added to some of the items made in Japan (Pls. 63–65). As it seems most improbable that such quantities of articles would have come in from abroad, one can conclude that they were chiefly made in Japan either by immigrants or by Japanese craftsmen working under their influence or guidance.

In spite of the influx of foreign elements, indigenous traditions and forms remained important. For example the *magatama*, a uniquely Japanese form, obviously imported to Korea from Japan and not vice-versa, remained an outstanding symbol of some superior force. In the latter part of the period, there seems to have been growing reliance upon the efficacy of numbers—to the detriment of artistic quality. The group of glass *magatama* from the Ōtani Tomb in Wakayama city (Pl. 52) is but one example of this new value placed upon repetition. Another is a cache of several hundred steatite *magatama* discovered in a Middle Tomb period burial in Nara Prefecture.[2] Furthermore, even though the idea of erecting large tumuli may possibly have had its source on the continent, its development in Japan was of a strictly local character. The large *zenpō-kōen* mounds are unique, and the *haniwa* are unlike anything known in Korea or China.

The beginnings of occupational classifications, first noted in the Yayoi period, were elaborated long before the end of the Tomb period in diverse hereditary professional groups known as *be*. From the *Nihon Shoki* we learn that these *be* included such groups as potters, brocade weavers, bronze and iron workers, carpenters, painters, saddlers, archers, stewards. Glassmakers were classed in the *tamatsukuri-be* (jewelmaking, or beadmaking, *be*). Considering the quantity and variety of extant beads, and the veneration felt for them, the *tamatsukuri-be*, and the glassmakers in particular, must have held a position of considerable prominence. Beadmakers lived in many localities, serving various regions; perhaps every district had its group to supply its needs.

Although 552, the year Buddhism was officially introduced from Korea, is often used as the terminal date for the Tomb period, in certain areas for some decades there was a continuation of Tomb period traditions and artifacts, while new trends in crafts characteristic of the following Asuka period appeared at the same time. This results in a chronological overlapping in styles.

GLASS IN THE TOMB PERIOD

The output of small glass items in this period is uncalculable, as is even an estimate of those that have survived. The large increase in production, new and varying types of glass beads, the inherent beauty of the glass metals, the greater variety in colors and uses in ornamentation, all are witness to the progress of glassmaking in Japan at this time.

Both lead glass and soda-lime glass were produced throughout the period. The lead glass often has a very high oxide content, up to approximately seventy percent.[3] The new and wide range of colors was caused by the conspicuous admixture of previously unused, or not commonly used, metallic oxides. Some specimens of raw materials for the fabrication of glass objects have been found in Izumo (Sup. N. 15, 16) and at Miyajidake Shrine in Fukuoka Prefecture (Pl. 48).

EVIDENCE OF EQUIPMENT, MATERIALS, AND TECHNIQUES

No glassmaking site of the Tomb period has been discovered that might indicate what raw materials (except as noted above), equipment, and implements the artisans used and just how the glass was fused, and no molds for glass casting have been found. However, some suggestive remains have been located that may, indirectly, shed some light on manufacturing methods. The industry—primarily of beadmaking—must have been largely of the small and part-time "cottage" type, undertaken in farmers' homes, even as has been done in modern times.

Since no glassmaking site of the Tomb period has been discovered, conclusions must be drawn about the beadmaker's equipment from the remains available, although these are often of questionable purpose or date. Since equipment and techniques vary according to the bead type, they are discussed below under the various bead type headings.

The first need in the making of beads—aside from the essential finding and assembling of the raw materials, which, lacking data, cannot be touched upon here—was for some sort of simple furnace and crucible in which the raw materials could be melted and fused into glass. The Tomb period artisans who produced beads were not independent craftsmen but members of a *be* working under supervision. The beadmakers may not have made the glass metal themselves; it may have come from a central site in the community, or even from farther afield, doled out to the individual workers by a supervisor. However, there is no direct evidence of any such central site of this time. Certain items, brought forward in recent years as Tomb period glassmaking equipment, are now generally discredited as such and thought to be from a later time and possibly for ceramic glass.[4] Fragments of a small, primitive clay crucible from Tamatsukuri seem more plausible for this period (Sup. N. 12).

A complete cup-crucible (Sup. N. 13) and the fragments mentioned suggest that the beadmakers may have prepared glass metal in small quantities or at least remelted raw glass in some container, very likely on ordinary household clay cooking stoves such as have been excavated. However, if glass was distributed in the form of rods, a crucible would be unnecessary for coiling, as the beadmaker would melt the end of the rod directly over a flame.

The broken slab and other fragments recovered from burials in Kyushu (Pl. N. 48) are authentic glassmaking metal of the Late Tomb period. The fact that other fragments of the same glass have been found at various localities in the same general area (Sup. N. 18, 19), may bear out the theory that glass was made at some central spot and portioned out to individual glassworkers for their use.

Kyushu still remained the main entrance to Japan from the continent, and, since the horse trappings excavated at Miyajidake Shrine show close similarities with Chinese and South Korean designs and workmanship, it might seem that a supply of this green glass could have been brought in from abroad. But the lead content, so much higher than any encountered on the continent, precludes a foreign source. The relatively late date of this burial (perhaps about 600 A.D. or a little later) suggests that local glassmakers were supplied with working material of domestic origin. This is supplemented by the fact that many beads, of similar metal (Pl. 58), were found with the slabs in the Miyajidake Shrine burial. Even the beads from Yoshimatsu-mura (Sup. N. 26) may also uphold such a theory, since their quality, color, and specific gravity bear such a striking likeness to the Miyajidake Shrine glass slab.

In addition to prepared glass metal, a crucible, and fire, the maker of glass beads would have needed the following:

1. Possibly a bellows for inducing a higher temperature from the charcoal fire. According to the *Nihon Shoki* the artisans working on wondrous things to entice the Sun Goddess from the cave to which she had retired made a "Heavenly bellows" of flayed deerskin,[5] an instance that must reflect an ancient custom. Further, a tuyere was found beside a pit near a shellmound in Fukushima Prefecture, together with traces of a furnace, much charcoal, and ash. "Foot bellows were apparently used on a large scale" for iron working.[6]

2. A small supply of glass metals in various colors, whether prepared by the beadmaker

himself or elsewhere. Today these are in the form of rods, but in the Tomb period they may have been small rod shapes (Sup. N. 17) or even irregular lumps (Sup. N. 15, 16); or possibly even in larger quantity, as the glass slab at Miyajidake Shrine.

3. Metal rods or wires (or their equivalents, such as twigs or small bones) to be dipped in a clay solution and dried in preparation for coiling glass threads about them.
4. Some arrangement whereby finished *marudama* or *kodama*, still on the rods, could be either thrust into a bed of warm straw ashes to cool and anneal, or "hung up to dry" on a line (Pl. 146 illustrates an eighteenth century method).
5. A smooth level surface, for marvering.
6. Simple tools, such as tongs or pincers (see Sup. N. 22 for a glass *magatama* that seems to have been grasped by such a tool).
7. In the Early Tomb period, perhaps molds for *magatama*.
8. Whetstones (Pl. 50) for the grinding of *magatama*, in the later years of the period.
9. An iron awl, for drilling bores when necessary.

BEADS

The old province of Izumo looms large in the mythology and history of Japan; and the tradition of beadmaking there traces back, indirectly, to the "Age of the Gods," when the deity Toyo-tama, or Ama no Akaru-dama, is said to have made beads as one of the offerings to entice the Sun Goddess out of the cave into which she had retired. He is said to have accompanied the Heavenly Grandchild down to earth; and his descendants purportedly later settled in Izumo.

A reference in the imperial annals of the Engi era (901–22; the *Engi-shiki*, in an entry of 905), mentions sixty strings of *ōn-fukidama* ("august blown beads")[7] as the annual tax allotment expected from the Kambe village, Ōu-gun, Izumo. It is largely on the basis of this, plus finds in the area, that the reputation of Izumo as an important glass-making center in antiquity developed. Remains of some dwelling sites near Kasenyama in Tamatsukuri are thought, locally, to have belonged to glass beadmakers, but, if so, there is at present no way of identifying their chronological place. A few examples of beads, excavated in Tamatsukuri by the Archaeological Research Institute of Kyoto University, can be authenticated by comparison with similar beads from Tomb period burials in other parts of Japan.

The most common bead of this period was a translucent, dark purplish blue *marudama* —a type found also on the continent. As this kind has been recovered from various parts of the Chinese empire of the Han dynasty, from its peripheral colonies, and from southern Korea, it would seem that the formula for their production was of continental origin; but the vast quantities excavated in widely separated areas of Japan are an argument against importation. The same holds true of other beads in different colors, found in quantity in the Chinese tombs at Lo-lang in northern Korea, and also in Southern Korea. Quite probably the coloring methods may have been brought into Japan by immigrant artisans.

As regards shape, in addition to the *magatama, kudatama, marudama,* and *kodama* of the preceding Yayoi period, several new forms made their appearance: variations of the *marudama,* such as the *tombodama* of two or more colors (Pls. 60, 61); the *kuchinashidama* or *mikandama* (Pl. 62); the *natsumedama* (Pl. 52, right); a new opaque brownish red *kodama* (Pl. 59); and also the *kirikodama* (Sup. N. 30). These are discussed individually below.

From many localities, all over the islands, hundreds of thousands of glass beads in varying shapes, sizes, and colors have been recovered. A growing multiplicity of form, size, color, nature of the glass, and method of forming became conspicuous characteristics of the Tomb period. Beads were not only worn in strings as personal ornament, with doubtless some special meaning, but were applied to various objects either worn or in common use. From the tremendous number found, we may be assured that beads were considered to exert some effective spiritual force. Whatever the original Japanese feeling for the *tama*—the symbol of spirit, the precious substance, the jewel, the bead— it must be remembered that these *tama* from the tombs were never "just beads" but cherished treasures symbolic of some superior power.

There is no doubt that the *magatama*, whether of stone or of glass, played an important role in the spiritual concepts of the time, a role that was never to disappear entirely, although in later periods changing circumstances were to diminish its use. It should also be remembered, and this may account in part for its endurance, that, since the beginning, the *magatama*, the sacred jewel, was one of the three imperial regalia of Japan, the other two being the sword and the mirror.

Magatama

It has been seen that in the Yayoi period, handsome *magatama* were made of green lead glass. Cast in a mold, they have rounded "fleshy" bodies, sometimes with incised grooves on the head, together with circular bores, more or less in the center of each side of the head, suggesting eyes. This gives those *magatama* a peculiarly lifelike aspect (Pls. 39, 49), suggesting an imitation of some form in the animal kingdom—a species of shellfish, or some familiar pupa—rather than the animal teeth to which they have been persistently linked by modern authors.

During the course of the Tomb period this delicately conceived realistic shape underwent transformation. The subtle contours of the early examples eventually became deformed, even squarish at times; the plump bodies often became flattened on the sides; and sizes were reduced. Precision in the placing of bores was neglected, and frequently the incised grooves were omitted or misplaced. An appearance of carelessness crept in. Certainly the reason for this was not lack of skill, since some still show sensitivity to form and detail, and other forms of glass show increasing deftness. Was it perhaps due to a growing belief in the greater efficacy of quantity? Whatever the cause, the large numbers that were mass produced were far removed from the exquisite perfection of form and finish seen in the fewer and more choice early examples.

Whether or not mold casting was continued in this period is difficult to say. But two other means of achieving the *magatama* form are evident. One is the procedure followed by the lapidaries who formed *magatama* from the semiprecious stones of Japan, such as jaspers and agates. In this process the artisan would start with a small lump or block of glass, grinding it down to shape, on two kinds of whetstone: one prepared with rounded concave grooves for forming the outer curve and another with convex ridges for shaping the inner curve. Such whetstones have been found in ancient beadmaking sites. (Pl. 50 shows a modern lapidary of Tamatsukuri in Izumo employing the same type of whetstone used there for centuries). A master glassmaker would turn out a handsome and carefully finished product; others, less skillful or under pressure for mass output, would produce cruder results.

That the form illustrated in Plate 51 was not produced by molding or by the friction method seems obvious. Its shape hints at the coiling method used for the production of glass *marudama*. There are other *magatama* whose head contours resemble such a coiled form.

Although a few *magatama* of this epoch are badly corroded, as are the Yayoi ones, the majority are in good condition, and the color and quality of the glass can be clearly seen. This is due apparently to (1) the discontinuance of burials in moisture-collecting urns in which phosphorus in bones combines with lead glass to form a lead-phosphate coating on the glass or (2) perhaps also a greater use of soda-lime glass. The predominant yellow-green lead glass of the Yayoi period was now gradually replaced by green of a darker tone, and new colors are found—a variety of greens, dark blue, pale blue, and even a clear, colorless type (Sup. N. 21). The glass may be nearly opaque, translucent, or transparent. This new coloration and quality has a counterpart in the stone *magatama*, which now, in addition to the green jade or nephrite of the Yayoi period, may be made of the darker green jaspers, of red agates, or of other colored stones. This might suggest that the new, diverse colors in glass were in deliberate imitation of the new diversity in the stone varieties, or, perhaps, it was simply the natural consequence of increased skill in the use of coloring agents.

Kudatama

Kudatama of the Tomb period were, like the *magatama*, made in jasper, agate, and other semiprecious stones; but, unlike the *magatama*, they were more rarely of glass. The *kudatama* from Mukaiyama, Mie prefecture, illustrated in Plate 53, have straight-walled bodies of uniform diameter, with ends softly and symmetrically rounded. This rounded contour of many *kudatama* reflects an outstanding characteristic of glass—its ductility when heated—for the harshness of what might otherwise be a straight-cut plane can be softened when reheated, as these seem to have been.

The production of glass tubes from which modern *kudatama* (as well as some *marudama* and *kodama*) are cut is done with mechanical help, resulting in great speed and uniformity;[8] but it was not always so, and we must think of the early Japanese method as being more primitive, although following basically the same principle.

Let us imagine a Japanese glassmaker of the Tomb period having before him some sort of primitive stand or stove with a charcoal fire, and, on it, a small crucible for melting the glass. Imagine him dipping an iron rod into the molten glass in the crucible and bringing out a very small gather of glass. Rolling this back and forth on a smooth surface (marvering it), he could then penetrate the free end with a small iron rod or wire that had been coated with clay to prevent the glass from adhering to it and, upon withdrawing it, obtain a hollow cylindrical form. If the cylinder were slim enough and his rod fine enough to approximate the bore of a *kudatama*, he might stop there and simply cut his little tube into a few beads. However, he might go further, and, by pulling simultaneously on two irons at opposite ends, he could stretch the tube into a longer length. If he had an assistant, the latter, holding the projecting end of one rod and moving away rapidly, could pull the cylinder out to a greater length and smaller diameter, before it cooled and hardened. Many *kudatama* could then be cut from the resulting tube. The *kudatama* of Plate 53 seem to have been made in this manner.

It seems possible, however, that these early glassmakers may have followed an even simpler method for the *kudatama* with rounded ends. A modern beadmaker can very quickly and easily form a glass *kudatama* by taking a *marudama*, still on its wire and still hot and soft, and marvering it back and forth on a smooth iron surface. It elongates into a cylindrical form, becoming a *kudatama*, with no sharp ends. This is a natural, rapid, and uncomplicated development from the making of simple round beads. If such *kudatama* were fire polished, the soft, rounded feeling would be emphasized.

For the polishing method of modern times we may refer to the explanation by Mr. Kōzō Kagami, an eminent glassmaker, who speaks of removing all cutting traces from *kodama* and polishing to a fine surface by first coating the cut beads with moistened clay to prevent adhesion to each other, then heating them in a revolving container, and finally shaking them in a bag with bran to remove the clay.[9] The smooth surfaces and glossiness of unweathered beads points to the skill of the ancient beadmakers in achieving a polished surface without the aid of the modern mechanically revolved container.

Tomb period *kudatama* seem to differ from other beads of the era in that they are rarely transparent or even clearly translucent, although some show translucence in the bores when held toward a light.

Since little scientific investigation has as yet been directed to the glass *kudatama* of the Tomb period, it is impossible to comment upon their composition. Perhaps the publication of the joint investigations of Dr. Umehara and Dr. Yamasaki, when it appears, will throw light in this direction.

Marudama AND *Kodama*

"Round beads" (*marudama*) and "small beads" (*kodama*) are found in great quantities. Whatever the origin of their mystic significance, they first appeared in Japan, primarily as *kodama*, in Yayoi burials. During the Tomb period the custom expanded, and both *marudama* and *kodama* became an ever-present accompaniment to human burials. It is not rare for thousands of these round beads to be found in a single tomb. Many are of beautiful glass.

The essential difference between *marudama* and *kodama* is a matter of size. The point of division is a bit vague, but it may be considered that *marudama* are approximately 0.5 centimeter or more in diameter and the *kodama* anything smaller than that. The largest *marudama* considered here are over 1.6 centimeters in diameter, but they are comparatively few.

About 115 large *marudama*, in the predominant dark blue glass of the period, were excavated from Chaosuyama Tomb in Fukuda-no-Ota, Amagi city, Asakura-gun, Fukuoka Prefecture. They were found with an oversize iron corselet in good condition, a large iron helmet, iron arrow fragments, horse ornaments, and an unusually large stone *magatama*. The shapes vary, and they are rather roughly formed, of slightly translucent glass. They are kept in the Asakura High School in Amagi city, Fukuoka Prefecture. Other large dark blue examples from Nishi-Miyayama, Tatsuno city, Hyōgo Prefecture, are in the Kyoto National Museum (No. 8080). It would seem that this larger size, like the similar but decorated type known as *tombodama*, were produced in the latter part of the Tomb period. In Korea hundreds of oversized beads in dark blue were found in the famous Gold Crown Tomb at Kyŏngju.

From the very large *marudama* the sizes range downward to such tiny *kodama* as those excavated in December, 1959, from the Zuian-zuka, Okusaka, Sōja city, Okayama Prefecture, and now preserved in the Kōkokan of Kurashiki. These are but 0.1 centimeter high and 0.15 centimeter in diameter, in a translucent, bluish gray green. But such minute beads are rare. The great bulk fall within a medium range in the two groups.

Marudama and *kodama* were formed primarily by two processes: the coiling method and the cut-tube method. If any molding was in use at this time, there is no evidence of it. Nor have beads made by the folding method found in the West been recognized among the beads of this period (except for the *kirikodama* of Sup. N. 30). Some beads, as mentioned, may have been ground to shape from rough lumps of glass and then drilled for the hole.

The most common mode for forming *marudama* and *kodama* seems to have been by coiling. This process has been in continuous use in Japan up to recent times, when economic pressure has largely displaced handwork.

To create a bead by this mode, the maker, holding in his left hand a clay-coated metal rod or wire, uses the right hand to heat the end of a rod or lump of glass over a flame. When a thread of melting glass runs down, he connects it to the metal rod, which he is revolving in the fingers of his left hand. The thread of soft glass at once coils itself around the revolving rod, building up with each revolution an increasingly rounded bead. In a few seconds, when the proper size has been attained, the glass source is deftly separated. This process is repeated until his rod is filled with finished beads. The rod is then either placed in a box of warm straw-ash to cool and anneal, or hung on a suspension line. Later the beads can be easily slipped off the clay-coated metal rod, for the contraction of metal is greater than that of glass, so that, in cooling, the diameter of the rod becomes smaller than the bores of the glass beads.

Sometimes, when the temperature was not sufficiently high, or perhaps the twirling of the rod not sufficiently rapid, the beads show a ridged or corrugated body as seen in a bead in the eighth century Shōsō-in, shown in Plate 92, lower left. Plate 54 demonstrates what happens when the thread of glass at the end of the process became too cool for complete fusion.

Often, especially in the small *kodama* and the smallest *marudama*, which cool more quickly than do the larger beads, a tiny peak was left on the body of the bead where the glass source was lifted away. The tiny thread, pulled away from the mass of warm glass, hardened too rapidly to permit the severed end to sink back entirely into the body. At times this peak is so minute as to be inconspicuous, except upon close examination (as with the *kodama* of Pl. 56, upper right).

If contact between the source of molten glass and the revolving bead was not completely broken after the forming of the bead, the glass trailed along the rod for a short distance, resulting in a double bead. If the two bodies were cut apart, a low collar would remain where the cutting was not ground down.

The cut-tube method has been described for *kudadama*. Not many glass *kudadama* seem to have been produced during the period, but numerous *kodama* and small *marudama* were made by this method. The opaque brownish red bead of Plate 59 is of this nature, as is evident not only from its general appearance but from the minute longitudinal dark stripes that were drawn out in the glass when the tube was formed. *Marudama* and *kodama* made by this method are in fact short *kudatama*. The diameters of the bores, in beads cut from the same tube, are naturally uniform, but the heights and shapes of the beads may be of many varieties. It is not surprising that a single bead, in fact, should show unevenness in height, giving it a lopsided look, for the makers of small beads in this period must have worked by eye and could not precisely control small measurements. Further, if quantity was important, they could not be too meticulous. This is not to say that all cut beads are crooked, for many are delicately and accurately formed. Such variety in shapes is typical of beads made by both processes, but the coiled process often results in perfectly proportioned shapes, especially in the larger *marudama*, perhaps due to natural surface tension in the glass as well as to the more easily controlled larger size.

The smooth and brilliantly shiny surfaces of many of the beads of the Tomb period show that the glassworkers had access to efficient methods of polishing, such as were described above, but we do not know definitely what they were. Perhaps they shook or stirred them over their charcoal fires in a receptacle containing hot sand, or rice husks, or other matter. Such reheating would have tended to soften the contours of cut beads or even make some of them look a little bulbous, removing the cut look and confounding any attempt to classify by method. It would also give them the characteristic high polish.

Though loosely termed "round," the *marudama* is not necessarily spherical, but has a more or less circular periphery. Heights vary, so that there is a wide range of forms from a shallow circlet to a nearly, or truly, globular shape, or even one approaching the cylindrical. The *kodama*, of course, display the same shapes.

The geographical range covers all of Japan. Colors, which are monochrome, range practically throughout the spectrum, but with a notable absence of red, except for the opaque brownish red beads, which are here treated separately. Included are the blues, varying from a dark midnight blue through purplish and sky blue to a very pale aqua; greens in many tones and intensities; a wide variety of yellows and browns; and less frequently, a violet with a harmonious reddish or bluish tone. Opaque black and a transparent or translucent colorless glass are also found, but less often. Qualities vary from transparency to complete opacity. The advanced technical skill in glass manufacture is clearly manifest in this broad range.

Opaque Brownish Red Beads

The special opaque, brownish red beads (Pl. 59) mentioned previously are of the *kodama* type but have individual characteristics that set them apart. In some of the better specimens, as those from Oku-chō in Okayama Prefecture or those from Tsushima in Nagasaki Prefecture, the surfaces are quite glassy. A distinguishing mark usually present in these beads, but in the smallest seen only under a magnifying glass, is the presence of longitudinal lines. Sometimes a bead displays a whole series of faint parallel lines, with only one or two standing forth in darker tone. These lines look generally black or occasionally brown but are in reality streaks of transparent glass caused by the oxidation of the cuprous oxide coloring agent in small areas of the original melt (see Appendix, p. 451). When a small gather was drawn out into the tube form from which these beads were cut, the transparent colorless areas were also drawn out along the length of the tube. The deeper the transparent area, the darker it appears. These lines have heretofore been described as "black."

According to the author's present information, the presence of these beads in Japan is limited to Honshu and to the island of Tsushima lying between Japan and Korea. They have been found on Tsushima, in Nagasaki Prefecture (Pl. 59);[10] Oku-chō and Kamoson, both in Okayama-Prefecture;[11] Matsue city, Shimane Prefecture;[12] in Fukui Prefecture;[13] in two tombs in Wakayama Prefecture: the Ōtani Tomb in Wakayama city[14] and one in Tomiyasu, Yukawa-mura, Hitaka-gun.[15] They were also found beneath a late sixth century Buddhist pagoda at Asuka-dera, Nara Prefecture (Sup. N. 38).

Dr. Sueji Umehara owns beads of similar appearance from China, but they are devoid of the dark stripes; others of the same general type, with stripes, known as *mutisalah*, have been excavated at Kakao Island, Takuapa, in South Thailand[16] and at several sites in the Malay Peninsula, notably Pengkalan Bujang and Kuala Selinseng, Perak; they have also been found in Sumatran megalithic sites. It is of interest to note that in 1965, at Arikamedu, near Pondicherry, South India, beads of this type were found with many fragments of working material of opaque red with dark parallel striations, and that similar, but small fragments, were found at Pengkalan Bujang, Malaysia, in 1961.[17]

The Anthropological Museum of the University of Michigan possesses some almost identical to the Oku-chō examples, but excavated from various sites in the Philippines. In The Corning Museum of Glass (No. 62.6.61) are a few tiny beads of 0.1 centimeter in diameter that are of this variety, although less glossy and less elegant of finish than the larger specimens. Professor H. Otley Beyer of the Museum of Archaeology, Manila, who sent them to the author, reported that they came from a large Stone Age burial jar at Narciso, Bondok Peninsula, Quezon Province, Luzon, a site considered to date from about the first century A.D. From Philippine burials there have also come opaque beads with "black" stripes, which are of the orange tone of ripe persimmons. Among the finds at Okinoshima, in northern Kyushu, there are also persimmon colored beads with stripes. From a burial excavated in Toyokawa-mura, Osaka Prefecture (Sup. N. 31) came orange red beads with inconspicuous darker lines.[18] At Taxila, in present Pakistan, such red and orange beads were found at the Sirkap site; and in the Bhir Mound one orange bead and red ones, colored by metallic copper, were found.[19] Similar beads have doubtless been found in many areas, for they are not uncommon among the so-called trade beads that were carried throughout the Orient for purposes of barter. Such beads from South Indian graves have often been mentioned as coming from Kambe, India.[20]

The wide geographical range of the opaque brownish red glass beads may be significant in suggesting a foreign source for the ones found in Japan, especially since red is otherwise unknown so early in Japanese glass. On the other hand, since red (from copper) is their distinguishing color, and since copper was plentiful in Japan, as elsewhere, and used widely in the production of bronze and as a coloring agent of other beads, it is possible that these beads could be of local manufacture.

Tombodama

Beads that have other colored glasses inserted in the main body are known as *tombodama*. The *tombodama* technique in its simplest form was a natural consequence of that by which *marudama* were made, since this bead is but a decorated *marudama*. There seem to have been several methods of adding the extra color. In some Japanese *tombodama* the spots have irregular, jagged outlines and must have been merely fragments of glass that were pressed into the heated body of the bead. In others, the inserts, which are more smoothly rounded (Pl. 60), were added by holding a formed *marudama*, still soft and still on its rod, over the flame and applying in one quick, brief dab a touch of a molten glass thread of the desired color. The new color would sink into the body of the bead, fusing with it and becoming an integral part. Occasionally one sees a *tombodama* in which the glass was insufficiently heated, so that the new color rises slightly, in a hump, above the bead's body. However, when this technique was employed by a more competent artisan, the spots were thoroughly fused and often placed symmetrically in a design of sorts; usually four nearly uniform spots in a single color or in two alternating colors were spaced around the waist of the bead. Others, perhaps of a more experimental stage, vary in size and seem arranged in a hit or miss fashion; in a few cases these colored inserts, not well integrated into the mass, have fallen out.

Most of the *tombodama* of the Tomb period have a dark blue, nearly opaque base, with spots of opaque yellow glass, opaque pale green glass, or, more rarely, an opaque pale blue glass, used singly or in alternating combination. Now and then the base color varies; a *tombodama* in the Archaeological Research Institute of Kyoto University has a gray blue ground with several inserts of pale yellow, while another in the Tokyo National Museum (No. 6950) has a translucent turquoise blue body with pale yellow inserts.

An unusually elaborate example, far more developed than other known *tombodama*, and probably an import, is shown in Plate 61. An example from Oku-chō (Sup. N. 28) is also exceptional. The *tombodama* technique, of course, has manifold potentialities in the way of design, although it was not until centuries later that they were exploited. One very simple maneuver of this time, but not common, was the inserting of a continuous band of very even width around the waist of the bead.

Another type, quite different in both technique and appearance, is also referred to as a *tombodama*. This is not a spherical *marudama* form, but is almost straight walled with level top and bottom, obviously cut from a glass tube. The technique is more complicated and, though the bead is not unique, it is very unusual for the Tomb period.

Although the *tombodama* is, in general, not rare in Japan, extant examples are not numerous. Nevertheless, the specimens that can be considered of Japanese origin, crude though some are, represent a distinct advance in glass technology, in that two or three colors are combined.

Natsumedama

The *natsumedama* ("jujube bead"), resembling the fruit of the jujube, is now seen for the first time in Japan. It is like a slightly elongated *marudama* incised in the fashion shown in Plate 52, upper right. A natural form, it is known also on the continent, and since Japanese examples are not numerous at this time, the idea was perhaps imported.

Kuchinashidama

This, a new form for Japan (Pl. 62), was known throughout the ancient world, so that it may not have been a spontaneous development here, although that is possible. In the West it is known as the "melon bead." In Japan it suggested the seed of the cape jasmine, or gardenia (*kuchinashi*) from which it derived its name. In modern times it has suggested the lobed form of a peeled tangerine and thus is also known as *mikandama* ("tangerine bead"). There is no proof of the process, although the lobes of some examples seem to have been formed by tooling, either while soft by indentation with a pincer or by rolling over a ridged surface, or by cutting after cooling. One grooved bead in the Archaeological Research Institute of Tokyo University shows clearly the end of a glass thread coiled around at one end, suggesting that, however the grooves were formed, the bead itself was orginally a coiled *marudama*, cancelling out the possibility of molding.

Kirikodama

Literally "faceted bead," it was shaped by working from the middle of a long bead, or of a rough lump of material, toward the ends, cutting the surface usually into twelve facets and giving the ends an hexagonal form. Exceptionally, octagonal *kirikodama* (Sup. N. 30) are also found. Commonly cut from rock crystal, ancient examples in glass are rare.

APPLIED ORNAMENT

As proficiency in both metalworking and glassmaking progressed during the Tomb period, craftsmen began combining the two media, embellishing silver and gilt-bronze objects with glass beads or insets. This seems to have arisen in the Middle Tomb period.

The least intricate ornamentation appears on the gilt-bronze crown and shoes recovered from a tomb at Mizuo, Shiga Prefecture (Pl. 63). In addition to this example of the use of beads, there also survive small beadlike globules of glass that were formed especially for applied ornamentation. Some are very simple, such as those found on bronze horse-trappings at Toyokawa-mura, Osaka Prefecture (Sup. N. 31), while, in the ornaments from the Ōtani Tomb in Wakayama city (Pl. 64), the mountings display special skill and complexity. The gold ear pendants from Uryū-mura, Fukui Prefecture, (Pl. 65) imply an even greater proficiency.

Whence came the idea of using applied glass in Japan? The great tombs of southern Korea are rich in fine items of pure gold (which was plentiful there), and many among these carry glass decoration, usually as insets or inlays. Most of these tombs date from the latter part of the Japanese Tomb period, but glass beads had been produced in the Korean peninsula long before that. Although the sumptuous gold crowns of Korea have *magatama* and golden discs attached by wires, the simple attachment of glass beads in the Japanese Mizuo crown and shoes finds no counterpart in Korea. It was an infrequent method in Japan and not continued. The combination of budlike, or fruitlike, globules of glass (not beads) and tiny metal leaf or petal forms was uncommon in the Tomb period, but it was gaining a foothold. Unique examples come from the Ōtani Tomb. These forms show that another forward step had been taken, which was to be perfected in succeeding periods.

BRACELETS

From the Tomb period, bracelets of shell, stone, and metal remain, but, as in the preceding Yayoi period, only one fragmentary instance is known in glass. It is from Mie, Omiyamachi, Naka-gun, Kyoto Prefecture and is now in the Tokyo National Museum (No. 1845). Heavy corrosion makes it difficult to judge the method of manufacture, but presumably it was cast, like the metal ones. Some glass bracelets of this time are known from Korean burials.

VESSELS

During this period glass vessels first appeared in Japan. Only one noted here has been assigned to a Japanese origin. It is a bottle of rather thick brown glass discovered in Shiga Prefecture, to the north of Lake Biwa. No specific date has been assigned to it, but a group of large *magatama* of similar glass, excavated in Nara Prefecture, suggests Japanese fabrication with imported raw materials.[21] This author has not had the opportunity to study any of these items, but it might be remembered that blown glass for beads was not unknown in this period, and beads, it would seem, need not be considered to have been made of foreign metal.

Three glass vessels from two imperial tombs (Pl. 1; Sup. N. 32) were discovered when storms damaged the tumuli. Their presence in royal tombs reveals the esteem in which they were held at the time. The high quality and the Sassanian characteristics of the only one of these available for study—the "Ankan Bowl" (Pl. 1)—are indicative of the high standard of living then attained and of the court's foreign contacts.

Whence, when, and how these objects reached Japan is today a matter of conjecture. We know that fairly frequent missions passed between China, Korea, and Japan, and that gifts ("tribute" the records call them) always accompanied the missions. For instance, in the *Nihon Shoki*, in an entry of 334 (by the old traditional reckoning, in the reign of the Emperor Nintoku), it is recorded that the Korean kingdom of Silla, after being prodded for a lapse in sending tribute, "presented 1460 pieces of tribute, fine silks and miscellaneous objects of all kinds—in all eighty shiploads." Again, in 370, the "Land of Wu [China] and the Land of Koryŏ [in northern Korea] together attended the Court with tribute." These two missions came to the court of the Emperor Nintoku, and in 534 (old reckoning) "Paekche [in southern Korea] sent tribute" to the court of the Emperor Ankan.[22] No doubt the glass vessels from the imperial tombs of Nintoku and Ankan, and perhaps the bowl of the Shōsō-in (Pl. 105), were part of such "tribute" from abroad, carefully preserved at the court until such time as they were dedicated in the tombs and in the Shōsō-in. Their origins and dates are discussed in the Notes.

Recently, in the excavation of the Senzuka Tombs at Niizawa in Nara Prefecture, two glass vessels—a bowl or jar (Pl. 2), and a plate—of types otherwise unknown in Japan were found.[23] The bowl, 7 centimeters high, is of transparent colorless glass, with a band of concave cut motifs, similar, it is said, to three vessels excavated in the last decade on the outskirts of Canton, China.[24] The Niizawa plate, about 14 centimeters in diameter' seemed to have served, in the burial, as a "saucer" for the cup. It is dark blue, on a foot, with a hollowed center around which is a painted design, now scarcely discernible, of a person with outstretched hand, a horselike animal, and trees. Full data on this tomb has not been available to the author, but it is reported that the glass is of soda-lime composition.[25]

Fragments of another bowl, characteristic of the glass of Sassanian Persia, were found on Okinoshima, a shrine island in the Genkai Sea north of Kyushu.[26] The implication of increasing foreign relations suggested by these glass vessels serves as a portent of changes to come.

Several glass items from tombs dating from the end of the Tomb period have been included in the next chapter because they exhibit characteristics of the early Asuka period (Pls. 68, 74).

1. Ryūsaku Tsunoda, Wm. Theodore de Bary, Donald Keene, *Sources of Japanese Tradition*, Introduction to Oriental Civilizations, New York, Columbia University Press, 1958, p. 11.

2. Illustrated in *Sora kara Mita Kofun* [Ancient Tombs seen from the Air], Tokyo, Asahi Shinbun Shashin Bukku [Asahi Newspaper Photographic Book], No. 17, 1955, p. 18.

3. *SGZC*, p. 77.

4. Since these have been published as Tomb period equipment, this seemingly erroneous attribution is mentioned here. The pieces are: 1) a broken crucible with glass adhering in the bottom and lumps of glass of corresponding shape, owned by Mr. Manjirō Saino, Tottori Prefecture; and 2) several jars and large fragments of glass or glaze owned by Mr. Manjirō Muraoka of Hawai-son, Tottori Prefecture, who had been told they were found in Tamatsukuri, Shimane Prefecture, and were considered to be very ancient. The largest jar is very heavy, weighing over 75 kilograms (23 *kan*); it is lined with a smooth creamy glassy glaze with one area of greenish blue, and on the exterior are broad brushstrokes of color, like glaze, which sweep across the body.

5. Aston, *Nihongi, op. cit.* (see n. 1, p. 45), I, p. 47.

6. Takao Tsuchiya, "An Economic History of Japan," *TASJ*, Second Series, XV, Tokyo, 1937, pp. 37–38.

7. "August blown beads" signifies blown beads to be offered to a deity, in this case to the Imperial Household. "Blown," in this context, refers perhaps not to blowing glass but to blowing a fire with some sort of bellows to produce sufficient heat. This suggests that the beads were of an artificial and ductile substance—that is, glass.

8. For this process the "Guide for Foreigners" visiting the famous Murano factories at Venice is interesting in regard to the mid nineteenth century mode in practice there; see Dominique Bussolin, *Les Celebrés Verreries de Venise et de Murano*, Venice, 1847, pp. 9–16.

9. *Kagami, *Garasu no Seichō* [Development of Glass], p. 318. The clay prevents the softened glass surfaces from blending together; the bran removes the clay and imparts a polish.

10. Seiichi Mizuno, Takayasu Higuchi, Takashi Okazaki, *Tsushima*, "An Archaeological Survey of Tsushima Island in the Korean Strait Carried Out in 1948," *Archaeologia Orientalis*, Series B, VI, Tokyo and Kyoto, Tōa Kōkogakkai, 1953; English summary, p. 17.

11. Oku-chō examples are preserved in the Oku-Kōkokan, Oku-chō and in The Corning Museum of Glass; those from Kamo-son, in the Kōkokan of Kurashiki, Okayama Prefecture.

12. Collection of the History Department, Shimane University, Matsue, Shimane Prefecture.

13. Excavated by Mr. Y. Saito of Fukui Prefecture; they are very small and lack the parallel lines.

14. Collection, Education Committee, Wakayama.

15. Collection of the Archaeological Research Institute, Tokyo University.

16. Alastair Lamb, "Miscellaneous Papers on Early Hindu and Buddhist Settlements in northern Malaya and southern Thailand," *Federation Museums Journal*, VI, New Series, Museum Department, Federation of Malaya, Kuala Lumpur, 1961.

17. Alastair Lamb, "A Note on Glass Beads from the Malay Peninsula," *Journal of Glass Studies*, VIII, Corning, 1966, pp. 80–94, Fig. 6. This article discusses the *mutisalah* type beads, the Sumatran, South Indian, and Penkalan Bujang finds, and also cites other less extensive references.

18. Collection of the Archaeological Research Institute, Kyoto University.

19. Sir John Marshall, *Taxila, An Illustrated Account of Archaeological Excavations Carried Out at Taxila under the Orders of India Bewteen the Years 1913 and 1934*, Cambridge, Cambridge University Press, 1951, II, p. 690; Horace C. Beck, "Beads from Taxila," *Archaeological Survey of India*, Memoir No. 65, Cat. Nos. 955, 956 and 962. Mr. Sana Ullah, *Archaeological Survey of India, Report 1922–1923*, p. 158, gives analyses and likens the beads to the *haematinum* of the Romans.

20. Mohammed Sana Ullah, "Excavation and Exploration," *Revealing India's Past* (ed. Sir John Cummings), London, India Society, 1939, p. 197. However, see Alastair Lamb's reference (*op. cit.*, n. 16) to raw materials for such beads found in quantity at Arikamedu, South India, and to a lesser extent at Pengkalan Bujang, Malaya.

21. *Umehara, "Shinshutsudo Hari-ki. . . . ," Frontispiece and pp. 4–5.

22. Aston, *Nihongi, op. cit.* (see n. 1, p. 45), I, pp. 284, 296; II, p. 28.

23. *Kōichi Mori, "Garasu-ki wo Shutsudo. . . ."

24. *Masuda, "Kandai no Garasu-yōki," p. 22.

25. *Yamasaki, "Garasu," p. 398.

26. *Okinoshima. . . . , II, English summary, p. 29. For another, Western type fragment, see also *Fukai, "Giran-shū Shutsudo. . . ."

ASUKA AND HAKUHŌ PERIODS

THE YEAR 552, usually cited as the beginning of the Asuka period, marks the presumed official entry of Buddhism into Japan. At that time, from the king of the Korean state of Paekche, the emperor received as a gift Buddhist sutras, a Buddhist image, and accessories, accompanied by a eulogy of the new religion. The event did not result in any immediate official sanction of Buddhism. Quite the contrary, in fact, for there was intense political dissension over the matter for some years. Not until the reign of the Empress Suiko (592–626), under the regency of Crown Prince Shōtoku, did Buddhism really become a living force at the Yamato court. Nevertheless, the date of 552 signifies the first official entering wedge of a new element, which was to be a determining factor in much of the future life and culture of the Japanese people.

As discussed above, there had been a deep Korean trend in the crafts of Japan during the Tomb period. In the industrial arts, the new influences dominating the Asuka period, and the increased influx of Koreans into the country, simply enlarged a tendency that had been growing for many years. However, the special buildings, paintings, sculptured figures, and the unfamiliar character of the accessories of various ritual ceremonies that the practice of Buddhism required were all until then alien to the Japanese culture. Thus, more and more, Korean artisans were encouraged to settle in Japan, to erect the first temples and prepare the unfamiliar appurtenances of the new religion. It is consequently not surprising that the art of the Asuka period was often strikingly Korean in character. Ango-in, or Asuka-dera temple (part of Hōkō-ji temple), the oldest Buddhist temple known in Japan, was constructed by Korean craftsmen ("carpenters"), who started the work in 588. Close contacts with Korea continued for several centuries, and before and after the fall of the Paekche kingdom in 668 many emigrants settled in Japan. The nobility (sometimes seventy at a time) were given aristocratic rank and honored with privileges, as were some skilled artisans, while plebeians in great numbers were settled in special districts.

Chinese influences were also conspicuous. Turbulence in China prior to the stabilizing influence of the Sui regime had sent many Chinese from the country; some reached Korea, and a few probably emigrated thence to Japan. An entry in the *Nihon Shoki* for

540 notes that ". . . emigrants from the various frontier nations were assembled together, settled in the provinces and districts and enrolled in the registers of population. The men of Ts'in [that is, China] numbered in all 7053 houses."[1] Furthermore, the Japanese court had invited Chinese artisans to Japan.

Despite complex foreign influences containing elements from most of eastern Asia, and despite the tremendous effect of Buddhism and Buddhist art at the Yamato court, the native culture remained strong, and Shintō rituals and their accessories were neither lost nor was their vigor impaired. The sacred ceremonies of purification and thanksgiving, for instance, continued with their usual supreme importance throughout the period.

Although 552 is used here as the opening of the Asuka period, simplified tombs and some characteristic tomb furnishings continued into the seventh century, while at the same time new aspects and objects became conspicuous. Thus there was a cultural overlap, which accounts for the discrepancy herein between the terminal date of the Tomb period and the opening of the Asuka period. The discontinuance of tumuli must have been due partially to an article of the Taika Reform edict of 646, patterned on a Chinese passage, which prohibited the erection of burial mounds except for the immediate imperial family; even the imperial tombs were to be reduced in size.[2] In the Abu-san Tomb, Takatsuki city, Osaka Prefecture (Pl. N. 68), the chamber was merely inserted in the side of a hill and was so reduced in size that it barely accommodated the sarcophagus, while the Kegoshi Tomb chamber (Pl. N. 74), though larger, was merely carved out of the end of a small hill.

The Suiko era (592–628), with Shōtoku Taishi serving as regent for the Empress Suiko, his aunt, stands out culturally as one of the bright intervals in Japanese history. His accomplishments were many, and even today he is an honored and beloved ideal. The empress and he made Buddhism a state religion; he was a student of Chinese literature and sent various scholars to China to study all aspects of Chinese civilization and organization and resumed relations with the Chinese court by sending envoys; Buddhist temples (the Shitennō-ji, Hōrin-ji, and Hōryū-ji among others) were established; he lectured eloquently on the Lotus Sutra (while lotus petals drifted down from heaven about him!); established a university at Hōryū-ji; founded charitable institutions; and promoted the arts. To him personally are now credited various art works (too many to be credible), and he is often regarded as a "patron saint" of artistic endeavor.

Perhaps one reason for the ready acceptance of Buddhism at this time was the fact that the doctrine of the Lotus of the Perfect Truth, which Shōtoku Taishi promoted, centered on this flower as the symbol of purity and perfection. This was easily compatible with the Shintō heritage, which was also centered on purity.

Shōtoku Taishi seems to have instigated some reforms at the court, but he did not live to see the eventual improvement in governmental and civil conditions. It was with the accession of the Emperor Kōtoku, in 645, that the official reformation had its beginning. The following Hakuhō period was also culturally brilliant. Some scholars include it in the succeeding Nara period, but since much of it was devoted to experimentation, with regulations based in part at least upon the hopes and aspirations set in motion by Shōtoku Taishi, it is treated here as an extension of the Asuka period. The new era was named Taika ("Great Change"), and in the year 646 an imperial code, the *Kaishin-no-Chō* (Code of Reform) was announced. After many experimental legal codes and revisions during the seventh century, the *Taihō Ritsuryō* ("The Taihō [era] Code" of criminal and civil laws) was promulgated in 702, near the close of the Hakuhō period. Although now lost, the *Taihō Ritsuryō* was the basis of the *Yōrō Ritsuryō* code issued in 718, which still survives, in part, in the *Yōrō Shokuinryō* ("The Yōrō [era] Code for Personnel") section. The part of that code of particular interest in this discussion is that regarding the Imono-no-tsukasa,[3] or Casting Bureau, which included glass.

The outstanding monument remaining from the period is the Hōryū-ji temple. A few of its Asuka-Hakuhō period buildings, though much repaired, have survived to modern times: the Chūmon ("Central Gate"), the Go-jū-no-tō ("Five-Storied Pagoda"), the Kondō ("Golden Hall," the main hall of worship; this burned in 1949, and its priceless wall paintings were irreparably damaged), and parts of the Cloister, which surrounds the Sai-in, or "Western Compound" as it is called. Whether these were of the Asuka period, the late Hakuhō period, or, as some have thought, of the first years of the Nara period, has been a matter of controversy for many years and still remains a problem. As the dates of the Kondō and the pagoda are pertinent to this study, details regarding them will be considered in the sections dealing with their glass (Pl. N. 70, 71).

GLASS IN THE ASUKA-HAKUHŌ PERIODS

Tomb burials of the transitional decades of this period, though fewer and altered, co-existed with the new customs and new techniques in glass, its uses, and significance. The overlapping of tombs into the Asuka period presents some seeming inconsistency. For example, the burial of Miyajidake Shrine (see Pl. N. 48) was so dominated by the old customs that it is included in the previous chapter. On the other hand, the burial on Abu-san (Pl. N. 68) and the Kegoshi (or Asagao) Tomb (Pl. N. 74) are so notable for the changes in their stone chambers, for a new type of lacquer coffin, and for the nature of their glass that they seem unquestionably to belong to the later period.

In the survey of extant glass of this period it will be seen, therefore, that old forms often mingle with the new, but that sometimes there is nothing but the new.

DOCUMENTARY EVIDENCE OF GLASSMAKING

Though the *Taihō Ritsuryō* is dated 702, some of the government bureaus and officials mentioned must have been operating long before that time. This would include the Imono-no-tsukasa (Casting Bureau), which produced, among other materials, glass. The first extant mention of the Imono-no-tsukasa comes from the *Yōrō Shokuinryō* of 718. It is known, however, that the Imono-no-tsukasa was definitely in operation in 702 because the *Ryō-no-Shūge*, a collection of legal interpretations compiled about 880, quotes *Koki* ("Ancient Documents") of 738 as mentioning the Imono-no-tsukasa in reference to the Taihō Code. In 662 an *Ōmi-Ryō* ("Ōmi [era] Code") had been issued on order of Emperor Tenchi. This was revised under Emperor Tenmu (672–86) and in 689, during the reign of Empress Jitō, it was "distributed to government offices."[4] This revision dealt, in part, with the matter of ministries and the responsibilities of officials. It seems likely that the Imono-no-tsukasa of the Taihō Code, issued thirteen years later, had already been active in Emperor Tenmu's time and probably in earlier reigns. In fact, it has been suggested that the Imono-no-tsukasa was the result of a merger of two large *be* of pre-Taika times (that is, pre-646), the *kanetsukuri-be* (the metalworkers' *be*) and the *tamatsukuri-be* (the beadmakers' *be*).[5] Indeed it does seem that some sort of official casting center must have existed during the Asuka-Hakuhō period, judging from the tremendous output of superb Buddhist cast bronze sculpture and temple accessories at the court-sponsored Hōryū-ji temple alone.

An article in the *Yōrō Shokuinryō* describing the Imono-no-tsukasa occurs in the section dealing with various officials, ministries, ranks and duties of officials; it is found in the portion entitled "Ōkura-shō" ("Ministry of the Treasury"), among whose responsibilities was the receiving and dispensing of taxes in kind from the various provinces, the oversight of government storehouses, and the production of treasures for governmental use. The passage reads:

> CASTING BUREAU [Imono-no-tsukasa]
> 1 Director
> Who controls the casting of gold, silver, copper, and iron, and the making of lacquer [?, *toshoku*], glass [*ruri*] (this is the so-called *kasei-ju* ["jewel made with fire"]),[6] and matters concerning the registration of beadworker and artisan families.
> 1 Secretary, or Assistant Director
> 1 Senior Clerk
> 1 Junior Clerk
> 10 Artisans in various fields [*zakkō-bu*]
> 10 Servants
> 1 Watchman
> Working households [*zakkō-ko*][7]

The number of personnel seems small for a government bureau of casting at a time when cast works of all kinds were in great demand, but the terminal listing of "working households" may have been quite large, including home industries or small factories in scattered localities. This aspect of the matter is discussed more fully in the next chapter.

The words *toshoku* and *ruri* have puzzled many scholars. *Ruri* means today, as it meant in ancient times, "glass"; *toshoku* now means "painted (daubed, smeared, lacquered) decoration." At the time of the code, could these terms possibly have meant colored glass? Or could they have meant lacquer and glass in the sense of glass combined with the lacquer production?[8] There is no doubt that glass was intended, both from the word *ruri* and from the explanation that it was produced by fire. But did the *ju* of *kasei-ju* mean "bead" or did it in those days have the significance of *gyoku* (*tama*), as "precious substance"? In other words, was the meaning limited to glass beads or could it have referred to the production of glass metal? The fact that glass containers for Buddhist *shari* were produced domestically in this period would support a belief that both glass metal and glass objects were produced in the Imono-no-tsukasa.

From the use of the term "beadworkers and artisans" it has sometimes been held that beads were the only glass produced in the Casting Bureau. But during this period beads were also made from various natural substances, semiprecious stones, steatite, and pearls, and the techniques would have been radically different. The makers of glass beads perhaps had to produce the artificial substance as well as create the final product and might therefore well have been classed among the artisans rather than among the beadworkers. Or, there may have been two types of glass workers: the fabricators of glass metal and the makers of beads from that glass.

In addition, could not such an Imono-no-tsukasa have been the center for distribution of the glass metal to glass workers in the various *tamatsukuri-be*? The glass slabs of Miyajidake Shrine (Pl. 48) suggest such a distribution, while the "cloisonné" of the Kegoshi Tomb, and new types of beads and beadwork, all testify to an advancing familiarity with glassmaking such as might have been sponsored by a governmental agency.

EQUIPMENT, MATERIALS, AND TECHNIQUES

There is little extant evidence to indicate what equipment and tools were used for glass production. Blowpipes must have been in use, since the Buddhist reliquaries of Plates 70 and 71 and the cinerary urns of Plates 3 and 4 are of blown glass. The slabs of Miyajidake Shrine and vicinity and two small fragments (Sup. N. 34) are representative of the material used, which included both soda-lime and lead glass.

Beads were coiled or tube-cut, and there are some new types (Pl. N. 68; Sup. N. 40, and the *nejiredama* noted below); and an entirely new technique suggesting cloisonné enamel (Pl. 74) appears for the first time.

BEADS

Only one fragmentary *magatama* from the Asuka-Hakuhō period can be mentioned. It was found with the *shari* installation of Asuka-dera. Similarly, *kudatama*, never very numerous in glass, seem to have fallen into disuse and disappeared. Again, only one small fragment has come to notice—also in the *shari* installation of Asuka-dera.

Marudama AND *Kodama*

Although elaborate tomb burials were being given up, quantities of glass beads were still associated with religious rites. Beads in Korea and Japan (and possibly in China) must still have been symbols of potent spiritual significance since they are included among the *shōgongu* ("embellishments to give solemnity and grandeur") in the *shari* interments beneath Buddhist pagodas; and the protective, and perhaps propitiatory, nature of the *shari* interments seems to have been related to some quality in the beads used in them. That the beads of the Tomb period were placed in tumuli as appeasement of earth spirits has not been suggested here, since there is no Tomb period evidence to support this as a pre-Buddhist practice. But in the clay platforms of some eighth century Buddhist altars in Nara have been found offerings known as *chindangu* ("altar implements to pacify"), such as beads, mirrors, and swords, which were definitely placed as offerings to the Buddhist deities and to appease the spirits of the soil (Pls. 79–81). The beads of the *shari* installations, primarily *marudama* and *kodama*, may have served the same amuletic protective purpose, especially as they are found both inside and outside the immediate containers of *shari* reliquaries.

OPAQUE BROWNISH RED BEADS

In one instance only have these been found in the Asuka period. They come from the *shari* installation of Asuka-dera temple (Sup. N. 38). This installation is a curious combination of the old and the new, since artifacts associated with it follow the tomb burial tradition. It is the earliest *shari* interment recorded in the *Nihon Shoki*.

Tombodama

Only three are recorded, and they come from the same early *shari* installation at Asuka-dera (Sup. N. 39). One is different from the older type in that it has copper-wire inlays instead of spots of green or yellow glass.

Tsuyudama

A new form of pendant bead, the *tsuyudama* ("dewdrop bead"), appeared in the Asuka-Hakuhō period (Sup. N. 40). In this period it was a simple globular *marudama* shape, but in later years it became elongated into a slightly pointed shape. The perforation penetrated the glass for only a short distance and was large enough so that a wooden plug could be inserted to wedge the suspension device in place.

Nejiredama

In 1963 the sites of the Kondō and pagoda of the Chūgū-ji nunnery, Ikaruga, Ikoma-gun Nara Prefecture (near Hōryū-ji) were discovered and investigated. At what was assumed to be the central foundation of this Asuka period pagoda, about 2.7 meters beneath the surface, two gold rings, a small lump of gold, gold thread, and beads of amber, crystal, and glass were found. Among the latter were glass *nejiredama* ("twisted beads") 0.7 centimeter in diameter. Previously this type was unknown from before the eighth century Nara period (Pl. 7). This somewhat sophisticated glass form in an Asuka period context indicates that a Casting Bureau may have been producing glass.

COMPLEX BEAD STRINGING (Yōraku)

The stringing of beads developed into complex forms in the Asuka-Hakuhō period. The

Kojiki, the *Nihon Shoki*, and other sources all include passages alluding to the earlier stringing of beads for use as hair and ear ornaments, necklaces, armlets, anklets; and they are so represented on the *haniwa* of Plate 47.

> Like a string of jewels
> Worn on the neck
> Of the Weaving Maiden
> That dwells in Heaven—
> Oh! the lustre of the jewels. . .[9]

However, according to the *haniwa*, these were but simple strings of *magatama*, *kudatama*, *marudama* or *kodama*; tales in the *Nihon Shoki* show that they were strung on thread or cord. In the Asuka-Hakuhō period, in the bead pillows of the tomb of Emperor Tenmu (see below) and the Abu-san tomb (Pl. 68) silver wire replaces thread, and patterns develop in the stringing, or weaving together, of the beads. These complex combinations (usually suspended) of beads and/or small metal forms are known as *yōraku*. From this time forward the craftsmen found many uses for *yōraku*. In later times they are seen repeatedly on architectural forms, in Buddhist sculpture, represented in painting, combined with textiles, and employed for many common uses.

It was recorded in 1235 that after thieves had broken into the tomb of Emperor Tenmu (673–85), known as Hinokuma no Ouchi no Misasagi, a round mound in Nara (Yamato), the councillor Fujiwara no Tametsune was sent to make a thorough investigation. The following data is taken from his account.[10]

The coffin, which had been covered with a square pall, was of red lacquer, with a wood cover. Among the remains was a drum-shaped (hourglass-shaped) pillow (*gyoku-chin*), "enriched with gold, silver and jewels, apparently of Chinese workmanship and magnificent beyond description." No sketches exist, but, since glass beads were often spoken of as "jewels," no doubt some, if not all, of the "jewels" were of glass. The suggestion that it "was apparently of Chinese workmanship" may be taken with skepticism, since the report was written in the thirteenth century when glass production had declined, and it would, no doubt, have been difficult for the writer to imagine the fashioning of such "magnificence" in Japan at that time.

In the Kondō of Hōryū-ji there are three elaborate canopies suspended over the altar, two of which are originals and one a replacement of the Kamakura period. Almost all of the beads forming the fringes are varishaped and glazed green and yellow, interspersed with red-dyed nuts. Among them are a few beads of glass. It is not known whether these are the remains of a larger original number or whether they were added later.

VESSELS

The most revered item of Buddhist glass was the *shari-ki*, or *shari-yōki* (receptacle for *shari*), also known as *shari-tsubo* ("*shari* jar"), *shari-bin* ("*shari* bottle") or *shari-tō* (a "pagoda"-shaped *shari-ki* or a pagoda-shaped reliquary for the *shari-ki*).

Shari (see Glossary) are not only symbols for veneration and devotion, but are also considered to have the power of protecting a temple. The custom originated with the Buddhist emperor of India, Asoka (reigned 273–32 B.C.), who is credited with having had the earthly remains of Gautama Buddha divided and deposited in eighty-eight sacred places. Later, perhaps because the dispersion of such relics was, after all, limited, it became an equally pious act to revere the shari of Buddhist saints, or even to use imitative pebbles or pellets of stone or of glass, dedicated to that purpose. In India, a stupa was erected over the buried śarīra (shari); the spot was holy ground and honored as such. In China, Korea, and Japan, the stupa became the pagoda, the holy guardian spot of a temple compound.

Glass reliquaries are presumed to have been used in China, but it is in Korea and Japan that material and literary evidence attests both to the manner in which these temple treasures were installed and to the tremendous reverence accorded them. Some of the Korean shari-ki were of glass. In Japan they are most frequently in the form of a small jar, sometimes of rock crystal but more often of glass. The pure and jewellike nature of these two substances made them particularly suitable for such a purpose.

The shari-ki, though entirely new to Japanese culture, was welcomed and found a ready place. Perhaps the Shintō veneration of lineage and ancestors provided the basis for its quick acceptance. It continued to be employed in ever varying artistic forms throughout the history of Buddhism in Japan, and glass, in one way or another, continued to be associated with it.

The earliest shari installation thus far discovered is that of Ango-in, the only remaining part of Hōkō-ji temple (known popularly as Asuka-dera) at Asuka-mura, Takaichi-gun, Nara Prefecture, the earliest known temple remains in Japan. This shari-ki was of gilt bronze, very likely brought from Korea, but later shari-ki of the Asuka period seem to have been almost invariably made of glass, so far as can be ascertained from the sources at our disposal. They may be correlated to a possible early Imono-no-tsukasa or its prototype. Most, and perhaps all, of these glass shari-ki differed from those of China and Korea in that they are of heavy, thick glass, while known continental examples are thin and delicate. Since Buddhism at this time was primarily court sponsored, it seems at least plausible that these glass shari-ki were made under official patronage and that there may have been some sort of official glass workshop or shops at that time.

Although the shari-ki of Asuka-dera was of gilt bronze, rather than glass, a few words regarding the manner in which it was buried and the veneration accorded it, seems advisable. In the spring of 588, according to the Nihon Shoki, the Emperor Bidatsu received from the Korean king of Paekche three Buddhist priests, Buddhist "relics" (that is, shari), and various artisans, including "two temple carpenters." Asuka-dera is known to have been founded in that year, and its buildings constructed by two Koreans from Paekche, who, no doubt, were these "two temple carpenters." On the fifteenth day of the first month of the reign of the Empress Suiko (593) a shari-ki (probably the item listed as "Buddhist relics") was dedicated and interred with accompanying offerings; the following day the central pillar of the pagoda was erected over it.[11]

In 1957, when the Nara Research Institute of the Commission for the Protection of Cultural Properties was investigating the vestiges of this temple they discovered this *shari* installation. The investigation showed that the installation had first been discovered in 1197, after a fire that, the previous year, had destroyed the main hall and pagoda, neither of which was rebuilt. At that time the objects were placed in a new wooden box (with inscriptions in the style of the day) and replaced in a niche in the foundation stone of the former pagoda pillar, where they remained until their discovery in 1957.

The central pillar of the pagoda of Asuka-dera temple (Ango-in) rested upon a two-meter-square foundation stone of granite, two meters below the ground. The reliquary was laid in a stone chest housed within the foundation stone. There the treasure was intended to remain forever, hidden, secret, safe, protected, and protective. On the top of the foundation stone were various small items of gold, silver, and jade, as well as larger items of iron and bronze suggestive of the Tomb period and having no Buddhist significance. Although the architects of the buildings were Korean Buddhists, the Japanese authorities themselves must have determined that these offerings accompany the holy treasure. Within the niche housing the box containing the reliquary, and within the box itself, hundreds of beads of glass and other materials (Sup. N. 35, 36, 38, 39) were found.

Except for the interment at Asuka-dera, a nested arrangement of gold, silver and bronze containers for the glass *shari-ki*, accompanied by beads, fragrant incense woods, cloves, and other small articles, was common for the Asuka-Hakuhō period.

The *shari* installation of the abandoned Yamada-dera temple (Jōdo-ji), erected in Asuka in 674, was evidently similar to that of Hōryū-ji but is known only through a document, the *Hōōteisetsu*, where it is thus described: "Eight *shari* in a green [or blue?] glass bottle installed in nested containers of gold, silver, and gilt bronze, with beads heaped about them in a large metal bowl with lid."[12] A fragment of a green glass *shari-tsubo*, very thick in some areas and thin and semitransparent in others, was one of a number of glass beads and fragments found beneath the Yakushi image of Yakushi-ji temple (on top of the pedestal) when the figure was moved during repairs a few years ago. A similar fragment came from the clay altar-platform of the Kondō of Hōryū-ji; this is of lead glass with a specific gravity of 4.5.[13] The *shari-ki* buried beneath the foundation of the pagoda of Hōryū-ji is the glass treasure of the Asuka-Hakuhō period. It is considered so sacred that, during a recent repair of the structure, an academic investigation (termed by the temple a "purification") was permitted only with the greatest reluctance, under protest by the temple, before the treasure was ritually reinterred, resealed, and covered with concrete (see Pl. N. 70).

Glass cinerary urns for the burial of cremated human remains are also known. One example, dating from the seventh century, is preserved at Miyajidake Shrine, Fukuoka Prefecture (Pl. 3). It is a vessel of blown glass, with lid, and seems to be of Japanese manufacture. Another important specimen, from the very end of the Hakuhō period, contained the ashes of a general, Fumi-no-Nemaro (Pl. 4).

These occurrences testify to the ever increasing use of glass, and to the new Buddhist custom of cremation, marking a great simplification over previous burial customs. Since this use of glass urns seems to have been short lived, there are but these two examples to present.[14]

VESSELS REPRESENTED IN PAINTINGS

Glass was considered worthy of use for the most holy treasures of Buddhism, the *shari*, and for preserving the ashes of the dead. Glass vessels now appeared in a usage new to Japan—associated with Buddhist deities in temple paintings. A wall-painting in the Kondō of Hōryū-ji (Pl. 73) shows the high status of glass, treated as a pure "jewel."

This new development, indirectly related to the glass history of Japan, appears first at the end of the Asuka-Hakuhō period. Since painting of this type was a continental custom introduced into China and Korea with Buddhism, and thence to Japan, the vessels included in these early Japanese paintings in all probability conformed to continental Buddhist canons and, for that reason, should not be considered as necessarily representing glass forms known in Japan in the seventh and early eighth centuries.

A CLOISONNÉ-LIKE TECHNIQUE

For the first time there appears, in the ornament from the Kegoshi (or Asagao) Tomb (Pl. 74), a technique consisting of filling spaces decoratively with colored glass—not as insets or inlays but by a process that, for lack of any other concise term, is here called cloisonné, since its appearance is very much the same. This example, the only one known in Japan from so early a date, is rather elementary, but it seems to be the forerunner of the elaborate enamelwork on the mirror in the Shōsō-in (Pl. 12).

1. Aston, *Nihongi*, *op. cit.*, (see n. 1, p. 45), II, pp. 38–39.
2. *Ibid.*, II, pp. 217–220.
3. *Ryō-no-Shūge*, 859–877 (ed. Nagamoto Koremune in the Engi era, 901–922), a commentary on the civil codes, gives the pronunciation as either Imono-no-tsukasa or Imoji-no-tsukasa.
4. G. B. Sansom, "Early Japanese Law and Administration," *TASJ*, Second Series, IX, December 1932, p. 69.
5. *Takigawa, "Imono-no-tsukasa. . . .," p. 3.
6. *Ryō-no-Shūge*, *op. cit.*, (see n. 3), quoting from an older work, says, "*Kaseiju* is dark blue," which is interesting considering the prevalence of dark blue among Tomb period glass beads.
7. From *Koji Ruien* [Encyclopedia of Ancient Matters], Tokyo, Koji Ruien Kankōkai, 1914, XIV, "Kan-i-bu, I, Ōkura-shō" [Section on Official Ranks, I, Ministry of the Treasury], pp. 967–968.
8. *Takigawa, "Imono-no-tsukasa. . . .," p. 2. There was also a bureau of lacquering in the Ōkura-shō; it would seem, therefore, that lacquer pro-

duced in the Imono-no-tsukasa, if any, must have been subsidiary and used in conjunction with other processes. *Yoshimura, *Shippō* [Cloisonné], p. 8, suggests that *toshoku ruri* "may well refer to the cloisonné technique." He also quotes Yukio Kobayashi (*Zoku Kodai no Gihō* [Ancient Techniques, Second Series], Hanawa Shōbō, 1959) as defining *toshoku* as gold and silver plating and *ruri* as glass "gems." Both definitions seem pertinent to Plates 12 and 74.
9. Aston, *Nihongi*, *op. cit.* (see n. 1, p. 45), I, p. 75.
10. *Aoki no Sanryō-ki* [History of the Aoki *Misasagi*], translated from *Koji Ruien* by Richard Ponsonby-Fane in "*Misasagi*: The Imperial Mausolea of Japan," *Transactions and Proceedings of the Japan Society*, London, 1921, XVIII, p. 35.
11. Aston, *op. cit.* (see n. 1, p. 45), II, pp. 121–122.
12. Quoted in *Hōryū-ji Gojū-no-tō. . . .*, p. 34.
13. *Yamasaki, "Garasu," Chart I, p. 399.
14. A similar glass lid was once found (present whereabouts not known to this author), so there were, it seems, at least three urns.

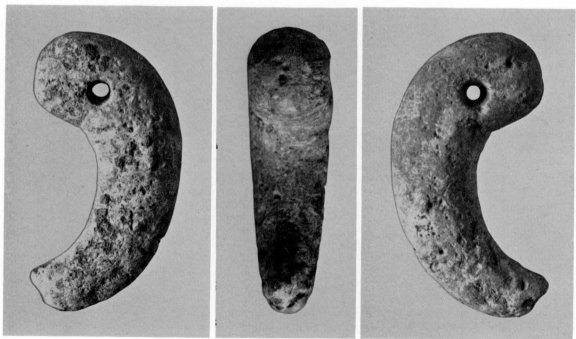

38. *Suigyoku* · possibly Latest Jōmon period · Sumiyoshi Shrine, Shimonoseki · H. 3.5 cm.
39. *Magatama* · Middle or Late Yayoi period · Suku-Okumoto site, Fukuoka Pref. · L. 5.3 cm.

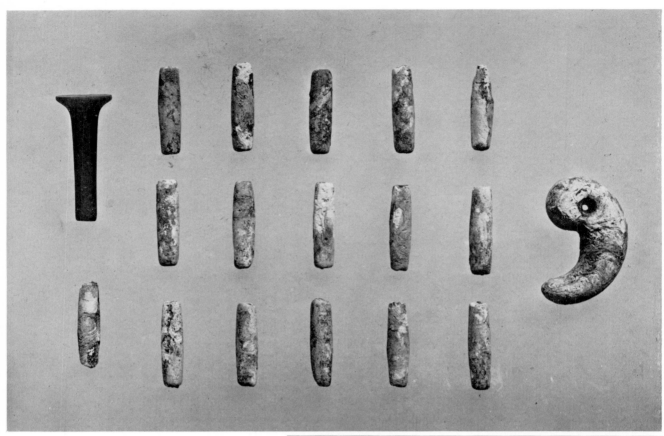

40. *Magatama*, *kudatama*, and a Chinese funerary object • Middle or Late Yayoi period and Han dynasty •
Suku-Okumoto site, Fukuoka Pref. • *magatama*, L. 3.2 cm.

41. Half of a mold for casting glass *magatama* • Late Yayoi period • Yanagabaru site, Fukuoka Pref. •
3.2 × 5.3 cm.

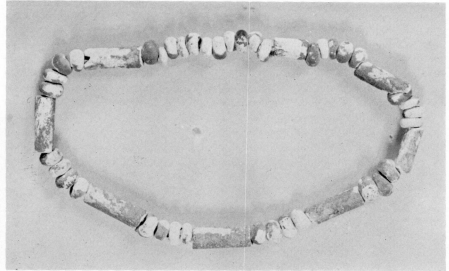

42. Fragments of glass bracelets • Late Yayoi period. • Maebaru site, Fukuoka Pref. • max. L. 2.3 cm.

43. *Kudatama* and *marudama* • Late Yayoi period • Maebaru site, Fukuoka Pref. • *kudatama*, max. L. 2.20 cm.

44. *Kodama* • Middle Yayoi period • Numa site, Okayama Pref. • D. 0.45 cm.

45. Interior, East Tomb, Monjuin, Nara Pref.

46. *Zenpō-kōen* tomb of Emperor Nintoku • early 5th century • Osaka Pref.
47. *Haniwa*: shrine maiden in festive attire • 6th century • H. 68.5 cm.
48. Glass slab • late 6th or early 7th century • Miyajidake Shrine, Fukuoka Pref. • 17.8 × 10.6 cm.

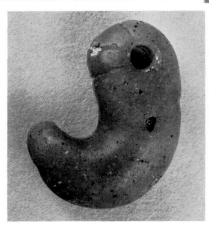

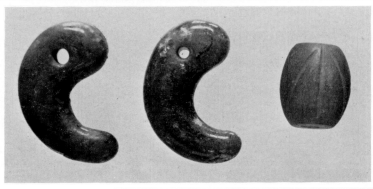

49. *Magatama* • Middle Tomb period • Nishisue site, Okayama Pref. • L. 5.65 cm.

50. Shaping a *magatama*, Tamatsukuri, Shimane Pref.

51. *Magatama* • Late Tomb period • L. 1.85 cm.

52. *Magatama* and *natsumedama* • second half, 5th century • Ōtani Tomb, Wakayama Pref. • max. L. 2.9 cm.

53. *Kudatama* • Tomb period • Mie Pref. • max. L. 2.1 cm.

54. Coiled *marudama* • Middle Tomb period • Shusenda Tomb, Okayama Pref.

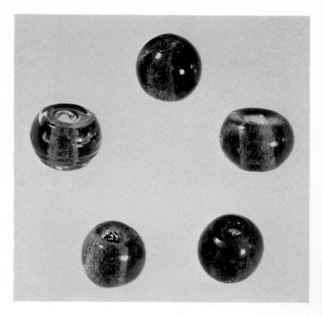

55. *Marudama* • Middle Tomb period • Shusenda Tomb, Okayama Pref. • D. 0.6–1.1 cm.

56. *Kodama* • Middle Tomb period • Shusenda Tomb, Okayama Pref. • D. 0.39 cm.

57. *Kodama* • Middle Tomb period • Shusenda Tomb, Okayama Pref. • D. 0.3–0.4 cm.

58. *Marudama* • late 6th or early 7th century • Miyajidake Shrine, Fukuoka Pref. • D. 1.75 cm.

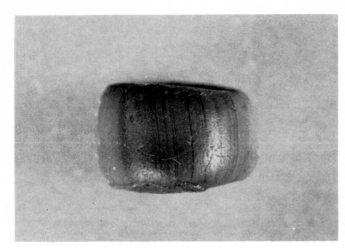

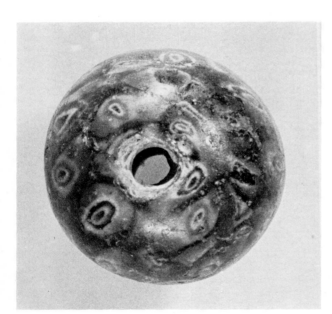

59. Opaque brownish red *kodama* • Middle Tomb period • Tsushima, Nagasaki Pref. • D. 0.25 cm.

60. *Tombodama* • Late Tomb period • Tamatsukuri, Shimane Pref. • D. 1.65 cm.

61. *Tombodama* • Middle Tomb period • Kagawa Pref. • D. 2.05 cm.

62. *Kuchinashidama* • probably 5th or 6th century • Gumma Pref. • D. 1.75 cm.

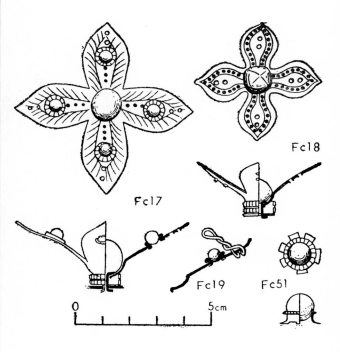

Fc17

Fc18

Fc19   Fc51

0   5cm

63. Ornamented gilt-bronze crown • early 6th century • Kamo mound, Shiga Pref.

64. Glass ornamented silver floral forms and diagram of parts • second half, 5th century • Ōtani Tomb, Wakayama Pref.

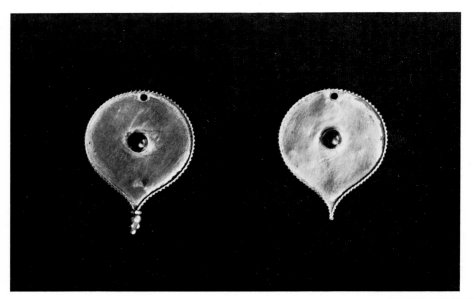

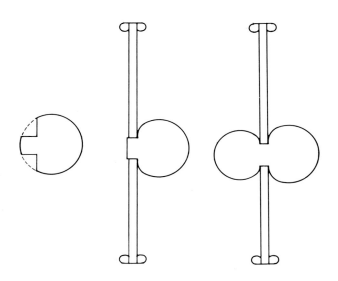

65. Gold ear pendants and construction diagram • Tomb period • Nishi-zuka, Fukui Pref. • L. 3.7 cm.

66. Gold ear pendant • Korean • Three Kingdoms period.

Asuka-Hakuhō Periods

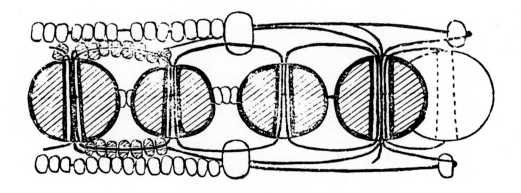

67. Cut glass bowl · Sassanian · 6th or 7th century · H. 8.9 cm.
68. Stringing diagram of *gyoku-chin* (jewel pillow) beads · 7th century · Abu-san tomb, Osaka Pref.

69. Five-storied pagoda, Hōryū-ji • late (?) 7th century.

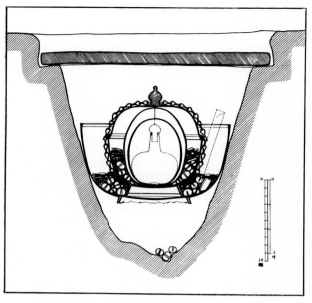

70. Shari installation beneath the Hōryū-ji pagoda · late (?) 7th century · glass, H. *ca.* 7.42 cm.

71. Fragments of a *shari-tsubo* • late (?) 7th century • Hōryū-ji • T. 0.25 cm.

72. Fumi no Nemaro cinerary urn, mouth, lid, and bottom (see Pl. 4).

73. East wall-painting of the Kondō, Hōryū-ji • late 7th or early 8th century • (photographed before the 1948 fire).

74. Cloisonné-like bronze ornament · 7th century · Kegoshi Tomb, Nara Pref.

NARA PERIOD

Aoni yoshi
   Nara no miyako wa
   Saku hana no
   Niou ga gotoku
   Ima sakari nari.

Beautiful Nara!
The imperial city of Nara,
Come now to full bloom
With the brightness
Of blossoming flowers.
          Ono-no-Oyu—*Manyōshū*

The adoption and official sponsorship of Buddhism in the Asuka period by Empress Suiko and her regent, Crown Prince Shōtoku, establishing a new faith, together with the stabilization in China's affairs and the development of the great T'ang empire, had far-reaching effects upon Japan's less developed civilization. The exchange of envoys, their enthusiasm upon returning from the T'ang capital, the preaching of Chinese priests who came to Japan, and the presence of many foreign scholars and artisans, who continued to immigrate, hastened the rapid progress of Buddhism and of civil and social affairs. While the Asuka period had been influenced by Korean Buddhist art and skills, the Nara culture flourished under the impact of the great T'ang empire.

The idea of constructing a permanent capital in the likeness of the Chinese capital at Ch'ang-an was realized in 710, when the government was moved to a new site in the Yamato plain. There, over twelve hundred years ago, a large city was conceived and built in the well-organized Chinese style, a city that was to house a population of one-half million. Buddhism expanded and gathered force. Emperor Shōmu (724–48) and his Empress Kōmyō became devotees, and their ardor, instigated and fed by foreign and native priests, brought together the legacies of Shintō ideals, Buddhist doctrine, Confucian thought, and many old and new skills, blending them into a culture that was to impart an astonishing brilliance to the Nara period.

It was the desire of the sovereigns to erect in Nara a great image of the Rushana Buddha. Before doing so, however, they felt compelled to ascertain the will of the Shintō Sun Goddess enshrined at Ise. An emissary was dispatched to Ise and returned with an assuring oracle in which, we are told, the Sun Goddess declared herself one with the great Buddha. Meanwhile, the emperor himself had a vision in which the Sun Goddess appeared and identified the sun with Rushana, the Buddha of Eternal Light. Thus the foreign doctrine was reconciled with the indigenous religion, and thus was born a closely interwoven and enduring mingling of Shintō and Buddhism. The great Buddhist project of the emperor went forward under the aegis of the abiding Shintō faith and under official state sponsorship.

The idea was prodigious—to construct, in cast bronze, a gigantic image of the seated Rushana Buddha more than eighteen meters high. Space cannot be given to the history of this difficult enterprise. It was fraught with obstacles, delays, and failures. The statue that exists today (known as the Daibutsu, "Great Buddha") cannot be accepted as an expression of the original, since fires and crude repairs have altered its appearance. Yet one can sense the enormity of such an undertaking and the high level of craftsmanship that it implies. The remaining original petals of the large bronze lotus seat, intricately incised with depictions of Buddhist deities symbolizing the vastness of the kingdom of the "Unifier of the Universe," reveal some of the beauty of the original image. The huge seated figure was covered with gold, discovered in sufficient quantity in Japan at that time, and was housed in a protective "Great Buddha Hall," the Daibutsu-den. The present Daibutsu-den, a seventeenth century replacement, is about one-third smaller than the original. It cramps the image as the original building could not have done.

On the ninth day of the fourth month, 752, all Nara was astir with festive anticipation, for the time had come for the Eye Opening Ceremony. The Emperor Shōmu, who by this time had abdicated in favor of his daughter, in order to devote himself solely to the Buddhist religion, the new Empress Regnant, Kōken, the Empress Dowager Kō-myō, and Shōmu's mother, the Grand Empress Dowager, led a tremendous procession to the hall. The imperial family, numerous members of the court, and thousands of Buddhist prelates with musicians and dancers in attendance, all wearing colorful ceremonial clothing, must have made up a memorable congregation. The abdicant Shōmu, attired in imperial robes of silk and wearing the majestic crown that now lies in shattered elegance in the Shōsō-in (Pl. 87), stood on a platform some thirteen meters above the assembly, and, to complete the image and release the life within, painted in the pupils of the eyes.[1] Long, streaming silken cords, attached to the large brush he used, were held by those below, enabling them to participate in this moving ritual.

The emperor, in making the vow to construct and dedicate this image, had declared himself, as the ruler of the nation, to be the earthly counterpart of the Rushana Buddha, ruler of the universe; thus, the temple that housed the great statue, the Tōdai-ji, was the national "cathedral," the mother temple of Japan, and had a branch monastery (kokubun-ji) and nunnery (kokubun-niji) in every province.

The interest in new ideas and tendencies was not confined to religion. It permeated the life of the court, where the new and exotic was sought. An eagerness for change and improvement was a basic element in the development of Nara culture. It took the form not of mere acceptance of imports, but acted as a stimulant for domestic efforts.

Artistic expression in the Nara period had a firm foundation upon which to grow. The many Chinese and especially Korean scholars and artisans, familiar with the requirements, traditions, and working skills needed for Buddhist art, assured initial success in still somewhat unfamiliar fields, while the requirements of Buddhism itself—a fervor and zeal to offer the best for the glory of the Buddha—assured rapid advance. The foreign influences that attended Buddhism were not derived from China and Korea alone. Heritages from Byzantium, from Syria, from Mesopotamia and Persia, India, Central Asia had swept across the vast continent in the wake of tremendous migratory, military, and trade movements from east to west and from west to east. They were especially strong in the cultural life of T'ang China. Some of these influences can be recognized in the many and varied treasures of Nara.

Yet these influences alone could not have produced that exquisite, almost indefinable spirit of the time that set Nara's cultural, aesthetic flowering apart from the continental expressions. Aside from the Shintō emphasis upon sincerity and purity, the temper of Japan itself—the gentle climate of Yamato, the poignant beauty of quiet and fertile valleys, the verdant hills, the contrast of her smaller, embracing vistas as compared to the harsher vastnesses of the continental scene, the overall peaceful conditions as against the continental political turmoils—all must have had cumulative effects not only on the native Japanese but on the numerous immigrants. From surviving temples and their treasures and from the collections of the Nara National Museum this spirit still emanates, but nowhere does it radiate so convincingly as in the carefully protected and venerated Shōsō-in, discussed in the second section of this chapter.

Buddhism became increasingly a political force after Emperor Shōmu's reign. The great complex of Tōdai-ji, with its branch temples in every province, grew powerful, as did the other important temples of Nara, exerting ever stronger political pressures. During the reign of Shōmu's daughter, first as the Empress Kōken and later as the Empress Shōtoku, ecclesiastical inroads became unbearably strong. A reaction set in, but the power of the priesthood remained unbroken, and this, it is traditionally thought, may have been the reason for the removal of the capital from Nara in 784 to the environs of the present Kyoto.

The earlier half of the eighth century saw the budding and the flowering of the Nara spirit; mid century saw it at full bloom, nurtured by the spiritual exuberance of the Emperor Shōmu, the Empress Kōmyō and their daughter, Empress Kōken. The pervasive influence of the Nara spirit spread to all the provinces, distilling the Buddhistic culture throughout the land. But the heart was in Nara, and it is there that art in general, and glass in particular, rose to a new height.

GLASS IN THE NARA PERIOD

The close and frequent diplomatic and religious contacts with T'ang China, which had begun in the Asuka-Hakuhō period, not only brought many objects of superb artistry to Nara, including some glass, but provided a stimulus for more creative indigenous work and refinements in design and workmanship. It was a period when the "new" was desirable, and inquiring minds and experimenting hands developed many fresh styles and techniques.

The construction of great temples and colossal images, of which the Daibutsu is the largest, was a powerful stimulant to the arts. There was a governmental department, Zōji-no-tsukasa (Bureau of Temple Construction), for the management of government-supported temple construction, and each new temple had a temporary office of its own, a *zōbutsu-sho* (office for buddhist construction). Some of the important *zōbutsu-sho* seem to have had their own workshops, such as an *imono-no-tokoro* (casting office), or equivalent. While glass was not an essential part of Buddhist images in this period, there were numerous subsidiary uses that called for it in fine quality and considerable quantity.

Most of the temple construction offices operated only while the temple was being established, but that of Tōdai-ji, the great state temple, with its various subsidiary temples, was larger and operated longer, from 748 to 789. Being the national "cathedral" (of the Kegon sect), Tōdai-ji was under government patronage. The size, importance, and activity of the Imono-no-tokoro (Casting Office) of the Zōbutsu-sho of Tōdai-ji may be estimated by its recorded personnel in 762 or 763:

> 2 *bettō* [stewards or high commissioners]
> 1 *hangan* [junior official]
> 1 *shisei* [under official]
> 3814 *tōkō* [employees]:
> 75 *shoryo* [foremen]
> 1352 *zakkō* [skilled artisans]
> 150 *shicho* [servants]
> 2237 *yatoi-ju* [perhaps artisans working in their own localities][2]

It is not known how many of these persons were directly concerned with glass.

In addition to their own personnel, the temple workshops were at times augmented by experts loaned by government bureaus. According to documents in the Shōsō-in, experts in calligraphy, at the behest of the Empress Kōmyō, were sometimes sent by one of the government bureaus to help temple offices with the copying of Buddhist scriptures. Thus it has been suggested "that perhaps the technique of making glass at the Zōbutsu-sho was that of the Imono-no-tsukasa."[3] Many documents preserved in the Shōsō-in bear the heading "Tōdai-ji Zōbutsu-sho," or that of one of Todai-ji's subsidiary temples. The Zōbutsu-sho seem to have been concerned with the architectural construction of the temples and with furnishing all of the prerequisites for worship and services. That the standards of these offices were high and demanding may be inferred from one document in the Shōsō-in concerning the Sutra Copying Office, which discloses that any scribe making an error or an omission was fined, the amount being payable to the person making the discovery.

It may not be superfluous to examine briefly the social and economic background affecting workers in the glass industry. The official personnel list for the Imono-no-tsukasa was discussed on pages 66–67. The director was responsible for the operations of the bureau and for the registration of the workers and their families. In Japan registration was required for the allotment of land and of occupational duties, for taxation of products, and for assigning individuals to public works or military service. The industries of this time could be described as family industries, of which there were two general types.[4] One was the enterprise of a "family" of some fifty to two hundred members, which may be comparable to the small factories of modern times; these people lived at home but sent to the capital a portion of their products as "taxes in kind."[5] The other were "special industries," in which families produced entirely for the government and the imperial family, under state control. In *Ryō-no-Shūge*, in a section concerned with dyeing and weaving, workers are said to have been scattered in the provinces of Ōmi and Yamato, weaving in their homes for the government weaving bureau, with only a few actually in the office in Nara.[6] One may suppose the same, perhaps, to have been true of workers of the Imono-no-tsukasa, and especially the makers of glass beads.

The Imono-no-tsukasa controlled some of the specialized glass work. But little is known of it aside from the listings in the regulations and brief references in commentaries and fragmentary documents. For instance, *Ryō-no-Shūge* states that "Forgers and makers of weapons and various artisans who came from Kokuryŏ, Paekche, and Silla [in Korea] are assigned to this bureau."[7] Since Korea had produced glass for royal burials, for *shari* installations, and for the ornamentation of gold items, glass craftsmen must have been included among these artisans. The *Seishiroku*, a kind of peerage of Japan, compiled in 814, lists a total of 1,177 families, of which 160 were of Chinese descent, 172 of Korean descent, plus 45 of doubtful origin—a total of about thirty percent foreign born.[8] Many of these immigrants were skilled artisans and, in the "family system," passed on their trades to their Japanese descendants.

The *zakkō* (skilled craftsmen) working in the Imono-no-tsukasa seem to have been assigned to it because of their special knowledge. Those of foreign origin were given land grants and, not infrequently, titles; taxes and corvée service were remitted for a period of ten years, revealing the esteem in which they were held. For the native *zakkō*, promotion came slowly. After continuous service for eight years they might be granted a rank of the lowest (eighth) class, and every eight years thereafter could receive a further promotion, step by step. They were given a stipend twice a year. If one who had not achieved any rank committed any crime that ordinarily required punishment by exile, he was to be given, instead, "One hundred beatings with a stick for a near exile, 130 for a mediumly near exile, and 160 for a far exile, and were subject to three years of servitude at home."[9] Their status was certainly not enviable.

The still lower classes, the "servants" and "slaves," though even more miserable, were not without some chance of reward. In 715 "all servants who had served over twenty years were given promotion in recognition of their services."[10] One Hida, a slave descended from a Paekche Korean, was proficient in beadmaking. He had discovered emery powder in Yamato and used it no doubt for drilling and polishing the beads. For this he was freed from slavery, granted citizenship, and given the name

Ōtomo.[11] The record does not say whether he worked in glass or other materials, but the story discloses recognition of individual worth.

Pieces of raw glass preserved in the Shōsō-in (Pl. 76) constitute important evidence, for they corroborate details in the *Zōbutsu-sho Sakumotsuchō* mentioned below, and seem identical in substance to the glass in finished objects preserved in the Shōsō-in, thus virtually proving local manufacture.

During the middle years of the eighth century, the peak period of temple construction, glassmaking activities reached their height, and a material of refined quality was produced, as demonstrated in the examples preserved in temples and in the Shōsō-in. With the passing of the Emperor Shōmu and his immediate successors, prosperity declined and the arts withered. Few new temples arose, and even the Casting Bureau was abolished. In 774 the Imono-no-tsukasa of the government's Ōkura-shō was transferred to a newly established Takumi-ryō ("Bureau of Skilled Work").[12] Glassmaking waned and, for the next eight or nine centuries, was not to regain a similar level.

Until recently it seemed that all glass vessels in Japan that were in any way related to the Nara period were those preserved in the Shōsō-in. However, in the last few years a number of examples have been excavated at various sites. They will be referred to in appropriate contexts.

DOCUMENTARY EVIDENCE OF GLASSMAKING

The section in the *Yōrō Shokuinryō* (Personnel Regulations of the Yōrō Era) setting forth the functions and personnel of the Imono-no-tsukasa (Casting Bureau), where glass was made, shows the continuation of glassmaking in the Casting Bureau, which had been active at the time of the *Taihō Ritsuryō* of 702 and presumably for many decades before that (see pp. 65–66). In addition there is the interesting record known as the *Zōbutsu-sho Sakumotsuchō* ("Record of Things Produced in the Buddhist Construction Office") (Pl. 75). It is only one of many fragmentary documents preserved in the Shōsō-in whose texts are given in the *Dai Nihon Komonjo* ("Ancient Documents of Japan").

BEADS

In the Nara period, beads seem to have been used, as far as can be determined, not to be strung for their own sake but for the enhancement of other items. How much of this was due to their decorative charm and how much to their amuletic content cannot always be judged.

Although no longer required for tomb use, beads continued to be produced in vast quantities. The great bulk of beads surviving from this period are preserved in the Shōsō-in, or have been excavated from temple sites as *chindangu* (see p. 68). Their main characteristics are superb quality of material and great variety in shape. A published chart shows that crystal and glass were used for ten different types, amber for nine, and agate for eight.[13] Other materials, limited to special types, include gold, silver, gilt copper, jasper, jadeite, glass, obsidian, white stone, black stone, pearl, coral, ivory, deer antler, sandalwood, wood, and several nuts and seeds. The most general type, the *sashidama* ("pierced bead"), used in sixteen different materials, seems to be the same as what up to this point has been discussed as *marudama* and *kodama*. This word appears repeatedly in the Nara records, both as *ō-sashidama* and *ko-sashidama* ("large and small *sashidama*").

The terms *natsumedama* and *kirikodama* for forms known in previous periods appear in some of the Nara documents, but no examples are known to the author.

The *Zōbutsu-sho Sakumotsuchō* contains evidence that *sashidama* were made in molds. It is known from some extant examples that others were made by the coiling method and possibly by the cut-tube method. A few were blown. But most of the beads, especially those in the Shōsō-in, were so skillfully made that it is difficult from their appearance to tell which method was employed.

The committee that studied the Shōsō-in materials in 1953–54 reported a broken bead that showed, in addition to many bubbles, a series of continuous circular lines, indicating that the bead was made by the coiling process. The coiling method is easily observable in the *tombodama* of Plate 79, right. In the *Kenmotsuchō* (Deed of Gifts Dedicated to Tōdai-ji), among the items recorded as presented to the Rushana Buddha in 754, are listed 669 *futago-dama* (double, or "twin," beads), a term applied to a pair of coiled beads that were joined in the making and had not been cut apart. It seems that these *futago* beads were made by coiling, although it might have been possible to copy the shape in a molded form. No examples from this period have yet been identified.

Evidence for the productivity of glass workshops in the Nara period appears in document fragments that are preserved in the Shōsō-in, as, for example:

Tempyō 6 [734]	Received by messenger, various colored glass beads	243,590 items.
Tempyō 6 [734]	Received various colored beads	255,996 items.
Tempyō 19 [747]	Beads—2 *kan* [about 7.5 kilograms] including glass as well as gold and rock crystal.[14]	

Quantities of beads were used on crowns, both religious and imperial. They were used as *yōraku* on Buddhist utensils, as *shōgongu*, and to give solemnity as well as added beauty to imperial sashes, cloth shoes, and perhaps other accessories. *Hankyūdama* were inset in sword handles and sheaths, in furniture, in Buddhist utensils and accessories. It is no wonder that beads were delivered from the workshops in lots of several hundred thousand at a time.

Magatama

Magatama of semiprecious stones are seen in fair numbers, evidence of the continued use of this amulet in the Nara period; but the author can cite only one example in glass. Now broken, it is in the crown of the Fukūkensaku Kannon image in the Hokke-dō (Sangatsu-dō) of Tōdai-ji temple (Pl. 77).

Kudatama

Glass *kudatama* were found in the Yayoi and Tomb periods, but these are different—not long and tubular but short and somewhat irregular. There are so few, one hardly knows whether they were accidents, experiments, or imports.

Marudama AND Kodama

Marudama and *kodama* continued to be the simplest and the most numerous of the beads. However, in the hands of the skilled artisans of Nara they reached a perfection lacking in examples of the Tomb period. Their use seems unlimited; they are found adorning all sorts of apparel and objects. Often one wonders if their function had become purely ornamental. However, in the case of the tiny *kodama* of various colors, interwoven in a sash so unobtrusively as to pass undetected except by close inspection, it seems that their function must have been primarily symbolic (Pl. 5).

Tombodama

Only a few examples are preserved, from the Gangō-ji temple (Pl. 79) and in the Shōsō-in (Pl. 7). Although usually referred to by writers as *tombodama*, these Nara examples are different in appearance from those of the Tomb period. Instead of spots of color applied here and there over the body, a thread of softened glass of contrasting color was applied, encircling the bead once or twice; sometimes the second encirclement crosses over the first. A descriptive term, occasionally applied to such a technique, is *tsumiage*, a "piling up," even when the "piled up" thread sank into the soft, heated body of the bead and fused with it. In most Nara period *tombodama* the added glass is well fused in the body, but occasionally it remains in slight relief on the surface.

Tsujidama

The term *tsujidama* refers to *marudama* whose bores are intersected by extra transverse bores, permitting the stringing on threads or wires to pass in all four directions. They were thus important in constructing the more elaborate *yōraku*, making possible rather complicated designs. This type of bore occurs in a number of *tombodama*, which were used at the intersections of beadwork ornaments, as in Plate 92. The *tsujidama* are not treated here as a separate class.

Nejiredama

These "twisted beads" present another advanced step in glass manipulation. The color varies slightly from the other beads and from some of the unworked materials in the Shōsō-in. This is perhaps due to differences in the heating and handling required for pincering and twisting the glass. Usually the *nejiredama* are monochromatic, but there exists at least one in the Shōsō-in that has an irregular applied stripe of brownish purple running around the "equator" area; and still another has a narrow stripe of opaque pale green wound around it, before twisting.

Until the recent discovery of *nejiredama* at the seventh century site of the Chūgū-ji nunnery, it was thought that this bead form was developed only in the eighth century.

Tsuyudama

The *tsuyudama*, literally a "dewdrop bead," lent itself excellently to a terminal form in bead strings (Pl. 93) and in *yōraku*. New in the Asuka-Hakuhō period, it was used with increasing frequency in the Nara period.

Hankyūdama

"Hemispherical beads" seem to have been new in the Nara period. They were frequently employed as insets, as can be seen from the many inset objects in the Shōsō-in. The sutra box of Plate 78, though now in deteriorated condition, suggests the richness that the colorful insets could add to an elegant object. The fact that glass insets were used in such a way, and their combination with pearls and semiprecious stones, shows that glass was considered a "jewel."

Hiradama

Literally "flat beads," both *hiradama* and *mentoridama* ("beads having faces") were used for game pieces. Some were also found as *chindangu* (see p. 68) offerings beneath an altar of Kofuku-ji temple in Nara (Pl. 80). As they are not truly beads, since they remain unpierced, both game pieces and the Kōfuku-ji *hiradama* are treated separately here.

BLOWN GLASS BEADS

Blown glass seems to be an entirely new technique for beads. Evidence of such a process is seen in Plate 85; there are a number of these blown beads in the Shōsō-in, and fragments were found also in the altar platform of the Hōkuen-dō, Kōfuku-ji, erected in 721.[15]

INSETS

Allied to the use of beads applied to other objects is the insetting of glass *hankyūdama* and other forms in glass. Here again it is difficult to know how much of the custom was merely a decorative device. Since the sutra box of Plate 78 held sacred treasures and the scepter of Plate 95 was used for Buddhist rituals, these glass inlays may have served some ritualistic purpose. But whether the inlays on the Chinese style sword (Pl. 94) could also have been considered of spiritual value, who can say?

Chindangu

Chindangu literally means "instruments to charm the spirits of a dais" and refers to a set of dedicatory objects interred in the clay platform beneath a temple altar to appease the spirits of the soil who may have been disturbed. Sometimes *chindangu* are spoken of as "purifying the earth." Usually they occur in the form of beads (Pl. 79), pearls, mirrors, swords (Pl. 81), and other items of gold, silver, bronze, semiprecious stones, and glass. The *shari* buried under Buddhist pagodas in pre-Nara times were usually accompanied by similar objects.

To the *chindangu* practice, which flourished at this time, is due the preservation of many treasures that further illustrate the quality of glass manufacture during the Nara period.

VESSELS

The installation of *shari* beneath the foundation, or in the foundation pillar, of Buddhist pagodas, was general during the Asuka-Hakuhō period. In the Nara period the practice seems to have almost died out. There is only one Japanese instance for this period, the installation found at the pagoda site of the Sūfuku-ji temple (Pl. 6). Another *shari-tsubo* was brought from China by a priest, Ganjin (Chien-chen), in 734 (Pl. 82). The contrast between this and the thick-walled Japanese examples is striking.

A glass vessel that has only recently come to the attention of scholars is a gourd-shaped bottle about 37.4 centimeters high purportedly excavated about 1932 from a grave in Fukuoka Prefecture in northern Kyushu.[16] The nearly transparent soda-lime glass is weathered, with the upper part broken and repaired.[17] On the basis of similarity with other gourd forms of the Sui and T'ang dynasties, a foreign provenance has been suggested.

A brown glass bottle, 14.5 centimeters high, is cited as of Japanese origin; by inference it has been assigned to the Nara period.[18] It was found a few years ago in Shiga Prefecture, and its mouth-rim is related to the piece in Plate 6. The author has had no opportunity to see either of these.

Other examples are the six famous glass vessels in the Shōsō-in, five of which present no evidence of domestic origin; one, at least, must have come from Iran. In addition, a few fragments of glass vessels have been found in the "debris" of the Shōsō-in.

Tōsu

Tōsu are small knives and other small implements fitted with sheaths so they could be worn suspended from the belt. There are many in the Shōsō-in. Some are inlaid with glass *hankyūdama*, but the examples in Plate 83 are different; the hilts are entirely of glass, ground to shape. This grinding of a special shape from a block of glass, even if this form was first roughly shaped in a mold, is a new departure.

THE SHŌSŌ-IN

THE Shōsō-in is an unique and precious monument to the Emperor Shōmu, treasured and inviolate for over twelve hundred years. The abdicant emperor died in the fifth month of the year 756. He was the first sovereign to be cremated and the first to be buried with Buddhist, not Shintō, rituals. The funeral ceremony accorded him was as expansive and expressive of the time as had been the Eye Opening Ceremony of the great Rushana Buddha image.

On the forty-ninth day after his death, an all-important Buddhist anniversary, elaborate ceremonies took place, carefully planned by the Dowager Empress Kōmyō, who proclaimed: "Each day my grief grows deeper and sadness weighs ever heavier on my heart. To supplicate the earth or to cry out to Heaven brings me no solace. I have therefore resolved, by the performance of good deeds, to give succour to his august Spirit. To this end, and in obedience to the will of his late Majesty, these his relics, . . . that in truth are National Treasures, I donate to the Tōdai-ji by way of an offering to the Buddha Vairocana, for the repose of the Emperor's soul. . . ."[19]

The quotation is taken from the preamble to a deed of gift known as the *Kenmotsuchō* ("Record of Things Offered"), which is preserved in the Shōsō-in.[20] It contains a long descriptive inventory of the gifts, is stamped with nearly five hundred imperial seals, and carries the witnessing signatures of five court officials, together with the date. In conclusion it contains a passage to the effect that all these things were either treasures that had been handled by the deceased emperor abdicant or utensils that had served him in the palace. To the original gift were added numerous individual gifts dedicated to the same purpose by various members of the court.

The collection was housed in two log-cabin style storehouses of Tōdai-ji, which were then known as *sōsō* ("pair of repositories"), a name that later became Shōsō-in ("Chief Repository"). The date of the original *sōsō* is uncertain. Some think they may date from the establishment of Tōdai-ji, when the Great Buddha image was created; others that they were built especially to receive the imperial gift of 756.

The Shōsō-in proper, now known as the Shōsō, is a three-part building about 33.2 meters long, with an overall height of 13.9 meters (Pl. 84). Its three rooms rest upon forty stout pillars rising about nine feet above ground. A single massive tiled roof with bronze fittings covers the whole. There is also difference of opinion as to when the third room and the roof were added to the original two storehouses. Those two units still stand intact, as the north and south parts, displaying on the exterior three of their four outside walls, which were constructed of log sections of cypress wood with the ends of the triangular wedge-shaped timbers interlacing alternately and projecting where they meet at the corners. The outer walls of the central room, however, are of plain boards instead of logs, filling the space between the two log units. This is the chief argument for a later date for this central unit. It is known that in 950, when two similar storehouses of the Kensaku-in of Tōdai-ji were damaged in a storm, their contents were brought to the Shōsō-in and stored in the South Section. But whether this Middle Section was constructed at that time, or whether it had existed before, is not known. At any rate, from at least 950 the three sections were treated differently. The North and Middle sections, presumably containing only the dedicated gifts, were under the jurisdiction of the Imperial Household and were continuously sealed by the emperor's signature, while the South Section, containing the material brought from the Kensaku-in, was under the control of, and sealed by, the three highest ranking priests of Tōdai-ji. This distinction continued until 1894, when the entire Shōsō-in came under the charge of the Imperial Household. At present it is administered by the Imperial Household Agency, a quasi-independent bureau of the Prime Minister's Office.

In 1880 "some cases with shelves were constructed." In 1882 "shelves were completed and objects arranged on them and catalogued; in the same year imperial sanction was given for the annual opening of the treasury." In 1892 "A bureau was established for the purpose of arranging in order the Imperial Treasure of the Shōsō-in." In 1894, following an offer by Tōdai-ji, the South Section "was completely taken over by the Imperial Household Department."[21] The bureau was not abolished until 1905, and it is conceivable that between 1894 and 1905 the South Section also underwent thorough inspection and rearrangement.

Ordinarily there was no access to the Shōsō-in, but at the special times of opening, a high platform with central steps was erected across the front of the building. In the past, openings were infrequent and sporadic, but from the Meiji era annual airings took place in the dry autumn season. Inspections were made, investigations undertaken, and any necessary steps taken for preservation. Until 1962, for a period of three days during this interval, persons fortunate enough to receive permits were free to spend one of those three days among the Shōsō-in treasures.

There are two floors in each of the three sections. Except during the short openings the objects were kept in the cases and were shrouded with white material. Each section had one entrance and no windows. Hence, it was always necessary to carry a strong flashlight to inspect the objects closely. However, in recent years, for some two weeks during the airing period, a varying selection of treasures has been on public display in the Nara National Museum.

Whether by intent or coincidence, the log construction of the buildings provided superb atmospheric conditions within, for in dry weather the timbers shrink sufficiently to admit a gentle inflow of dry air and in wet weather they expand, shutting out moisture. This, together with devoted care over the centuries, preserved the treasures well.

However, the construction that had been contributing, for centuries, to the excellent preservation of the contents, in modern times endangered them since, with the relatively free flow of air, car exhaust and other forms of pollution gained easy admittance. So critical was the situation that two reinforced concrete buildings, with controlled air, now house the treasures and the old Shōsō has become an empty monument.

Each of the three doors of the Shōsō was locked with a large and ancient key. Over the lock was the signature of the reigning emperor, wrapped tightly in coverings of paper and bamboo and wound securely with yards of heavy cord; to this was added, on the outside, the signature of the imperial messenger who was always present at openings and closings, and over all was placed a protective wooden boxlike cover. No attempt to desecrate this imperial sealing has been known. On two occasions, however, thieves did break into the building by burning or cutting a hole in the floor.

For the autumn airings, the imperial envoy came from Tokyo and in a private, silent, and moving ritual, attended by a small group of officials, removed and inspected the signatures for any signs of tampering, placed them in a black lacquer box bearing the golden imperial chrysanthemum crest, which was then wrapped in royal purple silk, and the envoy returned to Tokyo to present them to the emperor. When the Shōsō-in was officially closed again, at the end of the airing period, the envoy returned with new signatures and the ritual proceeded in reverse, resealing the building for another year.

The removal of any object from the Shōsō-in, and often its later return, were meticulously noted. Furthermore, nothing has ever been discarded, and some 150 wooden chests were made to receive damaged or separated items, even "dust" from disintegrating textiles and from broken glass.

Elsewhere ancient treasures have been recovered by excavations, whereas only in Japan were they preserved, from emperor to emperor, as an imperial heritage. This is the uniqueness of the Shōsō-in.

Aside from their intrinsic worth, the collections in the Shōsō-in have many interesting facets: some are undoubtedly of foreign, even far distant, origins, and others show foreign influences, while still others are unmistakably local products. It was long considered that a large majority were direct imports from abroad; a frequent expression in older writings (particularly in respect to glass) has been that "of course at that time such fine things could not have been made in Japan!" As more scholarly and scientific investigations are undertaken, it is becoming increasingly clear that many more objects were made in Nara than had previously been thought possible. Nevertheless, it must be remembered that numerous craftsmen of foreign birth or foreign descent were active in the Nara workshops, bringing talents from the highly developed cultures of the continent. Then, too, Japan's diplomatic relations in eastern Asia must not be forgotten— with the Korean peninsula, with P'o-hai, north of Korea, and with China. Furthermore, to the Chinese capital at Ch'ang-an came envoys, and goods, from Central Asia, Persia, and other Asian countries, for China was the eastern terminus of the Silk Road. Many of the items in the Shōsō-in may easily have been secured in Ch'ang-an by exchange, or have come as gifts from diplomatic or religious envoys, or from returning Japanese, or come as trade in Korean ships from China. There were, however, also the steady cultural developments in Japan, many of which had little to do with foreign imports, except as some provided the original stimuli.

Datings, or attributions of origin, are difficult for some of the Shōsō-in treasures, excepting those listed in the various *kenmotsuchō* and those that bear identifying labels. Presumably the contents of the North Section represent the original gift, but some of the treasures brought from the Kensaku-in in 950 (the original list has been lost) and thought (or probably at the time *known*) to have been associated with the emperor were removed to the imperially sealed sections; so there is some confusion about a number of items. The *Nansō-Gyōbutsu Mokuroku* inventory of 1117 mentions the removal of some Kensaku-in items to the imperially sealed sections. "Thus, offerings of the people to the Daibutsu came to be mixed in the Repository with those of the imperial families."[22]

One cannot understand the eighth century Shōsō-in without some inkling of the nature and range of its contents. No one knows the total number of objects preserved, for, although far over five thousand items have been counted, many of these "items" consist of large groups of objects, such as "eighty bundles of arrows" including 2,187 well-made arrows; or "twenty-nine quivers," which contain 1,516 equally fine arrows. In addition, there are items not even noted in the shelf list, such as thousands of glass beads. The categories are too numerous to list in toto, but among them are floor coverings, low tables and stands, chests and boxes of all sorts, braziers, mirrors, swords, spears, bows and arrows, Buddhist utensils and robes, censers, rosaries, receptacles for flower-scattering, banners, costumes, crowns, girdles and girdle ornaments, shoes, saddles, luxurious walking sticks, musical instruments of various kinds, screens, armrests, brocade pillows, writing materials, cherished examples of handwriting, incense and fragrant woods, medicines and drugs (roots, stalks, buds, flowers, seeds, minerals, bones), masks for exotic dances, scepters, game boards and equipment, tools, dishes, ewers, paintings on hempen cloth, and textiles of silk, hemp, linen, and gauze variously woven, dyed, embroidered or braided. Many crafts are represented: metalwork of many types, weaving, cabinetwork and marquetry, lacquer, intricate inlays, basketry, ivory, papermaking (much of it patterned), carvings, and glass. In some instances tools and materials attest local manufacture. Many items seem undeniably foreign, and even many local products show foreign influences in details of form and in exotic materials from abroad. Supplies of some of these materials are preserved; for instance, rhinoceros horn, cinnabar, and fragrant woods.

Among all this array glass is somewhat prominent, either in its own right or as decorative addition to objects of other materials, and one may perceive a striking advance in the knowledge and appreciation of glass and in the skill of its manufacture.

GLASS IN THE SHŌSŌ-IN

It would be difficult to estimate the number of items in the Shōsō-in that are either made of glass or have glass attached or inlaid. An attempt has been made to select such examples as are representative of the quality, variety, and uses of glass at the Nara court. These, it is true, represent only a small portion of the vast treasure, and yet clearly indicate the high place held by glass in this period. Often the selected items or groups of items are merely representative of many similar examples stowed away in chests (as, for example, the stock of some seventy-five thousand large beads, which were still unused at the time of placement in the Shōsō-in.)

The glasses of the Shōsō-in were thoroughly investigated by a committee of four specialists[23] who worked during the airing periods of 1959, 1960, and 1961. It has been possible to quote, where appropriate, from their report and from the findings of an earlier (1953–54) and larger committee appointed to study the various substances that appear in the treasures. The earlier committee reported finding glass of little or no lead content (Sp. Grav. 2.50–2.60) and glass of high lead content estimated in some cases at over seventy percent.[24] Some of these studies confirm data set forth in the *Zōbutsu-sho Sakumotsuchō*, discussed in Plate Note *75*.

BEADS

In addition to hundreds of glass beads that ornament other objects, there are an estimated seventy-five thousand beautifully formed and perfectly preserved large glass beads of several types strung together in some 250 strings of from one hundred to three hundred beads each; a very few of these beads represent items that have been investigated and classified according to shape, use, and quality.[25] In addition, there are two chests of glass "debris."

The beads include a few blue ones of soda-lime glass (Sp. Grav. 2.47) and, in much greater quantity and in other colors, lead glass (Sp. Grav. to 5.55) with lead content estimated as just above or below seventy percent.[26] Beads were not only cast in molds, according to the *Zōbutsu-sho Sakumotsuchō*, but also coiled and blown. Among other evidence, the high lead content, not known in the West and higher than that of China, places the origin of such pieces in Japan. The high quality of the glass and skill in forming the beads of the Shōsō-in are so notable that it must be assumed that the official Imonono-tsukasa commanded the cream of the skilled workers of the country.

The differing types of beads include what are now called *kudatama* (a few only), *marudama* and *kodama*, *tombodama*, *tsuyudama*, and *nejiredama*, together with *hiradama* (as in game pieces) and *hankyūdama* (for insets). Truly colorless transparent beads are noticeably few. The paucity of truly colorless beads is considered due to 1) impurities in the raw materials; 2) poor pulverization; and 3) lack of knowledge in the use of decolorizing methods. For these reasons the authors of *Shōsō-in no Garasu* (*SnG*) propose (p. *53*) that the few colorless examples may have been imports. However, too little is known about contemporaneous continental beads. Colorless beads are not mentioned in the *Zōbutsusho Sakumotsuchō*.

Red seems lacking except as an opaque reddish brown in some of the beads with intersecting bores. It was evidently impossible at that time to produce a clear red, and as a substitute *kirinketsu* was painted on the surface of some yellow beads when red was called for. Dark purplish blue, very common in the Tomb period, seems to have disappeared except for a few *marudama* in rosaries and several tiny *kodama* and small *kudatama*. The authors of *Shōsō-in no Garasu* (*SnG*) point out (p. *56*) that the components of the blue soda-lime glass differ from those of all other types, indicating recognition by the Nara glassmakers of the difficulty of obtaining this color in lead glass, thus revealing the high level of their technical skill.

Colors, specific gravities, and chemical ingredients of Shōsō-in beads of eleven classifications are given in *SnG*, Chart 3, page *55*. Qualities range from transparency through translucency to a rare opacity in "white" ones. The "opacity" of these beads is considered due to numerous unmelted quartz crystals; further, ten percent lime may have been added purposely to both the white and green "opaque" beads. The glass is rich and handsome. Colorless, transparent beads from the ceremonial crowns are considered imports.

Certain larger beads, a quasi-*tsuyudama* shape (Sup. N. 44), in a way suggest the thirty-nine *magatama* of the Ōtani Tomb (Pl. 52). It has been proposed that the larger *tsuyudama* may have been attached to curtains as weights.[27]

There are various examples of blown glass ornaments among the loose fragments of "broken beads" that were removed for investigation. No doubt there may be still others associated with other objects and unrecognized in the dim light of the Shōsō-in. At present the examples known are too few to draw any conclusions as to the extent to which the glassblowing technique was used in producing these small items, which to all intents and purposes resemble beads but are in reality hollow spheres with no bore but an open mouth.

The hundreds of thousands of glass beads from Nara workshops found varied uses both at court and in the temples. The two bead-decorated brooms (Pl. 86) for ceremonial use by the empress during the New Year season were in imitation of a Chinese ritual. But would such a broom have been embellished with small glass beads in China? Or is this strictly a Japanese idea? The ritual apparently did not fit into the Japanese way of life, for there seems to be no later evidence for either ritual or broom. *Yōraku* of glass beads strung on silver wire were found in the seventh century and occur in a number of instances in the Shōsō-in. In many of the bronze banners beads were impaled on projecting spikes (Pls. 90, 91). Beads are also found as decorations in ceremonial crowns (Pl. 87) and wearing apparel (Pls. 5, 93; Sup. N. 45).

INSETS

Insets of glass *hankyūdama* were also used profusely. These are of the same high quality as the beads. Their decorative use occurs either as single insets or as sets in elaborate designs worked in precious metals or other materials (Pls. 78, 94–97). The inclusion of such insets primarily on Buddhist sacred objects again speaks of the value and esteem held for glass.

GAME PIECES

In the Shōsō-in there are a number of game boards of handsome inlaid work, as well as counters, ivory dice, and an elegant dice shaker (Pl. 98). Glass *hiradama* were used as game pieces of especially fine quality. Only a few are illustrated in Plate 98, and since they are shown with the much larger equipment for the game, their unusual beauty is not obvious.

SASH ACCESSORIES

Just as the Japanese government had been organized along Chinese lines, so were certain ceremonial court costumes of this time strongly influenced by Chinese practices. One such practice determined some of the accessories that were worn suspended from the sash. There is the Chinese-style jeweled sword slung by cords from a girdle (Pl. 94), but smaller items were also worn from the waist, such as the small sheathed knives of Plate 99, the fish-shaped tallies of Plate 8, and the small linear measures of Plate 100.

In China fish tallies are said to have denoted rank and served for identification when the wearer visited the palace. They were made in pairs, one being retained at the palace. Since the custom seems never to have been practiced in Japan or was not "taken up," these fish forms were merely worn for their ornamental and exotic appeal.[28]

Jiku-tan

Jiku refers to the rod to which the inner end of a long manuscript or painting on silk or paper is attached so that it may be rolled up as a scroll; it includes the two ornamental cappings known as *jiku-tan* ("*jiku* ends"). The rod itself is usually, if not always, of wood; to it the left end of a horizontal scroll, or the lower end of a vertical scroll, is attached (Pl. 101). In Japan, the *jiku-tan* project out beyond the scroll's edges and thus not only serve a decorative purpose but a more practical one as handgrasps in rolling the scroll. *Jiku-tan* may be of any material—wood, ceramic, ivory, glass, semiprecious stones. Some are rather plain in shape; others flare out at the outer end. They may also be of various colors and qualities, and may even be decorated, as with lacquer. In the Nara period, when there was as yet no demand for scroll paintings, *jiku* were used for Buddhist sutras and important records (such as the *Kenmotsuchō* of the Shōsō-in dedications), which at that time, before the development of the book form, were in the nature of handwritten scrolls.

The need for their manufacture was great. The great Buddhist activity, not only in Nara but in all the branch temples throughout the country, required large numbers of scrolls. It is said that in the middle of the eighth century the Sutra Copying Office at Tōdai-ji turned out about one thousand scrolls per month, embracing about thirteen thousand books of the sacred scriptures. This would require some two thousand *jiku-tan* per month, of which only a relatively small number, however, must have been of glass.

The document fragments preserved in the Shōsō-in contain numerous references to both *jiku* and *jiku-tan* in relation to the Sutra Copying Bureau and the temple offices. These often read "received from the Casting Bureau," or "transferred to the Zōbutsu-sho." Many of the *jiku* are described as of pear wood, white wood, or black persimmon wood; some references mention glass *jiku-tan*. One records "gem *jiku*" as "received and kept," including "sixty-seven light blue, sixty-four deep blue, twenty-six deep green, seventeen black, fifteen red, eight white." The red may have been of some other material, but at least the blues and greens may have been of glass. This particular group was received from the administration office on the seventeenth day of the month, and there is a notation to the effect that they were "already returned before the first day of the month"; perhaps one may assume that the *jiku* had been received by the Sutra Copying

Office for the completion of sutra scrolls, and when this was accomplished, in less than two weeks, the completed scrolls were sent back to the administration office and a "returned" notation added to the original record of receipt.[29]

VESSELS

Most widely known of the glass preserved in the Shōsō-in are six glass vessels of varying shapes, sizes, and techniques (Pls. 9–11, 16, 105, 108). Much has been said and written about their probable origins, but, for the most part, theories of their sources, and even dates, remain rather tentative. Full discussion of each will be found in the Notes. One of the six Shōsō-in glass vessels is of later date (Pl. 16).

One other item, known only from a documentary source, is a "large windbell of dark blue glass," whose apparent removal (?) was officially recorded in a document fragment referring to the twelfth day of the sixth month of some unknown year.[30]

The fact that the types and the shapes of the vessels in the Shōsō-in are isolated examples, that nothing like them, either intact or fragmentary, is so far known in later years in Japan, seems in itself to point to a foreign source. For, if Japanese glassmakers had achieved such sophisticated work, one wonders how they could have refrained from continuing to create them. After the death of the Emperor Shōmu the building of new temples in Nara declined and the great activity in the craft gradually diminished by 774; even the official casting bureau, where glass was made, was absorbed by another bureau. However, the many references to glass vessels in the literature of the Heian period seem to indicate a domestic source either in the Nara period (from which they would have been survivals but probably less elegant than the Shōsō-in examples) or in the Heian period. Archaeological excavations and scholarly research may substantiate some instances of local manufacture or definitely corroborate importation.

CLOISONNÉ

The Japanese term *shippō* refers in modern times to true cloisonné. But its use in the literature of ancient Japan is ambiguous, as is that of *ruri* (glass). Often the two seem to have been interchangeable. Therefore, it seems convenient to borrow the Western terms "cloisonné" and "cloison" to denote a method of glass ornamentation that suggests cloisonné.

An incipient cloisonné-like glass ornament was first noted for the seventh century (Pl. 74). The example in the Shōsō-in (Pl. 12) is much more sophisticated, but in some specific ways related. For instance, the size and gilding of the "cloisons" are identical in the two pieces. Also, the glass of the ornament was clearly flowed into the petal compartments of the flower design from a molten glass source, as manifest in two minute peaks left on the surface when the source was withdrawn before the cooling glass could completely sink into the glass already flowed in. In the mirror there is no such visible evidence; however, since fairly thin sheet silver (0.05 centimeter thick) comprises the foundation of the design units, the gradual flowing in of molten glass—rather than heating the entire unit sufficiently to melt pieces of glass or glass powder—would have lessened the possibility of melting the thin silver in the process.

This mirror is outstanding proof of the technological advance achieved in the Nara period and of deeper understanding of glass potentials.

1. For a detailed description in English of this ceremony, see Sir Percival David, "The Shōsō-in," *Transactions and Proceedings of The Japan Society*, London, XXVIII, 1932, pp. 19–20.
2. Takeshi Kobayashi, *Nihon Chōkoku* [Japanese Sculpture], Nihon Rekishi Suisho [New Treaties on Japanese History], Tokyo, 1960, p. 29.
3. *Takigawa, "Imono-no-tsukasa. . . . ," p. 11.
4. Goichi Sawada, *Nara-chō Jidai Minsei Keizai no Suteki Kenkyū* [Study of Civil Administration and Economics in the Nara Period], Tokyo, 1927, pp. 575ff.
5. According to a record in the *Engishiki*, III, Section "*Rinji-sai*" (special festivals for which no fixed dates are set), *Koji Ruien* (n. 7, p. 72), Sangyō-bu, I, in Vol. 40, p. 614, beadmakers of Izumo (modern Shimane Prefecture) are examples of this. For reference to artisan groups working in their own provinces, see Tsuchiya, *op. cit.*, (n. 6, p. 62), p. 52f.
6. *Takigawa, *op. cit.*, p. 24.
7. *Ryō-no-Shūge*, *op. cit.* (see n. 3, p. 45), IV (Personnel).
8. Aston, *Nihongi*, *op. cit.* (see n. 1, p. 45), II, p. 133, n. 1.
9. *Takigawa, *op. cit.*, p. 7.
10. *Shoku Nihongi* [Continuation of the *Nihongi*], *TASJ*, Second Series, XIV, June 1937, p. 270 (J. B. Snellen, tr.)
11. *Takigawa, *op. cit.*, p. 7, quoting *Shoku Nihongi*, entry of Tempyō 15 (743).
12. The record is quoted by Kiyonori Konakamura, *Nihon Kanshoku Seido Enkakushi* [History of the Development of Japanese Governmental Organization], Tokyo, Benkyōdo, 1901, p. 139.
13. *Ishida, *The Use and Variety of "Tama". . . . ,* Table I, opp. p. 3.
14. *DNK, I, pp. 574, 577; II, p. 646.
15. *Oda, "Nara Jidai no Garasu. . . . ," p. 23.
16. *Umehara, "Arata ni Shirareta Furui. . . . ," pp. 29–30.
17. *Umehara, "Arata ni Shirareta Kodai. . . . ," p. 8, citing Kazuo Yamasaki's examination of a fragment.
18. *Umehara, "*Shinshutsudo Hari-ki*. . . . ," pp. 4–5.
19. David, *The Shōsō-in*, *op. cit.* (see n. 1), p. 28.
20. There are later supplementary *Kenmotsuchō* also, but they are usually referred to by some modifying phrase. "The *Kenmotsuchō*" refers herein to the original Deed of Gift.
21. *ECTS, p. 180.
22. *Ibid.*, p. 6.
23. The four members were Dr. Yoshito Harada, Emeritus Professor of Archaeology, Tokyo University; Mr. Jō Okada, then Chief Curator of Tokyo National Museum; Dr. Kazuo Yamasaki, Institute of Inorganic Chemistry, Nagoya University; and Mr. Kōzō Kagami, President of the Kagami Crystal Glassworks, Tokyo. Their official report is titled *Shōsō-in no Garasu, herein abbreviated to SnG.
24. Their report *Shōwa Ni-jū-hachi Ni-jū-kyu Sanjū Nendo. . . . , herein abbreviated to SGZC.
25. *SGZC, pp. 75–81; and especially the more recent *SnG.
26. *Asahina and Oda, "Shōsō-in Hagyoku. . . . ," p. 2, Table 1.
27. *SnG, p. 24.
28. *DNK, XIII, p. 248.
29. *Ibid.*, XXV, Supplement, p. 146.

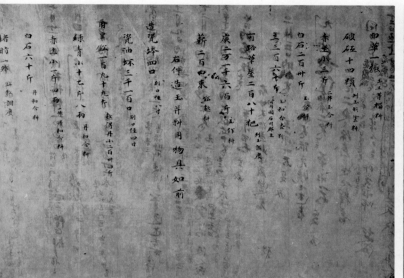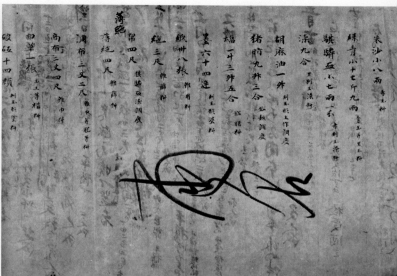

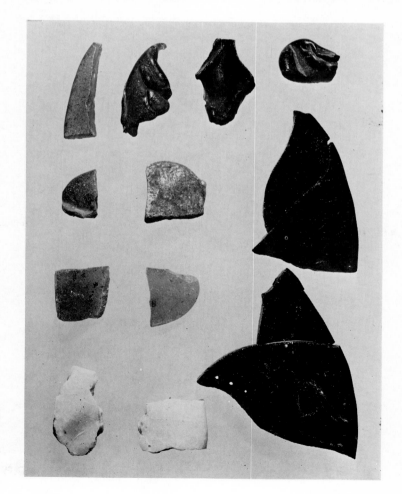

75. *Zōbutsu-cho Sakumotsuchō* • 8th century •
Shōsō-in.

76. Fragments of unworked glass • 8th century • Shōsō-in.

77. Crown of a Fukūkensaku Kannon image · mid 8th century · Hokke-dō, Tōdai-ji, Nara.

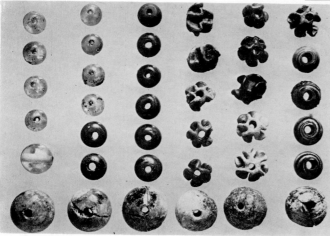

78. Sutra chest inset with glass and pearls • 8th century • glass, D. 0.7 cm.

79. *Chindangu* • 8th century • Gangō-ji, Nara Pref.

80. *Hiradama* from *chindangu* • 8th century • Kōfuku-ji, Nara Pref. • D. 1.1–1.5 cm.

81. Sword hilt fragment from *chindangu* • 8th century • Tōdai-ji, Nara Pref.

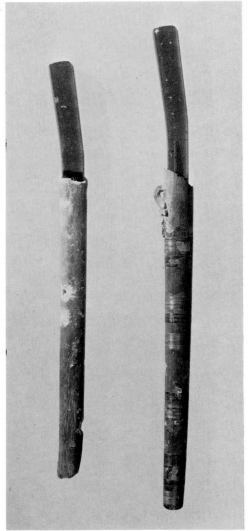

82. *Shari-tsubo* brought from China · T'ang dynasty (?) · H. 9.2 cm.

83. *Tōsu* with glass hilts · 8th century · max. L. 21.1 cm.

84. The Shōsō-in, Nara.

85. Glass remains from the "debris" • 8th century • Shōsō-in.

86. Ceremonial broom with glass beads • mid 8th century • Shōsō-in • H. 65.0 cm.

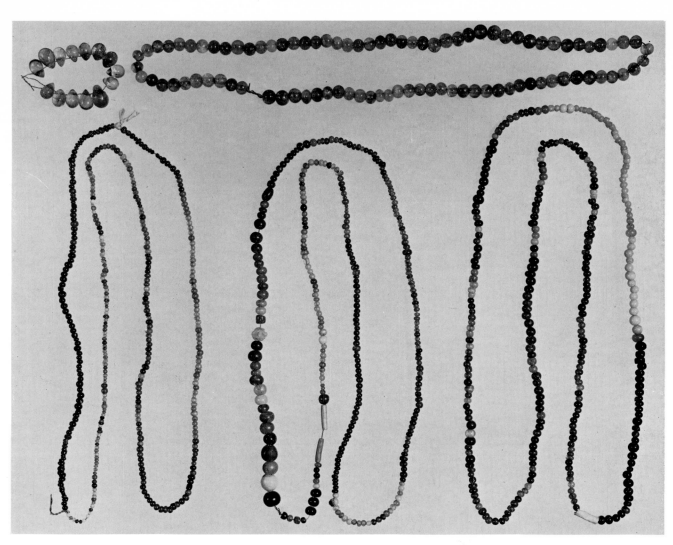

87. Beads from imperial crowns · mid 8th century · Shōsō-in.
88. Gilt-silver platter · probably 8th century · Shōsō-in · D. 61.5 cm.

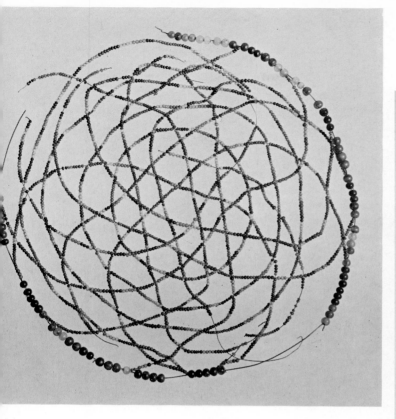

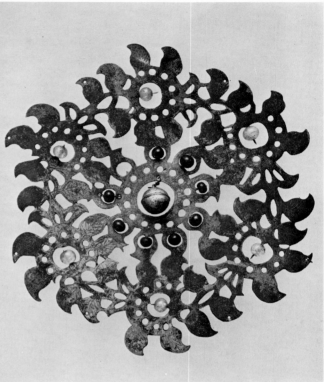

89. Flower basket • 8th century • Shōsō-in • D. *ca.* 36.0 cm.

90. Plaque with apricot-leaf pattern • 8th century • Shōsō-in. • D. 30.2 cm.

91. Plaque with impaled beads • 8th century • Shōsō-in.

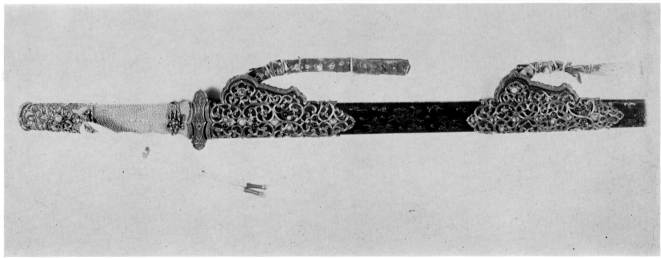

92. Beads strung on silver wire · 8th century · Shōsō-in.

93. Sash decorated with beads · 8th century · Shōsō-in · W. 6.5–7.0 cm.

94. Chinese style sword · 8th century · Shōsō-in · 98.0 cm.

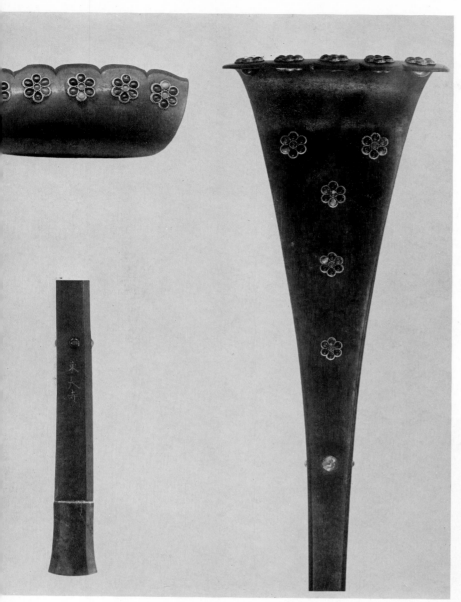

95. *Nyoi* (ceremonial scepter) • 8th century • Shōsō-in • L. 77.0 cm.
96. Handled censer • 8th century • Shōsō-in • L. 39.5 cm.

97. Yellow brass receptacle · Chinese (?) · 8th century · Shōsō-in · H. 15.9 cm.
98. *Sugoroku* set · 8th century · Shōsō-in · counters, D. 1.4 cm.

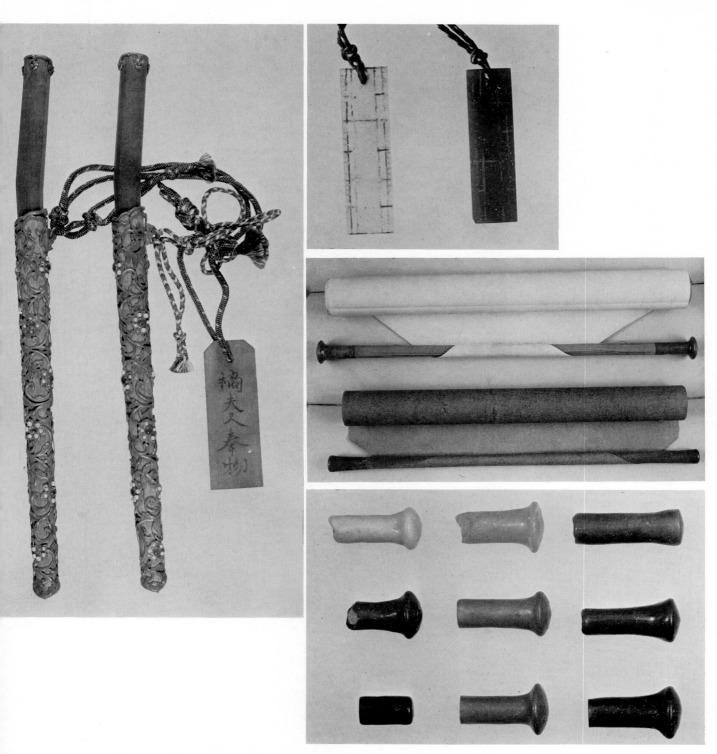

99. Pair of *tōsu* · 8th century · Shōsō-in · L. 23.0 cm.

100. Small linear measures · 8th century · Shōsō-in · max. L. 6.95 cm.

101. *Jiku* and method of attaching scroll · 8th century · Shōsō-in · 30.0 cm.

102. *Jiku-tan* fragments · 8th century · Shōsō-in.

103. Ewer, top and bottom (see Pl. 9).
104. Ewer • Nehawend, Iran • H. 16.5 cm.

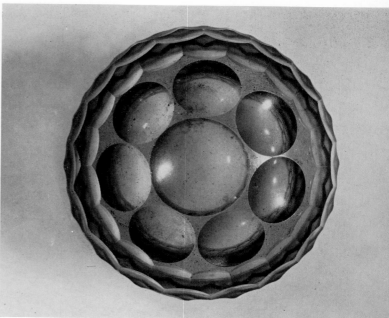

105. Cut glass bowl • Sassanian • 4th to 6th century • Shōsō-in • H. 8.5 cm.
106. Cut glass bowl • Sassanian • 5th or 6th century • H. 8.2 cm.

107. Twelve-lobed bowl, side view (see Pl. 10).

108. Footed vessel · Chinese (?) · 8th century (?) · Shōsō-in · H. 10.5 cm.

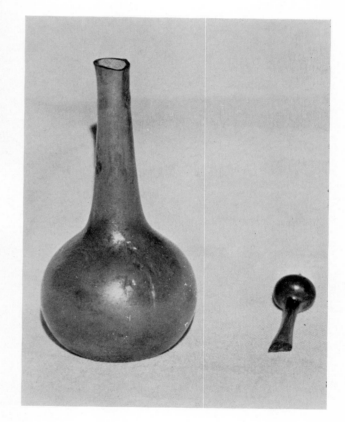

109. Yellow green cup in shrine • Korean • late 7th century • Songyim-sa temple • D. 8.1 cm. (see Pl. N. 11).

110. *Shari-yōki* • Korean • late 7th century • Songyim-sa temple • H. 6.3 cm. (see Pl. N. 11).

111. Vessel • probably Korean • 7th century • Sōbong-chong tomb (see Pl. N. 11).

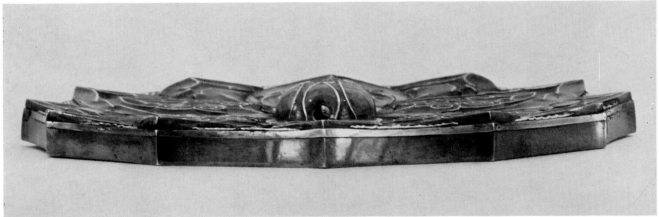

112. Bowl · probably Korean · 7th century · Kumyong-chong tomb (see Pl. N. 11).
113. Cloisonné-backed mirror, profile (see Pl. 12).

HEIAN PERIOD

ONE OF THE CHIEF reasons for the removal of the capital from Nara was the growing arrogance of the priesthood, which first became noticeable in the reign of Empress Kōken. In 784 the Emperor Kanmu removed the court to Nagaoka, near the present site of Kyoto, and started construction for a new capital; but after ten years, and before the buildings were completed, plans were suddenly cancelled and the site abandoned, apparently for circumstances thought to cast an evil influence upon the site. In 794 the capital was removed to an entirely new site nearby, and a new epoch, the Heian period, began.

The blossoming at Nara had lasted for less than a century. Then, except for the temples and temple activity, the old capital became but a ghost of its former self, though nostalgia for it lingered on, as evidenced in some poems in the *Manyōshū*. Although its glory was brief, the city has never lost its hold upon the hearts of the people, even to modern times.

The new capital, Heian-kyō ("Capital of Peace"), later known as Kyōto, was laid out according to the Chinese grid system, with the imperial palace as its heart. The situation was ideal, with protective mountains on the north (whence evil influences were thought to approach) continuing south on the east and west, thus enclosing the valley on three sides. Southward the valley broadened out, its several rivers joining in the Yodogawa, which empties into the eastern end of the Inland Sea at Naniwa (modern Osaka). It was an auspicious site from a geomantic point of view; the river provided easy access to the sea; and beyond that, it was beautiful. Here Emperor Kanmu established a capital that, as Miyako or Kyoto, was to remain the imperial seat for over a thousand years and that is still the cultural center of Japan.

Contacts with Korea were less close than they had been. Official relations with China continued during the early decades of the Heian period but they became chiefly religious and economic rather than diplomatic, and, as conditions in China became more and more disrupted, contacts declined still further. Meanwhile the Japanese had come to realize, officially, that many of the Chinese organizational methods they had welcomed so eagerly and incorporated in their official codes were, in many ways, not applicable to local conditions, and, as a result, supplemental regulations and interpretations of the laws continued to appear. However, the firm foundations of the past three centuries of assimilation of Chinese culture remained, Chinese learning was still highly respected, and Chinese objects admired and sought after; but the Japanese temperament gradually discarded many of the imported ways, and during the latter two centuries of the Heian period—referred to as the Fujiwara era because of the political domination of the Fujiwara family—asserted itself to the extent that all phases of life became increasingly enveloped in an aura that was distinctly Japanese but with persisting continental accents. This Heian environment provided fertile soil for creative expression freed from outside influence. Art production was prolific, pervaded in the ninth century by elements from the new, rather stern and exotic Buddhism brought from the continent, but in the tenth, eleventh, and twelfth centuries by the gentle qualities of the Japanese temperament.

One of the Buddhist priests of Nara, Saichō (Dengyō Daishi), had withdrawn in protest against the corrupt political practices into which the Nara temples had fallen, and established himself on Mt. Hiei, the commanding northeastern peak in the mountain ranges encircling the Heian-kyō valley. During a sojourn in China, he became imbued with the tenets of the new Chinese T'ien-t'ai Buddhist doctrine, which sought to syncretize the essential elements of different sects. This was entirely acceptable to the Japanese nature, which had already evinced its tolerant character in welcoming Buddhism and harmonizing it with the native Shintō. When Saichō returned he founded the Japanese Tendai sect, at his own site on Mt. Hiei; as Enryaku-ji, the temple grew to be a powerful Buddhist center and the fountainhead of a number of modified sects. Saichō emphasized the necessity of meditation and of long ascetic discipline for the attainment of wisdom and salvation, and was largely responsible for the movement that took Buddhist temples away from the cities into the peace and quiet of the mountains.

Another revered priest, Kūkai, known by his posthumous name, Kōbō Daishi, also went to China, and returned to found another branch, the Shingon (True Word) Sect. While on the continent he had come under the influence of a somewhat different type of Buddhism, a complex system based on secret formulae and rites. The esoteric Shingon faith centered in the majestic concept of Dainichi (Vairocana), Lord of the Universe and source of all its myriad aspects. But gradually there also developed among the masses a greater emphasis upon the various deities who symbolize those aspects, so that the component lesser deities sometimes came closer to the everyday experiences of the people than did the lofty ideal of Dainichi. The emperor established Tō-ji (Kyōōgokoku-ji) temple in Kyoto for Kūkai, and Kūkai himself founded a retreat on the high plateau of Kōya-san (Mt. Kōya), which later expanded into a tremendous complex of some three thousand temples, which, although now shrunken, is still the holy of holies of the Shingon sect.

In the latter part of the period new elements in Buddhism seem to have brought the religion closer to the people, developing finally (as one phase) into an ecstatic belief in Amida, the compassionate, omnipotent Buddha of Mercy. The concept of Amida and his Western Paradise was neither new nor confined to any one sect, but became especially widespread through the Pure Land Sect (Jōdo-shū). Genshin (942–1017), abbot of Eshin-in and known as Eshin Sōzu, did much to promote it through his *Ōjō-Yōshū* ("Essays on Rebirth in the Pure Land") and through his large paintings of a golden Amida appearing over the mountains or coming from the clouds at the hour of a believer's death to receive the departing soul, accompanied by his two attendant Bodhisattvas, Kannon and Seishi. The gist of this doctrine is that Amida Buddha will hearken to all who call upon his name in sincerity, even at the hour of death, and will come to welcome the dying believer into his paradise, where that soul would itself be reborn as a Buddha. The doctrinal simplicity of this, in contrast to the sterner concept of enlightenment through austerities and prolonged meditation, had great appeal to the minds of the masses. Furthermore, during this Fujiwara era the capital was often struck by famine, pestilence, and natural catastrophies, and by constant conflicts between armed Kyoto and Nara priests. The consequent sorrows of the people, both high and low, made the merciful Amida concept the one bright hope in life. The devotion thus engendered, supplementing the refinements of court life, is reflected in the Buddhist art of the Fujiwara era, especially toward its close. In it both the aristocratic and the religious were united. Fujiwara artistic expression at its best became a delight in grace, beauty, and hope.

In spite of the seeming Buddhist dominance in this period, continuity of the native Shintō belief remained evident. The all-important Grand Shrines of Ise (Kōdai-jingū), where the spirit of the Sun Goddess is enshrined, appears often in Heian history and literature; the Kasuga-taisha shrine in Nara, the family shrine of the Fujiwara, grew more important; the Kamo Shrine in Kyoto, and others, were also important to the life of the nation. The diary of the regent Fujiwara no Kanezane in 1180 notes: "The safety of our country now rests with the will of the Great Gods of Ise, Hachiman, and Kasuga."[1] It was in this period that a noticeable amalgamation of Shintō and Buddhism, the seed for which had been sown with the construction of the great Daibutsu image of Nara, took place in certain institutions. This assimilative trend displayed features of both religions and is called Ryōbu Shintō ("Dual Shintō").

The changes in Buddhist art were at first rather gradual. Figures eventually took on a more delicate and human, and, in the end, an almost feminine, quality. They were often of normal human size, although the ideal five-meter height was frequently used for temple figures, and the prime minister, Fujiwara no Michinaga, ordered for the Hōjō-ji temple, which he constructed, a colossal image of Dainichi over ten meters in height.

Nowhere today can one find the Fujiwara exuberance more fully expressed than in the Konjiki-dō of Chūson-ji temple at Hiraizumi in northeastern Honshu, where the Fujiwara feudal lords were powerful and exceedingly rich. Their high cultural standard is evident from the architecture and other arts that found expression there, especially in Chūson-ji, whose numerous structures were sponsored by Fujiwara no Kiyohira and his successors, Fujiwara no Motohira and Fujiwara no Hidehira. Practically all of the Heian buildings at Chūson-ji were destroyed by fire, only two remaining. One, the Konjiki-dō, is the "Golden Hall" built in 1124 as the mausoleum of Fujiwara no Kiyohira and later used also for his son and grandson (Pl. 114). In at least one of the coffins beads of glass, crystal, and amber have been found (Sup. N. 49), and glass was included in the architectural decoration (Pl. 115).

The Konjiki-dō and all its parts are imbued with the graceful feeling of Heian art. The conception is that of an Amida-dō (Hall of Amida) surpassing in elegance the numerous other halls of the Heian period. Beneath the central, forward altar, which supports figures of Amida and attendants, was interred the mummy of Fujiwara no Kiyohira. Originally this altar must have stood alone, since the two rear altars (the tombs of the son and the grandson), though similar, show some differences in details. Architects, sculptors, painters, metalworkers in bronze, silver, and gold, woodworkers, lacquer artisans, and craftsmen experienced in the use of mother-of-pearl and glass all contributed their skills. It is said that inside and out the building was covered with lacquered cloth covered by gold foil; and that the roof was sheathed in tiles of wood that had been gold lacquered. No wonder it was also called the Hikaru-dō (the Radiant, or Shining, Hall). In 1288 it was incased in an outer shell, which preserved it over the centuries.

As the Fujiwara clan in Kyoto gathered power unto itself, very largely it seems through the wedding of their daughters to young emperors and through regencies for child emperors, the Fujiwara regents practically became dictators. The nobility came to concentrate upon the aesthetics of life, devoting themselves to literary pursuits and the arts, to the niceties of court etiquette and dress and to a romanticism that expressed itself in architecture, sculpture, painting, the crafts, literature, beautiful gardens, music, and the dance. Thus, within the circles of the court the spirit of the time became ultrarefined and the art of the Fujiwara era evolved into an unique and pure concentration of delicate sensitivity. So profound it was, and of such strength, that much of the Fujiwara spirit survived to influence the cultures of all succeeding periods.

The literature of the time preserves some of the beauty of the Heian spirit. The era's great novel, *Genji Monogatari* (*The Tale of Genji*), was written in the early eleventh century by Murasaki Shikibu, a Fujiwara and lady-in-waiting to the Empress Akiko. This work gives detailed vignettes of life at the court and the customs of the day. That the descriptions in the *Genji Monogatari* and diaries of the time were based on personal experience and observation seems obvious from their nature.

The customs described in the novel are corroborated by the personal diaries of Murasaki and other ladies of the court. Some of them clarify the role of glass in this culture.

The refined courtiers seem to have had little inclination for law enforcement or military duties and relied upon warrior retainers from provincial clans. The two uppermost clans were the Taira (or Heike) and the Minamoto (or Genji). Under such circumstances the influence of the Fujiwara leaders weakened, the two clans became proportionately more powerful, and their rivalry grew. It was in this situation, in the twelfth century, that seeds of military rule were sown. The Taira defeated the Minamoto in 1160 and for some twenty years thereafter wielded the power. The office of chancellor, the highest, was granted by the emperor to Taira no Kiyomori, who often seems to have abused his power and entirely ignored the court. At the same time he displayed great piety and a perceptive appreciation of the arts, rivaling or even surpassing that of the court. In the east, grimly determined to avenge their earlier defeat, the Minamoto were recovering their strength. Kiyomori's political ineptness, together with deplorable conditions in the capital, gave the Minamoto their chance.

In 1180 Yoritomo, the eldest of the surviving sons of the former Minamoto leader, emerged with his two younger brothers, intent upon avenging their father and restoring the clan's influence. Thus began the struggle against Taira dominance, which later became famous in Japanese history, literature, drama, and art as the Genpei (the Genji-Heike) War and ended with the defeat of the Taira and the reputed drowning of the infant emperor in 1185. Yoritomo then returned to his stronghold in Kamakura to consolidate his position before attempting to assume supreme power.

The Heian period, the "Period of Peace," scarcely lived up to its name in the latter years. The impression we have of a gentle, luxurious life within court circles belies the conditions then prevailing throughout the country. Minor revolts, which were often brutally suppressed; the militant activities of the powerful priests on Mt. Hiei, who often raided the city to press a point; violent fighting between the Kyoto and Nara priests; conflict between provincial warriors; epidemics, famine, and various natural calamities all brought grief. Kiyomori died in 1181, and, with the downfall of the Taira at Dan-no-Ura in 1185, power fell into the hands of the strong, ambitious Minamoto. This ushered in the supremacy of the warrior class, which was to continue until 1868. Thus the delightfully sensitive Fujiwara era came to an end.

GLASS IN THE HEIAN PERIOD

The lack of extant examples has led past writers to state that glassmaking ceased in the tenth century. Recent archaeological and other discoveries, and study of Heian literary references, show this to be an exaggeration. Glassmaking, though evidently diminished, was far from obsolete in the Heian period.[2]

Provenances are difficult to ascertain. Considerable trade was carried on with the continent, but knowledge is lacking as to what proportion of the imported items were of glass. Frequently passages in Heian literature refer to certain objects and customs as being from this country or that. But not one of the glass references describes the item as coming from abroad.

Further evidence that glassmaking had not disappeared may be found in a Chinese record of glass exported from Japan to China in the eleventh century.[13]

> Through our southern traders at times Japanese productions find their way to China. In the 5th year of Hi-ning [1072] a priest named Ch'êng-Sün came to T'ai-Chow and stopped at the Kwoh-ts'ing Monastery of T'ien-t'ai and wanted to stay. The authorities reported the facts, and his majesty ordered him to be sent to the Palace [then at Nanking]. Ch'êng-Sün offered a silver incense-burner, mukorossi berries, white glass, five scents, crystal, red sandal, amber-mounted telling beads and dark colored staffs. . . .[4]

The Chinese phrase "white *liu-li*" may apparently, in present-day Chinese, mean either "white glass" or "white glaze." Interpreting it in the eleventh century, as white glaze coming from Japan, would seem strange. *Liu-li* has been defined as "an opaque, glasslike substance; porcelain,"[5] which in the above context, would seem equally strange. The Japanese use of the Chinese characters "*liu-li*" (Japanese, *ruri*) appears in eighth century Shōsō-in documents, clearly meaning "glass." And "white" glass has usually carried the meaning of "colorless."

For the Heian period, there is nothing comparable to the Shōsō-in of the Nara period, One must seek out Heian glass here and there, in the provinces as well as near the capital. The extant examples seem to have been primarily for religious purposes, but it must be kept in mind that fires, storms, and fighting brought violent destruction to palaces and other buildings. From the literary references cited below it is clear that glass objects of secular and religious nature were not rare.

In the Buddhist field, glass continued to be used for *shari-tsubo*, for beads, and for some decorative purposes.

Little is known of the use of glass in Shintō shrines, the only mention being of glass inlaid in the lacquer of sacred shrine palanquins (*mikoshi*) and the use of glass beads in the trappings of horses used in festival processions (see pp. 135 and Pl. N. 121). Perhaps *magatama* and other items of glass exist, but if so they are protected from prying eyes by their sacredness. It is a fact that in some instances of *go-shintai* (sacred enshrined symbols) even the priests may not know their appearance or nature, for their brocaded or silken covers have never been removed; when an outer cover shows signs of wear, a fresh one is simply added over the old. Furthermore, the custom at the Grand Shrines of Ise of renewing everything every twenty years and burying the old treasures has kept many ancient objects secret and inviolate. How many may have included glass is uncertain, but two later reproductions, the originals of which may have been Heian (or pre-Heian) products are illustrated here (Pls. 116, 121).

The glass items of the Heian period, as a rule, have an originality either in form or in use that seems but the natural outcome of diminished foreign influence and of the peculiarly fastidious tastes of the court. Certain of the author's tentative attributions may be questioned; her reasons for assigning such items to this period, and to a Japanese origin, are outlined in the Notes.

It is noticeable that the lead content in Heian period items for which there are estimates is much less than the seventy percent so conspicuous in Japanese glass of preceding periods. The various estimates range from 33.5 to 55 percent. Just what this may mean is not clear, but the demise of the Imono-no-tsukasa doubtless had something to do with it.

DOCUMENTARY EVIDENCE OF GLASSMAKING

Research is handicapped by lack of precise records of glassmaking for the Heian period. The *Engishiki* ("Regulations of the Engi Era"), of 905, stipulated that as tax in kind

"Izumo Province is to offer sixty strings of *ōnfukidama* (Thirty-six strings shall be for the three festivals of fixed date; twenty-four strings shall be for special festivals). Every year before the first day of the tenth month the beadmaking clan of Kambe [?] in Ōu-no-gōri is to make them and have a messenger come and offer them [i.e., in Kyoto]."[6] *Ōnfukidama* were "august blown beads" to be offered to Shintō deities or to the emperor. Considering that there are blown glass beads in the Shōsō-in (Pl. 85), perhaps one should not question this term. However, since blown items were certainly not common among ancient beads, and only relatively few examples are known, it might be questioned whether the practice of blowing beads had extended to the provincial workshops at the time; in fact, the "blowing" may refer to a blowing up of the fire with a bellows to achieve heat sufficient to melt or soften a ductile material, which would be glass. This distinguishes the artificial "blown" bead from the stone beads cut from "cold agates," jaspers, and crystal of Izumo Province. Modern writers seem to use the term *fukidama* for "glass bead."

The controls and functions of industrial art production of the period, including glass, as mentioned by one writer,[7] seem to be the same as those outlined in the *Yōrō Shokuin-ryō* (718), but one cannot assume that for glass the regulations of the code were still enforced without modification. It is known, for instance, that in 774 the Casting Bureau (Imono-no-tsukasa) was transferred from the Ōkura-shō to the Takumi-ryō (see p. 94), which was perhaps a kind of demotion in prestige, or at least in activity. Whether the rise of wood as a sculptural medium was the cause or effect of this change is not known, but certainly the day of great bronze-cast Buddhist images was on the wane. Glass production, being a function of the Casting Bureau, would also be affected by a decline in official governmental casting activities.

Due to the Shōhei-Tenkei civil war of 935–40 the custom of sending in beads from Izumo for tax purposes was abolished; in later periods "people used Chinese beads." It is true that a certain kind of bead, different from the Japanese glass beads, and which may be assumed to be of Chinese origin, did come into use somewhat later, but nothing of the sort is noticeable until sometime after the Heian period. Also it is known that glass beads were made in the Tsukumo-no-tokoro in Kyoto (the office for producing utensils and various wares for the imperial palace), and that this glassmaking, too, was abolished from the time of the Shōhei-Tenkei War. This source also mentions that, after the decline in beadmaking, there were good beadmakers among the priests;[8] perhaps this was a survival from the days of the Zōbutsu-sho of the Nara temples, kept alive by the priest-craftsmen in the temples. And perhaps the priests had never developed the high lead content used in imperial workshops.

BEADS

In spite of lack of physical evidence of glassmaking, it is known, both from extant examples and their continual representation in Heian paintings, and from some literary references,[9] that glass beads were still familiar adjuncts in the life and thought of the

Japanese. They were used prolifically, in the traditional manner and in a number of new ways. It is said that in 1184, when the Emperor Go-Toba was preparing to give a party, he invited distinguished craftsmen to create many articles for use at that entertainment.[10] Beadmakers were included, but it is not known who they were nor whether glass craftsmen were among them, though it is suspected that the latter were present.

Magatama and *kudatama* are rare among extant specimens. *Marudama* and *kodama* were apparently still turned out in great quantities, sometimes with very wide bores (Pl. N. 119; Sup. N. 49); but the modified forms, such as *natsumedama*, *kuchinashidama*, and *kirikodama*, are not in evidence, and *tombodama* can be presented here only in the rosaries of Supplementary Note 50; the latter may be of a later date.

There is at least one new bead form not observed in any pre-Heian examples (see Pl. N. 119; Sup. N. 53); it seems to be an extended form of a coiled bead but wider at one end, giving it a jar shape.

In general, it seems that the glass beads of this period were predominantly, or perhaps exclusively, of transparent and translucent glass, and that they were not as precisely made as the best of the tomb beads or the beads of the Asuka, Hakuhō, and Nara periods. The bores seem conspicuously wider than in the majority of the earlier beads. There are a few authenticated examples showing that beads were still made in the traditional way by coiling (Pl. N. 118–120). Molded and tube-cut beads cannot be ascribed to this period with any certainty.

Few individual specimens are presented here, but fortunately there are beads employed in *yōraku* and in other applications that tell much about the beads themselves and about the Heian temperament. For instance, imprints of two rows of beads left in the wrist skin of Fujiwara no Hidehira's mummy at Chūson-ji attest to the use of rosaries (Hidehira had taken Buddhist vows).

BEAD-WRAPPED SWORDS

In the *Engishiki*, in the section dealing with Shintō affairs, there is an undated listing of "Twenty-one Kinds of Sacred Treasures" (at the Kōdai-jingū, the shrine of the Sun Goddess at Ise). These are swords with gilded copper mounts. One is described as a *tamaki-no-tachi* with beads of five colors wound around thirteen times.[11] The *Naigū Chōryaku Sōkan-fu Dajōkan-fu* ("Orders of the Chōryaku Era [1037–39] Concerning the Inner Shrine: Orders of the Prime Minister") also lists twenty-one kinds of sacred treasures (all swords with gold-covered copper mounts), including the same sword, described as "wrapped with three hundred beads."[12] In 1869, during excavations for a sacred enclosure northeast of the north gate of the shrine, three swords of sumptuous craftsmanship were found buried in the ground. Two had delicate metal rings attached to the hilt; in one, small bells were attached to the ring, and wound around the sheath was a string of three hundred beads of precious stones in five different colors.[13] The choice of colors in all probability has symbolic meaning.

Every twenty years everything at the imperial shrine in Ise is renewed—not only the buildings but the treasures and ritual equipment. New, and therefore ritually immaculate, items replace the old, which are then ceremonially buried. A few replacements, reportedly replicas of originals, may to some extent reflect objects no longer available. In 1958 it was reported to the author that the ancient sword no longer existed and that only one made in 1909 was known (Pl. 116). It must be assumed that the excavated ancient one was reburied. There is no evidence to indicate when it was made.

The modern sword seems to be a stylization of those described in the two Heian texts quoted above. It does not have a string of beads "wound all around," but in its place there are insets of glass in five colors arranged in the pattern of a bead-string wound in what may have been intended as thirteen rounds, although this is partly obscured by metal mounts. The sword is preserved in the Jingū Chōkokan as "the finest ancient treasure at Ise."

NEW USES OF *Yōraku*

Yōraku were cited for the Asuka-Hakukō and Nara periods. In the Heian period they became more frequent.

In Buddhist art, the Buddhas themselves are portrayed in the simple robes of the monastic order, but attendants, especially the saintly Bodhisattvas, who have vowed to forego Buddhahood until all mankind has been saved, may be clothed in the royal apparel of the Indian tradition, complete with luxurious crowns, necklaces, armlets, and long festoons made up of beads of precious substances, metal medallions, and pendants. In images of the Asuka, Hakuhō, and Nara periods these regal ornaments were an integral part of the sculpture, as they had been in India and China, depicted in metal casting, in wood carving, in clay, and in lacquer. Now in the exuberant and human art of the Fujiwara era, the images, although still represented in a mystic and holy spirit, take on more human forms. They gradually acquired an ideal aristocratic femininity, often entirely losing their masculine traits. In Heian paintings, garments, delineated in color and in minutely cut strips of gold foil, simulated the sumptuous clothing of the Fujiwara court, and the *yōraku* was now fabricated separately and hung upon the body of the image as real jewelry. Naturally this latter provided a new outlet for the symbolic glass beads. But, not being an inherent part of the image and easily added (or easily removed), it is often difficult to determine whether the *yōraku* of a sculptured figure is original Heian work or a later replacement.[14] For this reason no examples of *yōraku* are included here, although many are available. Further investigation and comparisons between these and beads of later eras are needed before the matter can be clarified.

However, representations of *yōraku* in paintings of the period can be accepted as reliable simulation of the types and customs of the time. As such, a few typical examples are included here (Pl. 117; Sup. N. 51). Obviously they can be considered only as types. In paintings of the latter part of the Heian period, when the Pure Land doctrine of the Western Paradise of Amida was developed, there was an extravagant use of glass beads. It is as though the painters' fervor had led them to dream of the regal jewels of the heavenly beings in Paradise. If there were not a plentiful output of glass beads in the Fujiwara era, surely they would not appear so profusely in the art of the time.

Though *shari-ki* were still reverenced, the general practice of interring them in pagoda sites seems to have faded out. A new custom somewhat resembling the old *shari* burials sprang up during the Fujiwara period. When inscriptions exist, they are either of the latter part of the eleventh century or the first half of the twelfth century. *Kyō-zuka*, or sutra mounds, have been discovered in many regions, in each of which was installed a holy Buddhist sutra, or portion thereof, and sometimes other treasures. The sutra scroll was rolled and encased in a decorative cylinder of ceramic ware, bronze, or silver. Some cases are plain columnar shapes with a simple overhanging cap cover; others are more complicated, with compound spreading bases and rooflike lids. Often the bottom is a thin bronze mirror-shape with decorative floral or other motif typical of Fujiwara bronze mirrors. The lobed lids of many of the metal cases are gracefully conceived, surmounted with a *hōshu* knob, the "flaming jewel," and supplemented at the eaves with vertical strands of glass beads, or of glass beads intermingled with metal pendants (Pl. 119). In other sutra cases the cylindrical body becomes the main part of a simple, single-roofed pagoda form, generally surmounted by the usual tall pagoda finial, with wires extending from the top to the four corners of the eaves, and sometimes strung with a few glass beads (Sup. N. 52).

As in *shari* installations, other objects of a dedicatory nature may be found associated with the sutra cases: Buddhist statuettes, mirrors, earthernware jars, and in several instances fragments of what were evidently glass *shari* containers (Sup. N. 55, 56). Glass beads are always conspicuous. When beads are not actually found, punctured holes in the lid, or in the roof eave, with bits of wire or thread clinging to them, or possibly a single remaining bead, bear witness to their original presence. These sutra burials present one of several instances indicating that the spiritual significance of beads, and perhaps of the glass substance from which they were fabricated, was still respected.

Commonly the cylinder was buried a number of feet underground in a carefully prepared pit, with six stones forming, roughly, a small chamber around it, with one stone each for top and bottom and four others for walls. The arrangement of Plate 118 is somewhat different, with one base slab only, on which the sutra case was placed, with a wide-mouthed earthen pot inverted over it for protection; in this instance the excavated pit was filled in with charcoal, over which was a three- or four-layer covering of boulders and earth.

Often the beads from mounds in provincial areas are of lesser workmanship than those found nearer the capital. No doubt they are the products of priests or cottage craftsmen less carefully trained and supervised than those near a cultural center, where both skill and supervision may have been on a higher level. That the glass metal itself is of high quality may indicate the distribution of raw glass from some glassmaking center.

In the Tokyo National Museum are two bead-decorated, pagoda-shaped *shari* containers, expressing a use of beads for architectural ornament. The simpler of the two came from Naraharayama, Nibukawa-mura, Ochi-gun, Ehime Prefecture. The other, formerly at Hōryū-ji,[15] is larger and is adorned with a much more elaborate *yōraku* that contains a new, jarlike type of bead (Sup. N. 53).

Suggestive of the *yōraku* of these two containers, but much more elaborate and with some innovations, is the *yōraku* embellishing a shrinelike frame enclosing a sculptured image of Shōtoku Taishi as a child (Pl. 120).

NEW USES OF BEADS

Further, beads were ingeniously used to adorn the tails of bronze peacocks on altar panels in the mausoleum of the Fujiwara lords of northeastern Japan, the Konjiki-dō of Chūson-ji temple (Pl. 115). A similar use of glass beads in peacock designs is seen at Jōmyō-ji temple in Wakayama Prefecture.[16] In both instances, few of the beads remain.

Together with these, the use of beads in the lantern of Plate 13 also seems to express the imaginative taste of the artisans of the Fujiwara era.

Again, there is evidence that glass beads were used rather extensively in saddles and harnesses during the Heian period. Among the dedicatory offerings recovered from the earlier tombs are elaborate saddles, stirrups, and harness accoutrements, some with simple glass added, but it was in the Nara or the Heian periods that elaborate ornaments of glass beads were added. A Heian description of a procession of court nobles states that "The young princes and courtiers who rode with the procession had vied with one another in the magnificence of their accoutrement. Such gorgeous saddles and trappings had rarely been seen. . . ."[17] It is said that horses equipped with saddles decorated in the manner of the Sui and T'ang dynasties of China were first used when foreign envoys visited Japan in the eighth century; but that, later, ministers rode them in the festival processions of the Kamo Shrine in Kyoto. Remnants of a once handsome saddle and trappings remain in the Shōsō-in (*SGM* 349–352) but at present no beads are attached. Similar accoutrements were used for the sacred horses of Kasuga, Ise, and other Shintō shrines as well. A picture, reputed to have been painted at the time of construction of Kasuga Shrine in Nara during the Emperor Sanjo's reign (1068–71), shows a horse so equipped;[18] an elaborate throat ornament consists of a perforated bronze cap inside of which is hung a metal bell containing a rolling pellet for sound; hanging from the bottom of this cap are many strings of glass beads forming a long and complete circular fringe. A similar ornament hangs from the throat of the sacred white elephant upon which the Bodhisattva Fugen is shown seated in the Heian painting of Plate 117. An example of such a throat ornament, but of the Kamakura period, is shown in Plate 127. Two horse models at Ise wear this type of ornament; one is shown in Plate 121.

The Kasuga Shrine painting shows an *uzu*, a complex ornament at the joining of harness straps on the horse's rump. In this painting the *uzu* displays three Buddhist "flaming jewels" (*hōshu*). The published reproduction is too indistinct to determine whether the flame rays are made of glass beads, but it suggests such a form. It might be inferred that it was so, from the two horse models preserved in the Jingū Chōkokan of Ise, which, although later in date, presumably retain the ancient trappings style. Modern paintings on the *ōn-maita* (the wooden screens connecting the four small shrines of Kasuga-taisha) reveal, in general, the same custom, but some of the details differ.

NEW USES OF GLASS

Glass inlays and the application of beads for ornamentation have been cited previously, but Plate 14 exemplifies a different and seemingly unique method of using glass: transparent glass applied over the title of one of the sutra scrolls donated by the Heike rulers to the Itsukushima Shrine at Miyajima, Hiroshima Prefecture.

Somewhat different, although the literary reference calls them simply "glass" (*ruri*), are decorative *kugikakushi* ("nail concealers") used to cover nails driven into woodwork. "Where a nail is driven, it is covered with a piece of *ruri* to hide the mark left by the nail and also to serve as ornament."[19] In later centuries these were of metal or ceramic; sometimes they bore cloisonné (Pls. 17, 132). Confusion abounds in this period over the use of the terms *ruri* (always "glass' only? Or sometimes "cloisonné"?) and *shippō* ("cloisonné" only? Or sometimes merely "glass"?). In either case the two terms involve glass, and their appearance in the Heian period is significant.

INSETS AND INLAYS

The use of "jewels" as insets in other materials, common earlier, was continued in the Heian period. There are the already noted glass insets in the sword of ancient type at the Grand Shrines at Ise (Pl. 116). Now, however, not only are inset *hankyūdama* found, but sometimes pieces of colored glass cut to fit a design. Insets and inlays were used to enhance all sorts of objects of daily use, such as boxes and swords.

During the Fujiwara era Japanese lacquer craftsmen made further advances, developing, for instance, the *ikakeji* technique of dusting gold powder onto a still moist lacquer, which, when dried, gave the effect of a gold ground. With this they frequently associated mother-of-pearl inlays, known as *raden*, and bits of glass.

It is recorded that in 1029 the Emperor Go-Ichijō moved into the residence of Fujiwara no Yorimichi, Minister of the Left, who is said to have dedicated the glass lantern of Plate 13 to Kasuga-taisha shrine. Among the furnishings of that palace were many lacquer wares of *ikakeji* with *raden* inlay (perhaps including glass?), illustrating scenes of foreign countries. It is also recorded that when the retired Emperor Shirakawa, who had reigned from 1072 until 1085, moved to the Oi Palace he installed a two-story shrine of *ikakeji* lacquer with foreign scenes in *raden*.[20] In the *Ruijū Zatsu Yōshō*, a lacquered box is described as being in the *ikakeji* technique, inlaid with, among other motifs, a chrysanthemum branch in *raden* and glass; the leaves were of green glass, and the flowers of white and yellow glasses.[21] In 1146 an official ordered a box inlaid with blue and yellow glass for his daughter's wedding.[22]

Mikoshi (portable palanquins for transportation of a deity's spirit) were now decorated with lacquer, inlays, and "jewels." That of the Kumano-Hachiman Shrine in Wakayama Prefecture, a national treasure of Heian origin, is described as having the wooden members of its "couch" lacquered in *ikakeji* technique with floral designs in *raden* and glass.[23]

The glass inlays in lacquer seem now to be ornamental in nature, used for their interesting color and texture. Whether they were fashioned from newly manufactured glass or whether they were merely made with pieces of broken vessels from which the proper small shapes were cut is unknown. At least the pupils of the eyes of the cats and sparrows in the fine Kasuga-taisha shrine sword of Plate 15 (*if* of glass, as they seem to be) might have been especially fabricated for this purpose. In this sword, as in a sutra box at Daigo-ji temple, a double inlay was employed: glass set into mother-of-pearl, which was inlaid in lacquer.

Glass inset as an architectural ornament is found in the horizontal beams over the central dais of the Konjiki-dō of Chūson-ji. These beams are doubled, and in the centers and at the corners where pillars support them they are covered on the exterior by "flowing" applications of elaborately pierced metalwork (Pl. 114). Those portions on the uppermost beam are centered about an eight-petaled floral motif whose heart is a circular mount originally inset with glass—in one case blue (or green?) glass 3.0 centimeters in diameter,[24] and in another instance a "thin sheet of yellowish glass."[25]

GAME PIECES

Since game pieces of glass were found in the Nara period in the Shōsō-in, it is not surprising to find them also in the Heian period. Although the author knows of no extant examples, a literary reference describes dark blue glass game pieces used with some of white stone.

> Lines were drawn in gold and silver on a board of aloes wood, and game pieces of white jade [? *gyoku*] and dark blue glass were put in a silver container for the game of *go*. These were presented to a Minister by a Captain of the Guard.[26]

VESSELS

Knowledge of glass vessels in this period comes from three sources: extant examples; glass as represented in paintings; and glass mentioned in Heian documents and literature. Although extant vessels are few, and chiefly fragmentary, this need not imply that little glass actually existed, for literary evidence attests a familiarity with, and use of, glass jars, vases, wine cups, and other forms. Frequent calamities and devastation by violence and fire plagued the capital, and fragile glass, in fragile structures, would have been particularly vulnerable.

The dark blue glass spittoon of Plate 16 is evidently the one recorded as a gift to Tōdai-ji in 1021 and seems without doubt to be an importation. Since it was preserved in the Shōsō-in, it is in prime condition.

Fragments of several glass *shari-tsubo* were excavated at Nodayama, Hongo-machi, Hiroshima Prefecture (Sup. N. 55).[28] A similar *shari-tsubo* came from a *kyō-zuka* at Kō-ryū-ji temple on the outskirts of Kyoto (Sup. N. 56). A complete *shari-tsubo* (Pl. 122) is so like these two that it also is presented here, although it has at times been called early Kamakura. All three jars have a common type of stopper not noticed previously in Japan —a type that continued at least as late as the Edo period, if not later. It is uncertain whether these Heian examples were imported, which is possible, since there was some trading with the continent at this time, or whether they present a new local conception. No comparable examples in continental glass of the same period (Sung dynasty China) are known by the author. If a comprehensive study of the stoppers of contemporaneous glass jars in China were possible, it might indicate definitely whether this is solely a Japanese characteristic. The three stoppers have a hollow lid with a long wide open neck, which fits within the mouth of the jar. The same stopper type is seen in a less prominent form in a small Korean enameled silver needle case dating from around 700; this lid has the same type of knob as the examples of Supplementary Notes 55 and 56.

The many glass fragments found within the Shaka image of Seiryō-ji temple (Sup. N. 57) are the remains of several imported vessels. Both the nature of the glass metal and the shapes reconstructed from the larger fragments are unlike anything else known in Japan. They suggest western Asian forms.

It is said that when Kūkai (Kōbō Daishi) (see p. 126) returned from China he brought with him the following glass items for use in a Buddhist memorial service for the dead:

> 2 bowls of light blue glass [*heki-ruri*]
> 1 bowl of amber [amber colored glass?]
> 1 bowl of white glass
> 1 pair of chopsticks of dark blue glass.[28]

These would have been treasured utensils for ritual use, but their later history is unknown.

In Volume VII of *Tōhō-ki* ("Record of Treasures of *Tō-ji*"), a *shari-bin* is illustrated, shown as a gourd-shaped bottle. At present this reliquary, or one like it, bears an imperial seal and cannot be inspected, but from the shape and size of the bag in which it is contained it seems to be a tall, narrow object over 10.0 centimeters high. A glass receptacle of Ryūkō-in at Kōya-san is said to preserve relics of Kōbō Daishi, but it is not stated whether the object might be an import.

VESSELS REPRESENTED IN PAINTINGS

Most of the paintings in which glass vessels appear are so similar to paintings from the continent, and the figures who carry the glass so like figures of Chinese paintings of the time, that one must suppose these particular concepts to have been borrowed from Chinese prototypes, or from one of the guides to the painting of Buddhist deities that were brought from China for use in Japan. The *Tō-ji Reihō Shū*, published by Tō-ji temple in Kyoto, reproduces sketches that the temple owns; in one figure a transparent spherical bowl with wide mouth is held on an uplifted left palm, and in another a transparent lobed bowl is held, which contains a single opening lotus bud. These are line drawings deriving from some imported guide for artists. The figure at the lower left in the Senju Kannon scroll (Sup. N. 51) is an example, for although the bowl might conceivably have been a Chinese import, the figure itself and the details are so thoroughly Chinese that the artist must have been following a Chinese Buddhist canon.

The representation of glass vessels in the eastern wall painting of Hōryū-ji (Pl. 73) has been cited. Such representations appear more frequently in the Heian period; two are illustrated here (Pls. 123, 124). Representations include broad transparent bowls, or large transparent jars with tall necks, containing flowers whose stems show clearly through the glass, which is often blue. These shapes seem to have no counterparts in Japanese glass of the Heian period. Among Japanese paintings not catalogued here is the *Shaka Kinkan Shutsugen* ("Śakyamuni Rising from His Golden Coffin") once owned by Chōhō-ji temple, Kyoto, and dating from the late eleventh century; in it at least one glass vessel appears in light blue. Another is a late Heian, or very early Kamakura, copy of an earlier *Kegon Engi* ("History of the Kegon Sect") owned by Kōzan-ji temple in Kyoto and recounting the experiences of the two founders of the sect in Korea.[29] The pictures are ascribed to Jōnin, a priest-painter of Kōzan-ji; in one scene a darkish blue vase is seen, with the flower stalks showing through the transparent glass.

Representations of flying angelic forms carrying aloft flat receptacles for flowers occurred at Hōryū-ji. These recur in the Heian period, as in the Amida-dō of Hōkai-ji temple, Kyoto, where a transparent plate clearly represents glass.

VESSEL REFERENCES IN LITERATURE

Literary mentions of glass corroborate a familiarity with glass vessels. There is the record of the blue glass spittoon, discussed in Plate Note 16. References in Heian romances and tales must be accepted, for there are enough descriptions of customs of the period and enough substantiation in diaries of the time to confirm that these references to glass sprang from their authors' knowledge and experience.

Often, in the *Genji Monogatari* or other sources, objects or customs are specifically described as of foreign origin or style, as, for instance, in these excerpts:

> At the Feast of the Red Leaves dance after dance was performed, both Korean and of the land beyond the sea.
> . . . on a piece of very fine Chinese silk he made a number of rough ink sketches. . .
> . . . writing it on a *kurumi-iro* paper from Korea . . .
> . . . on Kanya paper backed with Chinese silk . . .
> . . . over which was thrown a cover of Chinese brocade . . . the carpet on which the boxes stood was of Chinese fine silk . . .
> The carpet was of Korean brocade . . .
> . . . a cushion bordered with Chinese brocade from Loyang . . .[30]
> [The prime minister's wife rode] in a Chinese carriage.
> . . . costume made completely of Chinese materials.[31]
> . . . with a stylish Persian quiver across his shoulders.[32]

Glass vessels are not so described, but are brought in casually—as, a "glass bowl," a "white glass vase," a "glass jar"—as if so familiar that nothing further need be said. A reference in *Tsutsumi Chūnagon Monogatari* merely states that a young girl came running forward carrying a glass jar containing shells.[33]

At the poetry loving court of the Fujiwara era, and among all the nobility, it was customary to exchange frequent letters and poems. A missive was assessed by the recipient according to its original and pertinent content, for its appropriate allusion to the classics, the quality of paper and calligraphy, and the beauty and aptness of the flowering or evergreen branch (or ornament simulating one) that often accompanied it, perhaps with a gift attached. In a number of instances glass is mentioned as the accompanying gift. The following are a few examples:

> Two incense jars of glass were put into boxes of aloe wood; in them were placed large pieces of incense. For the dark blue glass jar a twig of five-needled pine was selected; for the jar of white glass a plum branch. Also, the cords used to tie them were very elegant.[34]

> Prince Genji went to a mountain temple. On his return the priest presented him with [several things] including a rosary, which Shōtoku Taishi had had brought from Korea, and a Chinese style box also brought from Korea. He put them in an openwork bag and attached *goyō* pine to it. Then putting the medicine into dark blue glass jars, to which he further attached wistaria and cherry, he presented them to him.[35]

> The wine cups and bottle were of dark blue glass.[36]

> They placed a golden mandarin orange on a blue glass jar and putting it in a blue bag, attached a branch of five-needled pine.[37]

> Chinese pinks, bellflowers, etc., put in a glass jar.[38]

CLOISONNÉ

The present-day Japanese term for the enamelwork that we call cloisonné is *shippō*. This word appears often in Heian writings, but to assume that it meant then precisely what it means now would be erroneous. Literally the term means "seven treasures," having its origin in the Indian Buddhist concept of seven precious substances, such as gold, silver, ruby, emerald, crystal, lapis lazuli, and pearls (or some other slightly varied group). But in Japan, and perhaps in China as well, where precious stones such as rubies and emeralds and lapis were not found, it came to mean something different and seems to have referred to objects having something of the quality and beauty of the original seven precious treasures. Perhaps it was first applied to the semiprecious inlays of Japan, such as agate, crystal, pearls, mother-of-pearl, glass, and by a natural transfer came to mean enamel suggesting inlays. The terms are confusing; they are *ruri*, *shippō*, *ruri-shippō*, *ruri-shippō-dama*, *shippō-nagashi*, the last signifying, in later times at least, "*shippō* ware," although it means literally "*shippō* flowed on." Even as late as the Momoyama period a building at Zennō-ji temple, near Sendai, became popularly known as Shippō-ji, apparently because it had some sliding doors with sheet glass. Sometimes one can surmise from the context of a passage what type of glass is intended; at other times this seems impossible. For instance, in the very effusive description in the *Eiga Monogatari* of Hōjō-ji temple (built by the powerful prime minister Fujiwara no Michinaga), it states that "Flowers were made of *shippō*, and the ritual implements were also decorated with *shippō*."

Another writing, of 1150, uses the term in an equally ambiguous way in speaking of a "*shippō* pagoda," requiring ten men to transport, which was placed in the precincts of Sukiwata-dono by a man who hoped thereby to be born in Amida's Paradise.[39] Did *shippō* here refer to the technique, or did it simply mean something of brilliantly colored and rich appearance?

But cloisonné, whatever name was applied to it at the time, really did exist, as manifested in the ornamentation in the Hōō-dō (Phoenix Hall) of the Byōdō-in outside Kyoto (Sup. N. 58). This does not closely resemble the flowed-on glass "cloisonné" mirror of the Shōsō-in; it was achieved by applying molten glass, more like enamelwork, on the surface of bronze door mountings, giving cause for reflection on the continuing use of cloisonné and basis for thinking that perhaps certain of the references to *shippō* at Hōjō-ji—such as the "ritual implements" decorated with *shippō* or "flowers made of *shippō*"—may have referred to enamel.

As more factual evidence comes to light, from temples, shrines, and private treasure-houses, it may be possible some day to trace more clearly the path of *shippō* and *ruri* in ancient times. At least it is important to note the practice of a cloisonné technique in eleventh century Japan, as exemplified in at least one surviving example.

From the references and illustrations in this chapter, it seems obvious that the old and oft-repeated saying that knowledge of glass and glassmaking was "lost" after the early tenth century, not to reappear until European blown glass entered Japan after the sixteenth century, can no longer be justified. Certainly glassmaking was far from obsolete in the Heian period.

1. George Sansom, *A History of Japan to 1334*, Stanford, Stanford University Press, 1958.
2. *Jusei Sugie, *Nihon Garasu Kōgyōshi*, p. 40, felt that the decline in glassmaking after the Nara period was not only due to various social conditions but that the real and more fundamental reason lay in the absence of chemical knowledge.
3. Ma Twan-lin, *Sung-hui-yao*, Section 199, Pt. 7, "Barbarians."
4. E. H. Parker, "Ma Twan-lin's Account of Japan up to A.D. 1200 (Including the Japanese Chronicles as written down for the Chinese by a Japanese in China in A.D. 1000), "*TASJ*, XXII, 1894, p. 65.
5. R. H. Mathews, *Mathews' Chinese-English Dictionary, Revised American Edition*, Cambridge, Harvard University Press, 1956. Captain F. Brinkley, (*Japan*, Boston, J. B. Millet Company, 1897, Sect. VI, p. 137) also read this as "white glass."
6. *Engishiki*, op. cit. (see n. 5, p. 107), III, Section *Rinji-sai*.
7. *Soshū Watanabe, *Heian Jidai no* . . . . , pp. 25f.
8. *Kurokawa, *Kōgei Shiryō*, Pt. 2, p. 36; Pt. 4, p. 45; as usual in older writings, no sources are cited.
9. Such as the reference in the *Engishiki* to beads worn at throat, wrists and ankles, for the Festival of the Sacred Robe.
10. *Kurokawa, *Kōgei Shiryō*, Pt. 2, p. 36.
11. *Engishiki*, Pt. 4 of the section *Jingi*, p. 87 (in *Koji Ruien*, see n. 7, p. 72).
12. In *Koji Ruien* (see n. 7, p. 72), Sangyō-bu, I, p. 615. The work quoted is said to be a catalogue of utensils sent by the Imperial Household at the time

of the twenty-year renewal of the Kōdai-jingū in Chōryaku 2 (1038).

13. William Gowland, "Metals and Metalworking in Old Japan," *Transactions and Proceedings of the Japan Society*, London, XIII, 1914–15, Pt. I, pp. 59–60.

14. *Yamasaki, ("Garasu," p. 402) hints of the possibility that beads of such *yōraku* might have been manufactured in the Nara period.

15. In Meiji 11 (1878) Hōryū-ji, being in financial straits, transferred a collection of nearly three hundred art treasures to the Imperial Household in consideration of a cash donation, for repairs, from the Emperor Meiji of ten thousand yen (at that time a considerable sum). The bulk of these went to a museum, which later became the Tokyo Imperial Museum. In 1948 this became the Tokyo National Museum, and there the Hōryū-ji treasures remain, except for several that were returned to Hōryūji and several that remain in possession of the Imperial Household. In 1962 the Tokyo National Museum opened a subsidiary building to house these treasures only, known as the Hōryū-ji Homotsukan (Hall of Hōryū-ji Treasures).

16. Jō Okada, "Kii-shū Kishima no Jōmyō-ji—Shinkoji Junrei 15" [The Temple Jōmyō-ji at Kishima, Kii Province—Pilgrimage to Old and New Temples, 15], *Museum*, No. 39, June 1954, pp. 30–32.

17. Arthur Waley, *The Tale of Genji* (trs. from Murasaki Shikibu, *Genji Monogatari*), London, George Allen and Unwin, Ltd.; references used herein are from the Literary Guild of America Edition, New York, 1935, pp. 296–297.
For text and commentaries in Japanese refer to Kikan Ikeda, *Genji Monogatari Taisei* [Compilation of the *Genji Monogatari*], Tokyo, 1954; or Yoshinori Yoshizawa, *Taiko Genji Monogatari Shinshaku* [New Annotations on Comparative Texts of the *Genji Monogatari*], Tokyo, 1936.

18. *Nara*, No. 11, April 1929, p. 6.

19. *Eiga Monogatari*, Chap. 31, *Uta-awase*, entry of Chōgen 8 (1035), quoted in *Soshū Watanabe *Heian Jidai no. . . . , p. 321.

20. Shisui Rokkaku, *Tōyō Shikōshi* [History of Lacquer in East Asia], Tokyo, Yūsankaku, 1932, p. 81.

21. *Ruijū Zatsu Yōshō* [Collection of Sundry Important Matters], Vol. 4; a manuscript by an unknown author that explains and illustrates events, ceremonies, clothing, and furniture of the imperial court from mediæval times; taken from Hokiichi Hanawa, *Shinkō Gunsho Ruijū* [Revised Gunsho Ruijū], Tokyo, Naigai Shoseki K. K., 1928–1929, Vol. XX, p. 578.

22. *Kurokawa, *Kōgei Shiryō*, Pt. 2, p. 45.

23. *National Treasures of Japan*, Series 5, Applied Arts, Tokyo, p. 62.

24. *The Chōson-ji Temple*, Tokyo, Asahi Shinbunsha, 1959, p. 26.

25. *SnG, p. xvii.

26. *Utsubo Monogatari*, Chapter *Atemiya* from *Nihon Koten Bungaku Taikei* [Survey of Japanese Classics], Tokyo, 1957, II, p. 241.

27. Masana Murakami, "Aki-no-kuni Hongo-machi Kyōzuka Hōkoku" [Report on a Sutra Mound at Hongo-machi in Aki Province], *KKZ*, Vol. XLII, 4, March 1957, pp. 47–56.

28. *Soshū Watanabe, *Heian Jidai no. . . .* , p. 453; no reference source is given.

29. Illustrated in Jō Okada, "E-makimono ni Miru Kōgei Hin. . . . , II—Kegon Engi" [Craft Items Seen in Illustrated Scrolls—II—the *Kegon Engi*], *Museum*, No. 123, June 1961, p. 2.

30. Waley, *op. cit.* (see n. 17), Pt. 2 (*The Sacred Tree*), pp. 246, 268, 335, 338, 470.

31. Edward C. Reischauer and Joseph K. Yamagiwa, *Translations from Early Japanese Literature*, Cambridge, Harvard University Press, 1951, pp. 368, 369.

42. Waley, *op. cit.* (see n. 17), Pt. 4 (*Blue Trousers*), p. 544.

33. Reischauer and Yamagiwa, *op. cit.*, p. 217. Here the translators have given *ruri* as "lapis lazuli," a much rarer and more specialized meaning than the customary "glass."

34. Excerpt, translated from *Genji Monogatari Taisei op. cit.* (see n. 17), II, p. 977. Yoshizawa's comment, II, p. 223, refers to a previous annotation of the Edo period that, quoting from the *Kogetsu-sho*, uses the verb *eru* in the sense of "to select." *Eru* has usually been translated in its common present-day meaning of "to carve," which has led to confusion. Yoshizawa further elucidates "*kokoro-ba*" of this paragraph as "fashioned with cord or metal in the shape of plum or pine and attached to the gift boxes."

35. *Ibid.*, I, p. 167.

36. *Ibid.*, III, p. 1778. From the description of the Feast of the Wistaria, in which the vessels are listed. One text lacks mention of the wine bottle, *heiji*, and the phrase "dark blue," but these occur in the oldest text.

37. *Ochikubo Monogatari*, quoted by *Sōshu Watanabe, *Heian Jidai no. . . .* , p. 458.

38. *Eiga Monogatari*, quoted by *Takigawa, "Imono-no-tsukasa. . . . ," p. 12.

39. Fujiwara no Yorinaga, Minister of the Left, *Daiki* [Record by a Minister], Vol. 9: from *Shiryō Taikan* [Comprehensive View of Historical Materials], Tokyo, 1898, II, p. 302. Other titles of this work are *Ryaku-ki* [Chronological Record] and *Nichiji-ki* [Daily Record], but the text in *Shiryō Taikan* is based on the Sakakiyama Bunko (Sakakiyama Library) text, said to be considered the most reliable.

DIMINISHED GLASS PRODUCTION

KAMAKURA PERIOD (1185–1334)

After seizing control from the Taira, Yoritomo turned his attention to the court in Kyoto, since the spiritual power of the throne was still so strong that he could not hope to hold control without the emperor's sanction. The power of the imperial house to grant titles and carry on the national Shintō rituals was seemingly absolute and unchallenged. Without imperial appointment no political or military leader could hope for success, although the sanction might often be the result of coercion. Ostensibly inviolate, the emperors (with the exception of Go-Daigo) were actually helpless through the following seven centuries—virtually prisoners within their palace walls. The title coveted by Yoritomo—Sei-i Tai Shōgun ("Barbarian Conquering Supreme Commander")—was attained only after the demise of the retired emperor, Go-Shirakawa. It was finally granted in 1192 in the name of the twelve-year-old Emperor Go-Toba. Nominally the shogun functioned only by grace of the emperor; actually, thenceforth, the administration of the nation lay with the military alone.

Yoritomo maintained his capital at Kamakura; the regime is known as the *bakufu* or shogunate. Yoritomo lived only fourteen years after defeating the Taira, but during that time he laid foundations for an enduring feudal regime. At the time of his death, since his heirs were minors, a Council of Regents was formed, in charge of the Hōjō family; these regents became the actual power in the shogunate, just as the Fujiwara regents in Kyoto had been the actual rulers behind the emperor. Moreover, the political expediency of installing an infant or youthful shogun was taken over from the Fujiwara practice. For the most part, Hōjō regents seem to have ruled conscientiously and skillfully in an effort to establish law, order, and justice.

It had been the custom, at least since the time of the eighth century Emperor Shōmu, for sovereigns to abdicate in favor of an heir to the throne. Usually they took Buddhist vows—hence the term Hōō, "Cloistered Emperor." Since it became the custom for an emperor to retire in early youth in favor of a very young child, the first among them to have abdicated held seniority and was the only one who retained any power of decision in affairs of state. He remained an advisor and a power behind the throne in deciding such things as appointments and ranks, including appointing his own successor as senior abdicant.

The Emperor Go-Saga (emperor, 1242–46, and abdicant emperor until 1272), who seemed to favor a younger son over his oldest son, both of whom were also abdicants, died in 1272 without naming an abdicant successor. The dispute that arose immediately as to whether a descendant of the older or younger son should accede to the throne gave rise to a division between the "senior" and "junior" lines of descent, with accession going alternately to the two lines. The Emperor Go-Daigo of the "junior" line acceded to the throne in 1318. Being a mature person with ideals for administrative reform, he refused to retire in favor of a child sovereign. The results were civil wars that tore the country for years. When the shogunate attacked Kyoto, Go-Daigo fled, but accomplished a victorious return and, in the process, the power of the Hōjō regency in Kamakura came to an end. But by the end of 1333 Go-Daigo was again forced to flee, setting up a court in Yoshino, southeast of Kyoto, while a court of the senior line was established in Kyoto. By the end of the Kamakura period in 1334 the country was politically divided, with two imperial courts and with a new shogunate regime settled in Kyoto.

The Kamakura period was not a peaceful one, despite the fact that, at its beginning, the supremacy of the forceful Yoritomo and the establishment of a powerful temporal government based on administrative and political reform, contrasting with the laxness of the Heian period, brought some degree of stability. Violence, the frequent quelling of dissident factions, the struggle over the shogunate succession after Yoritomo's death, two attempted Mongol invasions, the imperial conflict after 1318, plus the usual natural disasters, fires and pestilence, all brought hardships to the country during much of the period. It is little wonder that the Amida religion of the Jōdo sect, with its certain promise of relief in the heavenly "pure Land of Bliss," continued strong. Other sects, such as Tendai and Shingon, and a new Nichiren sect, flourished also, but the Amida doctrine and some modifications had a great following.

Another new religious concept, akin to the Amida doctrine, entered Japanese Buddhism—the idea of Jizō Bosatsu, he who in compassion helps all, but in particular the souls of little children, in crossing the dark stream of death, and strives to alleviate their sufferings in the underworld. Representations of Jizō show him with a metal staff with loose rings with which to advise of his presence and to disperse the forces of evil. On his upturned left palm he carries a fragile vessel, symbol of some special and spiritual principal. In some instances, at least, this seems to be of glass (Pl. 130).

But heroic self-conquest rather than Amidism was the ideal that motivated the warrior class in power during the Kamakura period. It was developing an ethical code based upon self-reliance, bravery, and passionate, absolute loyalty to one's superior. Reinforcing this were two other factors: a renewed Confucianism introduced from China and a new type of Buddhism known in Japan as Zen, also introduced from the continent by the constant travel of priests to and from China. Confucianism, with its strong emphasis on ethics and human relations, was compatible with warrior ideals. Zen was a conscious return to the simpler tenets of the historic Buddha, Śakyamuni (Japanese: Shaka), a protest against the complex accretions of concept and worship that had altered those teachings over the centuries. Emphasizing deep intuitive meditation as a means of finding within oneself release from material bonds and the attainment of inner enlightenment, Zen, at first, had no general or immediate appeal to the masses, although eventually its characteristics influenced nearly "every nook and cranny" of Japanese culture. For the warrior class in Kamakura it had deep appeal, and influential Zen temples sprang up. The greatest impact, however, was to be promoted later by the Ashikaga rulers in Kyoto in the late fourteenth and the fifteenth centuries.

The military background of the new regime inevitably brought an element of heroic vigor and realism, which colored the culture and the art of the period. The new trend was in general forthright, less formal, and imbued with realism expressed in individualistic human terms. The new realism, however, coexisted with a gentleness and a love of details in pattern and texture carrying over Fujiwara grace and delicacy.

GLASS IN THE KAMAKURA PERIOD

There is a total lack of evidence of glassmaking methods and materials. However, one cannot say that there was no production of glass, because many beads and inlays exist that seem to be of local origin.

Although glass beads were still used in quantity, there are few single surviving examples, and beads can be presented here only in *yōraku*. Many Kamakura Buddhist images bear glass bead *yōraku*, ranging from simple ornaments (Sup. N. 59) to the profuse embellishment of Plate 125. In both capitals, Kyoto and Kamakura, there were manual workers who held special positions under the patronage of the shogun, Buddhist temples, and Shintō shrines. "In all cities and towns there were independent manual workers, most of whom paid service or tribute to the temples, shrines, and others, in return for their patronage."[1] Further, the *za* (a kind of guild system) is said to have had its origin in the late Kamakura period. Nothing is known, however, of the place of glassmaking in these activities. It seems strange that the making of glass vessels did not develop at this time. It is known that *shari-tsubo* were still made, in a new form but possibly always in rock crystal, and one may surmise that some of the references to glass vessels in Kamakura literature indicate domestic production. Why, then, did glass making not go forward to mature into a glass industry? Pottery, lacquer, and other crafts had been carried on for centuries. Was glass too expensive a process to compete with the old familiar ones? Or was the lack of chemical knowledge partly to blame?

It seems that, at this time, the history of Japanese glass is faced with a decline, if not extinction, except in the field of beads. Even the less valuable sources of knowledge— pictorial representations of glass and references in the literature—are scant and give no assurance of domestic manufacture. The most one can say is that glass, whatever its source, was rare and that, other than beads, it seems chiefly to have been imported.

BEADS

No beads from this period appear to have been scientifically studied, hence no data is available as to their chemical nature. Many are of rather thin, refined glass. In the past it was generally thought that, by this time, they all came from China (a theory now open to doubt). One late nineteenth century writer states that after the Mongol attempts at invasion, trade with China was interrupted for a time and, since beads were not imported, domestic beadmaking again became prosperous, chiefly at the hands of the priests. This implies that beads had for a time been primarily of Chinese origin, although this contention seems to have no supporting physical evidence. That beads of some sort were being made, even though glass is not mentioned, is evident from the fact that in Shōwa 4 (1315), when the Hiyoshi Shrine was built in Ōmi Province, the beadworkers employed for this venture are mentioned by name with the remark, "They are skilled men."[2]

Yōraku

The custom of *yōraku* for Buddhist images reached its height in the Kamakura period. While some figures show aesthetic restraint (Sup. N. 59), many exemplify such lavish abandon by pious donors that the sculptural quality of the figure is obscured (Pl. 125).

Reliquaries for Buddhist *shari* now take on a new form in which the glass beads, although subordinate to the elaborate quality of gilt-bronze work in the Kamakura period, still evidently played a significant role. Outstanding examples of gilt-bronze reliquaries are that of Supplementary Note 60, made to house an eighth century *shari-tsubo* (Pl. 82) brought from China, and that of Supplementary Note 61. Both of these *shari* containers are masterpieces of elaborate workmanship. It is assumed that the glass beads were added for some amuletic significance.

Mikoshi are the sacred palanquins of Shintō shrines in which the spirits of deities are transported at such times as shrine festivals. *Mikoshi* were also used by emperors. Previously mentioned were examples having glass in the *raden* (mother-of-pearl inlay) decoration of their interiors. The exterior walls were often hung with metal plaques and strings of glass beads and metal ornaments, as befitted a sacred equipage. Such a *mikoshi* is discussed under Plate Note 126.

Glass bead decorated horse trappings, especially the throat ornament, were used also in the Kamakura period. An ornament used for this purpose is discussed in Plate Note 127.

INLAYS

The custom of inlaying shaped pieces of glass in lacquer (Pl. 15) probably continued, since it is known again in the following period, but no examples can be presented for the Kamakura period. However, insets of *hankyūdama* were continued as before (Sup. N. 62).

Another method of adding glass, akin to this type of inlaying, was the impaling of globules on pins projecting upward from the surface to be embellished. This may be seen in the rows of pins, now empty, on the upper tier of the bases that support the lotus pedestals of the Kōdai-in images (Sup. N. 62). That these pins actually held glass was confirmed to the author by a scholar who had seen this trinity while some of the glass units still remained. Such a practice was evidently common in Buddhist art, if one may judge by Chinese and Japanese paintings, although it is not known whether glass was generally the medium intended; the gems are often represented in blue, which seems to indicate glass.

VESSELS

One very small vessel of this period is that of Plate 128. Although there is no record regarding its origin, it is assumed to be Chinese of the Sung dynasty, perhaps brought to Japan by Shōichi Kokushi who spent seven years in China.

The former type of Japanese *shari-tsubo* seems to have vanished. A new type of *shari* reliquary (a *hōshu*), a transparent ovoid form within a bronze "flame," mounted on a lotus pedestal, was promoted by the priest Eison of Tōshōdai-ji temple, who sponsored widespread worship of *shari* in the Nara temples. These *hōshu* are unquestionably domestic works, but it seems that most of the *shari* containers were of rock crystal.

The same uncertainty as to medium—that is, whether crystal or glass—applies to a modification of the form in the late Kamakura period, which was to lead to a more elaborate development in ensuing centuries. This is a small, flat, transparent form of flamelike contour, containing three *shari* and supported by a metal cap, like an acorn cup, all mounted on a flat, vertical surface.

As for bowls, vases, and the like, the sources of knowledge are representations in paintings and references in the literature, but generally there is no indication that any of these are domestic products.

VESSELS REPRESENTED IN PAINTINGS

Representations of glass vessels continued in paintings, but often in such distinctly Chinese settings that Japanese manufacture cannot be assumed. Buddhist priests were again studying in China and returning with books and other religious appurtenances. Trade with China, which had been advanced notably by Taira no Kiyomori and others in the latter twelfth century, further increased, and many Chinese works of art came into the country, especially paintings of the Sung and Yüan dynasties. Arhats and certain new forms of the Bodhisattva Kannon (Avalokiteśvara or Kuan-yin) are often depicted in Chinese and Japanese paintings. Frequently glass vessels appear among the details of the paintings; they are so often repeated that it seems some sort of pictorial guide must have been used. Such instances have already been noted for the Heian period. Types occurring frequently in Kamakura period paintings seem to be primarily flower bowls of transparent glass, or tall, Chinese style ewers holdings twigs of willow and themselves standing in bowls of transparent glass. However, paintings that illustrate these are so entirely in the Chinese tradition that the glass depicted must be considered also of Chinese manufacture. On the other hand, a few paintings by Japanese artists (Pls. 129, 130) have such distinctly Japanese feeling that the glass might be construed as Japanese.

The new cult of Jizō (Ksitigarbha) found expression in a standing figure, dignified and compassionate, holding in its uplifted left hand what has been described as the jewel of inexhaustible bliss and wisdom.[3] Sometimes this seems to be but an ethereal sphere of no substance; at others, it may appear as a globular glass jar with a metal cap (Pl. 130), or even a glass dish (Sup. N. 63). From the history of *shari-tsubo* in Japan it might be conjectured that the artist of the jar knew such glass shapes in Japan; but for the dish there is no such assurance.

VESSEL REFERENCES IN LITERATURE

In the literature of the Kamakura period there are various references to *ruri*, the term for glass that has become familiar in previous chapters. Sometimes these state definitely that the vessel was imported from China; in others one is tempted in infer that the vessels might be Japanese, but, again, the evidence is not complete.

In the diary of Fujiwara no Sadaie, a member of the State Council, is a description of a party:

> There was a party at the Nishi-ike-tei. A number of important persons were seated in one room. In an adjoining room to the west there were a white glass vessel [vessels?] with plum and cherry blossoms, blue [or green?] glass wine cups with a Chinese weaving beneath them, and beside them two small wine bottles. There was also a statue three feet high, a small table, some calligraphy, and a tall wine bottle.[4]

Since the woven textile is mentioned specifically as being Chinese, was everything else, including the glass, of Japanese manufacture?

The *Hyakuren-shō*, under, a date of 1250, refers to a glass jar at Ise:

> On the twenty-eighth of the second month at the palace of the Ex-emperor Go-Saga, they held a council and decided the matter of the dropping of the glass jar called 安宮 [?] *ruri-tsubo*, which had occurred at the time of the removal of the Geku [the outer shrine], and the matter concerning blood at the Western Treasure Hall.
>
> The regent, Sesshō Konoe Kanetsune, participated in this council.
>
> On the thirtieth day the priest of the Geku was summoned to the palace of the Ex-emperor Go-Saga and questioned about the matter.
>
> On the first day of the third month a divination was held. It was about the *ruri-tsubo* at the Geku and the blood. The Lord Keeper of the Privy Seal, Sanemoto, participated.[5]

No further details are given, but the matter had obviously been one of great importance. The *ruri-tsubo*, however, was perhaps not of Kamakura date but a treasure of previous times.

Mr. Yasuo Hagiwara, priest of the Office Instruction Section at the Grand Shrine

(Kōdai-jingū) of Ise, who kindly supplied the above translation from the original edition of the *Hyakuren-shō*, reported that the shrine has no record whatsoever concerning this jar, although it is supposed that it may have been a *shari-tsubo*. He further states that in a manuscript copy of the *Hyakuren-shō* kept in the library of the Grand Shrines the unintelligible characters describing the *tsubo* were corrected to read *tsuchi-no-miya* (土宮), a subsidiary building of the Geku.

In the *Azuma Kagami* ("History of the Eastern Provinces"), under the idate of the twenty-second day of the eighth month of 1189, there is a record that seems related to Yoritomo's relentless pursuit of Yoshitsune to Hiraizumi in the north:

> Yoritomo's warriors went to Hiraizumi, but the chief of the clan had fled and the house had been burned. There was no trace of any human beings and the house was completely ruined. Only a bleak autumn wind was blowing, and a curtain was making a forlorn sound. Also, rain was falling gently. In the southwest corner a storehouse remained intact from the fire. So Katsushige, Saburō, Kiyoshige, Kokuri, Jūrō, Shigenari and others were sent to investigate. There were a few shrines of Chinese woods such as red sandalwood and (?), in which there were bezoar, rhinoceros horn, a flute made of ivory, horn of the water buffalo, a scepter of dark blue glass . . . a crane of gold, a cat of silver, a glass lantern . . . numberless items.[6]

Since this episode occurred only four years after Yoritomo's ascendancy, the items mentioned may have been of Heian date. Whether the lantern might have been like the lantern of Kasuga-taisha (Pl. 13), or a Chinese lantern of glass panels in a wooden frame, is, of course, impossible to tell. Nor is there any indication of the nature of the glass scepter.

CLOISONNÉ

Thus far no example of cloisonné of the Kamakura period has been found. However, there are several literary references in which one may place some credence, remembering the coffin ornament from the Kegoshi Tomb (Pl. 74), the mirror in the Shōsō-in (Pl. 12), and the enamel decoration at the Hōō-dō (Phoenix Hall) of Byōdō-in (Sup. N. 58). At least two references to *shippō* are found in the *Heike Monogatari* (*Tales of the Heike*). One describes a large cart with *shippō*. The other speaks of a building, the Daigoku-den, made of *shippō* (or made to look like *shippō*?).[7] In the *Taiheiki* ("Annals of the Heike"; Chap. 24) this statement appears: "A white elephant with one head and six tusks . . . has on each tusk a lotus blossom in *shippō*." Surely this must mean an enamel decorative addition either on a carved figure or represented in a painting.

MUROMACHI PERIOD (1334–1573)

WHEN THE Emperor Go-Daigo established court in Yoshino, Ashikaga Takauji established a youth of the senior line in Kyoto as the Emperor Kōmyō, thus inaugurating the era known as the Namboku-chō (era of the Southern and Northern Courts). Emperor Kōmyō granted to Takauji the coveted title of Sei-i Tai-Shōgun, which Minamoto no Yoritomo had also held, and with this the period of Ashikaga dominance began. Such a situation was ripe for creating civil strife, which indeed lasted for many years.

In 1392, in the time of Ashikaga Yoshimitsu (1368–93), a reconciliation of sorts took place. The Southern Court returned to Kyoto, and both courts agreed to reinstate a system of alternating accessions. Thereafter, for a time, the capital became comparatively peaceful, but the prestige of the imperial house deteriorated, in sharp contrast to the rising ostentation and luxurious practices of the Ashikaga. In the provinces gradual decline in the authority of court-appointed representatives took place under the rising strength of Ashikaga provincial military officials. Dr. John Hall suggests that the continuous fragmentation of the large land holdings was a further factor in the breakdown of the balance of power between the civil and the military groups, with the military gradually taking over the civil administration of the provinces. These factors weakened the central shogunate in Kyoto, which gave its members time for the cultural pursuits that several Ashikaga shoguns followed so avidly.

The growth of Zen Buddhism, which had been introduced in the Kamakura period, contrasted to the political and military turmoil. Strong religious and commercial ties with China fostered this, introducing treatises and paintings expressing the ideals of this doctrine, which found a significant place in Japanese life and culture.

Japanese Zen taught simplicity, repose, silence, and detachment. Zen concepts were compatible with many ideals already expressed in Japanese culture, such as the Shintō ideal of purity and the pervasive recognition of beauty in natural forms and kinship with them. Thus they were suitable for application in daily life, as reflected in behavior, poetry, painting, gardens, the tea ritual, and in the philosophy, symbolism, and beauty of the Nō drama, which was particularly sponsored and encouraged by two Ashikaga shoguns—Yoshimitsu (1369–93) and Yoshimasa (1443–72). Visually, the Japanese gardens of Zen temples present this doctrine to us as an elegant, vital refinement, as do the ink paintings of the Zen painters.

Ashikaga Yoshimitsu erected an extravagantly rich "Flower Palace" (Hana no Gosho) in the Muromachi district of Kyoto and a monastic retirement retreat for himself, the famous Kinkaku (Golden Pavilion) of Rokuon-ji temple. He also made pilgrimages to various Shintō shrines and Buddhist temples, often accompanied by lavish processions, bearing rich gifts. His excessive expenditures were a drain on Ashikaga resources and created much uneasiness. The active and lucrative trade with Ming China, which he sponsored, was one means of compensation. Trade with China flourished also among the temples, shrines, and private sponsors, so that Japan benefited both by exports and by an influx of imports from the Ming empire.

Yoshimitsu's grandson, Yoshimasa (1443–72), obviously inspired by Yoshimitsu's Kinkaku, built the Ginkaku, or Silver Pavilion, at what is now known as Ginkaku-ji in Kyoto. This survives as a weathered gray building originally intended to be enhanced with silver foil; adjacent to it in the garden is an expanse of pure white sand and a truncated mound of the same popularly known as the "Moon-viewing Mound." In the Ginkaku the drinking of tea, advanced by Yoshimasa, was well on the way to becoming the now famous ritual. Ginkaku-ji was and is still noted for the skill of its abbots as tea masters.

Yoshimasa, who further promoted the evolution of the Nō drama, was likewise a patron of artists and also assembled a superb collection of Chinese paintings and porcelains. This stress on beauty in environment and in artistic activities marks the Muromachi period as one of the great aesthetic intervals in Japanese history.

During this period, when the central authority declined, various feudal lords throughout the country were consolidating and often extending their domains. After the decline of the strong Hōjō administration of the Kamakura period and during the ensuing conflicts, many of them emerged strong, independent, and ambitious. With this went a compelling desire for the "better things" of life—learning, literature, and the arts. Prior to the feudal periods, such interests had been largely limited to the court and religious centers. In the Kamakura period they had been taken up by shogunate circles, but now the enthusiasm and activities of Yoshimitsu and Yoshimasa spread, contagiously, to many of the distant feudal centers. This was especially true in Yamaguchi in western Honshu, where the Ōuchi leaders, wealthy from a lucrative trade with China, encouraged and promoted such interests. They sponsored the developing Nō drama, poetry, painting, and other aesthetic pursuits. Perhaps it was here that European glass, brought by Francisco Xavier, was first seen in Japan.

In about 1542 Portuguese merchantmen (and later Spanish ships) had begun to visit the harbors of Kyushu, the southern Japanese island. They were soon accompanied by Jesuit missionaries. The encouragement they received from various feudal lords had far-reaching results, for they brought new ideas from the outside world and incentive for further contacts abroad. The first ship arrived near Kagoshima, at the southern tip of Kyushu, blown thither, it is said, by the winds of a typhoon. Hearing of this new land, the captains of other foreign ships also took advantage of this unexpected trade potential; the welcome they received was probably largely due to visions of expanded trade. Soon other ports were likewise receiving foreign ships, such as Hakata, the old port on the northern coast of Kyushu. Nagasaki on the west coast was opened to the Portuguese in 1570—an event that was portentous for the future history of glass in Japan. Hirado, an island just off the coast of northwestern Kyushu, with an excellent harbor, also received foreign shipping, particularly from England and Holland.

No glass brought into the country by those earliest European visitors can be illustrated. Father Francisco Xavier, arriving in Yamaguchi in southwestern Honshu about 1550, presented Lord Ōuchi with, among other things, "crystal glass,"[8] but of the recipient's reaction there is no word, other than that he showed interest in the Father's gifts. The provenance of the glass is not known. It could have been Spanish glass or perhaps Venetian, picked up in Goa or some other Asiatic port, or even at Hirado, where a Portuguese ship had arrived just before Xavier stopped there enroute to Yamaguchi. One writer states that, at the close of the Tenmon era (1532–54), "elaborate glass was brought from Milan and Barcelona in foreign ships. Wealthy merchants and daimyo were much impressed."[9]

The Christian religion was at first welcomed, and Western products received with enthusiasm. A definite Western impress upon the crafts of the time is sometimes seen in works of the close of the Muromachi period, but there is no evidence that glass had as yet inspired any attempts at imitation.

Internal conditions in Japan during the Kamakura period, and more especially in the latter Muromachi period, were affected not only by foreign trade but by the increased domestic interregional trade, the development of roads and of means for financial transactions resulting in a growing awareness of the country as a whole. The seeds of ambition for overall control were being sown. The first obvious sign came in the second half of the sixteenth century when a young commander in Owari Province, Oda Nobunaga, achieved virtual control of much of the country, not only as a military dictator but as a civil administrator bent on reforms and projects to perpetuate his power. The close of the Muromachi period is traditionally ascribed to the year 1573, when Nobunaga, angered by the disloyalty of his puppet shogun, Ashikaga Yoshiaki, deposed him, ending the Ashikaga shogunate. The shogun title was not to reappear for thirty years.

GLASS IN THE MUROMACHI PERIOD

It seems strange that in this period of artistic excellence in so many arts and crafts, glass should have found no place. Not only is there a lack of glass specimens, but there seems to be no mention of it in various records of crafts, merchant guilds, and products. Research is needed in this aspect of economic history.

Perhaps the basic cause can be found in the discontinuance by the central government in the late Nara period of the official Casting Bureau, where glass had been fabricated, and to the apparently dwindling activity in the Heian and Kamakura periods when wood, to a large extent, was replacing bronze as the common medium for statues. At any rate, all techniques of manufacture of glass vessels seem to have been forgotten.

BEADS

Glass beads were certainly employed in some of the old ways, but their use was limited. Many surviving examples may be Chinese imports, although proof of this would require an extended study of glass and beadmaking in China during the Yüan and Ming dynasties.

Many of the beads show a carelessness in technique (Sup. N. 64) that is strangely unlike the skillfully made examples of earlier periods; and there is a new kind of smooth, opaque substance not observed before (Sup. N. 65). Even when the glass metal is of high quality, the execution is coarse.

Yōraku

The excessive use of glass beads in *yōraku*, so characteristic of the Kamakura period, seems to have nearly disappeared. This might be due either to the decline of beadmaking or to the rise of Zen Buddhism, which in general eschewed the use of religious images.

There are at least two small bead-decorated canopies known from this period (Sup. N. 65, 66). Although first used in the Kamakura period, this type of small canopy seems typical of this period. The immediate prototype may be the canopy of the image of Nyōirin Kannon of the Kōfuzō at Hōryū-ji, dating probably from 1258, when the image was repaired by Eison and "was completed with ornaments at that time."[10] It has a circular ceiling with foliated lacquer rim, from the underside of which hang long strings of beads and metal plaques. The two canopies referred to here are of this type.

The use of glass and small metal items as *yōraku* on *mikoshi* was continued (Sup. N. 67).

BEADS USED IN COSTUME

In addition to crowns, another item of imperial ceremonial wear, apparently used continuously from the Asuka-Hakuhō period,[11] is the *gyoku-hai* (jeweled bannerlike pendant hanging from the belt), which, worn one at the left and one at the right, were part of the formal attire of the emperor. Similar *gyoku-hai* were worn by high-ranking courtiers, but at the right side only. These were apparently always in the form of metal ornamental plaques strung together with five strings of differently colored beads (Sup. N. 68).

INLAYS

There is at least one example in this period of glass inlaid in lacquer (Sup. N. 69). Others may exist. The cutting and inlaying is Japanese work, but the fact that a small piece of glass was used does not necessarily suggest glassmaking. More likely the glass was a remnant of some treasured glass object that had been broken. However, its use suggests that glass was still considered a substance of beauty and worth.

GLASS USED IN COSTUME

Leather belts decorated with plaques of "precious stones" had been part of the formal court costume and for religious ceremonies since the Nara period, when the custom was taken over from China. One belt with plaques of lapis lazuli is in the Shōsō-in (*SGM* 414). In such belts the plaques were applied to the leather across the back, as can often be seen in paintings where courtiers are shown from the rear. The outer end of the belt bore a tip of the same material. The discovery of wooden remains of such belt tips set with glass *hankyūdama*, found among the "debris" of the Shōsō-in, makes one wonder if glass of some sort might have been applied across the back of that belt as well.

An early twentieth century writer mentions a belt of the Muromachi period as having been displayed in the Tokyo Imperial Museum.[12] The plaques were of green (or blue?) glass in place of the usual stone. This is described as part of a costume accompanying a group of musical instruments that had formerly belonged to the Amano Shrine at Kōya-san in Wakayama Prefecture. With the costume was a document bearing dates of the Eiwa era (1375–78) and the Kyōtoku era (1452–55); and a document relating to the musical instruments refers to the Bunan era (1444–48). Aside from the Shōsō-in belt tips, this is the only instance known to this author in which glass was used. Perhaps the belt was a treasure handed down from some earlier epoch (as was often the case with such costumes), or perhaps the belt, or the plaques, were Chinese imports. The present whereabouts of this costume is unknown.

Shari SHRINES

The *shari-zushi* (small *shari* shrines) began in a small way in the late Kamakura period and then were continued and elaborated upon during Muromachi times. The *shari*, placed on tiny narrow shelves behind a panel of glass, were often themselves small glass pellets of irregular shape (not beadlike), as though imitating natural *shari*. The glass panels, usually of circular or *hoshū* shape, were generally mounted in gilt bronze, which seems more often than not to have been of flame shape; the whole unit was then inserted in a flat wood panel. The shrine might be shallow—a mere panel with doors folding over it—or it might be a small four-sided shrine with *shari* installed on the sides as well as the front.

Such glass-protected *shari* units often occur in groups of three, arranged in a pyramidal effect, set among simulated sacred flames. One dating from this period is preserved at Tō-ji temple in Kyoto.

The *shari-zushi* are always of fine craftsmanship, as might be expected in the housing of such treasures. Where the flat glass came from is unknown, but since it seems that such glass was not produced in Japan, presumably it came from Holland or China or was possibly obtained from broken glass vessels.

VESSELS

Glass vessels seem to have been nonexistent among the domestic products of the Muromachi period. Even vessels of foreign production seem scarce. Therefore, the only knowledge is obtained from pictorial representations and literary references; in all of these, it seems, the scenes and the items are of Chinese types.

VESSELS REPRESENTED IN PAINTINGS

As in the Heian and Kamakura periods, there are a number of paintings either Chinese or in the Chinese style, which display as part of their detail vases with flowers or fruit or glass ewers containing willow sprays and standing in transparent glass bowls.

One scroll painting in a series of sixteen is attributed to the Japanese painter Minchō (1352–1431), who lived in Tōfuku-ji temple, Kyoto, and was an outstanding artist of his time; it shows an incense burner, which seems to be of bronze, standing in a fluted plate of blue glass.

A painting of a white-robed Kannon seated before a waterfall shows the deity holding on the palm of the left hand a small transparent bowl in which are lotus buds (?), which the deity touches delicately with the fingers of the right hand; this is the work of a fourteenth century Japanese painter, Ryōzen. There is no evidence, however, that the glass could represent a Japanese product.

One special representation of Kannon is the Yoryū Kannon (Kannon with the Willow), which shows the Bodhisattva seated in contemplation on a rock beside a waterfall. On the rock stands a vase, bottle, or ewer containing a willow twig; sometimes the vessel is set in a transparent glass bowl. This is seen in paintings of the Kamakura and Muromachi periods.

Vessel References in Literature

In the *Butsu Nichi-an Kōmotsu Mokuroku* ("Catalogue of Furnishings of the Nichi-an")[13] of Enkaku-ji temple, Kamakura, in an entry of 1363, is listed a *ruri-tōrō* ("glass lantern") brought from China, but no detail is given.

In the *Sanetaka-Ko Ki* ("Journal of Prince Sanetaka"),[14] a "glass vessel" (*ruri-ki*) and a "glass jar" (*ruri-tsubo*) are mentioned.

Cloisonné

Examples of enamelwork (*shippō, shippō-ruri,* or *ruri-shippō*) of the seventh, eighth, and early eleventh centuries have been cited. All this work existed before the assumed introduction of the European cloisonné technique into China in the Yüan and Ming periods. In the Kamakura period, only literary references can be cited, and these involve much confusion in terminology. For the Muromachi period, no extant examples are known, but from several literary references and from one published illustration one learns that *shippō-ruri* was apparently much prized for such items as jars and wine cups.

In the *Ōnryō-ken Nichiroku*,[15] a visit with Ashikaga Yoshimasa in the Shōsen-ken of of Shokoku-ji temple, Kyoto, is described as taking place in 1462:

> We visited the Shōsen-ken and before a sage green ceramic image of Kannon he burned incense. . . . He spoke and laughed and the time passed. . . . On his return home he sent us a pair of flower vases of *shippō-ruri* and a bronze hanging lantern. . . .

In a work by Sōami entitled *Kundaikan Sōchō-ki* (1511) there are several references:

> *Shippō-ruri* is no longer known at this time. It is admired no less than inlaid work. There is a mirror called *dojakudai*. On the copper base were placed substances of five colors which are very similar to *ruri*. Though they are clouded some are polished and can reflect the image of objects. This is valuable and rare.[16]

Although *shippō* (as cloisonné) is not actually mentioned, the description suggests that craft. An illustration in this work, advises "How to decorate your shelves." On the upper shelf, to the viewer's left, there is a wine cup that is labeled "*Shippō-ruri hai dodai*" (a *shippō-ruri* cup with its stand). As no detail is drawn in, we know nothing of its appearance, nor whether it is truly *shippō* in the enamel sense or simply a glass cup, as it seems in the simplified drawing. All of the items in this sketch seem Chinese.

MOMOYAMA PERIOD (1573–1603)

ODA NOBUNAGA was intent upon bringing order, restoring unity, and improving the economy of the country. By his death in 1582 he had gone a long way toward initiating the unification of the country, which the three dictators—himself, Toyotomi Hideyoshi, and Tokugawa Ieyasu—were, cumulatively, to accomplish during the period.

Nobunaga's chief occupations were military and political. He seems to have had some concern for architecture and erected a fortress-castle at Azuchi-yama on Lake Biwa as a lookout to protect Kyoto; the castle was the beginning of the bold art of the Momoyama period.

When Nobunaga died in a surprise attack, one of his generals, Hideyoshi, avenged his death and as victor in quelling other disturbances gradually gained supremacy. By 1585 he was well in command and had been appointed regent by the emperor. The following year he became chancellor. Since he was of lowly birth, a family name was granted him for the first time. Toyotomi Hideyoshi was a powerful military leader and an unusually astute administrator and organizer. He undertook land reforms, the disarmament of peasants and monks, and a census, with regulations restricting the change of residence from one place to another.

His campaigns against Korea, which he planned but in which he did not participate, though at first successful, ended in failure, at great cost to the country. Toward the end of Hideyoshi's life his one consuming obsession seems to have been that the succession of his beloved five-year old son, Hideyori, should be made secure beyond all doubt. Just before his death in 1598 he implored his council of elders, exacting from them solemn vows, to keep Hideyori's interests above their own; one, in particular, Tokugawa Ieyasu, was asked to guide the young Hideyori and to act as his regent until he should come of age. But Ieyasu was himself ambitious; conditions were unstable; and there were differences of opinion in the council. He eventually broke his promise to Hideyoshi.

During the near decade of Nobunaga's rule, and much of Hideyoshi's sixteen years, Christianity flourished, especially in Kyushu but also in Kyoto; and the Inland Sea port of Sakai became a strong Christian center. A report written in 1582 by Father Alexander Valignano estimated that there were some one hundred fifty thousand Christians in Japan at that time, and about two hundred churches; seven hundred thousand (about four percent of the population) have been cited for 1605.[17] Nobunaga received a number of missionaries in audience, and Father Valignano spent several weeks with him at his Azuchi Castle.

In 1582 four Kyushu samurai youths were sent privately by several Christian lords of Kyushu on a mission to Pope Gregory XIII in Rome, to Philip II in Spain, and to Portugal. The pageantry of their welcome in Rome was surprising, since their sponsors were neither powerful nor wealthy, their gifts simple, and the envoys were only youths and without funds.[18] They were feted, had their portraits painted, and their visit was commemorated by a papal medal "In Memory of the First Embassy and Obeyance from the Kings of Japan to Papal Rome"! On a long tour of Italian towns they visited Venice, where, it is said, a marble tablet in the Church of S. Maria della Carita commemorates their visit. The visit to Venice is recorded, as is a visit to the glassworks at Murano, where they were presented with "four large ornamented mirrors and two cases of glassware."

The youths returned to Japan in 1590. At Macao they heard of the proscription of Christianity in Japan. Nevertheless, Father Valignano and two of the young monks were permitted to visit Hideyoshi, who gave them a banquet, with some three hundred of the nobility present. Valignano's report of the youths' journey, adapted from their diaries, was published in Latin in 1590. All had become ordained priests. During their absence two of their Kyushu sponsors had died. One of the envoys was martyred, one apostasized, another died a natural death, and the fourth spent the rest of his life in Macao teaching Japanese in a Jesuit college.[19]

Hideyoshi was not at first antagonistic to Christianity. At times he was friendly and apparently eager for the trade that the foreign ships brought, while at others he issued orders to eliminate the foreign religion. His motives are not always clear, but in general he seems to have vacillated between periods of rage and intervals of indifference, or at least of nonenforcement of his edicts. It may not have been the doctrine itself that was distasteful, for the Japanese had always been tolerant of variety in religion, but rather the intolerance of many of the missionaries, their militant attitude toward Buddhism, the conflicts between Franciscans and Jesuits, and the threat of political subordination to Rome. There were other factors also, such as Hideyoshi's discovery in 1587 that the Portuguese owned most of Nagasaki[20] and that a slave trade was carried on, especially in Japanese children.

Little of Shintō appears during this period, but it continued at the heart of the nation, with the emperor as the high priest from whom even dictators received their titles.

The Momoyama interval, brief though it was, and marked by the consecutive rule of three strong generals, is another of those periods in Japanese history that displayed marked aesthetic characteristics. Nobunaga introduced a bold, ostentatious style and the use of much gold, but seems to have had no special inclination to sponsor cultural growth. Hideyoshi, though of low social origin and therefore not "to the manner born," took keen interest in such things. His pleasures and tastes were as flamboyant as his ambitions were grandiose. Furthermore, he was a great showman. His outdoor "tea ceremony," celebrating a military victory, was a tour de force to which all the public, both high and low, was invited from both Kyoto and Osaka—the only requisite being that each bring a mat to spread upon the ground and a teabowl from which to drink. It was of ten days' duration, with theatrical performances, dances, and a display of art treasures. On other more exclusive occasions the famous hundred painted screens of Hideyoshi were set up along the route of his processions. His Jūrakudai palace in Kyoto was sumptuous. His great fortified castle at Fushimi in the environs of Kyoto was, like the castle he erected in Osaka, an engineering feat, and the appurtenances were luxurious.

Gold and silver mining were flourishing at this time—Hideyoshi using some of the mines as his own personal resources—and gold became dominant in the art of the time. All this magnificence was far removed from the quiet, refined spirit of Zen art, which had permeated so much of Muromachi expression. And yet Hideyoshi's interest in the "tea ceremony" (perverted though it sometimes seems to have been), and his sponsorship of the great tea master, Sen no Rikyū, were direct reflections of Zen influence. Furthermore, these interests and his sponsorship of the arts associated with them brought out the talents of many competent artists and artisans.

Hideyoshi's successor, Ieyasu, was a more restrained aesthete, and during his regime design and color became more reserved. By the close of the period, before the death of Ieyasu in 1616, the efforts of the three individualistic and forceful warriors who shaped the character of the Momoyama period had brought unity and paved the way for a long period of peace under the Tokugawa shogunate, during which the arts would flourish. The new vistas opened up by Western contacts, restricted though they were, stimulated many new production techniques, among which glass would again play a role.

GLASS IN THE MOMOYAMA PERIOD

There is for this brief period no evidence for the domestic production of glass. However, European glass vessels were now first introduced and were to influence the revival of glassmaking. Cloisonné came to the fore.

BEADS

The use of glass beads seems to have been limited to ornamenting Buddhist images, to Shintō shrine use, and to court costumes. Specimens are scarce and none are considered here, since evidence concerning their origin is totally lacking.

The beads show little of the coarse quality of some beads from the Muromachi period, which were suggested as Chinese export, but whether this is indicative of Japanese manufacture, merely a different quality in Chinese beads, or whether they were Venetian beads imported from China[21] is impossible to ascertain without further study.

VESSELS

Knowledge of European blown glass first found its way into Japan during the second half of the sixteenth century. Foreign traders and missionaries sometimes included glass among their gifts to the Japanese military. Feudal lords, many of whom sponsored foreign trade, and even the emperor at times, offered to friends gifts of glass that had come into their hands.

The Jesuit Father Luis Frois is said to have presented to Oda Nobunaga candles and a glass flask filled with *kompeito* (a kind of sugar candy); and to Ashikaga Yoshiaki, silk and a glass vessel with a broken handle.

Nothing is known of the Murano glass that was given to the young Japanese envoys when they visited the island.

At one time Tokugawa Ieyasu wrote to Lord Kuroda in Kyushu, "Thank you for the foreign *biidoro* wine cup. I am glad to see it."

Yamashima Mototsune of the Imperial Household wrote in his diary in 1605: "Fine weather. I am very glad to have received from the emperor a *biidoro* glass."[22]

Though such vessels apparently interested the Japanese, there is no evidence that imitation was attempted.

CLOISONNÉ

Chinese cloisonné made according to the European method was imported during the Muromachi period. These examples were different from earlier Japanese enamels previously discussed. In the Momoyama period, during the invasion of Korea, many officers became exposed to the work of Korean craftsmen. Some of these, such as potters, were brought back to Japan and settled in feudal centers. Among them may have been artisans who were familiar with enamel techniques in the new Western mode, which involved adding metal cloisons to a metal base to form a pattern, filling the spaces between them with colored glasses (either broken up or powdered), baking them for fusion, and repeating the process until the molten glass completely filled the compartments, then polishing the surface flush. The result was a smooth design of fused glass and thin metal lines.

Surviving examples of Momoyama cloisonné seem to be chiefly *kugikakushi* (nailhead-concealing ornaments) and *hikite* (metal fingerholds for sliding wall panels) made for Hideyoshi's palace, the Jūrakudai in Kyoto. In one particularly large and fine example the design is a large plaited basket, such as would be filled with rocks to retain the banks of a stream, surrounded by waves. The woven bands of the basketwork are plated with yellow gold; the waves about it are in silver plating; and the flowing water is in blue *shippō*. Another example, also attributed to the Jūrakudai, is a *kugikakushi* in the form of a handwarmer (Pl. 132). Some of the examples attributed to Momoyama are so very much in tune with Japanese design that a foreign influence might be discounted. Further, they are, for the most part, different from the Chinese cloisonné imported at the time, and to some extent from the work of later Japanese artisans who reputedly learned from the Chinese.

Later, Tokugawa Ieyasu was to inaugurate a long line of *shippō* artisans, who, for generations, worked for the Tokugawa family. The first, Hirata Hikoshirō (Dōnin), has been erroneously credited with initiating the cloisonné craft in Japan, since the Jūrakudai items precede him. Hirata Dōnin was a metalworker who originally plied his trade in Kyoto. His birth date is given as 1591, whereas the Jūrakudai dates from about 1587. Where Dōnin learned his craft is still undecided.

1. Tsuchiya, "Economic History of Japan" *op. cit.* (see n. 6, p. 62), p. 129.
2. *Kurokawa, *Kōgei Shiryō*, Pt. 2, p. 37.
3. Masaharu Anesaki, *Buddhist Art—In Its Relation to Buddhist Ideals, With Special Reference to Buddhism in Japan*, Boston, Museum of Fine Arts, 1915, p. 44.
4. *Meigetsu-ki*, Tokyo, 1881, III, p. 21.
5. *Hyakuren-sho*, a chronology of events from 968 to 1299 A.D.
6. *Azuma Kagami* [History of the Eastern Provinces], a record in diary form of the Kamakura regime from 1180 to 1266; Vol. 9 in the original edition. From *Nihon Koten Zenshū* [Compilation of Japanese Classics], Tokyo, 1926, ed. 2, pp. 212–213.
7. *Heike Monogatari*, Chap. 6 (*Jishimpo*), cited in *Dai Nihon Kokugo Jiten* [Japanese·Language Dictionary], III, p. 89.
8. *Okada, *Garasu*, p. 56, mentions "a glass vessel, a mirror, and spectacles, and he became the first Japanese to hold European glass in the hand."
9. Chibiki Okamura, *Kōmō Bunkashiwa* [History of the Culture of the Dutch], Tokyo, Sōgensha, 1953, p. 263.
10. *Catalogue of Art Treasures of Ten Great Temples of Nara*, Tokyo, Ōtsuka Kōgeisha, 1933, VI, Pl. 5, English text, p. 5.
11. In the mausoleum of the Emperor Tenmu (673–685) there was found "a stone girdle resembling a *hiogo* chain, enriched with various gems and hung with two three-inch long stones something like rock-crystal and shaped as strings of cash; this recalled the "jewel girdle;" from *Aoki no Sanryō-ki* [History of the Aoki Misasagi] in *Koji Ruien* (see n. 6, p. 000), and quoted in translation by Richard Ponsonby-Fane in "*Misasagi*: The Imperial Mausolea of Japan," *Transactions and Proceedings of The Japan Society*, London, 1921, XVIII, pp. 20–78.
12. *Furuya, "Hompō Jōdai Garasu. . . . ," Pt. 6, p. 710.
13. Cited in Jō Okada, "Kenryū Garasu" [Ch'ien-lung Glass], *Museum*, No. 18, September 1952, p. 7.
14. "Journal of Prince Sanetake," Entry of the 10th day, 5th month, 1523. Quoted in *Okada, "Ruri Kirihame. . . . ," p. 12.
15. "Daily Journal of the Ōnryō-ken," Entry of the 14th day, 5th month from *Dai Nihon Bukkyō Zensho* [Complete Record of Japanese Buddhism], Tokyo, Bussho Kankōkai, 1912–1922, Vol. 134, p. 338.
16. *Kundaikan Sōchō-ki*, from Hanawa, *Shinkō Gunsho Ruijū* (see n. 21, p. 142), Book XII, p. 662, 674.
17. Masaharu Anesaki, *History of Japanese Religions*, London, Kegan Paul, Trench, Trubner & Co., 1930, p. 243.
18. For an English account, see Giuseppe Tucci, "Japanese Ambassadors as Roman Patricians," *East and West*, No. 2, July 1951, pp. 65–71. Also, Adriana Boscaro, "The First Japanese Ambassadors to Europe—Political Background for a Religious Journey," *KBS Bulletin—On Japanese Culture* (Tokyo, Kokusai Bunka Shinkōkai), No. 103, Aug.–Sept., 1970, pp. 1–20.
19. Shujirō Watanabe, "The Japanese and the Outer World," Chap. IX, *The Japan Magazine*, March 1928, p. 221. Inscribed on this monument is a letter of appreciation and avowal of faith on the part of the Japanese, with a promise to found in Japan a church dedicated to Santa Maria della Carita—a promise never fulfilled; also Boscaro, *op. cit.*, pp. 19, 20.
20. Robert K. Reischauer, "Alien Land Tenure in Japan," *TASJ*, Second Series, XIII, July 1936, p. 9. This was due to financial straits of local feudal lords, who gave surety in the form of mortgages.
21. Tome Pires had written, in the early sixteenth century, of Venetian glass and other merchandise exported as far as Southeast Asia, where Chinese trading ships also called; from *The Suma Oriental of Tome Pires, An Account of the East from the Red Sea to Japan, Written in Malacca and India in 1512–1515* (from the Portuguese MS), The Hakluyt Series, Second Series, London, 1914, p. 269.
22. *Okamura, "Nihon Garasu Kō," p. 16, diary entry of the 8th month, 26th day.

114. Interior of the Konjiki-dō, Chūson-ji • 12th century • Hiraizumi, Miyagi Pref.
115. Peacocks of the altar foundation, Konjiki-dō, Chūson-ji • 12th century.

116. Sacred sword of Ise · 1909, in an ancient style.
117. Fugen Bosatsu · Heian period.

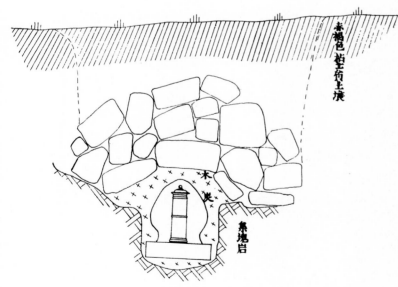

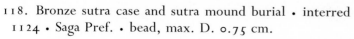

118. Bronze sutra case and sutra mound burial · interred
1124 · Saga Pref. · bead, max. D. 0.75 cm.

119. Bronze sutra case · interred 1123 · Shiō-ji, Fukuoka
Pref. · H. 37.5 cm.

120. Shrine and Shōtoku Taishi image • end of Heian period • Hōryū-ji • bead, D. 0.9 cm.
121. Model of a sacred horse of Ise • 1909, in Heian or earlier style.

122. *Shari-tsubo* • late Heian period • Denkō-ji, Nara • H. 3.45 cm.

123. Yakushi Nyōrai Trinity with Twelve Guardians • late
Heian period.

124. Rakan Panthaka Performing a Ritual for the Dead · Heian period.

125. Eleven-Headed Kannon • carved in 1316 • Hōkongō-in, Kyoto Pref.

126. *Mikoshi* · dedicated in 1196 · Konda Hachiman Shrine, Osaka Pref. · beads, D. 0.7–1.3 cm.

127. Horse's throat ornament · Kamakura period · beads, D. 0.4–0.5 cm.

128. *Shari-tsubo* • Chinese • early 14th century •
Ryōgin-an, Tōfuku-ji, Kyoto • H. 2.0 cm.

129. Subinda Worshiping *Shari* in a Vase • Early
Kamakura period.

130. Jizō Bosatsu · early 14th century.

131. Beadwork ornament • Chinese (?) • probably Ming dynasty • L. *ca.* 61.0 cm.
132. Cloisonné *kugikakushi* • Momoyama period.

EDO PERIOD

FOREIGN GLASS AND GLASSMAKING COME TO JAPAN

THE CONFLICTS and confusions that arose after Hideyoshi's death in 1598 culminated in the battle of Sekigahara in 1600, from which Ieyasu emerged the victor. In 1603 Ieyasu was granted the title of shogun by the emperor, and this date has been used here for the beginning of the Tokugawa period, although uncontested rule did not come until 1615, with the destruction of Osaka castle and the death of Hideyoshi's son Hideyori. Until his own death in 1616, Ieyasu worked to assure the strength of the Tokugawa line, which was to bring two and one-half centuries of freedom from internal strife.

Although Catholicism had first been tolerated, secret emissaries were sent by Ieyasu in 1607, and Hidetada, his son, in 1616, to Western centers (Macao? the Philippines?) to investigate its true nature.[1] The results emphasized the dangers of a religious practice that obligated allegiance to a foreign power (papal Rome). Ieyasu was eager for foreign trade and foreign knowledge, but the political danger that he saw in the foreign religion caused him, in 1614, to issue an interdiction against Christianity, "because the Catholic doctrine was considered inconsistent with home loyalties."[2]

Meanwhile the Dutch and English had appeared upon the scene, which gave the shogunate an opportunity to end the Portuguese and Spanish connections without losing entirely the benefits of foreign trade. The Dutch never became involved in religious matters. Neither did the English, although the "cross" motif on the ensign flying on their ships was the reason given by Sir Thomas Stamford Raffles for the coolness toward English trade.[3] Both English and Dutch had had free access to the harbor at Hirado, but after the final religious debacle the English withdrew and the Dutch were confined to the harbor at Nagasaki.

The third shogun, Iemitsu (1623–50), expelled the Spanish missionaries and traders in 1624 and the Portuguese in 1639 and executed Japanese "Kirishitan" who did not apostasize. The desperation of large numbers of Kyushu Christians brought about the rebellion of Shimabara in 1637, which ended with the mass execution of the insurgents. It was a time of tortures, burials alive, and crucifixions, and Christianity was ostensibly wiped out. But it had taken firm root in certain areas of Kyushu and western Honshu, and, although some converts apostasized, there were a few who eluded the authorities; they and their descendants kept their "Hidden Christianity" alive until the end of the proscription, a fact that came to light only after the Restoration of 1868.

In 1633 Iemitsu decreed that no Japanese ships were to sail abroad and that any Japanese then abroad would be prohibited from returning to Japan. The isolation of the islands was to be complete except for the strictly supervised entry of a few Dutch and Chinese ships.

To check possible recalcitrance on the part of the once rather independent daimyo (local lords) the shogunate established the *sankin kōtai*, under which each lord was required to spend certain periods of service in Edo. When the daimyo returned to his fief, his wife and children remained in Edo as hostages. This not only brought the daimyo under the surveillance of officials, but kept him in line when away from Edo; expense of moving his retinue to and from Edo and of maintaining two dwellings was a further deterrent to any subversive ambitions he might harbor.

As for the peasantry, they were held in check by rigid regulations and often by extreme poverty. The once lowly merchant class, however, which had profited by trading, by improved transportation, and by the development of monetary facilities in the Muromachi and Momoyama periods, although still rated as the lowest of the four classes (samurai, farmers, artisans, merchants), now rose to an enviable financial status. They were looked down upon by the samurai and the court aristocracy, but gained wealth and subtle power through their financial superiority.

Concentration of the daimyo with their families and retinues in Edo greatly increased the population and stimulated the economy. The population of Edo (now Tokyo) in the eighteenth century is said to have been between 1.3 and 1.4 million.[4] Then, as now, it was the largest city in the world. To meet the needs of so large a city, countless small shops and industries were established.

On a much smaller scale, industry grew throughout Japan. The feudal castles were no longer primarily fortresses, and in the castle towns that grew up around them handicrafts expanded and thrived as they could not during the preceding centuries of turmoil. Since Confucian ethics and regulations were emphasized in this period, the impulsive forces that had given birth to great religious art expression in the Nara, Heian, and Kamakura periods, and to Zen art in the Muromachi period, were restrained and formalized. The strictly regulated life under the Tokugawa shogunate produced a regulated kind of art; it might be delicate, beautiful, expert, but, except at the beginning of the period, it lacked the fire of new concepts. The popular *ukiyoe* art, which found its main expression in the famous woodblock prints and came into being during this period as an expression of the common people—just as the art of the traditional schools was for the aristocracy —has some vitality, but it, too, displays many of the signs of a craft rather than an inspired art. It is during this interval that glass gained ground.

The rise of the merchant class and the pastimes with which they amused themselves were, in a way, like a breath of fresh air. The puppet theater, and the new drama, kabuki, tended to democratize the theater even as the popular subject matter of *ukiyoe* paintings and woodblock prints depicting the luxurious life of the amusement world was a symbol of the slow breaking down of class barriers. But any overt, ostentatious display of wealth on the part of the merchant class, or defiance of prohibitions, was likely to arouse the authorities, because the offenders were preempting social privileges not in keeping with their station. Not unknown are instances of confiscations of property, or deprivation of name and status, even up to total social extinction.

The strict isolation of the country was broken only by a dribble of European goods and ideas, the few trading contacts with a colony of Chinese merchants and artisans in Naga-saki and with Dutch merchants. Nagasaki, in the long stretch of the Japanese islands, was like the eye of a needle. In the life of the country as a whole, what went on in Naga-saki was infinitesimal in quantity, but the qaulity of foreign knowledge and culture that was threaded bit by bit through that eye over the decades, and what the Japanese did with that knowledge, eventually became a potent force in Japanese culture. When the country awoke to the fact of Western scientific development, which made her by contrast a lag-gard nation, there sprang up a great furor to "catch up" and to be able to defend herself from the threat of the powerful Western nations that sporadically pressed for the opening of Japanese ports. The eighth shogun, Tokugawa Yoshimune (1716–44), being persuaded that the country was indeed in need of Western scientific skills, removed the ban on Western books in 1720, though retaining the prohibition of all books, whether Western or Chinese, that dealt with Christianity.[5] Then began the avid pursuit of the new scien-tific knowledge, primarily by a small group of retainers of the shogunate and the daimyo, who became known as *Rangakusha* ("scholars of Dutch learning"). Some went to Naga-saki to learn Dutch, others studied wherever they could find help. In 1808 the Yōgaku-sho ("Western Learning Institute") was established in Edo to provide translations from the Dutch; a Dutch encyclopedia was translated, and a dictionary published. Although not themselves technicians, the *Rangakusha* could pass on knowledge to those who were, and even initiate and supervise experimental undertakings.

Some scholars read translations of scientific treatises and strove, by trial and error, to master the techniques discussed or to assist artisans with their knowledge. With help from Dutch officials, or from interpreters in Nagasaki, or from *Rangakusha*, or at offices set up by some of the fiefs for study, as well as by study of imported objects, and, not least, by their own natural aptitudes, technicians succeeded in producing Western types. Thus began the "catching up" process, which was, in the end, to place Japan among the great powers of the world. This advance was made possible by the economic and social unity of the nation, which had developed during the years of isolation. Absolute political unification seems not to have been achieved, for such a powerful clan as the Shimazu in Satsuma, at the lower tip of Kyushu, was always rather independent. When the foreign menace increased in the mid nineteenth century, old factional antagonisms of Satsuma and other supporters of imperial sovereignty vis-a-vis the shogunate occasionally burst forth, with instances of bloodshed and disorders. The resignation of the fifteenth shogun, Tokugawa Yoshinobu, allowed the restoration of imperial leadership in 1868.

Mid nineteenth century confrontation with the demands of foreign shipping for port entry was a stimulus to Japan's original spurt toward mechanization and industrialism. Defense of the islands against the superior, armed ships of the West seemed the paramount duty and spurred the building of ships as well as the manufacture of artillery and arms. Ships needed protected signal lights, and this led to the production of colored glass, just as the production of chemicals had led to the need for acid-resistant glass bottles. In order to sustain the financial resources of their fiefs for the defense effort, many of the daimyo undertook the manufacture and processing of Western-style commodities, which they sold for profit. In this effort, for both defense and commercial gain, the manufacture of glass found a place.

IMPORTATION OF EUROPEAN GLASS

The earliest glass brought in by the Portuguese and Spanish was produced in southern European glass centers. Glass presented to Lord Ōuchi by Francisco Xavier has been noted in the previous chapter as being either Spanish or Venetian. A pair of Spanish glass candlesticks is now kept in Zuigan-ji temple near Sendai, one of the gifts brought back from a mission sent by Lord Date Masamune in the early seventeenth century to Spain, Rome, and Venice.

Glass from northern Europe was also brought in by the English and the Dutch. Much glassware of British origin came into the hands of Lord Matsuura of Hirado. In 1609 Jacob "Specx" of the Dutch mission, who had been commissioned to request permission to trade in Japan, presented to Ieyasu and Hidetada cloth, guns, gunpowder, and some small *glaese Flesschen* ("glass bottles") from Holland.[6] In the Tōshōgū Shrine atop Kunō-zan in Shizuoka Prefecture, where Ieyasu was initially buried, there are three small glass bottles reputed to be from Ieyasu's treasures.[7] They are of rather thin, greenish glass; two of the smaller type have a plain surface, but the larger one has a rounded square body with twenty-one vertical molded flutes. Can these be the *glaese Flesschen* of the report, or are they later in date?

Three late eighteenth or early nineteenth century European glass bottles (Pl. 133) were handed down in what seems to be their original European carrying box and treasured through the years by some Japanese family. The center one is gilded; the one on the left is undecorated; that on the right, though simple, is handsomely cut.

In the early years, foreign goods were sometimes smuggled ashore (in the capacious clothing of the officials, who enjoyed immunity from inspection). Before anything was formally offered for sale, the officials of Nagasaki selected from every new cargo those objects deemed by them to be suitable gifts for the shogun. It has already been noted that glass was a favorite among these gifts. It was, of course, a great day in Nagasaki when the new cargoes were displayed at special fairs "held three times yearly."[8] Until 1684 it was the custom for the representatives of merchants in Kyoto, Sakai, Osaka, Edo, and Naga-saki, to draw up a suggested price list for the articles. This was sent to the governor of Nagasaki, who, in turn, passed it on to the Dutch captain, "who then agreed to sell such of the goods as had prices affixed that came up to his ideas."[9] But after 1698 the Nagasaki Kaisho, a newly established government clearing house for imports and exports, handled all foreign business under close supervision.[10]

The European doctors (Dutch, Swedish, or German) who accompanied the Dutch trading missions to Japan often used medicine cases equipped with glass vials, as seen in some of the Japanese pictures of the time, such as a woodcut of about 1815 showing an arm amputation by a foreign surgeon—on the table an opened medicine case of this type is shown.[11] The Prefectural Library of Nagasaki owns such a case of mahogany, which was once the property of Dr. Philipp Franz von Siebold, who served in Nagasaki from 1823 to 1830. Each bottle has a flattened gilt stopper, gilt neck, and gilt decoration on the shoulder. The same library also owns some squat angular bottles with gilded ornamentation, used by Dr. von Siebold.

The Dutch ships that came to Nagasaki flew the ensign of the Vereenigde Oostindische Compagnie (Dutch East India Company) with the monogram oVc ("V.O.C.") often shown in Japanese pictures of Dutch ships (see Pl. 180, where it is corrupted to oVo). This monogram appears also on a number of items that may have been part of some ship's equipment. Plate 134 shows a large hanging glass lamp with such a monogram, suspended by glass-bead chains. Also with the monogram is a large punch bowl of transparent green glass sixty centimeters in diameter, in the Tokyo National Museum. Hanging lamps without the "V.O.C." but with bead ornamentation are seen in a number of prints of the time. A small hanging lamp has construction details similar to the "V.O.C." lamp of Plate 134, but is decorated with silk-strung beadwork and a long bead fringe. A label on its box reads: *Garasu Ō-tsuki-tōrō. Kenjō, Satsuma* ("Glass Hanging Lantern. Gift. Satsuma"). Satsuma would be a strange source, since the glass is inferior to Satsuma glass metal and this area was never known for bead production. Quite likely the lamp may have been a gift from someone in the Satsuma fief, or from the Satsuma lord, whose contacts with Nagasaki were rather close. The label also cites a Tanaka collection designated as Teiundō.

Dr. Nagamichi Kuroda, Tokyo, has a small collection of European glass of Bohemian types (Pls. 135, 136), which has been handed down in the Kuroda family since about the Bunka-Bunsei eras (1804–29), when the owner's great-grandfather was lord of the Kuroda clan of Fukuoka in Kyushu. An inscription on the packing box states that they came from Holland. The Kuroda clan shared alternately with the neighboring Saga clan the defence of Nagasaki (which was a shogunate domain) and thus had many opportunities to obtain European goods.

In addition to European glass imports, there were also some items of Chinese origin. It would be difficult to say whether these were imports from the mainland, or the work of Chinese glass artisans in Nagasaki. Chinese shipping was, like the Dutch trade, restricted. As there were no Japanese diplomatic relations with any country during this period, the flow of diplomatic gifts ceased, and fine gifts from Chinese imperial manufactories, which might otherwise have been received, did not come.

In the writing room of the Seisonkaku of the Maeda daimyo in Kanazawa, Ishikawa

Prefecture (Kaga), there are transparent glass panels of unusual technique. These are definitely of Chinese origin. Each panel is composed of layers: in the center layer are cut-out designs in an extremely thin brown paper(?), suggesting the flat donkey-skin shadow puppets of China; on each side of this decorative layer is a layer of transparent, colorless glass rods of minute diameter (forty rods in a space of about 3.7 centimeters) laid obliquely but at different angles in the two layers; and an outer layer, on each side, of transparent, colorless sheet glass. Some of the cut-out designs are naturalistic; one is a square vase with flowers; another is a Chinese poem. The date of these is unknown. The Seisonkaku was erected in 1863, but the panels are thought to antedate the construction of the building. In the same building are ten glass panels inserted in the woodwork below sliding paper-covered window panels; on each is painted a bird (Pl. 137). Tradition says these came from Holland, but their date is unknown.

Another example of the use of tiny rods of solid, colorless, transparent glass placed side by side is a curious hinged wooden case from abroad with six flower-vase tubes of thick, colored glass, held upright in holes cut in the hinged folding frame. At the base of each half of the frame is a paper painted with a flowering vine pattern in delicate rose and green, covered and yet not concealed by the minute glass rods, laid side by side, presenting a ridged transparent surface. The box is inscribed "Bunsei 2 [1812], by boat." It is in the Yamaguchi Prefectural Museum, Yamaguchi city.

In the Nijō Jinya, Kyoto, there are small panes of glass set in a sort of small dormer high up on the wall of the main room. The glass is amazingly thin, only about one-half millimeter thick. The Nijō Jinya was built in the first half of the seventeenth century by the son of one of Hideyoshi's faithful subjects, Lord Ōgawa Tosano, a daimyo of Shikoku. When Tokugawa Ieyasu came to power by beleaguering Hideyoshi's heir, Lord Ōgawa gave up his feudal rank rather than give allegiance to Ieyasu. He went to Kyushu as a commoner and became an import-export merchant, dealing with Korea and China.

According to tradition, the Ōgawa family returned to Kyoto after Lord Ōgawa's death and are said to have brought with them articles left over from the import trade. The high window is in the room reserved for visiting daimyo, and was perhaps placed there to admit light during troubled times, when solid wood sliding screens were drawn about the lower, open part of the room. This window is made up of a number of small panes of thin glass, each about 12.7 by 17.5 centimeters in size. A number of panes, each framed in wood, still survive in place; a fragment of a broken one, presented to the author by the present Ōgawa family, is in The Corning Museum of Glass (No.62.6.2). It is only 0.05 centimeter thick. There is no record as to the provenance of this unusual glass. Its extremely even surface, colorless fabric, and thinness suggest a considerably later date. It is included here only for the record. In the sliding doors of a small cabinet in the Nijō Jinya is a Chinese painting of a scholar in a garden; in the railings of the steps leading down into the garden of this scene are tiny, delicately painted landscapes, covered with a thin glass, which, it seems, is similar to the thin "window glass." Judging from the circumstances, it seems that this glass must be Chinese.

Heavier glass, this time very likely from a European source, was used by the daimyo

Date Tsunamune, in about 1688, in the sliding doors of his Edo mansion. After his death, the building containing them was donated to Zennō-ji temple in the Date domain, on the outskirts of Sendai in northern Japan. The empty frames that once held the glass are still preserved in the temple. It is said that Zennō-ji was also known locally as Shippō-ji because of this glass. The significance of this is two-fold: it suggests the high value placed on glass, since a temple was popularly named for it, and it discloses the confusion regarding the term *shippō*, which also means cloisonné.

A type of bottle that interested the Japanese for its novel shape was a tall gin container, four-sided at the base and rounding off at the shoulder to a tubular neck often mounted with pewter. Some were decorated on the shoulder with silver. Plate 138 illustrates a large gin bottle of transparent green glass, which was decorated in Japan with a painting of a Dutch *Kapitan* attended by two servants, one of whom, in Indian costume, holds a long-handled parasol over his master; among minor motifs is a strange word drawn in lines suggesting brushstrokes, which is evidently in imitation of some Dutch word.

A later bottle of similar shape but undecorated and obviously a commercial type, blown in a mold, bears on one side the molded Dutch name "V. Hoytema & C." The date is unknown.

Another example is a decanter of Irish type, of colorless transparent cut glass to which was added a delicate painting of what seem to be Japanese *nadeshiko* and other flowers, in colored enamels (Pl. 139).

Two dainty, stemmed wine glasses with white spirals in the stems are in a private collection in Tokyo.[12] These are gold rimmed, and have on the bowl a design of flowers and insects in gold, a decoration that seems to be Japanese rather than Western; the gold is darker and less glittery than usual, and the workmanship, the owner believes, suggests the gold lacquer technique of Japan. The inscription on the box notes that these glasses were brought from Batavia (the Dutch East India Company station on Java) by Captain Arend Willem Feith, and were obtained from him in the third month of Anei 3 (1774).

Some of the reports and writings of the time reveal what the Japanese liked or requested, and record actual importations. As early as 1577 the missionary Luis Frois wrote to Father Valignano that "sand-timers, glass vessels, eye-glasses and bottles containing confections" would be suitable gifts for the Japanese feudal lords.[13] Captain John Saris, who sailed from England in 1603, advised all English merchants to send to Japan "drinking glasses of all sorts, cans and cups, beere glasses, gilt beakers and looking glasses of the largest sort."[14] Sir Thomas Stamford Raffles, lieutenant governor of Java and its dependencies from 1811 to 1816, advised that "the Japanese are passionately fond of cut-glass of every description. A variety therefore should be sent from a plain cut glass rummer to a magnificent lustre. Coloured and plain liqueur bottles and glasses and ornamented smelling bottles are in great request.[15] British plate and common window glass will also be in demand. . . . Astronomical and optical instruments—An assortment of every description and of whatsoever may be useful in an observatory. . . . Clockwork—Watches and clocks of various descriptions, but expressly London make and bearing the London mark. . . ."

Many of the English items were sent from England to Batavia, where the Dutch took them over. The source just quoted comments on the strict watch kept on trade relations in Nagasaki; presents, "whether official to the Governor of Nangasaki or the Emperor [shogun] are of no great value, and rigidly limited by law and usage; and as the government of Japan is much stronger and more vigilant than that of China no such abuses can be ventured on at Nangasaki as those which esixt in Canton."[16]

Official lists and literary references reveal the variety and quantity of glass included in the foreign shipments. There were looking glasses, "which they break to make spy glasses and spectacles out of them;"[17] glass mirrors "big and small, the former measuring 2 × 3 *shaku* [60.6 × 90.9 centimeters] and the latter 4 or 5 *sun* by 1 *shaku* [12.12 or 15.15 × 30.3 centimeters];" glass utensils, vessels, novelties [*tsukuri no mono*]; eyeglasses of several kinds, such as "nose pinchers," "telescopes, magnifying glasses, multiplying glasses," "five-color glasses [prisms?]," "seashore glasses [?]," "*shokōku* about 30 centimeters long and consisting of a wooden box with a small rod of *biidoro* inside of which is water that rises and falls. . . ."[18] Other entries list such lots as: 18 looking glasses and 12 dozen glass bottles; 1,000 glass bottles; 60 glass bottles; 1 box with 53 spectacles; 1,000 glass bottles in a chest; 1 chest of glass instruments.

Other lists include: one large camera obscura, hanging vase lamps, glass waiters, clocks, musical table-clocks and silver pocket watches, mahogany liquor cases fitted with bottles of liquor and two liquor glasses, gold-flowered liquor decanters, gold-flowered small wine glasses, long and narrow wine glasses. There were also mirrors in gold frames, "Patent Lamps with reflecting diamond-cut mirror," "Organd's Patent Lamps."[19]

In a woodblock print of the interior of the *Opperhoofd*'s house on Deshima, made in 1788 by the artist Shiba Kōkan, the well-known exponent of Western style perspective, a "Great European Lamp" is shown hanging from the ceiling.[20] These chandeliers, and even portions of them, were among European glasses treasured by the Japanese. When Captain Ricord, of the Russian ship *Diana*, tried unsuccessfully in 1811 to put into port at Hakodate, he gave to each Japanese visitor who came aboard "a piece of fine red cloth, for making a tobacco bag, and two pieces of cut glass belonging to a chandelier. They regarded the latter as great curiosities."[21] A cut glass pendant from a European chandelier or candelabrum, which was at some time mounted in silver as a piece of jewelry, is preserved in a private collection in Saga city.

There are at least two sources (and very likely others) in which one can see sketches of glass vessels imported during this period. One is *Ransetsu Benwaku* by Otsuki Gentaku (or Bansui), published in 1799, purportedly consisting of his answers to questions about Dutch matters not well understood by them, and jotted down by one of his students. A section concerning glass vessels and their nomenclatures is accompanied by sketches and names. One presents, diagrammatically, a European saltcellar (Pl. 140). This sketch is of interest because of a similar European glass saltcellar in The Toledo Museum of Art (No. 53.156), which was found in Japan (Pl. 141). The Toledo example is colorless, thick and heavy, and 6.5 centimeters long, with twenty flutes around the lower portion.

The second illustrated source is a long, scroll-like *oboe* ("memorandum") of 1862 recording sales made by a dealer or broker in Nagasaki (Pl. 142). In this there are rough, but clear, outline half-sketches of glass vessels and a few other items, accompanied by their names, sometimes the name of the purchaser, and the price paid.

In addition to luxury types of glass, the Japanese in this period became acquainted with such useful articles as spectacles and telescopes, the hour glass, the barometer, the thermometer, and all sorts of scientific glass for laboratory use, such as retorts, and also with other items in which glass played either a primary or subsidiary role. The glass mirror of the West replaced the metal mirror previously used, and clocks and watches (with their glass covers) displaced the old water clocks and incense-burning devices for telling time. Japan was bombarded with a multitude of new ideas. What effect this influx had upon her own glassmaking efforts is discussed below.

BEGINNING OF FOREIGN TECHNIQUES

It would have been strange if the importation of European glass had not stimulated Japanese craftsmen to experiment with glass products of their own. This they did, as best they could, with some help from Chinese artisans in Nagasaki (chiefly makers of beads and other small articles), some guidance from foreigners and, later, with the help of European books.[22] It was not until after the end of the period and the lifting of the seclusion act that the Japanese could see European production procedures. But long before that they had acquired a technical skill of their own by which they produced glass vessels of fine quality, reaching a peak of excellence in the Satsuma workshops in the mid nineteenth century.

The changes brought about by the use of glass in Japanese life and by the ideas seeded in Japanese minds during the years of isolation were perhaps not very conspicuous in the overall culture of the time, which centered so strongly around traditional ceramics, lacquers, weaving, painting, and metalwork; but the techniques and forms that were assayed in this period helped Japan, when the isolation ended, to advance rapidly along the road to modern industrialization. It was not a matter of merely accepting European modes and forms. Dr. von Siebold recognized this when he wrote, "Japanese imitate how to make things, but the things made develop according to their customs."[23] Except for export wares, this has ever been true.

In Japan the *issen sōden* ("single line inheritance") had always been conspicuous in the crafts. A craftsman handed down verbally to his oldest son, or to a chosen disciple, the secrets of his trade, which were passed on by the pupil to his own successor in the same way. Furthermore the first *biidoro* makers in Nagasaki, having discovered what was then felt to be an exotic secret treasure, had further reason for secrecy. It will be noticed that in the early pictures of *biidoro* manufacture such matters as the raw materials and mixing the batch are never shown. Of those illustrated here, only the scroll of sketches, which is considerably later, includes the complete process (Pl. 147). The artists of the early pictures probably had no opportunity of seeing the preparatory steps.

Seemingly the earliest modern Japanese discourse on glassmaking is a section of the *Wakan Sanzai Zue*, an encyclopedia by Terashima Ryōan published in Osaka in 1713. In the following quotation, parentheses denote parenthetical clauses in the original; brackets denote editorial notes.

> *Biidoro* (The Chinese call it *po-li*. Commonly called *biidoro*, perhaps from a foreign language).
>
> *Biidoro* is considered to be *hari* [an ancient term for glass]. Originally it came from the *namban* countries. A citizen of Nagasaki-Hishū mastered the method and produced it. Recently it is produced in great numbers in Osaka, Sesshū. To make it, powdered silica and coarse niter are used. (Heat up by a small fire and remove the salt ingredient.) Put a jar in the furnace (a jar made of Karatsu pottery is suitable for this). Put lead in the jar; add sulphur and melt over a charcoal fire. Wait until the lead is melted, then put the powdered silicic stone and the powdered niter in and stir until it becomes like Korean gluten [gluten that looks like amber]. Attach a thin copper tube of about 62 centimeters in length and heat up and blow to make a form. Products round, oval, flat, and mortarlike in shape can be achieved according to the force of the blowing, the length of the blowing time and the skill of the worker. The original color is white [colorless], changing to wine color, purple, blue, or greenish yellow if powdered chemicals are added. However, real red is impossible (minium is changed by the heat). It is used in many rosaries and weights. It imitates crystal, amber, and lapis lazuli. It is beautiful when used for wine bottles, wine cups, and plates. It is a matter of regret that it is fragile. It is not inferior to crystal when used for eyeglasses. It permits complete transmission of sunlight. [It concentrates sunlight to make a fire]. Things that are made at present are produced from melted liquid and chemicals. . . . After a long time the taste of wine when poured out into a cup shows no change. Oil does not change for a long time. . . .[24]

An illustration from the *Haikai Azuma Miyage* ("Souvenir Poems of the East") (Pl. 143) of the Hōreki era (1751–63) shows a *biidoro* blower seated beside a simple stove, in the open top of which there seems to be a small crucible for his glass batch. Beside the craftsman is a tray of finished products, and on the rack above are hanging wind-bells and goldfish globes. It would seem likely that the blowing pipe is simply a glass tube called a *tomosao* (literally; a "mated pipe"), even today one finds them in use in some glass factories. This is a very simple portrayal of the glassmaking method, but is probably all that the public was allowed to see at the demonstrations of the middle eighteenth century, the time of publication.

Plate 144, taken from Miyake Yarai's *Bankin Sugiwai Bukuro* of 1732 shows a *biidoro* craftsman attended by an assistant. The furnace is shown, as is a wooden tub of water (perhaps a fire prevention precaution in a vulnerable Japanese building), and a number of finished wares. The artist has simplified his picture, not even showing the supply of glass metal. The accompanying detailed explanation is one of the earliest extant descriptions.[25]

Biidoro Blowing
It is understood that this is just like the Chinese craft. We knew it was a matter of

blowing but had no idea about the technique. Once a Nagasaki man secretly learned the Chinese process and the mixing of raw materials, and at last acquired the technique. He made it in secret. I do not know whether someone stole the technique, or whether he transmitted it to someone with the intention of perpetuating this secret process. Anyway, someone learned it, and nowadays artisans show the craft publicly, as at the time of Buddhist or Shintō ceremonies. They astonish people. (However, the mixture of the raw materials for *biidoro*, the apparatus of the furnace, are kept elsewhere and they make only the *biidoro* items in public). Because this is a very rare process, done by a secret method, they do not let people know the way of mixing the raw materials and other technical matters. This is understandable. When they blow *biidoro* vessels, there are some scraps remaining. These they break and put back into the crucible. They repeat this process again and again; so the materials when once mixed are used repeatedly.

Thus the artisans made *biidoro*, but only colorless ones; they could not demonstrate the making of indigo, amber, or light green. I will relate below the mixing of *biidoro*, the secret methods of coloring, the arrangement of the furnace, and the equipment. Those who try to practice what I say must follow it in detail, without omitting anything. The following is a secret, but I will explain it in detail. So please enjoy this secret; and I hope you will succeed.

After selecting *hakuseki-shi* ([quartz] from China), as transparent as rock crystal,[26] put it into a stone mortar, crush with an iron pestle, and sieve it through a silk screen. Then smelt Chinese lead of very excellent quality [presumably lead oxide], and pour into it the above mentioned quartz powder, little by little. The quantity is not uniform, since it varies according to the viscosity of the quartz. Anyway, pour the powdered quartz into a vessel containing the melted material, the lead. Test it with an iron spatula, and when it has the firmness of boiled rice, reduce the charcoal fire beneath the pan to a very low heat. Smooth it vigorously with the spatula, stirring from morning to night. Then fill a vessel with water and add the melted quartz and lead. Now it will look like zinc. Return this to the mortar and crush it with the iron spatula as described above.

Prepare potassium nitrate salts and mix in a pan with the above. Heat slowly on a charcoal fire for three days and three nights. If it boils and seems about to burn then boil water in a pot without salts and every hour or two pour one *shaku* [about 0.018 liter] of this into the mixture. Regardless of the amount of hot water you pour into this pan it will remain separated from the chemicals.

Now, I have a secret oral teaching about producing the salts of potassium nitrate. For instance, when we want to make one *kin* [now 0.6 kilograms] of this we must boil three *sho* [about 9.5 pints] of water in a pan with one *kin* of potassium nitrate. Add about ten *momme* [37.59 grams] of fragments of uncorroded copper ware, cover tightly, and bring to a boil. After one boiling up remove from the fire and cool in the pan. When cool enough, uncover, pour off the water, and dry the potassium in the shade. But if the mixture has not yet turned green from the copper, the salts have not yet formed. In that case, reheat in the same manner as above—again and again [if necessary]. The proper time will be known by the copper stain. If this process is performed badly, the potassium nitrate will sometimes catch fire. Be careful!

When the previously mentioned *biidoro* mixture has been heated for three days and three nights and you are ready to blow it, use an iron pipe about 75 centimeters long, which has been made beforehand, and put this iron pipe into the mixture that is very hot in the pan. Then take out the pipe and blow into it gently. A moderate amount of the mixture will have adhered to the end, and now it becomes globular like a ground cherry. Put the pipe into the crucible again and stir so that the first bit of *biidoro* has another layer. Take the pipe out, lowering the end, and blow the *biidoro* into a flask shape as shown in the picture. If we blow the flask shape slowly, the end curves and the flask takes on a curved form. So, move the pipe to and fro a little and make the shape round. If you cannot get a good shape, press it on a flat surface and reshape it without removing the pipe. Then you can make the bottom flat. With a metal knife break the *biidoro* away from the mouth of the pipe. The cut edge will not be beautiful, so you put the mouth edge in the fire and make it smooth with an iron spatula.

To make a chrysanthemum bowl, first prepare a clay mold in chrysanthemum shape, and blow into it. To make the handle of a writing brush or knotted hair ornament, one man should blow into the pipe with *biidoro* attached to the end, and another man, from the opposite end, pulls the *biidoro* out two or three feet, as desired, then cuts off the length desired. You can make the brush handle or the *kanzashi* [hair ornament] according to the extent of your pulling. The cut edge of the *biidoro* is made smooth with the spatula. For the knotted *kanzashi*, put the part you wish to knot into the fire again and, when heated, knot it.

This is the general idea of *biidoro* blowing.

Now as for the chemical preparations for the coloring:

If you want amber colored *biidoro*, add some powdered orpiment and pine resin in equal amounts. If you want a light green, use pine resin and copper sulphate, with slightly more of the latter. For dark blue color, boil white lead [basic lead carbonate] with *seitai* [indigo or cobalt?][27] and, when they are well melted, put the mixture in a crucible and set on a slow fire. Now put *biidoro* on the tip of your pipe and dip it into the mixture; then take it out and blow. Because you put the pipe into the crucible of low temperature in which the *seitai* liquid was not very hot, the *biidoro* layer becomes slightly cooled, and you cannot obtain a large bottle or flask; you can achieve only small saké cups, hair ornaments or handles of writing brushes. Since you work with white lead, these will not be entirely transparent. If you add pine resin to the white lead, you will get a deeper blue, and this also will not be transparent. *Seitai* has generally come from China. Things made with it and the white powdered lead ingredient added to the *biidoro* batch are chiefly such things as dark blue beads, or *ojime*, in imitation of an insect nest [a bead type so called because of many minute surface pits suggesting the tunneling of insects, and said to have been imported from China]. It is said that if you add *kimpaku no usuzumi* [?] to this indigo-colored *biidoro*, it will become quite transparent. I have not tried this as yet, but everything else I have written here is the result of trying the general methods.

However, if the temperature is not right, or the quality of the quartz not fine, or if the white lead is not well integrated and the mixture does not mature, the manufacture will not be satisfactory. So try the proper combinations three times, even five times, and after many, many failures you will naturally learn the secret of how to make it. If you are discouraged and give up after only one or two trials, you cannot master it.

I have written above the secret of carrying out the *biidoro* preparation, how to prepare the coloration, how to arrange the furnace and crucibles and the fire, and also how to blow. This is a rare modern technique. You must enjoy it!

The *Shokunin Burui* ("Various Types of Artisans") by Tachibana Minkō, first published in 1774, gives a one-page treatment of *biidoro* making, including a color illustration that shows the simple furnace, the master and his apprentice blowing, and beside them the trays of finished products (Pl. 145). The darker shading of some of the items suggests that colored glass was intended, possibly the popular indigo blue. The accompanying text reads:

Biidoro

This is not of Japanese origin. It is said that it came from a foreign country and was first brought by the *kōmōjin*. Its technique is splendid. They could make it in Nagasaki in the middle era, and it was transmitted to Kyoto and Osaka. That inaugurated the profession. Recently the occupation has been found in Tōto, [the eastern part of Edo], and the kinds of products and the large number of ornaments abound because of the truly peaceful imperial reign that extends to the four seas. We should be grateful, should we not, that we can assemble unrestrictedly even the production methods of foreign countries?

In the Nagasaki Municipal Museum there exists a set of seventeen manuscript volumes entitled *Nagasaki Kokon Shūran Meishō Zue* ("Drawings of Famous Ancient and Present-day Scenes in Nagasaki"). It is dated 1841. The "Picture of the Making of *Biidoro* Wares" is reproduced in Plate 146. It is one of the most complete early pictorial records of the equipment and methods of the period.

At the right is a square tank-type furnace with flames spurting from the opening at the top. As in other illustrations, the mixing of the batch is not shown. The craftsman sits on a bench before the "glory hole," into which he has inserted, for reheating, a *pokon-pokon* (or is it a bottle?), which he is just finishing; others rest on a tray beside him. Behind the worker stands a child blowing into a *pokon-pokon* (?, or could it be an assistant making one?). On the shelves above the furnace are various finished items.

In the left portion of the illustration a beadmaker is seated at his small furnace. The technique is essentially that of glass beadmaking in the Tomb period (pp. 51–57), although the equipment is more advanced. It will be noted that the artisan has a screen (of mica perhaps) for protection from the glare of the heat over which he melts the end of the glass rod before applying it to the revolving wire. The artisan uses his left fingers to revolve the wire. Finished beads are suspended above the worker.

The Tokyo National Museum owns a hand scroll made up of a series of amusing rough sketches by Suzuki Shige—, also dated 1841. These show the techniques, failures, and successes associated with *biidoro* manufacturing. In the scroll there are intervening sections of explanatory text. Translations of the pertinent passages follow.

Plate 147, left top

Once there was a man in the capital. He excelled in all matters, skillfully making even things called "glass," which had been transmitted from distant Western countries. He not only made it himself but also taught other people and had them make it. Among the various materials used he melted quartz and put it in water, then he put it in an iron mortar and pounded it well into a powder called "crystal sand." He ground mugwort to a powder and, putting it in an unglazed dish, heated it. As for the salt [nitrate], first he placed water in an iron pot and heated the salt in it; this he then separated from the water, put it in an earthen pot and roasted it, and so forth. Thus he taught exactly.

Caption at right: As regards the stone, that produced in Hitachi Province is excellent.

In upper center: If the fire is weak it will be difficult to make a flower vase.

At the left: How terrible! You had better add the salt little by little.

Plate 147, right top

He mixed all these chemicals together in an earthen pot, which he placed on the furnace, where it was heated for about — hours. When he thought it was completely melted, he took it off and poured it into water, then took it out and placed it in a jar. To it he added some of the boiled salts and heated it for — hours. Then it was finished.

Plate 147, left middle

When he thought it was completely melted, he inserted an iron tube and picked up some of it. Blowing it and making it flow as he pleased, he produced articles of various shapes. How wonderful that such things are created according to one's skill!

Caption at right: Let's pull! Let's pull!

At the left: I tell you it is harder than stone.

Plate 147, right middle

Now in order to make "something like spectacles" he began to grind and grind. Barely, and with difficulty, he succeeded in producing one. [Looking through it] everything becomes very large. It is astonishing and cannot be expressed in words. [Note: In this portion of the sketch the effects of the "something like spectacles" are illustrated—a magnifying glass and a multiplying glass.]

Plate 147, left bottom

He also made this *biidoro* into a "sun-catching lens" [*hitoridama*]; when you let the sun pass through it everything is scorched. In addition, he never failed to make anything he wished. Thus this *biidoro* became popular in society. People admired and appreciated it as a precious treasure. Thieves heard of it and wanted to steal the rare treasure at any cost, and watched for the opportunity. Once it happened that they met this man in the mountain. They wrangled among themselves as to which one should rob him, and the man seeing this, cried out "Rascals! Rascals!" Taking the lens out of his *kimono* he focused the sunlight on the robbers. It focused on their heads and clothes and burned them unbearably, so they fled precipitately. It is said that when one excels in something one can avoid an unexpected calamity.

Various captions: What is this?

Oh, it's nothing; it can't be anything serious.

Hot! Hot!

Plate 147, right bottom

The colophon:

Tempō 12 (1841), Kanoto Uma [the cyclical year], end of the tenth month.

When *hari* was made in the Kisei [Kishō?] Garden I wrote and illustrated this scroll for myself, and offered it to the lord. The pictures were drawn on lining paper, and the writing is on *hōsho* paper. The coloring is faint. I drew the pictures and wrote the text like those old illustrated scroll paintings. This was the first time that the best *hari* was produced by order of the lord.

Painted by Suzuki Shige—.

Since the Hitachi Province mentioned as the source of quartz was not far from Edo, one may infer that the author was perhaps from that city or possibly a retainer at Mito in Hitachi. As will be seen in the discussion of glass activities in Edo, the industry was thriving there since the late seventeenth century.

Mr. Yoshio Hiraishi of Nagasaki, ninth generation of a family of clockmakers, owns a clock and watch shop. His forefathers, he says, were interested in learning all they could about various techniques associated with clocks, such as metalworking, woodworking, glass, and enamel. Among their notebooks, and some others assembled since, are three dealing with glass. These are in manuscript form and undated, apparently notes written down from some lectures. When the Japanese of the Edo period wrote of glassmaking they often used Dutch terms, transcribed into the Japanese *kana* syllabary as they sounded or looked, to the writer. This sometimes makes translating difficult.

One of these notebooks carries the title *Atomareru*. After first stating that "the production of glass is old in origin; it was invented by the Egyptians but the date is not clear" and then giving the chemical symbols and their pronunciations written in *kana*, it proceeds with formulae for various kinds of European glass.

The second book is a continuation of the above, beginning with "Crown Glass." Here the writer not only gives formulae but expands into methods:

CROWN FLINT

Silica [*Kiisuru-shūru*]	300 parts
Soda [*kōshū sōda*]	250 parts
Calcium [*kōshū kalk*]	84 parts
? chloride [*Roto coroido*]	6 parts

When the stone materials are not pure, the glass may have some color. When producing flint and crown glass, the purest materials should be used. They should be put into the furnace little by little and, when melted, more should be added, with continuous stirring. After ten hours all material will be melted. Cool for eight days. The lower strata of glass will be heavy, and the upper strata light. If it is pure, it can be used as glass for astronomy.

> Note: Flint glass is white [colorless].
>
> Crown glass is in most cases greenish [bluish?].
>
> Flint glass should be polished convexly.
>
> Crown glass should be polished concavely.
>
> Crown glass should be used for the outer lens in a telescope.

Silica is a white stone; after roasting it completely, when you throw it into cold water it immediately breaks. But even if the outside seems to have been roasted, the inside is not easily heated, so you should roast it completely. Throwing the roasted stone in the water is called *shaki-ritsu-ken*. (We heat the stone in order to make it break easily.) After it is broken, the silica is ground in an iron mortar until it is so fine you do not feel the grains. This powder is then filtered through a cloth. When the filtered powder is put into water, a yellow substance rises to the top; this is iron. Remove the iron by washing the powder several times, drying it in the sun, and adding hydrochloric acid. (If there is no iron you need not add the hydrochloric acid.) When hydrochloric acid is added you should remove it also. You can do this by the same method as in dealing with sulphur chloride. After removing the acid, the powder should be dried in the sun, and you obtain silica.

Flat glass, which is used as the cover glass of a clock, necessarily requires much labor and cost if you grind it from glass, so you should prepare a mold of iron, copper, or whetstone, the shape of which depends upon the size of the clock. After cutting the flat glass into a round shape, put it in the mold and fire it in the furnace. You will obtain a glass in the shape of the mold. (This is because the glass melts.) You can polish it after this procedure. (By this process you save labor and money.)

From these passages one glimpses something of the difficulties that confronted the

Japanese artisan who wished to try out glassmaking. The *Atomareru* also deals with the laborious methods of preparing raw materials; it gives formulae and many admonitions, together with a number of alternatives. Then there are directions for manufacturing glass (including the crown glass quoted above), methods for preparing metallic oxides for color, for preparing enamel, and for painting on glass.

A letter of "Secret Instructions" written by a glassmaker in Kyoto, giving glass formulae, is quoted on pages 207–208.

Another extant manuscript of formulae for various colored glasses owned by Mr. Saichi Ōtomo of Kanazawa was written by Nakamura Benkichi, known as Ōno Benkichi. He lived in Ōno-mura, Kaga Province (Ishikawa Prefecture) and died in 1870, but it is not known whether he was actually a glassmaker.

Satō Nobuhiro wrote in 1827 of the varying glass imitations of precious stones, from what materials to produce them and how to do it—by grinding powder and mixing with an adhesive. Then he discussed the comparative qualities of glass:

> Domestic glass was at first produced in an incomplete way and had some dimness, cloudiness, and was not clearly transparent; it was very fragile and easily broken. So it could not be used for bead manufacture. But my grandfather, Fumi Ken-o, introducing the scientific method, found that silver ore, when refined into silver, was melted like a paste during the firing in a big furnace; so he and his disciple studied together the method of refining glass, and gradually improved the quality.[28]

He then discusses the difficulties encountered in improving the methods, so that gradually, step by step, they were able to produce a superior glass "remarkably clear and hard and pretty much like crystal." But it was still not equal to that made in London. So Satō and a friend, Ogino Shōminsai, "who was adept at manufacturing," began to study glass production and finally succeeded in achieving a satisfactory crystal glass.

In Edo, which was the center of Dutch learning in the early eighteenth century, a number of scholars helped glass establishments to develop and improve their glass by supplying them with European information, or by supplying European style forms (such as a retort), which were then copied. Their contribution will be discussed in the section dealing with Edo's production.

One should mention the comparative ease with which the first Nagasaki craftsmen learned the making of beads, lampwork ornaments, and other small and relatively simple items. Perhaps they imitated the work of Chinese artisans. When later they attempted to produce larger blown glass bottles and other vessels, or make glass bottles that would withstand the corrosive action of strong chemicals, and glass pure enough for optical use, there was no one to demonstrate, and only foreign books for guidance. By 1863, however, Sir Rutherford Alcock, the first British minister to Japan, could write: "They have attained no small skill in manufacturing glass for themselves, in great variety of forms, though I am not aware whether they have attempted window glass; but lamp chimneys, ground glass shades, bottles cut and molded, these they can manufacture at about English prices, and scarcely, if at all, inferior in material or workmanship."[29]

It has been generally conceded that the one thing not mastered in the Edo period was the manufacture of flat glass, but Dr. Thunberg's testimony in the 1770s is to the contrary.

> They are likewise acquainted with the art of making glass, and can manufacture it for any purpose both coloured and uncoloured. But window-glass, which is flat, they could not fabricate formerly. This art, they have lately learned from the Europeans, as likewise to make watches. . . . In like manner they understand the art of glass grinding, and to form telescopes with it, for which purpose they purchase mirror glass of the Dutch.[30]

If Thunberg was correct about flat glass, output must have been limited, for all evidence suggests little or no production before the mid nineteenth century. There is, however, a brief reference to flat glass produced at Sukagawa (see p. 233).

THE ROLE OF NAGASAKI

The early Portuguese and Spanish who came to Japan via Goa, the Philippines, Malacca, and Macao became known to the people of Japan as *namban-jin* ("southern barbarians") because they came from the southern ports. The *namban-jin* were the first Europeans to reach Japan, and from them emanated the grace of southern Europe manners and customs, which left a lasting influence after they had been expelled. The lighter-haired Dutch, who arrived a little later, looked different; they were called *kōmō-jin* ("the red-haired people"). Their impact upon Nagasaki and upon Japan was different and, because of its longer duration, sank even deeper into Japanese culture. Foreign ships, before the beginning of the Christian persecutions, were not confined to any special ports, and their personnel seem to have been free to move about within the country. Although the Portuguese were most active in Nagasaki, which had opened to them in 1570, they also sometimes used Hirado and Hakata, among others, for their trading operations. The English and Dutch both used the beautiful harbor at Hirado, where picturesque vestiges of their presence are still to be seen.

After the expulsion of the Spanish and Portuguese and the isolation of Japan, only the Chinese and the Dutch were permitted entry, and only to Nagasaki. Other ships (English and Russian, for example) occasionally appeared in coastal waters but were not welcomed, and nothing came of their efforts at establishing trade relations until after 1853 when Admiral Perry succeeded in breaking the isolation. During the years of isolation, the Dutch were closely restricted in Nagasaki, where they continued to bring to Japan not only the culture of Europe but of all the countries of southern Asia where they traded. The new foreign ideas permeated the life of Nagasaki and crept gradually throughout the nation. Mingled with these influences was that of China. At first the Chinese were quite free, but at the end of the seventeenth and for most of the eighteenth century they, too, were confined to a special walled quarter.

The Dutch ships, although restricted to calling but once, or at some periods twice or thrice, annually, laid over for some months disposing of their wares and negotiating for return cargo; their crews, it seems, lived aboard ship. Except for "visits of respect" to the shogun in Edo, the Dutch official responsible for operations, together with his staff, his medical advisor, and sometimes his family, lived throughout his term on Deshima, closely confined on that tiny walled, man-made island. Deshima was then connected with the city by a bridge, but is now encircled by so much new land that it is difficult to recognize it as ever having been an island. In later years, after the ban on Dutch reading was lifted, there was slightly more freedom within the city, but it was only with the lifting of the isolation that foreigners were really free. Traces of the Chinese presence can be seen throughout the old town.

The Portuguese, and to a lesser extent the Spanish, left an abiding impress upon Japanese life and culture, particularly in Nagasaki. Today many of the things they introduced are a common part of Japanese life, although their foreign origin is frequently overlooked except by scholars. The Japanese language is full of infiltrations from this time. *Tabako* is as ubiquitous in Japan as anywhere in the world. *Pan* (bread, from the Spanish *pan*) and *kastera* (sponge cake, from the Portuguese *castella*) are inextricably part of the modern Japanese diet. There are dozens of words that mark the influence of the foreigners.

The Portuguese word *vidro*, meaning "glass," was now incorporated into the Japanese language as *biidoro*, replacing popularly the *ruri* and *hari* of former periods. Since the southern European glass products imported by the Portuguese and Spanish were plain soda-lime glass, the term *biidoro* seems to have referred to the thin glass vessels with uncut surfaces, whereas a later term, *giyaman*, deriving from the Dutch *diamant* ("diamond") came to refer primarily to the heavier and thicker glass used for faceting—in other words "cut glass."[31] Goto Rishun wrote in his *Kōmō Dan* ("Tales of the Red-Haired Ones"), "*Giyaman* looks solid, like crystal; for carving a pattern on glass it is indispensable."[32] Though the real differences between the two terms are not always understood today, the mention of one or the other to older Japanese seems to elicit a response not exactly nostalgic but one of bright and warm animation. Frequently they remember a family treasure of either *biidoro* or *giyaman*. These two terms still have an exotic ring, but have all but disappeared from common usage, being replaced by the modern term *garasu*.

Anything that had to do with Dutch life in the "Little Holland" of Deshima found its way into pictorial art of the time. The furnishings and customs seen in Dutch offices and quarters—chairs, tables, chandeliers and candelabra, the wines and exotic foods, the tableware, glass decanters and wine glasses, the feasts, concerts, games and pastimes—are all shown (Pl. 149). The literature of the time also records the Dutch and their impact on the city.

One cannot review the life of the exotic city of Nagasaki without reference to Maruyama, the old amusement district on a hill above the harbor, which played so large a role in the assimilation of the foreign cultures. In some of the scenes of Deshima, the elegant entertainers of Maruyama in their elaborate kimono and coiffures are shown. The new-style glass decanters and wine cups must have found a ready market in Maruyama, where the flair was for the new and foreign. Two modern poets nostalgically voice the tradition of Maruyama and Nagasaki glass:

Maruyama no Kagetsu wa
Furuki biidoro ni morite
Motohoshi namban no sake.

Would that she of the
Kagetsu of Maruyama
Might bring me the *namban*
wine in an ancient *biidoro!*
Nobutsuna Sasaki

Giyaman no ōsakazuki wo
Te ni toreba kankatsu kokoro
Wasure-kane tsumo.

Taking the large *giyaman*
wine cup in my hand
I cannot forget the free spirit
of the olden times.
Isamu Yoshii[33]

The Chinese found pleasure on Maruyama, where they enjoyed the Japanese dances and performed Chinese dances and sang Chinese songs. Vivid reminders of those times remain in dances performed at the annual Okun'chi Festival of Suwa Shrine.

We understand very well that there was friendship between Chinese and Japanese people on those festival days. For example, the Chinese audience threw glass hair ornaments and leaden rings—both of which were precious things at that time—instead of bouquets, because they were so deeply moved by the skillful Karako-odori [Chinese dancing] by Nagasaki people.[34]

The Nagasaki trade (as all East Asian trade) was very profitable for the Europeans. According to Dr. Thunberg, writing of the decade from 1770 to 1780:

The traffic with Japan was formerly so very lucrative to individuals that hardly any but favorites were sent out as chiefs, and when these had made two voyages, it was supposed that they were rich enough to be able to live on the interest of their fortunes, and that therefore they ought to make room for others.[35]

In the early days when a sort of diplomatic immunity was observed for the Dutch officials, these emoluments were often achieved with guile, for Dr. Thunberg continues:

The captain therefore dressed himself in the blue silk coat, trimmed in silver lace, made very large and wide, and stuffed, and furnished in front with a large cushion. This coat has for many years past been used for the purpose of smuggling prohibited wares into the country, as the chief and the captain of the ship were the only persons who were exempted from being searched. The captain generally made three trips in this coat every day from the ship to the factory, and was frequently so loaded with goods, that when he went ashore, he was obliged to be supported by two sailors, one under each arm. By these means the captain derived a considerable profit annually from the other officers, whose wares he carried in and out, together with his own, for ready money, which might amount to several thousand rix dollars.

When the ruse was discovered, the order went out to search the captain also.

> It was droll enough to see the astonishment which the sudden reduction in the size of our bulky captain excited in the major part of the ignorant Japanese, who before had always imagined that all our captains were actually as fat and lusty as they appeared to be.[36]

Though glass was only one of the many commodities imported, it seems to have been a favorite. In the *Nagasaki Kokon Shūran Meishō Zue* ("Drawings of Famous Ancient and Present-Day Scenes in Nagasaki"), the title page (Pl. 148) shows the two sources of imports of the time: China and Europe. Two Chinese tables, in the illustration, stand amidst the waves of the sea; on one are laid Chinese books, and on the second, a tribute to its popularity, European glass.

How the foreigners reacted to Japan and to the Japanese may be gleaned from the reports sent home by missionaries before their expulsion and by the writings of foreigners attached to trading missions. Of the latter, Dr. Englebert Kaempfer's is the most detailed. He made two trips to Edo, in 1690 and 1691, as the Dutch commissioner's personal physician when the latter paid his annual respects to the shogun. Dr. Kaempfer, a botanist as well as a physician, collected plants wherever he went and made voluminous notes on botany and on everything his observant mind perceived—the Japanese never deterring him, apparently thinking his notetaking related entirely to his scientific studies.

Sir Thomas Stamford Raffles, although his information seems to have been obtained very largely through others, noted certain aspects of the Japanese character that seem to bear upon Japanese success in conquering the problems of glass manufacture. He wrote of the intelligence and polish of the Japanese, "considerably advanced in science, highly inquisitive and full of penetration."[37]

GLASS OF NAGASAKI

Traditions regarding the origin of glassmaking in Nagasaki are rather vague. In 1615 a trader (?) of Nagasaki, Hamada Yahei, set forth by sea and spent some time at foreign ports, where, among other things, he learned the technique of grinding lenses. Returning to Nagasaki, he taught the method to Ikushima Tōshichi, who is generally credited with having a number of pupils who spread the method of grinding crystal and glass lenses.[38] It is clear that Yahei did not learn how to produce glass metal—or at least could not produce optical quality—since the Japanese broke up European mirrors for the purpose. It has been stated that after the opening of Nagasaki in 1570, one or more foreign technicians came and taught glassmaking,[39] and that in 1730 a magistrate of Nagasaki was ordered to have Dutch traders teach the methods of manufacturing "*biidoro*, chintz, and cheese" to Nagasaki officials.[40] Since it is after this date that the Japanese pictures showing the blowing of glass vessels appeared, such an order may have initiated Western style glassblowing. However, shortly before, Nishikawa Tadahide (Jōken) had written in 1720, "Although the *ban-jin* ["barbarians"] imparted to us the secrets of their methods of manufacturing *biidoro*, it ceases to exist at this time. Rather, our many products that are manufactured by our own method are superior to the foreign ones."[41] Their "own method" was apparently a comingling of what the foreigners had taught them and of what had been learned from Chinese artisans. The superior quality of Nagasaki glass can be seen in such items as the graceful wine pot of Plate 21. It seems significant that the glass items of the Imauo-machi *kasaboko* (an umbrellalike "float" carried in the Okun'chi Festival) show a lead content ranging from sixty-three to seventy percent, about analogous to that of the Nara period. Scientific study of other Nagasaki glass products would no doubt reveal a similar high content.

The glass artisans were called *tama-kō* ("bead workers") and their small factory-shops, *tama-ya*. This seems to corroborate that they made things such as beads, lenses (which might also be termed *tama*) and other small items, although the *tama-ya* later handled blown glass and larger works as well.

Although the *tama-ya* of Nagasaki were very skillful, they did not learn to produce sheet glass. For all forms of flat glass they either used imported glass as it came or laboriously ground it down to the desired shapes. But an easier and cheaper method was devised in Japan (see p. 188) of roughly cutting a piece of sheet glass to fit a mold of desired shape, then firing to melt the glass and fill the mold. Toward the end of the period some Osaka makers of round hand mirrors used the bottoms of bottles.

Nagasaki was wealthy. There are numerous tales relating the extravagant use of glass, generally by wealthy merchants. For instance, in the Kanei era (1624–43) Itō Kōzaemon had a large "*biidoro* box" made as a goldfish tank, which he attached to the ceiling of his home; and on a hot summer's day, when he looked up, he saw "gorgeous creatures swimming about overhead and felt refreshed and cool."[42]

EYEGLASSES AND LENSES

The grinding of lenses, introduced in the late sixteenth century by Hamada Yahei, set the wheels in motion for a development that was eventually to place Japan in the top rank for optical glass. Spectacles "caught on" and became popular for their usefulness in aiding vision and also for the exotic and fashionable air they gave their wearers. Many examples in the pictorial art of the Edo period demonstrate the popularity of the new aids. The Japanese word *megane* is used in compounds to denote a dozen or more varieties of lenses that, in one way or another, aid or protect vision. Some of these varieties have already been mentioned.

BEADS

Beadmaking had by this time long been the prerogative of Buddhist temple and Shintō shrines. Hence, beadmaking in Nagasaki by lay craftsmen was indeed a new adventure.

Nishikawa Tadahide in *Nagasaki Yawasō*[43] credits the manufacture of beads at this time to both the Europeans and the Chinese. In Europe, both the Venetians and the northern Europeans were skillful beadmakers, and recent research has disclosed a seventeenth century glass factory in Amsterdam, where glass beads in the Italian fashion were produced, which may have been exported to Japan in cargoes of the East India Company.[44] Many Japanese representations of *namban-jin* ("southern barbarians"; i.e., Spanish and Portuguese) and *kōmō-jin* ("red-haired people," i.e., the Dutch) show Portuguese men wearing or carrying long European rosaries and wives of the Dutch officers wearing bead necklaces. The glass lantern of Plate 134 is suspended by chains of glass beads.

In the Edo period there was a prolific output of beads, in glass and in many other materials, but from all the extant examples it is virtually impossible to illustrate any indisputably made in Nagasaki as distinct from Osaka or Edo, except for certain ones added as embellishment to objects of Nagasaki manufacture.

The Japanese had long been accustomed to using Buddhist rosaries, some of them of glass in whole or in part, but now "All kinds of Chinese-style rosaries are made according to one's preference—such as purple, black, white, fragrant prayer beads, glass, and various others,"[45] The rosary makers, then as now, formed a profession and worked at a simple workstand in their own shops. They did not produce the glass beads themselves —they merely strung them.

At this time beads, other than those in rosaries, acquired a nonspiritual significance and were largely used either for utilitarian purposes or as ornament. An *ojime*, threaded on the cords of tobacco pouches and of medicine cases called *inrō*, was pushed down over the container for closure and stability (see Pl. 150). Other beads, woven on wire into beadwork borders or other portions, formed decorative networks added to all sorts of objects.

The various types of beads in the Edo period will be treated in the section on glass in Osaka (pp. 204–206), which later became the outstanding bead center.

INLAYS

Previous to the Edo period, inlays had primarily taken the form of jewellike *hankyūdama* (as in the Shōsō-in), or small shapes of glass cut to fit into a lacquer design to enhance it. In the case of religious items the purpose seems often to have been to add a symbolic note of spiritual power. In the Edo period, however, when glass was a fascinating, newly rediscovered substance, a different sort of glass inlay came into vogue. It became popular to insert small *biidoro-e* (paintings on glass) into all manner of objects (see Pls. 18, 151). They were often set into black lacquerware boxes, and a service of ten lacquer soup bowls in the Mody Collection has ten small round *biidoro-e* of different landscape scenes inset, one in each lid.[46] *Biidoro-e* are another instance of the adaptation of a foreign form, but the inlay of tiny or medium-sized plaques seems to have originated in Nagasaki.

VESSELS

The first modern blown glass vessels of Japan were made in Nagasaki under a triple stimulation: imported European glass, possibly infrequent help from Europeans, and the work of Chinese artisans. Just when the first vessels were blown cannot be stated, but it must have been rather early in the period (see Pl. N. 154). The Chinese used a soft lead glass, and the Nagasaki craftsmen seem to have worked in this material,[47] as they did with the glass for the festival display of Imauo-machi, various parts of which have a high lead content (Pl. 157).

An early, documented bottle of blown glass (Pl. 154) is clear yellow, but the most common color for Nagasaki glass is a slightly purplish dark blue, richer in tone as the shape increased in size (see Pl. 21, 155).

The earliest documented example of blown glass seems to be that of Plate 152. Possibly related to this is a set of cups, one of which is discussed in Plate Note 153. The glass metal of a set of five covered bowls, one of which is discussed in Plate Note 156, seems strikingly like that of the cups, though less delicate.

GLASS AND THE OKUN'CHI FESTIVAL

Nothing is more revealing of the ancient character of Nagasaki than the Okun'chi Festival of the city's Suwa Shrine. For the student of glass it has special significance.

Japan is undoubtedly one of the most festival-conscious nations, every one of its thousands of shrines and temples observing a number of special days each year. And yet, this festival is unique in Japan. It is said to have been depicted in Chinese prints and paintings of the Ch'ing dynasty and referred to in Chinese literature.[48] In Europe it was known through the reports of the Dutch missions in Nagasaki.

Tradition dates the origin of this festival to the suppression of Christianity and the consequent cessation of the colorful Catholic processions, which the Japanese had enjoyed. The priests of the city's Suwa Shrine decided to replace the Catholic processions with an elaborate annual Shintō festival.[49] The time chosen was the propitious "double nine" day (the ninth day of the ninth lunar month)—hence, the name of Okun'chi (Felicitous Ninth Day). In 1690 Kaempfer described it as follows:

> All sorts of diversions and publick shews, dancing, plays, processions, and the like (which they call *matsuri*, or an offering, and *matsuru*, that is, making an offering) so greatly divert and amuse the people, that many chuse rather to lose their dinner, than to give over sauntering and staring about the streets till late at night.[50]

Thunberg, writing about a century later, noted:

> The inhabitants of each street vied with each other in magnificence and invention, with respect to the celebration of this festival, and in displaying, for the most part such things as were characteristic of the varied produce of the mines, mountains, forests, navigation, manufactures, and the like, of the province from which the street derived its name, and whence it had its inhabitants.[51]

Nagasaki had eighty-eight "street" divisions (*machi* or *chō*), of which eleven are now chosen, in rotation, to take part every year.

The outstanding performance, aside from the carrying of three sacred palanquins (*mikoshi*) down the long steep stone stairs of the shrine, is the Ja-odori, or Dragon Dance, evidently derived from the Chinese New Year procession. This part of the festival is included annually, without rotation. The long, flexible, snaky dragon, with crimson and golden scales and magnificent large head, is manipulated by men in Chinese style costumes, who support the dragon form on long upright poles, making it slither and writhe in realistic undulations in its effort to capture the golden ball kept always just out of reach as drums sound and cymbals clash. At times the dragon rests, but even then so lifelike is it that one is carried away by the illusion, seeming to sense the nostrils quivering, and, as the head is turned sharply this way and that, the large, glass balls, painted on the back side and inserted in the eye sockets, seem, by magic, to possess a restless, penetrating glance. At the end of the performance, the bearer holding the golden ball aloft breaks away and runs from the scene, with the undulating dragon in hot pursuit. The realistic, protruding, and reflecting eyeballs are major contributors to the realism of the performance.

One of the early features of the festival (now lost) was the float of Edo-machi, on which effigies of the Dutch *Kapitan* (the *Opperhoofd*) and his lady sat in chairs under an arbor whose ceiling imitated the grape trellis in the yard of the *Kapitan*'s house on Deshima. The purple grapes were clusters of glass forms, said to have presented a beautiful sight and to have sounded "*chyarin-chyarin*" as the float was drawn over the pavement.

Besides the grape trellis float, many *kasaboko* (festival "floats" carried somewhat like umbrellas) included glass in one form or another (Pl. 157). One is said to have shown in *biidoro* the process of papermaking; and others had glass pine trees. One had what is called a "*biidoro* mosaic." The curtain of another was embroidered with figures of fish with glass eyes.

The entire Okun'chi Festival, with its many and varied scenes, comprises a synthesis of the Chinese, European, and Japanese aspects of Nagasaki. It is still one of pomp and extravagant display.

THE GLASS SOUND TOY, *Pokon-Pokon*

Originally a Chinese toy, the *pokon-pokon* was perhaps first made in Japan by the Chinese glass artisans of Nagasaki. Later it became popular all over Japan, surviving into the early twentieth century. The scene illustrated in the *Nagasaki Kokon Shūran Meishō Zue* (Pl. 146) portrays a *biidoro* maker, and perhaps a young assistant manufacturing them (or a child blowing the toy?). By the late eighteenth century it was sufficiently popular in Edo to appear in woodblock prints and in illustrated books of the time. Plate 158 shows an unusually large and handsome example, probably made in Nagasaki.

The toy consists of a small funnellike form whose closed bottom is very thin and hence flexible. When air is blown in, this flexible glass bends outward with a slight clicking sound, and as the air is drawn back the glass springs back with a snapping sound. This gave rise to various onomatopoetic names for the toy, according to the hearer's interpretation of the sound. It was perhaps most universally known at the *pokon-pokon* or *pekon-pekon*, but it had many other names. The *Geien Nisho*[52] uses *kyokoro*. The same reference also quotes two older sources. In one, the toy was said to be found in glass shops and commonly call *toeki*. The other, *Ganzan Zakki,* gives one method of manufacturing a *koto*: "First, blow glass into a gourd shape. Heat the bottom part to make it concave. Then smooth it to an even thickness, though it will remain a little uneven. Another name for *koto* is *kyokoro*."

The toy was made in colored and in colorless glass enameled in colors. The designs were sketchy (Pl. 158), for these toys were cheap commercial products sold at stalls during temple and shrine festivals. As may be imagined, the *pokon-pokon*, with its paper-thin bottom, was an expendable toy. Scarcely ever could a child preserve his souvenir long. Many older people nostalgically remember it as one of the joys of their childhood. The *pokon-pokon* is one phase of the leaven of Nagasaki that spread through Japan.

> For me there is the unforgettable memory of a cool evening when the swinging lanterns were lighted and I, a child in a *yukata* with white ground, walked along holding on to a parent's sleeve with one hand and clutching carefully in the other a *koppen*.[53]

Early in this century its manufacture diminished and died out. According to Mr. Yoichi Kojima of Fukuoka, *champon-champon* were, for safety, later made (in Fukuoka only?) of thin steel covered with a coat of tin.

COMBS AND HAIR ORNAMENTS

The striking hair ornaments of tortoiseshell worn in the elaborate coiffures of the Edo period are well known through the woodcuts of the time. But the ornamental combs, (*kushi*) sometimes set with glass panels, and the glass *kanzashi* (barlike hair ornaments), seem to be known only through extant examples, and they are not easily found today. A favorite type of comb, considered exotic and chic in Nagasaki, had, inserted in the usual tortoiseshell frame, a panel of fairly thin, transparent glass on which was engraved a bit of seascape with a Dutch ship prominently shown (Pl. 161). As these combs were worn upright, near the front of the coiffure, the design in the transparent glass showed up well and no doubt brought prestige to the wearer. One unusually large comb owned by Mr. Y. Yezaki of Nagasaki is of horn, 13.0 centimeters wide, with a high glass panel engraved with an unusually complicated view. The glass panels of these combs were very likely imported, but the engraving was Japanese after the manner of Dutch engraving. Other combs were later made in other places, but the style was modified, and different motifs were used (see Pl. 23).

The small glass hairpins (known as *kōgai*) were made by simple lampwork techniques. Like the *pokon-pokon* (Pl. 158), they were sold as souvenirs at stalls on festival days. Usually the *kōgai* had a small round stem ending in a point, with an ornamental head or a small ornament applied at the other end; sometimes there were even dangling pendants. This fashion also caught on quickly in other parts of Japan.

TOBACCO PIPES

The traditional pipe of Japan (*kiseru*), somewhat similar to the Chinese and Korean varieties, but always short and small, developed after the Portuguese introduction of tobacco. It was essentially a tube, with a small metal bowl just large enough for "three puffs," and a metal mouthpiece. In Nagasaki, where everything unusual and exotic was desired, the *kiseru* were sometimes made by the lampwork technique. Plate 20 is an example that is not only larger than was customary but unusually handsome in its proportions, delicate shaping, and colors.

QUAIL CAGES

The quail is a favorite in Japan, as evidenced in paintings and poetry and as witnessed in such a quail cage as that of Plate 22. The cages were usually of wood or bamboo, but some happy craftsman had the delightful thought of using transparent glass rods to replace the bamboo—another instance of the Nagasaki flair for using glass in new and pleasing ways.

FLY REPELLERS

In the early nineteenth century, very likely as a development of the resourceful Bunka-Bunsei eras, it was the custom to hang from the ceiling brightly colored shining spheres of glass on the assumption that flies or other unwanted creatures (in the open, unscreened house of Japan) would be repelled by the glitter. Supplementary Note 70 describes a notably large example.

Biidoro-e

Small *biidoro-e* used as inlays have been cited. *Biidoro-e* (today usually called *garasu-e*) were, in general, larger sheets of glass painted on their reverse sides with landscapes, Biblical and Christian subjects, portraits, and domestic scenes. The idea was inspired by the glass paintings, probably executed in China on sheet glass imported from Europe, seen in the quarters of the Dutch on Deshima. One author mentions the artist Shiba Kōkan's visit to the office of the *Kapitan* on Deshima, where, in a twenty-mat room, (one mat is approximately 1 × 2 meters) he found that "On all sides framed pictures painted on *biidoro* were hanging, with chairs beneath them." The author adds that "those who painted *biidoro-e* were something like our modern *penki-ya* (painters of advertisements). They were not great artists, but among *biidoro-e* we may find some that are very tasteful."[54]

CLOCK COVER GLASSES

A type of painting on glass allied to the *biidoro-e* are the glass covers for clocks, which were painted with ornamental enamel designs. Two techniques for producing the circular glass for this purpose were mentioned in one of the Nagasaki notebooks on glassmaking—one a laborious grinding down of mirror glass, and the other a short-cut process of fitting a roughly shaped piece of sheet glass in a mold of the desired shape and size and firing it until the softened glass had filled the mold. Mr. Yoshio Hiraishi, the owner of the notebooks on glassmaking, also owns about a dozen of these decorated cover glasses. Some have radiating designs in gold; some have little European girls in rose-trimmed bonnets; one, larger, has a clear center with a floral band for border. The owner considers these to have been produced in Nagasaki, and, since one of the note-books explains the enameling process, this explanation seems reasonable.

Cloisonné

Aside from the elementary enamelwork on the cover glasses and on the *pokon-pokon* sound toy, cloisonné enameling of the variety seen in other periods seems to have been ignored in Nagasaki.

The Spread of Glassmaking—Merchant Craftsmen

It would have been unnatural to expect that the manufacture of such rare and attractive products as *biidoro* and *giyaman* could long be confined to Nagasaki, but just when the first glassmaker left the city to practice his trade elsewhere is not known.

Osaka

Sakai, the ancient port at the eastern end of the lnland Sea and the port that had served the two imperial capitals—Nara and Kyoto—as well as nearby Osaka, was an important center for domestic and foreign shipping. Before the proscription it was an important Christian center, renowned for its cultural and artistic life.

Osaka, the major city only a few miles away, became independent and enterprising, characterized by free, exuberant popular expressions formalized in the new *ukiyoe* school of art. It was here that bunraku (Japan's famous puppet theater) originated, and kabuki (the popular theater) saw its early development. By 1703 it had over three hundred fifty thousand residents, and some say it rose in the eighteenth century to one-half million. Its merchant class, by virtue of its financial powers, was often given to ostentation beyond their low social rank.

In the Genroku era (1688–1703), a retired millionaire merchant, Okamoto Saburōe-mon, of the financial house of Yodoya, built a house that is described as magnificent beyond words.

> No chamber even in the Imperial Palace can compare with Yodoya's magnificent dwelling. . . . No residence of any daimyo or other noble can compare. . . . The parlours are gilded with gold and the gold-gilded screens bear paintings of the flowers of all the seasons drawn by famous artists. His garden has a splendid pond, bridges spanning it, as well as trees of all descriptions gathered from all places in Japan and China. The so-called summer chamber has sliding doors made of glass.

There are glass cases lining the upper part of the walls just below the ceiling, which are filled with water in which goldfish can be seen swimming.[55]

Because of this and other "unrivaled luxurious things," he incurred the anger of the *bakufu*, his property was confiscated and the family deprived of their name. Among the items confiscated were ships with "glass ports," whose value could not be estimated, and ninety-six crystal (glass) sliding doors.[56]

The story is indicative of Osaka's social and economic climate, with its wealthy mercantile barons, who often, with impunity, ignored the government and overstepped old class limitations. It was the freshness in outlook and the city's wealth that gave impetus to the glass industry and to the output of the *biidoro* and *giyaman* artisans.

GLASS OF OSAKA

The area now known as Osaka Prefecture (Osaka-*fū*), parts of which were known as Izumi, Sesshū, Sennan, and Kawachi, had an ancient glass tradition, especially in bead-making. Large amounts of glass beads have come from the area's tombs, and here, too, were the tombs of the emperors Nintoku and Ankan, which have yielded glass vessels probably imported during the Tomb period. But, as elsewhere, whatever productive skill and activity had anciently existed seem to have vanished. By the Edo period the traditions were largely forgotten, so that *bidoro* was virtually new.

The *Waken Sanzai Zue*, published in Osaka in 1713, states that *biidoro* "was also made in Osaka."[57] One repeatedly runs across the statement that *biidoro* artisans had set up their stalls at festival fairs in Osaka, Kyoto, and Edo in the Kyōho era (1716–35) to demonstrate their trade and "if requested" to sell their products.

The earliest name we have for an Osaka glassmaker is Harimaya Seibei (whose real name was Kume Seibei), a merchant who is said to have learned the technique from the Dutch in Nagasaki. In the Hōreki era (1751–63) he opened a *tama-ya* before the entrance to the Tenman Tenjin Shrine, where he manufactured wine cups, toys, hairpins, and other small items, which he sold in the marketplace. He is regarded as the first *tama-ya* to be known by name and is generally referred to as the "father of the Osaka glass industry."[58] Seibei taught his secrets to several pupils, including Yorozuya Shōzaburō.

In 1830 Itō Shōzaburō, the third generation after Yorozuya Shōzaburō, ventured upon a joint enterprise with Watanabe Kihei, and, by enlarging their business and training a number of apprentices and journeymen, they brought prosperity to a lagging industry. The apprentices, one by one, gained independence and became managers of their own factories. Kihei was the third son of a certain Watanabe who was in the service of the daimyo of Sasayama in Tamba Province; he had moved to Osaka and became an apprentice of Kazariya Kahei. Eventually he became a *giyaman* craftsman. In 1830, the same year that he and Shōzaburō joined forces, he set up his own shop and was known as Kazariya Ki. He made glass for the daimyo of Kii Province and became an influential glass manufacturer. In the precincts of Osaka's famous Sumiyoshi Shrine, there was said to be a pair of stone lanterns that had been dedicated in 1828 and that bore the names of fourteen glassmakers and dealers as donors, including the names of Shōzaburō and Kihei.[59] This is evidence of a notable growth in glass manufacture in Osaka by the first quarter of the nineteenth century. Most likely the list of fourteen did not include all the glass craftsmen of Osaka, but only a select group of the most prosperous.

In the Bunsei era (1818–20) an artisan named Kyūbei of the Kagaya shop in Edo was put in charge of the shop's new department of *giyaman* manufacture. He requested that he be sent to Osaka to study the technique there, since in Osaka "glass manufacture was more advanced than in Edo."[60] He became an apprentice to Izumiya Kahei and after a year of study returned to Edo to manufacture *giyaman* wares for Kagaya. Hence, the reputation of Osaka as a major glass center was by now well established.

The production of this area was large, considering the conditions of the time. It is said that the daily output of various kinds of bottles and small items such as the popular *poppen* (*pokon-pokon*) was at the rate of 150 per person per day, and that one hundred hair ornaments could be made daily by one worker.[61] From the Anei era (1772–80) onward, glass of various sorts was displayed at such places as pleasure resorts. Plate 181 represents the broadside advertising such a display in Edo. Plate 182 shows another by an Osaka craftsman. There is also reference to one Burakusai "who came from Osaka and from January to autumn exhibited at Higashi-Ryōgoku [in Edo] a large *giyaman* landscape."[62]

Much of the production was carried on in villages surrounding Osaka and particularly in Izumi Province. For beads, Shinoda-mura must be mentioned, and for mirrors, Minato-mura. Iwasaki Sembei, who made such things as weights, lanterns, dishes, and invented a telescope, was from Izumi. Since he trained no heir, his process for making optical instruments was lost.[63]

At the end of the Edo period in 1868, after Commodore Perry had negotiated the treaty with the United States, the kerosene lamp was introduced, and two Osaka glass men, Kume Chōbei and Itō Shōzaburō, began to produce lamp chimneys, but the time was not ripe, since the imported kerosene was prohibitively expensive. Itō Shōzaburō had, it is said, opened a factory in Osaka in 1835 producing *usumono* ("thin wares") and, like his ancestor of the same name, the first Itō Shōzaburō, he trained many apprentices.[64]

MIRRORS

It has been stated that the Japanese could not make sheet glass before modern times. They could not, therefore, make mirrors of the European type except by using imported glass, which was expensive. But in Izumi they could, and did, make a circular hand mirror. "The first looking-glasses of Japan were produced by putting mercury on Yoshino paper, which was then pasted to the glass. The glass was inserted in a frame of wood; afterward a lid was added. The majority of these looking-glasses were small and they were extremely breakable."[64] The popular name for such a mirror was *mage-kagami*, *mage* referring to the topknot or chignon styles worn by both sexes. The *mage-kagami* was really a pair of mirrors. They were mounted in circular wooden frames. One frame was slightly larger and fitted over the other as a cover when not in use. For viewing, one mirror could be held toward the back of the head to reflect the image of the coiffure into the second mirror, which was held in the other hand (Pl. 162). Some seem to have been mounted in lacquered frames, but many of those made in Osaka were of *kiri* (paulownia) wood with flower sprays, birds, or reeds painted in rough colors on each wooden back.

The glassmaking process is described as follows. The raw material for glass was quartz from Tosa Province. This was calcined and then ground into powder with a waterwheel. Lead and niter were added, and the mixture was reheated. When it had melted, it was poured into a mold, to form sheet glass. Yoshino paper was then pasted on a piece of tin, and, after applying mercury to the paper, it was attached to the glass. Charcoal was used in the process, "but only the *bincho* charcoal of Tosa Province was used, because of its heating power."[65] The mercury was poured over fine uncrumpled tinfoil and left until it amalgamated. In 1843 the back of the glass was plated with silver nitrate; this was called *gimbiki* ("coating with silver").[66]

These mirrors, it is said, were often made from the comparatively thin bottoms of glass bottles, because of which they were also called *bin-kagami*, or "bottle mirrors." The village of Minato-mura was a center for the production of these mirrors, and the competition, as seen from contemporaneous records, was keen.

Members of the Matsunami family, after considerable litigation, became the leaders of the mirror manufacturers.[67] As shall be seen in considering the modern period, the family still continues in the glass industry, although *mage-kagami* were discontinued when the manufacture of flat glass was introduced.

In the Edo period, Minato-mura was under the jurisdiction of the Tokugawa shogunate. The village had sixteen manufacturers of mirrors, with more than two hundred workmen. Since these mirrors, besides being a new fashion, were much less expensive and more practical than the old metal type, there was a great demand. Local records show that the *mage-kagami* were made in two sizes, large and small, and that their cases were decorated in color with such designs as the phoenix, the rising sun, cranes (dancing or flying), and plum blossoms. Annual production was about three thousand large mirrors and forty thousand small mirrors.

Labor difficulties were not uncommon and led to the enforcement of strict regulations, protecting employers among other things, against "the workmen's laziness." The rules of the trade association that was formed stated:

> If workmen come from other provinces and secure a job, they must obtain agreement from the workmen already employed. If violated they cannot be employed.

> No workmen may engage in the work of a retail business without permission from our organization, unless they deal with wholesalers in Sakai and Osaka.

> Members of the organization should arrange the retail prices. No member shall bargain regarding sales without permission of the organization.

If there is a new man who wishes to join this organization, he must first obtain approval of the organization.

All members are requested to pay the organization fee without delay.

Those who wish to leave the organization, or who change their personal seals, should report to the organization.

The mirrors were widely distributed throughout Japan, at first by Sakai merchants in Osaka. At the close of the period the chief broker for these mirrors was the Sakaman Shōten of Kuhōji-machi in Osaka.[68]

Many things were produced by the *biidoro-* and *giyaman*-makers of Osaka—beads, hair ornaments (though these were at one time frowned on by the conservative authorities), toys, *jiku-tan, sudare* (curtains), lanterns, eyeglasses, telescopes, wine cups, wine bottles, and *mage-kagami.* By the end of the Edo period, even though conditions were unsettled and the country was adapting to changes fostered by Western influence, the glass industry of Osaka had solid foundations.

BEADS

The output of glass beads became quite prolific in the Edo period. They were used in various ways. Some were added to *kanzashi*, or even, occasionally, to a comb. *Sudare*, or door curtains, were sometimes made up of strings of glass beads. A bead formed the slide on the *inrō*, and on tobacco pouches and purses. The fashionable *inrō* was formed of small compartments, three or more, strung together on silk cords and fitting closely together. The topmost unit was the cover, and a bead, the *ojime*, with both cords passing through it, could be pushed down to create an adequate closure. The bead might be of any material—gold, silver, copper, coral, ivory, crystal—but many were produced in glass of various colors, often in imitation of semiprecious stones. The *netsuke*, or toggle, which completed the device, was only rarely of glass (Pl. 185).

Beads were sought after for their novelty, their unusual designs, and color combinations. Some new types came in from China and from Europe. These were long thought to be primarily from Venice, but it may now be considered that they may also have come from Amsterdam (see n. 44). They were expensive, they were rare; their owners gained prestige from wearing particularly fine examples. It was not long, however, before the Osaka craftsmen were imitating the foreign ones, and they became quite common. Since glass beads were made in Nagasaki and Edo and no doubt in many other places, provenances are extremely difficult and precise dating virtually impossible to asceratin.

In Shinoda-mura, in Osaka Prefecture, farmer families spent their leisure hours making beads in a "cottage industry" with the simplest of equipment and from glass rods provided from a central source. This is still the case to some extent today.

The glass beads of the Edo period in Japan often pose problems other than where in

Japan they were manufactured. Some belong definitely to a foreign design tradition, but if they are imports from Venice, Chinese in the foreign manner, or Japanese in imitation of foreign styles is difficult or impossible to decide. The only Venetian beads that the author has had the opportunity of viewing—and none probably earlier than the nineteenth century—all seem inferior to the examples included herein, for the latter exhibit a skill and precision missing in the Venetian beads. In view of this, it seems wise, in the relevant instances, merely to cite the similarities to a foreign designs.

Among the beads of this period certain types suggest so-called trade beads found from East Asia to the African continent. Some of the examples shown in Plate 163 are possibly not all of domestic manufacture.

Sujidama

Sujidama are "line beads" (Pl. 163, upper left), in which stripes in different colors are inserted in a monochrome opaque body. The source of this idea, if not of the beads themselves, was surely foreign, probably Venetian.

Gangidama

Gangidama are "zigzag beads" (Pl. 163, upper right), so called because the lines, in other colors than the ground, are often zigzag. The designs varied; sometimes very simple lines were used, but at other times a compound design is seen. Everything is usually opaque. *Kurokawa, in *Kōgei Shiryō* states that the method of imitating the imported *gangidama* was invented in Osaka.[69]

Tombodama

The *tombodama* (Pl. 163, second row) was known from the Tomb period, although it is not known by what term it was then designated. Now, however, it is a new type, evidently inspired by some European beads, and shows a technical perfection not known in earlier times.

They are found in a wide variety of designs. Some are assuredly imports, others definitely Japanese. The designs that were pressed into the body of the bead and the tiny slices from glass canes (patterned glass rods) that were inserted (sometimes only skin deep) never seem to have fallen out as did those of the Tomb period. The heat must have been high enough to assure complete fusion.

Sarasadama

This bead (Pl. 163, fourth row) derives its name from *sarasa* (printed cottons), which were imported from India. These beads, inspired by the delicate designs and coloring of the Indian textiles, have a peculiarly individual daintiness that sets them apart from other *tombodama*, although they were fabricated by the same technique.[70] Some are small *kodama* (Pl. 163, fourth row, right), and are then also called *nankindama* because they resemble small beads said to have come from Nanking. Some are monochrome in color, while others have typical *tombodama* units.

Kinsuishōdama

A "gold-crystal bead," appearing as an imitation of the mineral aventurine; it is said that the Japanese did not make it themselves but imported the material and then shaped it as needed; however, as cited in Plate Note 163, the glass was evidently made in Japan in the Edo period. Plate 163, lower row, illustrates the use of this material in both a bead and a hair ornament.

BEADS WITH OVERLAY DECORATION

Beads of this type, with colored glass threads laid on in loops over a white base, were definitely an importation from China; whether they were ever made in Japan is questionable (Pl. 163, lower right).

KYOTO

Kyoto, as the imperial capital from 794 to 1868, was the home of traditional national culture. Though considerably influenced by the impact of Western culture, it was not a city of new growth like Osaka. Nor was it like the teeming shogunate capital of Edo, even though the population had once reached about one-half million. The more tranquil atmosphere, coupled with aristocratic traditions and the presence of the imperial court, which, however powerless, was still the heart of the nation, tended to keep the city conservatively in line with its cultural lineage. Kyoto was a center for brocade weaving, for lacquer ware of high quality, for excellent ceramics, and for the quieter types of painting. One does not hear of any suddenly wealthy merchant indulging in extravagant display, and the new *ukiyoe* woodblock prints did not flourish as in Osaka and Edo.

In the eighteenth and early nineteenth centuries, when *inrō* (the compartmented medicine cases that men wore suspended from the sash) were the height of fashion, Kyoto lacquerers turned out superb examples and paid much attention to the accompanying *netsuke*. *Inrō*, *netsuke*, and *ojime* were all indicative of the taste and social station of the wearer. *Ojime* of glass are relatively infrequent, but when found with a fine *inrō*, their quality is appropriately high. Glass *netsuke* are also known, though rare (Pl. 190). The advertisement of Kagaya of Edo (Pl. 183) displays an entire glass *inrō* assemblage.

Conservative, aristocratic Kyoto evidently was not one of the areas where glass curiosities became fashionable to the extent of making the city a glass center. Although records speak of *biidoro* making as having spread "to Kyoto, Osaka, and Edo" in the Kyōho era (1716–35), it must have been a limited influence, perhaps confined in this imperial capital to artisans who set up stalls at festival time.[71]

FOREIGN GLASS IN KYOTO

Foreign glass was not unknown, despite the fact that it could not have been as plentiful as in Nagasaki or even in Edo, where many official gifts were presented. One of the "sights" of Kyoto is the Nijō Jinya, on Omiya-dōri, Oike-sagaru, built in the first half of the seventeenth century and already mentioned on page 178. There, the thin window glass that still survives in part stands witness to the interest in *biidoro*.

In a section of the *Kyōto-fu Chiji* entitled *Fushimi Ikken no Ben* ("Tales of Events in Fushimi"), mention is made of a building in cabinetwork style, where glass was placed in all the sliding doors. This window glass must have been imported.

A painting, attributed to Matsumura Keibun (1799–1843), a Kyoto artist of the Shijō school, entitled *Matsumura Keibun and His Friends*, shows eight members of the Shijō school of painting. One gentlemen, seated in a foreign chair, is holding a footed wine glass of the foreign type. A more shallow footed cup stands on the floor beside another artist. Both items are quite plainly of glass, but it is impossible to ascertain whether they represent foreign imports or Japanese products in the foreign style.

Recently several glass vessels were discovered, which tradition refers to as used at the Katsura Imperial Villa in Kyoto. One, a seventeenth century goblet (11.0 centimeters high and 8.5 centimeters in diameter), is probably Venetian. Two are German or Dutch hour-glass-shaped bottles of dark green glass (23.8 centimeters high).[72] A fourth, a transparent bowl (6.5 centimeters high and 13.0 centimeters in diameter), has been thought to be of domestic manufacture.[73]

GLASSMAKING IN KYOTO

In spite of the often repeated statement that *biidoro* production spread to Kyoto, Osaka, and Edo, documentation of any such activity in Kyoto seems nearly nonexistent. An exception is a memorandum, dated 1826, possibly from an unidentified *biidoro* maker, named Eijirō (or Eigorō?), of Kyoto to a friend in Nagoya, perhaps a former apprentice.

> Bunsei 9 [1826], tenth month.
> [From]: Kyoto, Nishi-Horikawa-dōri, Shimodachiuri-agarumachi [Street on the west side of Horikawa Canal, above Shimodachiuri Street, Kyoto] Eijirō [or Eigorō?] Biidoro [*biidoro* maker].
> [To]: Nōshu, [an old name for Nagoya] Majima-mura, Baba Rokuemon no Segare Toyojirō-dono [Toyojirō Esquire, son of Baba Rokuemon, Majima, Nagoya].
> Document of Secret Instruction for Making *Biidoro*
> Item: Put lead into a pan and melt thoroughly. Remove the scum and add zinc, stirring well. Again remove the scum. Then add the powdered stone and mix thoroughly.
> As regards the addition of zinc: thirty *momme* [approximately 113 grams] of zinc should be added to one *kan* [3.76 kilograms] of lead.
> As for the addition of powdered stone: seven hundred *momme* should be added to one *kan* of lead.
> Here in Kyoto that is the way.

As regards potash; three hundred and fifty *momme* should be added to one *kan* of lead.

Item: Method for amber color:
Twenty-five *momme* of red oxide of iron should be added to one *kan* of lead.

Item: Method for dark blue: twelve *momme* of zaffer should be added to one *kan* of *biidoro*.

Item: Method for pale green glass: Twelve *momme* of copper carbonate should be added to one *kan* of *biidoro*.

Item: Method for blue glass: Fifty *momme* of [?] should be added little by little to one *kan* of red lead.

There is, I vow, no error in the above.

The Kyoto temperament was different from that of other localities, and perhaps the itinerant *biidoro* makers who displayed their trade at the temple and shrine festival fairs found insufficient encouragement to detain them in the capital. This contrasted with the glassmakers in Osaka, who benefitted by the patronage of wealthy merchants and neighboring feudal lords.

Beads

Various records cite areas where beadmakers' shops were concentrated—such as Shijō-bomon, Goko-machi, and Miyaki-machi. Here beads in all sorts of materials were made, and it is, of course, quite possible that some of the shops, not yet documented, made glass beads. The fact that imperial crowns were generously decorated with beads (see Pls. 165, 166) suggests that the new enthusiasm for glass may have infected the beadmakers of Kyoto. On the other hand, the flourishing glass bead manufacture in nearby Osaka may have provided a convenient source of supply.

In the imperial crowns of Japan, whether of this period or earlier, glass beads had a prominent role; perhaps it would be correct to presume that the sanctity and amuletic nature of the bead was still traditionally in force for things imperial. On the other hand, restrictions against luxuries, as well as the need for economy at the impoverished court, may have led to glass as a substitute for gems.

There are several types of crowns. One called *ben* is illustrated in the *Wakan Sanzai Zue*, where the original Chinese form and the Japanese adaptation are shown. It is essentially a flat board shape that fitted down over the traditional court headgear. From two ends hung strings of beads. The Japanese type is more elaborate, having a low "fence" around the periphery and longer strings of beads; from the center arose an ornamental floral upright, and at the front a taller upright terminating in a rayed sun-symbol above a cloud shape.[74] The board type was evidently used for the crown of the Emperor Shōmu, now in fragments in the Shōsō-in (Pl. 87).

Plates 165 and 166 show the type beginning in the Heian period said to have been worn by emperors on the occasions of their coronations. This type invariably had a central padded body of black, stiffly lacquered gauze in three lobes bound with metal bands. Above and behind this portion rose two, or three, three-lobed metal frames filled in with stiffened black gauze. The surrounding outer foundation of the crown was a tall form, usually of gilt bronze, perforated with a flower-and-leaf scroll in the imperial chrysanthemum design. Attached on the outside were tall upright rods or heavy wires terminating at the top in sizeable "jewels," each mounted on a calyx, simulating a lotus bud. Similar floral units were attached to the lobed gauze form, of which the upper ones were most prominent of all.

These imperial crowns of the Edo period emphasize the impoverished state of the imperial court under the rule of the shogun. For instance, there are no natural jewels. They have been replaced by glass. Even jasper and coral were imitated by hollow glass balls coated on the inside with color, as in Plate 166. The glass beads are mounted on brass (instead of gilt bronze) wires whose ends are crudely exposed. In one crown the flower calyxes are not even of metal but of silvered paper.

INLAYS

Certain lacquer works of this period—boxes of all kinds, *inrō*, and other forms—are sometimes found with glass used in certain parts of the design. Sometimes it is difficult to tell whether an inlay is of glass or mica. The writing box of Plate 167 contains on the exterior of the lid a landscape in which the moon is reflected in a stream; the reflection is a disk of what seems to be glass. A writing box of the Genroku era (1688–1703), shows a waterwheel covered with a glass disk that is described as "apparently an early watch glass from Holland."[75] Its late owner wrote it "is supposed to be the original of this idea—a very valuable piece, therefore, and I have been told that quite a few imitations were made later on, probably for foreign consumption if not for Japanese nouveau riche, of which my second one would be an example."

An instance of very small mica inlays to represent glass occurs in a incense box by Ritsuo (1663–1747) in the Freer Gallery (No. 56.3), where a monkey, costumed as a human, inspects a scroll painting. He wears spectacles composed of mica inlays. That glass for inlays was available, whatever its source, is shown by its use in the Kasuga *shari-ki* described below.

VESSELS

There is no evidence that Kyoto made glass vessels in this period. A miniature lacquer shrine containing a tiny deer carved from white sandalwood, recumbent upon a cloud, is preserved in the Kasuga-taisha shrine in Nara. The deer is richly caparisoned. From the saddle rises a sacred *sakaki* tree, whose branches embrace a *shari* container. Although scarcely a "glass vessel," this *shari-ki* is formed of two glass discs 1.5 centimeters in diameter, which enclose between them three minute curving shelves of brass to which ten *shari* adhere. This may have been made in Kyoto.

Cloisonné

Although the term *shippō* was advancing toward standardization in the sense of cloisonné in the Western technique, there was still considerable confusion as to its meaning. *Shippō, shippō-nagashi, ruri-shippō*—what did each signify?

Shippō, in the modern sense, is closely related to the metalworking craft, and it seems inevitable that the *kugikakushi* of Plate 17 must have been the work of one of Kyoto's expert metalsmiths and a forerunner of Edo period cloisonné. The author, however, does not know of any Edo period work from Kyoto.

Mino and Owari Provinces (Nagoya Area)

Although this area during the Edo period had no large metropolis, it was one of the localities where *biidoro* and *giyaman* were produced. Today it is one of the glass centers. Owari had become the seat of the major branch of the Tokugawa family, which controlled the Edo *bakufu*, and their patronage aided the development of the glass industry. As was true of Osaka, there were a number of neighboring feudal lords who also encouraged the glassmakers.

The founder of the glass industry in this locality was Ishizuka Iwasaburō, born probably toward the end of the eighteenth century. He was the second son of Ishizuka Seisuke, a samurai in the service of the Kuze daimyo at Sekiyadō in Shimōsa Province near Edo. Iwasaburō, dissatisfied with his samurai status, left home in the Bunka era (1804–18) to assume the role of a *rōnin*, a samurai without allegiance to any lord. After wandering in various provinces, he arrived in Nagasaki, where glassmaking was at its peak, became interested in it, and learned the techniques from a Dutch craftsman.

On his homeward journey, Iwasaburō discovered that there were especially good sources of silica in Mino Province, so he decided to stay in that region. He established a factory in Toda-mura, Kami-gōri, (present Gifu Prefecture), and presented some of his products to the Tokugawa daimyo of neighboring Owari Province, who not only arranged for him to build a waterwheel for the grinding of silica but supplied him with lead and niter. This sponsorship assured the success of his enterprise. Iwasaburō supplied the daimyo in Nagoya with his glass products; he also sent them to the Kuze daimyo, whom he had once served. His products were chiefly hair ornaments, cupping glasses, toys, or trifles such perhaps as the *pokon-pokon*.

Before Iwasaburō's death in 1867, the output of his small factory was one or two *kan* a day—that is, from about eight to sixteen pounds. The work was continued by his son Ishizuka Bunzaemon, who was succeeded by his son, Iwasaburō II, who guided the industry into the new modes of the Meiji era and into the twentieth century.

A crucible used by Iwasaburō I was long preserved in Yusen-ji temple; in 1933 it was presented to Iwasaburō II, and it is now preserved in the office of the present Ishizuka company in Nagoya.[76] Plate 168 is a reproduction of sketches showing how it was used. On the exterior of the crucible, below the shoulder, there is an accumulation of dull opaque glass in grayed blues and honey color. It will be noted that charcoal was the fuel, the lumps being piled and ignited on the *top* of the furnace, just as they were in the illustration in the *Bankin Sugiwai Bukuro* of 1732 (Pl. 144). The lower of the two sketches shows the method used after the introduction of coal in the Meiji era.

Also preserved at the Ishizuka factory is an interesting document from the end of the Edo period. In those unsettled times the lords' treasuries were sometimes depleted and payments were slow. In this instance money had been advanced by the village for expenses connected with glass production. Money was at that time still calculated by weight, since there was no universal standard for coins.

Item: Gold, 3 *bu* 2 *shu*: silver, 3 *momme* 5 *bu*
   For 2 *kan* [about 7.52 kg.] of white niter.
   One *kan* of this is worth 28 *momme* in silver.

Item: Gold, 1 *ryō* 2 *bu*
   For 3 *kan* of lead.
   On the basis of 30 *bu* in silver per *kan*.

Item: Ditto, 1 *bu* 2 *shu*
   For borax.

Item: Silver, 6 *momme*
   For 200 *me* [*momme*] of zinc.
   This silver was for a purchase made in front of Inuyama in Bishū [Owari Province].

Item: Small coins [copper and iron], 1 *kan* of *mon*
   Wages to four coolies for digging a well attached to the furnace.

Item: Ditto, 318 *mon*
   Wage for one horseload of clay to build a kiln.[77]

Item: Ditto, 250 *mon*
   Wages for ten coolies to help when making glass.

Item: Ditto, 7 *kan* of *mon*
   Cash paid out en route, and expenses at inns, while on a trip.

Item: Ditto, 600 *mon*
   Expense of putting glassware in two boxes.

Item: Small coins, 748 *mon*
   Cost of 2 *kan* of whipped cotton.[78]

TOTAL: Small coins, 12 *kan* 200 *mon*
   This amounts to: Gold, 1 *ryō* 3 *bu* 2 *shu*
          Silver, 1 *momme* 8 *bu* 7 *rin*.
          In each 6 *kan* there are 400 *momme*.
    Alloy, 4 *ryō* 3 *bu*
    Silver, 3 *momme* 8 *bu* 7 *rin*

Regarding the above mentioned items, you were ordered by the new lord to blow glass. Further, as to the supervision, even before the work was begun there was an order to economize strictly and, therefore, while I was with them, the requisites already prepared with the money I had previously borrowed in advance in Nagoya were insufficient, and, unless we can manage to obtain additional supplies, we cannot get along at all. As the village was requested to advance the money, and as payments have been made for each item, exactly according to the document, you must exert yourself to the best of your ability in regard to the order; and when the appropriation comes please reimburse the village.

Several other glassmakers of Mino and Owari are known by name, although information concerning them is scant. Iwasaburō I, had, it is said, two apprentices—his son, Ishizuka Bunzaemon, and Heigorō. The former followed in his father's business, while the latter became independent, and set himself up in Okaido-mura, Nakashima-gun. [79]

Baba Toyojirō, son of Baba Rokuemon of Nagoya, to whom the *biidoro* maker Eijirō (Eigorō?) of Kyoto sent formulae (see p. 207), may have pursued the profession of *biidoro*-making in Nagoya, although there is only that one letter for evidence.

Kimata was another Mino artisan in the mid nineteenth century. He is said to have been located at Hidamura, Toki-gōri, Mino Province, and to have made glass for the Tokugawa family of Owari and for other nearby lords. Watanabe Yojirō was his apprentice. [90]

There is brief mention that Watanabe Yojirō established a factory in Tajima, in Mino Province. [81] Yojirō had been adopted into the Watanabe family. His descendants say he was a seventh generation *biidoro* craftsmen and was himself a glassmaker from 1855 or 1856. He used a number of crucibles in a row and made glass with *gairome* (a clay of the area, rich in silica) and lead, using the simple glass pipe (*tomosao*) for blowing. In the Meiji era he produced bottles and lamp chimneys. [82]

The region had thus made considerable progress in glass manufacture by the end of the Edo period, but no *biidoro* or *giyaman* articles produced in this area during the Edo period can be illustrated.

CLOISONNÉ

In the mid nineteenth century, production of vessels decorated with *shippō* (in the sense of cloisonné) seems to have developed in this area; previously it had been used for the embellishment of small items such as sword fittings, *hikite*, and *kugikakushi*, and sometimes for hair ornaments. It is said that Kaji Tsunekichi, the second son of a samurai, founded *shippō* production in Owari. [83] A quote from an "official record . . . furnished by one of the present representatives of the family," states that he settled in Hattori-mura, Kaito-gōri, as a metalworker, in the Bunsei era [1818–29]. [84] Another source refers to his having invented an original method of wired cloisonné, which was later handed down through Tsukamoto Kaisuke and then to the *shippō* artist Namikawa Yasuyuki of Kyoto [85]

133. Bottles imported from Europe · Edo period · max. H. 29.85 cm.

134. Hanging lamp from a Dutch ship • Dutch • 18th or 19th century.

135. Cut glass plate imported from Holland • Bohemian (?) • *ca.* 1800.

136. Cut glass bowl imported from Holland • Bohemian (?) • *ca.* 1800.

137. Glass panels in the Seisonkaku, Kanazawa · Dutch (?) · 19th century (?).

138. Gin bottle decorated in Japan · Edo period.
139. Bottle decorated in Japan · 19th century.
140. Illustration of imported salt cellar · from *Ransetsu Benwaku*, pub. 1799.
141. Imported salt cellar · Edo period · L. 6.5 cm.

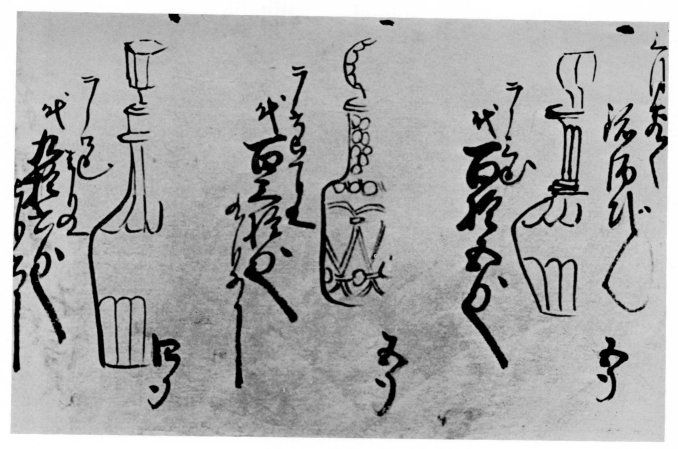

142. Importer's catalogue of foreign glass, Nagasaki • 1862.

143. Illustration from *Haikai Azuma Miyage* • Hōreki era (1751–63).

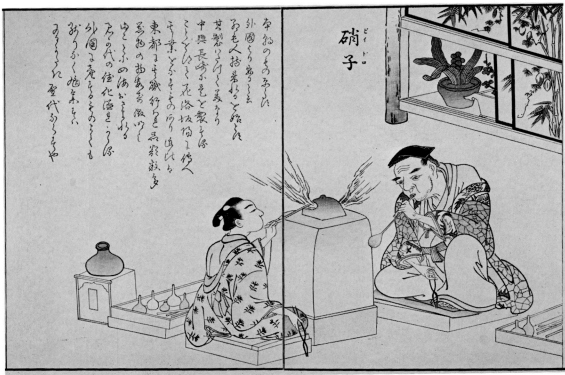

144. Illustration from *Bankin Sugiwai Bukuro* • 1732.

145. Illustration from *Saiga Shokunin Burui* • 1774.

146. Illustration from *Nagasaki Kokon Shūran Meishō Zue* • 1841.

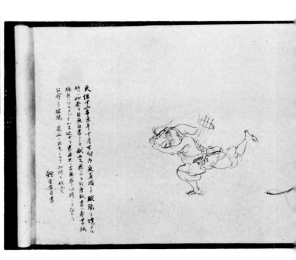

147. Illustrated scroll (details) by Suzuki Shige— • 1841.

148. Title page, *Nagasaki Kokon Shūran Meishō Zue* • 1841.

149. The Dutch quarters on Deshima, from *Nagasaki Kokon Shūran Meishō Zue* • 1841.

150. Lacquer *inrō*, signed Bunshin • Edo period.

151. *Biidoro-e* in a door pull • Edo period • *ca.* 5.1 × 3.5 cm.

152. Green cups • before 1746 • H. 6.6 cm.

153. Fluted cup • before 1746 • H. 5.6 cm.

154. Thin yellow bottle • 18th century • Nagasaki.
155. Thin, dark blue bottle • Edo period • Nagasaki • H. *ca.* 25.4 cm.
156. Covered bowl • Edo period • H. 8.8 cm.

157. *Kasaboko* of the Okun'chi Festival, Nagasaki • mid 19th century (?).

158. Enameled *pokon-pokon* sound toy • 19th century (?) • H. 14.0 cm.

159. Girl blowing a *biidoro*, woodblock print by Utamaro.
160. Child blowing a *biidoro*, woodblock print by Utamaro.

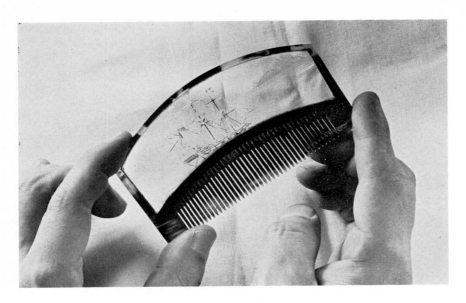

Edo Period—Merchant Craftsmen

161. Comb with engraved glass panel •
Edo period • Nagasaki • H. 4.0 cm.

162. Woman using a *mage-kagami*, woodblock print by Eishi.

226

163. Beads · Edo period · max. D. 2.1 cm.

164. Screen painting (detail) by Yanagisawa Kien · mid
18th century.

165. Imperial crown • Edo period.
166. Imperial crown detail • Edo period • beads, max. D. 1.9 cm.

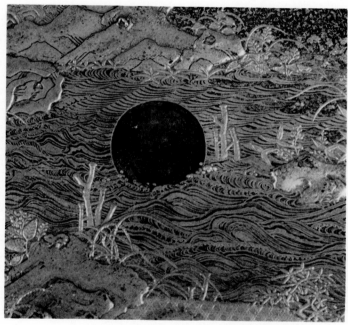

167. Lacquer writing box · perhaps 17th century · glass inlay, D. 2.9 cm.

168. Sketch of furnaces, Ishizuka glassworks • late Edo and Meiji periods.
169. Dark blue saké bottle • mid 19th century • Sukagawa • H. 25.0 cm.
170. Dark blue waste pot • mid 19th century • Sukagawa • H. 4.55 cm.

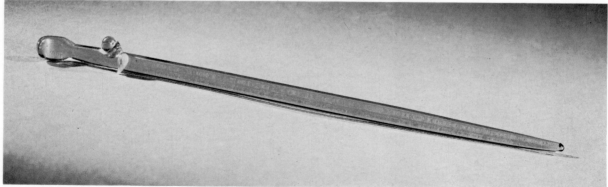

171. License issued to "glass artisan Shōkichi" • 19th century • Sendai.

172. *Kōgai* by Shōkichi • 19th century • Sendai • L. 16.0 cm.

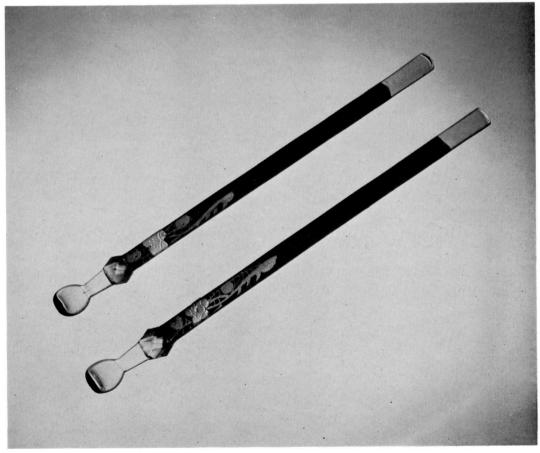

173. *Kanzashi* • 19th century • Sendai • max. L. 18.6 cm.

174. Decorated *kanzashi* • 19th century • Sendai • max. L. 16.5 cm.

SUKAGAWA, ŌSHU PROVINCE (FUKUSHIMA PREFECTURE)

When the pieces in Plate 169 and 170 were acquired by the author, she was told that Sukagawa was famous for exceptionally tall glass saké bottles (*tokkuri*), especially of dark blue or purple glass. However, glassmaking in Sukagawa, so far as now known, is substantiated by only one record, according to which Lord Matsudaira, in the Kansei era (1789–1801), engaged a glass technician who "manufactured sheet glass and other items."[86]

SENDAI AREA

Some sort of glassmaking activity in this area can be assumed for the Heian period, because of the glass in the Konjiki-dō of Chūson-ji (Pls. 114, 115). But there is little other evidence until the Edo period.

The wooden plaque of Plate 171 is a license tag of a glassmaker. The legend on the obverse side reads:

> Glass artisan Shōkichi
> Tenant of Wakakoya Kurazō

The seal on the reverse reads "Sendai fief commerce," with the signature below, "Merchant Hyakuri," written over some kind of seal.

The style of the license is thought to date from the Bunsei era (1818–29). When the present owner found it, the license was accompanied by some twenty-three amber colored glass *kanzashi* and *kōgai*. The *kōgai* of Plate 172 is one of the twenty-three. Amber or smoke-glass metal is common in glass attributed to Sendai.

It seems possible that the following quotation may refer to the glassmaker Shōkichi.

> In the Tempō era [1830–43]. . . . A *giyaman* craftsman came to Sendai from Nagasaki, established a factory at Minami-machi, and manufactured glass wares by order of the Sendai clan. He was much appreciated by many people for his *giyaman*, *kanzashi*, and *kōgai*, because under the law regarding luxury goods ordinary people were prohibited from wearing personal ornaments (including gold, silver, and tortoiseshell *kanzashi* and *kōgai*). This *giyaman* is called *kemuri garasu* ["smoke glass"] because of its somewhat murky color.[87]

A type of glass *kanzashi*, characteristic of Sendai work in both form and smoky amber color, is shown in Plate 173. This type of glass *kanzashi* is generally rather heavy and cumbersome and was probably inexpensive. For contrast, compare those of Plate 174, which are unusually delicate.

Until recent years glass *kanzashi* and *kōgai* could be found readily in Sendai, but now they have practically disappeared. Possibly a search in the records of the Date daimyo might uncover some pertinent data regarding Edo period manufacture of glass in the Date domain.

EDO

Dr. Engelbert Kaempfer, the German surgeon serving the Dutch East India Company in Japan from 1690 to 1692, wrote:

> It is scarce credible, how much trade and commerce is carried on between the several provinces and parts of the Empire! How busy and industrious the merchants are everywhere! How full their ports of ships! How many rich and flourishing towns up and down the Country! There are such multitudes of people along the coasts, and near the seaports, such a noise of oars and sails, such numbers of ships and boats, both for use and pleasure, that one would be apt to imagine the whole nation had settled there, and all the inland parts of the Country were left quite desart and empty.[88]

Edo, Ieyasu's old castle site, and chosen by him to be the capital of Tokugawa rule, must have been in many ways a city of absorbing interest. Kyoto, still the imperial, though almost impotent, capital, remained the conservative spiritual and cultural center of the nation. Edo, on the other hand, was the capital of the real force of the land, whose dictatorial grip was so strong that the Dutch continually referred to the shogun, in their reports and diaries, as the emperor, though occasionally some author used the term "secular monarch." They seemingly had little, if any, contact with the emperor and often no knowledge of him.

The Tōkaidō ("Eastern Sea Road"), the main artery from Edo to Kyoto, has been made famous in story, song, and art. Osaka, just beyond, and then the "rice-basket of Japan," kept the Tōkaidō and the coastal shipping busy with its transfer of rice bales and other commodities. Other roads and sea routes maintained connections with the more remote fief governments and with Nagasaki. Along this lifeline hurried the couriers of the shogunate, and at more leisurely pace came the colorful processions of the daimyo and their retinues, demanding, at sword's point, obeisance and servility from all along the route, as they returned to Edo for the *sankin kōtai* or went homeward after their tour of service was over. Along this artery came the less familiar Dutch envoys and their attendants, enroute for audiences with the shogun. As background were the ubiquitous tradesmen and coolies attending to the business affairs of the land.

> It is scarce credible, what numbers of people daily travel on the roads of this city, and I can assure the reader from my own experience, having passed it four times, that Tōkaidō which is one of the chief, and indeed the most frequented, of the seven great roads in Japan, is upon some days more crowded, than the public streets in any of the most populous towns in Europe.[89]

Kaempfer was deeply impressed by all that he saw as he journeyed to and from Edo. His description of the capital and of the highway leading to it and through it proves that glassblowing was a part of the city's industry in the last decade of the seventeenth century, antedating the Japanese records regarding the spread of *biidoro* making to Edo.

Of the five great trading towns, which belong to the Imperial demesnes, or crown lands, Jedo is the first and chief, the residence of the Emperor-Shōgun, the capital, and by much the largest city of the Empire, by reason of the many Princes and Lords, who with their families and numerous trains swell up the Imperial Court, and the inhabitants of the city, to an incredible number. . . . Jedo, properly the Capital of the whole Empire, and the seat of the secular Monarch, is so large, that I may venture to say, it is the biggest town known.[90] Thus much I can affirm from my certain knowledge, that we were one whole day riding at a moderate pace from Shinagawa, where the Suburb begins, along the chief street which goes a little irregularly indeed, to the other end of the town. . . . The throng of people along this chief and middle street, which is about fifty paces broad . . . is incredible. . . . On both sides of the streets are multitudes of well-furnished shops of merchants and tradesmen, drapers, silk-merchants, druggists, idol sellers, book-sellers, glass-blowers, apothecaries and others. . . . The city of Jedo is a nursery of artists, handicraftsmen, merchants and tradesmen, and yet everything is sold dearer than anywhere else in the Empire, by reason of the great concourse of people, and the number of idle monks and courtiers, as also the difficult importing of provisions and other commodities.[91]

With so many of the daimyo and samurai assembled in this capital, it is easy to imagine its high cultural level. There were likewise many wealthy merchants and craftsmen. The tastes, the costumes, and the pastimes of this new class found vivid expression in the paintings and the prints of the *ukiyoe* artists. Several of these are reproduced because of their representations of glass (Pls. 159, 160, 162, 175–178, 190, 191).

Biidoro and *giyaman* seem to have played an increasingly large role, both in serious scientific production of articles for the nobility and in such simple objects as windbells and *pokon-pokon*.

Under the paper lanterns suspended from the ceilings of the verandahs, there are often bells of colored glass, a long, slender clapper of metal supported by silk thread, or slip of colored or gilded paper. At the least movement of the breeze these bands of paper move, the metallic tongues swing and touch the glass bells, and their vibrations make a vague melody, like the sound of an Aeolian harp.[92]

Biidoro ya	The *biidoro*!
Kore mo fukimono	This also, breeze blown—
Aki no kaze.	The autumn wind.
	Yosa no Buson

Toward the end of the period, when Admiral Perry appeared off the Bay of Edo, the city's life changed, and notes of anxiety and of civil war marred for some years the peace of the city, until the isolation completely ended and disturbances finally died down. The emperor was "restored" to temporal as well as spiritual sovereignty in 1868, and Edo ceased to exist, supplanted by modern, progressive Tokyo.

FOREIGN GLASS IN EDO

As noted before, glass was a favorite commodity among the gifts carried by the Dutch envoys to the shogun in Edo. But foreign glass was also brought commercially. City merchants sent representatives to Nagasaki to acquire Dutch cargoes, and Ōsumi Gen-suke's broadsheet advertising his stock (Pl. 179) lists "imported wares" as well as domestic products. Some of the prints of Utamaro and others include representations of stemmed wine glasses, which resemble European types, but one cannot tell how many of these, if any, represent foreign items and how many are depictions of Japanese glasses made in the foreign manner.

Three years after a trade treaty between Holland and Japan had been signed in 1858, the Dutch government presented to Hotta Masaaki, Lord of Bitchū (in present Okayama Prefecture) and then minister of state in the Tokugawa government, a large cut glass vase consisting of four units—the vase itself, a circular traylike plate about 60 centimeters in diameter on which the vase stands, and a pedestal of two units. The total height of the ensemble is 77 centimeters. The provenance is considered British, but the tray and vase differ somewhat, both in appearance and technique, from the under parts and resemble Japanese Satsuma cut glass of the 1850s. This difference may be the result of breakage that necessitated replacement, to be made either by glass made in the Satsuma fief[93] or imported from abroad. The former seems unlikely since, with the death of Lord Shimazu Nariakira in 1858, the glass industry of the Satsuma fief quickly deteriorated. It is possible that the three-year delay between the treaty and the presentation was caused by the need to secure foreign replacements.

GLASSMAKING IN EDO

The *Rangakusha* (see p. 175) were not professional artisans in any sense, and yet it was through them that some of the more prominent of the *biidoro* and *giyaman* craftsmen acquired the technical knowledge that improved their skill and production. Among these scholars the most helpful was Sakuma Shōzan, who succeeded in producing glass of good quality and is said to have taught Kagaya Kyūbei to use borax so that his glass bottles might be sufficiently acid-resistant for chemical and laboratory use.

Sakuma Shōzan (or Zōzan) was a famous figure in the history of nineteenth century Japan. Born in 1811, he lived until 1864. He became a strong advocate of several principles: "Open the country in order to learn the Western techniques necessary for defense," "Unite the civil and military authorities to strengthen the nation politically," and in the cultural sphere, "Eastern ethics and Western sciences." Yoshida Shōin, who became famous for his participation in political struggles, was Shōzan's disciple.

Shōzan was born of a samurai family of the Matsushiro clan, Matsushiro-mura, Ueshima-gun, Shinano Province, or Shinshū (present Nagano Prefecture). Endowed with a brilliant mind, he was interested from childhood in reading and writing and decided at fourteen that he would make scholarship his vocation. Up to the age of twenty-three he studied with famous scholars of the clan, then for three years became a disciple of the Confucian scholar Satō Issai of Edo, an experience that convinced him of "the inseparability of knowledge and action."[94] After a three-year period back in the fief he returned to Edo in 1839, settling at Tamaike, to broaden and deepen his knowledge. Then he became more deeply acquainted with Dutch learning and pursued it avidly.

He made a telegraphic machine, a gyro compass, and analyzed the water of a hot spring. He cast guns and carried on other experiments on the basis of his reading. He is said to have acquired knowledge of glassmaking from a Dutch encyclopedia, extracts of which had been translated into Japanese under the title *Kosei Chimpen*. His interests led him to experiment in glass manufacture, and his success was recounted in letters to several friends. The correspondence is of such interest to students of glass history that pertinent parts are given here.[95]

> [To:] Tsukada Gengo
> All these are foreign books and show various kinds of methods for experiments. For example, if we proceed in such and such a way we shall be able to make fine *biidoro* just like crystal, or if we proceed in another way we shall be able to make grape wine, or if we do so and so we shall never fail in feeding silkworms. These things are outlined precisely in those books.
>
> I made *biidoro* according to these books, and could manufacture such a one as Japanese have never produced; it is just like those imported from Holland. I found this among sixteen Dutch books I bought this spring for forty *ryō* [for his lord]. In them I have found more useful things than I can count. . . . .[96]

Possibly among books read by Shōzan there may have been also two translations from European works, the *Seimi Kaisō* and the *Biidoro Seihō Shusetsu*,[97] both of which were useful to glass technicians before the Meiji era.

> 1845, third month, twentieth day.
> [To:] Takada Ikuta.
> I shall be well in a few days and will then call on you, bringing the glass that we made recently. I am sure that the glass is not inferior to those made in foreign countries. It is quite different from those called *giyaman* in our country. The quality is very solid and it is hard to work with, but it seems excellent. I wish to show it to you and to Mr. Mimura as soon as possible. I intend to make many such things, so every day I have my workman do various things. If we construct but a single furnace, I can make only a few, but if I have two or three furnaces I will invite you and show the products to you.[98]

> 1845, fifth month, fourth day.
> [To:] Takada Ikuta.
> You asked about the stone that becomes *hari* [glass], so I will tell you about it today. It is a kind of flint and slightly transparent. It is of a solid quality, and if we

strike it with steel, it gives out a flash. If we put potash and niter with the stone and melt them with a strong fire, they will become transparent glass. It is a natural and obvious fact that if we boil water it will become hot water, and if we fashion some clay and bake it, it will become a tile. In the same way we make transparent glass by combining some chemicals with a special kind of stone and melting them. As neither Mr. Tanomo nor others have knowledge of it, it is quite natural that you should find it strange. If you like, we will try it at your home. When burned, the stone's weight diminishes, and when it has become powdered, it will scatter. So I want you to assemble a little more than the amount desired in the end. Ten *kan* I think will be enough for an experiment, no matter how much weight is lost.

As I mentioned before, a kind of flint will be good. It does not matter whether it is white, black, red, or blue, since when melted and cooled it will be white, and so it is unnecessary to bring the stone from here. But the more solid it is, the better the glass will be. Peasants near your house often pick up this stone from the rice fields and use it daily to strike fire. That sort of stone is the most suitable, and if there is a large quantity, we can choose the best from among them. You had better order [your men] to collect many.

These are just a few lines to answer your question.

Postscript: The alembic that I showed you the other day is, in the beauty of its quality, the best thing, even compared to foreign articles, although bubbles are not completely lacking, because the vessel used for the chemicals was heated in a very small furnace [therefore not hot enough to dissipate the gas or air that forms bubbles].

People have thought that the same strong glass that is made in foreign countries could not be made in Japan. Among *biidoro* shopkeepers there are some who like curious things. They appealed to a Dutch doctor and tried making *biidoro* several times, but could not succeed. So I wondered what would they think, or what would they say, if they could see my glass. Yesterday I sent one of my messengers with this alembic to a large shop at Shio-machi, Yokoyama-chō, and had him request the same kind of thing. They were all amazed, and said that such a thing could not be made in Japan—that it must have been imported from Holland; and yet, they said, the workmanship seemed Japanese. Perhaps it came from Osaka, and yet even in Osaka it might be impossible to make such a thing. At another place all said it must be an import from abroad. If you doubt this, you or someone whom you trust may show this alembic to the *biidoro* shops in Edo and ask as I did. Then you will find that what I say is true.

To Mr. Takemura [Takemura Kingo] I will send one of my recent products, so you had better consult with him and do as you please.

Mr. Takemura told me in his letter that some official had inquired whether some merchant would undertake [an omission here], but in my opinion, if an official were to make a mistake, even though there were some wise man, he could not afterwards help him. So we had better confer about this.

If you will only inquire how much this alembic would cost if made in our country and whether there is someone who produces *sarube toru shuru* [?] then you will comprehend how great an effort it was for me to make this alembic. Be careful not to mention my undertaking! Of course, I will write also to Mr. Takemura, but I wanted to tell you, too, about this matter.

I will stop here.[99]

1845, fifth month, twenty-eighth day.
[To:] Fujioka Jinzaemon.
I read your letter that you sent at the beginning of last month. . . .

I think you have heard that at the order of the lord I made Dutch *giyaman*. We can find many different methods for *biidoro* making in the Dutch books. I chose the best method and can make any of them as I wish. When we keep nitric and sulphuric acids in glass bottles, if the glass is not of strong quality, cracks will soon appear, even though at first it seemed perfectly safe. The Dutch glass is not at all injured, no matter how long we may keep it. So I used that method and tried it for an alembic, and nothing has happened. When I used ordinary glass, the containers soon broke into pieces. Even by the best methods of the Japanese, the glass would not last long. But the glass made by the Dutch method is very solid, and because of that, our artisans do not like it, as they are accustomed to working with soft glass. It is just like working with iron when you are accustomed to tin. But the artisan whom I employed was very good, and his skill was splendid. The things that I ordered him to make were not ordinary items. Most of them were to be copied from imported ones. For the first few days he was troubled because he had had no such experience, but presently he was making them just as I ordered. A few days ago I had a green glass made[100] and will send it to you when opportunity arises. This would be a good chance to send glassware, as I would like to give you some, but there is nothing left, as I sent some to the lord and other persons. To Mr. Tanomo I sent, the day before yesterday, one made in imitation of an imported one. Perhaps he will take it to you, and you will then see it. In Japan, glass that cannot be affected by potassium nitrate has never been made. Some curious people who undertook Dutch studies tried to make some, but no one succeeded. Therefore, in order to store strong chemicals people have had to buy imported containers.

In my opinion, even the Europeans are not always infallible, nor are the Japanese incapable; so, if we Japanese read the books carefully and persevere in study, I am sure we can produce the same glass. I believed this when I undertook the work, and could do it without much difficulty, for which I am very glad. But as I cannot, in my rented grounds, make a strong fire, it takes much time to remove the bubbles. If you make it on a large scale at your place, using a large kiln just as the Europeans do, it will require almost the same time as the Europeans need. It is said that in Europe the strongest item requires twelve hours, but in my place it takes eighteen hours, and I still find some bubbles due to my limited scale.

I sent my messenger to a *biidoro* shop on the main street, with an example of my own glassware, but the master of the shop said that it was not made in Japan. Then he showed it at another shop, where the master said the material is from a foreign country but the craftsmanship seems to be of Japan, so maybe it was made in Osaka. But he wondered whether such glass could be made in Osaka.

Another example was taken by a member of the financial office to another *giyaman* shop. This master also said, "We cannot find this kind of glass in Japan." As for the green glass cup, no matter where I showed it, everyone said it must be an import. So I am very glad that I could introduce work that no one had ever done before. I began it for the lord. The reason why I started to make glass was that I had learned from Dutch books that black flint, which is called "quartz" in the Latin language, could be used to make the strongest *giyaman*. I want to make the strongest kind, which has not been made in Japan and export it to various countries to obtain much profit for our country. I also wish to make strong chemicals, and containers in which to keep them, so we will not be forced to depend on imported ones. I began to make things as an experiment. It took much time and labor, but is not useless, even if it requires three to five months, because it is something no one has ever mastered. But some people who do not understand my purpose think I am trying these things merely for my own profit. It is very foolish.

If you wish to have some glassware, please tell me so. Tomorrow Mr. Takemura is leaving here, so I wrote this letter and send it by him. At the same time I inquire for your health at this change of seasons. Since it keeps raining, please take care of yourself.

[From]: Shūri. Fifth month, twenty-eighth day.
[To]: Fujioka-sama.
Postscript: By the way, just for fun I will show you several examples of *giyaman*. You may test them by burning. Parts that come in contact with the fire will become rounded; that is because the quality is soft.[101]

It will be noticed that Shōzan did not mention specifically the use of borax to achieve the "hard" acid-resistant glass—a method that he had taught to Kagaya Kyūbei for his clinical and laboratory items. As borax is not found in Japan, it must have been imported and expensive.[102] Factors in Shōzan's success were his study of chemistry and experimentation, which gave him an understanding of his raw materials. He undoubtedly was a master of the craft.

EDO CRAFTSMEN

In 1691 Kaempfer had described glassblowers' establishments among the many small shops that lined the long route through Edo. As the years passed, many others sprang up to take care of the needs and luxuries of the great city. It would be impossible to identify all of them, but there are some meager references to individuals and localities.

Gennōjo is referred to as the first artisan to have made glass in Edo. In the *Kiyū Shōran* of 1830 it says: "There is a glassmaker named Nagashimaya Hanbei living at the present time in Asakusa. He is about seventy years old. His father was a man named Gennōjo, who was the first person to blow glass in Edo."[103] Since Hanbei was born in about 1760, it seems that Gennōjo must have begun to blow glass some time after Kaempfer's visits in 1690 to 1692.

Two areas in Edo where *biidoro* and *giyaman* shops flourished were Shiba to the west and Asakusa to the east, with various artisans sometimes referred to as living in other sections of the city. In the Tenna era (1681–83), beadmakers are specifically mentioned as residing around Nishima-machi, Shimmei-mae, and Minami-Tenna-chō in the Shiba district. Older people remember that some still operated there in the Meiji era.

Other shopkeepers and artisans mentioned by name are:[104]

Fukuda Yasoji	Asakusa, Sosenjimon-mae
Iseya Jisaku	Shiba, Shinmei-chō, Shindo
Iseya Kichibei	Shiba, Shinmei-chō, Shine-dōri
(a wholesaler)	
Koyama Seibei	Shiba, Mishima-chō
Minoya	Asakusa, Namiki-chō
Nishinomiya Tomejirō[105]	
[later called to Satsuma and subsequently to Hagi]	
Yamashiroya	Iwai-chō, Onarikōji
Yotsumoto Kametarō	Shiba, Shinmei-chō
[who was later called to Satsuma]	

In an entry of 1763, the *Bukō Nempyō* states that "recently many craftsmen in Tōto [eastern Edo] mastered its technique and produced various kinds of vessels, making the sale of glass their profession."[106]

In days when newspapers were nonexistent, the inexpensive woodblock print was a means of news distribution. This seems to have been the medium by which the *biidoro* and *giyaman* makers of the Edo period made their products known (Pls. 179–183). Since such broadsides (called *hikifuda*) are undated, one must fall back upon literary references to place them in a chronological setting. The *Nakasu Suzume*,[107] according to its preface, was published in 1777. Among all the attractions at Nakasu, the author writes:

The glass work is beautiful. It embodies many kinds of glass production, and people are astonished. Old and young together are so moved by it that they all ask themselves whether the Dragon Palace has not really come to view; it also makes them feel as though the Princess Otohime herself had come up to the water's surface and really existed in this world.

Plate 180 illustrates a woodblock broadside advertising the work of one glassmaker of Nagasaki. Unfortunately it is undated, and the glassmaker is not identified. The text announces that he will display glass "on the riverbank at Higashi-Ryōgoku." Ryōgoku was an amusement center in Edo from the eighteenth century, perhaps the date of the broadside. The inscription, noting that the craftsman had been making glass in Nagasaki, reads:

> Esteemed townsmen:
> I hope that you are in good health. For seven years I have worked in Nagasaki making *biidoro* products, such as Dutch ships and hanging lanterns. They caused a sensation, and people kindly took time to look at them. At the suggestion of my esteemed customers, I hastened to produce the aforementioned products, adding a device of moving dolls. I offer them for your inspection.
>
> Please come, one after another, on the opening day and see them. I will show them to you on the river bank at Higashi-Ryōgoku. I hope many, many customers will come.

Another such broadside is much more elaborate than the previous example (Pl. 181). It bears the heading *Giyaman Saiku* ("*Giyaman* Work") and illustrates a foreign ship:

> In the middle of this coming third month we shall start our display at Sengaku-ji, Takanawa, Shiba.
>
> The sailor's song is heard on the calm seas about Japan, in felicitation of the imperial reign.
>
> Many ships come on favorable winds, bringing tribute from all over the world. I drew in detail a ship from Holland. I made handiwork with *giyaman*, just like an oil painting. I made it minutely, from the dragonhead prow to the number of sails. And in order to amuse the children I made dolls representing three countries [India, China, Japan], which move by springs. . . .
>
> In connection with this miraculous affair, if you will come to see this display, the members of our guild will be very glad. We will feel as though flowers had bloomed on a dead tree.

From this it seems that this was a composite guild display, perhaps at festival time, since it was to be shown at Sengaku-ji temple in the Shiba district, noted for its glass shops.

This ship was perhaps rendered in a combination of wood, lacquer, and metal mounts, with the sliding windows, ropes, and other parts made up of groups of small glass rods. The beads at the upper left perhaps represent work by Shiba beadmakers.

Another broadside (Pl. 182) advertises a huge lantern to be exhibited at the Higashi-Ryōgoku amusement center in Edo. The maker seems to have come from Osaka, but unfortunately the spot where his name appeared is damaged. He says:

> Giyaman Ware. A Great Hanging Lantern.
> Height; about 10 meters, circumference, over 20 meters.
> Mechanical dolls—a wonderful feat!
>
> Please see it displayed at Higashi-Ryōgoku, from the early part of this coming seventh month.

I take the liberty of saying, "Gentlemen, I hope you are in good health." Now, I thank you for the unexpectedly large crowds when I displayed the large *giyaman* ship in the precincts of Asakusa. Eighteen years ago, when Asakusa was inaugurated, I displayed a large *giyaman* lantern, from Osaka, at Nishi-Ryōgoku, and many people came. I was much favored and encouraged by the people at that time, and that, together with the appreciation of the Osaka people, made me very happy. Now, as those same clients urged me to make the same kind of large lantern again, I have, despite my ineptness, made one twice as large as the one I made last year, adding some features of Takeda mechanical dolls. Please come, all of you, on the opening day—I beg it from the bottom of my heart.

The various participating artisans are named in explanatory notes and seals in the lower part of the picture. The design was drawn by Sadafusa Gokitei. The mechanical dolls were the work of Takeda Omi Daijo (a professional title) and his descendants (or pupils?): Nuidono-no-suke Seika, Kusumoto Tomiemon, and Kusumoto Iwajirō. The creator of the *giyaman* work was, it seems, mentioned at the lower left, where the paper is damaged. All that can be made out is "Osaka . . . . *shi* [perhaps part of *gishi*, meaning "technician]. In the lower right margin: "Owner of the woodblock, Moriya Jihei."

The lantern of the print is eight- or ten-sided, and in the Chinese style. Certainly these huge displays were not entirely of glass, but made up of glass panels and other glass parts assembled in a framework—often supplemented, as here, by small mechanical dolls; in the case of the ships represented, these dolls were sometimes made to run up and down the rigging, or to fire a miniature cannon. A lantern exhibited at Ryōgoku-Hirokōji was about seven meters high with a "landscapes of foreign cities on all sides."[108]

ŌSUMI GENSUKE

Practically nothing is known of this glassmaker but his name and address. However, his broadside (Pl. 179) shows that his production tended toward scientific-technical articles. The panel at the right of the advertisement lists: spectacles, surveying equipment, magnets, clocks, various articles of *giyaman* ware, imported wares, instruments of cartography, mirrors, and telescopes. Illustrations on the reverse include gauges of all sorts, compasses, scales, terrestrial globes, sextants, and a "thousand year lamp." The script advises that items will be made to order according to the customer's desire and will be given special attention, and that repairs are undertaken.

KAGAYA GLASSMAKERS

An artisan from Kaga Province is said to have established a shop in 1773 at Nihonbashi-dōri, Shio-machi, in Edo, where he produced and sold metal mirrors and eyeglasses. His name, and that of his immediate successor, are unknown, but it is presumed that he called his shop Kagaya after his native province. The proprietor of Kagaya in the Bunsei era (1818–29) planned to expand his business to include *giyaman* production and chose

Minagawa Bunjirō to head this new department. Bunjirō, in the light of subsequent developments, is called "the father of Kagaya glassmaking."[109]

Bunjirō requested that he be sent to Osaka, "where glass manufacture was more advanced than in Edo." There he spent a year as apprentice to Izumiya Kahei and became a *giyaman* craftsman. Returning to Edo, he became manager of *giyaman* manufacture for Kagaya. In 1839 Bunjirō was granted the Kagaya name in appreciation of his services, and became an independent craftsman, setting up his own shop in Oden-machi under the name Kagaya Kyūbei (popularly known also as Kaga Kyū). There seems to be much confusion over the name Kagaya, and perhaps there were numerous glassmakers in Edo by that name. Often an apprentice, when setting up shop for himself, would take the name of the shop where he had gained his training or would have the name conferred upon him, as had Minagawa Bunjirō. This, plus the custom of retaining one name for successive proprietors, makes it difficult to sift out historical data.

On his return from Osaka in 1834, Kyūbei devised a method for cutting designs on glass with emery powder as an abrasive. Later he learned how to make thermometers and hygrometers in the Western fashion.

Judging from the broadside (Pl. 183), the Kagaya output was predominantly tableware, lamps, and ornamental items, many of which were embellished with cut designs:

> We select the quality of the articles in order to attract the attention of our customers, and, also, we will produce them in beautiful appearance, suitable as gifts or souvenirs. . . . Regarding Japanese blown medicine bottles, our chief aim has been to make strong bottles, so we guarantee that there will be no leakage of medicine or other contents. Please kindly bring this matter to the attention of your friends.
>
> [Products:] Complete sets of vessels and blown items; small ornamental fittings; frames for oil paintings; bead screens; corals and varieties of beads; various kinds of precious stones and good beads; *biidoro* hair ornaments; *giyaman kanzashi*.
>
> We will take great care in repairing clocks and will provide cover plates to keep out dust, made in both foreign countries and in Japan.
>
> We also carefully polish, repair, and drill holes in coral beads, crystal, agate, and other kinds of precious stones, and varieties of *ojime*.

Regretfully, the broadside is undated, but since it suggests a well-established business, it was probably issued toward the middle of the nineteenth century and perhaps not until nearly the close of the period.

According to an unsubstantiated tradition, when Admiral Perry arrived in Uraga, near Edo, Kagaya Kyūbei was commissioned (by the shogunate?) to make cut glass bottles for presentation to the envoy, and the Admiral was "greatly astonished" and praised his skill. However, no glass of any sort has yet been found in the Perry Collection, and there is no reference to glass in family records.[110]

Kagaya Kyūbei (Minagawa Bunjirō) is said to have died in 1874. No doubt he trained many apprentices, who then expanded the profession in Edo. In the last years of the period, the shogunate had commissioned him to make signal lights for the ships that were being constructed for defense. His heir, Minagawa Kyūbei II, continued the business into the Meiji era.

KAZUSAYA GLASSMAKERS

Arihara Tomesaburō was born at Minami-Motomachi, Asakusa, Edo, where three generations of his forbears had made bottles.[111] In 1819 he opened a shop, Kazusaya, in Asakusa. His products were ornamental hairpins and windbells. In 1828 he set out to study glass in Nagasaki. Returning in 1834, he added ornamental vases and toys to his production. He also supplied glass metal to other *biidoro* artisans, since he and Kagaya Kyūbei were the only two craftsmen in Edo to produce their own glass metal.

In the Ansei era (1854–59), Kazusaya received an order for a retort with an attached bowl. This is considered to have been the first retort made in Japan. No doubt Kazusaya had received help from descriptions or illustrations in Dutch books. Like Kyūbei, Kazusaya also received orders for glass used in the defense ships under construction at the end of the Edo period.

The second and third generation from Kazusaya Tomesaburō inherited his name and continued to manufacture glass successfully until the second quarter of the twentieth century. It was only during World War II that the Arihara Glass Company, named for the founder, Arihara Tomesaburō, came to an end.[112]

The list of known glass types produced in Edo from the seventeenth century to 1868 is long, and contains all those mentioned for other areas, in addition to some new ones, but excluding sheet or plate glass. By the end of the Edo period, glass was produced in quantity and was within the reach of many.

It is impossible to attribute any specific examples to Kagaya, Kazusaya, or others. One can only compare surviving specimens to those illustrated in the broadsides of Ōsumi and Kagaya, mindful, in the shops' own words, that they also carried imported wares and that the same types were produced in other glass centers, often by migrating craftsmen.

BEADS

From the text of Kagaya Kyūbeu's broadside it is known that he produced beads, some of them glass. They appeared in the long fringes of lanterns, and in glass *sudare* (curtains). It is also known that there were beadmakers' shops in Shinmei-chō in Edo. It is likely, but impossible to prove, that some of those illustrated in Plate 163 may have been produced in Edo rather than in Osaka or Nagasaki.

COMBS AND HAIR ORNAMENTS

The combs of Edo differ from those of Nagasaki. Orchids or the combination of pine, bamboo, and plum, a favorite at the time of the New Year, were prevalent designs. In general, they are either fairly free floral subjects engraved in the glass or allover repeat patterns of cut-glass (*kiriko*), sometimes combined with cross-hatching, set into tortoise-shell frames (Pl. 23).

The four examples seen at the lower right in the Kagaya broadside (Pl. 183) are of the same "Sendai type" seen in Plate 173. It seems that this bar type was probably the "*giyaman kanzashi*" of the text, whereas the more delicate, pointed *kōgai* examples, Plate 172 and Supplementary Note 73, were of *biidoro*. The bar type was molded and sometimes cut, whereas the *kōgai* type was produced by lampwork. The bar type is said to have been unknown in Nagasaki; it became rather common in Honshu, probably in Osaka and, particularly, in Sendai and Edo.

Inrō AND *Netsuke*

Although an *inrō*, its *ojime* and *netsuke* all of glass would be a rare find, one is illustrated in the Kagaya broadside.[113] As it would have been heavy and impractical, perhaps only a dandy would have used it; conservative gentlemen adhered to the lightweight *inrō* of lacquer. A glass *netsuke* is shown in Plate 185.

VESSELS

Glass vessels were now a familiar sight in Edo. A glass bowl for ceremonial whipped tea (Pl. 186) presents an interesting aspect of glass adapted to Japanese use. The thin body and fluting suggest that it was made in Nagasaki, but it might be Edo work of the Tempō era (1830–43).

The wine cup of Plate 188 is known as a *choko* and is so labeled in the Kagaya broadside. With it is shown a wine pot labeled *kibisho*, a variant of which, with hoop handle, is seen at the lower left. The latter type must have been fairly familiar, since a number of examples exist in *biidoro* and *giyaman* cut glass.

One class of glass vessels popular in this period consisted of miniatures used as accessories for the Doll Festival. The carafe and wine glass set of Plate 189, mounted in a lacquer stand, is an especially good example.

There has been very little to say in recent chapters about glass *shari* containers. In the Edo period an entirely different type appeared. This is shown by the example excavated from the foundation stone of the five-storied pagoda of Tennō-ji temple at Yanaka, Ueno Park, Tokyo, which burned in 1957.[114]

This new type is essentially a rectangular case of gilt bronze in tower form, supported on a lotus pedestal and topped by a hip roof surmounted by a *hōshu* ("flaming jewel") finial. Each of the four sides has a small panel of flat glass intricately set into the gilt-bronze frame; the thickness of the glass varies from about 0.15 centimeter to about 0.2 centimeter. In the interior, clearly seen through the glass, is an upright bronze partition, to each side of which are attached three shelves. In the center of each is a tiny saucer holding a single glass *shari*. It is not known whether the glass panels were local or imported.

A similar reliquary was found at Taisō-ji temple in Yotsuya, Tokyo, installed in a Buddhist statue of Jizō. Others, somewhat similar but perhaps later in date, are known.

VESSELS DEPICTED IN WOODBLOCK PRINTS

Pictorial representations of foreign style stemmed wine glasses have been cited. But there are other woodcuts by *ukiyoe* artists that show their fascination with the new *biidoro* and *giyaman* wares—a fascination that (with the exception of the *pokon-pokon*) was probably largely due to the transparency and reflecting qualities of glass. Kitagawa Utamaro seems to have been particularly taken by transparency, for he depicted repeatedly the translucence of tortoiseshell, the transparent quality of nets, and the transparency of glass; he was also interested in images reflected from mirrors (Pls. 190, 191). Some of the forms shown in these plates have counterparts in the Kagaya broadside.

CLOISONNÉ

Hirata Dōnin (Hiroshirō) (1595–1646) had been a specialist in sword fittings. His work in cloisonné and that of his descendants in Edo seem to have been chiefly confined to small, delicate ornamental enamel units. A knife handle by the sixth generation Hirata, Narisuke (d. 1816), is discussed in Supplementary Note 77.

The boldness and vigor of conception, which had marked the Momoyama cloisonné style (Pls. 17, 132), became, in general, watered down in the Edo period into a skillful but lighter, daintier technique. The craft slipped into a more finicky manner, emphasizing small units, subdued colors, sometimes in minute allover patterns.

By the time foreigners arrived, the craft was on the decline, and items exported were, for the most part, totally unrepresentative of Japan's best workmanship. In the Meiji era there was a revival of *shippō*.

THE SPREAD OF GLASSMAKING—FEUDAL SPONSORSHIP

THROUGHOUT Japan there was now political and administrative unity, subject to the strict regulations of the shogunate. Socially, the *sankin kōtai* system played a large role in promoting closer contacts and even friendships between various daimyo and courtiers. Culturally, the presence of the feudal lords and their families in the busy and productive secular capital, and their pauses in Kyoto, the traditionally artistic imperial capital, were a chief factor in spreading throughout the land the aesthetic principles of the Edo period.

However, each fief was an entity in itself, characterized by differing local heritages, traditions, and influences, and fiercely eager to maintain its own individual character. Aside from the seven main roads, thoroughfares were practically nonexistent, and travel was largely by foot (with passports often required), thus perpetuating the relative isolation of each individual fief.

As the nineteenth century brought knowledge of Western scientific superiority and an appreciation of the menace it presented to a defenseless Japan, a few of the more perspicacious and enterprising daimyo strove to develop the means to meet the threat. Defense meant guns, ammunition, ship building, and all of the attendant manufactures. At first, action was slow, but after 1853, Japanese leaders awoke to the urgency.

Just as, in the Yayoi period, glassmaking seemed to come with the smelting of ore, introduction of Western scientific methods brought significant advances in glassmaking in those provinces where the feudal lords were alert to the potentialities of the age and financially able to promote new developments.

Saga (now Saga and Nagasaki prefectures) was the first to succeed in constructing a workable smelting furnace. Satsuma (now Kagoshima Prefecture) in southern Kyushu was particularly successful in iron smelting and casting. Others followed. These enterprises required capital, which was beyond the means of small fiefs, and difficult even for the larger ones. Some of them established commercial ventures to bring in revenue.

In the large cities (which were often domains of the shogunate) the glass producers were independent, unless they belonged to guilds. They may have had patrons among nearby feudal lords, but their establishments were run as private business enterprises. In the fiefs things were different; there were no privately owned factories. Large or small, they were formed and run by order of the daimyo as a fief activity.

In the following pages, the glass activity of four fiefs—Satsuma (Shimazu clan), Saga (Nabeshima clan), Fukuoka (Kuroda clan), and Hagi (Mōri clan)—will be considered.

SATSUMA FIEF

Satsuma (including both Satsuma and Ōsumi provinces) occupied the southern tip of Kyushu. The Shimazu clan had ruled the area since the eleventh century and was strongly entrenched. The fief was not only far from the capital at Edo, but it was largely surrounded by sea and, in the sixteenth century, like a few adjacent fiefs, it was not a vassal of the Tokugawa. Kagoshima city (the stronghold of the Shimazu) and Kagoshima Bay faced southward toward the sea and the Ryūkyū archipelago. Satsuma carried on trade with the islands, and even with China and Formosa, sometimes illicitly, sometimes with *bakufu* acquiescence. Much of Satsuma's wealth came through this trade.

Shimazu Shigehide, the twenty-fifth lord of Satsuma, and his descendants Narunobu, Narioki, and Nariakira, were forward-looking, perhaps because of the example of Shigehide, whose avid interest in the newly permitted Dutch studies began the trend toward industrial development in the fief. It was Narioki, however, who transformed this interest into action. He nurtured orchards and a horticultural garden of domestic and imported foreign specimens.[115] He built a refinery at the military training grounds in Nakamura, where gunpowder, steam engines, furnaces, sulphuric acid, hydrochloric acid, bleach, wine, and sugar were produced—all new to Japan. The chemical institute, known as the Seiyaku-kan ("Institute of Western Chemicals") was here. The first glass vessels made in Satsuma were containers for sulphuric and hydrochloric acids.

Yotsumoto Kametarō, a well-known Edo glassmaker of Gensuke-chō, was enlisted to develop these containers.[116] He succeeded in 1851, and production began. No trace of this factory survives, though some remains, now lost, appear to have been found during the building of a road shortly after World War II.

When Narioki retired, he was succeeded by his son Shimazu Nariakira, who, like his predecessors, had a keen interest in Western science. He had the thirty chapters of a book on chemistry and physics translated, a *Semi Dokuhon* ("Chemistry Reader"), which, with various others, he read assiduously. Nariakira realized clearly the precarious position of isolated Japan in a world where great advances had been made through scientific discoveries. It was his wish to master the new sciences, less for their facination than for their role in warding off a foreign threat.

Like others, Nariakira had many setbacks, but even when advised of a failure he considerately sent his workers a letter of encouragement, telling them that since the Saga fief had experienced some eighteen trials in perfecting a smelting furnace they could not expect to succeed "with only a few attempts." After all, both Westerners and the people of Saga (who had succeeded) were but human beings like themselves. Hence through perseverence how could there be such a thing as failure?[117]

All of Nariakira's interests and activities cannot be listed here, but a few will show the versatility of his mind and the diversity of his enterprises: production of metal type in Chinese, Japanese, and European languages; photography; papermaking; vaccination; building of steamships; mines for defending Kagoshima Bay; a telegraph; Satsuma porcelain and pottery (an amateur potter, he produced a series of ceremonial teabowls now on display in the Shimazu collection in the Shūseikan at Iso); and successful glass shops, which produced admirable glass. He suggested the advisability of having a national flag, and designed the Rising Sun flag familiar today.

Nariakira did much for his fief, reforming the government, increasing education, and exploiting natural resources. He was also a statesman on a national scale. The *bakufu* sometimes asked and took his advice. He was an ardent loyalist and did all he could to advance the return of sovereignty to the emperor; his efforts were influential, but he died in 1858 before the realization of his goal.

All these ventures were a drain upon the Satsuma coffers, but many were undertaken precisely for the purpose of refilling the depleted treasury. Many products were sold throughout the country and some exported abroad, via the Ryūkyū Islands. His soy sauce, for which ceramic containers were made, his sugar and various other products, all brought in revenue, as did the porcelain and the cast iron. One of the main sources of revenue, however, was the luxurious Satsuma glass. Considering the character and achievements of Shimazu Nariakira, the success of his glass was to be expected.

By the time the production of a strong acid-resistant glass had been developed, there grew a need for red glass for signal lights on ships. Enatsu Jūrō, Ushuku Hikouemon, Nakahara Yusuke, and Ichiki Shōuemon were appointed to develop a suitable glass. After months of experimentation, a red glass was produced. At first a dark red glass had been obtained by using copper dust. Then, by adding gold, a lighter, transparent red was made. During these experiments, methods were found to make blue, purple, yellow, and white glass, and various other tones. Elegant vessels of many shapes, sizes, and uses were then made.[118] Nariakira presented some of these to the family of the shogun and to friends among the daimyo. Cut glass was made, and it was cherished for its skillful designs and fine polish.

Flat glass had, at that time, been produced evidently only in the form of small cast circular pieces for mirrors. The first real plate glass was apparently made for ships in Satsuma. Several pieces are now preserved in the Shūseikan at Iso, which seem to be suitable for that purpose (Pl. 192).

The *Iso Ō-chaya Ōn-torisoeji e Hansharō narabini Kiritōshidai Sonohoka Go-zōritsu Go-nyumokuryō Motobari Sōchō* ("Total Record of Payments Advanced for the Construction of the Reverberatory Furnace, the Boring Machine, and other Equipment at the Annex to the Iso Tea House") lists items produced in the glass factory with their costs ("glass-making plus wages"). Since the old monetary terms give little comprehension of present-day values, they are omitted in the quotation given below, but it is interesting that the costs of "casting" are low in relation to the costs for polishing, the latter being from four to nine times greater than the casting costs. The rate for labor is given as three *ryō* per head for six glassmakers. Original Japanese sizes have been converted to centimeters.

    3 pieces glass plate: 31.8 cm. long by 25.76 cm. wide.
    4 circular glass plates: 24.24 cm. in diameter.
    6 circular glass plates: 20.30 cm. in diameter.
  28 circular glass plates: 20.30 cm. in diameter.
  29 pentagonal glass plates
    2 pentagonal glass plates
  17 pieces glass plate: 26.06 cm. long by 22.12 cm. wide.
  18 pieces glass plate: 26.06 cm. long by 19.09 cm. wide.
  18 pieces glass plate: 22.12 cm. long by 17.57 cm. wide.
    4 pieces glass plate: 31.82 cm. long by 25.76 cm. wide.
  12 pieces glass plate: 29.09 cm. long by 24.85 cm. wide
    4 round bottles, with *tsuba* [probably a projecting flange or flanges in the neck]
    3 hexagonal amber glass bottles, same as above
    1 round white bottle
    1 round dark blue bottle
    1 hexagonal blue bottle
    1 large round bottle
      same, 1 bottle
      same, 2 pair
    1 cut-glass bowl with lid.

Were the "glass plates" produced in the "kiln for plate glass" or in one of the several kilns "for the manufacture of ordinary lead plate glass," which are noted in the quotation cited below?

This plate glass, and the handsome cut-glass vessels, brought in much revenue. In the *Go-Nai Yōkin Hombarai Sashihiki Sō* ("Total Financial Receipts and Disbursements of the Lord"), an entry for 1855 lists:

Item: Gold: 127 *ryō* 3 *bu* 3 *shu*
Item: Small coins: 1 *kan* 178 mon

This money was sent from Edo as payment for plate glass, Chinese cotton and horseshoe-shaped silver, requested by Lord Date Tōtōmi.

In the same year the glass factory was moved to a section later known as the Shūseikan, to the east of the city, where reverberatory and blast furnaces were already located. This complex was to include all the workshops. In *Niirō Hisamochi Fu* ("Personal Record of Niirō Hisamochi") this entry appears for the eighth day of the tenth month of 1855: "I went to inspect the smelting furnace in precincts of the annex at Iso, and for the first time met Fukusaku Sukehachi and other staff members. Moreover, glassblower Kametarō began the blowing today, so congratulations were offered by the lord. We have entrusted the management of the factory to Sukehachi. . . ."

In the new glass factory there were:

2 kilns for dark red color—that is, melting kilns for the red glass used in ships' lanterns, which emits a red color from the use of copper dust.
2 kilns for transparent red glass, which emits a red color by the production of cassius purple from gold.
1 kiln for the manufacture of crystal glass.
1 kiln for the manufacture of plate glass.
Several large and small kilns for the manufacture of ordinary lead plate glass.
These have been established and widely extended.[119]

The unceasing efforts to improve glass production are suggested in a report to Nari-akira by Enatsu Jūrō in 1856:

While following your orders regarding the glassmaking, I have gradually devised the means of preparing potash. Since I heard that the ashes of the stems used in making indigo dye are particularly good, I wanted to have them used, so I consulted Tōgorō about having them for glassmaking. This I indicated to Sukehachi and Tokurō, and we arranged that all the ash be sent to the glass factory. . . .

We asked the Dutch in Nagasaki how to prepare glass, and after studying the literature in foreign books, according to your oder, we have at last been able to construct a kiln, and I think that from now on we can make glass and fill orders. We are all working very hard because it is your order. . . .

While searching out the techniques for glass materials we found the properties of lead very good. We tried to wash the fragments of stone with citrus vinegar [*ponzu*], as in crystal glass, and endeavored to find some substitute. Now it is the season for plums, and with Naosuke and Shōuemon I tested and found that the acid in the plums can dissolve iron and is good.[120] We are also trying to find a method for removing salts and one for elutriation, and are attempting to make glass that is as good as the foreign wares. I will let you know when we succeed.[121]

It may be worthwhile to consider the raw materials available in Satsuma. Pure quartz was quarried in Ōsumi Province. There were also ample sources of gold, silver, copper, lead, and tin. But there was no local soda and no cobalt.

It is said that a German artisan was invited to Kagoshima to teach the *kiriko* (cut glass) technique, but there is not even a whisper of this in the *Satsuma Garasu no Enkaku*, where, if true, it would surely have been noted. Possibly this was after Nariakira's death, but that seems doubtful because of the "retrenchments."

It has been suggested that the blanks for cut glass may have been imported, with only cutting done in Satsuma. However, this seems contradicted by the quotations given above, by the following report of Dr. C. Pompé van Meedervoort, and by the Japanese forms produced.

Various materials were used for polishing—stone, iron, and willow-wood wheels, various grades of emery, and an especially fine and delicate hardwood charcoal, known as *hosumi*, which was used in stick form with water.

The success of these efforts is revealed in the writing of a European visitor, Dr. C. Pompé van Meedervoort from Nagasaki, who was a passenger on the *Nippon Maru* when it touched at Kagoshima in 1858. He described the glass factory in some detail:

> There is a glass factory in which more than one hundred and twenty glass craftsmen are working. . . . In this factory there are: a melting shop; a blowing shop; and a large stone mortar. The products were uncolored wares, brilliantly colored ones, and together with the elaborately luxurious ones there were both refined and coarse items. Furthermore, there were practical, durable ones necessary for daily use. I noticed that this factory was kept in good order. I hear that coloring of glass was commenced only recently in Europe. In spite of this the Lord of Satsuma has manufactured glass with up-to-date methods. I was given some as specimens to take to Deshima in Nagasaki. Those glasswares were as fine as wares displayed in exhibitions in Europe. Therefore it is easy to imagine how this industry may develop in the future. I believe that his kind of glass industry may become the chief manufacture in Japan. . . .[122]

What pride and delight Nariakira took in his glass products is seen in an incident recorded in the memoirs of Mitsukuri Gempō, whom Nariakira met at Yoshida in Chōshū Province in 1854, while enroute to Edo. In the course of their conversation Nariakira brought out a small glass bottle, explaining that it had been made in Satsuma and had withstood all damage when filled with nitric acid or with powerful oil of alum. "By this process," he said, "I have also made 'patento' glass and am also making *hari*."[123]

His widespread generosity in presenting glass to various other daimyo is shown in a letter from Kuroda Nagahirō (a Shimazu who had been adopted into the Kuroda family) to the Date daimyo of Uwajima in Shikoku:

I hear that you received a red glass vessel from the same person. I, too, received one. He is very proud of the glass vessels, but in my opinion the red color is not really scarlet or bright red but a kind of red. Although the material is cassius purple, it turned red because of improper firing. If properly fired it would have been bright red. But in my factory, a red color cannot yet even be produced, so I cannot criticize their technique. Production of a bright red color is very difficult; but if I can make it later on, I will give you one. However, since there has recently been the incident involving the foreign barbarians, I cannot engage in such a thing. . . .[124]

So great is the variety in the Satsuma output, so diverse its shapes and colors, its designs and uses, that it is difficult to summarize. In the Shūseikan in Iso Park, Kagoshima, are housed about three hundred specimens. Others are presented in the Kagoshima Municipal Art Museum and in various Japanese collections.

Since the blowing, molding and cutting techniques were offsprings of the Western methods, learned from books and from looking at imports, early types of glass were naturally patterned after foreign models. Differences in detail or in design application are often noticeable. Many examples of Satsuma cut glass are colorless, like the bowl of Plate 194 or the wine glass, Plate 195. Two examples of red-overlay glass are evidently early: a cup, still uncut (Sup. N. 78) and a cut glass bottle (Sup. N. 82); the uneven mottled distribution of the red color attests to early difficulties in perfecting the technique. Other examples are clear red.

In some, the dark copper red (*inkoshoku*) is only translucent or semitransparent. Other examples of thinner glass, and of lighter tone and fully transparent, were produced by adding minute quantities of gold to the batch. A handsome cut-glass perfume bottle of this delicate "red," preserved in the Shūseikan (No. 1354/3), is faceted on eight sides and has a crosshatched stopper with a border of clear twisted lobes. The hatched center is colorless but takes on a rose tone from a bit of colored glass inserted below in the mass of clear glass. A deep plate in the Shūseikan (No. 1456/174) is of this same delicate transparent red, with gold-band decoration added.[125] Another variety of red glass is shown in Plate 201.

Dark blue for luxury wares was no less popular than the red. Early examples, it seems, are Plates 196 and 197, in which the cutting is comparatively "soft" and not highly polished. Plates 27 and 28, sharply cut and highly polished, must be somewhat later.

Molded glass was also produced. A handsome specimen is shown in Plate 198. The molded bowl of Plate 200, and other similar bowls, are assigned to Satsuma, but do not equal the handsome covered dish of Plate 198.

A ceremonial teabowl attributed to Nariakira (Sup. N. 84) gives every indication of being an attempt to throw glass on a potter's wheel—an extraordinarily unconventional approach, which, though doomed to failure, attests to the search that was constantly being pursued.

After Nariakira's death in 1858, a temporary retrenchment reduced the work force to about twenty persons. The responsibility for glassmaking was transferred to the superintendent of iron casting, and only five glassmakers remained.[126] Production still remained skillful, as is seen in the report by Imai Teisuke, from Tosa Province (present Kōchi Prefecture), who visited the factory in 1859. He was shown a book, *Hari Seikō Zensho* ("Handbook of Glass Technology"), by Hanai Kazuyoshi, which he copied, and was given a glass bottle made in a variety of colors: blue, green, red, and violet.[127] In 1860 the iron-casting department was abolished and its activities combined with the Shūseikan. The same year Nishinomiya Tomejirō left Satsuma and undertook glass production under Lord Mōri in Hagi.

In 1863 the British, in revenge for the death of an Englishman at the hands of Satsuma warriors, bombarded the city and destroyed the Shūseikan. When it was rebuilt in 1864, Satsuma activities were concentrated on steel, lumber and, at another site, on cotton spinning with British looms. Glass production first declined to such things as "toys," and finally became extinct.

There are a number of puzzling glass items said to be from the Satsuma factory. All bear, somewhere on the object and sometimes repeated a number of times, the Satsuma crest, very lightly incised on the surface. Since many of these seem incompatible with what is known of glass production in Nariakira's time, they have been included in the Meiji era. A few of them (as Pls. 213, 214) suggest something of traditional Satsuma elegance, but others (Sup. N. 86, 87) are heavy and stolid, quite out of tune with the glass of Nariakira's time. An often illustrated example in the Shūseikan is a vase of very dark overlaid blue (purple in transmitted light), which had three plain uncut roundels on the body; each roundel now bears a Satsuma crest clumsily and superficially scratched on the surface. The bottom is flat, smooth, and unpolished. The piece has the appearance of an authentic Satsuma item that remained unfinished and to which the crude crest was added by someone at a later date.

It has been said that dealers, in later years, added these crests in order to promote sales. This might explain examples such as in Plates 213 and 214. Mr. Tadashige Shimazu, the grandson of Nariakira, did not remember seeing crests on any of the family's glass. A number of pieces are in Kagoshima collections; a few in the Shūseikan collection were acquired from the large collection of "Satsuma glass" assembled by the late Mr. Kino-suke Edamoto. All seem out of keeping with what is known of glass produced in Nariakira's time. Later activities of the factory are touched upon below on page 286.

SAGA FIEF

Saga, in northwestern Kyushu (now Saga and Nagasaki prefectures) was, with the Kuroda fief of Chikuzen (now Fukuoka Prefecture), responsible for the defense of the port of Nagasaki. The lord of Saga, Nabeshima Kansō, was among the first to promote Dutch studies and industrial activities within his fief. With official approval, he planned for the fortification of Nagasaki Harbor and started iron smelting and casting. It was a pioneer affair, beset with problems and entirely based on translated Dutch texts and their illustrations. In 1852 the first successful cannon was produced. By 1856 two hundred more (probably in addition to those needed for Nagasaki) were supplied for the defense of Edo Harbor.[128]

Nabeshima Kansō was, like Shimazu Nariakira, an enterprising and farseeing lord. He sponsored Dutch studies and fostered the development of heavy industry. Although defense was the prime motivation, he also developed commercial enterprises to create revenue. The list of his ventures is strikingly like those of Satsuma—photography, spinning, telegraphy, sugar refining, the famous Arita porcelain, steamship building, the production of acids, soda, alkali, electricity, gunpowder, fuses, incendiary arrows, metallurgy, coal mining. After the treaty with the United States was consummated, two men from Saga were included in the *bakufu*'s mission to the United States in 1860.

Very little specific data has been found and very few authentic examples survive of Saga glass. One of a pair of large Nabeshima glass fishbowls is shown in Plate 203.[127]

According to historical records at the Saga Prefectural Library, a small glass factory was operating in the Ansei era (1854–59). Sanō Tsunetami was put in charge of the glass factory, where lamp chimneys, tableware, and cut glass are said to have been made. Some suggest that glass was made as early as 1848, while others push the date up to 1860. One informant stated that glass was cast in molds in 1851.[129]

The picture of glass production of Saga is thus vague and incomplete, yet the factory was not without influence upon later glassmaking in Japan. One reference speaks of Komatani Shinshichi, who had been trained in the Saga factory and later went into service to Lord Tōdō of Izumi (Osaka Prefecture); there he was able "to greatly expand the glass industry."[130] Fukutani Keikichi and Fujiyama Tanehirō, both of whom learned the glass technique in Saga, became famous in the Meiji era as leaders in the European-oriented Shinagawa Glassworks in Tokyo.

Fukuoka Fief

Saga and Fukuoka fiefs shared a joint responsibility for the protection of the port of Nagasaki. The tenth lord of Fukuoka, Kuroda Narikiyo was an enthusiastic and sophisticated scholar, and it was but natural that his adopted son, Kuroda Nagahiro, should likewise be enthusiastic about the advanced knowledge of the West.

Nagahiro, a younger son in the Shimazu family, had been adopted into the Kuroda family, and thus later became the eleventh lord of the Fukuoka fief. He established a research station in Fukuoka and in 1847 constructed a smelting furnace. Like other forward-looking lords, he produced defense materials and developed commercial enterprises as well.

The city of Fukuoka already had a glassmaker who called himself Biidoroya Uhei,[131] whose glass activities date back to 1832. He seems to have been adventuresome, and he became a small merchant of sorts, moving between Hakata (the port of Fukuoka) and Kyoto and Osaka, buying and selling, and sometimes carrying out in Osaka financial transactions entrusted to him by Hakata merchants. A friendly person, he made acquaintances easily. One of these was Uemon, a glassmaker from Edo, who returned to

Fukuoka with Uhei and taught him the glass trade. In 1832 Uhei built a kiln in his elder brother's yard and succeeded in producing glass. Uemon returned to Edo, but Uhei continued with his glass production. Among other things, he made and sold *pimpon* (*pokon-pokon*). Previously these had been imported from Nagasaki and sold at rather high prices by the merchants of Fukuoka, who therefore opposed a cheaper, local production. However, Uhei survived their antagonism and established a shop at Najima-chō in Fukuoka, which bore the sign Biidoroya Uhei.

Kuroda Nagahiro became interested and invited Uhei to be the head engineer of his new glass factory, but Uhei felt inadequate to the task and went to Nagasaki to seek suitable technicians. Meanwhile, Nagahiro had become interested in Uhei's son and sent him to Nagasaki to study glass techniques.

Uhei continued producing. His *pimpon* were especially popular, particularly during the annual festivals of the Hachiman Shrine at Hakozaki. He died in 1861, having been made prosperous from the sale of this toy.

There is considerable confusion regarding the development of Kuroda glass and the identity of those responsible for its management, but it is known that members of the Mizuno family were prominent and that they remained in control of the property when the factory ceased to operate in 1892.

When the Mizuno family home was burned during World War II, their records and glass collection were lost, with the exception of one small paperweight (Pl. 204).

Mrs. Mitsuyo Mizuno (born in 1894) recalls seeing in her home many strange "curved glasses" of various sizes, which she thinks were made in the Tempō era (1830–43). These were perhaps retorts or other laboratory equipment. Some were semitransparent, some "like stone."

Among materials for the Kuroda kilns, the oak used for charcoal fuel and the basic ingredients for the glass batches were obtained locally, but lead and other chemicals are said to have been brought from Nagasaki. A popular product was a translucent yellow bead.[132] The factory was also known for its excellent cut glass and a manganese-colored ware.[133]

A large variety of glassware is mentioned as having been produced at the factory: bottles, saké cups, water glasses, bowls, plates, toys, *kanzashi*, *kiseru*, lenses, candlestands, and toward the close of the period, lamp chimneys and oil pots for lamps. Surviving examples are few. The paperweight of Plate 204 is a particularly skillful work for its time. The tentative attribution of the saké cup, Plate 205, is supported by its unusual violet-blue tone.

A type of footed goblet engraved with grapevine designs has often been attributed to the Kuroda factory, but without any documentary basis. Two of these are in The Toledo Museum of Art (Nos. 56.4 A & B).

HAGI FIEF

The southwestern area of Honshu, the main Japanese island, was prominent in Japanese history from ancient times. It was the closest point to the Korean peninsula. In the Muromachi period, under rule by the Ōuchi clan, the city of Yamaguchi and the surrounding region became powerful and culturally imitated and rivaled Kyoto. In the civil wars of the late Muromachi period, the Ōuchi were destroyed, and their lands fell to the neighboring Mōri clan, who, for a short time, controlled a large part of western Honshu until Tokugawa Ieyasu deprived them of much of it. From that time forward they controlled only the southwestern end of Honshu.

That area, under the Ōuchi, had an active trade with China and Korea. It was in Yamaguchi that Father Francisco Xavier spent some time, and the Christian community that ensued felt some European influence. The tradition of foreign contacts came to an end when the area came under the control of the Mōri, who proscribed Christianity and all travel and contacts abroad.

After the order banning Western books was rescinded, the Mōri lords were among those who encouraged the study of Western science and who sent men to Nagasaki for that purpose. The center of Mōri rule was the relatively small castle in Hagi, situated on one of the most beautiful castle sites in Japan. Toward the end of the period, Mōri Takachika moved his residence to Yamaguchi city, probably a more convenient site from which to operate during the disturbances preceding the Meiji Restoration, in which "men of Chōshū" played a prominent role.

Mōri Takachika (Keishin; 1819–71) acceded as daimyo in 1837. Though a reformer, striving to improve the administration and activities of the fief, he was conservative, for he resisted the entrance of foreigners into Japan; yet he was interested in taking advantage of the new Western techniques. Cannon and arms were manufactured, but not to such an extent as at Saga and Satsuma. Additional enterprises included an old salt industry converted to new methods, paper making, ship building, production of wax and of indigo. A medical school was formed, and medicinal herbs grown commercially.[134] Eventually a glass factory was established in 1860.

Hagi maintained a research office in Nagasaki, to which promising men were dispatched to study European scientific methods. Upon returning to the fief, these men set up various manufacturing processes. One of them was a person of astonishing curiosity, imagination, and ability—Nakashima Jihei, son of Nakashima Saburōemon, who held an important position at the shipping headquarters. Jihei is of special interest here, having been appointed as superintendent of the glass factory when it was inaugurated in 1860. His petition to the clan written in 1863, apparently for support of further studies, reveals the inquiring spirit of the time and the vigor with which new knowledge was acquired and applied:

> In the first year of Ansei [1854] American warships called at Uraga; hence the nation must live amid fear and insecurity. My father, Saburōemon, thought it was time for him to do something good for the lord and the people who had favored his family over the years.
>
> With the permission of the fief government he sent me to Nagasaki in the third

year of Ansei 1 1856] to become a competent interpreter. At Nagasaki I studied chiefly under Namura Hachiuemon, a great interpreter. Besides the language, I had interests in chemistry and ironwork. Later I translated a small booklet of Harudes [Haldes?].

In the first month of the fifth year of Ansei [1858] I received silver as a special scholarship from the fief, at the rate of four *momme* a day.

In June of the same year, cholera broke out in Nagasaki, and Dr. Pompé thought it might spread rapidly throughout the nation. I learned the preventives against it, and sent a detailed report to Hagi, which was highly appreciated.

In the tenth month of the same year Kurihara Ryōzō and others came to Nagasaki as officially appointed students; I also was treated as an official student.

In the spring of Ansei 6 [1859], I studied chemical analysis, sheep husbandry, and wool dyeing, and made reports on them. In that year we received a letter suspending aid for students. As for me, with my work half done, I submitted a petition to the fief government to continue my studies.

In the seventh month of that year I returned to Hagi, by official order.

In Manen 1 [1860] I was appointed to the staff of the Analytical Experimental Center.[135]

In the tenth month of that year I went to Kagoshima and Nagasaki on official business, accompanied by Jikiyokome. Stayed in Satsuma several days. Everything turned out well, and I bought a locomotive and a steamboat.

In Bunkyū 1 [1861] on the first day of the fourth month, the locomotive engine ran for the first time, in the presence of the lord in the castle grounds. The steamboat was first sailed by Hōjō Genzō. I helped him in firing the engine.

In the fourth month of Bunkyū 2 [1862] I taught a new technique of dyeing to the dyers of Yamaguchi.

As a staff member of the Analytical Experimental Center, I often made medicine for the lords and their families.

In addition, I also engaged in teaching and in translating books.

As mentioned above, I have been serving the lord and the fief. My father is given two *koku* and four *to* of rice for his salary, which is not enough to send his son away to study.

I sincerely hope you may give generous consideration to our situation and the work I have done.

[Signed] Kōhei, son of
Saburōemon

Bunkyū 3, fifth month [1863]

In Satsuma he studied the reverberatory furnace, glass, and weaving. His versatility seems to have been almost unlimited. He was reputedly a good calligrapher, made lacquer, did woodcarving, and made cameras.[136] All of these activities, however, seem to have overshadowed his interest in glass.

The first notations regarding glass thus far found among records in the Yamaguchi Prefectural Library are dated 1860. Following are excerpts:[137]

> Nishinomiya Tomejirō, a man of Edo, maker of glassware.
> The above-mentioned person has been brought to the fief on fief business. It is the lord's order that he stay in Hagi.

> Nishinomiya Tomejirō, a man of Edo, maker of glassware.
> The above-mentioned person has been invited and has come, by order. Therefore, kindly let him pass the front gate and the three gates at east, west, and rear, with his equipment.

> MEMORANDUM [Plate 206]
> Nishinomiya Tomejirō, a man of Edo, maker of glassware.
> The factory repairs in Hatchō having been completed, you are instructed to go there from tomorrow. The lord has ordered me to inform you.

Thorough preparations went ahead to secure the needed materials, and the official announcement was made. A second glassmaker was engaged.

> Since the Okonandō [official in charge of fief products] has now been ordered to manufacture glass, crystal stone from Efunayama, Saiban, is needed. The local office should be notified, so that all preparations may be made to excavate and transport the crystal stone.
> Offices in all the counties are instructed to collect and present samples of stone. If, after testing, they prove suitable, orders will be issued for quarrying and delivering the stone. The county officers are instructed to avoid any disturbance until further notice is received on how to excavate the stone.

> MEMORANDUM
> Chōzō, of Osaka, glassmaker, pupil of Nishinomiya Tomejirō.
> Referring to the above mentioned person's coming to the fief at this time, he requested permission to stay for the time being at the glass factory in Hatchō with Tomejirō. This is so ordered by the lord.

Although Tomejirō is listed as a citizen of Edo, he had come from Satsuma, where he had worked for an unspecified period. He asked permission to go to Kagoshima to fetch his wife and children. Since he was a citizen of Edo, he could not be given a Hagi passport. Evidently the matter was resolved by giving him a letter of identification.

> Nishinomiya Tomejirō, glassmaker, citizen of Edo.
> The above-mentioned person, who was invited to the fief for fief business and who, by the lord's order, lives in the Hyakusō-en, asks permission to travel to Kagoshima on business. His travel is hereby authorized, estimating a round trip for forty days.

Nakashima Jihei and Ukichi Jikiyokome were ordered to go to Satsuma at the same time to observe glassmaking and other things. Jihei's activities in the glass field are not emphasized in the records, but it is clear that he was put in charge of the factory when it opened in 1860.

His notes incorporated in a series of manuscript notebooks preserved by his grandson Keichi Nakashima clearly reveal that he was familiar with the details of glassmaking. Plate 207 reproduces pages from this manuscript. It is of interest that the unusual square-footed cup form drawn in the upper left margin is duplicated in the cup of Plate 210.

There is a considerable amount of old glass owned in Hagi city, but how much was made in the Hagi factory is uncertain. A few items are known to have been brought from Nagasaki, either made there or imported from Europe. A covered glass jar of European manufacture is owned by the Umeda family of Hagi. When Umeda Nobufusa, a samurai, was in Nagasaki around 1800 to study the new scientific method of cannon making, he was told by his Dutch hosts that if he could drink this jar full of saké, it would be his.

In the Kikuya collection in Hagi a handsome covered box (Pl. 208) shows characteristics of both European and Satsuma glass and yet seems to have an individuality of its own. Since Tomejirō was well versed in Satsuma techniques, he may have been the maker.

The unsettled political circumstances that occurred in 1862 appear to have curtailed glassmaking in the feudal domains and especially in Hagi.

Colored glass seems to be lacking in the Hagi collections,[138] and it is likely that the bulk of the output was transparent, colorless glass. Perhaps the factory was not equipped to prepare the metal oxides needed as coloring agents, or operated too briefly to have fully developed the necessary techniques. Certainly it was not for lack of knowledge, since Jihei's manuscript shows familiarity with the methods.

The glassware produced in Hagi included bottles, Western style footed wine glasses such as in Plates 209 and 210, and Japanese style saké cups (Sup. N. 85). A year after the factory was started, Mōri Takachika presented to the emperor a set of glass items including "fifteen saké cups, one cup stand, three bowls, and twenty small plates."[139] A rosary of glass beads and a glass *jikutan* on a small scroll are said to have come from the Hagi factory. Doubtless there were other types as well.

In all fiefs, glassmaking operations were discontinued owing to the political and military uncertitudes of the 1860s. After the Restoration of 1868, the tremendous Western influences, and the upheavals in which the daimyo and samurai lost their powers and much of their wealth, the fiefs were integrated into the central new government. Under the circumstances, locally sponsored glass manufacturing operations suffered and, except for a last fluttering in Kagoshima, faded from the picture. Another phase of glassmaking in Japan had come to an end.

1. Shūjirō Watanabe, *op. cit.* (see n. 19, p. 160), pp. 87–88.
2. Sansom, *op. cit.* (see n. 1, p. 141), p. 404.
3. Sir Thomas Stamford Raffles, *Report on Japan, to the Secret Committee of the English East India Company*, Kobe, 1929, J. L. Thompson & Co., Ltd., p. 21.
4. Sir Rutherford Alcock, *The Capital of the Tycoon*, (2d. ed. ?), London, 1893, I, p. 73.

5. Charles Peter Thunberg, *Travels to Europe, Africa and Asia Performed between 1770 and 1779*, 3d ed., London, 1796, III, p. 12: "On this day all the Prayer Books and Bibles belonging to the sailors were collected and put into a chest, which was nailed down. The chest was afterwards left in the care of the Japanese till the time of our departure."

6. Okamura, *op. cit.* (see n. 9, p. 160), p. 264.

7. *Okada, *Garasu*, p. 56, refers to the tradition that they were filled, by Ieyasu's order, with drugs from the medicine garden below Kunōzan.

8. Thunberg, *op. cit.* (see n. 5), p. 50.

9. W. A. Woolley, "Historical Notes on Nagasaki," *TASJ*, IX, 1881, p. 137.

10. E. S. Crawcour, "Some Observations on Merchants, A Translation of Mitsui Takafusa's *Chonin Koken Roku* [Record of the Contribution of Merchants], *TASJ*, Third Series, VIII, December 1961, pp. 104, n. 12, 110, n. 35. This was an 18th century work.

11. C. R. Boxer, "Jan Compagnie in Japan, 1672–1674, or Anglo-Dutch Rivalry in Japan and Formosa," *TASJ*, Second Series, VII, December 1930, pp. 138–205.

12. Illustrated in *Shibui, "The Story of Glass in Japan," p. 115.

13. *Okada, *Garasu*, p. 62.

14. A. M. Wallace-Dunlop, *Glass in the Old World*, London, 1882, p. 103.

15. In the Shūseikan in Kagoshima, which now houses treasures of the Shimazu family of Satsuma, there is a group of such "smelling bottles."

16. Raffles, *op. cit.* (see n. 3), pp. 165–167.

17. Engelbert Kaempfer, *The History of Japan, Together with a Description of the Kingdom of Siam, 1690–1692*; first English translation by J. G. Scheuchzer, London, 1727, Book IV, p. 353. Another ed., Glasgow, 1906.

18. Kyūrinsai (Joken) Nishikawa, *Kai Tsūsho Kō* [Treatise on Commerce with the Chinese and the Barbarians], Kyoto, 1695; from Seiichi Takimoto, *Nihon Keizai Taiten* [Compendium of Japanese Economics], Tokyo, 1928, IV, p. 342.

19. Raffles, *op. cit.* (see n. 3), pp. 47–50, also p. 167, referring to the Argand tubular-wick lamp invented by the physicist Ami Argand about 1780.

20. Illustrated in Boxer, *Jan Compagnie in Japan, op. cit.* (see n. 11), opp. p. 122.

21. Capt. V. N. Golownin, *Japan and the Japanese*, rev. ed., London, 1853, I, p. 72.

22. In *Tanahashi, "Kinsei Nihon ni okeru. . . . ," II, the belief of Mr. Tetsuya Koshinaka is cited that, with no records of glass before 1624, uncolored glass was first produced after that date, probably around 1643 (on the basis of a business account-book recording the lineage of glassmaker Rokuemon) and that the making of colored glass

was mastered about a century later. In this respect refer to the dates in Plate Notes 152 and 154.

23. Philip Franz von Siebold, quoted in *Ono, *Doro-e to Garasu-e*, p. 194.

24. Quotation from *Sugie, *Garasu*, p. 57.

25. Parts of this work have been discussed in detail in *Tanahashi, "Kinsei Nihon ni. . . ." Pt. II; on page 253 the lead mentioned in *Bankin Sugiwai Bukuro* (and in *Nihon Kinsei Kōgyōshi*) is referred to as fused metallic lead rather than minium.

26. "White stone," quartz. Tadahide Nishikawa (Joken), in *Nagasaki Yawasō* [Night Tales of Nagasaki], 1720, refers, however, to a beach near Nagasaki as the only place for obtaining it; included in *Nagasaki to Kaigai Bunka* [Nagasaki and Overseas Culture], Nagasaki, 1926, Municipal Office, Pt. 2, p. 69. Dr. Masao Mine advised that *hakuseki* is a pure quartz sand, now called *Nagasaki shiro* ("Nagasaki white").

27. *Seitai*, a blue coloring agent. Since China is given as its source and it gives an indigo hue, could it have been the "Mohammedan Blue" cobalt from Iran used in Chinese ceramics? *Tanahashi ("Kinsei Nihon ni okeru Garasu. . . . ," II, pp. 273–274) carried out experiments according to this treatise, using white lead with indigo as the coloring agent, but without success as the color was impermanent.

28. Nobuhiro (Shin-en) Satō, *Keizai Yōroku* [Extracts Regarding Economics], written in Bunsei 10 (1827), but not published until Ansei 6 (1869), Tokyo, Iwanami ed., 1928, IV, p. 55.

29. Alcock, *op. cit.* (see n. 4), II, p. 329.

30. Thunberg, *op. cit.* (see n. 5), IV, pp. 59–60.

31. But in *Sugie, *Biidoro*, p. 60, it is stated that high-class *biidoro* was called *giyaman* even though not cut, whereas ordinary work was called *biidoro*. The spelling "giyaman" was noted in early books and is so used in this publication; later, "giaman" became common.

32. *Sugie, *Garasu to Seikatsu*, p. 19.

33. *Hayashi, "Nagasaki no Biidoro to Giyaman," p. 24.

34. Tokutarō Nagami, *Namban Nagasakigusa* [Namban Grass of Nagasaki], Tokyo, 1926, p. 67.

35. Thunberg, *op. cit.* (see n. 5), III, p. 13.

36. *Ibid.*, p. 17.

37. Sir Thomas Stamford Raffles, *Memoir of the Life and Services of Sir Thomas Stamford Raffles, F.R.S.* (By his Widow), London, John Murray, 1830, p. 231.

38. In *Okada, *Garasu*, p. 217, there is mention of "rosaries, garden lanterns, *sudare*, etcetera" also made by Tōshichi.

39. *Kurokawa, *Kōgei Shiryō*, Pt. 2, p. 45.

40. Okamura, *op. cit.* (see n. 9, p. 160), p. 266.

41. Nishikawa, *Nagasaki Yawasō*, in *Nagasaki to Kaigai Bunka*, *op. cit.* (n. 26), Pt. 2, p. 69. *Tanahashi,

"Kinsei Nihon ni. . . . ," II, p. 239, quotes *Ko-shinaka, "Garasu-kō," p. 7, that glass was seemingly first made in Nagasaki around 1643. *Koshinaka, "A Five-coloured *Biidoro* Bowl," p. 85, expresses the thought that colored glass and cut glass were produced a century later. *Tanahashi, I, p. 254, quotes a record of 1676, regarding contraband trade with Cambodia, including mention of a "Japanese glass hanging vase," together with glass saké bottles and brush holders (both non-Western types), as well as some *Oranda* [Dutch] items.

42. *Hayashi, "Nagasaki no Biidoro to Giyaman," p. 26.

43. *Nagasaki to Kaigai Bunka*, op. cit. (n. 26), Pt. 2, p. 59.

44. W. G. N. Van der Sleen, "A Bead Factory in Amsterdam in the Seventeenth Century," Man, LXVI, 1963, pp. 172–174; *Notes on Ancient Glass Beads*, p. 265; *A Handbook of Beads*, Liège, Musée du Verre, 1967. The Dutch beads are alleged to contain "over 20% potash" whereas Venetian products were "nearly always" of soda glass. This opens up a new field for investigation of beads imported into Japan in the Edo period.

45. Nishikawa, *Nagasaki Yawaso*, op. cit. (n. 26), p. 62.

46. *Mody, *A Collection of Nagasaki. . . .* , Pl. 214.

47. The *Bankin Sugiwai Bukuro* of Yarai Miyake quoted above outlines the use of potash with the lead.

48. *Tourist*, XVII, No. 108, September 1929, p. 1.

49. Paske-Smith, *Western Barbarians in Japan and Formosa in Tokugawa Days, 1603–1868*, Kobe, 1930, Thompson (J.L.) Ltd., p. 296.

50. Kaempfer, op. cit. (see n. 17), II, p. 28.

51. Thunberg, op. cit. (see n. 5), IV, pp. 48–49. It has been common in Japan for people of one area, when moving to another, to group themselves together, their street division then taking the name of the place from which they came or their profession. Nagasaki abounds in such names.

52. Kōtei Murase, *Geien Nisho* [Extracts Regarding the Crafts], Edo, 1808. VII, p. 2.

53. *Matsumoto, "Biidoro wo Fuku Musume," p. 12.

54. Nagami, op. cit. (see n. 34), p. 285.

55. Eijirō Honjō, *The Social and Economic History of Japan*, Kyoto, Nihon Keizaishi Kenkyūsho, 1935, pp. 264–265.

56. Yosaburō Takekoshi, *The Economic Aspects of the History of the Civilization of Japan*, London, 1930, II, p. 251.

57. *Terashima, *Wakan Sanzai Zue*, p. 651.

58. Data in this and the following paragraph are taken from *NKYS, pp. 5–6. No reference sources are cited in this work, and tracing such sources is extremely difficult due to the devastation of World War II.

59. *Sugie, *Nihon Garasu Kōgyō-shi*, p. 82. A visit by the author to Sumiyoshi Shrine in 1960 to see these lanterns was fruitless, although officials of the shrine were most courteous in trying to find the lanterns or to locate some record of such a dedication.

60. *Shiota, "Garasu", p. 397.

61. *NKYS, IV, p. 6.

62. *Bukō Nempyō* [Chronology of Events in Edo of Musashi], Edo, 1763; from *Koji Ruien*, (see n. 7, p. 72), *Sangyō-bu*, 1, p. 8.

63. *Yamada, *Nihon Garasu Sangyō no Seika*, p. 18.

64. *NKYS, IV, p. 6.

65. *Aizawa, "Sennan Garasu. . . . ," p. 442.

66. *Sugie, *Garasu*, p. 228.

67. For data regarding Minato-mura and the Matsunami factory, see *Morihira, *Matsunami Garasu.* . . .

68. *Ibid.*, pp. 8–10.

69. *Kurokawa, *Kōgei Shiryō*, Pt. 2, p. 46.

70. The *Tōki Daijiten* [Dictionary of Ceramics], p. 61, under *sarasadama* gives an alternative, *inkadama* (bead inset with flower motifs), "made in Nagasaki and Edo in the Tokugawa period." They were probably also made in Osaka.

71. But for mention of several glass artisans in Kyoto, see *Tanahashi, "Kinsei Nihon ni. . . . ," III, pp. 37–40.

72. *Okada, *Garasu*, p. 56, gives the present location as the Manshū-in, Kyoto, and dates them as probably 17th century. See also, Pls. 75, 76.

73. *Shibui, "The Story of Glass in Japan," p. 121.

74. *Terashima, *Wakan Sanzai Zue*, p. 373.

75. U. A. Casals, "Japanese Art Lacquers," *Monumenta Nipponica*, XV, Nos. 1–2, April–July, 1959, p. 3 and Pl. XIII.

76. According to the late Mr. Kuranosuke Iwaki, these crucibles were pottery tea storage jars whose sizes were designated by the weight of tea leaves they held. *Terashima, *Wakan Sanzai Zue*, referred to the jars of Karatsu, famous ceramic center in Kyushu, as being best for the purpose.

77. In *Yamada, *Nihon Garasu.* . . . , p. 26, a written character in the original document, meaning "horse", is misprinted as the character (高), "height," which made the phrase meaningless. Mr. Yasumasa Oda of the National Diet Library, Tokyo, suggested the correct character.

78. *Uchiwata*, supposedly for packing glass.

79. *Yamada, *Nihon Garasu.* . . . , p. 26.

80. *Shiota, "Garasu," p. 399.

81. *NKYS, p. 11. Mr. Ishizuka remembered a small hotel in Tajima called the Biidoro-ya.

82. *Meiji Bunkashi*, VIII, p. 285.

83. Katsumi Kuroita and Masao Endō (eds.), *Aichi-kenshi* [History of Aichi Prefecture], III, Tokyo, Yoshikawa Kobunkan, 1939, p. 455.

84. *Bowes, *Notes on Shippō*, pp. 34–38.

85. *Okada, *Japanese Handicrafts*, p. 97.

86. Tei Nishimura, *Nihon Shoki Yōga no Kenkyū*, Kyoto, Zenkoku Shōbō, 2d ed., 1946, p. 359. Quoted in *Tanahashi, "Kinsei Nihon ni. . . . ," III, pp. 41–42.

87. From the catalogue of an exhibition, "Cultural History of Tōhoku" (the northeastern provinces of Japan) held in 1949 at the Mitsukoshi Department Store, Tokyo.

88. Kaempfer, *op. cit.* (see n. 17), Book II, p. 335.

89. *Ibid.*, p. 429.

90. Comparative figures for about 1700 show Paris, the largest metropolis of Europe (pop. 600,000–720,000), and London (pop. 600,000), both lagging behind Edo's estimated 1,000,000 as based on a population of about 500,000 by census, exclusive of the samurai. Further, the general standard of living was then comparatively high in Edo; see Neil Skene Smith, "Materials of Japanese Social and Economic History: Tokugawa Japan (1)," *TASJ*, Second Series, XIV, June 1937, pp. 35–37. Population data for the Edo period are not absolute, but estimates for the year 1787, give Edo a population of 2,225,000; see Neil Skene Smith, "An Introduction to Some Japanese Writings of the 18th Century," *TASJ*, Second Series, XI, December 1934, p. 36.

91. Kaempfer, *op. cit.* (see n. 17), pp. 521ff.

92. Bayard Taylor, *Japan in Our Day* (compiled from writings of Sir Rutherford Alcock and N. Humbert), New York, 1872, Scribner, Armstrong and Co., p. 166.

93. Jō Okada, in *Hakubutsukan Niyusu* [Museum News], Tokyo National Museum, No. 146, July 1959, p. 1, illus.

94. Tsunoda, de Bary, and Keene, *op. cit.* (see n. 1, p. 61), pp. 603, 606–607.

95. Personal data is from *Zōzan Zenshū*, Nagano, Shinano Mainichi Shinbun, 1934–35 (original ed. 1913), Vol. III.

96. *Ibid.*, Letter 69, 1913 ed., II, pp. 138–139. Letter 127, 1934 ed.

97. *Seimi Kaisō* [Fundamentals of Chemistry] tr. by Yōan Udagawa, Edo. 1837, from a Dutch edition in turn translated from a German translation of a work by the English chemist, William Henry, about 1800. *Biidoro Seiho Shusetsu* [Explanation of Glass Manufacture], tr. Sanjurō Baba, Edo, 1810.

98. *Zōzan Zenshū*, *op. cit.*, Letter 78, 1913 ed.; III, pp. 172–173.

99. *Ibid.*, Letter 81, 1913 ed., II, pp. 181–184, Letter 146, 1934 ed.

100. Shown in the exhibition, *Edo Jidai no Kagaku* ("Science in the Edo Period") at the National Science Museum, Tokyo, November 1932. Its owner is given as Keinoshin Haneda, at whose death the cup was sold; its present location is unknown.

101. *Zōzan Zenshū*, *op. cit.*, Letter 83, 1913 ed., II, pp. 169ff. Letter 149, 1934 ed.

102. Kaempfer, *op. cit.* (see n. 17), Book IV, p. 353, listed "lead, saltpetre, borax and alum" among other materials brought by the Dutch from "Bengale and Siam."

103. Nobuyo Kitamura, *Kiyū Shōran* [Pleasures for Your Consideration], Tokyo, 1940 (original ed. 1830), quoted by Okumura, *op. cit.* (see n. 9, p. 160), p. 266.

104. *Sugie, *Nihon Garasu Kōgyōshi*, p. 267.

105. Data concerning Nishinomiya Tomejirō comes from Hagi fief records.

106. *Bukō Nempyō* (see n. 62), ed. of 1925, p. 22.

107. *Nakasu Suzume* [Sparrow at Nakasu], a light account of the amusement center near Ryōgoku, with restaurants, tea-houses, theaters and side-shows. From *Nihon Bungaku Taikei* [Compendium of Japanese Literature], pp. 209–216.

108. *Sugie, *Nihon Garasu Kōgyōshi*, p. 80.

109. Data concerning Bunjirō from *Sugie, *Nihon Garasu Kōgyōshi*, p. 82. *NKYS* gives the name Hisashi Kaga.

110. Dr. Mendel L. Peterson and Mr. Robert Elder of the Smithsonian Institution, Washington, D.C., searched for such a gift, but they "found no glass of any sort in the Perry Collection and no reference in the records of that collection."

111. *Shiota, "Garasu," p. 398.

112. *Sugie, *Nihon Garasu Kōgyōshi*, p. 74.

113. *Mody, *A Collection of Nagasaki. . . . ,* Pl. 219, Figs. 3 and 4, show a glass *inrō* and an *inrō* with a woven glass bead cover.

114. *Yajima, "Tokyo-tō Yanaka no Go-jū-no-tō. Hakken. . . ." and "Tokyo-tō Yanaka no Go-jū-no-tō Soseki. . . . ," both illustrated.

115. See *Sappan no Bunka* [Culture of Satsuma Fief], Kagoshima Cultural Commission, Kagoshima, 1935, pp. 157–183.

116. *Satsuma Garasu no Enkaku*, p. 5. Other references say he came from Shinmei-chō in Edo, and that he was a pupil of Bunjirō Kaga.

117. Futarō Ōyama, "Bakumatsu ni okeru Yōshiki Seitetsu Jigyō" [Western-style Iron Industry Enterprise in the Closing Years of the Bakufu], *Researchers in Economic History*, XX, 1938; quoted on p. 19. Stanleigh A. Jones, "Early Industrialization in Japan: The Example of Sagahan," Columbia University East Asian Institute Studies, No. 6, "Researches in the Social Science on Japan," Vol. Two, New York, June 1959, p. 19.

118. *Satsuma Garasu no Enkaku*, p. 5. The great variety of their achievements may be sensed in the glass collection in the Shūseikan.

119. *Ibid.*, pp. 5–7, 10–15.

120. In order to produce clear transparent glass the iron in the raw material had to be removed.

121. *Enatsu Jūrō Kanke Monjo* [Documents Concerning Jūrō Enatsu], quoted in **Satsuma Garasu no Enkaku*, p. 8.

122. *Viff Jaren in Japan* [Five Years in Japan], quoted in *Kagoshima no Oitachi* [The Growth of Kagoshima], Kagoshima, 1955, p. 172.

123. **Satsuma Garasu no Enkaku*, p. 7.

124. *Ibid.*, p. 6. When the American ships appeared in coastal waters, all daimyo had to contribute financial and material aid for defense, hence many other activities were curtailed.

125. There is also an elegant dish cut with lotus-petal design; collection of Professor Motoyoshi Higaki, Fukuoka.

126. *Takeshita Seiemon Nikki* [Diary of Seiemon Take-shita], quoted in *Satsuma Garasu no Enkaku*, p. 16.

127. **Satsuma Garasu no Enkaku*, pp. 16–17, quoting *Nangoku Iji* [Anecdotes of the Southern Country].

128. Jones, *op. cit.* (see n. 117), pp. 12–27.

129. Several other examples are now known and have been published. See *Okada, Teshigawara, Kunimitsu, *Garasu*, Illus. 35 and 36.

130. *Yamada, *Nihon Garasu. . . . ,* p. 39.

131. Data on Uhei primarily from *Biidoro Uhei Den.

132. *Meiji Bunkashi, VIII, p. 285, refers to artisans invited to Kuroda fief in the Tempō Era (1830–43), who produced "eye-glasses, bottles, and toys" and were especially skilled in semitranslucent beads.

133. According to Professor Motoyoshi Higaki of Kyushu University, manganese was discovered at neighboring Noma-mura, Tsukushi-gun.

134. Keiji Misaka, *Hagi-han no Zaisei to Buiku* [Finance and the Benevolent Government of Hagi Fief], Tokyo, 1944, Chap. 7.

135. *Horie, "Nakashima Jihei to. . . . ," p. 139, states that it dealt chiefly with the manufacture of glass and that it was generally referred to as "the glass manufactory." Jihei was its director. In a detailed petition he proposed that it be expanded to include physical sciences and especially all forms of chemistry and medicine.

136. This—and other data not gleaned from cited sources—was transmitted from Jihei's grandson, Mr. Keichi Nakashima. Mr. Nakashima possesses "relics" of Jihei, including glass used by him, and the book of notes on glassmaking partially reproduced in Plate 207.

137. Courtesy of the Yamaguchi Prefectural Library, which preserves, in the Mōri Collection, the daily handwritten records of the Mōri clan.

138. However, *Okada, *Garasu*, Pl. 94, illustrates a saké bottle of purple glass, with a bird motif painted in gold, assigned to Hagi. It is owned by an old family in Hagi, and an inscription on its box records it as a gift from Lord Mōri.

139. Yahachi Tokiyama, *Mōri no Shigeri* [Extracts from Official Records of the Mōri clan], rev. ed., Tokyo, Shinkōsha, 1932, p. 411.

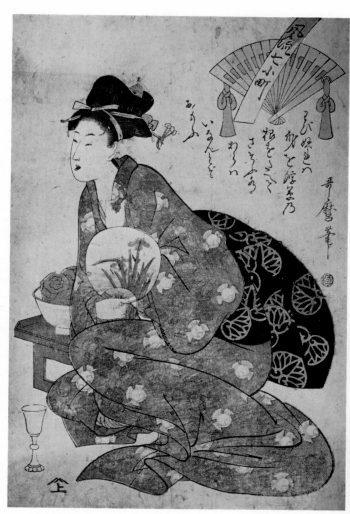

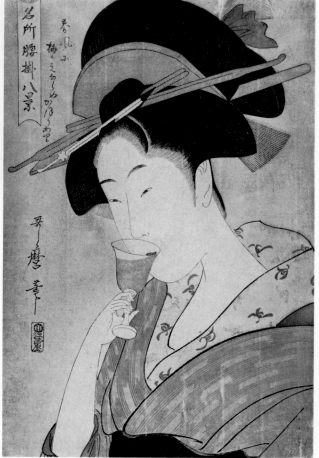

175. Seated woman, woodblock print by Utamaro.
176. Beauty drinking from a wine glass, woodblock print by Utamaro.

177. Beauty with a goldfish bowl, woodblock print by Eishō.

178. *Woman peeling a peach*, woodblock print by Utamaro.

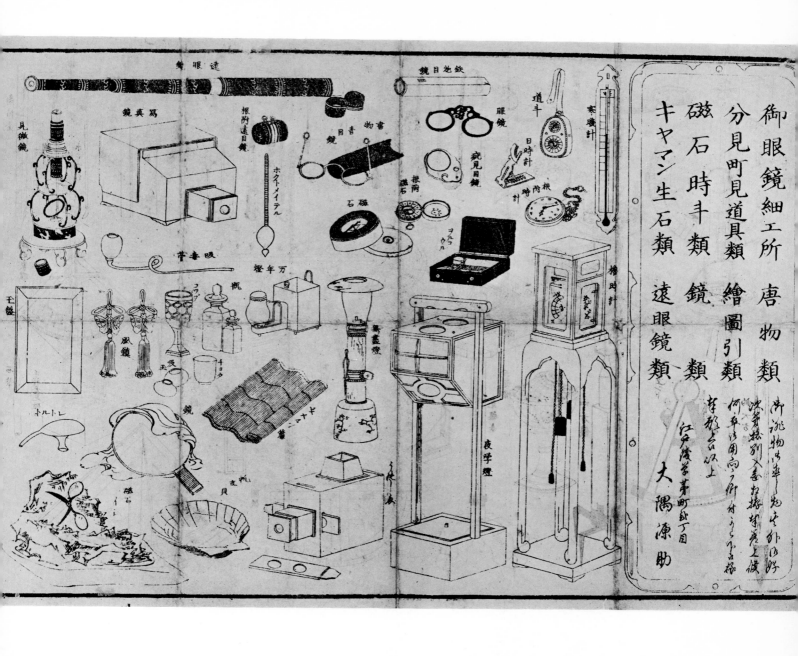

179. Broadside of glassmaker Ōsumi Gensuke • early 19th century • Edo.

180. Broadside of a glass ship display • late 18th or early 19th century • Edo.

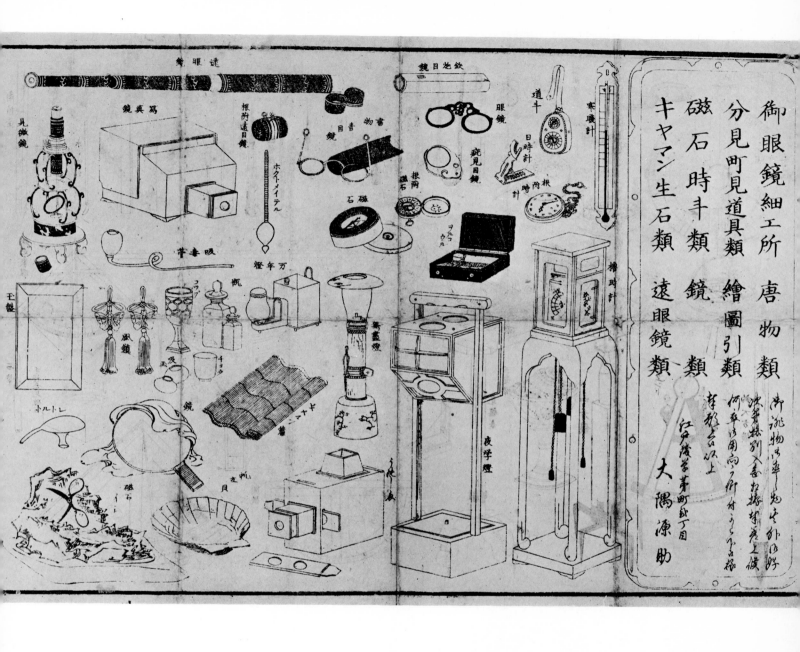

御眼鏡細工所　唐物類

分見町見道具類　繪圖引類

磁石　時手類　鏡　類

キヤマシ生石類　遠眼鏡類

大隅源助

179. Broadside of glassmaker Ōsumi Gensuke · early 19th century · Edo.

180. Broadside of a glass ship display • late 18th or early 19th century • Edo.

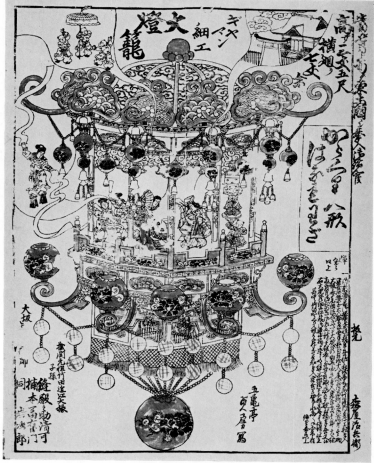

181. Broadside of a glass ship display · late 18th or early 19th century · Edo.

182. Broadside of a colossal glass lantern display · probably late 18th century · Edo.

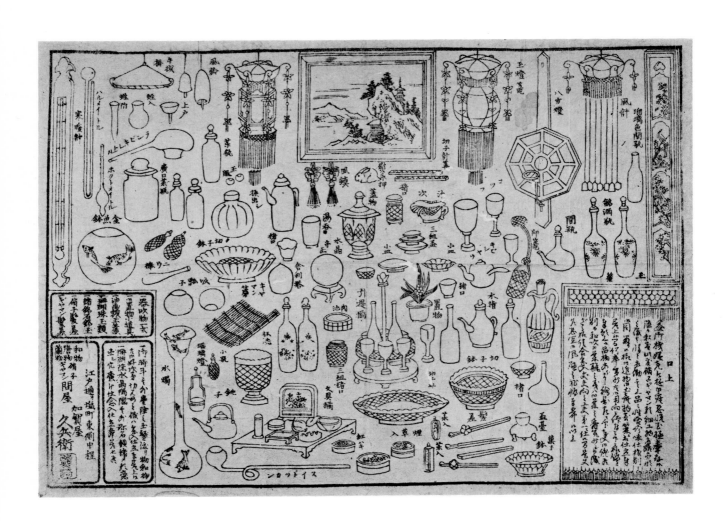

183. Broadside of glassmaker Kagaya Kyūbei • 19th century • Edo.

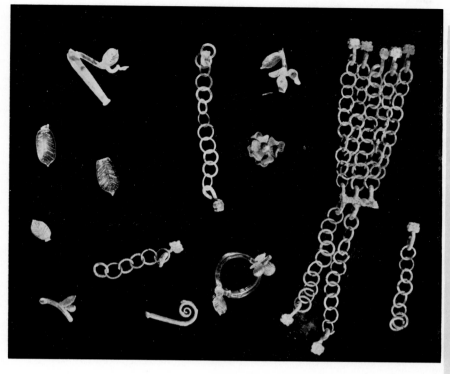

184. Glass hair ornament fragments • mid 19th century • leaf forms, L. 2.2 cm.

185. Dark blue, gourd-shaped *netsuke* • Edo period • L. 5.1 cm.

186. Ceremonial teabowl • 19th century • D. 13.7 cm.

187. Small covered dish, Irish style • Edo period • H. 10.7 cm.

188. Green saké cup • Edo period • H. 3.2 cm.

189. Miniature wine set for the Doll Festival • Edo period • decanter, H. 5.5 cm.

190. Mirror reflections, woodblock print by Utamaro.
191. Mirror reflections, woodblock print by Utamaro.

192. Plate glass · perhaps *ca*. 1853 · Satsuma · 29.4 × 32.0 × 2.4 cm.
193. Mound-shaped glass · perhaps *ca*. 1853 · Satsuma · D. 21.1 cm.
194. Cut glass bowl · *ca*. 1856 · Satsuma · D. 22.2 cm.

195. Cut glass wine glass · 1856–58 · Satsuma · H. 8.5 cm.

196. Cut glass covered jar, blue overlay • *ca.* 1856 • Satsuma • H. *ca.* 7.15 cm.
197. Cut glass wine glass, blue overlay • *ca.* 1856 • Satsuma • H. 15.85 cm.
198. Covered dish with molded design • 1857–58 • Satsuma • H. 11.4 cm.

199. Fluted cut glass bowl • 1857–58 • Satsuma • H. 12.0 cm.
200. Covered bowl • perhaps 1858 • Satsuma • H. 9.2 cm.
201. Tall red tumbler with cut design • 1859 or later • Satsuma • H. 15.1 cm.

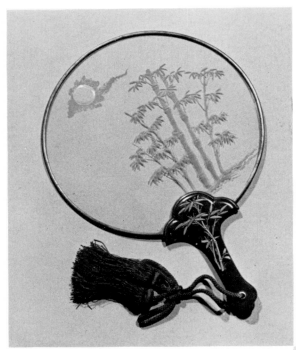

202. Round fan of engraved glass • *ca.* 1867 • Satsuma • D. *ca.* 26.0 cm.
203. Large goldfish bowl • 1848 (?) • Saga • H. 30.4 cm.

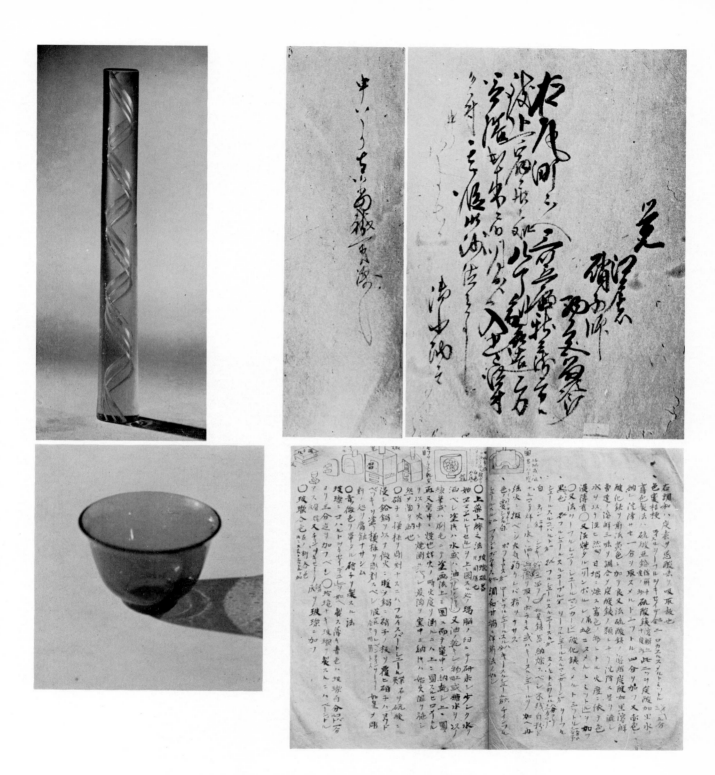

204. Paperweight · attributed to Mizuno Chōbei (d. 1869) · Fukuoka · L. 14.3 cm.

205. Violet saké cup · mid 19th century · Fukuoka (?) · H. 4.1 cm.

206. Hagi Fief order to glassmaker Nishinomiya Tomejirō · 1860.

207. Notes on glassmaking, by Nakashima Jihei · dated 1863.

208. Cut glass covered box • *ca.* 1860 • Hagi.
209. Cut glass wine glass • *ca.* 1862 • Hagi • H. 10.5 cm.
210. Cut glass wine glass • 1861–62 • Hagi • H. 10.9 cm.

MODERN PERIOD

THE COMING OF Admiral Matthew Perry with American warships in 1853, carrying a letter from President Fillmore requesting refueling and supply rights, struck fear into the hearts of the Japanese and awakened them to their own defenseless condition. When Perry departed with the admonition that he would be back in a year's time and would then expect an answer, severe controversies broke out, intermingled with efforts to restore full powers to the emperor. Factional outbreaks were to continue even after the foreigners had been admitted. Perhaps no one was really anxious to admit the strange "barbarians," but there were those like Sakuma Shōzan, Shimazu Nariakira, and others who realized that the end of isolation was inevitable. The shogun also felt that it would be useless to try to oppose the foreign countries.

Perry's return in 1854 resulted in a "Treaty of Peace and Amity between the United States of America and the Empire of Japan," often referred to as the Kanagawa Treaty. In 1858 this was followed by a detailed agreement concerning the opening of ports, commercial relations, duties, and arrangement for military aid. Meanwhile, there were treaties with Britain, the Netherlands, and Russia. Nagasaki, Kōbe, Kanagawa, Niigata on the Japan Sea, and Hakodate in the north were the ports opened to foreign shipping. The arrangements were not favorable to Japan, for the foreigners demanded extraterritorial rights and the authority to determine import duties, a privilege that was retained by the United States until 1876 and by others until 1899. The signing of foreign treaties did not prevent xenophobic feelings, which manifested themselves by occasional violent antiforeign outbursts and murders. The last Tokugawa shogun, Yoshinobu, resigned in December, 1867, leaving the way open in 1868 for the restoration of imperial rights to the eight-year-old boy-emperor, who was to become revered and known posthumously as the Emperor Meiji.

With the restoration of the emperor's sovereignty, the imperial capital was transferred to Edo, which then became known as Tokyo, the "Eastern Capital." But the imperial palace in Kyoto was maintained, and it is there that coronations still take place. The period under discussion, which already spans a century, is divided into three eras: Meiji, 1868–1912; Taishō, 1912–26; and Shōwa, 1926 to the present.

The transition from a feudalistic society to a semidemocratic monarchy, and the transformation of a feudal ruling class into members of a democratic and self-supporting society was rife with potential social dangers. Many of the samurai became influential in the new government, but not all had the political or financial acumen to meet these changed circumstances. On the other hand, many samurai of lower rank, with some practical experience, had the opportunity to come forward as political or economic leaders in government, banking, railroading, and industry.

At the close of the Edo period, glassmaking in the fiefs had been curtailed. For private glassmakers in the towns, conditions were somewhat different. Shops like Kagaya and Kazusaya in Tokyo, judging from the advertisement of Plate 216, must have continued much as before. Some Kagaya glass was taken to the Trade Fair in Vienna in 1878, where it received an award. The great change, however, came with the growth of large industrial enterprises. With this growth came the need to master new techniques for mass production of window glass, pressed glass, and mold-blown glass.[1]

Western architecture, which was newly adopted for public buildings, necessitated glass windows and glass lamps. When domestic glass production got underway, private individuals wanted glass to replace their paper windows. At first, a single small pane about four inches square inserted in the paper window was looked upon as a luxury. The poet Shiki Masaoka mentions, in a dairy written in 1900, when he was bedridden with illness, that he had a paper window replaced with glass so that he could look out. What a surprise! He could see clearly even an insect outside; therefore the glass plate must be made by a god, not by man. But he missed some of the sounds that the glass seemed to shut out. A pupil, after visiting his home, wrote two poems about the glass he saw there. In fact, glass is mentioned in many poems of the time.

In surviving examples of domestic architecture one often encounters window panels of Meiji glass with border designs or allover patterns in frosted lines. This type continued to some extent through the Taishō era. Today glass panes are mostly clear.

The new railways required glass for signal lights, lamps, and windows. Until people became familiar with this strange, invisible substance, there were serious accidents in rural districts where country people, thinking the window spaces open, shoved their heads through the glass. To prevent this, a stripe of white paint was often applied to the panes.[2]

As early as 1877, colored glass was used for windows or doors. Evidently it took some courage to enter a place that displayed such a thing:

> He fearfully entered the butcher shop, which had colored glass, with such determination as though he were jumping from the balcony at Kiyomizu Temple [a favorite spot for suicides]. With equal determination he tried beef, and was surprised to find it better than he had anticipated.[3]

Kerosene lamps, then gas street lamps and the lamplighter who went about with his ladder, and finally the electric arc light—all with protective glass covers—were a fascinating change from candles and lanterns. The first arc light was installed on Tokyo's

Ginza in 1882. Some woodblock prints of the period depict crowds of people in the street gazing up at the brightly shining light. The caption on one reads, "Nothing brighter can be compared to this light except sunlight."[4]

This barely scratches the surface of the widespread fascination with the exotic things of the West in early Meiji. It reminds one of the similar fascination in Nagasaki in the seventeenth century. The mass introduction of Western customs, increased by the presence of numerous foreigners who used tables and chairs, oil lamps, glass tableware, and other appurtenances, drastically affected the way of life and the manufacture of glass.

The importation of such glass commodities as lamp chimneys, dishes, light bulbs, and window glass was expensive, and the need to produce them domestically was urgent. Equipment and materials (all imported at first) were also expensive; there were no technicians familiar with them, so foreigners had to be engaged to teach the methods; and as one writer has commented, the past traditions of the Japanese were not conducive to the physical energy and rapid action required by the machines; in the early days this is said to have been particularly applicable to sheet glass manufactured by the then current Western technique of flattening large cylinders. All told, the first decades were years of toil, disappointments, and financial failures. The wonder is that the point of equilibrium was found so soon and with such overwhelming success.

Before turning to the new industries, let us first glance at the old glass centers of the Edo period and see how they fared in the new industrial age.

SEQUEL TO TRADITIONAL GLASSMAKING

NAGASAKI

With the opening of other ports to foreign trade, and the closing of the no longer needed Dutch missions, Nagasaki became less important politically and culturally. Glassmaking did not die out, but now it had little national significance.

Yahachi Matsushita of the old Tamaya *biidoro* shop continued to make *pokon-pokon*, windbells, and *kanzashi* as souvenirs of the summer festival. He also took up manufacture of lamp chimneys (which he exhibited at a Nagasaki Fair of 1879), until electricity ended the need for kerosene lamps; he then changed his occupation.[5]

Kosone Masaki founded a plant to make, among other things, lamps and ink bottles, which he also exhibited at the 1879 fair. This plant closed in 1887. He is said to have made dishes of combined red and colorless glass[6] and to have made contributions not inferior to those of Nishimura Shōzan and Itō Keishin in Tokyo and Osaka.[7] He and Tsuneyoshi Iwane, both former artisans of the Shinagawa factory in Tokyo, are said to have been called to Nagasaki and to have introduced the new techniques to that city.[8] The fish form of Plate 211 is thought to be Nagasaki work of early Meiji.

Several small factories were eatablished, which worked until World War II: the Nagasaki Glass Company, making vials, fishing lamps, fishnet floats; the Fukai Factory; and the Umeda Factory, making medicine bottles, fishing lamps, and buoys. These shops employed, for a time, the old hand methods, but their output was practical and commercial. Vanished was the high quality artistic glassblowing of former days. In the post-World War II era, some modern commercial glass was produced on a small scale.

OSAKA

One may suppose that the old glass shops of the Osaka area continued until their products were displaced by newer necessities. For instance, with the appearance of sheet glass on a fairly wide scale, the old industry of the *mage-kagami* (see p. 202) was disrupted and businesses discontinued. The last evidence of activity in this field was the medal awarded to Tōshichi Matsunami for a mirror at the first national industrial fair of 1877. He moved his shop to Kishiwada in 1886 and produced glass toys, *sudare*, and *kanzashi*, in addition to sheet glass. His son Sadakichi Matsunami was commissioned by the Naval Ministry to manufacture lenses for telescopes; later he made a study of glass for microscopes, and after much experimentation, by 1904 produced a nearly perfect lens. The following year he received a medal at the Osaka fair commemorating the victory in the Russo-Japanese War. This lens was sold in Japan and was exported to America in 1905; during World War I it replaced for a time the no longer available German lenses.[9] Today the Matsunami Glassworks, Ltd. of Kishiwada is successfully manufacturing glass of great clarity and exporting scientific supplies, slide covers, and pipettes. This company illustrates the fluctuations in glassmaking attendant upon the transitional changes.

KYOTO

Kyoto had never been a glass center, and the Meiji activities there seem to have been short lived. The governor of the prefecture, Masanao Kamimura (Uemura?), established a chemical institute for research in pottery, dyestuffs, soap, and glass, with Dutch and German technicians as instructors. The glass section produced lamps, tableware, and red running lights for ships. In 1881 it was sold to the chief of the chemical bureau, who was compelled to close it in 1883[10]—another instance of the difficulties that beset private enterprises in the earlier part of the Meiji era.

In 1887 Shoso Nakao established a factory at Kawaramachi-Kiyamachi, whose chimney can still be seen. Its main products are not known to this author.

A comment in the report of the Fourth Trade Fair of 1895 mentions "watch glasses of Kyoto,"[11] but no data has been found. Today, so far as could be ascertained, there is no glass activity in Kyoto.

NAGOYA

The activities of Ishizuka Iwasaburō I and his son Bunzaemon in the latter Edo period were discussed on pages 210–212. In the Meiji era *kanzashi* and *suidama* were first made; and the first bottle, for eye lotion, was produced in 1877. Iwasaburō Ishizuka II spoke of being the first to use a tank type furnace for medicine bottles, and two glass factories in Osaka sent technicians to learn his technique. He was also the first to use ten crucibles in one large furnace, but the furnace broke, and he gave up the use of crucibles. In addition to colorless glass for medicine bottles and lamp chimneys, colored bottles for beer and soft drinks were also produced; and a small factory was later established in Java. Products made in Toda-mura were sent to Nagoya by cart, and raw materials were brought back in the same way. Since that was a laborious way of operating, the factory was moved to the city in 1888. After a number of subsequent moves, it settled on its present location, where a modern establishment turns out bottles for milk, yogurt, whiskey, and ink. Some are exported to Southeast Asia.

A number of small new factories opened in Nagoya in the first decade of the Meiji era, chiefly for making oil containers and chimneys for kerosene lamps—so many, in fact, that a glass manufacturing union was formed.

In 1885 the Ishizuka factory began using soda ash, and the former whetstone molds were replaced by metal molds. In 1937, automatic machines were installed. In 1946, after rehabilitation from war damage, the factory expanded, and later, high-speed bottle making machines were added.

SENDAI

Although there had been at least one glassmaker recorded in Sendai in the Edo period (Pl. 171), the area was not a significant production center, but manufacturing continued into the Meiji era. One Shōbei Utsushima (Uchishima?) is listed as a manufacturer of sheet glass, bottles, and lamp chimneys, which were sold to Kotarō Takai, a wholesaler. Four other names are associated with glass factories in Sendai—Bunraku Nakamura, Eiji Satō, Ekisaburō Satō, and Enaji Satō[12]—but nothing is known concerning their activity.

There is a type of bead in which one or more tiny red goldfish forms, or flowers, were inserted in a transparent body, with the addition of spiraled dark blue threads either within the bead or on the exterior (Pl. 29). The body is usually colorless, but there is one that is of a transparent dull green.[13] Tradition in Sendai suggests that such beads, and some other types, were made for sale to the Ainu women of Hokkaido. Since similar beads are found in western Japan, no doubt it was a general type of the time, with the Sendai variety finding a ready market in Hokkaido.

The amuletic beads worn by Ainu women (Pl. 212) present a subject in themselves. They were not made by the Ainu but obtained, by traders, from the Japanese and from the tribal people living around the mouth of the Amur River on the Asiatic mainland, who in turn got them from Peking, via Manchuria. Perhaps these traders reached Hokkaido via Sakhalien (Karafuto), since the beads were sometimes called *Karafuto-dama*. Some of the beads look suspiciously like the "trade beads" seen in Southeast Asia. Although many Ainu beads are certainly of Japanese origin, sources and dates are hard to identify, and manufacture in Sendai, although likely, is difficult to pinpoint.

Uncolored, transparent glass beads are the most recent and are said to have been manufactured up to 1887 or 1897 around Okachi-machi, Tokyo.[14]

Local traditions suggest that the Ainu people believed their ancestors obtained the beads from Russians and Chinese;[15] and, again, that local traders sometimes took advantage of the Ainu, telling them that the beads came from China.

SATSUMA

Lord Nariakira's death in 1858 disrupted glass activities at the Shūseikan. It is difficult to learn just what happened after his death. A company was founded by Ichiki Shōuemon, one of Nariakira's retainers who had been close to him in various ventures. The company was called the "Kaibutsusha,"[16] but where it was located, or how it was financed, is not clear. When, in 1872, the Emperor Meiji visited Kagoshima "Governor Ōyama presented to the emperor a set of cake plates made of glass; this was accepted with admiration." At the end of that year the Imperial Household Ministry ordered three sets of bowls with lids,[17] which were also presented. One wonders if these bowls might have been of the molded type of Plate 200.

An advertisement in a trade publication indicates that a glass company called Fujimura Shōten, owned by Heitarō Inouye, was established in Kagoshima in 1890. It is not clear whether this was only a shop or a combined shop and factory. At any rate it is stated that Heitarō invented a machine for applying frosted patterns to glass and "satisfied the demand." His wares were glass vessels, lamps, sheet glass, bottles, lanterns. At the end is a cryptic remark not yet clarified: "He purchased the Kokuminkan of the Shimazu family in 1910 and succeeded in making the suburban area very prosperous."

None of this documentation sheds any light on the identification of those puzzling objects with the shallowly incised Satsuma crest.

SAGA

Glassmaking in Saga had declined, but its influence was still felt in the Meiji era. Tsunetami Sanō, who had supervised the glass factory, was a conspicuous figure in the economic affairs of the Meiji government. He had been appointed director of the government's Shinagawa glass factory in Tokyo and was responsible for employing two Saga artisans, Tanehiro Fujiyama and Keikichi Fukutani.

According to documents in the Saga Prefectural Library, it seems that two other men went to Tokyo, under the auspices of the Ministry of Trade and Commerce, and studied glass techniques. Returning in 1891, they organized a factory and produced glass cups, chimneys, and lampshades. Nothing further is known of this factory.

FUKUOKA

There seems to be little information about glassmaking in Fukuoka in the Meiji era. The shop in Najima-chō established by Ōgawa Uhei is still selling sheet glass today, chiefly to Kyushu University.

THE EDO TRADITION IN TOKYO

Before going forward with the new aspects of glassmaking in Tokyo, let us consider Plate 216, to see how Kagaya (the famous glass shop of Edo whose earlier broadside is shown in Plate 183) fared under the new circumstances. There was surprisingly little change in the new broadside, except that more pharmaceutical equipment was crowded in, and we have the proprietor's word that he prospered. No date is given, but the name Tokyo has replaced the former Edo. The text, in part, reads as follows:

> I hope you are very well.
> I have manufactured *giyaman* products as my profession, and have been fortunate indeed, as business is very prosperous. There is no one in more favorable circumstances than I at the present time.
> In particular, we are expending our best efforts to manufacture containers for strong chemicals. We will also wrap those items beautifully for gifts and souvenirs. We will make any item in any size, both large and small, according to your preference. We hope that orders will come in from our customers.
> As we have again issued a print at this time, illustrating samples of our commodities, please call this to the attention of your friends.
> Complete sets of vessels and blown items.
> Complete sets of medical equipment.
> Several items for the Doll Festival.
> Glass trays.
> Glass ornaments.
> Frames for oil paintings.
> Bead *sudare* of various stones.
> Glass-bead *sudare*.
> We will make glass plate for ships' windows in an extremely beautiful way.
> We guarantee to repair clocks carefully: cover glasses for clocks, both imported and Japan made, to suit your preference.
> Vaccination ampules.
> Complete sets of twelve bottles or six bottles in a leather-covered case. The strength of the medicine is guaranteed by strong medicine bottles.
> Sand clocks to measure seconds.

The name is given as "Kagaya (Kumazaki Yamutarō)."

It is said that, at the suggestion of Tsunetami Sanō, who headed the government's delegation to the Austrian Trade Fair in 1873, this Kagaya sent "a set of stationery" and received an award.[18] No doubt this was like the set of desk accessories seen in the broadside.

Although there is no proof of the prosperity of the Kazusaya shop, it seems that it must have prospered, since it continued until World War II, although its name was changed to Arihara Garasu Seizō-sho (Arihara Glassworks).

What happened to all the other smaller glass shops during the distressed times of the 1860s and early 1870s is not sure. Some people remember seeing glass shops in Shiba. One speaks of a deserted glass factory, which he remembers from his childhood in the Mukō-Yanagihara district of Tokyo, where he used to see a ball of glass still attached to a blowpipe. He also recalls that glass was fairly common in those days.[19]

NEW INDUSTRIES—THE MEIJI AND TAISHŌ ERAS (1868–1926)

NEW customs introduced in the Meiji era necessitated economic and industrial changes. For instance, bricks were needed for the new public buildings. At first they were imported from England, until the Shinagawa glass factory hired Dr. Gottfried Wagner to teach brickmaking. Sheet glass was also needed for windows, but importation was expensive, so there was great urgency in developing the large-scale production of cylinder glass. Kerosene lamps had replaced candles and lanterns, but the oil pots and chimneys were expensive to import and the breakage rate high, so factories all over Japan began to produce them, reducing the cost by more than half.[20]

The Meiji government, realizing the obstacles encountered by the new industries, embarked upon a far-sighted program of assistance to private enterprises. The goal was to reduce dependence upon imports.

Product improvements were mandated. In 1893 a police edict prohibited the production of such dangerously thin items as the *pokon-pokon*, and the glassmakers had to evolve a method of producing a sturdier and safer material. Furthermore, loading and transport facilities were sometimes inadequate, resulting in much loss through breakage.

TOKYO

SHINAGAWA GLASSWORKS

In 1873 a glass factory, known as the Kōgyōsha was established by Masatsune Niwa, as administrator, and Mishinosuke Murai, technical chief, in what is now Kita-Shinagawa, Tokyo. This is said to have been the first glass factory in European style (Pl. 217). All materials—such as clay for crucibles and firebrick for furnaces—were at first imported from England, and glass technicians from Tokyo and Osaka were employed under the supervision of an Englishman, Thomas Walton.[21] The first sheet glass was produced here. Some rock crystal from Yamanashi Prefecture was used in the batch in the belief that it would increase transparency.[22] But the venture failed.

Under the government's assistance program the bankrupt Kōgyōsha was taken over in 1877 by the Ministry of Industry. It was then renamed the Shinagawa Garasu Seisaku-sho (Shinagawa Glassworks).[23] The buildings (Pl. 217) were constructed of imported red bricks and originally had imported glass in the windows. The fan-shaped frames for door transoms and windows were of a characteristic Meiji type found in a number of places in Japan.[24] Some of those surviving at this factory are of glass made by Takijirō Iwaki, which Mr. Kuranosuke Iwaki was able to identify.

In 1873 the government had dispatched Tsunetami Sanō to the international trade fair in Austria with a delegation of technicians, including the craftsman Tanehiro Fujiyama, who had been trained in Saga. In the report of this tour, Tsunetami Sanō wrote that he had instructed Fujiyama to study sheet-glass production and the mixing of glass batches at the Stolzenfels factory in Austria. He further recommended that Fujiyama, now competent in the industry, be employed at the Shinagawa plant, and even be sent abroad for further study, to the end that Japan might compete economically with the imports upon which she was then forced to depend.[25]

Another glass craftsman from Saga who came to Shinagawa was Keikichi Fukutani, who is said to have been administrator, with Magoichi Shimada as technical chief.[26]

In 1877 the land upon which the factory stood, and which had until then been leased, was purchased from Tōkai-ji temple together with additional space, and expansion was planned. Tanehiro Fujiyama became a glass craftsman, and colored glass for ships' sidelights was manufactured.

In 1879 the government invited an English technician, James Speed, to the factory, and new techniques for the manufacture of tableware were introduced. Takejirō Miyazaki learned from him the art of engraving. In the same year an experimental station of the College of Industry was developed, and, under another Englishman, the manufacture of scientific and medical equipment began.

In 1882 Emanuel Hauptmann was brought from England to teach cut glass techniques. He is mentioned as having produced "fine glass with cut and frosted patterns."[27] Chibiki Okamura's reminiscence must have been written about this time:

> My father visited the factory when I was a small boy and bought a cup of red glass with a grape pattern cut on it. I remember it was a beautiful cup. However, there are few things that remain at present as products of the Shinagawa factory.[28]

The two brush holders of Plate 218 are products of the factory, and show rather unskillful spiral decoration. The paperweight of Supplementary Note 89, with a similar lack of control, suggests attribution to this factory.

As the sheet glass section had run a deficit, it was discontinued. In 1884, due to financial troubles, the factory was leased to Katsuzō Nishimura to be run as a private enterprise. Nishimura ran it as four departments: for water and medicine bottles; lamps; tableware; and physical and chemical equipment. Nishimura visited Europe and sent one of his technicians to study there. He studied the Siemens tank and adopted it; he also brought back models of molds, and two glass technicians. Wood molds were added in addition to the previous stone and clay molds, and later cast iron ones were introduced.[29] Nevertheless the factory failed and closed in 1892.

The same pattern can be followed in other new factories during the first decades of the Meiji era. Not only had technical and financial difficulties to be overcome, but the people's standard of living was not ready for mass production; one month's production, it is said, was sufficient to meet one year's demand! Altogether it was disheartening. "We finally came to realize how difficult it is to manufacture sheet glass!"[30]

A major contributor to the glass industries of Tokyo and Osaka was Kenkichi Koide, at one time a skilled artisan at Shinagawa. When the government invested in foreign equipment and lent to private enterprises, he was assigned to oversee the distribution. He often altered and improved the imported machinery to make it more suitable to Japanese capabilities.[31] It is said that he made the glass windows of the Imperial Palace.

Although the Shinagawa Glassworks failed repeatedly, it was nevertheless the pioneer in modern glassmaking in Japan. It trained many technicians, some of whom like Takijirō Iwaki in Tokyo and Magoichi Shimada in Osaka became pioneers in the management of successful enterprises and contributors to the development of new methods and new products. Some artisans stayed in Tokyo to develop the industry, others fanned out to spread the new types of glassmaking to Nagasaki, Osaka, and other places. Hence, the Shinagawa enterprise should be honored as the initial inspiration of today's highly developed Japanese glass industry.

IWAKI GLASSWORKS

In December, 1881, Takijirō Iwaki (Pl. 222), whose previous name was Takinosuke, resigned as foreman of the Shinagawa factory and established his own factory in Shinei, Kyōbashi, Tokyo.[32] It is said to have been the first completely private glass enterprise with no outside participation. The first products were lamp chimneys, tumblers, and flytraps.[33] The glass was melted in a tank furnace, and the pressing technique was introduced.[34] Acid-etched designs are said to have been used on lamp chimneys. Later, cut glass, chemical glass, and colored glass for ships' lights were produced, and around 1897 a searchlight reflector about 1.5 meters in diameter and slightly over 6 centimeters thick was produced for the Naval Ministry.[35]

After the Sino-Japanese War of 1894 there was an increased demand for window glass, and Takijirō went to the United States to study the process. Upon his return, about 1900, he took over the former Shinagawa factory, made his own firebrick and built his own furnace. His first sheet glass was approximately 60 centimeters square; railway signal lights were also produced. He evolved a blowpipe combining the iron pipe of the West and the Japanese *tomosao* (glass blow tube). In the second or third industrial exhibition he exhibited a large set of stacked boxes (*jūbako*) of cobalt-colored glass.

Financial difficulties were considerable. The government no longer gave assistance to private enterprises, except for lending machines and equipment. State participation was discussed in the Diet, and a report was sent to John Hay, U.S. Secretary of State, by the Secretary of the American Legation in Tokyo, with the thought that some American engineer might wish to assist.[36] The matter was forestalled by the Russo-Japanese War of 1904. Takijirō Iwaki died in 1915 and was succeeded briefly by Iwatarō Iwaki. Upon the latter's death his second son, Kuranosuke Iwaki, took charge.

Kuranosuke Iwaki had been to the United States, studied in the Bureau of Standards in Pittsburgh, and visited plants of the Corning Glass Works. Upon returning to Japan, he successfully undertook improvements in the manufacture of parabolic reflectors and was associated with the Japan Optic Company. Kuranosuke's leadership of the Iwaki Glassworks lasted until the company was taken over six years after World War II and the production emphasis changed.

OSAKA

The glass industry in Osaka, the great mercantile city of the Edo period, encountered the same problems as those of other centers during the first decades after the Restoration: difficulty with new equipment and techniques, lack of skilled workers, expense of importing equipment and supplies, no experience of business on a large scale, the slow growth of demand, and the depressions attending the Sino-Japanese War of 1894–95 and the Russo-Japanese War of 1904–05.

The president of the Koshida Glass Manufacturing Company related that to develop the skill necessary to meet foreign competition, workers were required to tie their right hand behind their back and work with the left hand until it became as proficient as the right. Thus, being ambidextrous, the workers greatly increased their production rate.

NIHON GLASSWORKS

The story of glassmaking attempts in the early Meiji era is somewhat confused, with published accounts occasionally at odds with each other. It seems clear that Itō Keishin pioneered Western techniques in Osaka, establishing a plant at Kawasaki-mura in 1875. This later became incorporated as the Nihon Garasu Seizō Kabushiki Kaisha (The Nihon Glassworks, Ltd.). After many difficulties, a successful red glass for ships' lights was produced. Then the Osaka mint ordered bottles for sulphuric acid, and retorts. An Englishman named Scidmore, who had been at the Shinagawa factory in Tokyo, worked there in 1881 to develop crucibles. Financial troubles and finally policy disagreements lead to the retirement of the chief engineer, Magoichi Shimada, who had worked at Shinagawa under James Speed.

Although Keishin Itō repeatedly had financial failures, he was a key figure in the early development of the Osaka glass industry, contributing to its eventual success through his emphasis on research. After his retirement, the company continued until it was bought by Magoichi Shimada in 1893. He used coal for fuel and then changed to gas to reduce costs. He also experimented with quartzite sand and found that, after being crushed in a watermill, it required less refining and was therefore more economical. In 1903 his sheet glass was entered in the Fifth Inter-Japan Trade Fair and was awarded a prize. In the following year it was available on the market.[37] Gaining confidence, as well as profits, Magoichi Shimada then went to study in America and Europe.

ASAHI JOINT STOCK COMPANY

When Magoichi Shimada returned in 1905, Toshiya Iwasaki of Tokyo invested in the company, which then became the Osaka Shimada Garasu Gōshi Kaisha (The Shimada Glass Joint Stock Company of Osaka). As the plant was too small for the large-scale production of sheet glass, a new factory was constructed in nearby Amagasaki in Hyōgo Prefecture, between Osaka and Kobe. It was called the Asahi Glass Company, Ltd. The old factory was renamed Asahi Gōshi Kaisha (Asahi Joint Stock Company), and it was there that fine glass vessels and tableware (Pls. 31, 32, 219) were manufactured until 1913. Then it was decided to concentrate solely upon sheet glass, and this factory was liquidated. In the Second All-Japan Ceramic Exhibition, 1911, this company's cut glass and colored glass was judged "excellent."

At first Osaka products had been primarily oil containers, lamp chimneys, and glass for ships' lights. Later, when electricity came into use, light bulbs, globes, and shades were made for domestic consumption, although kerosene lamps were still produced for export to Asia. Tableware was produced in quantity, as was scientific glass, medical glass, watch glasses, marbles, spectacles, and mirrors. The Osaka area, particularly the village of Shinoda-mura, became the center of a prolific manufacture of glass beads and bracelets for export; they are still important export items today.

In spite of the enlarged scope of glass production in the new industrial era, some of the whimsical and imaginative spirit of the *biidoro* and *giyaman* age remained. In 1902, for instance, a great exhibition was held in Osaka. The glassmakers all contributed their various products, which were then assembled and intermingled—tubes, rods, sheet glass, lamps, dishes, light bulbs, shades—to form an archway to the main entrance.[38]

World War I caused a depression because soda could no longer be imported from England, and the export of luxury goods fell off. After the war, however, there was a "boom," especially in bottles of all kinds—for mineral water, *ramuné* ("lemonade," a soft drink), saké, beer, milk, medicines, toiletries—and the new vacuum bottles, which were and still are called "magic bottles."

The devastations of World War II seriously hampered research, because glass and documents were destroyed wholesale. The collection of Waichi Yanase, a glass merchant of Osaka, consisting of three or four thousand examples of ancient and modern glass, some of which were made in Osaka, was entirely lost.

Now the Government Industrial Research Institute in Ikeda city—combining the Tsūshō Sangyōsho Kōgyō Gijutsu-in (Industrial Engineering Institute of the Ministry of Commerce and Industry) and the Ōsaka Kōgyō Gijutsu Shikensho (Osaka Experimental Institute for Industrial Arts)—is constantly experimenting to improve the quality of Japanese glass, among other materials, and developing new formulas and techniques for scientific and commercial wares.

VESSELS

Few examples of modern Osaka glass vessels survive, or if they do, their identity has not been recognized. Fortunately, the main office of the Asahi Glass Company in Tokyo owns a small collection of fine vessels from the Asahi Gōshi Kaisha of Osaka, designed by Hideo Miyamoto, before the company's dissolution in 1913. Plates 31 and 32 are of particular interest, for their "agate" technique, rare in Japan except for this company's work and the more recent products at the Fukuoka Tokushu Garasu Kabushiki Kaisha. Other examples in the collection include lustered, crackled, and monochrome wares, the latter enhanced by variation in tones. An example of cut glass produced by the Asahi Gōshi Kaisha is shown in Plate 219. A tall vase of orange-gold color obtained by selenium is in private possession.

The Bead Industry

Beadmaking, which had a long history in the Edo period, after the Restoration advanced technically and commercially and became an important export product.

Sakubei (Tokujirō) Ōi, who started production in the early 1870s,[40] is said to have been the first of the modern beadmakers. He went abroad to study and improve methods of manufacturing *hikaridama* ("shining beads"), said to have been imitations of Austrian examples.[41] Later he managed a factory in India that had been taken over from the Germans. Upon returning, he manufactured glass bracelets, by coiling and pressing, which he exported to India. He also produced imitation pearl beads, whose surface was covered with a fish-scale base mixed with an adhesive.

Although beads are said to have been made in the port of Sakai, the center of production was Shinoda-mura in Osaka Prefecture. Tradition has it that a villager learned the technique from a craftsman at a Sakai temple where beads were made. It was a primitive technique, carried on by the villagers in their homes. No financial outlay was required, and the villagers worked at it in their leisure time. About ten factories are said to have made up bars of colored glasses, which were then distributed to the villagers as working materials. At first each bead was made individually in the old manner, but in 1884 or 1885 Tokichi Nakamichi devised a way to increase the output by mold-blowing them in series.[48]

Initially, silver powder or small pieces of mica were applied to the surface of *hikaridama*, but later fish scales were used. In 1923 a wax coating was developed, which added weight and preserved the bead. Eventually color was applied, and some were gilded. *Hikaridama* were exported in quantity to Asian countries.

Some beads were still used for domestic purposes, especially for Buddhist rosaries, *kanzashi* beads, and *negake* (beads for the coiffure). Now their chief output is necklaces of glass beads; they also make some small amulets of glass. At first the beads were made by the coiling method. The current president of the company has patented a machine using a two-part mold through which a glass ribbon is run; when the two parts clamp together they cut the beads apart. Tiny *kodama*, for bead purses, are now produced from a mechanically drawn and cut tube, then revolved with carbon powder in a rotary furnace for fire polishing (previously an ordinary frying pan was shaken by hand over a fire—a slow and laborious process). The factory produces about 650 pounds per day.

Although necklaces, and costume jewelry (a new custom), are popular in Japan and are found in all stores, the chief activity of the Yoneda Wakamatsu Shōten is for export, sixty percent going to New York City, for distribution throughout the United States.

The bead of Plate 220, once thought to have been an accessory of the "Hidden Christianity" of the Edo period, has been identified as a type made by this company. Somewhat similar, but inferior ones, were exported after World War II to India (Pl. 221).

Many beads are still produced by a cottage industry in a number of localities, though production of coiled beads has been eased and speeded up by the introduction of a treadle, which revolves the wire mechanically, leaving both hands free for work. The wire has a clay coating, and the burner, now fueled by kerosene, has a blower to augment the heat. Otherwise the method of manufacture is traditional. The beads are made into earrings, necklaces, and other accessories, many for export to Asian countries.

Thus, the age-old cottage industry of Japan has kept step, in its own manner, with the modern trends of an industrialized age, and become an international affair.

KYUSHU

Kyushu is another active center for modern glass production. In 1914 a branch of the Asahi Glass Company was established at Tobata-machi for the manufacture of sheet glass by the Pittsburgh process. In 1917 a second branch was opened at Yahata city. Aside from emphasizing the historical significance of these large-scale industrial developments in northern Kyushu, they will not be discussed.

HIROKICHI NAKASHIMA

When Hirokichi (Shōsei) Nakashima worked at the Asahi Gōshi Kaisha in Osaka in 1907, they were producing artistic wares of high quality, such as those of Plates 31, 32, and 219. When the factory closed in 1913, he was apparently transferred to the Asahi Glass Company, where he was able to study various colored glasses, although they were not marketed. In 1919 he left the Asahi Glass Company and set up his own manufactory of various mixed-colored glasses, in Ueki, Fukuoka Prefecture (Sup. N. 90). He managed it for two decades, producing such things as flower vases and ashtrays.

STAINED GLASS

Stained glass has been a relatively recent development in Japan, dependent upon Western style architecture and introduced in the Meiji era by artisans who had studied in Europe and America.

In 1886 Tatsuo Unosawa (formerly Yamamoto) went to Berlin to study stained glass techniques. Returning in 1889, bringing "materials" with him, he produced for a limited time a number of windows for various government buildings in Tokyo, none of which apparently survive today.[43] A few years later his adoptive father, Tatsumi Unosawa, reinstituted the factory, where he taught some apprentices. In 1912, one of the latter, Shichirō Beppu, became a partner in a joint company, which lasted but a short time. Later, it is said, Shichirō Beppu, Shintarō Kiuchi and others, established a stained-glass factory in Osaka.

At the turn of the century, Takijirō Iwaki, founder of the Iwaki Glassworks in Tokyo, went to the United States to study sheet-glass manufacture and while there learned about stained glass, which was much in vogue. After returning to Japan he exhibited stained glass in the fifth exhibition in Osaka in 1903. He produced all of his own materials and may be said to have been the first truly Japanese pioneer in stained glass, although he did not pursue it extensively. Only one example of his work is known today—a window in a stairway in the mansion of the late Count Chiaki Watanabe in Takanawa, Tokyo.[44]

Another craftsman, Sanchi Ogawa, who had graduated from the Tokyo Art Academy in 1904, spent eight years in the United States, studying first at the Art Institute of Chicago and later visiting stained glass ateliers. On his return he was active in the Taishō era, producing windows in floral and landscape designs.[45]

Examples of stained glass windows exist today in a number of buildings, but it is not known who produced them. In the main dining room (now the Banquet Hall) of the Miyako Hotel in Kyoto, are glass panels with colorful processions above the sliding doors. Those of the south side represent the famous Aoi-matsuri (Hollyhock Festival) of the Shimogamo and Kamigamo shrines of Kyoto; those on the north, the equally famous Jidai-matsuri (Festival of the Epochs) of the Heian Shrine in Kyoto. These, done in 1927, are the work of Shintarō Kiuchi of Osaka.

There are other remaining examples, but stained glass of that period seems to attract little attention today, other than nostalgia. There has been some contemporary production, but largely pseudo-Victorian panels used as atmosphere decorations for coffee shops. The technique is still alive, and the future may see increased activity in creative, modern stained glass design.

CLOISONNÉ

In the early Meiji era, Dr. Gottfried Wagner was invited to Japan to teach chemistry. From 1874 to 1878, at the request of a foreign firm in Tokyo (Allens? or Arends?; Japanese, *Arensu*), he did research in enamels. The company established a factory, employing Kaisuke Tsukamoto, Sōsuke Namikawa, and Hikoshichi Muramasu. The combination of Western science and Japanese technical experience was a stimulant to the improvement in the production of cloisonné. However, in 1878 Dr. Wagner was called to the Bureau of Chemistry in Kyoto, and the factory closed.

Dr. Wagner was no doubt influential, although Yasuyuki Namikawa had already established a factory in Kyoto in 1871, and in 1875 had won a medal at the Kyoto Industrial Exposition for a flower vase of fine technique.[46] He concentrated on improving old techniques and produced cloisonné with fine cloisons and improved colors. He is said to have been invited to Tokyo as Sōsuke Namikawa's technical expert.[47]

Cloisonné in general was improving; gold and silver largely replaced the former brass wires; and new translucent enamels came into use. Denshichi Mikiyama and Sōbei Kinkozan of Kyoto applied cloisonné to porcelain, as did Chūbei Takeuchi and Kichisaburō Ōta, but this did not develop. Takeuchi also experimented with cloisonné on glass.[54]

Sōsuke Namikawa, in Tokyo, seemingly at Dr. Wagner's suggestion, began a new method, *musen shippō* (literally "no wire cloisonné") in which cloisons were used only temporarily, until the enamels had been placed in the cells. Removal before firing meant that adjacent colors met softly instead of being kept rigidly apart by the metal wires. Sōsuke was violently attacked by some critics for having destroyed the true nature of *shippō* by injecting a pictorial effect belonging to painting.

Sōsuke's decorative floral designs in *musen shippō* are found in the old banquet hall of the Akasaka Detached Palace in Tokyo (for some years used for the Diet Library), which was constructed between 1899 and 1909; This *musen shippō* technique was to be carried forward by others, notably the Andō Cloisonné Company of Nagoya.

CONTEMPORARY GLASS ACTIVITY—THE SHŌWA ERA (1926–   )

IT IS obviously difficult to draw any strict line of demarcation between the glass activities of the Meiji era and the later ones that flowed directly therefrom. However, the tremendous activity that has developed in the Shōwa era, especially since World War II, deserves special attention; yet the foundations of this activity, which seems destined to expand into even wider areas in the future, rest upon a few men whose careers go back into the prewar decades.

It is not intended to introduce in this work a lengthy discussion of modern activity in glass manufacture, evidence of which can be seen throughout the country. So prevalent, indeed, is glass of all types that Dr. Pompé van Meedervoort's prophecy, "I believe that his [Shimazu Nariakira's] kind of glass industry may become the chief manufacture in Japan," seems not so far from fulfillment!

Not included here are many glass craftsmen and glass companies who have come to the fore in Tokyo and elsewhere since World War II. They, too, are constantly widening and advancing the range and skills of glass production. Many deal with the primarily commercial aspects of glass—plate glass, light bulbs, T.V. glass, optical glass, foam glass, and numberless other products. Less dominant numerically, but equally important, are the producers of fine glass tableware and luxury glass, of whom only a very few can be included here.

IWAKI GLASSWORKS

Continuing the work that his father had pioneered, Kuronosuke Iwaki went on to produce sheet glass, safety glass, heat and chemically resistant glass, cut glass of high quality, etched and sandblasted glass, and even stained glass. Even custom-made glass eyes were produced in quantity for soldiers injured in World War II. This pioneer work was continued until 1951, when the company was taken over by the Asahi glassworks and all fine art glass operations were discontinued.[49]

About 1920, someone taught Kuranosuke how to make *pâte de verre*, which a number of artists who had been to France considered valuable as an industrial art. A sophisticated technique was developed, and Jūhei Ogawa, a sculptor, designed molds. The portrait bust of Takijirō Iwaki (Pl. 222) was produced by this method. This process was continued by the company until it merged with the Asahi Glass Company in 1951.

SOTOICHI KOSHIBA

Sotoichi Koshiba, who helped develop the process but is now an independent craftsman, still makes *pâte de verre* (Pl. 33) and is said to be the only man in this line in Japan. However, there is little interest in this process. Sotoichi also became interested in glass mosaic murals; his panels of 1960 may be seen in the ground floor of the Yokohama Marine Tower. His sons, Kōichi and Shirō Koshiba, are specialists in architectural decoration utilizing glass mosaic, tiles, and blocks, and have organized their own company, of which Shirō is president and Kōichi the designer.

IWATA INDUSTRIAL ART GLASS COMPANY

Tōshichi Iwata, painter, sculptor, and glass craftsman, is a graduate of the Department of Metalwork (1918) and Department of Painting (1923), Tokyo School of Fine Arts.[50] From 1931 to 1936 he trained in glass at the Iwaki Glassworks. Afterward he founded his own company and developed his own styles quite independently from any previous tradition. He speaks whimsically of his three periods: an "Egyptian period" (Pl. 34), a "Chinese and Asian period," and a more recent "Jōmon period" referring to modeling reminiscent of pottery of the Jōmon period. He also appears to have had a Venetian period. His factory turns out a great deal of commercial ware, seen today throughout Japan. But his heart has always been in carefully executed handwork, which perpetuates his own imaginative spirit. These are often flower vases, "because flower arrangement is an art in Japan and there is need for complementary containers to set off the flowers." His work has been described as having a "sensual warmth that makes best use of the plasticity of blown glass."[51] Mr. Iwata has also worked with flat glass panels, which he calls "Colorart." In recent years his son, Hisatoshi Iwata, and his daughter-in-law, Itoko Iwata, have handled the management and design activities of the company (Pls. 35, 227).

KAGAMI CRYSTAL GLASS COMPANY

Kōzō Kagami's approach to glass is entirely different. He manufactures principally colorless crystal glass, some plain, some cut or engraved.

He has been closely associated with glass since his youth. He graduated from the Tokyo Higher Technical School and in 1920 he studied glass engraving under Professor Willhelm Eiff at the Kunstgewerbeschule in Stuttgart, then visited Czechoslovakia and learned Bohemian methods.[52] Returning to Tokyo in 1931, he trained a group of pupils in the engraving techniques and in 1934 inaugurated the Kagami Kurisutaru Seisaku-sho

(Kagami Crystal Glassworks). He began to enter his works in various exhibitions and has since continued to win awards (see Pls. 36, 228, 229).

To support his artistic production, a line of commercial products of high quality was developed: lenses for lighthouses, automobile headlights, covers for light meters, architectural ornament, and lighting units. Kagami tableware and luxury items may be seen practically everywhere in Japan. In the beginning, some colored glass was produced, but now the output is mostly of colorless soda-lime and lead glass. The company has produced glassware for the Imperial Household, and a cherry-blossom pattern was made for Japanese embassies throughout the world.

A pioneer in modern techniques, Kōzō Kagami has also written on glass, and was one of the committee of four appointed to study the glass in the Shōsō-in.

His son, Mitsuru Kagami, is continuing in the family business but has developed his own designs, which reveal an independent character (Pls. 230–232).

Another associate, Junshirō Satō, is designer and managing director for the company. He is a graduate of the Tokyo School of Fine Arts (1934). He is especially interested in drinking glasses and has frequently written about them. In addition to the more or less familiar types of cut glass (Pls. 233, 234), he has produced glass pictures, architectural mosaics, and sculptural forms (Pl. 235).

SASAKI GLASS COMPANY

This company was one of thirty-eight prize winners in the Tokyo Industrial Exhibition of 1907.[53] Today its main products are widely sold hand-blown wares, pressed wares, and machine-blown tumblers. Three factories are in operation, but the products of other companies are also handled for the wholesale trade. About twenty percent of the business is for export, chiefly to the United States and Southeast Asia.

HOYA CRYSTAL GLASSWORKS

The Hoya company, established since World War II, turns out a tremendous amount of tableware, both plain and cut, flower vases, cut glass chandeliers, optical lenses, and photo filters, for home consumption and for export, especially to America, Europe, and Australia. Standards are high, and fine design is emphasized. Hoya glass was awarded the Grand Prix at the 1958 World's Fair in Brussels.[54]

The author recalls her delight at coming upon a small, but choice, exhibition of Hoya glass flower containers at the Tōyoko Department Store in Tokyo. Each had its own simple flower arrangement, harmonizing with the individual shape and with the clear purity of the glass.

AWASHIMA GLASS COMPANY

Masakichi Awashima, a graduate of the design department of the Japan Art School, was a designer for the Kagami Crystal Glass company from 1935 to 1946, and chief designer of the Hoya Crystal Glassworks from 1946 to 1950, when he established his own Awashima Glass Design Institute, later to become the Awashima Glass Company. Among his products are practical household items (evidently the backbone of his production), which he himself terms "lower than my design level." Other more luxurious items are definitely in what the modern Japanese call the "good design" category. A patented design is the *shizuku* ("dripping water") pattern (Pl. 236). Mr. Awashima strives to capture the simple beauty emanating from transparency, textures, and the soft, rounded quality of old Japanese ceramic froms. His molds, into which the glass is blown or poured, are of clay, stone, occasionally of plaster, and of metal. He seeks a "homespun touch" (his words), accented by gleams of diffused reflection. At present his work shows great versatility in design, arising from his interest in and studies of many different crafts (see Pl. 37).

SHIBATA HARIO GLASS COMPANY

Two companies carry the Shibata name. The Shibata Kagaku Kika Kōgyō K.K. (The Shibata Chemical Appliance Manufacturing Company, Ltd.) is said to be the largest manufacturer of scientific glass equipment in Japan. The Shibata Hario Garasu Kabushiki Kaisha (The Shibata Hario Glass Company, Ltd.) produces borosilicate scientific apparatus and, in the last decade, has also produced handmade table- and housewares, some of which bear the trade name "Hiromu."

Hario tableware is fairly recent. A particularly notable form is a double walled tumbler, ideal for hot or iced beverages. This new Hario tumbler contains dry air of low pressure in the space between its double walls.

FUKUOKA ART GLASS COMPANY

In 1937, one of Hirokichi Nakashima's (see p. 294) deep bowls was awarded a prize in the Paris World's Fair. In 1939, with financial aid from Fukuoka Prefecture, a new company was established, the Fukuoka Tokushu Garasu Kabushiki Kaisha (Fukuoka Art Glass Company, Ltd.), and a new factory was constructed. It was there that a stable manufacture of cased art glass developed. It is now known all over Japan as *murutigarasu* ("multi-glass," abbreviated from "multiple-layer glass"). During World War II the government placed the factory in the *gijutsu hōzon* ("preservation of techniques") category, exempting it from total war effort. Hence, production of art wares, in small quantity, continued uninterrupted.

Fukuoka multiple-layered glass, now manufactured in a new, up-to-date factory, is seen in shops everywhere in Japan and is exported to Australia, Africa, Mexico, and the United States. The Hattori-Wako company now owns the factory. Products carry the label "FTG," the trademark of Fukuoka Tokushu Garasu. Examples of this ware are illustrated in Plates 238 and 239.

Each "multi-glass" piece is in three layers, the inner being of thin soda-lime glass; the center layer (a sandwich filling) is a special glass of high lead content; and the exterior, a thicker casing usually of transparent and colorless glass. The outcome is not precisely predictable, so no two pieces are ever exactly alike.

New ideas, techniques and designs are continually being tried out, so that the range in color and shape is wide, as may be observed in the factory's small museum. Nobuyuki Nakashima, son of the founder, showed the author, in 1960, a lightweight, soft-glass bowl he had just produced.

CLOISONNÉ

ANDŌ CLOISONNÉ COMPANY

The first Andō was Jūbei, who used as a trademark a conventionalized form of the character *jū*, 十, which is still in use today. The Andō Cloisonné Company was established in Nagoya in 1880, with Tsunekichi Kaji as chief craftsman. Since then the company has steadily progressed technically and artistically. The following information regarding the company's various kinds of *shippō*, and their techniques, comes partly from a small pamphlet produced by the company and partly from conversations at the factory.

1. *Yusen shippō*, or *shippō* with wires—the traditional type.

   The metal base, of silver or copper, is shaped and the desired design drawn on it.

   Small and thin fillets, usually of silver but sometimes of gold or brass, are placed on edge on this base following the lines of the design, the adhesive being powdered orris root moistened with cold water.

   The cells so formed are filled with a compound of silica, niter, lead oxide, and borax, with metallic oxides added for color. The first firing takes only ten to twenty minutes at 800–1000° C.; a longer period would melt the silver. The precise nature of the metallic oxides is, as usual among artisans, a family secret, handed down from generation to generation.

   Two more fillings and firings are required, until the enamel completely conceals the cloisons. The object is then ground down on a revolving wheel with powdered whetstone under a thin stream of water. Powdered pumice, wrapped in rice straw, is used for the final polishing, the pumice working its way out through the interstices of the straw wrapping.

2. *Musen shippō*, or cloisonless *shippō*

   In this technique the cloisons are attached only temporarily and are removed after the enamel paste has been placed in the cells. The cloisons are then replaced for each subsequent refilling and refiring. Although in the Company's small museum one sees old works entirely of *musen shippō*, the practice is now used only for portions of a large design—as, for example, Mount Fuji and clouds in the distance worked in the soft *musen shippō* manner, while the foreground, perhaps a forest scene, is done with cloisons.

3. *Zōgan shippō*, or "inlaid *shippō*"

   This is enamel of the champlevé type.

4. *Tsuiki shippō*

   In this, the metal base is hammered over a form into a design in relief, and the enamel is brushed onto the raised portions.

5. *Totai shippō*

In this technique parts of the metal base are cut out in a design, and the enamel applied in such a way that it fills these open areas, appearing in the finished item as transparent glass. This is an intricate process, and is said to be particularly difficult when combined with solid opaque areas.

6. *Shotai shippō*, or baseless *shippō* (Pl. 240)

In which, after firing, the metal base is removed with nitric acid, leaving the object transparent or slightly translucent.

7. *Tōmeiyū shippō*, or transparent *shippō*

The metal base is engraved with a design that shows through transparent enamel.

8. *Nambutetsu shippō*

Enamel decoration on a base of Nambu iron; so called from the area of northern Honshu where famous cast iron tea kettles for the tea ceremony are made.

Of course, there are variations, but these are the basic techniques. For a characteristic transparent "pigeon blood" red enamel of today, gold is added.

The cloisonné industry has now become a kind of assembly-line operation, with each worker trained (in a three-year apprenticeship) for one aspect of the work only. One is the designer; another fabricates the metal form; a third attaches the cloisons; another applies the enamel (using a brush for the background, a small bamboo tube for small cells); one fuses and fires; still another grinds and polishes; and, finally, one adds the rims, usually of silver. This works well for mass production, but tends to leave the worker devoid of creative fulfillment, since he never sees the work as an entity of his own creation. The process has been likened to an "assembly of cripples, each knowing only a part, though the whole has the aspect of a fine cooperation."[55] Economic realities are, of course, partly responsible for the manner of production.

Much of the Andō output goes to the tourist trade—necklaces, pendants, earrings, cuff links, brooches, tie clips, ashtrays, boxes, smoking sets, paperknives, besides the usual receptacles of all kinds, sizes, and prices. Framed pictures in enamel are now available also.

In the museum displays at the main office and at the factory in Nagoya there are items that could not be duplicated today. Some have delicate surfaces with small allover patterns—extremely difficult to accomplish. Among these is a six-lobed cup whose exterior is covered with minute silver wires like a tiny punched design; inside there is an allover pattern of the most minute butterflies, in white, grayed blue, and dull red. Others are masterpieces of technical perfection and subtle feeling. One turns away with a sense of regret that the freedom of the craftsman to work out his own visions has been forced into divisions of labor that deter the artisan who is working on one small part from "seeing it whole."

INABA CLOISONNÉ COMPANY

In Kyoto another enterprise in cloisonné, the Inaba Cloisonné Company, produces objects similar to the ones just described.

Modern cloisonné is in sharp contrast to that of the Edo period. Sir Rutherford Alcock wrote in 1878, that the Japanese used bright colors so sparingly in their cloisonné that they were conspicuous by their absence, and spoke of the drab lilac, dark blue, and somber green tones.[56] Now the dominating impression is of harmonious rich greens and yellows, and the vibrant "pigeon blood," which contrast strongly with soberer early colors.

1. For details regarding glassmaking in the Meiji era refer to *NKYS.

2. Basil Hall Chamberlain, *Things Japanese*, 5th ed. rev., London, John Murray, 1905, p. 407.

3. Kon Shimizu, "Okamoto Ippei Den" [Tales of Okamoto Ippei], *Chūō Kōron*, January 1962, p. 313.

4. *Nihon Bunkashi Taikei* [Historical Survey of Japanese Culture], II, Tokyo, Shogakkan, 1956, p. 365.

5. *Hayashi, "Nagasaki no Biidoro to Giyaman," p. 31.

6. *NKYS, p. 118.

7. Yamada, *Nihon Garasu Sangyō.* . . . , p. 37.

8. *Itō, "Shinagawa Garasu Seizō Nempyō," p. 6.

9. *Morihira, *Matsunami Garasu.* . . . , pp. 10 11.

10. *NKYS, pp. 22–23.

11. *Shiota, "Garasu," p. 289. However, *Ōsaka no Garasu Kōgyō*, p. 10, states that in the Meiji era watch glasses were achieved by merely polishing fragments of broken fishbowls.

12. *NKYS, p. 93.

13. The Corning Museum of Glass (No. 63.6.84)

14. *Sugiyama, *Ainu Tama*, p. 64.

15. John Batchelor, *The Ainu and Their Folk-lore*, London, Religious Tract Society, 1901, p. 154.

16. Mr. Taruo Kurokawa, Chief of the Chemical Division of Kagoshima Prefecture Experimental Industrial Institute, stated that when the new industrial center had been established by Nariakira Shimazu at Iso, suggestions were sought for naming the center. One of the eliminated entries, *Kaibutsukan*, was then applied to an analytical laboratory in the castle. Possibly this name was the origin of the Kaibutsusha.

17. *Ichiki-shi Kiroku* [Records of Mr. Ichiki], quoted in *Satsuma Garasu no Enkaku*, p. 18.

18. *Shiota, "Garasu," p. 1451.

19. *Shibui, "The Story of Glass in Japan," p. 119.

20. Chamberlain, *op. cit.* (see n. 2), p. 298; the reduction was from 12 *sen* to 5 *sen*.

21. *Itō, "Shinagawa Garasu. . . . ," p. 4. Unless otherwise noted, data regarding this factory are taken from this article.

22. *Yamada, *Nihon Garasu.* . . . , p. 30.

23. A study of this historic factory was undertaken by graduate students in the College of Architecture, Tokyo University; it is to be hoped that the final results will be published. A summary chronology of the factory's history appeared in *Itō, *Shinagawa Garasu.* . . .

24. Similar lunetted windows of brightly colored glass survive at Arita, Saga Prefecture, in the reception room of the Koransha and in the early Meiji foreign style home of Mr. Tashirō Kinichi. Hōzanji at Ikoma, Nara Prefecture, has similarly shaped but uncolored lunettes over doors in a second-floor reception room. The cupola of the gate at Oyama Shrine, Kanazawa, has all four walls glazed in red, green, blue, and yellow; these are brighter than the other examples and are said to be modern replacements. Original colored glass panes at the Ōtomo-rō, an old restaurant in Kanazawa owned by Mr. Saichi Ōtomo are similar and said to have been produced in Tokyo.

Curiously enough, Mr. Sekio Iwanaga of Nagasaki owns a confection box of gold lacquer, also of the Meiji era, with a border of colored glass panels in amber, green, blue, and a violet red, which are strikingly reminiscent of these Meiji era colored windows.

25. Quoted by *Shibui, "The Story of Glass in Japan," pp. 119–120.

26. *Yamada, *Nihon Garasu.* . . . , p. 3. Magoichi was later prominent in developing glass manufacture in Osaka.

27. *Yokoi, *Nihon Kōgyōshi*, p. 301.

28. *Okamura, "Nihon Garasu Kō," p. 22.

29. *Shiota, "Garasu," p. 301.

30. Taiji Maeda (ed.), *Japanese Arts and Crafts in the Meiji Era*, Tokyo, 1935, Pt. 3, p. 135.

31. *NKYS, p. 221.

32. Not to be confused with a short-term enterprise led by Eichi Shibusawa and Sōichirō Asano in Meiji 20 (1887) at Onahama Beach, Fukushima Prefecture, which had to be abandoned because a harbor planned by the government did not materialize and the breakage of glass in the buffeting of the cargo ships by strong winds and high waves hampered operations; *Shiota, "Garasu," pp. 427–428.

33. Data regarding the Iwaki factory, except as otherwise noted, are used by courtesy of the late Mr. Kuranosuke Iwaki, son and successor of Takijirō Iwaki. Kuranosuke Iwaki was, in his own right, a contributor to the progress of modern Japanese glassmaking.

34. *Shiota, "Garasu", p. 438.

35. Told by Mr. Kikujirō Ōno of Osaka, who had trained from early boyhood in the Iwaki factory. In his nineties, in recognition of his knowledge, he was called "The Glass Treasure," by Osaka glassmakers.

36. From The National Archives, Washington, D.C., Record Group No. 59.

37. *Shiota, "Garasu", p. 432.

38. As told by Mr. Iwabei Yoshida, son of Iwakichi Yoshida, who was a manufacturer of many kinds of glass and inventor of a new device for producing glass wind bells. Iwakichi also ingeniously used bamboo molds for lamp chimneys, the natural oil of the bamboo coming to the surface when the hot glass entered the mold.

39. This unusual piece was once in the collection of the late Mr. Shigeta Kanashima, Kami-Takeda-son, Mitsu-gun, Okayama Prefecture.

40. *NKYS, pp. 77, 81, gives 1875 as the date; *Osaka no Garasu Kōgyō, p. 7, gives 1871.

41. *Osaka no Garasu Kōgyō, p. 7.

42. *Ibid.*

43. Two of these are in The Corning Museum of Glass (No. 61.6.41 a–b).

44. Hironao Izumi, in *Nihon Bunkashi Taikei, op. cit.*, XII, p. 318.

45. Jō Okada, in *Nippon Times*, Tokyo, July 16, 1955.

46. *Kisha, "Kagami Kurisutaru. . . . ," p. 44.

47. *NKYS, IV, p. 129.

48. *Kokusai Shashin Jōhō* [International Graphic], Vol. 32, No. 5, May 1958, carried a well-illustrated article on Hoya glass.

49. *Meiji Bunkashi*, VIII, p. 289.

50. Now the home of the son, Chifuyu Watanabe; illustrated in *Space Modulator*, No. 6, (1961), p. 21.

51. See *Nihon Bunkashi Taikei, op. cit.* (see n. 4), Vol. II, Pl. 721.

52. *Meiji Bunkashi*, VIII, pp. 280, 281.

53. *Okada, *Japanese Handicrafts*, pp. 97–98.

54. *Meiji Bunkashi*, VIII, p. 282.

55. *Noma, "Shippō Zuishō," p. 41.

56. Rutherford Alcock, *Art and Art Industries of Japan*, London, 1878, p. 180.

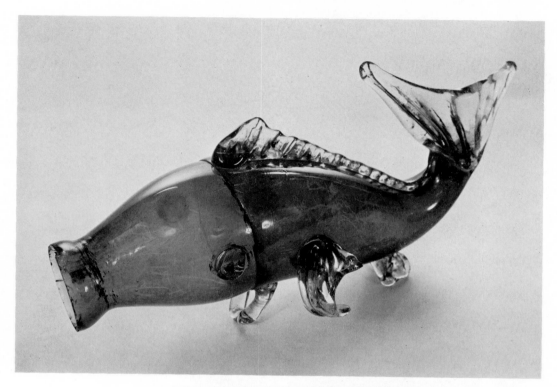

211. Hollow fish form • *ca.* 1877 (?) • Nagasaki • L. 26.0 cm.

212. Glass beads of the Ainu women • Japanese and continental • 19th–early 20th century.

213. Stemmed wine glass • probably early Meiji era • Kagoshima • H. 12.7 cm.
214. Stemmed wine glass • probably early Meiji era • Kagoshima • H. 10.9 cm.
215. Engraved covered bowl • Meiji era • H. 5.6 cm.

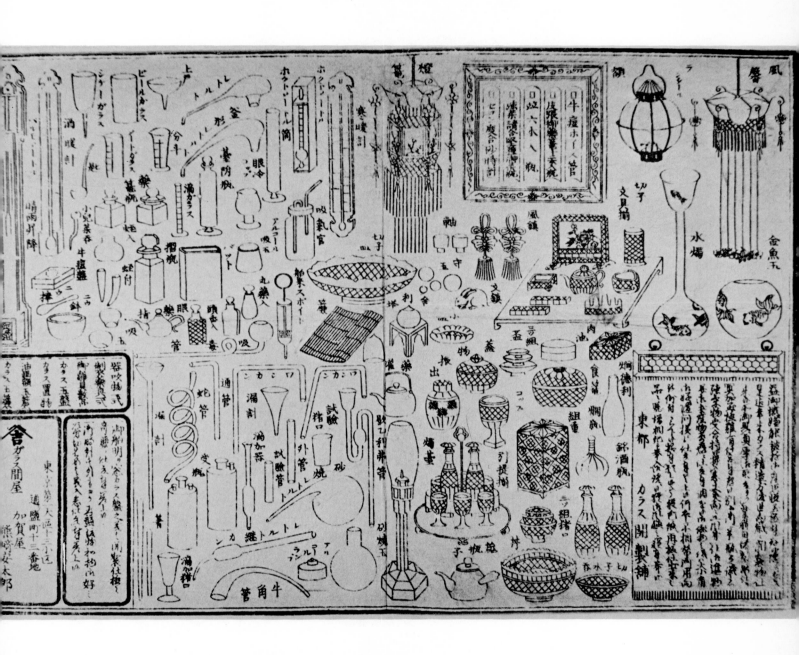

216. Broadsheet of glassmaker Kagaya Kyūbei · early Meiji era · Tokyo.

217. Shinagawa glass factory, Tokyo • early Meiji era • demolished in 1962.
218. Brush holders • early Meiji era • Shinagawa glass factory, Tokyo • max. H. 16.5 cm.

219. Cut glass bowl • between 1908 and 1913 • Asahi Joint Stock Company, Osaka.
220. Bead with cross motif • early 20th century (?) • Yoneda Wakamatsu Shōten, Osaka Pref. • H. 1.2 cm.

221. Beads with cross motif • post-World War II • Yoneda Wakamatsu Shōten, Osaka Pref. • H. 1.0 cm.

222. *Pâte de verre* portrait bust of Takijirō Iwaki • 1935 • H. 30.5 cm.

223. Cut glass bowl and goblet for the Imperial Household • before 1941 • Iwaki Glassworks.

224. Whiskey glasses • before 1941 • Iwaki Glassworks.

225. Vase by Tōshichi Iwata • 1937 • H. 29.0 cm.

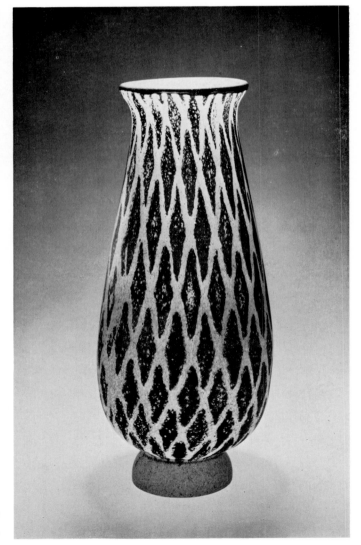

226. Vase by Tōshichi Iwata • 1956 • H. 20.6 cm.
227. Vase by Hisatoshi Iwata • 1971 • H. 38.0 cm.

228. Engraved vase by Kōzō Kagami · *ca.* 1955 · H. 19.4 cm.
229. Bowl by Kōzō Kagami · 1955 · H. 11.0 cm.

230. Vase by Mitsuru Kagami • 1955 • H. *ca.*
43.0 cm.
231. Monument by Mitsuru Kagami • 1970 • H.
2.1 cm.

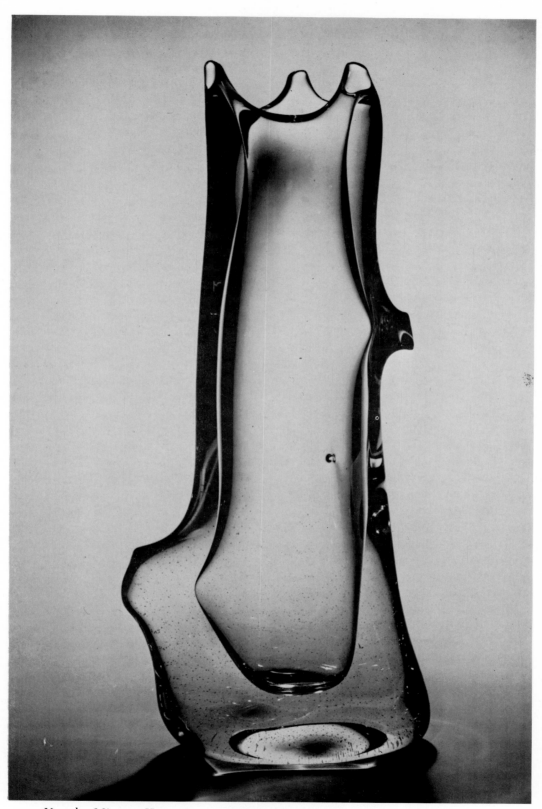

232. Vase by Mitsuru Kagami • 1968 • H. 30.0 cm.

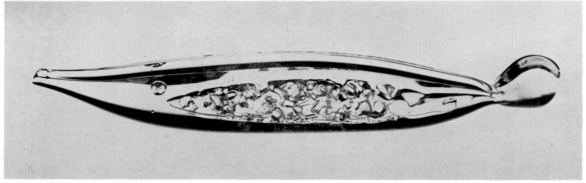

233. Vase by Junshirō Satō • before 1955 • H. 28.0 cm.
234. Bowl by Junshirō Satō • *ca.* 1955 • H. 7.1 cm.
235. Fish by Junshirō Satō • 1972 • L. 29.5 cm.

236. Tumblers by Masakichi Awashima • produced since 1950 • max. H. 10.6 cm.

237. Agate ware bowl • modern • Fukuoka Art Glass Company.

238. Bowl • *ca.* 1952 • Fukuoka Art Glass Company • D. 17.15 cm.

239. Bowl by Nobuyuki Nakashima • 1960.

240. "Baseless" cloisonné bowl • 1960 • Andō Cloisonné Company • H. 4.8 cm.

CONCLUSION

In Retrospect

WE HAVE NOW come to the end of this survey of the development of glass in Japan. We have followed its vicissitudes from the beginning, when Jōmon man was slowly advancing toward the discovery, or introduction, of glass. During the days of Yayoi man, glass seems to have had its beginning in Japan. The following period of the Great Tombs was marked by quick progress in production of glass beads and globules. In the Asuka-Hakuhō interval of the seventh century we found locally produced vessels, sacred *shari* containers of blown glass, which were interred, with beads, beneath Buddhist pagodas. We encountered the first attempts at a new cloisonné-like process, which in the next century became a richly developed form. The striking beauty of the glass in the eighth century, in Nara, declined in the Heian and Kamakura periods, and glass practically disappeared in the Muromachi and Momoyama periods.

Then came the Europeans, and we saw a revival, especially in the town of Nagasaki, where we found a different kind of glass—large objects blown in the European manner. The Japanese there and throughout the land, awakened to new ideas during the Edo period, adopted and adapted new customs and methods. Later, after the Edo period, Japan opened to the new forces of the industrial age and mass production methods.

And what of the future? Will Japanese glass develop some inherently Japanese qualities, as did her lacquers, ceramic wares, metal, textiles, paintings, and prints? Will there be independent advances in technology and design to set Japanese glass apart from other glass in the world?

Already, at the time of this publication, there seems to be an explosion everywhere in the Japanese glass field. Not only has the popularity of glass increased, not only have ist forms and uses multiplied, but the emphasis upon design in glass has burst into full bloom. Whereas for the older glass craftsmen the prime interest centered upon the manipulation of glass as a material—upon its purity, transparency, and reflective qualities, its ductility, and often also its color potential, it seems that the approach to glass today is from the avenue of design rather than craft.

Outstanding in this later aspect is the development of glass for decorative architectural use, as in the many handsome achievements of the Kagami Crystal Glass Company (Pl. 231) and in the immense and superb decoration in the lobby of the new Imperial Hotel, "The Wall of Light—Dawn," a broad and two-story-high rendition of morning light shining on and through ocean waves. Conceived by the designer, Miss Minami Tada, and produced in 1970, the component glass tiles of this wall present a wide spectrum of color, texture, and technique. Each translucent tile is backed with an aluminum sheet, which contributes a special soft, luminous quality.

Glass mosaic, decorative glass panels (Pl. 35), windows, and dividers are popular and widely used for both public and private structures. It is interesting that women have also come to the fore in the designing of contemporary glass. The new Nihon Garasu Kōgei Kai (Japanese Association of Industrial Art Glass), organized in April, 1972, promises to give further impetus to present-day trends.

Furthermore, the forthcoming Tenth International Congress of Glass, to be held in Kyoto in 1974, should increase the domestic interest in glass and likewise focus the attention of foreign glass specialists upon the vigor and quality of Japanese glass activity.

Japanese culture is an amalgamation of qualities from centuries past—from Jōmon times to the present—all now blended into a homogeneous whole whose individual parts may sometimes be difficult to distinguish. Two main factors, however, stand out: the influences from without, which have been powerful stimuli at times but never overwhelming; and the tenacious continuing of indigenous ideals. The two, like the raw materials of glass, have been fused over long centuries into what today constitutes the unique culture of Japan. Rice culture, the casting of metals, and the potter's wheel in the early days; the assimilation of thousands of Koreans and Chinese into Japanese life; the myriad facets of Buddhist influence; various forms of Chinese intellectualism; the industrial mechanizations of the West; two world wars, with their ensuing upheavals— all these have left a deep impression on Japanese culture. But these alone, without the binding power and strength of national ideals and ideas, could never have produced the peculiarly individual complex that we know today as Japan. Moreover, the intimate topography of the islands, their comparatively gentle climate and the surrounding, protective seas, intervening in the past between all that was foreign, must have been potent elements in forming and maintaining the vigor of the national character.

In earliest times glass was an esteemed treasure, suitable for the most sacred uses. With the production of glass vessels, from the Asuka-Hakukō period on, a new and more utilitarian prospect began to creep in, albeit glass was still rare and reserved for the upper classes. With the coming of Western processes in the Edo period, glass came down to the level of the "common man." Although still admired and used in certain sacred ways, it became primarily utilitarian, or was still sought after as an exotic curiosity.

Today glass is no longer an exotic curiosity. The focus now is on design, form, color, and other qualities appealing to the senses in terms of beauty. Exhibitions of fine glass are frequent. Glass has invaded both shop and home, enjoyed for its cleanliness, delicacy, shimmering reflections, coolness, and visual beauty.

Research Needs for the Future

As the reader already must have sensed, this history of glass in Japan is rife with insufficiencies and suffers from a dearth of definitive data. No glassmaking sites, even in the cities and feudal domains of recent times, have thus far been found, and hence little is known of their tools, equipment, methods and materials. In many instances we lack surviving examples upon which to base any conclusions, and documentation from other sources is also scarce.

The author has been unable to pursue or even approach many avenues of research. The history of glass in China and Korea, and literary sources of many kinds in both countries, need further probing. Trade relations with East Asia await further investigation. Widespread examination of Japanese archives and literature may reveal nuggets of value in filling in gaps. The scientific study of Japanese glass has begun. Notable contributions to an understanding of glass chemistry have been made by Dr. Tei-ichi Asahina, Dr. Masao Mine, Miss Sachiko Oda, Dr. Kazuo Yamasaki, and others. Staff members of the Bunkazai Kenkyū-sho (Institute for Research on Cultural Properties) are also contributors.

Meanwhile, neither archaeology nor other investigative sciences are standing still. More palaeolithic sites are being uncovered. More Jōmon and Yayoi sites are being discovered. Newly found records and artifacts of later times are coming to light, and Japanese scholars seem to be emphasizing less the influences from without and giving greater recognition to developments from within. Undoubtedly the dedication and thoroughness of the Japanese, attested to so often throughout this volume, will eventually lead to the new discoveries that some day will enable someone to fill the gaps that are all too visible in this work.

CHRONOLOGIES

CHRONOLOGY OF JAPANESE GLASS

Jōmon Period (*ca.* 10,000–*ca.* 250 B.C.)
    Possibly Latest Jōmon or Early Yayoi (Pl. 38)

Yayoi Period (*ca.* 250 B.C.–*ca.* 250 A.D.)
    Suku-Okamoto site (Pls. 39, 40; Sup. N. 1–5)
    Yanagabaru site (Pl. 41)
    Maebaru-machi jar burial (Pl. 42, 43)
    Kadota shellmound (Sup. N. 6–10)
    Numa dwelling site (Pl. 44)
    Toro dwelling site (Sup. N. 11)

Tomb Period (*ca.* 250–552 A.D.)
    Equipment, Materials, and Techniques (Pls. 48, 50, 54, 56; Sup. N. 12–19, 22)
    Beads (Pls. 49–62; Sup. N. 20–30)
    Applied Ornament (Pls. 63–66; Sup. N. 31)
    Vessels (Pls. 1, 2, 67; Sup. N. 32, 33)

Asuka-Hakuhō Periods (552–710)
    General (Pl. 69)
    Beads (Pl. 68; Sup. N. 35–40)
    Vessels (Pls. 3, 4, 70–73; Sup. N. 41)
    Cloisonné (Pl. 74)

Nara Period (710–794)
    Documentary Evidence (Pl. 75)
    Equipment, Materials, and Techniques (Pl. 76)
    Beads (Pls. 5, 77)
    Insets (Pl. 78)
    Chindangu (Pls. 79–81)
    Vessels (Pls. 6, 82)

CHINA
Simplified and Approximate

Prehistoric and Protohistoric	before 2205 B.C.
Hsia dynasty	2205–1766 B.C.
Shang dynasty	1766–1122 B.C.
Chou dynasty	1122– 221 B.C.
Ch'in dynasty	221–206 B.C.
Han dynasty	206 B.C.–220 A.D.
Six dynasties	220–589 A.D.
Sui dynasty	589–618 A.D.
T'ang dynasty	618–906 A.D.
Five dynasties	906–960 A.D.
Sung dynasty	960–1279 A.D.
Yüan dynasty	1279–1368 A.D.
Ming dynasty	1368–1644 A.D.
Ch'ing dynasty	1644–1912 A.D.
Period of the Republic	1912– A.D.

KOREA

Prehistoric and Protohistoric	before 108 B.C.
Period of the Four Guns (Chinese), North	108 B.C.–4th century A.D.
Period of the Three Kans, South	(?)–1st century B.C.
Three Kingdoms	1st century B.C.–668 A.D.
Koguryŏ	*ca.* 37 B.C.–668 A.D.
Paekche	*ca.* 18 B.C.–663 A.D.
Silla	*ca.* 57 B.C.–668 A.D.
United Silla	668–935 A.D.
Koryŏ dynasty	918–1392 A.D.
Yi dynasty	1392–1910 A.D.
Period of Japanese Domination	1910–1945 A.D.
Republic of Korea	1945– A.D.

NOTES TO THE PLATES

1. CUT GLASS BOWL FROM THE TOMB OF EMPEROR ANKAN

Important Cultural Property

This tumulus is at Furuichi, Kawachi, Osaka Prefecture. In the Genroku era (1688–1703), a glass vessel was washed out of the sandy soil of the mound. "A servant of Mr. Kamiya, the village master, found the bowl in the earth. It was the property of the Kamiya family for over one hundred years and was donated then to Sairin-ji."[1] The bowl was first illustrated, with a misleading drawing, by Fuji Sadamiki in his *Shūkozu* ("Collected Illustrations of Ancient Things"). A publication of the year 1806, the *Kawachi Meisho Zue* ("Illustrated Survey of Famous Places of Kawachi"), in the section on Sairin-ji, mentions as a treasure of that temple a "*gyoku-wan*" ("bowl of precious substance"), adding that the nature of the *gyoku* was unknown, and that the bowl had "circular motifs linked together over the entire body and bottom like stars." It is further stated that the bowl had come out of the Emperor Ankan's tomb about eighty years before, during flood damage to the tumulus.

Later Sairin-ji was abolished, and the bowl's whereabouts became unknown until about 1950, when a bowl found in a family storehouse and taken to Mr. Mosaku Ishida for an opinion proved to be this very bowl. On the interior bottom of the box there is an inscription in gold lacquer revealing this to have been dedicated to the temple in the third month of 1796. On the exterior bottom, written with a brush, is the information that this had been donated to Sairin-ji by Shohō Genzaemon of the ninth generation of the Kamiya family.[2]

- *Collection*: Tokyo National Museum.
- *Provenance*: Although no one seems to have thought it could have been made in Japan at such an early date as the tumulus, some leaned in the past toward a theory of Chinese origin, but since more and more bowls of this type have come to light in Iran, scholars now think of this example, and a very similar one in the eighth century Shōsō-in (Pl. 105), as having originated in the Amlash area in Iran, near the Caspian Sea. Vessels of comparable size and pattern have come from sites in northwestern Iran, although somewhat similar work has also come from graves in south Russia, and numerous fragments of hollow-ground glass were found by Sir Aurel Stein along the eastward route across Asia.[3] China, during the Han dynasty, had extended her territories into this region along the famous transcontinental Silk Road, and the trek of cultural ideas and treasure from the west moved into the great Chinese empire for some centuries. It is not strange, then, to think that, among all the importations from Iran, such glass bowls also found their way along that route.
- *Date*: Some time prior to the death of Ankan, which would be later than the recorded 535—

perhaps the latter part of the sixth century. If, as now seems most likely, the bowl came from Iran, some interval would have elapsed before it reached Japan.

- *Size*: H. 8.2 cm.; D. at lip, 12.2 cm.; T. of the rounded lip, 0.45–0.525 cm.
- *Color*: Originally probably colorless, now it has a brownish tinge; transparent.
- *Bubbles*: Elongated horizontally and obliquely, some only slightly so, some emphatically so. There are at least two spiraling striae with which the oblique bubbles are associated.
- *Composition*: Soda-lime glass without lead. Weight, 409.89 grams; Sp.Grav.: 2.52; Refr. Ind.: 1.52.[4]
- *Technique*: Free blown; then cut. The exterior bottom consists of a single, irregularly circular hollow a little off center.[5] The design on the exterior wall above this, with only a narrow uncut space left at the rim, is made up of rows of adjoining hollow-ground units. The lowest row has but seven, whereas the four upper rows have eighteen each. Thus, there is a total of eighty cut units. The shape of the bowl is not entirely symmetrical, due to an irregular start in the cutting of the bottom hollow; one "side" bulges out noticeably, which is more conspicuous when the bowl is inverted.

It is of interest to note that the Ankan bowl and the Shōsō-in bowl (Pl. 105) have not only the same number of tiers of these units, but corresponding numbers in each tier, whereas the bowls excavated in western Asia vary in this respect.

The cutting of the hollows is quite irregular, some being circular, some circular with a point at the top, and some being unevenly hexagonal. In the fourth row from the bottom, which is just about at the point of greatest diameter, the cutter apparently did not calculate his space in advance, so that there is an appreciable space between two of the units. The fact that the plain uncut space at the top varies two or three millimeters in height seems due to the off-center position of the bottom hollow and indicates that the cutter worked from the bottom upward.

- *Condition*: Broken and repaired with lacquer, a few gaps also being filled in with lacquer. The interior surface is smooth; the exterior slightly roughened, with a thin film.
- *Remarks*: The various problems of provenance and date will be discussed in greater detail in the paragraphs pertaining to the strikingly similar bowl in the Shōsō-in in Nara (Pl. 105). For further remarks and literary references concerning the history of this bowl, see *Shōsō-in no Garasu*, pages 4–5.

References:
1. *Fujisawa, "Ankan Tennō. . . . ," p. 304.
2. *Ishida, "Shiryō Shōkai—Sairin-ji. . . . ," pp. 52–57. This summarizes documentary evidence regarding this bowl.
3. Sir Aurel Stein, *Serindia*, Oxford, The Archaeological Survey of India, Clarendon Press, 1921; *Innermost Asia*, Oxford, The Archaeological Survey of India, Clarendon Press, 1926; *Archaeological Reconnaissances in Northwestern India and Southern Iran*, London, MacMillan & Co., Ltd., 1937.
4. *Asahina, "Kodai Garasu. . . . ," p. 70.
5. *SnG*, Fig. 5, p. 10, illustrates the probable process, and the authors suggest that the single hollow was off center because the cutting began with grinding away of an imperfectly placed pontil mark.

2. CUT GLASS BOWL FROM NIIZAWA

From one of the Senzuka ("Thousand Tomb") group at Niizawa, Nara Prefecture. Since the author had no opportunity to study this bowl, only the data presented on page 61 can be made available here.

References:
*Mōri, "Garasu-ki wo Shutsudo. . . ."
*Yamasaki, "Garasu," p. 398.

3. CINERARY URN, MIYAJIDAKE SHRINE

National Treasure

From a burial in the precincts of Miyajidake Shrine excavated in 1938; discovered accidentally. An outer case, consisting of two pottery vessels, one inverted over the other, is reminiscent of the old Yayoi jar burials. It was badly broken by the spade that struck it. The inner case, a lidded container of bronze, was filled with clear water when found—that is, there was no cinnabar as in earlier burials. Within it the glass urn, deeply weathered from the water, contained the cremated remains of the deceased.

- *Collection*: Miyajidake Shrine, Miya-tsukasa, Tsuyasaki-machi, Munakata-gun, Fukuoka Prefecture.
- *Provenance*: The thick wall favors a Japanese provenance.
- *Date*: Uncertain; probably 7th century.
- *Size*: Body, H. 9.5 cm.; D. 12.7 cm. Collar, at mouth, H. *ca.* 1.0 cm.; D. 5.3–5.75 cm.; T. 0.6 cm.
- *Color*: Rich dark green; transparent. A color match is difficult because of corrosion, but the clearest shows IH.D.Refl.: Ch 13, 12-4-14; IH.D.Trans.: Ch 13, 12-5-17. By Munsell system, approximately 10GY5/8.[1]
- *Bubbles*: Not discernible; perhaps obscured by weathering.
- *Composition*: Lead glass. Sp. Grav.:5.[1] Refr. Ind.: 1.577.[2] For analysis, see Appendix, Table VII.
- *Technique*: Free blown and cut. The concavity of the bottom is about 0.5 cm. in depth; there is no pontil mark. The straight-walled neck was unevenly cut at the top, leaving a sharp, thin edge (Pl. 3), but otherwise the urn's wall is rather thick.
- *Condition*: Thick encrustations except on the bottom; slightly less on the interior; a few areas are rather clear.

References:
1. *Oda, "Miyajidake-jinja. . . . ," p. 20.
2. *Umehara, "Nihon Kodai no Garasu," p. 28.

4. CINERARY URN OF FUMI NO NEMARO (see Plate 72)
National Treasure

A covered urn of heavy glass. Discovered in 1831 at Yataki, Uchimaki-mura, Uda-gun, Nara Prefecture. When a bronze chest that had been struck by a farmer's hoe was investigated by the village authorities, it was found to contain a bronze jar with lid and an inscribed tablet citing the name of Fumi no Nemaro and the date Keiun 4 (707). The jar contained a green, covered urn, which the report stated "may be of glass; the ashes inside look like lime; there are no bones." The items were subsequently buried in front of Ryūsen-ji, but in 1877 they were disinterred and sent to the Imperial Museum in Tokyo. Monuments were later erected at both the site of the grave and at Ryūsen-ji.[1]

- *Collection*: Tokyo National Museum.
- *Provenance*: Probably Japanese. Except for the inscribed name and date this urn is undocumented and its origin is therefore doubtful. The various circumstances noted below seem to indicate local manufacture. The amateurish, irregular shape and execution are not sufficient to assert a local provenance, but they suggest the work of an inexperienced artisan, whereas vessels that have been attributed to this period in China display more skill in handling. The similarities of technique and metal between this urn and the Miyajidake Shrine urn (Pl. 3) may support a local origin.

Some years ago it was reported[2] that a glass lid similar to those of the Miyajidake Shrine and Fumi no Nemaro burial urns had been discovered in Ōe-mura, Otokuni-gun, Kyoto Prefecture. This was of blue green glass with a thick layer of silvery iridescence and about 3.64 cm. in diameter.

From a superficial comparison with a lidded glass vessel in the Eumofopoulos collection, thought to have a Chinese T'ang provenance,[3] these two examples seem to resemble each other. But details differ. The Chinese for instance, has a "kick" in the bottom; the neck is sharper and flares outward at the rim; and the lid, instead of overhanging the neck, has an extended stopper form that fits down inside the neck.

We must remember that the date of this burial lies six years after the issuance of the Taihō Code, which showed that the Imono-no-tsukasa, the Casting Bureau where glass was made, was definitely in operation by that time. Fumi no Nemaro, according to the inscription, was a descendant of the famous Korean scholar, Wani, who had come to the Japanese court, and Fumi no Nemaro himself had given such distinguished military service to Emperor Tenmu that he was granted posthumously the Senior Fourth Rank. Perhaps with the granting of this rank the court may have felt some responsibility for the burial, in which case the urn might have been made to order or taken from the court treasury.

- *Date*: Before 707.
- *Size*: Irregularities make measurement difficult. H. 17.0 cm.; D. at bottom, 5.7 cm.; T. at rim, 0.35–0.55 cm. The body wall varies in thickness, probably accounting for the variations in color tone.
- *Color*: Varying tones of green; translucent. IH.D.Trans.: difficult, due to corrosion, but close to Ch 12, 11-5-16, a yellowish green. The lid, by IH.D.Refl. differs slightly, being Ch 13, 12-4-14. Visual similarity of the glass of this urn to that of the flat glass specimens at Miyajidake Shrine (Pl. 48) is striking.
- *Bubbles*: Numerous, minute, and circular in shape. At one point on the exterior, just below the neck, there is a small smooth depression (0.35 × 0.25 cm.), which suggests a large broken bubble.
- *Composition*: Lead glass. Sp. Grav.: approximately 4.[4]
- *Technique*: It is difficult to determine the general method of manufacture, partly because of repairs and partly because of thick encrustation. The base is approximately level; there is no concavity and no pontil mark. The body is globular and irregular, so that the urn does not stand straight. There is a rudimentary neck (Pl. 72), indicating work by an artisan who had not yet learned to use a punty, but let the vessel cool and then shaped the mouth rim by cutting, as was the case in the urn at Miyajidake Shrine (Pl. 3). This lip is sharp except for one area, at the thinner side, where it feels smooth to the touch. The thick, heavy glass of the lid, where visible, is rounded, smooth, and glossy on the upper side, as though molded, but the underside is level, with a perpendicular collar, the rim of which shows grooves as of cutting. The *hōshu*-shaped solid knob of the lid, broken at the tip, seems to have been formed separately and added.
- *Condition*: Badly broken during the original excavation; repaired, with some missing parts replaced by wood. Smooth olive green and brown weathering on body and lid. This is now broken away in many places, disclosing the underlying green glass.

References:

1. Suenaga, Masao, *Yamato no Kofun* [Old Tombs of Yamato], Kyoto, 1950, pp. 252ff.
2. See *Umehara, "Nihon Kodai no Garasu," p. 27; also, *Kyōto-fu Shiseki Meishō Tennen Kinenbutsu Chōsa Hōkoku* [Report of the Investigation of Historical Monuments in Kyoto-fu], X, Kyoto, Kyoto City Council, Illus. 12 and p. 28.
3. Illustrated in W. B. Honey, "Early Chinese Glass," *Burlington* Magazine, No. 416, Nov. 1937, p. 217 and Pl. I-B.
4. *Yamasaki, "Garasu," p. 399, Chart I.

5. FRAGMENT OF A *KUMI-OBI* WITH GLASS *KODAMA* AND PEARLS

Important Cultural Property

Kumi-obi are belts of braided threads worn, in court dress, for the suspension of the ceremonial sword. They were slipped through two suspension loops on the sword-sheath and tied about the waist as a girdle. The glass beads, and a lesser number of pearl beads of the same size, are not applied but *woven* in, each bead having been threaded onto a strand during the weaving. The belt was formerly considered to be unique, but a small fragment of a similar belt was discovered in the textile "debris" of the Shōsō-in; it is illustrated in *Shōsō-in no Garasu*, Plates 65 and 66, Plate 66 being an enlarged detail that shows clearly this extraordinary technique.

- *Collection*: Tokyo National Museum. Formerly owned by Hōryū-ji.
- *Date*: 8th century. Because of its likeness to similar weavings (minus the beads) in the Shōsō-in, and because of the quality of the beads, it must have been made in the mid eighth century.

KODAMA:

- *Sizes*: H. 0.2 cm.; D. 0.2–0.3 cm.
- *Colors*: Greens: dark, bright, and light grayed; translucent. IH.D.Refl.: close to Ch 13, 12-3-17, 12-4-13, or 12-5-15.
Amber: both darkish and pale; translucent.
Yellow: translucent. IH.D.Refl.: Ch 9, 8-4-16.

Blue: translucent. IH.D.Refl.: Ch 4, 15-1-15 or 15-3-13.

Violet: translucent. IH.D.Refl.: Ch 12, 23-3-11.

Dark: indeterminate (gray, red, or green?). White: Seems opaque but under magnification proves to be colorless translucent glass crowded with minute "bubbles," which are apparently a multitude of unmelted bits of quartz.[1] This type of bead has also been noted in the Shōsō-in.

- *Bores*: D. *ca*. 0.1 cm.
- *Composition*: Sp. Grav.: 2.5 for the violet and 4.87 for all others;[2] therefore soda glass for the former and lead glass for the latter. This is also borne out by spectrographic analyses.[3]

Condition: Excellent.

References:

1. *Oda, "Nara Jidai. . . . ," p. 23, and Table III, p. 24, where reference is made to the great quantity of silica in opaque white beads in the Shōsō-in as compared to other beads.
2. *Asahina, "Kodai Garasu no Kenkyū," p. 68.
3. For spectrographic analyses see *Oda, "Nara jidai. . . . ," p. 24, Table III.

6. *SHARI-TSUBO* FROM THE PAGODA OF SŪFUKU-JI

National Treasure

From the pagoda ruins of a former temple, Sūfuku-ji, at Mise, Shiga-no-Sato-chō, Ōtsu city, Shiga Prefecture. In 1940 the foundation of the pagoda was discovered about 120 centimeters underground. In the south side of the foundation an arched cavity was found, which had been closed with a stone slab; in it was set out a *shari* installation. In addition to nested chestlike containers of gold, silver, and bronze for the *shari-ki*, fragments of amethyst, glass beads, an unusual iron mirror with a floral design worked in its gilt-bronze back, coinlike items of silver, two copper bells, and a few stone beads were found.

The really jewellike quality of the rich green glass *shari-tsubo* is supplemented by a plain, close-fitting cap of smooth, thin yellow gold. To preclude damage a supporting "seat" for the glass was fashioned in gold in a perforated floral design and attached permanently to the floor of the gold chest. The rectangular gold chest has thin walls and is expertly made, having a removable lid that fits over the rim of the box with a wide bevellike slope downward. An ingenious device in the center of each long side locks the lid in place; a pierced protrusion on the lid slips down between two matching protrusions on the body, and a gold pin then slips through all three. The silver container is similar but, of course, slightly larger. The gilt-bronze chest is also of similar construction, and again slightly larger, but it is more elaborate, having an added open pedestal base.

The fact that glass was used in connection with such delicately refined work is an indication that this medium continued to be regarded as appropriate for the most sacred uses.

- *Collection*: Ōmi Shrine, Ōtsu city, Shiga Prefecture.
- *Date*: 8th century. There has been difference of opinion over the date of this installation, because of historical problems connected with the temple. Sūfuku-ji was established by the Emperor Tenchi in the seventh year of his reign (667), when the capital was temporarily in Shiga, and some have thought that the *shari-ki* dates from that time.[1] The fact that the placing of *shari* beneath pagodas is rare for the Nara period is one element in favor of this opinion. Also, the comparatively low lead content is not typical of Nara period glass. But other scholars hold that the *shari* installation dates from the late Nara period and was associated with the temple, Bonshaku-ji, built on the ruined site of Sūfuku-ji in 785.[2] A strong argument in favor of the Nara date is the character of the gold, silver, and bronze nested reliquaries, which resemble chests, boxes, and other objects with similar locking devices preserved in the Shōsō-in. It is not impossible, of course, that the glass vessel itself was a temple treasure of the earlier date, reinstalled during the Nara period in the enclosing chests. However, when this dedicatory group was designated a national treasure, a Nara period date was assigned to it.
- *Size*: H. *ca*. 3.0 cm.; D. 3.2–3.4 cm.; mouth rim, T. 0.1–0.25 cm.
- *Color*: Rich yellow green; translucent. IH.D.

Refl.: Ch 12, 11-5-15; IH.D.Trans.: Ch 11, 10-2-16 or 10-1-17.

- *Bubbles*: Many small circular ones that spread upward from the bottom in spiral lines and near the mouth become somewhat elongated. Two large round bubbles and one large oblique one protrude a little from the surface, as does a large oval one on the bottom.
- *Composition*: Lead glass with lead oxide content of about 30%, determined by Beta-ray back scattering investigation.[3]
- *Technique*: Free blown. The mouth rim was cut off level, interrupting the bubbles at that point and leaving open pits on the cut surface. The glass wall is very thick for so small a receptacle.
- *Condition*: From the viewpoint of preservation, excellent. However, at some time since its discovery it was broken and repaired.

References:
1. *Umehara, " Ōmi Shiga-no-sato. . . ." and "Sūfuku-ji no Mondai. . . ."
2. *Ishida, "Sūfuku-ji no Tō. . . ."
3. For explanation of the method used see *Asahina, Yamazaki, and Yamasaki, "Investigation of Antique Relics. . . ."

7 (right). *MARUDAMA*

These are evidently the *sashidama* of the *Zōbutsu-sho Sakumotsuchō* (see pages 96).

- *Former Location*: Shōsō-in, Middle Section. No *STM* listing.
- *Date*: 8th century.
- *Sizes*: Various. Sample, H. 0.8 cm.; D. 0.95 cm.
- *Colors*: Greens: pale, bright, dark, and almost black.
  Yellows: pale, medium, and brownish yellow.
  Browns: yellowish brown and dark.
  Blues: pale, medium, and dark.
  Colorless: very few; and "black."
  Some are nearly transparent, some translucent, and others seemingly opaque due to unmelted material.
- *Bores*: Various. Sample, 0.1 cm.
- *Bubbles*: Numerous; seen in the nearly transparent examples.
- *Composition*: The blue beads are of soda-lime glass; all others of lead glass.[1]
- *Technique*: According to the *Zōbutsu-sho Saku-*

motsuchō some may be molded; others are coiled or blown; many retain a black substance in the bores, which by X-ray proved to be lead oxide, indicating coiling.[2]
- *Condition*: Perfect, except for the breakage of many in the "debris."

References:
1. *SnG, p. 56.
2. *Yamasaki, "Garasu," p. 404.

7 (center). *TOMBODAMA*

- *Former Location*: Shōsō-in, Middle Section. No *STM* listing.
- *Date*: 8th century.
- *Sizes*: H. 1.1-1.5 cm.; D. 1.3–1.8 cm.
- *Colors*: A wide range of hues and tones.
  Greens: pale, medium (IH.D.Refl.: Ch 13, 12-4-16), dark, "black," grayed green, olive green thickly flecked with white (particles of unfused quartz).
  Yellows: pale, brownish yellow.
  Browns: yellow brown, medium, reddish brown—all varying in tone; IH.D.Refl.: Ch 2, 1-2-11, 1-4-12, 1-5-12; Ch 13, 24-4-11.
  White: white and pale greenish white; opaque.
  Black: seemingly dead black, and a dark greenish black; opaque.
- *Bores*: D. 0.4–0.5 cm. Some are simple perforations; some have an added transverse bore. The latter were used in rosaries or decorative beadwork where the wire had to pass in more than one direction. This type of bore appears especially in *tombodama* with crossed threads of applied glass on the exterior, and occasionally in examples with single thread decoration.
- *Composition*: Sp. Grav.: 4.5; lead content, *ca.* 70%.[1]
- *Technique*: Coiled, as manifested by the presence of a black coating in the bores and by the applied coiled thread. Transverse bores, when present, must of course have been drilled.
- *Remarks*: A curious feature of several of these beads is that the two contrasting colors have bled into each other at their points of contact; this seems to indicate a higher temperature than usual.

Reference:
1. *Yamasaki, "Namari Garasu to. . . .," p. 20.

7 (left). *NEJIREDAMA*

- *Former Location*: Shōsō-in, Middle Section. No *STM* listing.
- *Date*: 8th century.
- *Sizes*: *SnG (p. 42) refers to 168 *nejiredama* with diameters of about 2.3 cm. for the largest and 1.1 cm. for the smallest.
- *Colors*: Greens: pale, medium, deep bright, grey green, turquoise green.
  Yellows: pale and medium.
  Browns: pale and reddish brown.
    In general, most are almost opaque; others, translucent or, in the flanges, semitransparent.
- *Bubbles*: Numerous.
- *Composition*: Sp. Grav.: 4.5; lead content *ca.* 70%.[1]
- *Technique*: Could these beads have been first molded? Or were they perhaps formed from *marudama* by heating and pincering to form the flanges (Pl. 7, left)?[2] The final step was a twisting motion that distorted the beads into the forms seen in this Plate. It is said that these twists are always S shaped, never Z shaped.[3] Some twistings are slight, some elaborate.
- *Condition*: Covered with a rough film, although the glass was obviously clear from the start. This would seem to be the result of reheating and handling, bringing about a very slight devitrification of the surfaces. *SnG (p. 42) questions whether this could have been a deliberate attempt to suggest the wrinkled surface of seeds.
- *Remarks*: The term *nejiredama* seems to have been used in the Nara period as well as today. However, a tag bearing a Meiji date (1893) calls them *kongō-shu* (*kongō* "gems"). Seeds of six angular parts from a tropical fruit, called *kongō-shi*, were greatly valued for use in rosaries.[4] Perhaps these twisted glass beads were substitutes for the exotic and precious seeds, which may have been difficult to obtain. It has also been suggested that the beads suggest flower forms.

References:
1. *Yamasaki, "Namari Garasu to. . . . ," p. 20.
2. *Kagami, "Kodai Garasu no Kakō," p. 17 and Illus. 18–21, explains the probable process

as one of fusing four colored rods to a hollow tube and cutting the whole into slices, which were then worked to produce the twisted quality. *SnG, p. 42, however, explains the simpler method suggested herein.
3. *SGZC, p. 80.
4. *SnG, p. 42.

8. GLASS FISH-FORM TALLIES

Six of a total of seven tallies, the seventh being fashioned from rock crystal. Rotund forms, with mouths, eyes, and gills incised. In China such incisions were painted with either gold or silver according to the rank of the wearer. Suspension cords of silk were threaded through perforations near the mouth; traces of some still remain.

- *Former Location*: Shōsō-in, Middle Section. *STM* No. 515.
- *Date*: 8th century.

a. *Size*: L. 6.7 cm.; T. 1.1 cm.
- *Color*: Green; translucent. Munsell, 10GY 5/8.
- *Composition*: Lead glass.
- *Technique*: Grinding and incising.
- *Condition*: Excellent.
- *Remarks*: Details outlined in silver paint. Remains of silk cord in bore.

b. *Size*: L. 6.4 cm.; T. 1.25 cm.
- *Color*: Dark green; translucent. Munsell, 7.5GY3/6.
- *Composition*: Lead glass, inferred by weight.
- *Technique*: Grinding and incising.
- *Condition*: Excellent except for a crack across the head.
- *Remarks*: Details outlined in silver paint.

c. *Size*: L. 6.2 cm.; T. 2.4 cm.
- *Color*: Yellow; translucent. Munsell, 10Y 7/10.
- *Composition*: Lead glass, inferred by weight.
- *Technique*: Grinding and incising.
- *Condition*: One tail fin slightly damaged.

d. *Size*: L. 6.3 cm.; T. 1.4 cm.
- *Color*: Blue; translucent. Munsell, 5B4/6.
- *Bubbles*: Numerous, as well as broken-bubble pits on the surface, which is probably true of all, the pits being the result of grinding.
- *Composition*: Soda-lime glass, inferred by weight.

- *Technique*: Grinding and incising.
- *Condition*: Excellent.
  Remarks: Eyes outlined in gold paint; remains of silk in the bore.
e. *Size*: L. 8.2 cm.; T. 1.4 cm.
- *Color*: Green; translucent. Munsell, 10GY 5/8.
- *Composition*: Lead glass, inferred by weight.
- *Technique*: Grinding and incising.
- *Condition*: One tail fin broken.
- *Remarks*: Details outlined in gold paint; has silk cord attached.
f. *Size*: L. 7.2 cm.; T. 1.3 cm.
- *Color*: Dark green; translucent. Munsell, 7.5GY3/6.
- *Composition*: Lead glass, inferred by weight.
- *Technique*: Grinding and incising.
- *Condition*: One tail fin broken.
- *Remarks*: Incised eyes and gills outlined in gold paint; has silk cord attached.
Reference:
SnG, pp. v, 26–28. Catalogue, Shōsō-in Exhibition, Nara National Museum, 1959, Item 56.

9. WHITE GLASS EWER (see Plate 103)

The body of the ewer is like a greatly enlarged *tsuyudama*, the "dewdrop" jewel, with a coil base.

- *Former Location*: Shōsō-in, Middle Section. STM No. 305.
- *Provenance*: When Dr. M.T. Mostafavi, former Director of the Iranian National Museum in Tehran, accompanied His Imperial Majesty, the Shah of Iran, to Japan in 1958, he was said to have chosen eight articles in the Shōsō-in as being definitely Iranian, in his opinion. These were four textiles, three metal objects, and this glass ewer.[1] As basis for his opinion of the ewer he cited a smaller glass ewer found in Nehawend, western Iran, discovered about twenty years before (Pl. 104). Dr. Mostafavi is also quoted as saying that, judging from photographs, the other glass vessels in the Shōsō-in must also be of Iranian origin.[2]

The applied leaf-shaped, or so-called bird beak, mouth of this piece suggests, rather, a development from the Greek pottery oenochoe ewers, and adds grace; this is similar to the mouth of the Iranian ewer of Plate 104, but is lighter and more graceful. The handle of the Shōsō-in ewer is also lighter and seems much more sophisticated and skillful than the Iranian example. The forthright slant of the handle and the strong support given where the applied glass of the handle is coiled up closely beneath the mouth rim are likewise different. This hugging of the neck and mouth rim is reminiscent of some so-called Roman glass of the early centuries of the Christian Era and is not like that of the Nehawend ewer, nor is it typical of ewers of the Islamic period.[3] In the Islamic examples, handles usually take on more of the arched-curve proportions. The Shōsō-in handle is reminiscent of pre-Islamic Iranian examples dating from the second to the seventh and eighth centuries, such as exist in The Corning Museum of Glass. The angle is somewhat suggestive, however, of a well-known dragon-handled Chinese ceramic ewer of the T'ang dynasty in the collection of Mr. Moritatsu Hosokawa of Tokyo.

It is said that in the official *Kenmotsuchō* of the Shōsō-in this ewer is listed as a *kobin*, the character for which means "foreign bottle," a term used at the time in China to designate a vessel of this type from Western Asia, presumably from Iran.

- *Date*: Uncertain. The authors of *Shōsō-in no Garasu* (p. 15), among others, infer an Iranian origin during the Sassanian period.
- *Size*: H. 27.0 cm.; greatest D. 14.0 cm.; for further detail see *SnG*, Figure 7.
- *Color*: Colorless in effect, but with a slightly greenish tinge at points where the glass is thicker, as at the handle joinings; transparent. The committee investigating materials in the Shōsō-in, who presumably studied this in strong daylight, classified the color as matching IH. D. Ch. 9, 8–4–18 (olive yellow). In *SnG* it is given as Munsell 7.5GY7/4.[4]
- *Bubbles*: Numerous, and of many shapes and directions; in the handle are extremely long drawn-out ones, attenuated at the ends. There are several stones in the glass. Vague spiraling striae swirl upward from left to right, with a very slight suggestion of blue near the top.

- *Composition*: On the basis of the Beta-ray back scattering, the ewer is assumed to be of soda-lime glass. Under ultraviolet the ewer is said to give forth a yellow fluorescence.
- *Technique*: Free blown, with mouth, handle, and foot-rim shaped separately and applied. There is no "kick" in the interior bottom of the ewer, which is flat. On the exterior bottom the pontil mark remains rough.[5]

In contrast to the general refined aspect of the ewer, some of the working details seem inept. For example, the mouth, as seen from above (Pl. 103) is uneven and lacks a uniform thickness in the rim. Handsome as is the handle, it was awkwardly applied, slanting off to one side, out of line (Pl. 103). On the bottom, the pontil mark is not centered, and the foot-rim curve and joining are not skillfully done.

- *Condition*: Excellent.
- *Remarks*: There are in Japan and elsewhere a number of ewers with some of the characteristics of this one. They are of metal, lacquer, and ceramic. Some are supported by a circular pedestal-type foot; some have a mouth, and often a cover, simulating a bird or dragon head. Most have curved handles; none seems to have quite the shape, the harmony of proportion, or the elegant handle, that characterize this ewer.[6]

References:

1. *Asahi Evening News*, Tokyo, June 10, 1958.
2. *Museum*, No. 88, July 1958, p. 13.
3. But the same sort of close, upholding support occurs in a metal ewer with dragon-head mouth in the Tokyo National Museum formerly owned by Hōryū-ji. Suggestive of the straightness of the Shōsō-in handle are three handles illustrated by Anton Kisa, *Die Antiken Glaeser der Frau Maria von Rath*, Bonn, 1899, Pl. XXXI, 12–14.
4. *SnG, pp. iii, 13.
5. *ECTS, p. 24.
6. For illustration of some of these see *SnG, pp. 12–13, Figs. 6, 8–11. It was once reported that there was discovered in Japan in the early Edo period a glass "bottle with crane neck" similar to the Shōsō-in ewer. According to an inscription on its box, it was an item in a sale held by the Maeda family of Kaga Province. "Because it was of glass no one at that time considered it to be an antique of the

Tempyō era;" see Akahori, Matajirō, "Machin Hatsukō" [Fragrance from Buried Dust], *Nara*, No. 12, 1929, Pt. 3, p. 85.

10. TWELVE-LOBED GREEN BOWL (see Plate 107)

A shallow oval dish of heavy glass decorated on the exterior with a cut design. The shape is an intricate twelve-lobed form, with pronounced rounded areas and deep grooves on the exterior. This exterior is carved with a design that has been variously interpreted. Dr. Mayori Kurokawa, a member of the commission to "arrange" the Shōsō-in collections in the Meiji era and who therefore presumably had opportunity to inspect the bowl closely, is said to have described the motif carved at each side, near the rim, as a rabbit.[1] Later, however, it was considered to represent a fish among water grasses; this was the interpretation in the official catalog, *Tōyei Shukō*, of 1908 and in the *Shōsō-in Gyobutsu Mokuroku*, which was begun in 1928. In recent years, seen under good lighting conditions, it has been recognized as an animal form, probably a rabbit. The mouth and prominent eyes do suggest a fish motif, perhaps fortuitously, and the adjacent foliage suggests water grasses, but what seem to be haunches, long ears, and a short tail are suggestive of the animal kingdom. The legs are folded close under the body, but it is difficult to know whether the animal is hopping or resting; it is not shown running at great speed, as is the case with all other rabbit forms depicted on various Shōsō-in treasures, where the position of the hare is that of the conventional so-called "flying gallop" of Asian art, in which all four feet are off the ground, extended fore and aft and more or less parallel to the earth. The only other example known to the author, of this "resting rabbit" motif is a small carving (approximately 1.5 cm. high and 2.52 cm. long) said to have come from a Chinese tomb of the Han dynasty at Lo-Lang in North Korea.[2]

The quality of the cutting varies. The small leaf sprays are well executed, and quite naturally; but the angular lines of what is called a tulip design, in the center, are awkward and faulty in alignment. They suggest lack of experience on the part of a cutter trying to adjust a design to a curved surface. Unless the bowl is inverted, these deficiencies are, of course, not visible. The surface is not highly polished.

- *Former Location*: Shōsō-in, Middle Section. *STM* No. 398.
- *Provenance*: Dr. Nakao, in 1931, considered it to have been made in Japan.[3] *SnG*, p. 20, suggests a possible Chinese Han dynasty date; *Okada, in *Garasu* (p. 212), thinks it probably Chinese of the T'ang dynasty.
- *Date*: 8th century.
- *Size*: H. 5.0 cm.; L. 22.5 cm.; W. 10.7 cm.
- *Color*: A bright deep green ("malachite green"); translucent, nearly transparent. Munsell, 7.5G4/8.
- *Bubbles*: Elongated lengthwise, with greatest diameter of 1.0 cm. and a smallest diameter of 0.4 cm. Numerous broken-bubble pits on the surface from polishing.
- *Composition*: On the basis of the Beta-ray back scattering dispersion rate, this is inferred to be lead glass of 55% lead oxide content, colored by copper.[4]
- *Technique*: Because of the nonuniform direction of the bubbles, it is judged to have been mold cast and later cut. Mr. Okada thinks the cutting method was probably that in use in China for centuries by lapidaries, employing a drill with a tiny wheel at the end.[5] In *SnG* (pp. iv and 18) mention is made of a red powder existing in the pits on the surface, which it is suggested may be garnet dust, indicating that garnets were used for polishing. There are garnets in the Shōsō-in.
- *Condition*: Excellent.
- *Remarks*: Among lobed vessels a twelve-lobed one is rare; most have only eight or ten lobes. There is one in silver with twelve lobes and an elaborate ornamentation of human figures, animals, and floral scrolls now in the Czartoryski Museum, Krakow, Poland.[6] There are, in various collections, a number of lobed vessels similar to this in form but raised on a low, and lobed, base rim. There are three in the Shōsō-in of gilt-bronze, but of eight lobes only and not decorated. In China and Korea, low, oval

cups with "ears" at the sides suggest a prototype of this form; they were known in lacquer from the Han dynasty or earlier, and there are a number of lobed silver-gilt examples from the T'ang dynasty, as well as excavated gilt-bronze cups.

In the Museum of Fine Arts, Boston, there is a low eight-lobed bowl of translucent pale green glass, called Chinese. It has many bubbles, singly and in clusters. It is smaller than the Shōsō-in dish, and the somewhat irregular shaping of the lobes contrasts sharply with the symmetry of the Shōsō-in example. Since only this and the Shōsō-in example seem to be known in glass, it might be conjectured that the Shōsō-in bowl is also Chinese. But the Chinese were so skillful from long experience in cutting designs on jade and other hard materials that it is difficult to imagine a Chinese cutter slipping up so badly in the spacing of the "tulip" design. The craftsman had evidently not had long experience in the difficult process of maintaining a symmetrical semirealistic design on a hard, segmented, curved surface. The lobed shape itself is very well handled, which, if one were to assume a possible Chinese or Japanese source, would not be surprising considering the skilled experience of artisans in both countries in the production and use of molds for casting.

Dr. Gallois, after saying that this dish could be Chinese of the T'ang dynasty, added that "chance of this piece being also Egyptian or Syrian must be reckoned with."[7] There has also been talk of porcelain lobed dishes.[8] Dr. Yoshito Harada, who has discussed various aspects of this problem, champions an Oriental rather then Western "feeling" in this Shōsō-in bowl and suggests a T'ang date.[9] A possible Chinese source is suggested by the 55% lead content, which is considerably less than the 70% of the Nara period glass.

The green glass metal of this Shōsō-in bowl looks very much like that of the green flat glass slab of Miyajidake Shrine (Pl. 48) and the glass objects there, as well as the three beads from Kumamoto (Sup. N. 26), the *magatama* from Nishisue (Pl. 49), the *magatama* from Fukui

Prefecture (Sup. N. 20) and the *shari-tsubo* from Sūfuku-ji (Pl. 6). Although this approximate color is probably common in many regions, and although the lead content is not uniform in all, it would nevertheless perhaps be of value if this bowl and the green glass raw materials of the Shōsō-in could somehow be brought together with all those other specimens of similar glass from the Tomb period onward, for close comparison and thorough scientific investigation.

References:

1. *Kurokawa, *Kurokawa Mayori Zenshū*, pp. 376–381.
2. *Chōsen Kōko Zuroku, I—Shirakami Hasayoshi Shi Kanshū Kōkohin Zuroku* [Illustrated Record of Korean Archaeology, I—Illustrated Record of Archaeological Items in the Collection of Mr. Hisayoshi Shirakami], *Chōsen Kōkogaku Kaikan*, Pl. IX, 2.
3. *Nakao, *Shōsō-in Gokō. . . .*, p. 28; based on his opinion that it was green lead glass similar to other items in the Shōsō-in.
4. *SnG*, pp. iii, 17, 18.
5. *Okada, "Shōsō-in Garasu-ki no Gihō," p. 22.
6. Harada, Yoshito, "The Interchange of Eastern and Western Cultures as Evidenced in the Shōsō-in Treasures," *Memoirs of the Research Department of the Tōyō Bunko*, No. XI, 1939, p. 57.
7. Dr. H. G. Gallois, "About T'ang and Ta Ts'in," *Transactions of the Oriental Ceramic Society*, London, 1935–1936, p. 49.
8. As, for instance, in William Willetts, *Chinese Art*. Penguin Books, Harmondsworth, Middlesex, 1958, II, pp. 459–463.
9. *Harada, Yoshito, "Shōsō-in Garasu wo Megutte," p. 5.

11. DARK BLUE CUP

A glass cup supported, goblet fashion, on a silver pedestal. Smooth on the interior but decorated on the exterior with twenty-one applied coils of the same glass, eight coils in each of the two upper tiers and six in the narrower lower tier where the contour curves in toward the base. The rounded bottom of the cup rests in a perforated calyxlike form of gilded silver, whose six points project upward into the intervals between the six lower coils. The calyx is a "restoration" of the Meiji era; in 1905 another gilded silver calyx, said to have

been the original, was found; it had an open "honeysuckle" motif derived from Chinese Buddhist art. The flat circular base of the foot is incised with an intricate Chinese design of two dragon forms; when it was added to the cup is unknown.

- *Former Location*: Shōsō-in, Middle Section. STM No. 394.
- *Provenance*: Probably Korean.[1]
- *Date*: Late 7th or early 8th century.
- *Size*: Overall H. 10.8–11.2 cm. Cup, H. 8.0 cm.; D. at lip, 8.6 cm.; T. at lip, 0.3–0.4 cm.; D. of coil, 1.7–1.85 cm.; W. of the coiled thread, 0.3 cm.[2]
- *Color*: Dark blue; transparent. IH. D.: Ch 6, 17-4-12.[3] Munsell, 5PB3/6.839 The color quality derives from a somewhat impure cobalt ore, so it is not such a strong bright blue as the glass of the spittoon, Plate 16; iron and manganese impurities are mentioned.[4]
- *Bubbles*: Minute bubbles, some of which seem to follow in curving lines; a few, slightly oval, both transverse and longitudinal, especially near the rim, where they are horizontally elongated.
- *Composition*: Inferred, by calculation of Beta-ray back scattering, to be soda-lime glass, with no lead content.
- *Technique*: Mold blown, "as indicated by small uneven traces on the surface." The decoration consists of short sections of glass rods that were heated and bent to form circles, which were then applied, by heat, to the cup's body; the incompletely fused ends are clearly visible at the bases of the coils.

   Lacquer was used as an adhesive to join the two units, and a small rivet at the interior body of the cup attaches it firmly to the base.
- *Condition*: Excellent.
- *Remarks*: The shape of this cup suggests to the Westerner a chalice form; and yet this form was known in East Asia long before the Nara period. Of course, it is a natural shape and therefore common in many areas. The silver pedestal base, with its incised dragon design, is decidedly Chinese, whatever the origin of the cup itself.

   Relevant to this piece is a similar glass cup

(Pl. 109) with a bit of crude clay to steady it (instead of a metal base), which was discovered in 1959 during repair to the brick pagoda of Songyim-sa temple in the Tsilkok district of North Kyongsang Province in South Korea, not far from the provincial capital, Taegu.[5] That cup was the focal point of a *shari* installation judged to date from the late seventh century. The Korean cup is very like the cup of the Shōsō-in, but the glass, instead of being dark blue, is a transparent yellowish green (IH.D. Refl.: Ch 12, 11-4-15 or 5-16). Since the cup fits closely in the shrine and cannot be taken out, this color match may not be entirely accurate. Likewise, all measurements could not be taken. The diameter at the lip is 8.1 cm. The cup is well formed and a very handsome work. The exterior decoration consists of twelve applied coils of the same green glass, arranged in three tiers of four coils each; the coils of the center tier are spaced between those of the upper and lower tiers. On the average, the overall diameter of the coils is about 1.4 cm., slightly smaller than those of the Shōsō-in cup. In thickness, the glass coils are approximately the same. The ends of a few, like those in the Shōsō-in, meet neatly but are not fused completely, while the ends of others are fused to the point of showing an excrescence at the point of juncture. These end joinings occur at the right sides of the coils.

(The author would like to take this opportunity to correct a slight misunderstanding in *SnG* [p. 16] regarding her calculation of a coil of glass in Korea. That coil was *not* a coil "which had fallen from" the Korean cup, but an isolated, although identical, coil found in the National Museum of Korea in Seoul.

She would also like here to admit that at least several of her specific gravity calculations made in Seoul and published by Dr. Kim [see Reference 5] are not to be relied upon, due, it seems, to an unnoticed stirring of the air in her place of work, which evidently upset the delicate balance of the scales and produced an incredibly high lead content for some of the specimens.)

A startling difference is the unique embel-lishment added within each coil of the Korean cup. In the center of each coil a rounded rectangular set of semitransparent honey-colored glass was affixed with adhesive; in each set tiny bubbles of various sizes cluster together in the center of the upper face. Surrounding each glass set is a circlet of what may be small pearls, now deteriorated.

When the shrine was taken from the stone chest of the *shari* installation into the air these additions fell off; they had been attached with a reddish brown substance. All were replaced before photographing.

Among Korean excavated relics are several glass items that give clues to the source of production for this Korean cup. These are:

a. A coiled ring of glass identical to the coils on the Songyim-sa cup. Site of excavation unknown.
- *Collection*: National Museum, Seoul.
- *Provenance*: Korea.
- *Date*: Probably late 7th century.
- *Size*: D. 1.4 cm.; W. of coiled thread, 0.2–0.3 cm.
- *Color*: Yellow green; transparent. IH.D. Refl.: Ch 12, 11-5-15.
- *Bubbles*: Minute and not numerous; a few slightly oval, both transverse and longitudinal.
- *Technique*: Curving a section of softened glass rod and joining the ends.
- *Condition*: Excellent.
b. Fragment of a glass vessel, with applied coil of the same glass. From a chest in the stone pagoda of Punhwang-sa temple, Kyŏngju. Associated with other glass fragments, glass beads, and other small items.
- *Collection*: National Museum, Seoul.
- *Provenance*: Seemingly Korean.
- *Date*: Installed in 634.
- *Size*: Coil D., 1.5 cm.
- *Color*: Yellow green; transparent. IH.D. Refl.: Ch 12, 11-5-16 or 17.
- *Technique*: Coil formed by curving a softened glass rod, joining the ends and fusing to the glass body.
- *Condition*: Good.
c. A coiled ring of glass, from Kyŏngju.

- *Collection*: National Museum, Seoul.
- *Provenance*: Korean.
- *Date*: 7th century.
- *Size*: D. 1.3 cm. Coil, W. 0.25–0.3 cm.
- *Color*: Glossy opaque black, but by transmitted light shows translucent brown.
- *Technique*: Curving a softened glass rod and joining the ends; slight widening of the coil at point of joining.

The presence of such items, perhaps all from Kyŏngju, the old Silla capital, suggests the manufacture of coiled glass rings in southern Korea. The Songyim-sa cup and the fragment from Punhwang-sa narrow the date to the seventh century. Moreover, the coincidental existence of the Songyim-sa cup, the fact that its two accompanying small bottles are of identical glass, the isolated coil identical to the cup's coils and the fragment of another vessel of the same color with an applied coil practically the same as those of the cup seem to add up to evidence of local manufacture for all.

Additional factors support a theory of local production for the Songyim-sa cup. The thousands of fine glass beads found in Korean tombs, while not closely related to the production of glass vessels, indicate a knowledge of glass and competence in producing the glass metal; various broken-off metal rods occasionally found in bead bores bespeak local manufacture. The prolific use of glass insets in gold jewelry and other objects; the fragments of yellow green glass; and "thousands" of glass beads found in the *shari* installation of Hwangbok-sa in Kyŏngju, installed in 692;[6] a *shari-yōki* fragment of translucent green glass from Asan, South Chung-chong Province, in the National Museum in Seoul (No. 98.94); and a piece of glass in the National Museum in Kyŏngju that seems to be glassmaking material—all point to a lively activity in Kyŏngju, and perhaps elsewhere, in the manufacture and use of glass.

In addition, a number of glass cups with applied colored glass threads, suggesting Western types, have been excavated from Korean tombs (among them, Pls. 111 and 112).[7] Not all scholars consider them to be of Western origin; the Japanese seem to lean to a Chinese origin. There are some half dozen or more of the type of Plate 111 from Kyŏngju. The discovery of so many in one small area of South Korea suggests domestic production. There should be little doubt that the Songyim-sa cup was a domestic product. Hence, why should not the Shōsō-in cup also be either: (1) an imported gift from Korea; or (2) a cup made by a Korean craftsman at the Imono-no-tsukasa in Nara?

References:

1. *Teshigawara, Kunimitsu, and Okada, *Garasu*, p. 212, Mr. Okada considers both this and the similar cup from Korea as probably Chinese of the T'ang dynasty.
2. Shōsō-in records; courtesy of Mr. Junsei Matsushima.
3. *SGZC*, p. 76.
4. *SnG*, pp. iii, 16, 57.
5. Chewon Kim, "Treasures from the Songyim-sa Temple in Southern Korea," *Artibus Asiae*, XXII, Nos. 1/2, July 1959–June 1960, pp. 95–112.
6. Chewon Kim, "The Stone Pagoda of Koo Huang Li in South Korea," *Artibus Asiae*, XIII, Nos. 1/2, 1950, pp. 25–38. Dr. Kim prefers the name Koo Huang Li (derived from the village name) since proof is lacking that the temple of this pagoda was called Hwangbok-sa.
7. Several vessels of the same threaded type are authenticated as Chinese, from a tomb of the Sō family of North Wei.

12. TWELVE-LOBED CLOISONNÉ MIRROR (see Plate 113)

A silver mirror with cloisonné-like back of glass, gold and gold-plated silver, elaborately designed in a conventionalized floral pattern of a type popular in T'ang China. Although this is not true cloisonné in the modern technical sense, it is called so for lack of any other term and because the effect is that of cloisonné.

The complex character of the mirror makes a concise description difficult. The body, its reflecting surface, is of silver beautifully shaped with a simple twelve-lobed perimeter. This face is not usually seen, since it is always the decorated back that is displayed. The silver base is 0.8 cm. thick and is surmounted, toward the "back," first by a rim of gold about 0.2 cm. thick and then by the various elements of the decorative design on the reverse face of the mirror.

A description of the elements of the decoration on the back of the mirror begins in the center with the silver knob through which a silken cord or bit of silk cloth was threaded as a handgrasp. This knob is about 3.0 cm. in its greatest diameter. The cord aperture at its base is gilded at the two openings. The body of the knob underlying the sepals of the design is thinly covered with a transparent brilliant green glass. The "cloisons," as is true throughout, are barely 0.05 cm. in thickness and are of gilded silver. The translucent, light golden brown glass shows glints of much brighter yellow.

The areas of medium brown glass are opaque, and the brilliant green glass is transparent. The very dark green glass is opaque. The points of the six large leaflike forms coincide with six of the twelve points of the silver base. The tips of six other large leaflike forms coincide with the remaining six tips of the silver base. Filling in the intervening spaces between all twelve tips, and conforming to the periphery of the silver mirror, are twelve triangular sections of pure gold about 0.05 cm. thick, with an allover "dewdrop" design in relief, adding another 0.05 cm. The "dewdrops," or nipples, were formed by punching them up from the back, as is easily seen at the exposed edges. These twelve gold sections were cut to fit from a larger plate, as may also be noted at the exposed edges, where some of the "dewdrops" were bisected in the cutting.

The resulting ensemble, when viewed outside the case and in proper daylight, is one of great beauty in its seminaturalistic ordered form and in the striking contrasts of its colors and materials. This is true not only of the complex reverse face just described but also in the simple profile view (Pl. 113), where the thick band of the silver body is topped by the narrow band of the gold rim, and these in turn by the whole decorated top seen in profile as an alternating series of nippled gold areas and the rising "cloisons" of the tips of the large leaf forms. Plate 113 also shows the downward slope of the leaf forms, the depression around the knob, and the rising bud form in the very center.

- *Former Location*: Shōsō-in, South Section. *STM* No. 702.
- *Provenance*: Japanese.

Theories have been advanced assigning the mirror to a foreign provenance, ranging from Byzantium and Iran to China of both the T'ang and Yüan dynasties,[1] and Japan from the eighth to the seventeenth century "or later."[2] This author, for combined technical and stylistic reasons outlined in a previous article,[3] feels strongly that it was produced in eighth century Nara rather than in any foreign country or in later times. The authors of *Shōsō-in no Garasu (p. 26), after suggesting certain stylistic resemblance to Chinese T'ang designs, add: "However, from the point of view of glass coloration and of substance, there exists doubt as to whether, together with such objects as the small linear measures [Pl. 100] and the jiku-tan [Pls. 101, 102], this was not likewise of Japanese manufacture."

- *Date*: 8th century.

The time when this mirror was placed in the Shōsō-in is not known, but in modern times, at least, it has been kept in the South Section, and it is not impossible that it was included among the contents of the two treasure-houses of the Kensaku-in of Tōdai-ji when they were housed in the South Section after the typhoon of 950 had damaged the Kensaku-in storehouses. The inventory of this transfer is lost, and a new inventory made in 1117 (which does not include this mirror) is said to be incomplete, so there is no corroborating evidence of either the presence or absence of this mirror in the South Section in 950 or 1117. This, however, is not essential in regard to the date of manufacture, since the mirror might have been treasured at Tōdai-ji (if it came from there) for a considerable period before placement in the Shōsō-in. A great many of the ritual utensils in the South Section, for instance, which were presumably there in 950, are clearly eighth century types, and some are regarded as used in the Eye Opening Ceremony for the Great Buddha in 752. There is also, in the North Section, one documented treasure, the "Red Lacquer Cabinet" (STM No. 46), which the Kenmotsuchō specifically describes as having been bequeathed down through a succession of sovereigns. In the same manner the mirror could have been preserved for some time.

It is not beyond possibility that the mirror, in modern times located in the South Section, could have been in one of the imperially sealed sections of the Shōsō-in in ancient times. There are known instances of transfers from one section to another; for example, the glassmaking record (Pl. 75) is marked in ink "South Section" but was kept in the Middle Section. Also, from time to time, on occasions of building repair, items in one section were temporarily sealed in another. As one instance, in 1193 the contents of both imperially sealed sections were moved to the South Section, where they remained for nearly eight months; again, in 1230 the contents of the North and South Sections were moved for a time into the Middle Section.[4] One assumes that great care would have been taken on such occasions, but there could always be a possibility of some error. However, the important consideration lies in the activities of the bureau appointed in the Meiji era, which have been outlined in the discussion on page 100.

In the North Section there are eighteen mirrors, which, with one exception, are documented in the original Kenmotsucho of 756.[5] Since all the other thirty-seven mirrors of the Shōsō-in (all undocumented, and including this cloisonné-backed mirror) were displayed together in the south wall case on the upper floor of the South Section, it seems not unlikely that they were all assembled there during the "arrangement in order" of the Meiji era, as a matter of interest and homogeneous classification. This theory is upheld by the placement of the six glass vessels of the Shōsō-in in one case, as discussed under Plate 16, Remarks.

The inference, it seems, can only be that, in the Meiji era, mirrors (except for documented examples in the North Section), as well as glass vessels, were assembled, like with like, in one place regardless of their original positions in the Shōsō-in or their dates of entry. This would mean that the modern position of the mirror, like that of the glass vessels, proves nothing either as to the date of placement in the treasury or the date of manufacture.

- Size: Mirror: H. overall, in profile, 1.3–1.4 cm.; D. from tip to tip, 18.5 cm. Further measurements are given in the descriptive paragraphs below.
- Glass colors:

  1. Brilliant green; transparent. Munsell, 10GY 4/8.[6]
  *SnG (pp. 25, 57) attributes this to copper oxide. This glass is so permeated with the the bright tints gleaming through from the silver beneath that it cannot be matched precisely on the IH color chart.

  2. Dark green; nearly opaque. Munsell, 7.5GY2/2.[6]
  This is so close to black that it cannot be matched precisely on the IH color chart. *SnG (pp. 25,57) attributes this to copper oxide; the suggestion is also made that the opaque portions were probably the result of incomplete melting.

  3. Medium brown; opaque. This easily corresponds to IH. D. Refl.: Ch 5, 4-2-14, termed a "gray-brown." Munsell, 10YB3/6.[6]
  *SnG (pp. 25, 57) attributes this to a probable low iron content.

- Bubbles: In general not conspicuous. There are several open pits in the opaque glass; and on the knob where some glass is broken off, numerous minute pits are visible with a magnifying glass.
- Composition: If one may assume that the stable, close adhesion of the glass to the metal predicates the presence of lead, a necessary element in glass for adhesion to a metal surface, then this is lead glass; the authors of *SnG so list it (p. 57). If an eighth century product of Nara, then the lead content might be expected to be around 70%, possibly one reason for the excellent preservation of the mirror.

A side by side comparison of the glasses of the mirror with the lumps of unworked glass preserved in the Shōsō-in proved illuminating. The bright green glass of the mirror and certain green lumps, in their thinner sections, seemed to be the same. The very dark green glass of the mirror and the black-looking lumps with green tones, allowing for the much greater thickness of the latter, *may* be the same; and the translucent portions of the brown glass of the mirror are very like some of the brown lumps. These comparisons also contributed to the author's overall feeling that this mirror was fabricated in Nara in the eighth century. She also feels sure that if many of the small items of glass and glass beads and insets that are preserved in the Shōsō-in could be compared, side by side, with the glasses of this mirror, other analogies would be found. The authors of *SnG (p. 25) say that the green coloration is close to that of a green glass linear measure (Pl. 100), green *jiku-tan* (Pls. 101, 102), and various green beads.

- *Technique*: Here, again, analysis is a complex task—one must take the mirror apart, mentally, to understand how it was put together. One would naturally presuppose that the silver mirror body had been cast, but it is said that investigation has shown this not to be so, at least for the finishing stages. It is possible that it was first cast or forged and then turned on a lathe or wheel (a technique in which the Japanese were masters at this time), for there are wheel marks seen beneath the knob aperture, and the body itself is slightly concave toward the knob (Pl. 113). There is also a protruberent circular section in the center just under the silver knob. How the knob was formed is uncertain, for there is no visible evidence of any means of attachment. Dr. Toshihiko Gotō (who has set forth these details) thought it might have been soldered.[7]

To the upper surface of this plain silver mirror body, probably with the silver knob already a part of it, there was then affixed (as with the knob, there is no visible adhesive) a narrow peripheral rim of gold about 0.2 cm. thick. This rim, rising above the silver body like a low curb, formed a shallow hollow with the knob rising from the center. This hollow was coated with a reddish brown adhesive of lacquer admixed with something resembling a coarsely powdered grain; the appearance of this adhesive, where seen, is slightly reddish, rough, and grainy.[8] Into this bed of lacquer were pressed the finished "cloisonné" parts—the eighteen leaflike units—and the twelve sections of gold. As these were pressed down, the displaced fresh lacquer oozed up around the edges, and can be easily recognized along the bases of all these units, except only in the profile view, where the gold rim hides it.

A seemingly unique technique is purported to have been employed in preparing the decorative units—that is, the eighteen leaf forms and the twelve gold sections—which were set into the lacquer bed. This has been described in detail by Dr. Toshihiko Gotō and Mr. Hironobu Aida as leaf shapes cut from sheet silver, whose edges were then bent up to form shallow pans, with the walls (0.05 cm. thick) forming the "cloisons". The cloisons forming the inner coils of the leaf motif, being of the same width as the outer ones, would seem to be simply strips of silver cut in narrow fillets from the same sheet silver from which the pans were cut; stood on edge and affixed in place, they would then have formed true cloisons. There is no assurance as to the method of attaching these silver cloisons to the beds of the silver pans, but it might be assumed that lacquer could well have been the medium, or possibly solder, or perhaps a simple temporary vegetable adhesive was used, which would have served until the glass had hardened. Since there has been no loosening of any parts, there is no place where this can be determined by inspection.

The silver pans, with their added silver cloisons, must first have been filled with the molten colored glasses (or, less likely, with small fragments of glass, or powder?), which were then fused by heating, and cooled, although this might have resulted in some melting of the silver. Both the glass-filled pans and the triangular gold units were subsequently placed on the freshly prepared bed of the lacquer mixture, pressed down, and thus became secure parts of the mirror back as the lacquer dried and hardened. This process, so far as the author is aware, is entirely different from any Western technique, so that it alone, and especially because of the lacquer, would indicate an East Asiatic provenance.

All silver cloisons are gilded on their upper surfaces, and the lines of the design consequently stand out in gold. Only in some areas near the up-curving leaf tips has this gold worn off slightly, revealing the silver ground beneath.

Next, how were the individual silver units of the design filled with glass? In true cloisonné, the ground is usually of one piece, with metal wires, or thin bands, applied to form the compartment walls of the design. These compartments are then filled with pulverized enamels, fired, and as many times as necessary refilled and refired until the compartments are entirely filled, or slightly overfilled. Later all are ground down to the level surface and polished. There is no evidence whatever to suggest that the use of glass powder was practiced this early in East Asia, whereas there is evidence—in the small ornament of Plate 74 and in one or two Korean ear pendants—that melting glass was sometimes flowed in to fill a compartment.

The glass of this mirror does not fill the compartments, and apparently no attempt was made to add to the shrunken glass after it contracted in cooling. The glass clings to the cloison walls, but away from the walls it slopes down into slight concavity. The cloisons rise above even the highest point of the glass, thus standing out in high relief in the design.

The small ornament from the Kegoshi Tomb has been presented (Pl. 74). Although of the seventh century, it is strikingly like this mirror in the width of the cloisons and in their gilding. In that ornament the outer background of opaque (deteriorated?) creamy white glass is flat and somewhat sandy; but in the central rosette motif, where the filling is a translucent reddish brown, the surfaces of the petals are rounded over as though a little melted glass from one end of a heated glass rod (as in the beadmaking process) had been allowed to flow into each small petal compartment but had cooled too quickly to settle into a flat surface and, by surface tension, remained slightly rounded. Further, under a magnifying glass, two minute humps or peaks are observable in one area, where the glass thread was evidently disengaged. Obviously the glass was too cool to settle into a smoothly fused surface, just as happens sometimes in coiling glass threads to form beads.

A thin thread of melted glass allowed to flow into a small compartment is seen also in at least one or two of the many glass-embellished gold ornaments from Korean tombs.[9] The similarities between the Korean ornaments and the Kegoshi Tomb ornament, and between the latter and the Shōsō-in mirror, are too incomplete to suggest any direct connection, but the simple experimental technique of the smaller items may have led to the development of the more sophisticated one of the mirror. The flowing of molten glass onto a silver ground occurred in Korea in a silver needlecase found in the pagoda of Punhwang-sa temple, Kyŏngju. It is covered with transparent or translucent green glass. No cloisons were used, the entire face of the case being of continuous glass except for the stopper and base. A migrating Korean artisan could easily have brought these ideas into Japan, where, in the Nara period, and under governmental sponsorship, the technique could have advanced into a more skillful performance. Whether the larger, flatter surfaces of glass in the mirror could have been achieved by flowing molten glass into the compartments either from a melting glass rod or from a small crucible could probably be determined only by microscopic examination or by experimentation.

• *Condition*: In general, excellent. The brilliant green glass is slightly crackled, due to the different expansion rates of glass and silver. A few long cracks follow the contours of the cloisons, with a few transverse cracks between them. The medium brown glass is only slightly crackled.

The very top of the knob and one of its sepals show damage, where a little of the glass was broken away; this, being the highest point, was naturally the most vulnerable. Some of the gilding on the cloisons in the comparatively high leaf tips has worn off slightly, disclosing the silver base, but this is not conspicuous. The silver base is relatively untarnished, and all of the individual parts of the mirror and its decoration are still firmly united.

The silver of this mirror is thought to contain some gold. It is said that an addition of five to ten per cent of gold to a silver content retards the oxidation of silver over a long period. Silver dust preserved in the Shōsō-in was found to have a 1.14% gold content.[10]

• *Remarks*: The possibility of a Western provenance for the mirror is precluded by the use of the typically East Asiatic lacquer for the adhesive medium and by the design, which is suggestive of an arabesque motif prevalent in the seventh and eighth centuries in East Asia and reminiscent of some lotus-petal arrangements of the period. If any West Asian glassmakers among the foreign artisans said to have been active in Ch'ang-an in China were involved in such a technique, they must have been under the influence of China sufficiently to have absorbed these two factors.

One object, attributed by Dr. Umehara to the Chinese T'ang dynasty,[11] which suggests an incipient cloisonné, is a gilt-bronze pedestal for a Buddhist statuette preserved in the Archaeological Research Institute of Kyoto University. However, in that, the lotus petals, hollowed on their upper surfaces, are filled with an opaque, blue, glasslike substance; but the process is quite unlike that of the Shōsō-in mirror and more like Western champlevé enamel, for the filling is like a glass paste and shows evidence, in tiny ridges near the edges, of having been tamped down into the cavities with some flat-headed implement rather than flowed in as molten glass or even placed there as pulverized enamel and subsequently fused.

Various writers have disagreed with the author's opinion that the mirror is a Nara product of the eighth century. Mr. Ralph M. Chait assigned a Chinese provenance of the Yüan dynasty.[12] Sir Harry Garner, on the other hand, believed the mirror to have been made in Japan, but "in the seventeenth century or later."[13] For this author's reaction to the arguments advanced by these two gentlemen reference may be made to the *Journal of Glass Studies*, V, 1963, pp. 150–160. Sir Harry quotes Mr. Basil Gray as believing it to be Japanese of the late sixteenth century Momoyama period. In reviewing the Garner publication, Dr. John A. Pope expressed agreement with his theory of a Japanese provenance but felt that it was probably made long after the eighth century "but not as late as 'the seventeenth century or later'," and Mr. Soame Jenyns in a similar review suggests a Korean source.[14] Mr. Henry Trubner, in reviewing the Garner book, agreed that the mirror is not Chinese, but withheld further comment. The authors of *Shōsō-in no Garasu* (p. iv) state that "It does not seem reasonable to date this mirror to the seventeenth century, as some Western scholars do," and, as noted above, they question if it may not be eighth century Japanese. Mr. Okada labeled his illustration as "Chinese T'ang."[15]

This author feels that numerous considerations militate towards a Japanese provenance. There is the identity with the cloisons of the seventh century ornament from the Kegoshi Tomb burial (Pl. 74); there is the similarity of the leaf design motif to other works known to be from Nara workshops of the eighth century —notably the dry lacquer decoration on the pedestal of the Fukūkensaku Kannon image of the Hokke-dō of Tōdai-ji; there is the convincing similarity of the three glasses of the mirror to some of the surviving glassworking materials preserved in the Shōsō-in, which bear out the compositional nature of glass batches noted in the section on glassmaking in the *Zōbutsu-sho Sakumotsuchō* document in the Shōsō-in (Pl. 75); and there is the existence of the Imono-no-tsukasa, the official casting bureau, recorded as in control of work in gold, silver, glass, and lacquer—the latter probably for some minor uses, since there was also a bureau for lacquerwork. Furthermore, there is the fact that the Imono-no-tsukasa employed some Korean craftsmen, plus the existence of the Korean needlecase with brilliant green enamel, as well as two small Korean ear pendants into whose cavitylike areas molten glass had been flowed.

Against a possible Korean provenance, the Koreans of the seventh and eighth centuries were not mirror makers comparable to the Chinese and Japanese, although they were master goldsmiths, and the very few known Korean instances of enamel or enamellike items are elementary.[16]

None of these factors alone could constitute a definitive basis, but together they seem to this author an overwhelming aggregate substantiating a Japanese eighth century origin for the mirror.

Attention is called to an example of enamel-work used in the eleventh century in Japan, an architectural ornament in the Hōō-dō of the Byōdō-in at Uji. This, although not like the Shōsō-in mirror, seems to indicate a familiarity with enameling in advance of the dates usually assigned to its first use in other areas of East Asia.

Needless to say, the origin and early development of cloisonné in Japan is a conspicuous problem in the history of glass in Japan, needing clarification by intensive research.

Still to be published are papers discovered several years ago at Kanshū-ji temple in Kyoto Prefecture regarding the opening and sealing of the Shōsō-in by Prince Kanshū-ji Narichika, first son of the Emperor Reigen, in 1693. The papers are said to include also records kept by the Muromachi shoguns, the Toyotomis, and others, some three hundred documents in all. Hopefully, some light may be thrown by these papers upon the problem of the cloisonné mirror and upon other glass objects in the Shōsō-in.

References:
1. *Chait, "Some Comments on the Dating. . . ." See also *Chait, "Letters to the Editor."
2. *Garner, Chinese and Japanese Cloisonné . . . ., p. 99.
3. *Blair, "The Cloisonné Backed Mirror. . . ."
4. *ECTS, pp. 23–24, 176.
5. One of the eighteen does not tally with the remaining description in the Kenmotsuchō of a mirror that was taken out in 822 but whose return is not recorded; presumably this "extra" mirror was a replacement. See *ECTS, pp. 32–33.
6. *SnG, p. iv.
7. *Gotō, "Shōsō-in Gyobutsu Kinkō-hin. . . . ," pp. 70–73. *SnG, p. iv, describes the mirror as "probably first fashioned into a circular disk by hammering and then into the twelve-pointed shape by cutting the edge."
8. It is said in *SnG, p. 25, that this adhesive does not fluoresce under the X-rays, indicating that it is lacquer. In the Zōbutsu-sho Saku-motsuchō, in a section dealing with ingredients, komugi-ko (wheat powder) is listed in association with lacquer (DNK, I, p. 574). Hironobu Aida of the Osaka mint, in an article on this mirror that appeared in Geppō, the monthly organ of the Ōsaka Kōgyō Shōshikan, 1950, p. 3, mentioned the late Professor Shūshin Katori's remark in his Kinkōshi [History of Metal Work], that it was used as a strong adhesive in connection with the casting of the Daibutsu image of Tōdai-ji.
9. See *Blair, "The Cloisonné Backed Mirror. . . . ," pp. 89–90, Figs. 6–7.
10. See *Gotō, "Shōsō-in Gyobutsu Kinkō-hin . . . . ," p. 70.
11. *Umehara, "Shippō no Butsuzō. . . ." Mr. Soame Jenyns considers this of a later date.
12. *Chait, "Some Comments. . . . ," pp. 68–71.
13. *Garner, Chinese and Japanese Cloisonné . . . ., p. 99.
14. John Pope, review of Garner, Chinese and Japanese Cloisonné Enamels, p. 42. Soame Jenyns, in his review of the same work, in Artibus Asiae, XXV, No. 2/3, pp. 207–213, erroneously cites the Blair (*"The Cloisonné Backed Mirror") assignment of the mirror as to the Chinese T'ang dynasty; he misquotes again in his Chinese Art, Vol. II, 1960, pp. 162–163, 188. Henry Trubner, in the Journal of the American Oriental Society, LXXXIII, 1, January-March, 1963, p. 161, merely states that he agrees with Mr. Garner that the mirror is neither T'ang nor of Chinese manufacture.
15. *Teshigawara, Kunimitsu, and Okada, Garasu, Color Pl. 5 and p. 197.
16. Since this text was written, a discussion of early cloisonné in China has been published in *Umehara, "Chūgoku Shutsudo. . . . ," citing one small bronze fitting decorated with glass that was excavated in Korea, and several belt-mountings excavated in China. These Dr. Umehara attributed to a pre-T'ang date. One of the Chinese examples shows a rather complex design of a crouching human figure;

portions seem to have been glass-paste inlay, now much deteriorated, but in the limb areas is a semitransparent glass substance "of good quality" described as "molten glass poured in—that is, *shippō*." This is, of course, pertinent to the early development of cloisonné in China, but seems to this author in no way indicating that the Shōsō-in mirror must, therefore, have been produced in China.

13. GLASS LANTERN WITH *KODAMA*

Partially constructed of glass beads. Said to have been presented in 1038 by Fujiwara no Yorimichi to Kasuga-taisha shrine in Nara, the shrine of the Fujiwara family. In the catalogue of an exhibition held in the Tokyo National Museum in 1958, *Tōyō Kotōki Tokubetsu Kinretsu* ("Special Exhibition of Old Lighting Equipment") it was ascribed to the Kamakura period. The border line between much of Heian and early Kamakura art, especially in the field of crafts, is not always clearly demarcated. Certain types of Kamakura art had their foundations in the Fujiwara era, and this lantern, even should it be later than the year 1038, reflects the Fujiwara spirit.

The hexagonal frame is coated with black lacquer rimmed with vermilion and accented with white gesso. The roof takes the shape of an inverted lotus blossom surmounted by a bronze chrysanthemum blossom supporting a suspension ring and hook. Each panel immediately under the roof has a group of seven horizontal wires strung with translucent beads of a darkish blue tone. Each of the six main panels of the body of the lantern is a frame holding thirty-five vertical wires strung with the same beads, about seventy-five to each wire. When a flickering taper is lighted within this "glass lantern," the effect is soft and rich. Among the thousands of lanterns at Kasuga-taisha, this one is unique.
- *Collection*: Kasuga-taisha, Nara.
- *Date*: Ca. 1038.
- *Color*: Rich, darkish blue; semitransparent.
- *Condition*: It is said that many of the beads are replacements, but that the original style was maintained. The beads are, at any rate, in excellent condition.

14. PLAQUE OF GLASS ON ONE OF THE HEIKE *NŌKYŌ* (Sutras Dedicated by the Heike)
National Treasure

The last quarter century of the Heian period is sometimes called the Heike, or Heiji, era because of the ascendancy of the Heike (Taira clan). Taira no Kiyomori, its head, equalled the Fujiwara in his response to the refinements of the time. The *Heike Nōkyō* are Buddhist sutras, which were copied by members of Kiyomori's family and dedicated by him to the clan shrine, Itsukushima-jinja, a Ryōbu-Shintō shrine (a shrine including elements of Buddhism) in the Inland Sea. Copying of a sutra was believed to bring divine protection for the copyist or sponsor as well as for some deceased loved one in whose name they were often dedicated. Thirty-three scrolls were made under his supervision, the first in the series being his own work.

The papers of the scrolls, which are 35.5 cm. high, are dyed in delicate tones, painted with unobtrusive designs and sprinkled with filings, thin threads, and scattered flecks of foil in gold and silver. The written columns of sutra text are indicated in thin lines. The brushwork writing of the scroll included here is done in a variety of colors—ultramarine blue, a bright mineral green, and some accents of gold and silver. At the opening of each scroll is a frontispiece painted in color and illustrating some meaning of the sutra or some aspect of contemporary aristocratic life. This scroll shows the Princess of the Dragon Palace beneath the sea offering a *hōshu* jewel to the Buddha (significant of the meeting of Shintō and Buddhism in Ryōbu-Shintō and indicative of the role of Itsukushima as a sea shrine). It is Number 12 in the series and entitled the *Daiba Bon Kyō*.

The outer end of the reverse face is said to be of sheepskin; it is painted with a scene of fantastic whales, dolphins, and swordfish sporting in a blue sea. The remainder of this exterior surface carries decorative floral designs, changing with each of the joined lengths of paper backing: plum blossoms, lotus, mandarin orange, and chrysanthemums. The end edge is stiffened with a narrow silver band cut with a perforated motif and washed in part with gold. To this is attached a winding-cord of braided silk ending in a flat, silver lotus blossom terminal. Most of the scrolls have elaborate title plaques, usually of cast metal plated with gold or silver, and have delicately formed, elegant *jiku-tan*. This *Daiba Bon Kyō* has rock crystal *jiku-tan* in the shape symbolizing the five elements. A simply written title is covered by a plaque of transparent blue glass firmly but inconspicuously attached by a vegetable adhesive to a rectangle of dark blue paper crossed with gold border lines.

The standard of perfection and beauty achieved in these scrolls illustrates the artistic level of the Fujiwara crafts; the use of glass in one of them emphasizes that glass was still regarded as a precious substance.

GLASS PLAQUE:

- *Collection*: Treasure House of Itsukushima Shrine, Miyajima city, Hiroshima Prefecture.
- *Date*: Ca. 1164.
- *Size*: L. 5.495 cm.; W. 1.9 cm.; T. 0.2 cm.
- *Color*: Greenish blue; transparent. IH.D.Refl.: nearest to Ch 3, 14-5-13 or 14. This is quite close to the glass of the two knife handles, (Pl. 83) and almost identical to the glass *shari-tsubo* of Denkō-ji (Pl. 122).
- *Bubbles*: Only three are visible.
- *Composition*: Lead glass.[1]
- *Technique*: Uncertain, but it seems that the plaque was ground from a larger piece. The edges are wavy, and at several points there are minute chips or nicks. The plaque is almost imperceptibly curved, fitting the scroll closely when it is rolled. In that respect it would seem to have been shaped purposely. At the left edge the curved surface is slightly flattened and a trifle rough and irregular. The polished surface suggests reheating after grinding. In one area at left center there is a sort of waviness in the glass surface.

The knife handles of Plate 83 provide a similar instance in the Nara period of grinding from a glass block.

- *Condition*: Excellent. Recently these scrolls have been remounted and individually housed in special wooden cases to ensure preservation.

Reference:
1. *Yamasaki, "Garasu," Chart 5, p. 403.

15. SWORD WITH TWEEZER MOTIF
National Treasure

A slightly curved sword a little over 96 cm. long. The donor is unknown, but the sword was dedicated to Futsunushi-no-Mikoto, the Shintō deity of one of the shrines of Kasuga-taisha. On the hilt is a gilt-bronze ornament in the shape of Japanese tweezers (*kenuki*), whence the name. The ground of the hilt is of gold lacquer decorated in delicate relief with tiny birds and butterflies. The scabbard is covered with fine gold *ikakeji* lacquer with a design of cats and sparrows in a bamboo grove, inlaid with mother-of-pearl and glass. On the obverse side, at the left near the hilt, are three sparrows on bamboo branches, with a cat approaching from the right; in the center, a cat with a sparrow in its mouth and two other sparrows on a branch; at the right, five sparrows among branches, with a running cat chasing a sixth sparrow. On the reverse, three sparrows among the branches watch a reclining cat who eyes a flying sparrow.

The bamboo branches are of inlaid mother-of-pearl with hairline engraving. The leaves are of the same inlaid and engraved mother-of-pearl, in which are occasional inlays of green glass and black glass (or lacquer?). The irregular "calico" spots on the bodies of the cats are of glass, as are, perhaps, the pupils of the eyes of both cats and sparrows.

- *Collection*: Kasuga-taisha, Nara.
- *Date*: Late Heian period.

GLASS:

- *Colors*: Inlays on the bodies are green, which generally look dull and opaque except for one instance on the reverse of the scabbard where the green is more intense and either translucent or transparent. IH.D.Refl.: Ch 2, 13-4-13 and 14. In the cats' eyes the whites are mother-of-pearl; the tiny globular pupils are a glossy brown, which *seems* to be glass. The minute pupils of the sparrows' eyes are very dark and so tiny it is difficult to tell whether they are blue, green, or black—possibly they are dots of lacquer.

- *Bubbles*: One bright bubble is seen on the reverse in an area where the glass surface is clear.
- *Technique*: The globular eyes are solid. Where one has fallen out, the ground looks grainy and brown, evidently the remains of an adhesive. The "calico" spots and the inlays on the leaves are flat glass cut to shape and fitted into recesses cut in the mother-of-pearl. The "calico" inlays are thicker than the mother-of-pearl and the cut-out areas are skillfully done.
- *Condition*: The sword is in excellent condition. One glass on the reverse is so bright and clear as to suggest a possible replacement, but since it is on the reverse and would therefore have rubbed against the clothing when the sword was worn, or have been on the "under" side when the sword was stored, it may be original.

16. DARK BLUE JAR

A jar with a spherical body and widely flaring lip. The mouth opening is said to be barely large enough to admit a little finger, which seems strange for a vessel known as a spittoon (*dako*). The exterior bottom is concave in the center. The jar does not stand evenly and has usually been displayed upside down, for steadiness; this gave opportunity to view the rounded concavity at the bottom, and the graceful contour of the exterior neck, under the wide lip—neither of which show clearly in the illustration.

- *Former Location*: Shōsō-in, Middle Section. *STM* No. 396.
- *Provenance*: Chinese(?), or possibly Egyptian(?).[1]
- *Date*: Probably Sung dynasty.
- *Size*: H. 8.5–9.0 cm.; D. of the wide lip, 11.4–11.7 cm.; D. of body, 8.3 cm.; D. of base, 4.5 cm.
- *Color*: Deep dark blue, colored by a cobalt ore purer than that of Plate 11, and therefore brighter. Munsell, 7.5PB3/8.[2]
- *Bubbles*: Large, elongated ones, very much attenuated, following the line of the circumference on the wide lip flange. These suggest the same type of large bubbles in the high-footed vessel (Pl. 108), which is thought to be

of Chinese, or possibly Egyptian, origin. A large air bubble at the constricted neck extends into both upper and lower parts.

- *Composition*: Inferred from the Beta-ray back scattering to be soda-lime glass with no lead content.
- *Technique*: Free blown; a large bubble at the point of constriction, extending into both sections, indicates that this was made in one piece. A pontil mark is on the exterior bottom.
- *Condition*: Excellent.
- *Remarks*: An entry in the *Tōdai-ji Betto Shidai* ("Record of the Abbots of Tōdai-ji") for 1021, the first day of the tenth month, states that Taira no Munetsune, former head of the Palace Guard, dedicated a *dako* (spittoon) of dark blue glass.[3] Because this was dedicated to Tōdai-ji, which had jurisdiction over the South Section of the Shōsō-in at that time, and because no other glass "spittoon" is known in Japan, it is assumed that this is the item of the record. The spittoon seems demonstrably later in date than the other five glass vessels in the Shōsō-in. It may be Chinese of the Sung dynasty, or, less likely, Iranian or perhaps Egyptian. In those countries spittoons of glass, or of ceramic, bearing some points of resemblance, were used.

  In modern times this vessel was installed in the Middle Section. Since all six vessels have occupied the same glass case in the Middle Section, it seems they were placed there during the arrangement "in order," which took place from 1892 to 1905.

  It should be noted that the date of dedication of the spittoon provides only one terminus. The fact that the 1021 record calls for a spittoon indicates that such a form was known in the early eleventh century and was apparently used for that purpose. A Chinese example in pottery bears a brushed-on date of 841; it shows some resemblance to the Shōsō-in example.[4] A Chinese source states that when the emperor stepped out, an attendant carried a cuspidor.[5] Two glass examples from Rayy in Iraq are known,[6] but they are more like a deep basin with a wide mouth and are less directly related to the Shōsō-in *dako*.

An example in glass similar to the Shōsō-in jar was in the collection of the late George Eumofopoulos, London. The donor, the late Oscar Raphael, told the author he had found it in Egypt and personally considered it and the Shōsō-in example to have been made there. In this author's opinion it seems likely that the *dako* of the Shōsō-in, like the high-footed vessel of Plate 108, may have come from China as a Chinese product, or have been an importation there from a West Asian, or even Egyptian source.

The following passage is quoted in *SnG (p. 18):

> Glass cast in China is different from that of regions west of China. If cast in China, the color is very bright and the substance light and brittle, and if we pour in warm rice wine it explodes. Examples that are imported are slightly rough and dull and the color rather clouded. They are also different in that they withstand boiling water, as though they were made of silver.[7]

If this passage can be relied upon, the reference to a "very bright" color might seem to support the theory of Chinese origin.

References:

1. In *Yoshimizu, "Shōsō-in no Konruri Tsubo," English summary, a West Turkestan source is suggested.
2. *SnG, pp. iii, 17, Fig. 14.
3. "Tōdai-ji Betto Shidai" [Record of the Steward of Tōdai-ji], from Hanawa, "Gunsho Ruijū," in *Shinkō Gunsho Ruijū*, III, p. 271.
4. In the collection of Sir Herbert Ingram; see Willetts, *op. cit.* (n. 8, p. 337), II, pp. 485–486, Pl. 38a. A somewhat related form, in glass, is in the Benaki Museum, Athens.
5. *Takigawa, "Imono-no-tsukasa. . . . ," p. 13 (Appendix 2).
6. Carl Johan Lamm, *Glass from Iran in the National Museum*, Stockholm, 1935, Pls. 2D and 15K and L, dated 7th to 9th century.
7. From the section on glass in Volume III of Ch'eng Ta-Ch'ang's thirteenth century *Yen Fan Lu*, which is said to explain many terms used during the T'ang and Sung dynasties.

17. CLOISONNÉ *KUGIKAKUSHI*

- *Collection*: Mr. Ryō Hosomi, Izumi-Otsu city, Osaka Prefecture.
- *Date*: Momoyama period.
- *Size*: L. 10.2 cm.
- *Colors*: White, red, and green enamel; opaque.
- *Technique*: Probably enamel powders applied directly to areas of the design and fired. No cloisons were used to contain the areas of red flush on the petals. Brass ground.

For a more detailed discussion of Momoyama cloisonné, see Plate Note 132.

- *Condition*: Good.

18. *BIIDORO-E* PANELS INLAID IN A *JŪBAKO*

A *jūbako* is a series of nested boxes used for cold foods on such festive occasions as picnics or New Year's meals. This one, 22.0 cm. high and 18.5 cm. square, is of mulberry wood. The cover and the sides of each compartment are inlaid with glass panels painted on the back with landscapes, blossoming trees, fruits, flowers, birds, butterflies, geometric designs, and other motifs, in color; some areas are even iridescent, as though imitating mother-of-pearl inlay. A square frame, whose sides are of black gauze with gold-paper embroidery, is set down over the *jūbako* as a protection from insects. Such an object, it is said, was intended for use in the tea ceremony.

- *Collection*: Mr. Sekio Iwanaga, Nagasaki.
- *Provenance*: The scenes of the panels are in the Chinese manner, so it may be that they are the work of Chinese artisans in Nagasaki.
- *Date*: Edo period.[1]

Reference:

1. *Okada, *Garasu* (1969), Pl. 21, considers this technique to have been initiated about the Bunka era (1804–17).

19. GROUP OF DECORATED SAKÉ BOTTLES

- *Collection*: Mr. Noboru Azuma, Tokyo.
- *Date*: Late Edo, early Meiji periods.
- *Sizes*: Average H. 18.5 cm.
- *Colors*: Colorless; transparent. White; translucent. Blue; transparent. Purple; transpar-

ent. Decoration in silver, "gold," and red.

- *Technique*: Mold blown. Decorated with tin dust, what appears to be brass foil, and a red "enamel" over a lacquer ground, which was most probably applied with stencils. Some overpainting to emulate *maki-e* lacquer.
- *Condition*: Good, with some peeling of the lacquer.
- *Remarks*: These bottles were popular, mass-produced items in the late years of the Edo period and probably early Meiji. The work is gaudy, and the designs are all associated with felicitous occasions. The fish bottles display a rebus for the word meaning "felicitations"; the pine and crane motif is associated with happy occasions and is perhaps the most common motif used by Japanese saké companies today. A collection such as the one pictured clearly conveys the appeal these bright little bottles must have had at a time when glass was just beginning to assume a place in the daily life of Japan.

20. *KISERU*

This fine *kiseru* is larger and more elegant than usual, and would have lent prestige to its owner.

- *Collection*: Nagasaki Municipal Museum, Nagasaki.
- *Date*: Probably early 19th century.
- *Size*: L. 32.0 cm.; D. of bowl, 1.6 cm.
- *Colors*: Stem, dark blue; transparent; IH. D. Refl.: Ch 6, 17–5–11 and IH. D. Trans.: Ch 6, 17–5–12. Mouthpiece, colorless; transparent. Bowl, colorless with dark blue rim.
- *Technique*: Lampwork.
- *Condition*: Excellent.
- *Remarks*: In the Ikenaga Collection of the Kobe Municipal Museum there is a very similar *kiseru*, but slightly shorter, less elegant, and entirely of amber color; a second one in the same collection has a larger, upstanding bowl, more like a Dutch pipe. Most of the extant glass *kiseru* are probably of later date; they are shorter, monochrome, and usually opaque.

21. THIN, DARK BLUE WINE POT

A superb example. The thin glass metal is similar to that of Plates 154 and 155. The shape is refined, with its extremely long spout, the glass uprights on the shoulder, and the lightweight swivel handle of silver (with repoussé dot design), which fits into the uprights. The lid is reminiscent of the Heian period glass *shari-ki* of Supplementary Notes 55 and 56, with their *hōshu* shaped knobs, downward flaring form, and hollow necks.

- *Collection*: Mr. Shirō Tonomura, Nagasaki.
- *Size*: H. overall, 8.5 cm.; D. 12.0 cm.; L., including spout, 24.5 cm.
- *Color*: Very dark blue, rich and elegant; transparent. This is the typical dark indigo blue that appears repeatedly in the *biidoro* of Nagasaki. By reflected flashlight the solid knob on the lid shows a reddish cast.
- *Technique*: Free blown, with a slight rounded "kick" in the bottom; added spout and uprights.

22. QUAIL CAGE WITH GLASS BARS

The framework is of unlacquered black wood, with cut-out cartouche openings in the solid lower part, in which are floral scenes delicately painted on paper and protected by transparent glass. The open spaces above are filled in with upright ornamental glass rods of a triple-groove spiral pattern. The top is filled in with a netting of knotted gray green cord, with the ends twisted around the tops of the glass rods and tied around the wood frame at the corners. On one side there is a central section of the glass rods, which may be raised or removed; the opposite side, seen in the illustration, has a small opening for supplying food and water, the top of which is a thick ornamental form of uncolored glass.

- *Collection*: Mr. Sekio Iwanaga, Nagasaki.
- *Date*: Edo period.
- *Size*: Cage, H. 33.0 cm.; W. 23.5 cm.
- *Glass color*: Colorless; transparent.
- *Condition*: Excellent.
- *Remarks*: Such cages, it is said, were not merely for confinement of the quail, but to give a cherished pet a safe and airy place to lay and tend her eggs.

23. COMB
• *Collection*: Tokyo National Museum.
• *Provenance*: Edo.
• *Date*: Edo Period.
• *Size*: 9.17 cm.
• *Glass color*: Colorless; transparent.
• *Technique*: Engraved glass panel attached to tortoiseshell comb.
• *Condition*: Good.
• *Remarks*: Precision and finesse of workmanship is well displayed in the engraved glass panel of this comb. Some of the Edo combs in the Tokyo National Museum collection show a mastery of glass technique that contrasts surprisingly with the workmanship in Plate 24.
References:
*Okada, *Garasu*, Pl. 111.
*Teshigawara, Kunimitsu, and Okada, *Garasu*, Pl. 46.

24. CUT GLASS BOWLS WITH RED OVERLAY
Probably bowls for cakes or fruit. The shape is atypical for Japan and was probably inspired by foreign examples.
• *Collection*: Mr. Kōji Katō, Tokyo.
• *Provenance*: Edo.
• *Date*: 19th century.
• *Sizes*: D. 14.8 cm.
• *Color*: Ground, colorless; transparent. Overlay, red; translucent.
• *Technique*: Probably free blown, cased, and cut. Rim of upper piece scalloped.
• *Condition*: Excellent.
• *Remarks*: These two pieces show the soft, blurry design outlines found in some cut glass made in Edo. Satsuma cut glass does not display this quality, being sharp and precise. It is difficult to consider either piece, and the upper one in particular, as examples of a refined cut glass technique.
Reference:
*Okada, *Garasu*, Pls. 15, 17.

25. CUT GLASS BOTTLE WITH RED OVERLAY
One of the finest of several known bottles of dark-red Satsuma glass. The body is similar to that of Supplementary Note 82 and almost identical to the brush holder of Supplementary Note 83.
• *Collection*: Mr. Shirō Tonomura, Nagasaki.
• *Date*: 1856–58.
• *Color*: The cut overlay is in varying tones of red, from very deep to a lighter carmine; translucent. The uncolored ground is transparent.
• *Composition*: Not analyzed, but the coloring agent is copper.
• *Technique*: Free blown, cased, and cut. Highly polished.
• *Condition*: Excellent.

26. "RASPBERRY RED" STEMMED BOWL WITH GOLD DECORATION
The contrast between this Satsuma piece and the red Satsuma example of Plate 25 (also Sup. N. 80–83) is great; for this is thin and of a delicate tone, sometimes spoken of as "raspberry red" or "strawberry red," and is transparent—both qualities obtained by the addition of gold as well as copper to the glass batch. An orchid motif applied in gold decorates the bowl. There is a thin gold line at the rim, and the stem and foot are of colorless transparent glass with thin bands of gold added at intervals.
• *Collection*: Shūseikan, Iso-kōen, Kagoshima city.
• *Date*: 1857–58.
• *Size*: H. 20.3 cm.; D. at mouth rim, 15.2 cm.; T. of rim, 0.5 cm. The bowl is slightly crooked, being higher at one "side."
• *Color*: Bowl, light purplish red; transparent. IH.D.Refl.: Ch 13, 24-6-16. Stemmed foot, colorless; transparent.
• *Bubbles*: A few, small and circular.
• *Composition*: Not analyzed, but the color was achieved by copper and gold.
• *Technique*: Free blown, with attached foot.
• *Condition*: Excellent.
• *Remarks*: Several of these delicately tinted glass items, depending upon gold for their particular color and transparency, are known, but they are by no means common. Their rarity attests to the difficulty of controlling gold-containing glasses. In the Shūseikan there is a shallow

plate with decoration in gold in the center and on the walls. There is also an unusual and striking perfume bottle with an elaborately cut stopper and exterior base, which is preserved in prime condition in the Shūseikan. Its body is plain, cut in eight angular facets. A third outstanding example is a shallow dish obtained in Kagoshima by Professor Motoyoshi Higaki of Fukuoka, which has no gold decoration, but for beauty depends entirely upon the contour of the twelve curving facets of its wall and upon its color.

27. PAIR OF CUT GLASS WINE BOTTLES WITH DARK BLUE OVERLAY

Bright purplish blue and brilliant, polished cutting. The design is similar to those of Plates 196 and 197, although the technical perfection of these two bottles and their high polish suggest a later date.

- *Collection*: The Corning Museum of Glass (No. 55.6.18 A-B); gift of the Asahi Glass Company, Tokyo.
- *Date*: 1857–58.
- *Size*: H. overall 25.4 cm.; D. overall, 7.9 cm.
- *Color*: Ground, colorless; transparent. Overlay, dark purplish blue; translucent.
- *Composition*: Lead glass (ultraviolet fluorescence).
- *Technique*: Free blown, cased, and cut.
- *Condition*: Excellent.

28. SET OF THREE CUT GLASS SAKÉ CUPS WITH DARK BLUE OVERLAY

Sets of three graduated and nested saké cups, often with accompanying stand, were reserved for ceremonial occasions, as weddings and the New Year celebrations.

- *Collection*: The Corning Museum of Glass (No. 55.6.18 C-G); gift of the Asahi Glass Company, Tokyo.
- *Date*: 1857 or 1858.
- *Sizes*: Cups, H. 4.6 cm., 4.9 cm., and 5.2 cm.; D. at rim, 7.9 cm., 9.5 cm., and 11.0 cm. Stand, H. 8.4 cm.; D. 10.8 cm.
- *Color*: Ground, colorless; transparent. Overlay, dark blue; translucent.

- *Composition*: Lead glass (ultraviolet fluorescence).
- *Technique*: Free blown, cased, and cut.
- *Condition*: Excellent.

29. "AINU BEAD" WITH GOLDFISH

Known as a *kingyodama* ("goldfish bead").

- *Collection*: One of six in The Corning Museum of Glass.
- *Provenance*: Uncertain. In Sendai they are considered to be of local manufacture, but they seem to be have been made in other localities as well.
- *Date*: Meiji era.
- *Size*: H. 0.8 cm.; D. 0.95 cm.
- *Bore*: Seems to be lined with white.
- *Colors*: Colorless body; semitransparent. Blue glass thread spiraled beneath the surface; opaque. This type sometimes has the blue thread spiraled around the exterior.
- *Technique*: A coiled bead with spiraled thread of color and a red-gold fantailed goldfish insert.
- *Remarks*: For characteristic Ainu beads, see Plate 212. This particular bead shows unusual delicacy and clarity in the tiny goldfish form.

30. ENAMELED WINE GLASSES

Three of a large group of many designs.

- *Collection*: The Corning Museum of Glass.
- *Provenance*: The glasses are considered by some as probably of European origin, with the decoration added in Japan. However, an unusual, smooth convex rounding of the glass on the underside of the foot, immediately under the stem (in the position for a pontil mark), is the same as two engraved wine glasses produced by the Asahi Gōshi Kaisha, in the collection of the Asahi Glass Company, Tokyo. Thus, the enameled glasses pictured may also be products of that company. The tradition that Fusanosuke Kuhara (a Japanese political figure) used these at the close of the Meiji era ties in with this theory.
- *Date*: Probably between 1908 and 1913.
- *Size*: Glass with flower design, H. 11.5 cm.; D. at rim, 5.0 cm.
- *Color*: Glass, colorless; transparent. Enamel, polychrome and dark gold.

- *Technique*: Blown bowls; stems and feet added. The lead enamel fired on.
- *Remarks*: All three designs (flowers, butterflies, and carp) are extremely delicate, imbued with Japanese sensitivity, and executed with skill. The execution is so fine that it suggests the work of a *maki-e* lacquer artist. However, equally detailed work was being done in overglaze enamels on ceramics at this time.

31. AGATE WARE BOWL BY HIDEO MIYAMOTO

- *Collection*: Main office, Asahi Glass Company, Tokyo.
- *Provenance*: Produced at the Asahi Gōshi Kaisha, Osaka.
- *Date*: Between 1908 and 1913.
- *Size*: H. 8.3 cm.; D. inside, 17.4 cm.
- *Color*: Interior, gradations of olive green, with center area of brown; thin lines of green swirling upward. Rim, brown. Exterior, pale opaque gray overlay, sometimes nearly white or slightly bluish; the cut-away portions result in a design in the underlying opaque brown. Casing, colorless; transparent.
- *Composition*: High lead content with metallic oxides as colorants.
- *Technique*: So-called agate ware method of cutting through layers of colored glasses to form designs in color. Molded in lobes; on each lobe the gray surface was cut away to reveal, in the underlying brown, an abstract design whose edges spin out delicately in feathery scrolls. Delicate grooves, cut beside the lobes and crossing at the exterior bottom form a central starlike pattern.
- *Remarks*: This bowl and the box of Plate 32 manifest the eager outreach by Meiji period glassmakers for new ideas and techniques, and, furthermore, attest to the high degree of skill attained in the search.

32. AGATE WARE BOX BY HIDEO MIYAMOTO

- *Collection*: Main office, Asahi Glass Company, Tokyo.

- *Provenance*: Produced at the Asahi Gōshi Kaisha, Osaka.
- *Date*: Between 1908 and 1913.
- *Size*: H. 7.8 cm.; D. 9.9 cm.
- *Color*: Variations of color, chiefly brown, gray, green, blue, and purple, with an area of beige at the edge of the lid; opaque. Casing, colorless; transparent.
- *Composition*: High lead content, with metallic oxides as colorants.
- *Technique*: So-called agate ware method of cutting through layers of colored glasses to produce varicolored patterns. Molded and sharply cut into facets on both body and lid; further cutting on each facet brought out abstract designs in the various underlying colors.

33. INCENSE BURNER BY SOTOICHI KOSHIBA

- *Collection*: Anonymous.
- *Date*: 1970.
- *Color*: Body, blending of colorless, blue, and purple glasses; translucent. Foot, colorless; translucent, with a small area beneath the bottom surface of opaque dark blue rimmed with a trace of bright green. Lid, subdued green blended with colorless glass and surmounted by a colorless bird-shaped handle in which are an area of pink and a spot of opaque dark blue.
- *Bubbles*: Various shapes and sizes throughout.
- *Composition*: Lead glass, with cobalt, copper, and manganese as colorants.
- *Technique*: Pâte de verre, cast in outside and inside molds of refractory clay, which were broken to release the object. Since a too finely powdered glass will not fuse easily, a powder of 100 mesh was used.

34. VASE BY TŌSHICHI IWATA

- *Collection*: Mr. Kōzō Nakamura, Tokyo.
- *Date*: 1967.
- *Size*: H. 24.0 cm.; D. of rim, 23.3 cm.
- *Color*: Gold, suggesting lacquer.
- *Composition*: Soda-lime glass, with added gold.
- *Technique*: Blown, with foot and handles added.
- *Remarks*: The rounded contour suggests the

"soft" contours of the famous Nyōrin Kannon image at Chūgū-ji nunnery, Nara Prefecture, which the artist credits as his inspiration for this vase.

35. WALL PANEL BY ITOKO IWATA
- *Date*: August, 1971.
- *Size*: H. 105.0 cm.; W. 90.0 cm.
- *Colors*: Yellows, oranges, reds, and some brown and purple; translucent.
- *Composition*: Soda-lime glass.
- *Technique*: Molded. In two rectangular sections, made up of individual joined squares. Design, low relief with some concave units; Ground, plain.
- *Remarks*: Exhibited in a one-man show at Mitsukoshi Department Store, Tokyo, September, 1971.

36. VASE BY KŌZŌ KAGAMI
- *Date*: 1970.
- *Size*: H. 24.0 cm.; D. 15.0 cm.
- *Color*: Colorless; transparent.
- *Composition*: Lead glass.
- *Technique*: Free blown and engraved after the artist's own brushwork.
- *Remarks*: Besides being one of Japan's leading glassmakers, Kōzō Kagami is noted for the quality of his calligraphy. The rendering of the small figure of the priest Ryōkan (1758–1831) on this bottle is done in the *ippitsu* ("single brushstroke") style often seen in Zen painting. Ryōkan was a Zen priest famous for his poetry, calligraphy, and love of children. A rough rendering of the Chinese style poem reads: "Passing days among children, with a few balls in my sleeve. Idle, drunk—a peaceful spring." The shape of this saké bottle, the brushwork of the figure, and the imagery of the poem (balls, saké, spring) all tie together in a beautiful unity of conception.

37. HANIWA FIGURES BY MASAKICHI AWASHIMA
- *Date*: 1971.
- *Size*: Maximum H. 48.3 cm.; T. at bottom, 0.7 cm.
- *Colors*: Colorless, red, and blue; transparent.

- *Composition*: Soda-lime glass with selenium red and copper blue.
- *Technique*: Bodies, free blown and elongated. Heads, pressed. Arms, formed from rods softened in a kiln. Color sandwiched between two layers of colorless glass.
- *Remarks*: Typical of the artist's creative interest in new approaches and his pleasure in whimsy.

BLACK-AND-WHITE PLATES

BEGINNING OF GLASS IN JAPAN

38. *SUIGYOKU* (Hanging Ornament)
Two portions washed out of the soil separately in 1948 and 1949 in the precincts of Sumiyoshi Shrine in Shimonoseki, at the southwestern tip of Honshu. Many fragments of Yayoi pottery were also found close by.
- *Collection*: Sumiyoshi Shrine, Ichinomiya, Shimonoseki city, Yamaguchi Prefecture.
- *Date*: Possibly Latest Jōmon period? The glass of this *suigyoku* is so conglomerate, the surface so imperfect, and the shaping so elementary that it is difficult to think of it as the product of a later time when glass was handled with skill. The author has seen a number of primitive glass forms, including some human figures, which hint that there may be some surprising discoveries awaiting the student of earliest glass technology in Japan.
- *Size*: H. 3.5 cm.; W. 3.8 cm.; T. (maximum), 1.5 cm.
- *Color*: Dark blue, primarily opaque; varies in right and left portions and in the two faces. One face, a bright, clear, semitransparent greenish blue, very glossy in the break, although the surface is dull, with some reddish tones. Reverse face very dark, with some tones of the same blue color.
- *Composition*: Crude, nonhomogeneous glass metal; small unfused lumps of quartz are conspicuous. Sp. Grav.: 2.92.
- *Technique*: Primitive forming by hand, the mass apparently pressed into a kind of roll with narrowed ends brought almost together. At one end the glass seems to have been doubled over in the shaping. One face is rounded, one

flattened; the object seems to have been worked on a flat surface, or laid down on a flat surface, before hardening.

- *Condition*: Broken and mended; dull surface.
- *Remarks*: In 1967 Dr. Umehara published another primitive glass example similar to this one, reported to have come from an unknown site in northern Kyushu, together with several other equally primitive specimens.[1] He calls all *magatama*, single or double. The author has had no opportunity to study these and can present no other data beyond the fact that they, too, are of mixed dark blue tones, and opaque with impurities.

Reference:
1. *Umehara, "Hari no Magatama," Pl. I, upper left and right, Figs. 2, 3.

39. *MAGATAMA* WITH INCISED HEAD
Discovered in 1922 at the Suku-Okumoto site by Dr. Heijirō Nakayama in a square earthen chest beneath a large stone. Included were Chinese bronze mirrors and swords, and a tiny *kudatama* considered at first to be of deerhorn but more likely of corroded glass.

- *Collection*: Archaeological Research Institute, Kyushu University.
- *Date*: Middle or Late Yayoi period.
- *Size*: L. 5.3 cm.; W. at center, 1.6 cm.; T. at center, 1.45 cm.
- *Color*: Green, seen only at the broken tip; either translucent or transparent. Impossible to match on color chart because of the surrounding wall of decomposed glass. In areas where the white coating is thin, a pale greenish tone shows through.
- *Bore*: Drilled from both sides, narrowing at the center. D. at ends, 0.4 and 0.5 cm.; at center, 0.2 cm.
- *Composition*: Not investigated, but probably lead glass.
- *Technique*: Mold cast.
- *Condition*: Broken at tip; covered, except at the break, with whitish weathering, circular pitting, and some scars.
- *Remarks*: Three grooves incised on the head, and faint traces of another under the "chin." An unusually fine example from the point of

view of glass metal and subtle contour and proportions.

Reference:
*Nakayama, "Suku-Okamoto Shin-hakken. . . ," pp. 129–147; also *Nakayama, "Jigo Saishūseru Suku-Okamoto. . . . ," pp. 329–332.

40 (right). *MAGATAMA* WITH PLAIN HEAD
From a jar burial discovered in 1949 at Suku-Okamoto by the owner.

- *Collection*: Motochika Suzuki, Kokura city, Fukuoka Prefecture.
- *Date*: Middle or Late Yayoi period.
- *Size*: L. 3.2 cm.; W. at head, 1.4 cm., at center, 1.1 cm.; T. at head, 0.9 cm., at center, 0.6 cm.
- *Color*: Deep bluish green, seen only through the bore; translucent.
- *Bore*: D. 3.2 cm., with slight widening at the ends.
- *Composition*: Lead glass containing barium,[1] possibly from melting a Chinese *pi*.
- *Technique*: Mold cast.
- *Condition*: Complete, with white coat of lead phosphate, heavily striated[2] (see Pl. N. 41, Condition).

References:
1. *Umehara, "Nihon Jōko no Hari," p. 10.
2. *Yamasaki and Saitō, "Investigation of Corroded Ancient Glasses. . . . ," pp. 504–505.

40. (center). *KUDATAMA*
The illustration shows sixteen of thirty *kudatama* found in the same jar burial as the *magatama* preceding, the remainder having been dispersed.

- *Collection*: Motochika Suzuki. Kokura city, Fukuoka Prefecture.
- *Date*: Middle or Late Yayoi period.
- *Size*: L. 2.3 cm.; D. at center, 0.5 cm. Slightly smaller at the ends.
- *Color*: Where visible, bluish turquoise green.
- *Bore*: D. 0.2 cm. Diameters vary within the group; often they are larger at one end.
- *Composition*: Lead glass containing barium, possibly from melting a Chinese *pi*.[1]
- *Technique*: Evidently shaped by hand. The irregular contours, bulging in the center, and the narrowed, rounded ends, suggest forming

by pressure, or rolling, around a small cylindrical core. The fact that the bores vary in diameter, plus the fact that one end of the bore is often slightly larger than the other, suggests a lack of uniform rods for shaping, such as the wires of later times. Possibly tiny animal or bird bones were used for this purpose; in this connection note that from the Yayoi shell-mound in Oku-chō, Okayama Prefecture, described below, came three minute, slender needles made from bird bones. There is also a reference to *kudatama* made of bird bones.[2] It thus seems that bird bones were common material for small practical purposes and might well have served as cores for shaping these glass *kudatama*.

In one *kudatama* given to Mr. Shigeaki Nakahara of Fukuoka there is a longitudinal gap (not a break) where the glass wrapping did not completely meet over the original core, whatever that may have been.

- *Condition*: Corroded with white lead phosphate coating. It was chiefly from his X-ray examination of these *kudatama* and the above *magatama*, as well as the glass of Plates 42 and 43, that Dr. Kazuo Yamasaki discovered[3] that when glass containing lead was confined with human remains in the presence of moisture, the surface of the glass became transformed into lead phosphate rather than the usual lead carbonate, having been affected by the calcium phosphate of dissolved bones. Such lead phosphate coating is not found on glass buried under drier circumstances.

References:
1. *Yamasaki "Garasu," p. 397.
2. Seiichi Mizuno and Yukio Kobayashi, *Zukai Kōkogaku Jiten* [Illustrated Archaeological Dictionary], Tokyo, 1959, p. 272.
3. *Yamasaki and Saitō, "Investigation of Corroded Ancient Glass. . . ."

40 (left). CHINESE FUNERARY OBJECT

A long octagonal form with flaring circular end, discovered by the owner in a jar burial at Suku-Okamoto in 1957.

- *Collection*: Motochika Suzuki, Kokura city, Fukuoka Prefecture.
- *Provenance*: Chinese. Dr. Sueji Umehara has

expressed the opinion that a difference in composition between this item and the *magatama* and *kudatama* found at Suku is an additional point in support of probable importation from China.[1]

- *Date*: Han dynasty.
- *Size*: L. 3.3 cm.; D. at narrow end, 0.5 cm., at flaring end, 1.4 cm.
- *Color*: Dark greenish blue; translucent. IH.D. Refl.: nearest Ch 4, 15-5-14; IH.D.Trans.: nearest Ch 3, 14-6-17.
- *Bubbles*: A few, and some large and small surface pits.
- *Composition*: No analysis available, but considering that, although from a jar burial, it still has no lead phosphate coating, one may assume that this is soda-lime glass.
- *Technique*: Cut or ground from a solid rod, with the end shaped.
- *Condition*: Good.

Reference:
1. *Umehara, "Nihon Jōko no Hari," p. 9.

41. HALF OF A MOLD FOR CASTING GLASS *MAGATAMA*

From the site at Yanagabaru, Fukuoka city, Fukuoka Prefecture.[1] Discovered by Mr. Motochika Suzuki.

- *Collection*: Archaeological Research Institute, Kyushu University.
- *Provenance*: This is the earliest proof of domestic manufacture of glass to be found in Japan. The fact that the *magatama* conception is purely Japanese in origin precludes any thought that the mold could be an import. *Magatama* very similar to the form of this mold, although slightly smaller, have been found not far from this site.
- *Date*: Late Yayoi period.
- *Size*: H. 3.2 cm.; L. originally 5.3 cm. Overall L. of cavity for molding, 3.3 cm.
- *Color*: Brownish, with areas of dark gray on the exterior.
- *Composition*: Quartz sand, now solidified.
- *Condition*: Parts worn away; broken and repaired at one point. Corresponding half missing.
- *Remarks*: In the center of the head-part of the

hollow is a tubular depression about 0.5 cm. in diameter and equally deep. There must have been a corresponding depression, it seems, in the missing half of the mold. The two halves were perhaps held in place by a rod (probably of metal, since metal was now in use), which extended into the two depressions; when the melted glass was later poured in, the rod would form a bore in the head of the *magatama*. This would explain those *magatama* whose bores are of uniform diameter throughout but show no sign of having been drilled; but would not, of course, account for the *magatama* of Plate 39, the bore of which had been drilled from both ends.

Judging from molds for bronze weapons found in this region, Dr. Umehara assumed that a channel must have been provided for pouring in the molten glass. A sandstone mold for metal halberd heads was found in this same locality but, as Dr. Umehara has pointed out, no metal *magatama* have ever been found, so this *magatama*-shaped mold must have been used for glass.[2]

References:
1. *Seiki Watanabe, "Fukuoka-shi Hakken. . . ."
2. *Umehara, "Nihon Jōko no Hari," p. 12, refers to the dark gray areas as remains of glass; they are very thin and faint.

42. FRAGMENTS OF GLASS BRACELETS

From a jar burial at Futazuka, Higashi, Maebaru-machi, Itoshima-gun, Fukuoka Prefecture. Discovered in 1935;[1] aside from the glass, no other artifacts were found.

Considered to have comprised two bracelets of solid annular form, rounded on the outward face and somewhat flat on the inner.

- *Collection*: Tokyo National Museum.
- *Provenance*: It cannot be asserted definitely that these bracelets were manufactured locally rather than imported; but since a mold for glass *magatama* exists (Pl. 41) and since metal bracelets of similar type were cast, it seems likely that these simple annular bracelets of glass were produced in Japan.
- *Date*: Late Yayoi period.
- *Size*: Largest fragment, L. 2.3 cm.; W. 1.375

cm.; T. 1.0 cm. Dr. Umehara estimated an exterior diameter for the bracelets of 8.0 cm., which is about that of Yayoi stone bracelets.[2]
- *Color*: Deep green; translucent. IH.In.Refl.: Ch 12, 11-3-12 and 11-3-13.
- *Bubbles*: Broken pits visible.
- *Composition*: Lead glass, colored by copper oxide; the white corroded coating analyzed as lead phosphate.[3] Sp. Grav.: of the glass, 5.66; of the white coating, 5.75.[4]
- *Technique*: Mold cast.
- *Condition*: Irregular broken fragments; outer thin coat of rough chalky white substance tinged with a thin layer of red cinnabar.
- *Remarks*: Numerous shell bracelets have been found on the forearms of Jōmon skeletons, and burials of the Late Jōmon period disclosed bracelets of red-and-black lacquered wood.

References:
1. *Dairoku Harada, "Nihon Saikō no Garasu," p. 6.
2. *Umehara, "Nihon Jōko no Hari," p. 8.
3. *Ibid.*, quoting Dr. Kazuo Yamasaki.
4. *Asahina, "Kodai Garasu. . . . ," p. 69.

43. EIGHT *KUDATAMA*

From the same jar burial at Maebaru-machi as Plate 42. Now strung together with the *marudama* below.
- *Collection*: Tokyo National Museum.
- *Date*: Late Yayoi period.
- *Sizes*: L. *ca.* 1.15–2.20 cm.; D. *ca.* 0.6–0.7 cm.
- *Color*: Deep green; translucent. IH.: probably the same as Plate 42.
- *Bores*: D. 0.35–0.40 cm. Several bits of hemp remain in these bores.
- *Composition*: Doubtless the same as Plate 42.
- *Technique*: In later times glass *kudatama* were usually cut from long tubes of glass formed by extending a hollow cylindrical form, but it is doubtful that these were produced in that way, because the bores vary in size. Perhaps in each case a simple *marudama*, still on its rod and still soft, was marvered on a flat surface to produce the cylindrical form.
- *Remarks*: Now arranged as a necklace, together with the following thirty-nine *marudama*.

Traces of hemp in the bores indicate an original stringing.

43. THIRTY-NINE *MARUDAMA*
From the same jar burial at Maebaru-machi as Plate 42. There were originally seventy-eight *marudama* found.[1]
- *Collection*: Tokyo National Museum.
- *Date*: Late Yayoi period.
- *Sizes*: H. 0.3–0.5 cm.; D. 0.7–0.8 cm.
- *Color*: Deep green; translucent. IH.: probably the same as Plate 42.
- *Bores*: D. *ca.* 0.3 cm.
- *Composition*: Probably the same as Plate 42.
- *Condition*: Identical to that of the bracelet fragments and the *kudatama* preceding.
  Reference:
  1. *Dairoku Harada, "Nihon Saikō no Garasu," p. 6.

44. *KODAMA*
From the 1953 excavation of the dwelling site at Numa, Tsuyama city, Okayama Prefecture. Further excavations, in 1958, were carried out under the auspices of the city, directed by Dr. Yoshirō Kondō of Okayama University. The settlement includes a number of pit-dwellings and what are considered to have been a storehouse, or assembly room, and workshops. Found here were stone implements and arrowheads, an iron weapon, and much Yayoi pottery.[1]
- *Collection*: Kyōdokan, Tsuyama city, Okayama Prefecture.
- *Date*: Middle Yayoi period. The assignment of this *kodama* to the Yayoi period is indisputable, since it was found in the dwelling site beneath the remains of the charred thatched roof, which had fallen, intact, when fire burned out the framework supporting it.
- *Size*: Almost ring shape. H. 0.15 cm.; D. 0.45 cm.
- *Color*: Turquoise blue; semitransparent. IH.D. Refl.: Ch 3, 14-4-16.
- *Bore*: D. 0.25 cm.; very wide in proportion to the bead's diameter.
- *Bubbles*: Several.
- *Technique*: Coiling around a rod. All contours are slightly rounded, and one area is thicker than the rest.
- *Condition*: Excellent.
- *Remarks*: This bead bespeaks the skill of the Yayoi artisans. Attention is called to the similarity of this glass to that of *kodama* from the Suku area in northern Kyushu (Sup. N. 4).

Three glass beads and a fragment were found in the second excavation, from the storehouse site K and the dwelling site L. These, however, are of a different type, with straighter walls and slightly elongated bubbles. Two were evidently cut from a glass tube, but one seems to have been coiled, indicating that the Yayoi craftsmen understood both techniques.
Reference:
1. Yoshirō Kondō and Yasuhiko Shibuya (ed.), *Tsuyama Yayoi Jūkyo Ato Gun no Kenkyū* [Investigation of a Group of Remains of Yayoi Dwellings in Tsuyama], Tsuyama Kyōdokan Kōkogaku Kenkyū Hōkoku [Tsuyama Local History Museum, Report of Archaeological Research], II, Tsuyama, 1957.

48. GLASS SLAB, MIYAJIDAKE SHRINE
National Treasure
Discovered in a burial at Miyajidake Shrine, in Kyushu; excavated in 1938, although discovered in 1934. The burial lay just outside the corridor outlet of the Oku-no-in Tomb, a large circular stone-chambered tumulus. It is thought that the burial was originally inside the tomb but was later moved outside the entrance when a prayer altar was installed in the interior. Associated objects included remarkably fine artifacts: gold-plated bronze crowns (subsequently other crown fragments were found that seem to be gold-plated copper); a perforated and punched, gold-plated saddle-mount with stirrups; gold-plate horse trappings, exhibiting Chinese Six Dynasties characteristics; a bronze sword; many large glass *marudama* (Pl. 58) whose glass corresponds to the glass of the slab; and large fragments of the same flat glass, apparently remnants of other slabs.
- *Collection*: Miyajidake Shrine, Miya-tsukasa, Tsuyazaki-machi, Munakata-gun, Fukuoka Prefecture.
- *Provenance*: This slab, the sizeable accompany-

ing fragments and others found in neighboring areas are so nearly identical that one must assume a common source for all. It has been assumed by some scholars that this material must have been brought in from abroad, but present knowledge of glassmaking progress up to this time makes it difficult to believe that the glassmakers of Japan, so obviously skillful by now, had to depend upon foreign sources for their glass metal. The very high lead content is in line with Japanese glass; analyses of ancient Chinese glass show 15–35% less. Could this glass possibly have come from the government casting bureau, Imono-no-tsukasa, in Nara?

- *Date*: Late 6th or early 7th century.
- *Size*: L. 17.8 cm.; W. 10.6 cm.; T. 0.45 cm.
- *Color*: Rich, deep yellowish green; almost transparent. Among the associated fragments, however, this tone varies in intensity, probably because of variations in thickness. By Munsell system, approximately 10GY5/8.[1]
- *Bubbles*: Circular, some fairly conspicuous, others tiny. These occur also in the accompanying fragments.
- *Composition*: Lead glass, showing by direct analysis a lead content of 69–77%[2]; colored by copper.[3] Sp. Grav. 5.46.[1] Two of the accompanying fragments showed Sp. Grav. 4.86 and 4.93.
- *Technique*: The molten glass metal was poured out into some shallow container, as evidenced by the low perpendicular walls and by the surface appearance of the underside.
- *Condition*: The underface not only shows the usual surface quality of cast glass but also bears shallow swirling striae, while the upper face bears heavy swirling striae; What appears in Plate 48 to be a short curving break at the lower left is actually a deep groove, or injury. There is also heavy corrosion on the sides and top, with some patches of greenish white, mossy crystallization (similar to two green lumps in the Shōsō-in; see Pl. 76), some areas of slight iridescence, and a few rather clear areas.

References:
1. *Oda, "Miyajidake-jinja. . . . ," p. 20.
2. *SGZC, p. 77.

3. Information on coloring agents comes from *Umehara, "Nihon Kodai no Garasu," p. 26.

TOMB PERIOD

49. *MAGATAMA* WITH THREE INCISIONS ON THE HEAD
Discovered in 1907 at Tsukiyama, Nishisue, Osafune-chō, Miwa-son, Oku-gun, Okayama Prefecture. Ancient Chinese bronze mirrors were in the same find.

- *Collection*: Tokyo National Museum (No. 14279).
- *Date*: Middle Tomb period.
- *Size*: L. 5.65 cm.; T. at head, 1.95 cm.
- *Color*: Dull, deep green; translucent. IH.D. Refl.: Ch 13, 12-3-15.
- *Bore*: D. 0.3 cm.; seems to be drilled from both sides with one opening widened ovally.
- *Bubbles*: Small and scattered.
- *Technique*: Mold cast and incised.
- *Condition*: Good surface, but minutely rough grained. Broken and repaired; cracks.
- *Remarks*: The well-rounded form (and that in Sup. N. 20) shows close affinity in shape, color, and general size to the Yayoi period *magatama* (Pl. 39), although precise comparison is hindered by the corrosion of the Yayoi example.

51. SMALL DISTORTED *MAGATAMA*
- *Collection*: The Corning Museum of Glass (No. 61.6.58).
- *Date*: Late Tomb period.
- *Size*: L. 1.85 cm.; W. at head, 0.84 cm.; T. at head, 0.71 cm.
- *Color*: Green; semitranslucent, but with appearance of opacity.
- *Bore*: D. 1.9 cm.
- *Bubbles*: Broken bubble pits prominent on the surface. Under the surface the bubbles appear whitish; in the head they are elongated, ellipsoidal, toward the tail they are circular, but along the extended curve are longitudinally elongated.
- *Composition*: Lead glass. Sp. Grav.: 3.20.
- *Technique*: The appearance suggests a coiling technique in which the glass thread was coiled around the rod only long enough to give a

rounded shape at the head, then pulled out toward the worker and, with a twist, disengaged, leaving a curving tail. In order to do this, the glass thread would have been only semimolten, as in beadmaking. The elongation of the bubbles in the head also indicates coiling, but it cannot be known whether the shape was accidental or intentional. There are, however, other larger *magatama* whose head shapes are also reminiscent of coiling.

- *Condition*: Good.
- *Remarks*: This is a far cry from the realistic contours of early large *magatama* and may be the result of quantity demand in the latter centuries of the Tomb period, which inevitably led to quicker methods and more abstract forms.

52. *MAGATAMA* WITH PLAIN HEADS
Part of twenty-one from the Ōtani Tomb, Ōtani, Wakayama city, Wakayama Prefecture. Excavated by a joint group under the supervision of Professor Takayasu Higuchi of Kyoto University.[1] Finds included a stone coffin "shaped like a house"; iron scale-armor, helmet, weapons, and rare horse armor; gilded bronze saddle-mount and other items; bronze mirrors; bronze and silver belt plaques; gold ear ornaments iron tools; *haniwa*; stone beads, glass *kudatama*; over ten thousand glass *kodama*; opaque brownish red glass beads, and other glass item (see Pl. 69).

- *Collection*: Education Committee, Wakayama city.
- *Provenance*: The contents of this tomb are in some ways unusual and in some respects unique in Japan, with some stylistic affiliations with both China of the Six Dynasties and Korea. Perhaps the artifacts were produced by some of the many immigrant craftsmen who entered Japan about this time. Even the color and consistency of the glass are unlike typical Tomb period glass; whether this was due to a different, foreign technique or to the growing lack of technical fastidiousness in *magatama* making, it is hard to say.
- *Date*: Second half 5th century.
- *Size*: Average example, L. 2.9 cm.; W. at head, 1.2 cm.; T. at head, 0.9 cm.

- *Color*: Rich glossy blue; opaque or slightly translucent. IH.D.Refl.: near Ch 4, 15-5-14.
- *Bore*: D. *ca.* 0.4 cm.
- *Bubbles*: Small circular ones visible at fractures; pitted surfaces.
- *Composition*: Soda-lime glass colored mainly by copper and iron. Sp. Grav.: 2.4.[2]
- *Technique*: Ground, or molded? Apparently a relatively low temperature was used, for the glass looks incompletely fused and is somewhat friable. In this respect, these *magatama* suggest a kind of glass paste.
- *Condition*: Generally speaking, good; but some examples are fragmentary, with what seem to be new breaks.

References:
1. *Higuchi, Nishitani, and Onoyama, *Ōtani Kofun*.
2. *Ibid.*, p. 87, quoting Dr. Kazuo Yamasaki's preliminary investigation "by the combined results of qualitative analysis followed by spectrographic luminescent analysis."

52 (top). *NATSUMEDAMA*
From the Ōtani Tomb, Ōtani, Wakayama city, Wakayama Prefecture, a *zenpō-kōen* mound excavated in 1957–58 by a joint group under the supervision of Professor Takayasu Higuchi of Kyoto University.[1]

- *Collection*: Education Committee, Wakayama city.
- *Date*: Second half, 5th century.
- *Size*: H. 1.35 cm.; D. 1.1 cm.
- *Color*: Pale gray green; semitransparent. IH.D. Refl.: Ch 13, 12-2-16; IH.D.Trans.: Ch 12, 11-3-16.
- *Bore*: D. *ca.* 0.2 cm.; flattened and irregular.
- *Bubbles*: A few.
- *Technique*: Probably marvered from a *marudama* to give an elongated form; then incised with a few lines for naturalistic effect.
- *Condition*: Good.

Reference:
1. *Higuchi, Nishitani, and Onoyama, *Ōtani Kofun*.

53. *KUDATAMA*
Excavated at Mukaiyama, Mie Prefecture.

- *Collection*: Tokyo National Museum (No. 8916)
- *Date*: Perhaps Middle Tomb period.
- *Size*: L. 2.1 cm.

- *Technique*: Evidently cut from a glass tube.
- *Condition*: Good.

55. MARUDAMA

From a stone sarcophagus installed in the clay chamber of the Shusenda Tomb at Abe, Hosaki, Nishi-takatsuki-son, Akaiwa-gun, Okayama Prefecture. The name Shusenda is due to an unusual amount of cinnabar (*shu*) found in the sarcophagus. Dedicatory items were first removed in the Meiji era; an official excavation was carried out in 1933, when Dr. Umehara dated the find to the fourth century.[1] Locally it is now considered a little later. According to tradition, there were in the burial a few iron swords and spears; mirrors; *magatama*; and a multitude of glass beads such as have been picked up on the site over many years. Six of the smallest *kodama* (uncatalogued) are shown in Plate 56.

- *Collection*: The Corning Museum of Glass (No. 62.6.7. III). Formerly owned by Mr. Iwatarō Mizuhara of Tamano city, Okayama Prefecture, and Mr. Masaemon Iwatsu of Okayama city; the latter presented them to the author. Mr. Iwatsu owns others of the group.
- *Provenance*: The large number of recovered beads and the considerable number of similar beads from Oku-chō (Sup. N. 23, 24), as well as from other nearby sites, suggest a possible common source. Mr. Iwatsu, member of the Okayama Prefectural Commission for the Preservation of Cultural Properties, conjectures— because this area was an ancient center for sword-making and other craft activities and because of the large number of glass beads found here—that this site may have been that of the local *tamatsukuri-be*.
- *Date*: Middle Tomb period.
  BLUE *marudama* (lower right)
- *Size*: H. 0.8–1.0 cm.; D. 0.6 cm.
- *Color*: Rich dark blue; transparent. IH.D. Refl.: difficult, but nearest Ch 6, 17-4-11.
- *Bore*: D. 0.25–0.3 cm. Lined with reddish clay; has a tinsellike appearance as seen through the transparent glass wall.
- *Bubbles*: Few, and near the surface.
- *Composition*: Soda-lime glass. Sp. Grav.: 2.43.

- *Technique*: Coiled and highly polished. Ends are flat, where apparently cut from other beads.
- *Condition*: Excellent.
  FOUR AMBER *marudama*
- *Sizes*: H. 0.8–0.9 cm.; D. 0.95–1.1 cm.
- *Color*: Deep honey color; transparent. IH. impossible to match.
- *Bores*: D. 0.3–0.55 cm.; wider, in each example, at one end. Like the blue bead, the bores are lined with a rough, light reddish clay that appears tinsellike through the transparency of the bead.
- *Bubbles*: Few, and chiefly near the surface; some are elongated both spirally and longitudinally. Some circular pits on the surface.
- *Composition*: Soda-lime glass. Sp. Grav.: 2.43.
- *Technique*: Coiled and well polished. Note that one of these displays the coiling process conspicuously in its corrugated surface.
- *Condition*: Excellent.

Reference:

1. Sueji Umehara, "Bizen-no-kuni Nishi-Takatsuki-mura no Kofun—Okayama-ken Shimo ni okeru Shinzō Kofun Chōsaroku, I" [Tombs of West Takatsuki-mura in Bizen Province—Report of the Investigation of the Principal Ancient Tombs in Lower Okayama Prefecture, Part I], *Rekishi to Chiri*, XIII, 4, pp. 366–369.

57. FIFTY-TWO KODAMA

- *Collection*: The Corning Museum of Glass (No. 62.6.7, II)
- *Provenance*: The same as Plate 55.
- *Date*: Middle Tomb period.
- *Sizes*: H. 0.2–0.4 cm.; D. 0.3–0.4 cm.
- *Color*: Dark turquoise blue; semitransparent. IH.D.Refl.: nearest Ch 4, 15-4-15 and 15-5-15.
- *Bores*: D. 0.075–0.175 cm.
- *Bubbles*: Numerous, small, circular; broken-bubble pits on the surfaces.
- *Technique*: Seem tube cut.
- *Condition*: Good.
- *Remarks*: This glass closely resembles that of some *kodama* from Oku-chō (Sup. N. 23, 24).

58. MARUDAMA
National Treasure
Found in the burial in front of the Oku-no-in

Tomb at Miyajidake Shrine. This burial also contained the flat glass slab (Pl. 48) and fragments, which are of the same glass metal.

- *Collection*: Miyajidake Shrine, Miya-tsukasa, Tsuyazaki-machi, Munakata-gun, Fukuoka Prefecture.
- *Date*: Late 6th or early 7th century.
- *Size*: Largest, H. 1.6 cm.; D. 1.75 cm.
- *Color*: Pale, medium, and dark green. Some look almost black, although green can be seen through the bores; semitranslucent. Some parts check IH.D.Refl.: Ch 11, 10-3-16 and Ch 13, 12-6-15.
- *Bores*: 0.25–0.6 cm.
- *Composition*: Lead glass; Sp.Grav.: 5.0.[1] One bead, by direct chemical analysis, had a high lead content of 68–76%; the lead content of the glass (Pl. 48), from which these were evidently made, was found to be 69–77%.[2] An X-ray fluorescence test (in relation to platinum) was made by Mr. Yoshikime Emoto of the Tokyo National Institute for the Preservation of National Cultural Properties; for chart of this see *Oda, "Miyajidake-jinja," p. 20.
- *Technique*: Coiled? No clear evidence of coiling, unless in a broken section of one bead that seems to show the glass wound around in layers. However, the condition of the beads makes conclusive investigation difficult.
- *Condition*: Some beads are covered with thick white corrosion; some, deeply scored with threadlike striations. Some pale green corroded areas appear bronzelike.

References:
1. *Oda, "Miyajidake-jinja. . . . ," p. 20.
2. *SGZC, p. 77.

59. OPAQUE BROWNISH RED *KODAMA*

From the Shimo-hinata Tomb, Takahama, Kechi-chō, Shimoagata-gun, Tsushima, Nagasaki Prefecture.[1]

- *Collection*: The Corning Museum of Glass (No. 62.6.11).
- *Provenance*: Perhaps an import.
- *Date*: Middle Tomb period.
- *Size*: H. 0.175 cm.; D. 0.25 cm.
- *Color*: Dark brownish red with darker stripes.

Color due to cuprous oxide. IH.D.Refl.: Ch 2, 1-6-12.
- *Bore*: D. 0.15 cm.; proportionately wide.
- *Composition*: Soda-lime glass. Sp. Grav.: 2.64; Refr. Ind.: 1.52.
- *Technique*: Tube cut.
- *Condition*: Excellent.

References:
1. This site was reported by Mizuno, Higuchi, and Okazaki, *op. cit.* (n. 10, p. 62), but there is little mention of glass.

60. SIX *TOMBODAMA*

From Tamatsukuri, Tamayu-mura, Yatsuka-gun, Shimane Prefecture. Excavated in 1915 by the Archaeological Research Institute of Kyoto Imperial University.

- *Collection*: Archaeological Research Institute, Kyoto University (No. 4329).
- *Date*: Middle or Late Tomb period.
- *Size*: H. 1.9 cm.; D. 1.65 cm.
- *Colors*: Glossy deep blue bodies with inserted irregular green spots; opaque. IH.D.Refl.: blue ground, nearest Ch 6, 17-2-11; green spots, Ch 12, 11-4-15 and 4-16.
- *Bores*: D. 0.3–0.4 cm.
- *Bubbles*: Small circular pits discernible.
- *Technique*: Coiled bodies, with green spots applied from a thread of semimolten glass. Some spots were well received by the heated bead, becoming an integral part of it; others, perhaps partially cooling before integration, are slightly rounded above the bead's surface and have crawled away a little around the edges. These *tombodama* seem to be early experiments. The blue glass is ill fused, some areas being darker, some lighter. The beads are poorly shaped and the green spots are rather clumsily inserted. Surfaces, however, are very glossy.

61. *TOMBODAMA*

From Nagahigashi, Oku-shirakata, Shirakata-mura, Nakatado-gun, Kagawa Prefecture.

- *Collection*: Tokyo National Museum.
- *Provenance*: Probably an import. A somewhat similar bead is illustrated by Professor Seligmann as coming from a burial on Java, which he called "millefiori of a type well known in

the East Indies."[1] Similar beads were found in Kyŏngju, Korea.

- *Date*: Considered to be of the Middle Tomb period.
- *Size*: H. 1.825 cm.; D. 2.05 cm.
- *Color*: Ground color, from dark green at one end to blue at the other, merging; opaque. Composite spots of various opaque colors, including dark blue, pale yellow, red, and white.
- *Bore*: D. 0.25–0.30 cm.
- *Technique*: Although this type is usually called "millefiori" by Westerners, this example is a coiled bead of the "stratified" type, with touches of various colored glasses superimposed to form compound "eye" motifs. At one end of the bead (the "finishing" end of the coiling) the "eye" insets became elongated, converging toward the bore, probably due to the revolving motion of the rod, combined with surface tension.
- *Condition*: Good.

Reference:
1. C. G. Seligmann and H. C. Beck, "Far Eastern Glass: Some Western Origins," *Bulletin of the Museum of Far Eastern Antiquities*, No. 10, Stockholm, 1933, p. 15.

62. *KUCHINASHIDAMA*

Excavated from a tomb in Gōshi-mura, Sawagun, Gumma Prefecture.

- *Collection*: The Corning Museum of Glass (No. 58.6.8).
- *Date*: Probably 5th or 6th century.
- *Size*: H. 1.2 cm.; D. 1.75 cm.
- *Color*: Blue green; translucent. IH.D.Refl. and Trans.: Ch 3, 14-4-16.
- *Bore*: D. 0.4–0.5 cm.; slightly oval.
- *Bubbles*: Surface somewhat pitted.
- *Technique*: A *marudama* tooled while still hot into an eight-lobed shape, using a fairly sharp knife-edged tool.
- *Condition*: Excellent.
- *Remarks*: Also known as a "melon bead," or *mikandama* ("tangerine bead").

63. GILT-BRONZE CROWN ORNAMENTED WITH BEADS

From the Kamo mound (popularly known as Inariyama mound), Mizuo, Takashima-gun, Shiga Prefecture, discovered in 1902 and investigated in 1923 by the Archaeological Research Institute of Kyoto Imperial University.[1] Associated objects: a Japanese bronze mirror; iron sword and knives; gilt-bronze ornaments; deerhorn ornament; fragment of lacquered wood; silver ring; *iwaibe* pottery; *haniwa*; horse trappings in iron and bronze; bronze bells; beads; gold ear pendants inset with glass; gilt-bronze shoes.

The gilt-bronze crown and shoes are decorated with punchwork, and numerous small items are attached everywhere, including glass beads, circular tufts of silk floss, gilt-bronze fish, and flat discs. Each is secured by a single twist of wire inserted through one of the many holes in the punchwork.

- *Collection*: Archaeological Research Institute, Kyoto University.
- *Date*: Early 6th century.
- *Glass color*: Dark blue; translucent.
- *Condition*: Although the bronze is badly damaged and fragmentary, the beads are in fair condition; many of the beads are missing.
- *Remarks*: Although the construction of this tomb was simple, the artifacts found within are rich. The nature of the dedicated items shows strong Korean influence, but the use of simple glass beads attached by wire to the gilt-bronze seems not to have been practiced in Korea. Could it be that glass beads were of such significance in Japan that they were deliberately used as jewels instead of gold discs? Or was it simply a lack of goldsmithing that led to these substitutes? The beads themselves are no different from others in Japanese tombs.

Reference:
1. Kosaku Hamada and Sueji Umehara, "Ōmi-no-kuni, Takashima-gun Mizuo-mura Kame no Kofun" [The Wild Duck Tomb at Mizuo-mura, Takashima-gun, Ōmi Province], *KTDKH*, VIII, Kyoto, 1923.

64. GLASS ORNAMENTED, INCISED SILVER FLORAL FORMS

From the same site as Plate 52.[1]

- *Collection*: Education Committee, Wakayama city.
- *Date*: Second half, 5th century.
- *Size*: Larger central sets, D. 0.6 cm.; medium sized sets, D. 0.425 cm.; smallest sets, D. 0.3 cm.
- *Color*: Largest sets, a rich, dark blue; translucent. IH.D.Trans.: Ch 7, 18-2-11. Smallest sets, gray blue; translucent. IH.D.Trans.: Ch 6, 17-5-15. The larger sets not only have thicker walls but are set into rather deep collars with no light transmitted from beneath. The tiny ones are set into open holes with no collars of any depth and nothing to obstruct the transmission of light. This imparts to the small ones a gray blue, glinting, jewel quality, whereas the larger ones display a less lively but rich dark blue. No doubt they were all produced from the same glass batch.
- *Composition*: Soda-lime glass, colored by copper and cobalt; the same glass as that of many dark blue beads found in this tomb. Sp. Grav.: 2.5.[2]
- *Technique*: The sets are hollow drops, the smaller ones spherical and the larger ones more pointed. They are set into simple basic rings with four to six flanges, which were passed through holes in the silver leaves and spread out behind for secure fastening. Around the basic collars are wrapped coils of silver; for the large central glass sets these are triple and overlapping, for the medium-sized sets they are a single coil, and for the smallest sets they are omitted entirely. The sets stand up high above the silver leaves; the leaves are pertly and realistically curved, and their outlines are smart; the coiled bands around the collars (where they have not fallen off) add a note of elegance. These, together with the shining beauty of the glass, have all served to produce attractive, imaginatively conceived ornaments. The tiny open holes in the leaves perhaps provided the means for attaching the ornaments to cloth or clothing. However, since there are thin bronze plates beneath some of the items, and also beneath some isolated glass sets mounted in the same kind of rings, it seems probable that these ornaments were used to adorn a crown or some other metal object.

- *Condition*: The glass is well preserved, but, as may be observed, the ornaments have suffered greatly.
- *Remarks*: The importance of this tomb is witnessed by the superior quality of its dedicatory offerings. Many characteristics of the relics are similar to those of Chinese artifacts or of tomb burials in Korea. These silver mountings are especially reminiscent of the skill of Korean goldsmiths of the time, but the author can cite no counterparts from Korea in method, design of the mountings, or in the use of silver.

References:
1. *Higuchi, Nishitani, and Onoyama, *Ōtani Kofun*.
2. *Ibid*., p. 87, quoting Dr. Kazuo Yamasaki.

65. GOLD EAR PENDANTS INSET WITH GLASS

Found in Nishi-zuka (West Tomb), Uryū-mura, Onyū-gun, Fukui Prefecture.[1] Associated objects: fragmentary iron armor; helmet, swords, halberds, arrowheads; iron and gold-plated iron horse-trappings; small bells of copper and silver; small and large mirrors; jasper *magatama* and *kudatama*; glass *magatama* (Sup. N. 20).

- *Collection*: Archives and Mausolea Division, Imperial Household Agency (No. E 1–1/1).
- *Provenance*: It would be difficult to say whether these ear pendants from Uryū-mura were imports from Korea, whether made by a Korean craftsman in Japan, or whether produced by a Japanese artisan who had either learned from a Korean artisan or imitated an import from Korea. However, the purity and thickness of the gold and the quality of the glass suggest a Korean origin. Since the location of the tomb was on the western side of Honshu it is not unlikely that there were connections between that area and the Korean peninsula.
- *Date*: Tomb period.
- *Size*: Pendants, L. 3.7 cm. Glass on obverse side, H. above the gold, 0.5 cm.; on reverse face, H. above the gold, 0.45 cm.; D. 0.475 cm.
- *Color*: Light, grayed sapphire blue; semi-transparent.
- *Bubbles*: Many minute ones; a few larger.

• *Technique*: Apparently an unique method. At first glance the glass seems to be, in each pendant, two globules, one appearing on each side of the gold plate. But upon close inspection it was observed that the two globules were joined, as an integral unit, through a perforation in the center of the gold piece. Mr. Mosuke Ishida of the Archives and Mausolea Division, in discussion with the author, discovered that the glass had been slightly cut away on one globule at the level of the gold plate. Where this had happened a resultant tiny horizontal ledge in the globule on the upper face of the pendant rested on the gold; what was left of the glass globule below that point proceeded through the perforation to join the globule on the under side. The globule on one side of the perforation, that is the globule that had been cut, was obviously larger than that on the reverse side, making it both wider and higher by about a millimeter. Everything was tight and secure, with no looseness or disintegration whatever. Several possibilities for attaining this have come to mind, but only one seems flawless. If the craftsman had first cut away a small portion of a glass globule (Pl. 65, a) and had then inserted the cut end through the perforated gold sheet of the pendant (Pl. 65, b), he could then, by inverting the gold piece and holding the glass firmly in place, have touched the end of the cylindrical portion, or core, with a thread of glass from a heated glass rod. By surface tension a second globule of glass would have formed, firmly fused to the cut neck of the first globule (Pl. 65, c). The two glass globules, having thus become a single unit, would, barring breakage of the glass itself, remain permanently in place. The fact that no metal "seat" intervenes between the glass and the flat gold plate accentuates the contrasting beauty of both glass and gold.

• *Condition*: Excellent. The two leaf forms are of thick, pure sheet gold heavy enough not to have become misshapen during the centuries of burial.

• *Remarks*: Leaf-shaped metal pendants with tooled edges are common in Korean gold ear pendants, and a few have been found in Japan.

Some have merely a central threadlike line running the length from top to tip; but in at least one example, from Kumamoto Prefecture (Pl. 66), a central boss appears, which, though it is of gold, resembles in general the glass globules under discussion.

Reference:
1. Sanpei Ueda, "Wakaza-no-kuni Onyū-gun Uryū-mura Nishi-zuka" [The West Tomb at Uryū-mura, Onyū-gun, Wakasa Province], *KKZ*, VIII, 4, pp. 224–229.

ASUKA-HAKUHŌ PERIOD

68. *GYOKU-CHIN* (Bead or "Jewel" Pillow) From the burial on Abu-san, Takatsuki city, Osaka Prefecture. Discovered in 1934 and subsequently investigated by an appointed committee. The following data as well as this plate were obtained from the report by Dr. Umehara.[1] The body was apparently covered with a pall woven of gold threads, and a few items of the sort "kept by one's bedside at night" were placed nearby, but no dedicatory offerings were found other than the *gyoku-chin*. The investigation, however, was incomplete, since the authorities felt it improper to further disturb the spirit of this nobleman; after constructing a protective outer box for the coffin, everything was replaced in the tomb, with ceremonies of apology and prayer for the soul's repose.

The *gyoku-chin* consists of several hundred glass beads strung in a complex, repeat pattern on interwoven wires of almost pure silver. This lay within at least five folds of thin silk, forming a sort of cylindrical pillow. Found at the head of the coffin, it seems to have formed a symbolic cushion for the head of the deceased. It gives a possible clue to the nature of the *makura* (pillow) in the tomb of Emperor Tenmu discussed on page 69. The manner in which the beads were arranged to form a complex design attests not only to the growing skill of the beadmakers but to a budding awareness of the potentialities of design.

• *Collection*: Replaced in the tomb on Abu-san.
• *Date*: 7th century. The assigned date of the tomb is partly determined by the kind of sar-

cophagus used, a *kanshitsu* (dry lacquer) type, the exact nature of which was ascertained by study of fragments of similar coffins in the Kegoshi (or Asagao) Tomb of Nara Prefecture (see Pl. 74). Such coffins are constructed, layer by layer, of hempen cloth dipped in lacquer, the whole solidifying to the stiffness of a thin, lightweight board. The lacquered coffins of China and Korea are unlike these, since they have a wood base. These seemingly unique Japanese examples are referred to as *kyōchō* coffins (the meaning uncertain). In each instance the exterior of the coffin was further coated with black lacquer and the interior with vermilion lacquer. The coffin of the Emperor Tenmu (see page 69) was of red lacquer, but it is not known whether it, too, was of the *kyōchō* technique. It is recorded that the sarcophagi of Shōtoku Taishi and his wife belong to this class.[2]

Local tradition identifies the interred as the renowned statesman, Fujiwara no Kamatari, who died in 669, but a site in Kawachi is also claimed for that burial.

The glass beads themselves further corroborate the late date assigned to this tomb, for they are said to seem more related to seventh and eighth century glass than to beads found in earlier tombs.

- *Sizes*: Wire framework, over 30.3 × 9 cm. Larger beads, D. *ca.* 0.9 cm.; medium size beads, D. 0.6 cm.
- *Colors*: Larger beads, dark blue; medium size, dark blue and green; smallest beads, green.
- *Bores*: In the largest beads the bores are comparatively wide, increasing in size from one end to the other, indicating that they were probably drilled.
- *Composition*: Larger beads, soda-lime glass; smaller beads, lead glass with high lead content. Sp. Grav.: larger beads, 2.5; smaller beads, 5.1.
- *Technique*: If the bores were drilled, then the beads were seemingly molded.
- *Remarks*: For the record of another *gyoku-chin*, see page 69. The *gyoku-chin* idea was perhaps not unknown even in the late Tomb period in Japan. In the Ban-zuka, a *zenpō-kōen* tomb at

Karita-machi, Miyako-gun, Fukuoka Prefecture, a group of nearly two thousand glass beads (*marudama* and *kodama*)[3] was found at the position of the head, and it is thought to have served such a purpose. That burial antedates this one; its beads are of the usual Tomb period type.

The belief that the dwelling place of the soul is in the head points to the real significance of the *gyoku-chin*. Often, sarcophagi of the Tomb period have a hollow or a pillow carved in the stone for a headrest; in at least one instance the symbolic *magatama* is carved in such a headrest.[4]

The idea of concealing and protecting a rare and intricate design of beads such as this within layers of silk wrapping manifests the still continuing attitude toward the bead as something more than a mere decoration. This rich and secret arrangement can be construed only as being an amuletic offering charged with power to safeguard and bless the deceased in his tomb, an example of a still vital belief in some sacred spiritual potency lying inherent in the bead and possibly also in glass.

References:
1. *Umehara, *Settsu Abu-san Kobo*. . . . , pp. 5–37.
2. Sueji Umehara, "Shōtoku Taishi Isonaga no Gobyō" [The Mausoleum of Shōtoku Taishi at Isonaga], *Shōtoku Taishi Ronsan* [Studies Relating to Shōtoku Taishi], Kyoto, 1921, pp. 344–370.
3. Archaeological Research Institute, Kyushu University, Fukuoka city.
4. In a fifth century tomb in Kagawa Prefecture; see *Sekai Kōkogaku Taikei* [Survey of World Archaeology], Heibonsha, III, Fig. 316.

70. *SHARI-TSUBO* OF THE HŌRYŪ-JI PAGODA

Interred beneath the five-storied pagoda of Hōryū-ji, Ikoma-gun, Nara Prefecture.[1] This installation was discovered in 1926 during repairs, but because of its sanctity no report was made at that time.[2] The hollow was resealed and thickly covered with concrete.[3]

In 1949, as new repairs to the pagoda were in progress, scholars and the Education Ministry pressed for a thorough scientific investigation of the *shari* installation. The temple authorities maintained that since the treasures were the very life stream, the essence, of their Buddhist faith, it was inconceivable that they be disturbed. Nevertheless, after discussions by priests and parishioners of Hōryū-ji, there was final acquiescence, with the proviso that rituals of worship and prayers be held throughout the excavation and reinterment. The investigation was sponsored by the Hōryū-ji Kokuhō Hoson Iin Kai ("Commission for the Preservation of Hōryū-ji's National Treasures") under the leadership of Dr. Tōru Haneda.

Although the associated objects were carefully examined and some gelatin molds taken so that they could be reproduced in fascimile (now on exhibition in the Hōryū-ji museum), the glass *shari-ki* itself was considered so sacred that no reproduction was permissible—and no doubt it would in fact have been impossible to accurately reproduce the color and quality of the glass under the circumstances. As it was, the investigators themselves could only view the treasure as it was held before them at some distance by the abbot of the temple. Nonetheless, at some time during the proceedings a complete photographic record was made. It is the author's good fortune, through the courtesy of Abbot Ryōken Saeki, to be able to present illustrations from the official report of the investigation.

Plate 69 shows the pagoda. Its central wooden pillar penetrated somewhat more than one meter into the ground before resting on the foundation stone. Beneath it, in a stepped cavity covered by a circular metal lid, the *shari-tsubo* and its accompanying treasures had been interred. As befitted these objects' holy nature and the status of this great temple, the installation was elaborate.

The glass *shari-tsubo* was first encased in a handsome hinged oval reliquary of perforated sheet gold. These two were then encased in a slightly larger oval receptacle of sheet silver fashioned in the same shape and design as the larger gold one. These three were placed in a covered receptacle of bronze, together with many beads, incense woods, cloves, and other small votive offerings loosely piled about them. The lid of this bronze jar is surmounted by

a bottle-shaped knob suggestive of the glass *shari-tsubo* housed within; the lid was held securely in place by a chain of stout silver links. Finally, the whole was placed in the center of a large open bowl of bell metal, and around it were heaped more of the precious beads and other small offerings; among these there was placed, on edge, a silvery bronze Chinese mirror of the "grapes, birds, and animals" style, which Dr. Umehara, who examined it, felt might be of the Sui dynasty.[4]

• *Collection*: Reinterred beneath the foundation stone of the Hōryū-ji pagoda and further sealed beneath concrete.

• *Provenance*: Dr. Umehara has suggested a Japanese source for this *shari-tsubo*, on the basis of his experience that all known continental examples are of thin glass, while this one seems to be of thick glass, as were others found in Japan.[5] Further supporting evidence includes: the presence in this installation of two thick fragments of glass (Sup. N. 34); fragments of a small glass bottle of thick glass (Pl. 71) found in the lowest layer of the clay platform of the Kondō of Hōryū-ji; and fragments of a green glass *shari-tsubo* (very thick in some areas) which, during repair of the Yakushi image in the Kondō of Yakushi-ji temple, Miato-mura, Ikoma-gun, Nara Prefecture, were found beneath that bronze image, which dates from the late Hakuhō period.

• *Date*: Probably late 7th century. For discussion of the dating of the ancient Hōryū-ji buildings, see Plate Note 73. One of the important aspects of this installation is its dating. If the *shari-tsubo* was installed under a new pagoda after 670, an official casting bureau with a glass division, or even a glass office in a temple construction bureau, must certainly have been operating, and this *shari-tsubo* may well have been produced there. It is also possible that the installation was placed under the original pagoda about 607 and could have survived a 670 fire undamaged (as did those of Asuka-dera and Hōrin-ji). Although there were skilled glass artisans working in Yamato in the early seventh century as well as later, Dr. Umehara states that the particular type of openwork design on the gold and silver containers did not develop until the later seventh century, which therefore seems to substantiate at least a late seventh century date for the installation. The glass container *could*, of course, have been an earlier product.

- *Size*: From Mr. Kishi's measurements in 1926: H. 7.42 cm.[6] Dr. Umehara reported that, from the distance at which it was seen, it seemed to be of thick glass.
- *Color*: Green, presumed due to copper. One writer calls it a "bright" green; another, "dark" or "strong" green. Evidently it was rather intense, which calls to mind the intense green glass found at Miyajidake Shrine (Pl. 48). Mr. Kishi, who saw the container more closely in 1926, called it simply "green."
- *Composition*: Presumed, from the color, to be of lead glass.
- *Technique*: Blown glass. The *shari-tsubo* shape is globular; there seems to be a "kick" in the bottom, but how high it rises in the interior cannot be determined. The straight-walled neck tapers slightly toward the top. The stopper is of silver, which, as far as can be judged, is unusual if not unique in Japan, but it resembles somewhat the glass stopper used for the *shari-tsubo* of Songyim-sa temple in Korea (Pl. 110).
- *Condition*: Slightly deteriorated surface due to water seepage; otherwise in good condition. In one instance Mr. Kishi reported that no object was contained within, but in another he wrote of "clove fragrance and water; as regards the *shari*, it is unknown." Perhaps the *shari* became dissolved, over the centuries, in the water that had seeped in; or perhaps, due to restrictions, the matter was not investigated.
- *Remarks*: Although references to other pagoda installations of the period are available, they are either exceedingly brief or lack full scientific detail. The report of the committee of investigation of the Hōryū-ji installation, begun in 1949, is carefully detailed, even though close study of the glass *shari-tsubo* itself was prohibited. From the superb quality of the attendant gold, silver, and bronze containers, from the description of the strong color of the glass, and from its general appearance in the illustration, the high value placed upon this treasure and the care and skill expended in producing it can be inferred.

References:

1. For the official report, see *Hōryū-ji Gojū-no-tō.* . . .
2. Information from *Tamura, "Hōryū-ji Gojū-no-tō shita. . . . "
3. *Asahi Shashin Bukku* [Asahi Photographic Books], No. 38, Tokyo, Asahi Shinbunsha, 1957, p. 28.
4. Sueji Umehara in *Hōryū-ji Gojū-no-tō.* . . . , p. 37.
5. *Umehara, "Nihon Kodai no Garasu," p. 27. In the Archaeological Research Institute of Tokyo University there are, however, fragments of a small bottle assigned to Kyŏngju, the ancient Silla capital in Korea, which were purchased in Korea. Of very dark blue, or black, opaque glass, they are about 0.2 cm. thick, approximately twice as thick as the usual continental examples. Could they represent an import from Japan?
6. *Kishi, "Taishō Jū-go Nen. . . . ," p. 14.

71. FRAGMENTS OF A *SHARI-TSUBO*

Discovered after the fire of 1949 in the lowest stratum of the altar platform of the Kondō of Hōryū-ji.

- *Collection*: Hōryū-ji, Ikoma-gun, Nara Prefecture.
- *Provenance*: In general, similar to the thick glass metal of the *shari-tsubo* of Sūfuku-ji (Pl. 6), although this glass is neither so brilliant nor so beautiful as that one. Both are in contrast to thin Korean and Chinese *shari* containers, thus supporting attribution to domestic production.
- *Date*: On the basis of similarities, probably 7th century.
- *Size*: T. 0.25 cm.
- *Color*: Yellow green; translucent. IH.In. Trans.: Ch 12, 11-4-15.
- *Technique*: Blown glass; has spiral striae.
- *Composition*: Lead glass with estimated lead content of 68%. Sp. Grav.: 4.8. (K. Yamasaki)
- *Condition*: Surface condition good.

73. EAST WALL PAINTING OF THE KONDŌ OF HŌRYŪ-JI

Important Cultural Property

Hōryū-ji is said traditionally to have been

founded in 607, and many scholars believe that the ancient buildings that have survived to modern times date from that year. These buildings—the pagoda, the central gateway (Chūmon), the Kondō (the main hall of worship) and parts of the cloisters surrounding the courtyard—are part of the Sai-in, or Western Compound. However, in 670, according to the *Nihon Shoki*, "After midnight a fire broke out in Hōriū-ji. Not a single building was left."[1] Certain scholars believe that the Kondō and other buildings of the Sai-in were all destroyed and rebuilt in the same style and on the same site in 708—though no evidence of any scorched earth has ever been found there.

Other scholars hold that the fire took place in an earlier compound to the southeast of the present Sai-in, because in that area have been found traces of Asuka-style roof tiles and of scorching. All the intricacies of this controversy between scholars, priests, architects, and others cannot be discussed here, but it would be pertinent to know the exact date of the buildings associated with glass. Perhaps the record of 693 that three canopies were dedicated to Hōryū-ji by the imperial court in that year[2] may refer to the three canopies of the Kondō, in which case they must either have been a simple gift to an existing building or a special gift for one being newly rebuilt.

Another controversy involves the dating of this particular painting on the east wall of the Kondō. It was thought for a time that it might have been a repainting of the Kamakura period. Now, however, it is agreed that it dates from the end of the Hakuhō period, or the first year or two of the Nara period, after the reconstruction of the Kondō was completed.[3]

The interior of the Kondō was entirely lined with paintings of the Buddhas of the "Paradises of the Four Directions" and their attendants. In 1949 a fire broke out, and, before it could be extinguished, the wooden columns and the paintings were irreparably damaged. The charred remains served as an accurate guide in rebuilding a facsimile on the same site. The new Kondō was dedicated and opened in 1954 in an impressive Asuka style ceremony.

For glass, the most important is the east wall painting. Here is portrayed the Buddhist deity who reigns in the Eastern Paradise, the Buddha Yakushi Ruri-kō Nyōrai, or Bhaisajya-Guru Vaidūrya Prabhā (Master of Medicine of the Blue Jewel Radiance) who uttered, among twelve vows to aid mankind, one to cure the spiritual and bodily ills of men.[4] Yakushi is often depicted holding in his left hand a small medicine jar. In this painting one glass vessel is clearly indicated, and two others may have originally represented glass, although the condition of the painting, even before the fire, made this difficult to determine.

1. The Bodhisattva standing on the Buddha's left carries on the palm of the uplifted right hand a shallow, colorless, and fully transparent platelike vessel, through which, before the fire damage, could be seen the details of the supporting hand and part of the robes of the priest standing to the rear, the dark band of his inner robe being especially prominent. In the shallow glass dish are red lotus petals for strewing in adoration before the Buddha. Today the details of the glass may still be seen quite clearly, but the dark red of the petals is completely charred, and the dark band of the priest's robe has disappeared.

2. The Bodhisattva on the Buddha's right holds a small bottle or flask, which, at first glance, suggests glass. Somewhat closer inspection reveals a pattern that seems to indicate either some other material or applied threads of glass. Before the fire this seemed blue; it has been mentioned as a "jar of five colors."[5] It has also been said that by infrared photography the object seemed to be glass.[6] Since the fire, the shape of the jar and the curving lines on its surface are still clearly seen, but color is entirely gone. A cup or bowl of glass with similar configurations laid out in what seem to be applied threads of colored glass appears in a wall painting in a Buddhist cave temple at Qumtura in Central Asia. The bowl is described as being faintly white with a rounded yellow rim and design lines of a bright brown color.[7] Perhaps the

representation at Hōryū-ji was also intended to represent a glass bottle with applied threads of colored glass.

3. A possible third glass vessel is the "round object" that the Buddha holds in his left hand. From what is known about the iconography of this deity, the object would be the medicine jar symbolic of his vow to help the physical ills of man; but the condition of the painting, both before and since the fire, prevents accurate identification of the nature of the jar. Glass may have been intended. In a painting of the late Heian period this deity is shown holding a jar that is definitely represented as of blue glass (Pl. 123).

References:

1. Aston, *op. cit.* (see n. 1, p. 45) II, p. 293.
2. *Art Guide of Nippon*, Vol. I (Nara, Mie, and Wakayama Prefectures), Tokyo, Society of Friends of Eastern Art, 1943, p. 210.
3. For a resume of outstanding arguments (in English) see Ichimatsu Tanaka, *Hōryū-ji Kondō Hekiga Kaisetsu* [An Introduction to the Wall Paintings in the Main Hall of the Hōryū-ji Monastery], Tokyo, Ministry of Education, Cultural Properties Protection Commission, 1951. There is also a resume of the dispute in *Art Guide of Nippon*, pp. 212–216.
4. Formerly the deity represented here was considered to be the Buddha Shaka (Śakyamuni). For refutation, see Tanaka, *ibid.*, pp. 4–5. Iconographically, paintings of Yakushi and Shaka are often similar, and, frequently, especially in older writings, the deity of the east wall is referred to as Shaka.
5. *Sōshu Watanabe, *Heian Jidai. . . .*, p. 458.
6. Toichirō Naitō, *The Wall Paintings of Hōryū-ji*, tr. and ed. William Reynolds Beal Acker and Benjamin Rowland, Jr., *Studies in Chinese and Related Civilizations*, No. 5, American Council of Learned Societies, 1943, p. 127, n. 6.
7. A. von Lecoq, "Vessels of Glass Illustrated in Two Wall Paintings from a Buddhist Cave of the Eighth Century, in Chinese Turkestan," *Eastern Art*, I, Pl. IV, Fig. 4 and p. 135.

74. CLOISONNÉ-LIKE SMALL BRONZE ORNAMENT

This was found in the Kegoshi (or Asagao) Tomb, Asuka-mura, Takaichi-gun, Nara Prefecture. Only fragments of the coffins were found, but these were of the new *kyōchō* (lacquer-saturated hemp) type (see Pl. N. 68). As the tomb had been rifled, nothing remained in it except coffin fragments and several small items.

This ornament is a lozenge-shaped plaque of bronze with an outer wall enclosing a ground of opaque whitish glass surrounding a central six-petaled bronze rosette motif filled with transparent glass; all of the exposed top surface of the bronze walls, or "cloisons," were originally gold plated.

- *Collection*: Yamato Rekishikan, Kashiwara, Nara Prefecture.[1]
- *Provenance*: Probably Japanese. Until recently nothing similar could be cited from China,[2] nor from Korea, except that the glass-flowing technique may be noted in one or two Korean artifacts and may constitute the origin of this mode.[3]
- *Date*: 7th century.
- *Size*: L. overall, 4.6 cm.; W. 3.2 cm. Outer rim, H. 0.2–0.3 cm.; W. 0.075–0.5 cm. Inner "cloisons," W. *ca.* 0.05 cm.
- *Color*: The background is a light, slightly cream-colored glass; opaque. The petals of the rosette are filled with golden reddish brown glass; transparent. IH.D.Refl.: close to Ch 2, 1-4-12, but when seen at an angle, Ch 2, 1-5-12 or 13.
- *Bubbles*: In the whitish ground, numerous minute broken-bubble pits. In the glass of the central motif, circular bubbles here and there.
- *Technique*: Because of bronze corrosion it cannot, unfortunately, be ascertained whether the bronze outlines of the central petals are true cloisons (as in later cloisonné). Nor is it possible, if they are cloisons, to ascertain the manner of adhesion to the base. The filling in of the rosette was not done by the Western enamel technique, but by guiding a melting glass thread into each petal compartment of the rosette. This must have been done by a simple technique, such as that used when forming glass beads by hand. One end of a bit of glass rod would have been softened over a flame and the melting glass directed into each interstice of the rosette. Two tiny peaks in the rounded surface of one petal (seen under a magnifying

glass) indicate the lifting away of the glass rod with a twisting motion to free the glass thread; the glass left in the rosette compartment was not sufficiently hot to level off in the petal forms, but cooled in a somewhat rounded shape, with these two minute peaks as further clues to the method.

The appearance of this cloisonné ornament, taking into account both the manner of applying the glass and the size of the "cloisons," as well as the gold plating of their upper edges, provides an intermediate link between ornamental pieces in Korea, of perhaps the seventh century, and a very advanced example of similar technique preserved in the Shōsō-in (Pl. 12)

- *Condition*: The bronze is corroded and green; the light colored glass ground is weathered, covered with a crackled silvery white film; only portions of the central glass filling in the rosette remain, much having broken away; the gilding is largely worn off.
- *Remarks*: At the present moment, this ornament is still the earliest example known in Japan of what, for the lack of a better term, is here called cloisonné, although it differs from true cloisonné except in general effect.

References:

1. *Umehara, "Chūgoku Shutsudo no Hari-yū. . . . ," p. 22, gives the location in 1967 as the Nara National Museum.
2. Dr. Umehara, *ibid.*, speaks of this as Chinese of the T'ang dynasty and compares it with examples discovered in Korea and China and assigned to the Six Dynasties and T'ang dynasty. The author has had no opportunity to study these. He also describes a bronze belt mounting as Chinese, Six Dynasties, in parts of which glass was "poured in."
3. *Blair, "The Cloisonné Backed Mirror. . . ."

NARA PERIOD

75. FRAGMENT OF THE *ZŌBUTSU-SHO SAKUMOTSUCHŌ*

- *Collection*: The Shōsō-in. This is not listed in the official shelf-list catalogue of the Shōsō-in, but was kept in the Middle Section and is so marked on its face.

- *Date*: First day, fifth month of Tempyō 6 (734).
- *Provenance*: The *Zōbutsu-sho Sakumotsuchō* has long been thought to refer to the activities of Tōdai-ji; however, Dr. Toshio Fukuyama has made a somewhat tentative rearrangement of the fragments and relates this document to the construction of the West Kondō of Kōfuku-ji.[1] On the basis of a notation on a companion fragment of the *Zōbutsu-sho Sakumotsuchō*, he suggests that this was part of a draft that would presumably be discarded when the permanent record had been made. According to his theory, the *Zōbutsu-sho Sakumotsuchō* was a discarded record whose reverse side was used, after 743, for the keeping of accounts in the Sutra Copying Office (Shakyō-sho) of the construction office of the Konkōmyō-ji temple. It seems strange that a discarded record of the *Zōbutsu-sho* of Kōfuku-ji should have found its way into the Sutra Copying Office of another temple, unless, of course, the record could have been discarded not by Kōfuku-ji itself but by the overall supervisory Zōjibutsu-sho (the government's Bureau of Temple Construction) and, such being the frugal use of precious paper, was later doled out to another temple office when paper was needed there. According to Dr. Fukuyama, the formulae given in this document represent glass made in the Imono-no-tokoro of the Kōfuku-ji Construction Office. He further discusses the probable sources of materials, such as the Office of the Empress's Household, the Takumi-ryō (Imperial Workshop) and the East and West markets near Nara.

TRANSLATION

USE: *Koku-en* [black lead], 983 *kin*.
By heating it, 1158 small *kin* of red oxide of lead will be obtained.
Shusha [cinnabar], 9 small *ryō*
Material for red beads
Rokushō [basic copper carbonate], 17 small *kin* 9 *ryō*
Material for green and black beads
Kirinketsu [literally "blood of the *kirin*," a fabulous animal, but is a vegetable product], 7 small *ryō* 1 *bu*

For red *sashidama* [pierced beads]

Urushi [lacquer], 9 *gō*
 Dye for black *sashidama*

Goma-abura [sesame oil], 1 *shō*
 Requisite for clay molds for *sashidama*

Choshi [wild-boar fat], 9 *shō* 3 *gō*
 Requisite for roasting lead

Shio [salt, or salts], 1 *to* 3 *shō* 5 *gō*
 Material for roasting lead

Sumi [block ink], 64 pieces
 Material for molds for *sashidama*

Kami [paper], 38 *chō* [sheets?]
 Material for various uses

Tsumugi ["pongee"], 3 *shaku*
 Material for various screenings

Kinu [silk], 4 *shaku*
 Material for dyeing with *kirinketsu*

Usu-tsumugi [thin "pongee"], 4 *shaku*

Chōfu [a cloth woven as "tax"], 3 *jō* 2 *shaku*
 Material for house cloths and head coverings

Shōfu [a cloth woven for sale], 2 *jō* 4 *shaku*
 Material for cleaning cloths

Shirokawa [white leather], 1 *chō* [sheet?]
 Material for beadworkers' protection

Haga [broken tile], 14 *ka* [small round pieces]
 Material for coated molds for *sashidama*

Akatsuchi [red clay], 3 small *kin*
 Ingredient for 2 *shō* of beads

Hakuseki [silica quartz], 230 *kin*
 Material for beads

Tsuchi [clay], 360 *kin*
 Material for a crucible for melting beads. Clay from Ishikawa-gōri in Kawachi Province

Karosō no kuki [stalks of an unidentified plant], 280 bunches
 Requisite for *sashidama*

Sumi [charcoal], 21,600 *kin*
 Material for beadmaking [i.e., fuel]

Takagi [firewood], 204 bundles
 Requisite for roasting lead

The above list represents materials and equipment for beadmaking.

The two large characters brushed carelessly on this fragment read "Nan-sō" (South Treasure-House), but in modern times the document was stored in the Chū-sō (Central Treasure-House). When it was removed from the South Section to the Central Section is not known; perhaps during reorganization in the Meiji era.

• *Remarks*: According to the document, basic materials for the batch were red oxide of lead, prepared from black lead, and silica from quartz. Mr. Jusei Sugie calculated that the red clay does not exceed sixteen percent of the total, so it must be thought that it contained iron and was perhaps used as a coloring agent. He surmised that the "salt" must have been a flux, and estimated the ingredients as

Silica (SiO_2)	37%
Lead Oxide (PbO)	61%
Alkali (Niter)	2%

and compared this with the composition of heavy optical glass of today. Glass made from this formula was equal to a lead glass with a specific gravity of 5 and with a high refractive index—excellent for decorative purposes.[2] This is borne out in most of the fragments of glass in the Shōsō-in.

The authors of *Shōsō-in no Garasu* (pp. 48–49) consider the "black lead" of that time as metallic lead. They are surprised at the small quantity of red lead, or minium (1158 small *kin*, or 386 *kin*), and consider that there must have been inferior minium, or slag, which was not counted; there are, in fact, packages of minium preserved in the Shōsō-in with "superior," "medium," and "inferior" notations written in ink on the eighth century wrappings.[3]

Coloring agents are given as cinnabar, copper carbonate, *kirinketsu*, and lacquer. Cinnabar is said to vanish at fusing temperature, so it must have been finely powdered and applied on the surface. A small amount of copper would produce green, and a larger amount a very dark green, even black in appearance. Among the glass materials in the Shōsō-in, there are seemingly black ones, which, by transmitted light, show green tones. *Kirinketsu* is a reddish brown substance secured from plants in Southeast Asia, which today is mixed in varnishes and used in cosmetics; in Nara times it was probably imported from China.[4] *Shōsō-in no Garasu* (p. 34) explains it as "a coagulation of a fluid extracted from the fruit of a kind of wistaria distributed through the East Indies." (For examples of beads painted with an alcohol-soluble red substance, which, although not scientifically investigated, is considered to be *kirinketsu* due to its small amount, see Pl. N. 89, *Color*, and *Shōsō-in no Garasu*, Plate 12.) As for lacquer, it is difficult to imagine its combining with glass, or how it could have been used. There seem to be no beads with lacquer applied as decoration.

The sesame seed oil, according to Mr. Sugie, was kneaded with clay for the making of molds. The wild boar fat he thought was a fuel added to the firewood to intensify the heat, but Dr. Nakao describes it as added to powdered yellow lead oxide "to perfect it" and to produce red oxide of lead.[5] In the section in the *Zōbutsu-sho Sakumotsuchō* immediately following the glass document are details of pottery making, in which wild boar fat is listed as "for the lead extracting process"; in the same text "red earth" is designated "for mixing with a *shō* of lead oxide." The *sumi* (block ink) has been considered as a coating for molds.

The pongee (about 91.5 cm. of it) and the silk (about 122.0 cm.) were evidently used for fine screening of such materials as the *kirinketsu* and possibly the cinnabar. *Chōfu* was cloth woven in the provinces and sent to the central government as tax in kind. *Shōfu*, on the other hand, was cloth woven for personal use or sale. The white leather was perhaps used for aprons or for holders to protect body or hands from heat. The exact use of the unidentified *karosō* stalks is unknown, unless possibly for plant ash; it has been suggested that the pierced beads were temporarily "strung" in groups on these stalks for counting purposes, but in another section of the *Zōbutsu-sho Sakumotsuchō* there are listed, as purchases, "Yellow thread . . . material for stringing beads" and "arsenic sulphide or gamboge . . . material for stiffening the ends of strings for beads."[6]

From factors such as the exactness of quan-

tities listed, the silk used for fine screening, the white leather, and the care with which molds were prepared, it can be assumed that the technique of glassmaking was, at this time, a matter of considerable precision. Confirmation of this exists in the glass of the period, especially those glass items in the Shōsō-in.

The *Zōbutsu-sho Sakumotsuchō* is sometimes referred to in Japan as "the oldest known formulae for glass existing in the world." However, some Babylonian clay tablets, of various sources, predate this Shōsō-in document. For this, refer to A. Leo Oppenheim *et alii*, *Glass and Glassmaking in Ancient Mesopotamia*, The Corning Museum of Glass Monographs, Volume III, Corning, 1970.

Aside from the few items noted in the *Zōbutsu-sho Sakumotsuchō* there seems to be only one that might be identified as a tool. This is a smooth whetstone, with traces of scouring,[7] which was found in the Shōsō-in in a bundle of beads and fragments. Perhaps it was used for polishing or for the shaping of such small articles as the fish shapes (Pl. 8) and the small measuring scales (Pl. 100), which were formed by grinding.

References:

1. Toshio Fukuyama, *Nihon Kenchikushi no Kenkyū* [Studies in the History of Japanese Architecture], Kyoto, 1943, pp. 89–130.
2. *Sugie, *Nihon Garasu Kōgyōshi*, pp. 23, 25. There are in the Shōsō-in brown glass beads, reported as containing iron (*SnG*, p. 49); *SnG*, p. 50, quotes "a record" of red clay used for "greenish blue beads," and also "for blue beads and black beads," but the source is not cited.
3. Among the drugs and medicines in the North Section are twenty-eight packets of finely powdered *tan* (cinnabar minium) weighing *in toto* 101,846 grams. *M. Nakao, in "Shōsō-in Gokō. . . . ," p. 29, says that originally there was more, but some was withdrawn for use on tiles in the provincial temples; he thought it was used for flowing glass and/or glaze on the tiles.
4. *Sugie, *Nihon Garasu Kōgyōshi*, pp. 26, 27.
5. *Nakao, "Shōsō-in Gokō. . . . ," p. 31.
6. *SnG*, pp. 50, 51.
7. *Ibid.*, p. 46, Fig. 35.

76. FRAGMENTS OF UNWORKED GLASS
The only materials available for this period are

these in the Shōsō-in, which are placed here because they are applicable to Nara glassmaking in general.

It is notable that none are of truly colorless, transparent glass. Perhaps this was due to the absence of methods for counteracting impurities in raw materials, or perhaps to the fact that rock crystal was so readily available. The few colorless, transparent beads that survive are considered imports. Their specific gravity is only 2.5, indicating a light soda-lime glass.

- *Collection*: The Shōsō-in (not noted in the shelf list; from the chest of glass "debris").
- *Date*: 8th century.

a. *"Black" glass fragments.*

- *Size*: T. *ca.* 9.0 cm.
- *Color*: Although all seem black (faintly translucent), some, in transmitted light, show a kind of smoky green, and some of the thinner areas seem similar to the bright green glass of the cloisonné mirror (Pl. 12). Perhaps this is some of the glass colored by copper mentioned in the document as "material for green and black beads."
- *Composition*: The pieces are heavy and inferred to be of lead glass.

b. *Green glass fragments.*

- *Color*: Very dark; translucent. These fragments suggest the dark green glass of the cloisonné mirror (Pl. 12). One is a smoky green like the tone of some of the "black" pieces. Others are a bright, but dark, yellow green in transmitted light. Two are close to the "olive green" of IH. D.Refl.: Ch 10, 9-3-14. Two more are similar to IH.D.Refl.: Ch 10, 9-3-13; one of these is peaked, indicating the point where the flowing glass source was lifted away after the pouring. Another example is opaque, but very glossy looking where fractured; this is nearest to IH.D. Refl.: Ch 12, 11-3-18, a pale green. Two are like IH.D.Refl.: Ch 2, 13-5-17, a light but strong blue green. Two others, slightly lighter and with largish bubbles, have a whitish mosslike weathering somewhat like some of the flat glass at Miyajidake

Shrine (Pl. 48). Ten others are opaque, with a creamy tone, some more yellowish than others; they have many bubbles and there are broken pits on the surface.

- *Bubbles*: Numerous.
- *Composition*: All are heavy and inferred to be of lead glass.
- *Condition*: Some fragments are rough and bubbly on the surface; others, smooth and glossy.
- *Remarks*: It would be interesting to compare some of the green fragments with the green glass of Miyajidake Shrine (Pl. 48), taking into account the greater thickness of these Shōsō-in lumps. Comparative studies of the many artifacts of the seventh and eighth centuries that show similarity to the green working materials of Miyajidake Shrine and those of the Shōsō-in might shed light on the possible widespread use of a common formula—or the distribution of such glass from a central agency, such as the government's Imono-no-tsukasa.

c. *Brown glass fragments.*

- *Color*: Varying from brown through rosy brown to red brown; more translucent than *a* and *b*.
- *Composition*: Since these are heavy, presumably lead glass.
- *Condition*: Some flat, with rough surfaces; others smooth, uneven in thickness and swirled on the surface.
- *Remarks*: The translucent parts of the brown glass in the cloisonné mirror (Pl. 12) are very similar to some of these fragments.

d. *Yellow glass fragments.*

- *Color*: One is pale yellow, almost translucent. Another, honey color, is thickly translucent. Three others are between these two in color.
- *Bubbles*: Full of tiny bubbles.
- *Composition*: From their weight, inferred to be of lead glass.
- *Condition*: One fragment had been melted in one area, as though over a flame for coiling a bead or filling a small mold.

e. *Fragments of blue glass, but appearing black.*

- *Composition*: These, unlike all the others, are of soda-lime glass, with no lead content.
f. *Fragment with a small bit of adhering metallic lead.*

It is surmised that this may have been formed by combustion in a reducing flame when quartz and lead oxide were being fused into glass. Probably the iron rust took shape when the hot fused glass was poured out onto an iron plate.

77. CROWN OF A FUKŪKENSAKU KANNON IMAGE
National Treasure

Fukūkensaku Kannon (Amoghapāśa), is the Buddhist deity of infinite, unfathomable mercy. An heroic statue, about 3.4 meters tall, this is the principal image of the Hokke-dō (Sangatsu-dō) of Tōdai-ji, Nara. The image dates from the mid eighth century and was made in *dakkatsu kanshitsu*, a type of dry lacquer technique.[1] From this figure there emanates a majestic feeling and a refinement of detail with which the crown harmonizes admirably in its well-proportioned design and richness of detail. Basically a silver framework, elaborately composed, the crown is adorned with some twenty-six thousand beads of amber, jadeite, rock crystal, coral, pearl, and glass. At the front is a miniature figure of Amida in solid silver, standing on a pearl-encrusted pedestal.

The glass beads are both large and small, chiefly *marudama* and *kodama*, although *natsume-dama* are said to be included; using the Nara terminology, they are *sashidama* ("pierced beads"). Many of the *kodama* form ropes of five strands. At each of the arched bands at the sides of the crown's framework, and again at the back, an intricate arrangement of *marudama* and *kodama*, strung (as are all the beads) on silver wire, forms a floral rosette pattern. Extending from the perimeter of a large frontal screen-like halo behind the small flame-edged mandorla of the silver Amida are flower forms, from each of which hangs a rope ornament made up of large and small beads and terminating in a *magatama*. Only one of the *magatama* is

of glass and it is broken. A belt around the lower part of the frame has horizontally connected beads.

Other units in the crown are: the small silver halo behind Amida's head, from which radiate twenty-five silver rays; silver eight-lobed mirrors on larger perforated forms and backed by other silver rays; and intermingled silver arabesque and petaled flower forms.

There may have been a dual reason for the use of glass here—the beauty that the glass materials, colors, and shapes could in themselves contribute, and the protective force believed inherent in them.

- *Collection*: Hokke-dō (Sangatsu-dō), Tōdai-ji, Nara.
- *Date*: Mid-8th century.
a. *Magatama* (broken).[2]
  - *Size*: Present L. *ca.* 2.7 cm.
  - *Color*: Deep blue; opaque.
  - *Bore*: The bore penetrates directly through the glass, and there is no sign of damage at the ends.
  - *Composition*: Lead glass of high lead content; Sp. Grav.: 5.[3]
  - *Condition*: Aside from the break, good.
b. *Beads*.
  - *Sizes*: Various.
  - *Colors*: Blue, green, pale green, greenish yellow, yellow, "opaque" white (rare or lacking before the Nara period). Possibly like those in the sash of Plate 5?
  - *Bores*: Diameters unknown, but wide enough to accommodate silver wire.
  - *Composition*: Soda-lime glass; Sp. Grav.: 2.5.[3]
  - *Condition*: Excellent. Many of the "jewels" in the crown were lost, and, during the restoration conducted in 1952, beads remaining at the back of the crown were removed to replace those missing at the front and sides.
  - *Remarks*: The imperial crowns (Pl. 87) must have been equally impressive, and in general style possibly reminiscent of this one.

References:
1. *Katori, *Kinkōshi*, pp. 113–120.

2. *Umehara, "Tōdai-ji Sangatsu-dō Honzon Hō-kan. . . . ," p. 2.

3. *Asahina, "Kodai Garasu no Kenkyū," p. 7.

78. SUTRA CHEST INSET WITH GLASS AND PEARLS
Important Cultural Property
A chest for Buddhist scriptures, constructed from aloe wood veneered with thin panels of betel nut palm wood. These panels were originally painted in gold with maritime scenes. Strips of lacquered cedar border the panels; it is in these that the rich blue green glass *hankyū-dama* and the pearls were inset. Ingenious carved ivory plaques attached on the interior prevent the lid from slipping sideways.
- *Collection*: Tokyo National Museum. Formerly in possession of Hōryū-ji.
- *Provenance*: Boxes or chests painted with gold and silver were not uncommon in the Nara period; a number are in the Shōsō-in. Exotic imported woods were used for many items produced and were highly valued, especially the fragrant incense woods. Domestic production of this chest cannot be proved; it may have come from China or Korea. However, the evidence of imported woods and of many objects in which such woods were used, either as veneer or for marquetry, makes it quite possible that this is of Japanese manufacture.
- *Date*: 8th century.
THE GLASS SETS (*hankyūdama*).
- *Size*: D. 0.7 cm.; Chest, 18.2 × 34.6 × 10.8 cm.
- *Color*: Deep blue green; almost transparent. IH.D.Refl.: Ch 4, 15-5-12, or IH.D.Trans.: Ch 3, 14-5-13.
- *Technique*: Probably mold cast.
- *Condition*: The box badly deteriorated and many insets missing; those remaining are well preserved.

79. CHINDANGU FROM THE PAGODA FOUNDATION, GANGŌ-JI
Important Cultural Property
Although the custom of interring *shari* beneath Buddhist pagodas seems to have waned during the Nara period, a somewhat similar custom appeared: burying *chindangu* (see p. 97) beneath buildings, and particularly beneath, or in, the clay foundation platforms of altars in Buddhist temples.

In 1927 a technician of this temple at Shiba-Shinya-machi, Nara, making a survey of the pagoda ruins, found this treasure around the foundation stone about thirty-five centimeters underground.[1] Associated objects were fragments of bronze, copper and gold plating; a gold button; 124 coins of various years of the early Nara period; clay fragments with traces of gold leaf and inscriptions; ten green and brown *magatama*; one pearl; fragments of amethyst, crystal, and agate.
- *Collection*: Nara National Museum; owned by Gangō-ji.[2]
- *Date*: The pagoda was erected in 718.
  a. *Six large* marudama, *all encrusted* (lower row).
    - *Sizes*: H. 1.64–2.35 cm.; D. 1.8–2.0 cm.
    - *Colors*: All perhaps yellow; translucent.
    - *Bores*: D. 0.25–0.335 cm.
  b. *Twenty-six* marudama (17 pictured, left).
    - *Sizes*: H. 0.7–1.0 cm.
    - *Colors*: Green; translucent. IH.D.Refl.: some, about Ch 12, 11-4-15. Pale honey color, creamy tone. Color matching difficult due to deterioration.
    - *Bores*: D. 0.15–0.40 cm., with little relation to the bead size.
  c. *About 150* kodama (not pictured).
    - *Sizes*: Various, as are the shapes.
    - *Color*: Blue; opaque, and translucent. IH.D.Refl.: about Ch 3, 14-6-16.
    - *Bores*: Various sizes.
  d. *Four* tombodama *wound with creamy white threads* (far right).
    - *Sizes*: H. 0.925–0.95 cm.; D. 1.2–1.3 cm.
    - *Colors*: Black; opaque. Pale green; opaque (?). IH.D.Refl.: approaches Ch 11, 10-3-17.
    - *Bores*: D. 0.4 cm.
    - *Composition*: Lead glass; Sp. Grav.: 4.[3]
  e. *Eleven* nejiredama (right center).
    - *Sizes*: H. 0.9 cm.
    - *Colors*: Four items, pale green; IH.D.Refl.: close to Ch 11, 10-3-17. One item, dark amber, encrusted.

- *Bores*: Average D. 0.4 cm.
- *Composition*: Lead glass; Sp. Grav.: 4.[3]

References:

1. Sei Kitagawa, "Gangō-ji no Tō no Ato Hakkutsu Jōkyō" [The Status of the Excavation of the Gangō-ji Pagoda Ruins], *Nara*, No. 9, 1927, p. 46. See also *Gangō-ji Tō no Ato Maizōhin Shutsudo Jōkyō Hōkokusho* [Written Report of the Circumstances of the Excavation of the Dedicated Items from the Ruins of the Gangō-ji Pagoda], Nara-ken Shiseki Meishō Tennen Kinenbutsu Chōsa Hōkoku [Report on Historical Remains, Scenic Views and Natural Monuments of Nara Prefecture], II, 1930.
2. It is said that others are also preserved in the Tokyo National Museum (*SnG, p. xv).
3. *Oda, "Nara Jidai no . . . ," pp. 22, 23.

80. *CHINDANGU* FROM BENEATH THE ALTAR OF THE KONDŌ, KŌFUKU-JI

National Treasure

These *chindangu* were discovered in 1874, but no report was written. This was an unusually large dedication of some fourteen hundred objects, including bowls of chased silver and other metals; silver spoons; wine cups; mirrors; items of gold, silver, and copper; gold bullion and gold dust; beads of glass, crystal, and amber; swords and sword fittings; tweezers; and ritual implements. A division was made, some items being retained by Kōfuku-ji and some transferred to the Imperial Museum in Tokyo.[1]

HIRADAMA

Many *hiradama*, slightly flattened on the bottom.

- *Collection*: Tokyo National Museum.
- *Date*: Early 8th century.
- *Sizes*: D. *Ca.* 1.1–1.5 cm.; T. 0.55–0.70 cm.
- *Colors*: Dark green, green, light green, green yellow, yellow, yellow brown, brown, dark brown, suggesting a probable *ungen* (prismatic) color grouping.
- *Bubbles*: Few.
- *Composition*: 79% lead content. Sp. Gravities: 5.0–5.4.[2] Coloring agents: for the greens and yellows, chiefly copper; for the brown, chiefly iron.
- *Technique*: Mold cast; circular striations on some surfaces.
- *Condition*: Thinly encrusted with a smooth,

dull, somewhat brownish coating,[3] broken away in spots, where the glass surface is rough and minutely pitted. Some silvery iridescence.

- *Remarks*: At the time of the author's inspection, these *hiradama* were tightly sealed in a glazed frame, which of course hampered study.

References:

1. *Yajima, "Kōfuku-ji Kondō Shutsudo. . . . ," pp. 19–22.
2. *Oda, "Nara Jidai no . . . ," pp. 22, 25, 26.
3. *Ibid.*, where this is called "much adhesion of copper rust."

81. *CHINDANGU* FROM THE PLATFORM OF THE GREAT BUDDHA, TŌDAI-JI

National Treasure

Part of the *chindangu* of the clay platform beneath the Great Buddha image of Tōdai-ji. Discovered in 1907, during repairs, about 40.6 cm. below the surface. Associated objects included: fragments of swords and sword-fittings; mirrors; a large silver jar with incised scene of boar and deer; leather fragments; lacquered casket; crystal and amber beads. The dedication of the image occurred in 752, and it is thought that this group of *chindangu* may have been used ceremonially in the Eye Opening ritual of that dedication.[1] Since the objects were found in the outer rim of the great circular dais, it may well be that they were interred there after their use in the dedication.

a. *Pair of straight-bladed swords with glass-ornamented hilts and jeweled sheaths* (hilt fragment pictured).

The swords, certainly ceremonial, are decorated with gold filigree set with rock crystal, white agate, and three unusual glass insets, which seem to be unique in Japan.

- *Collection*: Tōdai-ji, Nara.
- *Provenance*: Although the hilt and scabbard decorations are similar in kind to those of various swords kept in the Shōsō-in, the glass insets in these swords seem unique. Their unique design has a slight foreign flair, but this may be fortuitous.
- *Date*: 8th century.
- *Size*: Each inset about 1.0 cm. long.
- *Color*: Dark blue; translucent.

- *Technique*: Mold cast.
- *Condition*: The swords were in fragments and badly disintegrated when discovered, but, except for an iridescent film, the glass is in excellent condition.

b. *Ninety-five beads of various shapes.*

The most unusual, a biconical bead, is apparently a new type in the Nara period. It is not angular as some biconicals are, but softly rounded at the center diameter. Today this type is used in the Japanese abacus (*soroban*) and is called *sorobandama*.

- *Collection*: Nara National Museum.
- *Sizes*: H. *ca.* 0.225–0.35 cm.; biconical bead: H. 0.7 cm.; D, at center, 0.65 cm.
- *Colors*: The tones vary, but many seem to be blue; translucent. IH.D.Refl.: Ch 6, 17-6-12 and Ch 7, 18-5-12. Green; translucent or semitransparent. IH.D.Refl.: Ch 13, 12-4-16 and 3-17.
- *Bubbles*: Small and circular, in some quantity. Some beads have a vertical row of four or five bubbles, or indefinite and fine vertical streaks of bubbles.
- *Technique*: Tube cut, in general, but some seem to have been coiled. The biconical form suggests individual formation, perhaps by molding.
- *Condition*: Surfaces look slightly rough and pitted under magnification.

c. *Fifty-four kodama.*

- *Collection*: Nara National Museum.
- *Date*: 8th century.
- *Sizes*: D. *ca.* 0.2–0.325 cm.
- *Colors*: Pale gray blue; semitransparent. Light turquoise green; translucent. Pale green.

Reference:

1. Sampei Ueda, "Daibutsu-den Sumidan-nai ni oite Hakkenseru Ihō ni tsuite" [Relic Treasures Discovered in the Altar Platform of the Daibutsu-den], *Nara*, No. 8, July 1926, pp. 67–72.

82. *SHARI-TSUBO* BROUGHT BY THE CHINESE PRIEST GANJIN

National Treasure

The priest Ganjin (Chien Chen) had been invited so that there would be someone of author-

ity to administer the Buddhist initiation rites; it was he who initiated Emperor Shōmu, Empress Kōmyō, and their daughter. He brought with him three thousand *shari* (recorded as relics of Gautama, the historic Buddha); it is said that when a sea demon attempted to obtain the *shari* a golden tortoise saved the holy treasure. In the Kamakura period Priest Eison of Tōshōdai-ji (Ganjin's temple) had some of the three thousand enshrined in gilt-bronze reliquaries, distributed throughout the temple precincts for use during daily prayers.[1] This *shari-tsubo*, with the remaining *shari*, he placed in an elaborate reliquary, which rested on a tortoise form (Sup. N. 60).

In modern times at least, this treasure was kept in the Shari-den (*Shari* Hall) of Tōshōdai-ji. Once a year the doors were opened so that parishioners might stand before the hall and worship in the holy presence. When the author was permitted to study this treasure, it was first necessary to lift it in its wrapping from the elaborate reliquary and then to remove, one by one, the series of stiff brocade covers that enveloped it. Each brocade piece consisted of two flaps that, secured with silken cords, encased the relic. They were used in pairs, the second one applied so as to cover any crevice left between the two flaps of the first one, thus permitting no light or contamination to reach the treasure. From time to time a new pair of brocades had been added without removing the previous ones.[2]

The neck of the glass *tsubo* is fitted with a gilt-bronze cap about the base of which is knotted a folded strip of silver paper bearing the imperial seal of Emperor Go-Komatsu (1382–1412). So deep is the reverence for this treasure, and for the emperor's seal, that the nature of the neck and mouth of the glass vessel remains unknown. Was the gilt-bronze cap merely a precaution against damage to the delicate glass? Was it added in China before the dangerous voyage? Or was the neck at some time broken and this cover added? Until the assignment of this *shari-tsubo* as a National Treasure even the bronze cap was not visible, since the entire top of the vessel had been covered over with a paper tied with cords. Removal of the paper disclosed a remnant of red weaving with silver threads, beneath which were papers bearing seals. According to the Commission for the Protection of Cultural Properties, these are of the Emperor Go-Daigo (reigned 1318–39), the Ashikaga shogun Yoshimitsu (ruled 1368–94), and the Ashikaga shogun Yoshinori (ruled 1426–41). There is also a notation that the sealing of the treasure by Emperor Go-Komatsu occurred in 1392.

- *Collection*: Tōshōdai-ji, Nara Prefecture.
- *Provenance*: Chinese. The glass of the *shari-tsubo*, it will be noticed, is thin and delicate, in contrast to the thick and heavier glass of examples made in Japan.
- *Date*: Brought to Japan in 754.
- *Size*: Total height unknown; H. to top of cover, *ca.* 9.2 cm.; to shoulder, *ca.* 4.5 cm.; D. *ca.* 11.01 cm.; D. of cover, 5.1 cm.
- *Color*: In the dim light of the temple this seemed to be a greenish yellow, but it has been traditionally referred to as "white" (colorless). The glass is completely transparent.
- *Bubbles*: Many small ones; one large oval one on the shoulder about 0.6 × 1.0 cm.
- *Composition*: Soda-lime glass, ascertained by measuring the Beta-ray back scattering dispersion rate with radioactive phosphorus 32 isotope "with maximum energy of 1.71 Mev."[3]
- *Technique*: Blown glass.

References:
1. *Iwanami Shashin Bunsho* [Iwanami Photographic Series], No. 95, p. 61.
2. There is also preserved at Tōshōdai-ji a woven silk-net wrapper for this *shari-tsubo*, which is thought to have been brought from China by Ganjin. It is a handsome circular weaving in dark blue, browns, and white, illustrated in the *catalogue of an Exhibition of the Ceramic Art of Sui and T'ang*. Kyoto National Museum, October-November, 1959, No. 294.
3. *Asahina, Yamasaki, et al, "Tōshōdai-ji Hakurui Shari-bin. . . .," pp. 14–18. Also, *Asahina, Yamazaki, and Yamasaki, "Investigation of Antique Relics. . . .," pp. 2–4.

83 (left). *TŌSU* WITH GLASS HILT, IRON BLADE, AND PLAIN SHEATH OF RHINOCEROS HORN

- *Collection*: Imperial Household Agency. Formerly owned by Hōryū-ji.
- *Date*: In the Shōsō-in there are a number of *tōsu* whose sheaths are inlaid with "jewels" of glass. Two others, similar to these in Plate 83, have hilts of obsidian[1] and of rock crystal, which were previously thought to be of glass. By comparison with those, the two pictured here are assigned to the eighth century.
- *Size*: L. of the glass hilt, 7.9 cm.; overall L. of the *tōsu*, 18.8 cm.
- *Glass color*: Blue; transparent. IH.D.Refl.: Ch 5, 16-5-13; IH.D.Trans.: Ch 5, 16-7-14.
- *Bubbles*: Fairly numerous but not throughout; chiefly circular, but one is slightly elongated longitudinally and one transversely.
- *Composition*: Judged, from the color and the Sp. Grav. of 2.3, to be of soda-lime glass.[2]
- *Technique*: Ground from a larger piece of glass and well polished. The lower end of the hilt was ground off flat, and in it an aperture was opened to receive the tang of the iron blade. At the free end of the hilt the corners were rounded. The slightly bent form provided a good grip.
- *Condition*: Excellent.
- *Remarks*: Little of the beauty of the blue glass of this and the following item can be sensed from the illustration. The careful and appropriate shaping of the glass, however, is evident for these two hilts.

References:
1. See *SnG, p. 38, for scientific reasons for calling this obsidian.
2. *Oda, "Nara Jidai no. . . . ," p. 23.

83 (right). *TŌSU* WITH GLASS HILT, IRON BLADE, AND CARVED SHEATH OF *MUKU* WOOD (A Kind of Elm)

The sheath is wound with bands of minute, slender strips of black and dark vermilion bark. It is now a little damaged but still expresses in its contour and in the minute detail of its tiny bark threads something of the delicate aroma of the Nara spirit.

- *Collection*: Imperial Household Agency. Formerly owned by Hōryū-ji.
- *Date*: 8th century (see preceding Note, *Date*).

- *Size*: L. of the glass hilt, 7.9 cm.; overall L. of the *tōsu*, 21.1 cm.
- *Glass color*: Blue; transparent. IH.D.Refl.; Ch 5, 16-5-13; IH.D.Trans.: Ch 5, 16-7-14.
- *Bubbles*: Tiny circular ones with larger one elongated transversely.
- *Composition, Technique, Condition, Remarks*: Same preceding Note.

SHŌSŌ-IN

The transfer of the treasures from the original building in the spring of 1962 made the old locations given in the official shelf-list catalogue, *Shōsō-in Tanawaka Mokuroku (STM)*, obsolete. They are, however, used here for reference, as they are the official numbers. All items in this section are in the collection of the Shōsō-in.

Note: Since this study was completed, three glass items, later found among the "debris," have been published. The author has had no opportunity to study them.

One (*SnG*, Pls. 65–66) is a fragment of a narrow sash with small glass beads woven in; similar to Plate 5.

The second (*SnG*, Fig. 28) is a pair of spool-like items of opaque green glass, 1.95 cm. high with end diameters of 1.9 cm.; they are referred to as lead glass. Their use is undetermined.

The third item (*SnG*, Pls. 70–72) consists of two end plaques for leather girdles. They are of *hinoki* (cypress) wood with painted designs in pigments, black ink, and gold leaf. In the center of one there remains a transparent green glass *hankyūdama* 1.8 cm. in diameter and 0.5 cm. thick, attached by two copper prongs, embedded in the glass, which pierce the wood and spread apart at the back. A complete leather girdle of the type these end pieces would be used for, worn by courtiers from the eighth century on, is preserved in the Shōsō-in; it is set with plaques and end-piece of lapis lazuli (see *ECTS*, Pl. LVIII, upper). In the glass *hankyūdama* of the newly found item there is an area at the base that is now red, due to reduction when the copper prongs were inserted in the hot glass. Otherwise the glass resembles

other glass in the Shōsō-in and is presumed to be lead glass (*SnG*, p. 39).

85 (center). *TSUYUDAMA*

The slightly elongated natural form of these beads makes them ideal for terminals of bead strings, as in the sash of Plate 93.

- *Former Location*: Middle Section, from a group of "broken beads." No *STM* listing.
- *Date*: 8th century.
- *Sizes*: Various, from tiny droplets to some over 4.5 cm. long.
- *Colors*: A diversity, similar to the various colors of the *marudama* and *kodama*; translucent and transparent.
- *Bubbles*: Many.
- *Composition*: Sp. Grav.: 4.5; lead content about 70%.[1]
- *Technique*: The beadmaker could dip a small clay-coated rod or wire into molten glass and bring up a small gather of glass. By rotating the rod slowly he could keep the glass in spherical form, which the force of gravity would modify to the somewhat elongated shape. When cool, the rod could easily be pulled out because of its greater contraction rate and its clay coating. This would leave a small cavity at the top of the bead into which the end of a suspension wire could be slipped and made firm by inserting a bit of wood, perhaps a bit of cloth, as a filler, or even a touch of lacquer. In some of the cavities there are remains of a muddy light brown substance and bits of wood and silk.[2]
- *Condition*: Excellent.

References:
1. *Yamasaki, "Namari Garasu to. . . . ," p. 20.
2. *SnG*, p. 44.

85 (left center). "BEADS" OF BLOWN GLASS

It is thought that these beads may have fallen from the embroidered ceremonial shoes of Supplementary Note 45.

- *Former Location*: Middle Section. No *STM* listing.
- *Date*: 8th century.
- *Size*: Sample, H. 0.9 cm.; D. 0.65 cm.; mouth D. 0.45 cm.

- *Colors*: Blues, greens, yellow green, yellow; and broken ones of pale gray blue glass, very light in weight and delicate. The same sample as above, IH.D.Refl.: Ch 4, 3-4-15.
- *Bubbles*: In one they are circular in the lower part; above that they begin to be elongated longitudinally (except for one that is slightly elongated horizontally just above center) and become larger at the mouth opening.
- *Technique*: Made with a small blowing pipe. In one example the mouth opening is wide and dips down inside to a ragged edge, where the pipe was broken away. This suggests, in miniature, the same dipping down and rough edges seen in the blown cinerary urns of Pls. 3 and 72.
- *Condition*: Good, aside from the fact that they are either discards or fragmentary.
- *Remarks*: These ornaments were evidently intended to be inverted as insets or topped with sepals.

In the collection of Mr. Yang-sun Kim in Seoul, there is a large blown glass bead 1.7 cm. in diameter, which shows at one end the typical rough breakaway from the blowpipe and at the opposite end a smaller opening with a short upstanding collar, as though a drop form (like that of Pl. 85, left bottom) had had the extended point cut off to make a "bore" for a bead.

85 (left bottom). HOLLOW BLOWN GLASS FORM LIKE A *TSUYUDAMA*
Found among the fragments, and most certainly part of a large *tsuyudama*. Toward the bottom (the top in the illustration) the glass-wall becomes thicker, ending in an extended drop.
- *Former Location*: Middle Section, in the "debris". No *STM* listing.
- *Date*: 8th century.
- *Color*: Deep yellow green.
- *Condition*: Fragmentary; otherwise good.

86. *NE-NO-HI NO HŌKI* ("Brooms for the Day of the Rat")
Brooms such as the two examples in the Shōsō-in were used in China at the time of the New Year, on the Day of the Rat, for symbolic sweeping out by the empress of silkworm chambers, in solicitation for a good silk year. Correspondingly, there is also in the Shōsō-in a pair of ritual ploughs to be used by the emperor in petition for a good rice harvest.

These two brooms of twigs of *medo-hagi* (*Lespedeza serica*) were originally bejeweled with glass beads of "yellow, light yellow, deep green, brown, light green, deep green, arranged in *ungen* gradation in the order given."[1] The handgrips are wrapped in purple leather; the broom illustrated has gold cord wrapped over the leather. The other had beads, strung on white thread, wound around the handgrasp, of which now only one row remains, with the positions of the other fourteen rows evident from dents left in the leather. Over the ends of the twigs glass beads were slipped individually. The brooms are also known as *tama-hōki*, "jewel brooms."
- *Former Location*: South Section. STM No. 747.
- *Date*: 758. A green silk bag carries the inscription: "Cover for stand of the *Ne-no-hi no Hōki*, Tempyō Hōji, 2nd year, [758], 1st month."[2] This year fell within the reign of Empress Kōken.
- *Sizes*: Brooms, H. 65.0 cm.; beads, H. of those on handgrip, 3.0 cm., D. 3.5 cm.; those on the twigs are small *kodama*.
- *Color*: The two beads remaining on the broom of Plate 86 are dark blue, and a light, almost greenish, gray blue. Those on the handgrip of the other broom are in *ungen* gradation of the "pale yellow to the green" and "brown to green" families.[3]
- *Condition*: Fair, except for the missing beads.
- *Remarks*: In the *Manyōshū*, Volume 20, Poem 4493, there appears this passage:

Second year of Tempyō Hōji [758], first month, third day.
A small page, attendant upon the Empress, summoned the court officials and seated them near the hedge of the eastern wing of the Palace. Then the Empress gave them a beaded broom [*tama-bahaki*] and held a banquet at which time the Uchi no Otodo,

Fujiwara no Ason, announced the imperial order requesting them to compose poems, Chinese or Japanese as they preferred. Thereupon each composed a Chinese or Japanese poem according to his own emotions.

Note: As yet I have not acquired any of the poems.[4]

This note is accompanied by the following poem, which is thought to have been written by Otomo no Sukune Yakamochi, compiler of the *Manyōshū* and himself the outstanding poet of time.

> Hatsu haru no
> Hatsu ne no kyō no
> Tama-bahaki
> Te ni toru kara ni
> Yuragu tama ho o.

Taking in the hand the bead-broom
 of today,
The first Rat Day of the new spring—
O, the tranquillity when the beads sway
Or when the spirit is moved.[4]

Since the inscribed date for the *tama-hōki* in the Shōsō-in corresponds to the day of this poem, it seems that this broom was the one used at the banquet.

References:
1. *SGZ, XIV, Caption of Pl. 10.
2. *ECTS, p. 139.
3. *SnG, p. vi.
4. Translated from *Kokka Taikan*, Tokyo, Chūbunkan Shōten, 1931, I, p. 813. Utsubo Kubota, *Manyōshū Hyōshaku* [Commentary on the *Manyōshū*], 2nd ed., Tokyo, 1956, XII, p. 372, makes this statement: "When a string of beads is shaken, it makes a sound—a sound that drives away evil. This is of significant importance. The mind is moved by the sound."

87. BEADS FROM IMPERIAL CROWNS

The cedar box for the emperor's crown is octagonal, that of the empress, hexagonal, indicating some difference in the form of the headdresses. Both cases contain cypress stands. There is also a case for the Empress Kōken's crown.

The *Tōdai-ji Zoku Yōroku* ("Supplement to the Tōdai-ji Yōroku") relates that in the year 1242, in connection with the enthronement of the Emperor Go-Saga, four jeweled crowns, including that of Emperor Shōmu, were borrowed from the Shōsō-in[1] and that when returned several days later they were in fragments.

According to the records, the emperor's crown was made up of black gauze (no doubt lacquered and stretched over a frame), gold and silver, jewels, and cords of deep violet; that of the empress bore gold phoenixes, gold and silver, jewels, and white cords.[2]

- *Former Location*: North Section. *STM* No. 205.
- *Date*: About 752. According to the *Shoku Nihongi*, the Emperor Abdicant Shōmu wore the new-style *benkan* type crown for the first time in 752.[3] The crowns are not mentioned in the Shōsō-in's *Kenmotsuchō*, but are thought to have been installed in the Shōsō-in around 770 to 780.[4] They appear in the inventories of the airing periods of 793, 811, and 856, and are recorded in the fragmentary *Reifuku Reikan Mokuroku* ("Catalogue of Imperial Robes and Crowns for Ceremonial Use"), which is considered to date from the Saikō era (854–56) and which was preserved in the North Section. Tags attached to red-lacquered cases in which the crowns were stored bear a date corresponding to 752, fourth month, ninth day, which was the day of the Eye Opening Ceremony, and designate the crowns as those of the Emperor Abdicant Shōmu and the Dowager Empress Kōmyō.
- *Bead sizes*: From minute *kodama* to fair sized *marudama*.
- *Colors*: A wide range of blues, greens, yellows, browns, colorless, opaque black, and both opaque and milky white. Except for the black and white, they are all either transparent or translucent.
- *Condition*: Although the crowns are damaged beyond repair, the beads are in excellent condition.
- *Remarks*: Extensive research might find analogies between the details of these crowns and the crowns and decorative jewelry seen in the arts of China, Central Asia, India, and Iran, as

depicted in wall paintings and sculpture. But it does not seem that the Japanese crowns were direct imitations of any continental examples. Since ceremonial crowns were perhaps an innovation, it is likely that the basic design was patterned after imperial crowns of T'ang China. Supporting this idea is the presence in the wooden case for the emperor's crown of post-like supports thought to have held up a flat boardlike upper portion similar to those of Chinese imperial crowns.[5] The *benkan*, or flat board part, worn over the basic crown, may have been something like the illustration in *Wakan Sanzai Zue*.[6]

References:
1. To serve as models for a new one (*SnG*, p. vii.).
2. *Shōsō-in Tenkan Mokuroku* [Catalogue of the Shōsō-in Special Exhibition], Nara National Museum, 1952.
3. David, *op. cit.* (see n. 1, p. 107), p. 21, n. 38.
4. *Treasures of the Shōsō-in—The North Section*, p. vi.
5. The supporting stand is illustrated in *Treasures of the Shōsō-in—The North Section*, Fig. d, p. 5.
6. *Terashima, *Wakan Sanzai Zue*, p. 373.

88. GILT SILVER PLATTER FOR FLOWERS

In the center of this large six-lobed platter of gilded silver, with a *yōraku* fringe, is a standing deer in high repoussé, with a spreading tray-like motif of flowers branching out from the skull. Each lobe of the rim carries a blossom-and-leaves motif, also in repoussé. Three leaf-shaped feet (replacements of the Meiji era) are secured with three bolts, whose gilded heads are seen on the surface of the platter. Many large and small colored glass beads and small bronze ornaments, strung on wire, make up the fringe; the largest beads, with two-way bores, were used as dividers.

- *Former Location*: South Section. STM No. 606.
- *Provenance*: The platter at least is believed to be Chinese. A similar embossed platter in China has a lion in place of the deer, and a different floral motif on the rim;[1] there are three feet riveted on, as in the Shōsō-in example. Another similar example, with a phoenix motif, was excavated near Hsian, China.[2] Whether the trays in China ever had beads attached, this

author does not know; in the one or two illustrations seen, no beads are indicated.

The curious deer motif of the Shōsō-in tray occurred in Central Asia and is usually referred to as of Sassanian origin.[3] This motif also occurs in one of the colored ivory measuring scales of the Shōsō-in.

- *Date*: The platter itself seems to be of the 8th century.
- *Sizes*: The beads are both large and medium sized *marudama* and *kodama*; the footed platter, H. 13.2 cm., D. 61.5 cm.
- *Colors*: Dark blue (or black?); semiopaque turquoise blue; transparent blue; green; yellow; brown; opaque black; and opaque white.
- *Technique*: Not determined, but probably coiled.
- *Condition*: The record of 1899 repairs reports: "Various bead ornaments fell off, and all the feet were lacking; now repaired."[4] How many, or whether all, of the replaced beads were originals and how many were new replacements is left uncertain. *SnG* (pp. 32–33) refers to the fact that in the Shōsō-in there exist working materials for the Meiji "repairs," which include some beads from melted-down ancient broken beads and some from newly fused glass, as well as slender glass rods of the latter. These are said to include all colors, both opaque and transparent. As they are remarkably like the present beads of the platter, the investigating commission concluded that the ornament as it now exists is made up from these Meiji supplies.

References:
1. Yoshito Harada, "Chōgoku Kōkogakuteki Shin-shiryō no Ni-san" [Several New Chinese Archaeological Materials], *Museum*, No. 80, Nov. 1957, Fig. 4, p. 20.
2. *SnG*, p. 32.
3. A similar motif appears in a wall painting in the Khan's Palace at Idyout, Central Asia; see Albert Grunwedel, *Altbuddhistische Kultstatten in Chinesisch-Turkistan*, Berlin, 1912, Fig. 665.
4. *Treasures of the Shōsō-in—The South Section*, p. ix.

89. FLOWER BASKET

One of two items. Although traditionally called

parts of hanging banners (several being hinged together to form a long ensemble), these are now generally considered to have been used as flower baskets (*keko*) for the scattering of blossoms during Buddhist services.[1] They are made up of various colored glass *kodama* strung on silver wires, which were plaited alternately over and under each other to form shallow circular basketlike receptacles. The final finish was a rim of the larger *marudama* strung on stronger wire.

- *Former Location*: South Section. *STM* No. 781.
- *Date*: 8th century.
- *Sizes*: "Basket," D. *ca.* 36.0 cm. *Marudama*, H. 0.8 cm. and D. 1.1 cm. *Kodama*, H. 0.3 cm. and D. 0.5 cm.[2]
- *Colors*: Light blue, and varying tones of green, yellow, and brown, together with black (or very dark green?). All are somewhat translucent, but some of the browns seem almost opaque and rather mottled. *SnG* (English text, p. vi) says: "Some of the yellow and light-brown beads in this piece retain a resinlike substance adhering to their surfaces (*SnG*, Color Plate 12). Investigation has proved that these beads were painted with a red substance soluble in alcohol, which is probably identifiable with what is termed "*kirinketsu* for painting red beads" in the *Zōbutsu-sho Sakumotsuchō* of 734. This red pigment was so used because at that time it was impossible to produce red glass.

The green beads of this basket sometimes seem very thin and delicate, almost like blown beads. The tones of all are soft, enhancing the *ungen* grouping in sequences of two, three, or four beads of one color but in different tones. The gradated shading of the prismatic *ungen* system of the beads of these baskets is explained in detail in *SnG*, p. 35 and Figs. 30–31.

- *Condition*: The beads are well preserved, although some show slight iridescence, and some of the reddish color has rubbed off a little. The baskets, obviously, have suffered damage.
- *Remarks*: Flower scattering was an essential part of Buddhist services in ancient times. There were many baskets in the South Section,

both for washing flowers and for scattering; but these are the only two involving glass.

References:
1. *ECTS*, p. 146.
2. *SGZ*, XIII, Caption of Pl. 37.

90. GILT-COPPER OPENWORK PLAQUE WITH APRICOT-LEAF PATTERN

Some sixteen plaques for banners exist, a few still hinged together in the original manner to form long temple banners. Some are of complex openwork with compound floral designs, or phoenixes *en face*, while others are quite simple (Pl. 91). Often, tapering metal spikes project into open spaces, and on them are impaled one or more large beads of rock crystal, agate, bronze, or glass. Many of the beads are now missing.

This plaque retains all but one of the original nine glass beads in the central apricot-leaf motif; the beads in the peripheral units are of rock crystal. The perforations noticeable in the outer leaves once held bronze bells attached by wire, like the one surviving bell in the center; a companion plaque still retains two such bells in position. The incising of such details as leaf veins occurs on both front and back surfaces, indicating that the banners were to be seen both from the front and from the rear.

- *Former Location*: South Section, from a chest of banner "hardware," group No. 165. No *STM* listing.
- *Date*: 8th century.
- *Sizes*: Plaque, D. 30.2 cm.[1] Beads, H. and D. 0.8 cm.[2]
- *Color*: Green, rather dark; slightly translucent. Beads in other plaques are of yellow or brown as well as green.
- *Composition*: Presumed to be of lead glass.
- *Technique*: Apparently coiled, judging, from their shapes.
- *Condition*: Good. One glass bead is missing, and one whose spike was broken off is now secured with wire.
- *Remarks*: There are various records of such banners being used for special Buddhist rituals. Surely they must have been employed for the Eye Opening Ceremony and for the anniversary

rituals of the Emperor Shōmu's death; banners are spoken of as carried in the emperor's funeral cortege.

References:
1. **SGZ*, XIII, Pl. 25.
2. **SnG*, pp. 39, 40.

92. *MARUDAMA* AND A *TOMBODAMA* STRUNG ON SILVER WIRE

Fifty-three small glass *marudama* strung on silver wire in a tripartite arrangement of three loops with a large glass *tombodama* as the parent bead, or divider.

- *Former Location:* South Section. No *STM* listing.
- *Date:* 8th century.
- *Colors:* Various.
- *Technique:* Variety in sizes and shapes suggests coiling; this is corroborated in a bead at the lower left that shows corrugations due to cooling before complete fusion of the coiled thread.
- *Condition:* Excellent.
- *Remarks:* The intended use of such an arrangement is unknown. Although the stiff wires seem impractical, it was possibly a rosary.[1] Other similar arrangements are preserved in the Shōsō-in, some with divider beads of bronze; all were kept in the chest of so-called banner "hardware."[2]

References:
1. Found in the tomb of Emperor Tenmu (673–85) was "a rosary of three rows of amber beads threaded on copper wire"; *Aoki no Sanryō-ki* (see n. 10, p. 72), p. 35. Although the "three rows" may indicate an entirely different arrangement, at least these also were strung on stiff wire.
2. **SnG*, p. 40.

93. SASH DECORATED WITH JEWELS

Only a portion of the long fragment is shown. Only one of four extant specimens retains the bead strings that adorn one edge. The foundation of the belt is plain, pale brown silk, over which is pasted a thin silk gauze of pale brown (the original color?). An allover embroidered lattice design simulates intersecting bead strings "in *ungen* shading represented in greens and blues with yellow at the intersections."[1] Within each lozenge of the lattice is a small five-petaled flower embroidered in red and purple threads. At each end, and at four places in between, palmettes cut from purple leather were applied with a buttonhole stitch. The edges of the belt are finished with two joined variegated braided strips, and along one edge are still attached at intervals strings of small pearls and excellent glass and rock crystal beads.[2] Each string terminates in a *tsuyudama*, which is sometimes of rock crystal and sometimes of dark green or dark blue translucent glass, but always associated with gilded sepals. The other beads are small pearls and glass *kodama*. In its original state, with all the attached strings in place, perhaps an *ungen* type of prismatic color gradation may have been evident here as well as in the embroidery.

- *Former Location:* Shōsō-in, Middle Section. *STM* No. 392 a.
- *Date:* 8th century.
- *Sizes:* Length of the fragment, 85.0 cm.; W. 6.5–7.0 cm.[3]
- *Bead colors:* Blue, gray blue, dark blue; pale transparent green, dark green; pale opaque yellow, a rich translucent brown, rose purple.
- *Condition:* Such of the glass beads as remain are perfectly preserved.
- *Remarks:* One wonders about the embroidered dots that imitate bead chains and form the lattices. Were these purely a design motif, or were they done to give the belt some amuletic significance?

References:
1. **SnG*, p. vii.
2. According to Jō Okada (**SnG*, p. 213), some of the beads seem to be replacements of the Meiji era.
3. **Treasures of the Shōsō-in—The Middle Section*, p. III.

94. CHINESE STYLE SWORD

One hundred swords are listed in the *Kenmotsuchō*, but other records show that ninety-three were removed in 760 and 764. Of the remaining seven, only three now exist. This one tallies with a detailed description in the *Kenmotsuchō*, but some later inventories do not mention it.[1]

The black lacquered decoration on the sheath is a design of birds, beasts, and clouds delin-

eated in gold embedded in the lacquer. Both hilt and scabbard are embellished with gold and silver work in perforated arabesque designs here and there; on the obverse face, with insets of green and blue glass and of rock crystal over painted vermilion.
- *Former Location*: North Section. *STM* No. 96.
- *Provenance*: The entry in the *Kenmotsuchō* calls it a "Chinese or Chinese style sword," but the particular lacquer method (*makkinro*) used on the scabbard has always been regarded as a Japanese technique; the same technique also appears on some arrows among the ancient treasures of Hōryū-ji.[2]
- *Date*: 8th century.
- *Size*: Sword L. 98.0 cm.[3]
- *Glass colors*: Dark and light green; dark blue; brownish (perhaps paint under rock crystal?); black (?).
- *Technique*: Probably molded.
- *Condition*: Excellent, brilliant; but some of the inlays are modern replacements. The white leather strap on the hilt is also new.

References:
1. **ECTS*, p. 35.
2. Jō Okada, *Shōsō-in no Hōmotsu* [Shōsō-in Treasures], *Gendai Kyoyō Bunko* [Modern Education Library], No. 257, Tokyo, Publication department, Research Institute for Sociological Thought, 1959, p. 30.
3. **Treasures of the Shōsō-in—The North Section*, p. xv.

95. *NYOI* WITH INSET DECORATION

The *nyoi* is a kind of scepter used in Buddhist rituals. This *nyoi* is carved from rhinoceros horn, and is decorated on both sides with five-petaled floral forms of gold-washed silver in which glass and amber *hiradama* are inset—a particular type of decoration said to have been introduced from T'ang China. The two high *hankyūdama* on the underside of the curved "fingertips," flanking the three floral forms, are of amber and rock crystal. On the long stem are insets of rock crystal placed over painted color; the tip of the handle is carved from a single piece of lapis lazuli.[1] Near the bottom of the stem "Tōdai-ji" was carved and filled in with vermilion. There is a plain black case on which the same inscription appears.

- *Former Location*: South Section. *STM* No. 669.
- *Date*: Probably 8th century.
- *Size*: Nyoi, L. 77.0 cm.; W. of head, 10.4 cm.[2]
- *Glass colors*: Rich and brilliant in several tones of green and blue, mingling with the red of amber. The order is not identical in all of the forms.
- *Condition*: Excellent, but has been partially repaired.
- *Remarks*: The *nyoi* of the South Section are of varying substances, from simple wood to whale fin, tortoiseshell, and rhinoceros horn. One is exceedingly intricate in design and variety of materials. A number have glass insets, but none so many as this example.

References:
1. Lapis lazuli is not found in Japan and was, therefore, like rhinoceros horn, an imported material. It is thought to have come from Afghanistan; see **Treasures of the Shōsō-in— The South Section*, English text, p. xi. In the Shōsō-in there is also a leather courtier's belt set with ten plaques of this stone (*STM* No. 414).
2. **Treasures of the Shōsō-in The South Section*, p. XV.

96. HANDLED CENSER

The body is of dark sandalwood, inset with gold, crystal, and glass, in a design of flower, bird, and butterfly motifs. Each flower form is centered with a small inset, sometimes of rock crystal, sometimes of glass. The lion in the full round at the end of the handle is of gilded silver; there is another lion form of gold-plated copper on the rim of the ashbowl. The black and yellow cords intertwined along the handle are modern; under them, the top of the handle is overlaid with brocade. At the juncture of handle and bowl there is mounted, horizontally, a delicately perforated, heart-shaped, silver-gilt plaque that acts as a background for two small silver lotus blossoms, in each of which, at the center, is set a *hankyūdama* of bluish green glass, flat side uppermost. At the point of this plaque is a single high inset said to be of rock crystal.

- *Former Location*: South Section. *STM* No. 605.
- *Provenance*: Japanese (?).

- *Date*: 8th century.
- *Size*: Censer, L. 39.5 cm.; H. 7.6 cm.[1]. Glass insets, D. 1.2 cm.[2]
- *Glass color*: The two sets, greenish blue, somewhat mottled.
- *Remarks*: One of the most elaborate and luxurious objects among the treasures of the Shōsō-in.
  References:
  1. *Treasures of the Shōsō-in—The South Section*, p. xv.
  2. *SnG*, p. 39.

97. YELLOW BRASS RECEPTACLE

Inlaid with glass. A spherical shape on a high foot, with lid surmounted by a five-storied pagoda form; both foot and pagoda top are riveted on. The metal is beautifully tooled in all the units, and it is said that each of the pagoda rings is decorated with gold and silver.[1] In three of the intervals between the pagoda roofs there were glass sets, six in each interval, of which only one now remains. Similar examples, without the glass, also exist in the Shōsō-in, and another, with layers of silver between the roofs but with no glass, is owned by the William Rockhill Nelson Gallery in Kansas City (No. 47.22). The latter is called Chinese T'ang, "eighth century or earlier."

- *Former Location*: South Section. *STM* No. 647.
- *Provenance*: Chinese?
- *Date*: Probably 8th century.
- *Size*: Overall H., 15.9 cm. Glass, D. 0.15 cm.[2]
- *Condition*: Excellent, including the one remaining glass set.
  References:
  1. *SGZ*, XII, Pl. 48.
  2. *SnG*, p. 38.

98. *SUGOROKU* SET

Sugoroku ("double sixes") is a sort of backgammon game for two, with fifteen game pieces and two dice, said to have been introduced into China from India in about the fifth century.[1] There is a record in the *Nihon Shoki*, under the eighth day of the twelfth month of Jitō 4 (689) that the game of *sugoroku* was prohibited,[2] but it was apparently revived and in good standing in the Nara period.

This collection contains eighty-five pieces, forty-six of which are of high quality glass (six are illustrated in Pl. 98). The rest are of amber and rock crystal, with some quartz for the game of *go*. They are kept in a box of black lacquered hide. These pieces are thought of as "horses," proceeding from a starting point with the enemy "camp" the goal.

- *Former Location*: North Section. *STM* No. 40.
- *Date*: 8th century.
- *Sizes*: Vary slightly, but the average D. is 1.4 cm. and average T. 0.7 cm.[3]
- *Colors*: Greens: pale, medium, dark.
  Blue: one only, a beautiful soft tone.
  Yellows: honey color, greenish yellow.[4]
- *Bubbles*: Small and so numerous that the glass, which was probably transparent, appears translucent; are these, rather, bits of unfused quartz?
- *Composition*: Except for the blue one, all are of lead glass; lead content of 69%, on the basis of a specific gravity of 5, arrived at by making a model and estimating the content as 0.84 cubic centimeters, disregarding the bubbles.
  "On the basis of the Beta-ray back scattering dispersion rate of the phosphorus 32 isotope, the lead content was estimated as 75%. . . . Allowing for accidental error in measuring, it is essentially a lead glass with lead oxide content of about 70%."[3] The one blue example is soda-lime glass.
- *Technique*: Mold cast, as *hiradama*; finely shaped and polished, bright and fresh although soft in tone.
- *Remarks*: Although the items shown in Plate 98 do not actually belong together as a set, they are usually exhibited so, illustrating the game.
  References:
  1. *Treasures of the Shōsō-in—The South Section*, p. xv.
  2. Aston, *op. cit.* (see n. 1, p. 45), II, p. 395.
  3. *Treasures of the Shōsō-in—The South Section*, p. xv; see further, *Oda, "Nara Jidai no. . . . ,"* Table I, p. 24.
  4. *Oda, ibid.*, p. 24.
  5. *SGZC*, p. 75.

99. PAIR OF *TŌSU*

In the Shōsō-in there is a group of sixty small

knives and other implements in some of whose elaborately ornamented scabbards glass insets appear. A wooden tag attached to this pair reads: "Dedicated by Lady Tachibana."

The hilts of the two *tōsu* are of rhinoceros horn; the scabbards, of wood stained a dark rose color. Completely encasing the scabbards are perforated silver frames in a running floral pattern, each floral rosette of which has a green glass inlay surrounded by eight petals inlaid with small pearls. The mounts by which the *tōsu* are suspended are of silver gilt.

- *Former Location*: Middle Section. *STM* No. 432-7.
- *Date*: 8th century.
- *Size*: *Tōsu*, total L. *ca.* 23.0 cm. Glass, D. 0.15 cm.[1]
- *Glass colors*: Blue, and strong green; translucent.
- *Condition*: Excellent, perhaps due to the repairs of the Meiji era; only a few of the glass sets are originals.
- *Remarks*: The shape of the hilts resembles those of Plate 83, which seems to be a common form for *tōsu*.

Reference:
1. *SnG, p. vii.

100. SMALL LINEAR MEASURES

Total of five small measures, four of which are of glass and one of mottled rhinoceros horn. Rectangular forms of glass pierced at one end, with a suspension bore of 0.2 cm. in diameter.[1]

Associated with lumps of raw materials (see Pl. 76) was a fragment of chrolite schist scored on the bottom. This is considered to be a whetstone, perhaps the one used to shape such items as these measuring scales and the fish forms of Plate 8.

- *Former Location*: Middle Section. *STM* No. 533.
- *Date*: 8th century.
  a. *Size*: L. 6.3 cm.; T. 0.45 cm.
    - *Color*: Green, due to copper. Munsell, 10GY4/8
    - *Composition*: Lead glass; translucent.
    - *Technique*: Grinding; broken-bubble pits on the surface.
    - *Condition*: Excellent.

- *Remarks*: Joined by a cord to the yellow example described in *b*. The scale (2 *sun* 5 *bu*) is indicated in gold paint on both faces, one Nara *sun* being equal to about 2.12 cm.

b. *Size*: L. 6.9 cm.; T. 4.0 cm.
  - *Color*: Yellow, due to iron; translucent. Munsell, 10Y7/10.
  - *Bubbles*: Many, small.
  - *Composition*: Lead glass.
  - *Technique*: Grinding; broken-bubble pits on the surface.
  - *Condition*: Excellent.
  - *Remarks*: Attached by a cord to example *a*. A scale of 3 *sun* (*ca.* 3.36 cm.) is painted in silver, now blackened, on both faces.

c. *Size*: L. 6.7 cm.; T. 0.4 cm.
  - *Color*: Green, due to copper; translucent. Munsell, 7.5 GY3/4.
  - *Bubbles*: Many, and one black stone.
  - *Composition*: Sp. Grav.: *ca.* 4.75, calculated from volume and weight; inferred lead oxide content of 68%.
  - *Technique*: Grinding; broken-bubble pits on the surface.
  - *Condition*: Excellent, but paint is gone.
  - *Remarks*: Traces only of a former 3 *sun* (*ca.* 3.36 cm.) in gold paint.

d. *Size*: D. 6.95 cm.; T. 0.4 cm.
  - *Color*: Yellow, due to iron; translucent. Munsell, 10Y7/10.
  - *Composition*: Sp. Grav.: *ca.* 4.7, calculated from volume and weight; inferred lead oxide content of *ca.* 68%.
  - *Technique*: Grinding; broken-bubble pits on the surface.
  - *Condition*: Excellent.

Reference:
1. All data from *SnG, v, pp. 26–28, 45, 57.

102. *JIKU-TAN* FRAGMENTS

- *Former Location*: Middle Section. No *STM* listing.
- *Date*: 8th century.
- *Sizes*: Various; wall thicknesses also vary.
- *Colors*: Dark blue, due to cobalt; IH.D.Refl.: Ch 5,16-3-11.[1]

Gray blue, due to copper? IH.D.Refl.: Ch 5, 16-3-11.

Turquoise blue, due to copper; opaque and glossy.

Dark green, due to copper; opaque.

Light greenish yellow, due to iron. IH.D.Refl.: Ch 9, 8-2-18.

Dull yellow, due to iron; opaque with glossy surface.

Extremely pale yellow, due to iron.

- *Composition*: All are of lead glass except the blue, which is of soda-lime glass. The first committee reported that on the basis of a specific gravity of 5.06, one pale yellow *jiku-tan* fragment was shown to be of lead glass, with an estimated lead oxide content of 70%. Also, the green color of another fragment is assumed to have come from copper, and the blue to have come from copper and cobalt.[2]

References:
1. All data from *SnG*, p. 57.
2. *SGZC*, p. 76.

105. WHITE GLASS BOWL

There has been confusion regarding this cut-glass bowl because it is almost identical to one interred in the sixth century tomb of the Emperor Ankan (Pl. 1). The difference in date between these two examples is not difficult to explain, for articles kept in imperial possession were sometimes handed down from one generation to another—as witness the red lacquer chest (North Section, *STM* No. 46) that is described in the original *Kenmotsuchō* as having been bequeathed by the Emperor Tenmu to the Empress Jitō, and then passed on to the Emperor Mommu, the Empress Genshō, the Emperor Shōmu, and finally to his daughter, the Empress Kōken, who contributed it to the dedication of the Emperor Shōmu's belongings.[1]

- *Former Location*: Middle Section. *STM* No. 397.
- *Provenance*: Probably Iranian. Although before the Nara period the Japanese were skillful in the grinding of various materials, including glass, and were masters of the lathe, no one seems ever to have thought of this bowl as a product of Japan. It was generally considered in Japan that it was of Chinese origin, wrought by a skilled Chinese lapidary. However, the appearance of numerous similar bowls, found since World War II in the Amlash region of northwestern Iran, has disproved this theory.

Another type is known in two instances: bowls from a tomb in Canton, China, which are said to have a band of hollow-ground units just below the rim;[2] and a bowl with two bands of circular units, from a tomb of the Senzuka group of Niizawa in Nara Prefecture[3] (Pl. 2).

The appearance of the Amlash bowls, together with the two bowls in Japan, presents a sophisticated design of contiguous hollows[4] in an allover pattern that gives the effect of a tortoise carapace, especially when the units become hexagonal.

In ancient Japan there was considerable intercourse with the continent in the way of embassies to and fro. There were also channels of trade to and from China along the overland Silk Road, and the Arabs carried on some maritime trade with Canton, China, while Korean mariners were purveyors, along the East Asian coastal areas, of both Chinese and Western goods from the Chinese cities. Since the quality of the two imperial bowls in Japan is high, especially that of the Shōsō-in example, it seems likely that they were diplomatic gifts ("tribute") perhaps brought by Chinese envoys.

The Japanese archaeologists feel that since all the Amlash bowls came from tombs, in an area where there were no palaces, houses, or temples, the bowls would not have originated in that immediate vicinity but may have come from some locality near the Caspian Sea.[5] Since all examples of hollow-ground ware found in and around the far-flung Roman Empire were of different design, perhaps this group of bowls with contiguous design units and the hollowed bottoms always surrounded by seven hollow units did actually originate in Iran, somewhere around the Caspian Sea.[6] Professor Fukai has suggested that the bowls may have been produced by glass artisans among prisoners brought by the new rulers of the Sassanian Empire to construct their capital.

- *Date*: Uncertain; 4th to 6th century.

- *Size*: H. 8.1–8.5 cm.; D. at mouth, 10.9–12.0 cm. D. at bottom, 3.8 cm.[7]
- *Color*: "White" in the title of this bowl is understood as "colorless." A very slight brownish tinge, due to iron impurities in the original raw materials; transparent. Munsell, 2.5YB 5/4.[8]
- *Bubbles*: According to the investigation committee, bubbles are seen in great quantity,[9] but since they are minute they are not noticeable to the observer restricted to inspection only through the glass case. Judging from a photograph in the Shōsō-in Office, they seem chiefly circular at the bottom but slightly oval above and occasionally even elongated horizontally. Near the top there are a few misty swirls in the glass.
- *Weight*: This is somewhat heavier than the Ankan bowl (Pl. 1), which is very nearly the same size—the Shōsō-in bowl weighing 75.2 grams more than the Ankan bowl. This difference is probably due to the fact that some broken glass is missing from the Ankan bowl and the lacquer repair is much lighter than glass.
- *Composition*: Soda-lime glass. Sp. Grav.: 2.52; Refr. Ind.: 1.52.[10] The bowl at one point contains fine crystals not unlike pine needles in shape, which are thought to be diopside ($MgO\cdot CaO_2 SiO_2$), indicating the presence of magnesium and calcium. It is perhaps of interest that a *magatama* of the Tomb period (Sup. N. 20) also contains diopside crystals.

It was formerly stated that the Shōsō-in bowl had an estimated 5% lead content. But this is now questioned as a possible error in the early use of the Beta-ray equipment, due to difficulty with curved surfaces. It is now concluded that there is probably no lead in the bowl.

- *Technique*: Mold blown and hollow ground.[11] At the exterior bottom a single large circular hollow is surrounded, on what one may call the second tier, by seven circular hollows (distorted to ovals in Pl. 105). Each of four upper tiers consists of eighteen contiguous hollow units, circular and hexagonal, with those of tiers five and six—being positioned at the point of greatest diameter—carefully separated by

thin spaces, although this is not noticeable at a general glance. The placing of the hollows does not show the somewhat haphazard effect apparent in the cutting of the Ankan bowl. The slight unevenness of the uncut area at the rim is due to the slight off-center position of the bottom hollow where the craftsman obviously began the cutting. *SnG* (p. 10) suggests that the single hollow at the base began in grinding away the pontil mark before the upper hollows were executed. The unevenness would, then, have been due to a slight miscalculation in attaching the pontil.

The rim of the bowl is smoothly rounded. Subtle niceties of form and the precise placing of the design units make this bowl a superior work, beautifully shaped, cut, and polished.

- *Remarks*: Four Amlash type bowls were brought to Japan by members of one of the Archaeological expeditions to Iran.[12] Numerous others are known. One, in The Corning Museum of Glass (No. 60.1.3) is a similar, but larger, example (H. 8.2 cm.; D. 12.9 cm.). The exterior is rough, and, in areas where a creamy deposit has come off, a mottled grayish surface is disclosed. There is slight iridescence. A brown film covers the interior, and it is quite impossible to ascertain the exact color of the glass body, although when viewed against the light it appears translucent and of no color beyond what is probably due to weathering.

Another example suggesting this type is a glass hollow-cut bowl in the Metropolitan Museum of Art in New York (No. 59.34) assigned to the seventh to eighth centuries. It is of thick green glass quite deep in tone at the rim and at the bottom, which sets it somewhat apart from the colorless or lightly tinted examples. Fragments from Kish in Iraq also carry forward this same configuration of tiers of closely joined hollows; these are assigned to a "fairly accurate date, 5th–6th century A.D."[13]

References:
1. *ECTS*, p. 24.
2. *Sei-ichi Masuda, "Kandai no Garasu-yōki."
3. *Mori Kōichi, "Garasu-ki wo Shutsudo shita Kofun," pp. 12–14. More recently illustrated in *Asiatic Art in Japanese Collections: Decorative*

Art, Tōyō Bijutsu VI, Tokyo, Asahi Shinbunsha, Pl. 104.

4. Dr. Yamasaki states (*SnG*, p. xvi) that the radii of curvature of the hollows of this bowl and those of the bowl from the Emperor Ankan's tomb are identical. In *SnG*, page 9, is reference to similar identity with the bowls from Iran.

5. *Fukai, "Shōsō-in Hōmotsu. . . . ," p. 412.

6. Dr. Axel von Saldern suggests a *circa* 6th century date for this type, and the central and northern Sassanian area as a possible locale ("Achaemenid and Sassanian Cut Glass," *Ars Orientalis*, V, 1963, p. 15). Egypt as a source has not been widely suggested, although some scholars in the past have lightly mentioned the possiblity and Mr. Fukai hints at it (*Fukai, *Study of Iranian Art and Archaeology*, English text, p. 10), assigning this bowl to "not earlier than the First Century A.D." Further investigation in this direction is needed.

7. *Treasures of the Shōsō-in—The Middle Section*, p. 3.

8. *SnG*, p. ii.

9. *SGZC*, p. 76.

10. *SnG*, pp. iii, 10.

11. In *SnG*, p. 10 and Pls. 16–22, attention is called to "countless minute marks" attributed to contact with a mold. In *Fukai, *Study of Iranian Art and Archaeology*, English text, p. 9, it is suggested that the "facets" of nine such bowls were cut with whetstone.

12. *Fukai, "Shōsō-in no Hōmotsu. . . . ," p. 407. See also *Masuda, "Iran Aruboruzo no Garasuki," pp. 35–38.

13. D. B. Harden, "Glass from Kish," *Iraq*, I, Pt. 2, Nov. 1934, pp. 131–136; in: S. Langdon, "Excavations at Kish and Barghuthiat," 1933, pp. 113–136.

108. WHITE GLASS VESSEL WITH HIGH FOOT

The wooden tag on a small lacquered chest kept in the Middle Section (*STM* No. 405) is inscribed: "Two agate cups, five crystal beads, one white glass vessel with high foot, six packages of miscellaneous incense, and eleven pieces of wrought gold;"[1] on the reverse is the date, "Ninth day, fourth month, Tempyō Shōhō 4 (752)," which was the day of the Eye Opening Ceremony for the Great Buddha image. If this refers to this vessel, as seems probable, perhaps it was used on an altar for some of the many offerings to the great Rushana Buddha. Its rimmed plate would be appropriate for such a use.

The workmanship is unskillful, the rimmed portion crooked and unsymmetrically placed on the foot, and the glass has a number of large bubbles.

- *Former Location*: Middle Section. *STM* No 403.
- *Provenance*: Probably Chinese—or possibly even Egyptian? Other similar rimmed glass plates on pedestal feet are known. These have come out of T'ang dynasty China, where footed vessels were popular in ceramics, metal, and, it seems, in glass. Two such glass examples from China, with rimmed plates surmounting broad pedestallike bases and considered to be of Chinese manufacture are owned by the Tokyo National Museum.

This example also suggests certain Egyptian vessels, especially footed and rimmed specimens. One wonders if it might have been brought from Egypt in one of the Arab ships trading with South China.
- *Date*: 8th century or earlier.
- *Size*: H. 9.1–10.5 cm.; H. of foot, 6.6 cm.; D. of upper unit, 29.0–29.2 cm.[2]
- *Color*: Though labeled as white, i.e., colorless, it has a brownish tinge, especially in the thicker areas; Munsell, 2.5Y6/4[3]; pale purple streaks follow the line of circumference. The hollow foot is of a deeper brown than the upper portion. The glass is transparent.
- *Bubbles*: Many large bubbles, long and attenuated, following a line concentric with the circumference; close to the joining with the foot is one large triangular bubble. A stone at the center.
- *Composition*: From Beta-ray back scattering, it is inferred to be soda-lime glass, with no lead content.[4]
- *Technique*: Free blown, with folded rim; two separate units fused together. For suggested method see *SnG*, p. 21, Fig. 20. A pontil mark within the stemmed foot.

References:
1. *ECTS*, p. 87.
2. *SnG*, pp. 21, Fig. 19.
3. *Ibid.*, p. iv.
4. *SGZC*, p. 77.

HEIAN PERIOD

114, 115. PEACOCKS ON THE ALTAR OF THE KONJIKI-DŌ, CHŪSON-JI

National Treasure

Elaborate decorative metal panels enhance the foundation walls of the altars in the Konjiki-dō of Chūson-ji at Hiraizumi-machi, Nishi-Iwai-gun, Iwate Prefecture. Each has a gilt-bronze peacock and flowering plants in relief, which are said to be riveted to a silver-plated ground. Surprisingly, each panel differs slightly from the others in its design. Two of the panels of the rear altars carried, in each heart-shaped perforation representing the "eyes" of the peacock feathers, a glass bead, attached by wire.

This is not an isolated example; similar traces remain in peacock altar decoration at Jōmyō-ji, Wakayama Prefecture.[1]

Reference:

1. Jō Okada, "Kii-shū Kishima no Jōmyō-ji— Shinkoji Junrei 15" [The Temple Jōmyō-ji at Kishima, Kii Province—Pilgrimage to Old and New Temples, No. 15], *Museum*, No. 39, June 1954, pp. 30–32.

116. SACRED SWORD WOUND WITH BEADS

This sword, apparently in imitation of an ancient one, has been discussed on page 132. The glass sets of the sheath, like the ancient beads, are in the traditional five colors, but do not here seem to follow any traditional order.

- *Collection*: Jingū Chōkokan, Uji-Yamada city, Mie Prefecture.
- *Date*: 1909, imitating an ancient treasure.
  GLASS:
  a. Glass insets of the sheath; set in high gilded mounts, apparently in imitation of an ancient sword with a long bead string wound around the sheath.
  b. Five glass inlays in large heart-shaped mountings.
     - *Color*: Purplish blue.
  c. On the *tsuba* (hand guard), round sets of purple blue and of amber colored glass.
  d. Two long and slightly flaring hexagonal glass pendants as terminals.

- *Color*: Dark purplish blue.
- *Condition*: Excellent.
- *Remarks*: Of course, the exact nature of the glass in the original sword cannot be judged from this sword of 1909. However, the sword preserves a continuing tradition that is partially corroborated in ancient records. Certain elements—the long straight blade, the loop handle—suggest an ancient Tomb period type. Whether the sword discovered at Ise in the excavation of 1869 was an original one from antiquity is impossible to know. Future discoveries may clarify this.

117. FUGEN BOSATSU (Samantabhadra)

National Treasure

A hanging scroll, painted in color on silk, depicts the Bodhisattva Fugen, whose vehicle is a white elephant. Here the artist has lavished upon the holy being the glass beads symbolic of suprahuman power. The figure is given long strands of beaded *yōraku* falling down over the pedestal, and the elephant is decked out with ornate harness ornaments of beaded *yōraku*. From the elephant's throat hangs an ornament of the type discussed in Plate Note 121; it consists of a metal cap from which hang numerous chains of glass beads.

- *Collection*: Tokyo National Museum.
- *Date*: Heian period.

118. BRONZE SUTRA CASE FROM A SUTRA MOUND

Discovered accidentally in 1957 by Mr. Matsuji Nakamura on a hillside of his property at Taku city, Saga Prefecture.[1] No dedicated articles; only the *Hokke-kyō* (Lotus Sutra) and a fragment of some black substance. The bronze case is plain. The lid, with its flattened *hōshu* knob, overhangs the simple cylindrical body bearing only two plain molded ridges. The base flares a little; in it was inserted, for a bottom, a mirror disc molded in a delicate low-relief design of sparrows amid rice plants heavy with ripened grain. Six perforations in the lid show where bead strings were attached, with the hemp thread still there, and one thread imbedded obliquely in the corrosion of the bronze body. Some seventy-nine glass beads were found beside the case, their threads having rotted.

- *Collection*: Mr. Matsuji Nakamura, Yamasaki, Taku city, Saga Prefecture.
- *Date*: Case inscribed Tenji 1 (1124).
  BEADS:
- *Sizes*: Average H. 0.35 cm.; D. 0.55–0.75 cm.
- *Colors*: Larger ones, green; translucent. Smaller ones, bright turquoise blue; translucent.
- *Bores*: D. 0.275–0.375 cm.
- *Bubbles*: Difficult to see because of weathering, but several show large broken-bubble pits, and broken fragments disclose many bubbles.
- *Technique*: Coiled; neither coiling nor shapes are precise.
- *Condition*: Badly weathered. Some broken areas show devitrification.
- *Remarks*: The glass metal is rich in color, but the rather amateurish shaping suggests a cottage type industry or provincial workshop.
  Reference:
  1. Koreji Kinoshita, "Yamasaki Kyōzuka" [Yamasaki Sutra Mound], *Shinkyōdo*, Saga Prefecture Bunkakan, No. 10, 1955, pp. 15–17.

119. BRONZE SUTRA CASE FROM SHIŌ-JI
Important Cultural Property

Discovered about 1940 in the ruins of Shiō-ji, Umi-machi, outskirts of Fukuoka city, Fukuoka Prefecture. Fragments of the *Hokke-kyō* (Lotus Sutra) were found in this case.

The tall, cylindrical form is about 37.5 cm. high, with the lid a hipped pagoda roof with nine-ringed finial. Beneath the eaves is suspended a simulated fringe in bronze, from the lowest points of which hang single glass beads, so placed that their bores face the viewer—a mode not seen previously. A flat metal piece, folded and evidently intended as a sepal, surmounts each bead. From each of the four corners of the roof hangs a *yōraku* pendant composed of larger and smaller glass beads and characteristic metal links. Four plain mirror shapes are suspended from the cast-metal loops on the underside of the roof.

- *Collection*: Mr. Hirosuke Uchimoto, Fukuoka city.

- *Date*: Inscribed Hōan 4 (1123).
  BEADS:
- *Sizes*: Various.
- *Colors*: The larger beads look opaque, but this may be due to weathering. The smaller beads are a delicate pale green; translucent.
- *Bores*: Wide, so that the beads are nearly ring shaped.
- *Technique*: Coiled; some of the beads not separated.
- *Condition*: The larger beads are corroded; the smaller ones bear some film.
- *Remarks*: The slightly amateurish appearance of these beads, as in those of Plate 118, suggests provincial work. The two sizes of beads differ in appearance. A new type of bead occurs here, as in the *yōraku* of Supplementary Note 53.

120. SHRINE AND SHŌTOKU TAISHI IMAGE
Important Cultural Property

This *yōraku* adorns a shrinelike frame for a sculptured seated figure of Shōtoku Taishi as a seven-year-old child. The wood figure is signed by the sculptor Enkei, and dated 1069. Whether the frame is contemporaneous or a work of the Kamakura period is not yet settled; since this bead *yōraku* resembles those of Heian metal sutra cases and a Heian *shari-tō* (Sup. N. 53) in some ways not characteristic of later *yōraku*, it is included here.

The upper part of this fringe, which extends around the three open sides of the frame, is of the lozenge design fundamental in much beadwork. The lower portion, however, is more elaborate than usual, having suspended strings compounded of four-petaled plaques of what is probably mother-of-pearl (or, less likely, opaque glass) about 2.1 cm. square; these are dividers for the wire-strung beads that form the lozenge-shaped openings of the design. The wires come out on the front of the medallions, through perforations, to make secure on each medallion a small sepallike metal form topped with a glass bead; the wires then proceed around the plaque, fitting into the indentations marking the petals. This technique, although more complex, suggests the metal medallions with beads in Supplementary Note 53. The strands suspended from the lower row of plaques are an intermingling of simple wire loops, of glass beads of various sizes, of metal sepals capping glass *tsuyudama*, and of metal pendant terminals in the shape of round bells and flat leaf forms.

- *Collection*: Hōryū-ji, Nara Prefecture.
- *Date*: Late Heian period?
  BEADS:
- *Sizes*: Largest beads, H. 0.9 cm.; D. 0.9 cm.
- *Colors*: The beads centered on the plaques are blue; others are green, both intense and pale, or honey color, or colorless, some of which look almost pearly because of reflections. A few of those strung between the plaques look possibly opaque, but this may be due to dust. All are beautiful in tone, either reflecting the light or transmitting it through transparency.
- *Bores*: Comparatively large, giving the largest of these transparent beads an almost hollow, blown look; however, bores are clearly visible.
- *Bubbles*: Some.
- *Technique*: Coiled: some of the smaller beads show corrugated ridges from coiling.
- *Condition*: The *yōraku* is in need of repair, but individual beads are well preserved.

121. MODEL OF A SACRED HORSE, KŌDAI-JINGŪ, ISE

Every twenty years everything at the Imperial Grand Shrines (Kōdai-jingū) at Ise is renewed —not only the buildings but treasures and ritual equipment. Entirely new, and therefore ritually immaculate, items replace the old, which are then ceremonially buried. A few such replacements have nevertheless been preserved at the shrine. As they are reportedly replicas of the old, it may be assumed that to a certain extent they represent former customs and objects.

This is one of two horse models, which are similar to the Heian painting mentioned on page 135; thus the throat and rump ornaments may be considered as representing the Heian style. Their general nature may be discerned in this Plate, but there is no way of knowing whether the quality and coloring of the glass

beads is true to that of Heian glass. An extant throat ornament of the Kamakura period is discussed under Plate Note 127. A similar throat ornament appears on the elephant depicted in Plate 117.

The ornament (*uzu*) at the rump of the Ise model has a flame motif made up of rows of metal pins on which many glass *kodama* are impaled, the heads of the pins forming the rim of the flame. This is so suggestive of the *uzu* of the Heian painting that one may assume this same use of glass beads in the Heian period.

In addition to these two main ornaments, small pendant chains, each of about five glass beads and a metal terminal, are attached to the bridle and the harness straps and to the ends of the brocade skirts of the saddle.

- *Collection*: Jingū-Chōkokan, Uji-Yamada city, Mie Prefecture.
- *Date*: A twenty-year replacement of the year 1900.

122. *SHARI-TSUBO* OF DENKŌ-JI
Important Cultural Property

This *shari-tsubo* was discovered within the body of an image of Jizō Bosatsu in Denkō-ji, Nara it contained two white *shari* and a tiny carved sandalwood figure of Yakushi Nyōrai less than 3.0 cm. high.

- *Collection*: Denkō-ji, Ozawa-machi, Nara.
- *Date*: The dedicatory scroll is dated as of 1222, but certain characteristics relate this example to *shari-tsubo* of the Late Heian period (such as those in Sup. N. 55, 56). Since the donor was a nun eighty-three years of age, she may well have possessed it since the Fujiwara era—the main image of the temple was also her gift and is mentioned as a treasure owned by her "for many years."[1]
- *Size*: H. overall, 3.45 cm.; body alone, 2.55 cm.; greatest D., 5.15 cm.; at mouth, 2.8 cm.; lid, 3.1 cm.; T. at mouth *ca.* 0.225 cm., but the body is thinner, perhaps 0.1 cm.
- *Color*: Blue; transparent. Matching tone on color chart, "greenish." IH.D.Refl.: nearest Ch 3, 14-4-13; lid rim close to Ch 4, 15-4-13. (see Pl. 14).
- *Bubbles*: Many tiny circular ones. Two large

ones below the rim on the interior are slightly concave. One small elongated bubble in the stem handle.

- *Composition*: On the basis of specific gravity and Beta-ray back scattering, 50% lead content; Sp. Grav.: 3.8.[2]
- *Technique*: Blown, a "kick" in the bottom. The rim of the lid and the stem-shaped handle were applied.
- *Condition*: Excellent but for the broken stem of the lid, part of which has been lost. The edge of the lid's neck is jagged, perhaps where broken from a blowpipe (?).

References:
1. Koboku Ōta, "Omoidasu no Butsuzō" [Recollections of Buddhist Images), *Omoide no Butsuzō*, No. 1, 1955, pp. 1–9.
2. *Asahina, *et al*, "Tōshōdai-ji Haku-ruri. . . . ," pp. 17–18; *Asahina, Yamazaki, and Yamasaki, "Investigation. . . . ," p. 4.

123. YAKUSHI NYŌRAI TRINITY WITH TWELVE GUARDIANS
Important Cultural Property

A silk hanging scroll painted in colors. The "medicine jar" held in Yakushi's left hand is a small squat bottle of dark blue glass. In shape, except for the wide-flanged mouth, it suggests some of the *shari-bin* known from earlier periods, such as that installed under the Hōryū-ji pagoda (Pl. 71). Its mouth is familiar from other containers often seen in sculpture from the Asuka period on. It seems likely that this glass bottle represents a form that was familiar to the artist and therefore was not necessarily an imported article.

- *Collection*: Yōchi-in, Kōya-san, Wakayama Prefecture; shown in the museum of Kōya-san, the Reihō-kan.
- *Date*: Late Heian period.

124. RAKAN PANTHAKA PERFORMING A RITUAL FOR THE DEAD
National Treasure

Rakan (arhats) were saintly disciples of Śakyamuni, the historical Buddha, who through spiritual discipline attained superhuman powers. They are often grouped in series of sixteen or of five hundred. Series of sixteen paintings are not uncommon. By the Heian period they had become a popular subject in Chinese painting, and for a time were also seen in Japan, in both imported Chinese and domestic paintings. In many series, one or more of the paintings include representations of fairly large glass vessels, usually for fruit or flower offerings. As the shapes of these vessels are generally familiar in Chinese glass and ceramics of the time, and as the general tone of the paintings is distinctly Chinese, one must conclude, with possibly a few exceptions, that the glass forms depicted were probably copied from examples in Chinese paintings or from some pictorial guide. The blue *shari-tsubo* shown in this Plate is one of the possible exceptions.

This painting of the Rakan Panthaka (No. 10 of the series) depicts him in priestly robes officiating on his knees before an altar whose main object of worship is a dark blue glass *shari-tsubo* emitting golden rays. In the foreground, before praying attendants, is an elaborate pedestal supporting a transparent pale blue glass filled with blossoms; the bowl is of typical Chinese form.

- *Collection*: Tokyo National Museum; formerly, Shōju-Raigō-ji, Shiga Prefecture.
- *Date*: Heian period, "not later than the 11th century."[1]
  a. *Shari-tsubo*.
  This bottle form suggests the smaller medicine pot discussed in Plate Note 123, except that this is obviously larger and has an added stopper of *hōshu* form, which is somewhat similar to the stopper of the *shari-tsubo* of the Hōryū-ji pagoda (Pl. 70). This author knows of no Chinese painting showing such a glass *shari-tsubo*, whereas flower and fruit vessels appear with some frequency. It seems possible, therefore, that the artist was reproducing a Japanese glass form with which he was familiar.
  b. *Flower bowl*.
  This form is so common in Chinese paintings that one cannot consider this glass as more than a borrowing of a Chinese type.

Reference:
1. *Okada, "Kōten Kaiga. . . . ," p. 8.

KAMAKURA PERIOD

125. ELEVEN-HEADED KANNON OF HŌKONGŌ-IN

Important Cultural Property

The temple authorities stated that the *yōraku* have never been restored and are the originals of the Kamakura period. Some portions are now missing and others incomplete; even so, the image is almost eclipsed by the dripping strands that adorn it, and by the sixteen elaborate *yōraku* suspended from its shrine ceiling, which encircle the head and shoulders of the image.[1] From the photograph, it is difficult to distinguish the complex detail and the ingenious manner of attachment. For example, beneath the figure is a circular metal plate from which horizontal bars project, bent upward just behind and over every other one of the innermost upper petals of the lotus pedestal; each ends in a "flaming jewel" form, and just below each of these are four hooks from which hang the elaborate *yōraku* strands draped over the outside of the pedestal. This is a device that is seen in other works of the Kamakura period as in the Amida Trinity of Supplementary Note 62. In the Kannon of Hōkongō-in, one glass bead with a metal pendant is attached to each of the projecting bars. In each of the outer petals is a large glass bead attached with a tripartite strand suspended from it (not seen in the photograph). The larger strands depending from the upturned bars cover the entire lower four rows of petals. The small lotus dais directly below also had complex, but smaller, strands from the petal tips. Beneath, an octagonal dais carries at each of its foliated feet other compound strands; a perforated bronze fringe also carries at each point a suspended glass bead.

The glass pendants from the frame of the crown are *tsuyudama* of glass with metal sepals. It was difficult to determine whether the insets at the very edge of the halo are of glass.

- *Collection*: Hōkongō-in, Hanazono-mura, Kyoto Prefecture.
- *Date*: 1316, according to an inscription on the back of the lotus pedestal and to writing deposited within the image.

BEADS:
- *Size*: Various; some are large, like marbles.
- *Colors*: Dark blue, deep, rich bluish green, honey color, and whitish; chiefly transparent.
- *Bores*: Very small.
- *Technique*: Coiled. In each of the eight panels of the octagonal plinth at the bottom is a square perforated bronze panel with a large glass *hankyūdama* inset at the center. No *tsuyudama* were seen except in the crown.
- *Condition*: Good, barring a heavy film of dust very difficult to remove; a number of the *yōraku* are now missing and others incomplete.

The beads are of excellent quality—good, clear glass metal, light in weight and of rich coloration. Data are incomplete, since the beads were too coated with dust to study *in situ*. Inspection was only of *yōraku* that had fallen off and from which the accretion could be at least partially removed.

- *Remarks*: The extreme elaboration of the *yōraku*-burdened image is expressive of the belief of the donors in the protective efficacy of glass beads. The number of beads on this figure attests to quantity production of glass beads in this period. There seems to be no reason for considering them to be other than of Japanese provenance.

126. *MIKOSHI* OF KONDA HACHIMAN SHRINE

National Treasure

This *mikoshi* was dedicated by Minamoto no Yoritomo when he sponsored the repair of Konda Hachiman Shrine. Its style and workmanship are in the Heian tradition. It seems to be the most ancient extant *mikoshi*, antedating by over thirty years the one of the Hachiman Shrine of Nakaban, Tomobuchi-mura, Naka-gun, Wakayama Prefecture, which dates from 1228 but is sometimes referred to as the oldest.[1]

This *mikoshi* has a hip roof, and from the eaves hang large *yōraku* of gold-plated plaques and hanging strands of glass beads. The lacquer framework carries some mother-of-pearl inlay decoration.

- *Collection*: Hachiman Shrine, Konda, Habiki

(formerly in Furuichi-machi), Osaka Prefecture.
- *Date*: 1196.
  BEADS:
- *Sizes*: Large *marudama*, H. 1.2 cm.; D. 1.3 cm.; small *marudama*, D. 0.7 cm.
- *Colors*: Deep blue; opaque. Sky blue, blue green, green, dark honey color, yellow, and uncolored; transparent. Brown; opaque.
- *Bores*: Large *marudama* sample, D. 0.3 cm. The bore rims are rough, where two beads were cut apart.
- *Bubbles*: Some have many bubbles.
- *Technique*: Coiled; some beads are almost corrugated, others quite smooth.
- *Condition*: Good.
- *Remarks*: The Teppō-zu Inari Shrine in Minato-machi, Chūo-ku, Tokyo, owns a *mikoshi* said to be an imitation of this one at Konda Hachiman but the details are quite dissimilar.
  Reference:
  1. *Nihon Rekishi Daijiten* [Dictionary of Japanese History], Tokyo, Kawade Shōbō Shinsha, 1959, XVII, p. 184.

127. HORSE'S THROAT ORNAMENT
National Treasure

Kubi-kazari ("throat ornaments") on animals are depicted in Buddhist art and were a part of secular horse trappings and the trappings of sacred horses at Shintō shrines. In the Nara and Heian periods, and probably in the Kamakura period, horses were richly caparisoned, and glass played a major role. This has already been touched upon in Plate Note 121.

This throat ornament was part of the accoutrement of a sacred horse of Tamukeyama Shrine in Nara, but there is no shrine record regarding it.

Such an ornament was suspended from the throat, swinging loosely in front of the chest (see Pls. 117, 121). Inside the bronze cap at the top there is a globular bronze bell, about three inches in diameter, with a loose pellet inside for sound. From the lower of the two bronze borders with leaf motif are suspended six *yōraku* strands, made up of connected bronze

plaques, strings of colored glass *kodama* and, as terminals, small bronze bells.
- *Collection*: Nara National Museum, Nara.
- *Date*: Kamakura period; so assigned by the Nara Museum on the basis of the bronze workmanship.
  KODAMA:
- *Sizes*: D. 0.4–0.5 cm.
- *Colors*: Dark blue and purple, dark green and pale green, honey color, clouded white. Some are transparent, some translucent.
- *Bubbles*: Small, circular.
- *Technique*: Coiled, but not conspicuously so.
- *Condition*: Good.
- *Remarks*: According to a priest of the shrine, not since the Edo period has a shrine horse been a part of any shrine procession.

128. *SHARI-TSUBO* OF TŌFUKU-JI

This was discovered in 1961 in the body of a wood statue of Mukan Fumon Zenshi, under whom Shōichi Kokushi, third abbot of Tōfuku-ji, had studied the Zen doctrine in China for seven years. It had been installed in the statue in company with an unusual "five-elements" form, *shari*, a copper ring, a fragment of incense wood, and an inscription.
- *Collection*: Ryōgin-an, Tōfuku-ji, Kyoto.
- *Provenance*: It is thought, without substantiation, that Shōichi Kokushi brought the jar, with *shari*, from the continent.
- *Date*: Early 14th century.
- *Size*: Present H. 2.0 cm.; T., except at the mouth opening, 0.05 cm.
- *Color*: Body of cobalt blue; solid lid, deep blue.
- *Technique*: Body is blown glass with a "kick" in the bottom. The lid is solid; "some other material seems to have been mixed with it."[1]
- *Condition*: Broken.
- *Remarks*: This tiny glass *shari-tsubo* is, except in size and in the thinness of the metal, remarkably reminiscent of the glass *shari-tsubo* of earlier epochs. The *shari*, which are not of glass, are now preserved in a small bronze tube.
  Reference:
  1. Shuno Fukushima, "Gozen Priests and Japanese Culture," KBS Bulletin, Tokyo, No. 55, July-Aug. 1961, p. 5. For details regarding

this *shari-tsubo* the author is indebted to Mr. Haruki Kageyama of the Kyoto National Museum.

129. SUBINDA, THE FOURTH *RAKAN*, WORSHIPING A *SHARI* IN A VASE

A Japanese painting in color on silk. The treatment of the *shari* detail is unusual, the single large *shari* being shown at the bottom of a transparent glass vase, with the rays that emanate from it shooting straight upward somewhat like the lotus or other stalks usually seen in such receptacles. The shape of the containing vase is also somewhat unusual, unlike vessels seen in other paintings of the period.

This painting apparently depicts a miracle—a holy *shari*, descending from heaven, which will come to rest in the four-lobed bowl on the lotus pedestal.

- *Collection*: Museum of Fine Arts, Boston (No. 11.6197).
- *Provenance*: Japanese.
- *Date*: Early Kamakura period.

130. JIZŌ BOSATSU

A painting on silk in color. Here the object held in the left hand is not what often seems to be an ephemeral vaporous sphere, but is an actual transparent sphere fitted with a metal cap, convincingly resembling a glass jar with lid.

- *Collection*: Museum of Fine Arts, Boston (No. 11.6185).
- *Provenance*: Japanese.
- *Date*: Early 14th century.

MUROMACHI PERIOD

131. BEADWORK ORNAMENT FOR AN IMPERIAL *MIKOSHI* (?)

Important Cultural Property

The panel length is about 61.0 cm. and the width 9.7 cm. The panel is entirely of woven beadwork, with a short fringe. The background is of opaque white beads; the inscription, of opaque black beads. The border is of translucent red, blue, yellow, and amber-colored beads; the fringe has translucent green beads in the center and otherwise semitranslucent rose-colored and opaque white beads.

- *Collection*: Tokyo National Museum. Formerly owned by Hōryū-ji.
- *Provenance*: Traditionally ascribed to the Chinese Ming dynasty, even though an inscription on the storage box reads "Ornament for the Palanquin of the Retired Emperor Shirakawa," who retired in 1086. Perhaps this contradiction in dates is due to use for storage purposes of a box with an old inscription. It may be that this so-called "*mikoshi* ornament" was never intended for such use.

The appearance of the beadwork, with strong red and green tones, combined with dominant opaque black and white, together with the coarseness of the bead technique and the style of the fringe at the bottom, is distinctly not Japanese. The red, rose, and green of the beads were popular colors in Ming China. The overall feeling is coarse and almost strident in comparison with usual Japanese beadwork; this contributes to the feeling that the panel is not of domestic origin.

- *Date*: Probably Ming dynasty.
  BEADS:
- *Size*: D. approximately 0.2 cm.
- *Colors*: Dark red; translucent. IH.D.Refl.: Ch 2, 1-5-12 or 13 and 1-6-11 or 12.
  Greenish blue; translucent. IH.D.Refl.: Ch 4, 15-4-13 or 14.
  Green; translucent. IH.D.Refl.: Ch 11, *ca.* 10-3-12.
  White; opaque.
  Black; opaque.
- *Bubbles*: Many, large and small; seen even in the opaque white beads—Or could these be unmelted quartz, as in the Nara period?
- *Technique*: Coiled carelessly; corrugated bodies and long, irregular projections where the glass source was drawn away.

MOMOYAMA PERIOD

132. *KUGIKAKUSHI* ("Nailhead Concealer")

Considered to have come from the Jūrakudai mansion of Toyotomi Hideyoshi.[1] In the oval form of a handwarmer, carved and hollowed out from *kiri* (paulownia) wood and fitted with a lid of perforated metal. The design of the lid includes the Toyotomi crest of *kiri* blooms and leaves in cloisonné beside a running stream and the interwoven gold-plated meshes of a *jakago*, the large basket which, when filled with rocks, was used for reinforcing the bank of a stream or pond. *Kugikakushi* were sometimes used to cover the heads of nails driven into wooden beams. In the main body of this simulated handwarmer the craftsman took full advantage of the wood grain. Above, a wave pattern in silver plate surrounds the metal lid, which fits over the hollowed part intended to contain charcoal.

Since this *kugikakushi* has not been studied personally by the author, catalogue data are incomplete, but from Plate 132 the bold character of the cloisonné technique, characteristic of Momoyama taste, may be recognized.
- *Collection*: Mr. Ryō Hosomi, Izumi-Otsu city, Osaka Prefecture. Previously owned by the former Baron Takashi Masuda (Don-ō), Tokyo.
- *Date*: Probably late 16th century.[2]
- *Color*: Flowers and leaves of the design are bluish green, on a gold ground.
- *Technique*: Cloisonné method.
- *Condition*: Excellent.
- *Remarks*: This example of *shippō* seems to differ from the techniques characteristic of Chinese cloisonné and from the meticulous, often minute, work associated with Japanese cloisonné as it developed in the Edo period. Perhaps this merely hinges on the broader nature of Momoyama work and the abundant use of gold, but relationship to Chinese cloisonné of the same time is not clear, and the source of the sudden Momoyama outbreak of *shippō* decoration is an enigma. Too little is known regarding any possible contemporaneous enamel activities in Korea to determine whether knowledge of the technique might have come thence as a by-product of Hideyoshi's invasion of the Korean peninsula. Could the old methods of enamel decoration as seen in the Kegoshi Tomb coffin ornament (Pl. 74), the mirror of the Shōsō-in (Pl. 12) and the architectural ornaments of the Hōō-dō of Byōdō-in (Sup. N. 58) have survived, to break out anew under the stimulation of Hideyoshi's extravagant

schemes? Certainly the field of pre-Edo cloisonné calls for intensive study (see also Pl. 17).

References:
1. *Hosomi, "Momoyama Jidai. . . . ," Pl. 2, p. 22.
2. For the owner's reasons for his dating, see *Ibid.*, Pl. 45–48.

Edo Period

Nagasaki

151. *BIIDORO-E* IN A DOOR PULL
An oval metal fingerhold for a sliding wall panel (*fusuma*), inlaid with a *biidoro* vignette landscape.
- *Collection*: The Toledo Museum of Art (Apparatus, 1956); Gift of Mr. Kaiichirō Tazawa, Tokyo.
- *Date*: Edo period.
- *Size*: Glass estimated as 5.1 × 3.5 cm.
- *Colors*: Blue, green, brown, and gold, with a pale blue sky and black tree trunks.
- *Technique*: Painted in reverse on the underside of a flat piece of glass.
- *Condition*: Excellent.

152. STRAIGHT-WALLED GREEN CUPS
Originally a set of ten. They emit a delicate tone when struck.
- *Collection*: The Toledo Museum of Art (No. 54.69 A-I).
- *Date*: An inscription inside the storage box reads: "Transparent green *biidoro* saké cups for ten people. Maruya Seibei. Lucky Day in the First Month, Year of the Tiger, Enkyō 3 (1746)." Perhaps "Maruya Seibei" indicates one of the early glassmakers of Nagasaki; no attempt has as yet been made to trace the name.
- *Size*: H. 6.6 cm.; D. at rim, 5.0 cm.
- *Color*: Deep green; transparent with a slight iridescence. One cup, IH.D.Refl.: Ch 13, 12-6-15; some others much darker.
- *Bubbles*: Some large ones; some pitting.
- *Composition* (one cup): Lead content 40.12%; Sp. Grav.: 3.0; Refr. Ind.: ND 1.634. For full analysis see Appendix, Table IX.

• *Technique*: Mold blown. Delicately pebbly "eggshell" surface. A slightly projecting lip is thin and rather rough. One mold mark.

153. FLUTED CUP
From an original set of five, fabricated of glass similar in nature to that of the cups of Plate 152. Thin and light in weight, straight walled with twenty-four softly rounded vertical flutes forming a delicately scalloped rim. Foot-rims are slightly rounded. The glass metal emits a musical tone when struck.
• *Collection*: The Toledo Museum of Art (No. 53.154 A-B).
• *Date*: Uncertain; possibly like Plate 152, before 1746.
• *Size*: H. 5.6 cm.; D. at rim, 5.9 cm.
• *Color*: Colorless, with faint greenish tinges; transparent.
• *Bubbles*: Numerous minute bubbles and pittings.
• *Composition* (of a cup of the same set): 45.28% lead content. Sp. Grav.: 3; Refr. Ind.: 1.645. For complete analysis see Appendix, Table X.
• *Technique*: Mold blown; the rims have thin, sharp edges.

154. THIN YELLOW BOTTLE
A graceful shape attenuated to a long slender neck with a mouth rim.
• *Collection*: Mr. Teruyo Yamada, Hirado city; formerly owned, it is said, by the daimyo of Kashima fief, Saga, who presented it to his vassal Hara in 1770. Exhibited in the Hirado Kankō Shiryōkan.
• *Date*: The legend on the storage box reads: "Meiwa 7 [1770], seventh month. Relic presented by the lord." If a "relic" in 1770, it must presumably already have had a history.
• *Size*: H. 23.5 cm.; D. *ca.* 10.0 cm.
• *Color*: Yellow; transparent. This is rare in Nagasaki glass.
• *Technique*: Blown glass.
• *Condition*: Excellent.
• *Remarks*: It seems that this may be the earliest preserved important specimen of Nagasaki glass (but see also Pl. 152).

155. THIN, DARK BLUE GOURD-SHAPED BOTTLE
A striking example of thin metal suggestive of that of Plates 21 and 154. In this case a ball-shaped stopper was added.
• *Collection*: Mr. Shirō Tonomura, Nagasaki.
• *Provenance*: It has been suggested that this is Chinese of the Ming dynasty. To the author it seems more likely, if Chinese, to have been made by one of the Chinese artisans in Nagasaki, but still more likely to be Japanese work.
• *Date*: Edo period.
• *Size*: H. *ca.* 25.4 cm.
• *Color*: Indigo blue, but lighter in tone than the wine pot of Plate 21; transparent.
• *Bubbles*: Several large ones.
• *Condition*: Excellent.

156. COVERED BOWL
From an original set of five. Rather thin glass with twenty vertical flutes, softly rounded. Emits a musical tone when struck.
• *Collection*: The Toledo Museum of Art (No. 53.155 A-B)
• *Date*: Edo period.
• *Size*: H. overall 8.8 cm.; D. at base, 4.1 cm.
• *Color*: Colorless but slightly greenish; transparent.
• *Composition* (of a bowl from the same set): 49.6% lead content. Sp. Grav.: 3; Refr. Ind.: 1.645. For complete analysis, see Appendix Table XI.
• *Technique*: Mold blown.
• *Condition*: Excellent.

157. *KASABOKO* OF IMAUO-MACHI
Kasaboko are conspicuous features of the Okun'chi Festival of Suwa Shrine, Nagasaki. In this instance the platform carries an assemblage of delicate glass parts simulating a fishnet hung on a bamboo pole to dry, water reeds, two sea bream in baskets, a white fish, and a lobster. All except the enclosing bamboo frame are of glass.

When the author visited Nagasaki in 1955 to see the once-in-every-eight-years appearance of this *kasaboko*, she was presented with broken remnants of the various elements; these provided most of the data given below. They are now in The Corning Museum of Glass.

- *Collection*: Imauo-machi Association. Although formerly packed away and stored during the eight-year intervals between showings, it has recently been on exhibition in "Mansion Sixteen," one of the historic buildings of Nagasaki.
- *Date*: Edo period, perhaps about 1853. Kaempfer, in his detailed description of the festival written in 1690, mentions the elaborate contrivances for some of the streets, but does not refer to Imauo-machi.[1] Although tradition has placed this *kasaboko* within the Kyohō era (1716–35) or the Tenmei Era (1781–86), Mr. Hayashi, quoting both the *Bakufu Jidai no Nagasaki* ("Nagasaki in the Days of the *Bakufu*"), published in 1903, and an inscription on the storage box, stated that it was thought to have been made in 1853 after the design of Tamisaburō Tamaya of Imauo-machi.[2]
- *Condition*: Much of the original glass no longer exists, due to severe damage during the festival "dances." One record states that Yonekura, in 1927, replaced the *tai* in one of the baskets with one made of raw materials from the Fukai Glass Factory of Imauo-machi.
- *Remarks*: Accompanying this *kasaboko* in the festival is a fishing boat float whose railing is draped with a net made of long purple glass beads. Were the green reeds on the boat's deck also originally of glass?

GLASS OF THE *kasaboko*:

a. *Bamboo pole.*

Fragments in The Corning Museum of Glass (No. 63.6.22).

- *Size*: H. of the pole, 160.0 cm.; D. 3.35 cm.; T. of the glass, *ca.* 0.1 cm.
- *Color*: Blue green; transparent. IH.D.Refl. and IH.D.Trans.: Ch 3, 14-6-15.
- *Bubbles*: Not many; minute, and chiefly attenuated longitudinally.
- *Composition*: Lead glass, colored by copper. See Appendix, Table XII.
- *Technique*: Drawn out as wide, open tubing.
- *Condition*: Partially broken.

b. *Fishnet and rope.*

(1) Rope coiled around the pole.
Fragment in The Corning Museum of Glass (No. 63.6.64).

- *Size*: W. 0.9 cm.; T. 0.75 cm.; T. of glass, 0.2 cm.
- *Color*: Typical Nagasaki "indigo" glass; semitransparent.
- *Composition*: Lead content about 64%; colored by cobalt.
- *Technique*: Drawn out into an unobtrusively spiraled tube. The spiraling takes the form of flat plane surfaces turning gradually to the right, an effective method to suggest twisted rope.
- *Remarks*: This same "rope" appears as reinforcements on the two fish baskets of *d*.

(2) Net
Fragments in The Corning Museum of Glass (No. 63.6.24). This is composed of more slender tubing of the same glass as above, so the purple blue seems less saturated, becoming a grayed indigo. Four lengths of this smaller tubing, threaded and tied together, form each single mesh of the net. Larger tubing forms the edging.

- *Sizes*: Tubing for the mesh, D. 0.1 cm.; tubing at the border, D. 0.3 cm.
- *Color*: Smaller tubing, purple blue; transparent. IH.D.Refl.: Ch 7, 18-3-11; IH.D. Trans.: Ch 7, 18-2-16.
- *Technique*: Same as that of *b*(1) except, being smaller, the plane-surfaced spirals are more delicate.
- *Condition*: Excellent.

(3) Simulated floats added along the border of the net.
Fragment in The Corning Museum of Glass (No. 63.6.23 II). At intervals along the edge of the net are lengths of tubing simulating floats on real fishing nets. The glass is identical to the two fish baskets (see *d*), except that the tubes are narrower. They are slightly flattened.

- *Size*: L. 12.0 cm.; D. 0.5 cm. and 0.4 cm.; T. of glass 0.16 cm.
- *Color*: Brownish yellow; IH.D. Refl.: nearest Ch 8, 7-4-16.

- *Composition*: Lead content about 70%; colored by iron.
- *Technique*: Drawn out into tube form.
- *Condition*: One conspicuous stone and several minute imperfections; good surface preservation.

c. *Reeds.*

Hollow tubing attenuated to solid tips.

(1) Stems and leaves.

Fragments in The Corning Museum of Glass (Nos. 63.6.18–19).

- *Size*: W. from 1.4 cm. or more in the main stalk to practically nothing at the tips.
- *Color*: Variable, from deep blue green; transparent. IH.D.Refl.: Ch 3, 14-6-15.
- *Bubbles*: A few minute, circular; some inconspicuous longitudinal air stripes.
- *Composition*: Lead content about 63%; colored by copper.
- *Technique*: Drawn out, narrowing to solid tips.

(2) Tassels of the reeds.

Fragments in The Corning Museum of Glass (No. 63.6.25)

- *Size*: D. at greatest width, 0.2 cm.; T. of glass less than 0.035 cm.
- *Color*: Grayed purple blue; transparent. IH.D.Refl.: nearest Ch 6, 17-4-17; IH.D. Trans.: Ch 6 17-2-17. Some are practically gray.
- *Bubbles*: None; one exceedingly slim, longitudinal air stripe.
- *Technique*: Hollow circular tubing drawn out to attenuated solid tips.

d. *Fish baskets.*

Fragment in The Corning Museum of Glass (No. 63.6.23, I) The entire plaiting of the baskets is of flattened, hollow glass tubing. The vertical ropes are of the same dark blue tubing as the rope of b(1).

- *Size*: Baskets, H. 25.0 cm.; D. 45.0 cm.; the plaited glass, W. 0.9 cm; greatest T. 0.3 cm.
- *Color*: Brownish yellow; transparent. IH. D.Refl.: difficult, but nearest Ch 8, 7-5-16.
- *Bubbles*: Some small and circular, with one continuous longitudinal air stripe.

- *Composition*: Lead content about 70%; colored by iron.
- *Technique*: Drawn out into flattened tubing, hollowed slightly in the center of both upper and lower faces.
- *Condition*: Good.

e. *Fish.*

Fragments in The Corning Museum of Glass (Scales, No. 63.6.21; tail rods, No. 63.6.118 a-i).

(1) The bodies are of papier-mâché, which, for the sea bream, is painted red; for the white fish, thin scales of white, clouded and somewhat shimmering glass—too thin to be measured—were added on the surface; most have fallen off. They have a lead content of about 69%.

(2) The tails are ingeniously formed of many slender, colorless and transparent glass rods of several diameters, arranged in varying lengths and held in place by a cover of thin, transparent membrane.

f. *Lobster.*

Partially of papier-mâché. The extremely long and delicate feelers, the legs, tail, eyes, and projecting points of the forepart are all of the same dark blue glass as the rope of b(1). The feelers are 62.0 cm. long. It is remarkable that they have remained intact; the lobster, however, occupies a protected position, low and just inside the basketwork enclosure.

References:
1. Kaempfer, *op. cit.* (see n. 17, p. 261), 1906 ed., pp. 135–142.
2. Mr. Genkichi Hayashi called the author's attention to drawings of this festival in *Nagasaki Kokin Shūran Meishō Zue*, 1841, which show very simple *kasaboko*; this would seem to indicate a later date for this elaborate one of Imauo-machi—that is, perhaps the 1853 date. Or were the drawings merely simplified?

158. ENAMELED *POKON-POKON*
- *Collection*: Nagasaki Municipal Museum, Nagasaki.
- *Date*: Middle 19th century (?).
- *Size*: H. 14.0 cm.; D. at base, 4.5 cm.; at mouth, 0.6 cm.

- *Color*: Colorless; transparent. Indistinct floral motifs daubed on in opaque red, green, and yellow.
- *Technique*: Blown glass, with flexible bottom; enameled.
- *Condition*: Excellent.
- *Remarks*: The woodblock print by Utamaro Kitagawa entitled *Biidoro Fuku Musume* (Pl. 159) depicts a young woman blowing a plain blue *pokon-pokon*. A second print by Utamaro (Pl. 160) gives some idea of just how "musical" this so-called musical toy is; its note is but a short popping sound, which may be of considerable volume.

161. COMB WITH ENGRAVED GLASS PANEL

A simple type with only a foreign ship and, at the right, a glimpse of a distant hilly shoreline engraved on glass, which is set in tortoiseshell.
- *Collection*: Ikenaga Collection, Kobe Municipal Museum, Kobe.
- *Date*: Edo period.
GLASS:
- *Size*: Glass, H. 4.0 cm.; W. 10.5 cm. Since the tortoiseshell is 0.3 cm. thick, the glass must be about 0.2 cm. or less in thickness.
- *Color*: Colorless; transparent.
- *Bubbles*: Minute, only noticeable under magnification.
- *Technique*: Wheel engraved, with both frosting and angular lines side by side. There is a slight hint of Western perspective in some details of the ship.
- *Condition*: Excellent.

MERCHANT CRAFTSMEN

OSAKA

163 (upper left). LARGE *SUJIDAMA*
- *Collection*: The Corning Museum of Glass (No. 63.6.71)
- *Provenance*: Of foreign style. The *Soken Kisho* illustrates a similar one, and the accompanying text states that this was known as an *Oranda fukimono* (Dutch glass bead—that is, one imported through the Dutch trade) and that the

imported ones had a dull surface, whereas the Japanese imitations were glossy, although this gloss was sometimes reduced with a whetstone.[1] It is said that Venetian beads had a glistening surface at the bore end,[2] as does this one.
- *Date*: Edo period.
- *Size*: H. 1.3 cm.; D. 1.6 cm.
- *Colors*: Black ground; opaque and dull. Six vertical stripes inserted in the order of red, white, and yellow, each varying slightly in width.
- *Bore*: D. 0.3 cm.; glistening at the ends.
- *Technique*: a *marudama*, reheated for insertion of the preformed stripes.
- *Condition*: Excellent.
References:
1. *Inaba, *Sōken Kishō*, VII, p. 24.
2. *Bowes, *Notes on Shippō*, p. 69.

163 (upper center). LARGE *GANGIDAMA*
In foreign style.
- *Collection*: The Corning Museum of Glass (No. 63.6.74).
- *Date*: Edo period.
- *Size*: H. 1.5 cm.; D. 1.75 cm.
- *Colors*: Body, dull terracotta red; opaque, IH. D.Refl.: Ch 3, 2-6-13. Bore ends, black; opaque. Encircling band, pale green with wavy white edges and central red line opaque and dull. Green, IH.D.Refl.: Ch 11, 10-2-19.
- *Bore*: D. 0.4 cm.; bore ends flat.
- *Technique*: Coiled, very skillfully done; reheated for decorating.
- *Condition*: Excellent.

163 (upper right). *GANGIDAMA*
In foreign style.
- *Collection*: The Corning Museum of Glass (No. 63.6.83).
- *Date*: Edo period.
- *Size*: H. 1.1 cm.; D. 1.15 cm.
- *Colors*: Black ground, white at the bore ends, and two zigzags of combined terracotta red and white; all opaque.
- *Bore*: D. 0.15 cm.
- *Technique*: Coiled, but not a spherical bead;

reheated for decorating. The surface is smooth but not glossy.
• *Condition*: Excellent.

163 (second row, left). CYLINDRICAL *TOMBODAMA* WITH FLORAL MOTIFS
In foreign style.
• *Collection*: The Corning Museum of Glass (No. 63.6.80).
• *Date*: Edo period.
• *Size*: H. 2.3 cm.; D. 1.1 cm.
• *Colors*: Dull gray green ground; IH.D.Refl.: Ch 11, 10-2-17; with conventionalized leaf motifs in blue, green, red, purplish brown, and white; all opaque.
•*Bore*: D. 0.45 cm.
• *Technique*: Apparently a *marudama* manipulated to produce a cylindrical form, which was then reheated to receive the inserts; or possibly first cut from a tube, reheated, and decorated.
• *Condition*: Good.

163 (second row, left center). SQUAT CYLINDRICAL *TOMBODAMA* WITH RUNNING LEAF DESIGN
Design in foreign style.
• *Collection*: The Corning Museum of Glass (No. 63.6.77).
• *Date*: Edo period.
• *Size*: H. 1.35 cm.; D. 1.3 cm.
• *Colors*: Dull ground, half black and half dark turquoise blue; opaque. IH.D.Refl.: nearest Ch 4, 15-5-17. Inserts red, dark purplish blue, yellow, green, and white; all opaque.
• *Bore*: D. 0.3 cm.; flat bore ends.
• *Technique*: Coiled, with inserts added.
• *Condition*: Good.

163 (second row, right). SEVEN-LOBED *TOMBODAMA* WITH HORIZONTAL STRIPE
• *Collection*: The Corning Museum of Glass (No. 63.6.79).
• *Date*: Edo period.
• *Size*: H. 1.3 cm.; D. 1.5 cm.
• *Colors*: Body, glossy black with a single white stripe edged on one side with narrow red and on the other with narrow green; all opaque.

• *Bore*: D. 0.4 cm.; ends seem to have been cut flat and reheated.
• *Technique*: Coiled, as a smooth-surfaced *marudama* with a stripe; later lobed by pressure, perhaps in a pincer mold.
• *Condition*: Excellent.

163 (center). LARGE NINE-LOBED *TOMBODAMA* WITH INSERTS
• *Collection*: The Corning Museum of Glass (No. 63.6.70).
• *Date*: Edo period.
• *Size*: H. 1.75 cm.; D. 2.1 cm.
• *Colors*; Black body; opaque and very glossy.
• *Bore*: D. 0.5 cm.
• *Composition*: Considering the heaviness, it must be of lead glass.
• *Technique*: A *marudama* with four added strips of copper, one of them folded over in a V shape. Lobes formed by pressure from some heated implement, perhaps a small pincer mold.
• *Condition*: Excellent.

163 (center right). *TOMBODAMA* SUGGESTING MILLEFIORI TECHNIQUE
• *Collection*: The Corning Museum of Glass (No. 63.6.75).
• *Date*: Edo period.
• *Size*: H. 1.5 cm.; D. 1.65 cm.
• *Colors*: Black with a conglomerate collection of small colored inserts packed close together and including dark blue, light blue, yellow, green, brown, white; all opaque. Glossy surface.
• *Bore*: D. 0.3 cm.
• *Technique*: Coiled (?). The colored bits must have been pressed into the glass body by rolling the bead over a group of the small fragments on some flat surface.
• *Condition*: Slight chipping, but otherwise good.

163 (fourth row, left). *SARASADAMA* WITH BROWN GROUND
• *Collection*: The Corning Museum of Glass (No. 63.6.82).
• *Date*: Edo period.
• *Size*: H. 1.35 cm.; D. 1.4 cm.
• *Colors*: Brown ground, with thin spiraling darker lines not obvious at a casual glance; IH.

D.Refl.: near Ch 5, 4-5-13; opaque. Bore ends inset with pale yellow, not matched on the color chart; opaque. Inserts, same yellow in the petals, with dot of green in the center; opaque.
- *Bore*: D. 0.15 cm.
- *Technique*: A coiled *marudama*, with yellow coil added at the bore ends and floral units, cut from tiny canes, inserted in the reheated body of the bead.
- *Condition*: Excellent.

163 (fourth row, left center). *SARASADAMA*
- *Collection*: The Corning Museum of Glass (No. 63.6.72)
- *Date*: Edo period.
- *Size*: H. 1.4 cm.; D. 1.45 cm.
- *Colors*: Body, bright dark blue; opaque. IH.D. Refl.: near Ch 6, 17-5-12. Bore ends pale yellow, not matched on the color chart. Floral inserts, white with red accents.
- *Bore*: D. 0.15 cm.
- *Technique*: A coiled *marudama*, with a yellow coil added at each end and minute floral inserts scattered over the body, perhaps by rolling the still soft bead over a group of tiny cane sections laid out on a flat surface.
- *Condition*: Chipped in a number of places.

163 (fourth row, center right). *SARASADAMA* WITH BAND OF CROSSED THREADS
- *Collection*: The Corning Museum of Glass (No. 63.6.81).
- *Date*: Edo period.
- *Size*: H. 1.4 cm.; D. 1.45 cm.
- *Colors*: Ground, very dark green (IH.D.Refl.: Ch 13, 12-3-12); opaque. Pale yellow at the bore ends; opaque. On each shoulder a stripe of delicate red thread on yellow. A central band has one thread of opaque pale yellow enclosed in two interlaced spiraling threads, one of opaque yellow and one of translucent pale green.
- *Bore*: D. 0.15 cm.
- *Technique*: Coiled; then decorated with two threads and a strip of cane in colors, added by coiling—an intricate and well-handled procedure.

163 (fourth row, right). STRING OF SMALL *SARASADAMA (NANKINDAMA)*
- *Collection*: The Corning Museum of Glass (No. 63.6.88).
- *Date*: Edo period.
- *Remarks*: As these are in general of the type described above, although in miniature, no data is given here. The smallest is 0.6 cm. in diameter.

163 (lower left). AVENTURINE GLASS BEAD
- *Collection*: The Corning Museum of Glass (No. 63.6.78).
- *Date*: Edo period.
- *Size*: H. 0.93 cm.; D. 1.26 cm.
- *Color*: Brown, gilt spangled.
- *Bore*: D. 0.2 cm.
- *Technique*: Perhaps ground from a chunk of aventurine glass and the bore drilled; or possibly formed from molten aventurine glass.
- *Condition*: Excellent.
- *Remarks*: See Plate 163, bottom center, for a block of aventurine glass used as the head of a hair ornament. Dr. Masao Mine advised that Dr. Kenji Nakanishi of Nihon Daigaku (Japan University) of Osaka once told him that aventurine glass was made in the Edo period but that the technique was later lost because a chemically pure iron sulphide, known in earlier times, was no longer found in Japan. On the other hand, Mr. Kikujirō Ōno of Osaka spoke of seeing this glass being manufactured in a factory in present Fukushima Prefecture in 1894 or 1895.

163 (bottom right). LARGE BEAD WITH OVERLAID LOOP DESIGN
- *Collection*: The Corning Museum of Glass (No. 63.6.69)
- *Provenance*: Possibly Chinese.
- *Date*: Edo period
- *Size*: Overall H. 1.65 cm.; D. 2.0 cm.
- *Colors*: Body, white; opaque. Overlays, dark purplish blue, turquoise blue, very pale blue, and white; all opaque but very glossy.
- *Bore*: D. 0.7–0.8 cm.

- *Technique*: Coiled, with overlaid coiling of colored glass threads.
- *Condition*: Excellent.

164. DETAIL OF A SCREEN BY YANAGI-SAWA KIEN

Depicting a glass vase with morning glories; part of a pair of screens showing various glass articles: flower vases; lanterns with some glass beads; glass bird-feeders or birdbaths attached to bird perches. All seem types of domestic manufacture.

- *Collection*: Mr. Riichi Yagi, Kyoto.
- *Provenance*: (of the represented glass): Since Kien was a retainer of the Lord of Koriyama, between Nara and Osaka, these representations possibly were based on Osaka products.
- *Date*: First half, 18th century. Kien lived from 1706 to 1758.

KYOTO

165. BEAD-DECORATED IMPERIAL CROWN

Some of the beads, and their calyxes, are mounted directly on the three-lobed padded form, but others are terminals on the brass rods, or pins, which stand upright around the perforated gilt-bronze body of the crown. A small gilded wood legendary animal form, the *kirin* (symbol of protection), is attached at the front. Full catalogue data for this crown cannot be given. The beads are large and well preserved. The crown is slightly less elaborate than a similar one also in the Tokyo National Museum (not reproduced here), which has three, instead of two, upstanding frames.

- *Collection*: Tokyo National Museum.
- *Date*: Edo period.

166. GLASS-DECORATED IMPERIAL CROWN

This crown, similar to Plate 165 but in damaged condition, is particularly interesting for the blown-glass spheres that decorate it. However, the perforated metal portion with the openwork chrysanthemum scrolls is not gilt-bronze but silver (or possibly silver-plated?). All petals in the calyxes are of heavy paper painted with silver, some perfectly plain with no simulated chasing.

- *Collection*: Tokyo National Museum.
- *Provenance*: The entire crown, including the glass, perhaps produced in Kyoto.
- *Date*: Edo period.

GLASS SPHERES AND BEADS:

- *Sizes*: Varying from 1.9 cm. in the single transparent globe at the top to *kodama* at the base of the silver foundation band.
- *Colors*: a. The topmost "flower" is an uncolored sphere of thin glass; transparent.
  b. The lighter colored spheres on the row of taller rods, and some attached to the padded form, are also uncolored transparent glass, but their interior walls are coated with opaque vermilion pigment, evidently to imitate coral. Strange curving lines, which at first glance seemed intentional, are simply cracks in the dried pigment.
  c. The darker spheres on the lower range of rods are also of uncolored glass, but their interiors are coated with a dull, dark olive green pigment, now in similar cracked condition.
  d. Small beads (*kodama*) on the silver band at the base of the crown are red.
- *Technique*: The globes are of thin blown glass. Except for the topmost, the interiors are coated with opaque pigments. Each globe has an uncoated tubelike transparent collar (seen at upper right and left in Pl. 166), which is evidence of their having been blown with a tiny glass blowpipe. The *tomosao* and the little globe would have been completely fused together, and instead of breaking the tube off at the juncture point, the artisan separated it at some little distance from the globe, leaving a neck or collar, which could be thrust through the center of a calyx. This procedure seems likely evidence of local manufacture, the *biidoro* craftsman and the crown maker working in collaboration.
- *Condition*: Though the crown is badly damaged, the glass balls, thin as they are, remain in good condition.

167. LACQUER WRITING BOX
A compartmented writing box containing ink-stone, ink, water pot, and brushes. The landscape design of the lid's exterior shows, in the stream, the reflection of the moon, represented by an inlaid disk that seems to be of glass. In the original, the reflection is more convincing than in the illustration. The box is by a lacquer craftsman of the Kōami school of Kyoto, thought to be Ozaki Ryōsei (died 1662).
- *Collection*: Museum of Fine Arts, Boston (No. 11.10163).
- *Date*: Edo period, perhaps 17th century.
GLASS INLAY:
- *Size*: D. 2.9 cm.

SUKAGAWA, ŌSHŪ

169. TALL, DARK BLUE SAKÉ BOTTLE
A saké bottle of the conventional type but exceptionally tall. The bottom has a wide but shallow concavity, and the interior "kick" is correspondingly low. The slightly flaring rim is very irregular.
- *Collection*: The Toledo Museum of Art (No. 55.63).
- *Provenance*: The place of manufacture seems likely to have been Sukagawa.
- *Date*: Edo period, 19th century.
- *Size*: H. 25.0 cm.; D. at base, 7.12 cm.
- *Color*: Dark purplish blue; transparent. IH.D. Refl.: Ch 7, 18-4-11; IH.D.Trans.: Ch 7, 18-5-13.
- *Bubbles*: Scattered, chiefly elongated vertically; spiraling striations.
- *Technique*: Free blown.
- *Condition*: Excellent.

170. DARK BLUE WASTE POT
It is problematical if this piece was a container for waste water or was used in rinsing saké cups. Since it accompanied the bottle in Plate 169, to which it was said to belong, the latter seems probable. It may also have served as a stand for a cup. The glass is much thicker than that of the bottle. Three motifs were applied in dull gold on the shoulder. The mouth rim is

level and dull gilt. The base is smooth and shallowly concave.
- *Collection*: The Toledo Museum of Art (No. 55.64).
- *Date*: Edo period, 19th century.
- *Size*: H. 4.55 cm.; D. 7.2 cm.
- *Color*: Dark blue, only slightly purplish; transparent. IH.D.Trans: Ch 7, 18-6-11.
- *Bubbles*: Numerous, circular.
- *Technique*: Free blown.
- *Condition*: Excellent.

SENDAI

172. *KŌGAI*
This accompanied the license of Shōkichi (Pl. 171) and is therefore considered to be his work. Near the head a small floral or fruit ornament, in the round, was applied, consisting of a globule with a coil around it and a small leaf attached.
- *Collection*: The Toledo Museum of Art (Apparatus, 1956); Gift of Mr. Sōshichirō Mōri, Ishinomaki, Miyagi Prefecture.
- *Date*: Second quarter, 19th century.
- *Size*: L. 16.0 cm.; W. 0.5 cm.; T. 0.3 cm.
- *Color*: Body, honey color; transparent. IH impossible to match. Flower (?), same as body. Leaf, greenish blue, opaque: IH.D.Refl.: Ch 4, 15-3-18.
- *Bubbles*: None.
- *Technique*: Lampwork.
- *Condition*: Excellent.

173. *KANZASHI*
All have ear-spoon heads and beveled edges on the bars, but the ornamental elements differ.
- *Collection*: The Toledo Museum of Art (Apparatus, 1956); Gift of Mr. Saburō Kuki, Tokyo.
- *Date*: 19th century.
- *Sizes*: L. 18.3–18.6 cm.; W. 0.95–1.4 cm.; T. 0.4–0.6 cm.
- *Colors*: Light to dark honey color; transparent.
- *Bubbles*: Longitudinal air spaces drawn out the length of the bars.
- *Technique*: Bars drawn; heads and ornaments molded.

- *Condition*: Excellent.
- *Remarks*: Included in May, 1949, in an exhibition, "The Cultural History of Tōhoku," at Mitsukoshi Department Store, Nihonbashi, Tokyo.

174. DECORATED *KANZASHI*
Decorated with application of thin gilt and silver in a floral design.
- *Collection*: The Corning Museum of Glass (No. 61.6.13 a-b); gift of Miss Grace Miriam Kinner.
- *Provenance*: In delicacy and refinement, these are in sharp contrast to the usual heavy "Sendai *kanzashi*" and perhaps belonged in the family of the daimyo or some high official in the fief, in which case it might be questioned whether they were necessarily made in Sendai, for they might have been brought from Edo.
- *Date*: From the character of the decoration, they seem to date from the end of the Edo period, or even from the early Meiji era.
- *Size*: L. 16.5 cm. and 15.8 cm.; both, W. 0.6 cm.; T. 0.3 cm.
- *Color*: Stems, deep purple glass, appearing black; semiopaque. Ends, light honey color; transparent.
- *Technique*: Stems, drawn; ends, molded. Thin gold and silver applied, probably with lacquer.
- *Condition*: Excellent.

Edo

184. HAIR ORNAMENT FRAGMENTS
From the tomb of the young wife of the twelfth Tokugawa shogun, Ieyoshi, among the group of Tokugawa mausolea in Shiba, Tokyo, which were much damaged during World War II. The ornament must have been exquisite, but has suffered from breakage and moisture; some of the coiled tubes that form the rings are remarkably slim and fragile. It is thought that pendants made up of these units were suspended at each temple, from a projecting bar.
- *Date*: Mid 19th century.
- *Size*: Leaf forms (at right center in the illustration): L. 2.2 cm.; W. 1.2 cm.; T. 0.15 cm. Ridged on the upper surface; plain beneath.

The petal forms are similar, but smaller, and rounded on the upper face. Larger rings, D. 1.1 cm.; the smaller ones, 0.8 cm. Diameters of the tubing forming the glass rings, 0.05–0.1 cm.
- *Color*: Colorless; transparent.
- *Technique*: Lampwork.
- *Condition*: Aside from breakage, the glass is in good condition. Cinnabar from the burial adheres.

185. GOURD-SHAPED *NETSUKE*
- *Collection*: The Corning Museum of Glass (No. 61.6.9)
- *Provenance*: The glass quality is reminiscent of Nagasaki *biidoro*, but the *netsuke* may well be a product of Edo. It was purchased in Tokyo.
- *Date*: Edo period.
- *Size*: L. 5.1 cm.
- *Color*: Dark blue; transparent. IH.D.Refl and Trans.: Ch 7, 18-3-11.
- *Technique*: Free blown, with metal mount added at the mouth.
- *Condition*: Excellent.

186. CEREMONIAL TEABOWL
A thin and delicately flared bowl of a form used especially in the summertime for ceremonial whipped tea. The thirty-five twisted flutings are rounded, inside and out. The glass is slightly iridescent.
- *Collection*: The Corning Museum of Glass (No. 58.6.2).
- *Date*: Assigned by the dealer as Edo work of the Tempō era (1830–43).
- *Size*: H. 4.9 cm.; H. of base, *ca.* 0.3 cm.; D. at rim, 13.7 cm.
- *Color*: Pale greenish yellow; transparent. IH. difficult to match.
- *Bubbles*: Minute, circular, mostly in the foot-rim; oval in the spiraled grooves; one, near the rim, vertically elongated. A number of small stones.
- *Composition*: Lead glass (ultraviolet fluorescence).
- *Technique*: Mold blown; very thin rim edge; shallow, rounded foot-rim.
- *Condition*: Several nicks in the rim.

187. SMALL COVERED DISH IN IRISH STYLE

The pattern is of interlocking quatrefoils and lozenges; the cutting is somewhat rounded except for the finial on the cover, which is angular and sharp. Upon closer inspection, the pattern proves to be not entirely symmetrical and the cover does not fit perfectly, having a slight overhang on one side. There is a six-pointed star motif on the bottom and also in the center of the cover.

- *Collection*: The Toledo Museum of Art (No. 55.69); gift of Mr. Fumio Asakura, Tokyo.
- *Provenance*: Traditionally considered an Edo product, with which the author concurs.
- *Date*: Edo period.
- *Size*: H. overall 10.7 cm.; L. at base, 7.1 cm.; W. at base, 6.15 cm.; T. 0.3 cm.
- *Color*: Colorless; transparent.
- *Bubbles*: Mostly circular; some impurities, including a large one in the cover.
- *Technique*: Mold blown and cut.
- *Condition*: Excellent.
- *Remarks*: Irish glass of this type, but not identical, was known in Japan, since it was illustrated, as an importation, on the title page of *Nagasaki Kokin Shuran Meisho Zue* (Pl. 149). Such joined motifs became popular in Japan.

188. SAKÉ CUP

Japanese cup for saké, known as a *choko*.
- *Collection*: The Corning Museum of Glass (No. 61.6.32).
- *Date*: Edo period.
- *Size*: H. 3.2 cm.; D. at rim, 6.1 cm.
- *Color*: Green; transparent and slightly iridescent. IH.D.Refl.: Ch 13, 12-5-15.
- *Bubbles*: Several, circular; also one stone.
- *Technique*: Mold blown; the rim is rough and rather sharp.
- *Condition*: Excellent.

189. MINIATURE WINE SET FOR THE DOLL FESTIVAL

Two miniature decanters and four miniature stemmed wine glasses, mounted in a gold-decorated black lacquer stand. They are unusually small miniatures but skillfully cut, their fine quality suggesting use in a wealthy and refined home. Such miniatures formed part of the annual Hina Matsuri (Doll Festival) display of small images of the emperor, the empress, attendants, musicians and sundry items of furniture and implements as used in the palace. They are installed on stepped shelves covered with red felt, and in front of this display the young daughters of the house, on the festival day, practice the courtesies of hospitality as they serve a special sweet wine and confections to friends.

- *Collection*: The Corning Museum of Glass (No. 61.6.11).
- *Provenance*: The design is typical Edo work.
- *Date*: Edo period.
- *Size*: Decanters: H. overall 5.5 cm.; D. at base, 1.4 cm. Wine glasses: H. 2.6 cm.; D. at rim, 1.0 cm.
- *Color*: Colorless; transparent.
- *Bubbles*: Very few and minute.
- *Technique*: Free blown and skillfully cut.
- *Condition*: Excellent.
- *Remarks*: It may be noticed that a set of this general type, but less refined, appears in the Kagaya advertisement of Plate 183. In fact, the author has seen other examples of this type, but none so small or so delicate as this one in Corning.

   Also in The Corning Museum of Glass there are other, larger miniature bottles and dishes relating to the Doll Festival.

FEUDAL SPONSORSHIP

SATSUMA

192. ONE OF SEVERAL PLATE GLASS SLABS

- *Collection*: Shūseikan, Iso-kōen, Kagoshima city (No. 650/2).
- *Date*: Perhaps *ca.* 1853.
- *Size*: 29.4 × 32.0 × 2.4 cm.
- *Color*: Colorless but with faint greenish tone; transparent.
- *Bubbles*: Scattered small circular bubbles.
- *Technique*: The rounded corners suggest casting in a mold. Bevels that are rough and frosted occur on both upper and lower edges.

- *Condition*: Excellent.
- *Remarks*: It is thought that such thick, heavy glass must have been used as skylights or windows on the new Western style steamships that were being built in the Satsuma fief. No other extant Satsuma plate glass is as yet identified.

193. SOLID MOUND-SHAPED GLASS
Could this have been the cover for a ship's signal light? The mounded section is highly polished. The basal disc is rough and frosted, with a beveled edge on the upper rim. The whole is extremely heavy.
- *Collection*: Shūseikan, Iso-kōen, Kagoshima city (No. 873/8).
- *Date*: Perhaps *ca.* 1853.
- *Size*: Circular base H. 2.8 cm.; D. 21.1 cm.
- *Color*: Pale green; transparent.
- *Bubbles*: Circular; with one area of elongated opaque bubblelike particles.
- *Technique*: Molded.
- *Condition*: Good.

194. CUT GLASS BOWL
A typical example of "Satsuma *kiriko*."
- *Collection*: Shūseikan, Iso-kōen, Kagoshima city (No. 1534/57).
- *Date*: Ca. 1856.
- *Size*: H. 9.7 cm.; D. at lip, 22.2 cm.; at base, 14.0 cm.; T. at lip 0.6 cm.
- *Color*: Colorless, but with grayish tone; transparent.
- *Bubbles*: Scattered; circular and oval. Near the base some larger ones, horizontally elongated; a few others, nearer the rim, obliquely slanted. A few minute opaque white stones.
- *Technique*: Free blown and cut. Includes deep angular cutting, deep half-moon-shaped cutting and areas of fine, regular and smooth-feeling cross-hatching, as well as a number of rather deep oval hollows. The cutting planes are all broad, and there is none of the later ultrasharp cutting. The exterior bottom is cut with an allover basket-weave design.
- *Condition*: Excellent.

195. SMALL STEMMED WINE GLASS
- *Collection*: The Corning Museum of Glass (No. 61.6.14); gift of Mr. Tadashige Shimazu, Tokyo.
- *Provenance*: Coming from the household of the former head of the main house of Shimazu, grandson of Shimazu Nariakira, the provenance of this glass cannot be questioned.
- *Date*: 1856–58.
- *Size*: H. 8.5 cm.; D. at rim, 4.6 cm.; T. at rim, 0.3 cm.
- *Color*: Colorless; transparent.
- *Bubbles*: Some, minute.
- *Composition*: Lead glass (ultraviolet fluorescence).
- *Technique*: Blown, with square, molded base.
- *Condition*: Excellent.

196. CUT GLASS COVERED JAR WITH DARK BLUE OVERLAY
The dark blue wares of Satsuma *kiriko* seem to have been as characteristic of the Shūseikan products as were the red, although far less famous, since far less difficult to achieve and more common. The color is usually a deep blue with a slightly purplish tone.
- *Collection*: Shūseikan, Iso-kōen, Kagoshima city.
- *Date*: Late Edo period, probably *ca.* 1856.
- *Size*: H. overall *ca.* 7.15 cm.; D. of lid, 10.8 cm.; T. at lip, 0.35–0.7, according to the cutting.
- *Color*: The overlay very dark blue, scarcely even translucent; the ground, where revealed by cutting, is transparent.
- *Bubbles*: Large ones, vertically elongated near the interior bottom of the colored portion.
- *Composition*: Because very heavy, the glass is presumed to contain lead.
- *Technique*: Body, free blown, cased, and then groove-cut and cross-hatched; the lid, molded, cased, and similarly cut; the base, molded and cut. Although deep, the cutting is not sharp, and since there is also no high polish, the effect is rather soft, seemingly characteristic of the early examples.
- *Condition*: Excellent.

197. TALL CUT GLASS WINE GLASS WITH DARK BLUE OVERLAY

- *Collection*: Shūseikan, Iso-kōen, Kagoshima city (No. 814).
- *Date*: Probably *ca.* 1856. The "soft" cutting and the yellowish base suggest an early date.
- *Size*: H. overall 15.85 cm.
- *Color*: Overlay, dark blue; translucent. IH.D. Refl.: approximately Ch 6, 17-5-11 but in effect seems slightly grayed blue. Mouth rim and stemmed foot, uncolored and transparent; the foot is yellowish.
- *Bubbles*: Some, vertically oval, clearly seen. Also some small stones. At the juncture of bowl and foot, numerous bubbles, elongated spirally.
- *Technique*: Free blown, partially cased and cut with diagonal lines, the resulting lozenges being cross-hatched. The cutting is not sharp, nor the relief high.
- *Condition*: Excellent

198. COVERED DISH WITH MOLDED DESIGN

A handsome specimen in thin glass. The traditional attribution to the Shūseikan is strengthened by the fact that the only other known example from this mold is owned by the Kagoshima Municipal Art Museum and is likewise attributed to the Shūseikan. The only discrepancy between the two is the very slightest difference in detail in the gold mounts beneath the lobed knobs of colorless glass. The design on the lids differs slightly from that on the bodies, but both include four floral sprays interspersed with vertical rows of graduated dots in relief.

- *Collection*: The Toledo Museum of Art (No. 55.29).
- *Date*: 1857–58.
- *Size*: H. overall 11.4 cm.; D. 13.35 cm.; T. of body wall, 0.15 cm.
- *Color*: Amethyst; transparent. IH.D.Refl.: Ch 9, 20-2-14.
- *Bubbles*: A few minute ones.
- *Technique*: Mold blown; polished rim on both dish and cover, with minute bevels at outer edges.
- *Condition*: Excellent.

199. FLUTED CUT GLASS BOWL

One of three bowls in graduated sizes, cut with fifteen, eighteen, and nineteen flutes respectively. These flutes are slightly irregular. It is interesting that Mr. Masanori Kawagoe of Kagoshima owns a single bowl of blue glass that is cut similarly, with the same irregularities.

- *Collection*: The Corning Museum of Glass (Nos. 58.6.7 A-C).
- *Date*: Probably 1857 or 1858.
- *Sizes*: 11.7–14.0 cm.; D. at lip, 17.5–22.2 cm.
- *Color*: Colorless; transparent.
- *Bubbles*: A few bubbles and a considerable number of stones.
- *Composition*: Lead glass (ultraviolet fluorescence).
- *Technique*: Free blown and cut. The rims are ground; the bases are solid discs.
- *Condition*: Nicked in several places.

200. LARGE COVERED BOWLS WITH CHRYSANTHEMUM DESIGN

A set of five, decorated in shallow, rounded relief with a running pattern of flowering twelve-petaled chrysanthemums. The glass is thin and resonant.

- *Collection*: The Corning Museum of Glass (No. 58.6.6).
- *Provenance*: Probably Satsuma ware.[1]
- *Date*: Late Edo period.
- *Size*: H. 9.2 cm.; D. at rim, 12.5 cm.; T. of the glass, 0.2 cm.
- *Color*: Colorless with greenish tinge; transparent and slightly iridescent.
- *Bubbles*: Some, very small and circular.
- *Composition*: Lead glass (ultraviolet fluorescence).
- *Technique*: Mold blown; a tiny indented dot (mold mark) on the bottom.
- *Condition*: Excellent.
- *Remarks*: Similar bowls seen in Japan have been called Satsuma ware. Could these be of a post-1858 date, like the "sets of bowls with lids" ordered by the Imperial Household in 1872? Or even of 1857–58 as some of the "ordinary" ware for everyday use mentioned by Dr. Pompé when he visited the Shūseikan?

Reference:
1. A similar bowl, apparently from the same mold, is illustrated in *Okada, Garasu, Pl. 83, as of Edo provenance.

201. TALL RED TUMBLER WITH CUT DESIGN

- Collection: The Toledo Museum of Art (No. 55.75); gift of the late Mr. Kinsuke Edamoto, Shigetomi, Kagoshima Prefecture.
- Provenance: Both the glass metal and the cutting of such tumblers is so far inferior to the usual Shūseikan glass that it seems they must either be the "coarse" ware or the "practical, durable ones necessary for daily use," of which Dr. Pompé wrote. They might also have been produced after Nariakira's death, in the days of glassmaking decline. On the other hand, they may even have come from one of the factories established in Kagoshima in the Meiji era. A considerable number are known, varying in both size and color.
- Date: Post-1859?
- Size: H. 15.1 cm.; D. at rim, 8.5 cm.
- Color: Orange red; transparent. IH.D.Refl.: Ch 3, 2-8-15.
- Bubbles: In the bottom several circular ones; in the wall they are elongated vertically.
- Composition: Not analyzed; the coloring agent is copper.
- Technique: Molded and cut; the rim was fire polished.
- Condition: Good.

202. ROUND FAN OF ENGRAVED GLASS

Perhaps this is the type called "circular plate glass" noted in the document quoted on page 188. It is bound in a brass frame and mounted in a handle of red sandalwood decorated with a bamboo motif in gold lacquer. The engraved design is of bamboo in moonlight.

- Collection: Itsuō Bijutsukan, Ikeda city, Osaka Prefecture; former owners: the Konoe family; the Fukuda family of Kyoto; Mr. Kinsen Kumekawa.
- Date: An accompanying document of the Meiji or Taishō eras state that this is Satsuma work just prior to the Meiji era.

- Size: D. ca. 26.0 cm.; T. esitmated as 0.2 cm.
- Color: Colorless; transparent.
- Technique: Plate glass with engraving and etching on the back side. The moon was hollow ground and highly polished; the cloud, acid etched; the bamboo, engraved and very slightly hollowed.
- Condition: Excellent.
- Remarks: In the catalogue of the museum's exhibition in 1958, it is stated that these decorating techniques were learned from a British person working in Satsuma fief. (At the close of the Edo period, when amicable relations had been restored between England and Satsuma [after the war in which the Shūseikan had been bombarded], British engineers supervised the spinning mills in which British looms had been installed by Shimazu Hisamitsu. Perhaps one of these engineers understood glass.)

SAGA

203. LARGE GOLDFISH BOWL

A plain vessel with wide-flanged mouth and three applied feet. In the center of the bottom a curious circular glass about 13.5 cm. in diameter is inset, which resembles a lens, slightly convex on both upper and lower surfaces; on its exterior face there is a rough groove, as though this area had been cut or broken from some other object.

- Collection: Mr. Naotsugu Nabeshima (great-grandson of Nabeshima Kansō), Saga city.
- Date: Late Edo period; the owner's attribution, 1848.
- Size: H. 30.4 cm.; greatest D. 34.0 cm.
- Color: Colorless; transparent.
- Bubbles: A number, in both bottom and wall; all are oval, except where elongated on the spiral and one or two that are large ovals with whitish streaks. Near the top, one conspicuous amber-colored spiral streak spins out into attenuated ends.
- Technique: Body, free blown; feet, by lampwork, each a little different.
- Condition: Excellent.
- Remarks: In the Shūseikan in Kagoshima there is one glass vessel with feet suggesting these,

and *Okada, *Garasu*, black and white Plate
35 illustrates a shallow Saga bowl with similar feet.

Fukuoka

204. PAPERWEIGHT
A paperweight in graduated rod shape. A
flattened area at the back permits it to lie flat.
Three parallel whitish lines spiral through the
interior, end to end. The ends are cut level and
polished.
- *Collection*: The Toledo Museum of Art (No.
56.43; gift of Mrs. Mitsuyo Mizuno, Fukuoka
city.
- *Date*: Late Edo period. Attributed to Mizuno
Chōbei of the Kuroda fief (died 1869).
- *Size*: L. 14.3 cm.; D. 1.4 cm. and 1.7 cm.
- *Color*: Colorless, but with slightly gray tone;
transparent.
- *Technique*: Twist-drawn from a lump of glass
metal with three applied spots of white glass.
- *Condition*: Excellent; near the wider end of the
weight, what appears to be an internal crack
follows the lines for a short distance.
- *Remarks*: Mr. Yoshio Arakawa of Kyoto, grandson of Tsukumo Mizuno, who has been interested in the history of the Mizuno family, said
without hesitation when shown this paperweight that it was certainly the work of Mizuno
Chōbei, rather than of the father, Hambei,
or the son, Tsukumo. It is not considered as
work done for Lord Kuroda, but something the
Mizuno craftsman may have made and brought
home for family use.

205. VIOLET SAKÉ CUP
- *Collection*: The Toledo Museum of Art (No.
56.42); gift of Mrs. Tomeno Kōto, Onoda
city, Yamaguchi Prefecture.
- *Provenance*: Uncertain. In the family of the
donor it was traditionally known as a work
from the Fukuoka fief. Mrs. Kōto received it
from her mother, who was the daughter of the
karō, or chief retainer, of the lord of Hamada
fief in Inami Province (Shimane Prefecture).
His name was Morie. Whether the cup was
brought by the Morie daughter when she mar-

ried into the Kōto family (in which case it
might well have been a gift from some samurai
of the Kuroda clan to the *karō* while in Edo for
the *sankin-kōtai*), or whether it had come down
in the Kōto family, is not known.
- *Date*: Edo period; probably mid 19th century.
- *Size*: H. 4.1 cm.; D. at lip, 6.1 cm.; T. at lip,
0.05 cm.
- *Color*: Bluish purple; transparent.
- *Bubbles*: Several pits on the outer surface. Very
slight spiral striations or ripples.
- *Technique*: Mold cast.
- *Condition*: Excellent.

Hagi

208. CUT GLASS COVERED BOX
An extremely handsome and brilliant example,
but undocumented. Unfortunately measure-
ments cannot be given.
- *Collection*: Kikuya family, Hagi city.
- *Provenance*: European, Satsuma, or Hagi, but
since Nishinomiya Tomejirō had been brought
to Hagi from Satsuma, the box may well be a
Hagi product.
- *Date*: Ca. 1860.
- *Technique*: Molded and cut; the cutting is fairly
deep.
- *Condition*: Excellent.

209. STEMMED WINE GLASS WITH SQUARE FOOT
The bowl is cut in an allover pattern; the
pedestal foot is plain, with a square base.
- *Collection*: Mr. Ashiyoshi Kumaya (Kumagai),
Hagi city.
- *Date*: Late Edo period; perhaps 1862.
- *Size*: H. 10.5 cm.; D. inside lip, 6.5 cm.; T. at
lip, 0.2 cm.
- *Color*: Grayish, especially in the foot; trans-
parent.
- *Technique*: Bowl free blown and cut, with base
molded and attached.
- *Condition*: Good.

210. STEMMED WINE GLASS
- *Collection*: Mr. Takejirō Tanabe, Hagi city;

formerly the property of Mr. Ishimitsu, Hagi city.
- *Date*: 1861 or 1862.
- *Size*: H. 10.9 cm.; D. at rim, 6.5 cm.; base 5.3 cm. square.
- *Color*: Colorless and clear; transparent.
- *Bubbles*: A few tiny ones, but only in the base.
- *Technique*: Bowl free blown and cut; stem, cut; base attached. The cutting, which encircles the body, forms oblique, leaflike unpolished grooves. The double foot is unusual and perhaps unique. The cup and its foot were mounted on a flat piece of glass, which was then cut off square so closely that the cutting penetrated the circular foot at four points. In the reproduction of Nakashima Jihei's notebook shown in Plate 207, the resemblance between the small sketch at the extreme upper left margin and this wine glass will be noticed, both having the same curious base.
- *Condition*: Good.

Meiji Period

211. HOLLOW FISH FORM
Probably a flower container to be hung on a wall, suspended by a cord attached around the neck; such a use is known in more recent times.
- *Collection*: Mr. Sekio Iwanaga, Nagasaki.
- *Date*: The date is uncertain. Mr. Tetsuya Etchū, of the Art and Science Division of the Nagasaki Municipal Museum, attributes it to about 1877.
- *Size*: L. overall 26.0 cm.
- *Color*: Violet body; transparent. Fins uncolored; transparent.
- *Bubbles*: Elongated lengthwise in the body; numerous in the uncolored portions, some very elongated.
- *Technique*: Blown body; lampwork additions. The curious hybrid form suggests a whimsy by some artisan, who joined parts of two bottles as the body and completed the suggested fish image by tooling and applying discs for eyes.
- *Condition*: Excellent. The mouth rim is rough, as though broken away from a blow pipe.
- *Remarks*: Mr. Iwanaga also owns similar fish

forms in transparent colorless glass and transparent brown glass. The Nagasaki Municipal Museum has two very short and stubby examples of uncolored glass. Some extant examples of this type, however, seem to be of blue glass, perhaps made elsewhere.

213. STEMMED WINE GLASS
- *Collection*: The Toledo Museum of Art (No. 55.66); gift of the late Mr. Kinosuke Edamoto, Shigetomi city, Kagoshima Prefecture.
- *Date*: Probably Meiji era. Professor Motoyoshi Higaki of Kyushu University, a student of Satsuma glass, feels that this may be a Meiji product; however, he has seen only a photograph.
- *Size*: H. 12.7 cm.; D. 5.5 cm., T. at lip, 0.2 cm.
- *Color*: Bowl, yellow green; transparent. IH.D. Refl.: nearest Ch 11, 10-5-18. Stemmed foot, colorless; transparent.
- *Bubbles*: In the bowl, some round, some elongated vertically; more in the foot.
- *Technique*: Free blown and cut, with attached foot. On the upper face of the base is a lightly incised crest of Satsuma fief.

214. STEMMED WINE GLASS
- *Collection*: The Toledo Museum of Art (No. 55.68); Gift of the late Mr. Kinosuke Edamoto, Shigetomi city, Kagoshima Prefecture.
- *Date*: Probably Meiji era.
- *Size*: H. 10.9 cm.; D. 5.4 cm.; T. at lip, 0.275 cm.
- *Color*: Bowl, "raspberry red;" transparent. IH.D.Refl.; Ch 13,24-8-15. Stemmed foot, colorless; transparent.
- *Bubbles*: Some small, horizontal and spiraling.
- *Composition*: Gold was an ingredient of the glass batch.
- *Technique*: Bowl, free blown; attached foot, cut; slight pontil mark smoothed. On the upper face of the base is a lightly incised Satsuma fief crest.
- *Condition*: Excellent.

215. ENGRAVED COVERED BOWL
In spite of the elementary decoration, there is

a crispness of contour not seen in earlier pieces; especially conspicuous in the foot-rims on bowl and cover.

- *Collection*: The Toledo Museum of Art (No. 54.67).
- *Date*: Meiji era.
- *Size*: H. 5.6 cm.; D. at rim, 10.3 cm.
- *Color*: Colorless; transparent.
- *Bubbles*: A few, minute; within the foot-rim, large spiraling bubbles.
- *Composition*: Soda-lime glass. Sp. Grav.: 2.4905; Refr. Ind.: 1.518. For complete analysis, see Appendix, Table XIII.
- *Technique*: Blown, with foot-rim hollowed by cutting.
- *Condition*: Excellent.

218. BRUSH HOLDERS WITH SPIRAL DECORATION

- *Collection*: Tokyo National Museum.
- *Date*: Early Meiji era.
- *Size*: H. 15.0 cm. and 16.5 cm.
- *Color*: Colorless and transparent, with spirals in indigo, light red, and milk white.
- *Technique*: Blown. Experimental introduction of spirals in color.
- *Condition*: Excellent.
- *Remarks*: Given Meritorious Awards in the "Second National Exposition for the Encouragement of Industry" in Meiji 4 (1871),[1] apparently on the ground that this technique had never before been attempted in Japan. However, see Plate 204.

Reference:

1. See *Okada, *Garsu*, p. 91, quoting from the catalogue.

220, 221. BEADS WITH CROSS MOTIF IN RELIEF

Both are probably products of the Yoneda Wakamatsu Shōten in Shinoda-mura, Osaka Prefecture; the beads of Plate 221 are those exported to India in recent years by this company. However, the single bead of Plate 220, although also lightweight, has a noticeably more substantial wall, and the color is an integral part of the bead, whereas the others are

gilt. It is also better made, the cross standing up in high relief, more carefully and sharply shaped than the beads of Plate 221, whose cross is shallow and less distinct in contour. The single bead is certainly considerably earlier than the string of beads.

- *Collection*: The Corning Museum of Glass (Nos. 63.6.66 and 67).

Pl. 220. *Single bead*.
- *Date*: Probably 20th century (?).
- *Size*: H. overall 1.2 cm.; greatest W. 0.8 cm.
- *Color*: The "gold" color (coppery in appearance) emanates from within the bead.
- *Technique*: Blown in a group mold and separated by cutting; the cut edges were not polished.
- *Condition*: Good.

Pl. 221. *String of beads*.
- *Date*: Post-World War II.
- *Size*: L. overall 1.0 cm.; greatest W. 0.7 cm.
- *Color*: Glittering gold color from a very thin film of gilt.
- *Bores*: D. 0.3 cm.
- *Technique*: Blown in a group mold and separated by cutting, with rough edges left unpolished.
- *Condition*: Good, but the beads are very fragile and easily broken.

CONTEMPORARY

222. HOLLOW GLASS PORTRAIT BUST OF TAKIJIRŌ IWAKI

The original model was the work of Yuhei Ogawa; the glass was executed by Sotoichi Koshiba, craftsman of the Iwaki factory.

- *Collection*: The Corning Museum of Glass (No. 61.6.69); gift of the late Mr. Kuronosuke Iwaki, Tokyo.
- *Date*: Inscription on the back at lower left: "Shōwa 10, [1935]. Autumn. The work of Yuhei")
- *Size*: H. 30.5 cm.; W. 22.2 cm.
- *Color*: Slightly tinted.
- *Composition*: Soda-lime glass.
- *Technique*: *Pâte de verre*. Blown in a mold made

of finely powdered refractory brick mixed with plaster.

223. CUT GLASS FOR THE IMPERIAL HOUSEHOLD

Two items from a complete set of many shapes of crystal glass for use at state dinners. Designed by Baccarat of France, but executed in the Iwaki Glass Company, which before World War II produced this ware in quantity.

- *Date*: Before 1941, when production ceased.
- *Color*: Colorless; transparent.
- *Technique*: Blown and cut, with engraved and frosted imperial chrysanthemum crest.
- *Composition*: Lead flint glass.

224. WHISKEY GLASSES

- *Date*: Before 1941, when production ceased.
- *Color*: Colorless; transparent.
- *Composition*: Lead flint glass
- *Technique*: Free blown and cut.

225. VASE BY TŌSHICHI IWATA

- *Collection*: Tokyo University of Fine Arts.
- *Date*: 1937.
- *Size*: H. 29.0 cm.
- *Color*: Black, white, and red; opaque.
- *Composition*: Soda-lima glass, with gold added to the red color.
- *Technique*: Blown glass, colorless and transparent; cased with flecks of opaque white; lower half cased in opaque black. Opaque white and ruby red glasses added, twisted, and trailed with an instrument to form the design, which suggests the ancient Egyptian coiled and hooked designs.

226. VASE BY TŌSHICHI IWATA

- Made by Mr. Iwata for the author as a gift to The Toledo Museum of Art.
- *Collection*: The Toledo Museum of Art (No. 56.54); gift of Mr. Tōshichi Iwata, Tokyo.
- *Date*: February, 1956.
- *Size*: H. 20.6 cm.; D. at rim, 10.5 cm.; T. at rim, 2.2 cm.
- *Color*: Colorless, transparent body with areas flecked with opaque white, and with curving rectangular areas of flecks of gold leaf.

- *Bubbles*: Some, small.
- *Composition*: Lead glass.
- *Technique*: Free blown; probably rolled in controlled areas of bits of opaque white, and flecks of gold leaf; cased in colorless transparent glass.

227. VASE BY HISATOSHI IWATA

- *Date*: 1971.
- *Size*: H. 38.0 cm.; D. 16.0 cm.
- *Color*: Body, translucent speckled white; design, dark blue. Rim, opaque black. Foot, pale blue.
- *Composition*: Soda-lime glass.
- *Technique*: Blown glass.
- *Remarks*: Exhibited in the artist's first one-man show, at Mitsukoshi Department Store, Tokyo, 1971.

228. VASE BY KŌZŌ KAGAMI

Floral Design.

- *Collection*: The Toledo Museum of Art (No. 56.22); gift of the Kagami Crystal Glassworks, Tokyo.
- *Date*: Ca. 1955.
- *Size*: H. 19.4 cm.; D. at rim, 19.2 cm.
- *Color*: Colorless; transparent.
- *Technique*: Free blown, engraved, and cut; foot added. Frosted in the engraved areas.

229. BOWL BY KŌZŌ KAGAMI

Thick, heavy glass, emphasizing the ductile nature of hot glass and its reflecting qualities when cooled.

- *Date*: 1955.
- *Color*: Colorless; transparent.
- *Technique*: Free blown and manipulated.

230. VASE BY MITSURU KAGAMI

- *Date*: 1955.
- *Color*: Colorless; transparent.
- *Technique*: Parts free blown and joined.

231. MONUMENT BY MITSURU KAGAMI

- *Location*: Sakae Underground Shopping Arcade, Nagoya.
- *Date*: 1970.
- *Size*: Glass only, H. 2.1 m.; D. 2.5 m. Base,

a dark mirror, H. 70.0 cm.; W. 3.5 m. × 3.5 m.
- *Color*: Colorless.
- *Composition*: Silica, 50%; lead, 30%; potassium carbonate, 15%; potassium nitrate, 3%; other, 2%. Weight, 5 tons.
- *Technique*: Fabricated of glass bricks, joined. Lighted from within and from the ceiling. Based on a dark reflecting mirror.

232. VASE BY MITSURU KAGAMI
- *Date*: 1968.
- *Size*: H. 30.0 cm.; D. 13.0 cm.
- *Color*: Colorless; transparent.
- *Composition*: Lead glass.
- *Technique*: Free blown and hand-shaped; a large decorative bubble in the bottom of the vase. The bubblelike unit in the body was formed by pushing out from the inside.

233. VASE WITH FLORAL DESIGN BY JUNSHIRŌ SATŌ
- *Collection*: The Corning Museum of Glass (No. 55.6.7); gift of the Asahi Glass Company, Tokyo.
- *Date*: Before 1955.
- *Size*: H. 28.0 cm.; greatest D. 9.8 cm.
- *Color*: Colorless; transparent, and frosted.
- *Composition*: Lead glass (ultraviolet fluorescence).
- *Technique*: Free blown, engraved, and cut.

234. BOWL BY JUNSHIRŌ SATŌ
- *Collection*: The Toledo Museum of Art (No. 56.23); gift of the Kagami Crystal Glassworks, Tokyo.
- *Date*: Ca. 1955.
- *Size*: H. 7.1 cm.; T. at rim, 0.3 cm.
- *Color*: Colorless; transparent.
- *Bubbles*: Few; scattered, small, and circular.
- *Composition*: Lead glass
- *Technique*: Mold blown; exterior etched vertically and cut with oblique leaflike design; the added foot is a solid, polished disc.

235. FISH FORM BY JUNSHIRŌ SATŌ
- *Date*: 1972.
- *Size*: H. 4.5 cm.; L. 29.5 cm.

- *Color*: Body, colorless; transparent. Eyes, partially pale green.
- *Composition*: Lead glass.
- *Technique*: Free blown; glass fragments inserted, after which the whole was drawn out lengthwise. Tail and eyes applied. Underside cut to form base.
- *Remarks*: Exhibited in the artist's first one-man show, Mitsukoshi Department Store, 1972.

236. TUMBLERS BY MASAKICHI AWASHIMA
Three tumblers of the patented *shizuku* ("dripping water") design.
- *Date*: This type has been produced continuously since 1950.
- *Size*: Largest, H. 10.6 cm.; D. 6.7 cm.
- *Color*: Colorless; transparent.
- *Composition*: Soda-lime glass.
- *Technique*: From two-piece metal molds. Originally, clay molds were used.

238. LOW BOWL OF ROUNDED SQUARE FORM
Multiple-layer glass.
- *Collection*: The Toledo Museum of Art (No. 54.66).
- *Date*: Ca. 1952.
- *Size*: H. 2.35 cm.; D. at rim, 17.15 cm.
- *Color*: Interior, dark brown center, shading in gradation to yellow under a black rim. Exterior, glossy black. A gray stripe at the rim.
- *Technique*: Free blown.

239. GLASS BOWL BY NOBUYUKI NAKASHIMA
- *Date*: November, 1960.
- *Color*: Gradations of rose and gray tones; opaque.
- *Composition*: Soft glass, light weight.

240. BOWL OF *SHŌTAI SHIPPŌ* (cloisonné without a base)
- *Collection*: The Corning Museum of Glass (No. 61.6.61).
- *Date*: 1960.
- *Size*: H. 4.8 cm.; D. at rim, 9.3 cm.
- *Colors*: Colorless ground, speckled. Design in

blues, greens, rose, brown; translucent.
- *Composition*: Lead glass (ultraviolet fluorescence).

- *Technique*: Produced by the usual cloisonné method, but with the copper base dissolved away with nitric acid after firing.

SUPPLEMENTARY NOTES

Sites in Kyushu

1. TWO FRAGMENTS OF A CHINESE GLASS *PI*

From a jar burial discovered in 1899 at "D Spot," Suku, Okamoto, Kasuga-mura, Tsukushi-gun, Fukuoka Prefecture. Included were fragments of Chinese bronze mirrors and daggers.

- *Collection*: Archaeological Research Institute, Kyoto University.
- *Provenance*: Chinese.
- *Date*: Han dynasty.
- *Size*: Ca. 1.5 × 2.2 cm.
- *Color*: Unknown because of white coating.
- *Technique*: Mold cast.
- *Condition*: Weathering coat, presumably of lead phosphate (see Pl. N. 40, *Condition*).
  Reference:
  Umehara, "Nihon Jōko no Hari," p. 4.

2. TINY GLASS FRAGMENT

From the same burial as Plate 39. Considered to be part of a Chinese *pi*.

- *Collection*: Archaeological Research Institute, Kyushu University.
- *Provenance*: Chinese.
- *Date*: Han dynasty.
- *Color*: Pale blue.
- *Composition*: Lead glass "essentially of the same components as many glass *pi* found in China."[1]

3. *KUDATAMA*

From an original group of six or seven from a pit grave found in 1949 at Suku-Okamoto by Mr. Masao Kaneko.

- *Collection*: Archaeological Research Institute, Kyushu University.
- *Date*: Middle Yayoi period.
- *Size*: L. overall 2.1 cm.; D. at center, 0.5 cm.; at narrowed ends, 0.4 cm.
- *Color*: Turquoise blue; opaque. IH.D.Refl.: Nearest Ch 2, 13-4-17.
- *Bore*: D. at one end, 0.2 cm.; at the other, 0.15 cm.
- *Composition*: Approximately 50% lead; Sp. Grav.: 3.83. (Dr. M. Mine)
- *Technique*: Shaped by pressing or rolling soft glass around some kind of rod of nonuniform diameter.
- *Condition*: Complete and excellent; although of lead glass, since it was not from a jar burial it has no corroded white coating. The unpolished surface has some small pits and a slight roughness.

4. TEN *KODAMA*

From an original 160 discovered by Dr. Heijirō Nakayama at Suku-Okamoto.

- *Collection*: Rekishikan, Minagi-mura, Asakuru-gun, Fukuoka Prefecture.
- *Date*: Considered to date from the Late Yayoi period, on the basis of Yayoi pottery of the Middle and Late Yayoi period found with the beads.

- *Sizes*: D. 0.25–0.35 cm.
- *Color*: Bright blue; translucent. The color and quality approximate those of a single bead found at the Numa site in Okayama Prefecture (Pl. 44).
- *Condition*: Good.

5. SMALL GLASS MIRROR SHAPE
From an unknown site in northern Kyushu.
- *Collection*: Formerly, the late Moriya Kōzō.
- *Date*: Late Yayoi period.
- *Size*: D. 4.0 cm.; T. 0.35–0.50 cm.
- *Color*: Deep yellow green; the condition prevents color matching.
- *Composition*: Lead glass.
- *Technique*: Mold cast.
- *Condition*: Broken and repaired. Has a patina that at first glance resembles bronze; clay-colored film on the bottom.
- *Remarks*: For ritual or funerary use. According to Dr. Umehara, this is a strictly Japanese mirror design, seen in Japanese bronze mirrors of the Yayoi period found in northern Kyushu.[1] The pattern brings to mind volute motifs incised on earthenware artifacts of the Late Jōmon period.

Reference:
1. *Umehara, "Nihon Jōko no Hari," pp. 15, 16, Pl. II (2) and Figs. 5, 6. For the bronze mirrors, see Sueji Umehara, "Nihon Jōko-shoki no Hōsei-kyō" [Mirror Adaptations of Early Antiquity], *Dokushikai Soritsu Go-jū Kinen (Kokushi Ronshu) Satsu* [Commemorating the Fiftieth Anniversary of the Association for Historical Studies Treatises on National History], pp. 263–282.

SITES IN OKAYAMA PREFECTURE

6. HEXAGONAL BEAD
The Kadota shellmound in Oku-chō, Oku-gun, Okayama Prefecture, is assigned to the Middle Yayoi period. It was excavated in 1934 by Mr. Kaoru Nagase, an amateur archaeologist. The mound is said to have covered about seven acres, with a depth of about one and one-half meters, and to have been one of about twenty shellmounds in the region, but the only one in which glass was found. Also found were: Yayoi pottery; stone, bone and shell artifacts, including five stone amulets (or weights?) three of which suggest an incipient *magatama* form; one *magatama* of green stone, among others; three rare, delicately fashioned needles made of the leg bones of tiny birds; a few stone beads.
- *Collection*: Oku-Kōkokan, Oku-chō, Okayama Prefecture.
- *Provenance*: The fact that lumps of glass wastes (Sup. N. 7–10) were also found in this site suggests local manufacture.
- *Date*: Probably Middle Yayoi period.
- *Size*: L. 1.6 cm.; W. 1.25 cm.
- *Color*: Rich grayed blue; almost transparent. IH.D.Refl.: Ch 6, 17-5-14 or 15, or 17-6-14. This is not very different in color from the glass lump of Sup. N. 7, though the latter is slightly lighter.
- *Bore*: D. 0.15 cm.; drilled from both ends.
- *Composition*: Seems to be soda-lime glass. Approximate Sp. Grav.: 2.40.
- *Technique*: Gives the appearance of having been roughly cut, with poorly indicated planes; the ends are cut off level and the bore drilled.
- *Condition*: Good; surface not polished.
- *Remarks*: A similar bead of dull, darker blue glass, just as crudely formed and with a bore that is not centered, is preserved in the Jingū Chōkokan of the Kōdai-jingū at Ise, but its provenance is not known. In color—IH.D. Refl.: Ch 6, 17-3-15 to 3-11 or 13—it differs but slightly from the Oku-chō bead. Both beads hint of what in later periods were to be truly faceted cut glass beads, the *kirikodama*.

7. GLASS LUMP
From the Kadota shellmound.
Excavated in 1950.
- *Collection*: Oku-Kōkokan, Oku-chō, Oku-gun, Okayama Prefecture.
- *Date*: Probably Middle Yayoi period.
- *Size*: 0.7 × 0.55 × 0.35 cm.
- *Color*: Gray blue; slightly translucent. IH.D. Refl.: Ch 5, 16-4-15.
- *Composition*: Untested; approximate Sp. Grav.: 3.
- *Condition*: Good, except for irregular fracture

patterns on the surface, probably due to lack of annealing.

- *Remarks*: This lump is of the same general color as the bead of Sup. N. 6, but is slightly lighter in tone. Compare with Sup. N. 8–10.

8. GLASS LUMP
From the Kadota shellmound.
In two fragments, excavated in 1934.
- *Collection*: Fragment "a" is in the Oku-Kōkokan, Okayama Prefecture. Fragment "b", a gift from the Oku-Kōkokan to the author, is in The Corning Museum of Glass. (No. 62.6.12)
- *Date*: Probably Middle Yayoi period.
- *Size of "b"*: 1.5 × 1.2 × 0.7 cm.
- *Color*: Colorless, with a slight grayed green tinge, due to vitrification near the surface; translucent.
- *Composition*: Soda-lime glass with a few impurities of minor and trace elements. An iron content of approximately 0.27% and absence of other colorants accounts for its colorless appearance. The lead content is approximately 0.001. The rounded surface and surface devitrification indicate that this glass was either accidentally fired or is waste from manufacturing (R.H.Brill).
- *Condition*: Good. Impurities and some adhering soil. One face, clear and glossy; the other has a thin, rough film.
- *Remarks*: Compare with Sup. N. 7, 9, 10. As there is no report of the excavation, other data are lacking, but if these four items are truly of the Yayoi period, they are unique in Japan and therefore valuable as the earliest known glass material in Japan. Should they be intrusions from the Tomb period (and many Tomb period glass beads have come from this area), they would still be important. However, none of the Tomb period finds at Oku-chō correspond to the glass of these lumps.

9. GLASS LUMP
Excavated in 1934.
- *Collection*: Oku-Kōkokan, Okayama Prefecture.
- *Date*: Probably Middle Yayoi period.
- *Size*: 2.2 × 1.85 × ca. 0.8 cm.

- *Color*: Green; transparent. IH.D.Refl. and IH.Trans.: Ch 13, 12-3-17.
- *Condition*: Good; film of clay on surface. Both contour and the depressions on the surface are softly rounded, possibly from accidental heating.
- *Remarks*: Compare with Sup. N. 7, 8, 10.

10. GLASS LUMP
- *Collection*: Oku-Kōkokan, Okayama Prefecture.
- *Date*: Probably Middle Yayoi period.
- *Size*: 3 × 2.3 × ca. 0.8 cm.
- *Color*: Very dark green; translucent. IH.D. Refl.: Ch 12, 11-2-16; IH.D.Trans.:Ch 12, 11-4-15. There are some areas of pale gray green.
- *Bubbles*: Numerous, especially in the lighter areas, where they are slightly oval.
- *Condition*: Good. The soft contour rounding probably due to accidental heating.

11. *KODAMA* FRAGMENT
From the site at Toro, Shizuoka city, Shizuoka Prefecture. A farming site dating from the Middle to Late Yayoi period. Discovered in 1943 and thoroughly excavated in 1947.[1] An extensive site of pit-dwellings, storehouses, and rice fields that were well preserved by inundation. Found here, in addition to glass beads, were stone implements, bronze and iron implements, much Yayoi pottery, a great deal of wooden equipment such as canoes, looms, spindle whorls and shuttles, stools, tools and utensils, some with painted decoration.
- *Collection*: The Corning Museum of Glass (No. 63.6.116).
- *Date*: Middle Yayoi period.
- *Size*: H. ca. 0.225 cm.; D. ca. 0.36 cm.
- *Color*: Turquoise blue; translucent. IH.D. Refl.: Ch 3, 14-5-17.
- *Bore*: D. 0.2 cm.; comparatively large.
- *Bubbles*: Fairly numerous; one or two slightly oval.
- *Composition*: Presumably soda-lime glass: Sp. Grav.: 2.13; Refr. Ind.: 1.492; coloration due to copper. (Dr. K. Yamasaki)
- *Condition*: Good.
- *Remarks*: Complete beads are preserved in

several places, as in the museum at Toro and in the Archaeological Research Institute of Tokyo University. Their colors include a bright blue (IH.D.Refl.: Ch 4, 15-7-15); a dark purplish blue (IH.D.Refl.: Ch 6, 17-5-11); turquoise blue; turquoise green; light grayed blue. All are translucent or semitransparent. Most have rounded contours, but some approach the tubular. Some have comparatively wide bores. All have bubbles. Some have one or more flattened places on the body of the bead, as though from pressure on a flat surface before the glass hardened.

Reference:

1. "Toro, A Report on the Excavation of the Toro Sites," ed. Nihon Kōkogaku Kyōkai, partial tr. Jirō Harada, Tokyo Mainichi Shinbunsha, 1949.

TOMB PERIOD

12. FRAGMENTS OF A CLAY CRUCIBLE
Important Cultural Property

Found in 1922 at Bessho-dani, Tamatsukuri, Tamayu-mura, Yatsuka-gun, Shimane Prefecture. The broken edge of the larger fragment is of a light-colored clay at the exterior, containing minute white pebbles. Adjoining this, at the bottom, is an indefinite layer of very porous glassy substance, probably actual glass that has penetrated the clay. Above this layer is smoother and better integrated dark blue glass, with small bubbles and bubble pits. Another fragment has a thin layer of glass, while a third has a very thick bubble layer.

- *Collection*: Tamatsukuriyu Shrine, Tamatsukuri, Yatsuka-gun, Shimane Prefecture.
- *Date*: Probably Tomb period. The porosity of the clay seems indicative of an early date, as is also the fact that the glass residue is in part darkish blue, the most common color of glass beads in the Tomb period.
- *Size*: Larger fragment, L. overall *ca.* 19.0 cm.
- *Composition*: Dr. Yamasaki, who examined a fragment of this crucible, found cristobalite and mullite, and believes a temperature of about 1200° C was used.

13. SMALL CUP-SHAPED CRUCIBLE OF UNGLAZED CLAY

Discovered at Asabaraguchi, Sogo-son, Tsukubo-gun, Okayama Prefecture. The exterior base shows marks of the potter's wheel; the exterior surface was hardened and refined by the heat of molten glass, some of which remains, solidified, in the crucible. In the very bottom some of the glass is missing, evidently broken away, and there the exposed bottom is covered with a dark, dull, rough, bluish gray coating. The glass residue remaining around this area is in some places colorless and in some amber colored; it is translucent and transparent. Above this the interior walls are completely covered with a more opaque, slightly grayish coating, which dribbled over the edge onto the exterior wall as though at some time the molten contents had been poured out. This coating has no transparency, is thin, smooth, and roughly crackled, almost like a glaze; in tone it is slightly bluish.

- *Collection*: Kibi Kōkokan, Onzaki Shrine, Yamate-son, Tsukubo-gun, Okayama Prefecture.
- *Date*: Uncertain; possibly Tomb period.
- *Size*: H. 5.1 cm.; D. at lip, 8.4 cm.; at base, 3.15 cm.
- *Composition of the glass residue*: Soda-lime glass; if lead is present at all it is less than 0.01%. (R.H.Brill)
- *Remarks*: Although this crucible seems small, even for the manufacture of small beads, it is not out of keeping with ancient glassmaking customs elsewhere in the world, for clay crucibles of no more than two or three inches in height were found in the ruins of Tel El Amarna of ancient Egypt. Alfred Lucas wrote that when these small crucibles were broken away they found colored glass, with a frothy upper surface caused by the escape of carbon dioxide and combined water, and a lower portion caused by dirt and impurities sinking to the bottom.[1] Perhaps these same causes account for the dark coating in the bottom of this small Japanese crucible and for the somewhat opaque (frothy) coating on the upper walls.

This part of Okayama Prefecture was the heart of the Kibi area, one of the cultural centers of early Japan. Significantly it is from the

Kibi locale that many glass beads of the Tomb period have been excavated.

Reference:

1. Alfred Lucas, *Ancient Egyptian Materials and Industries*, 4th ed., rev. by J. H. Harris, London, E. Arnold, 1962, p. 191.

14. METAL TUBE HOLDING A ROD-SHAPED GLASS FRAGMENT

The rather nondescript glass fragment in this metal tube has an irregular, chipped appearance. Whether the glass was inserted in the metal by intention or by some disturbance in the burial is not certain, but it has all the appearance of having been placed intentionally so that the metal would serve as a finger grasp. Since it was found with a small lump of glass waste and with several glass beads, it would seem to be a tiny bit of unworked glass metal too small to hold over the flame in the hand and was thus attached to a tiny handle. The small diameter of the piece suggests that it was used in the making of coiled *kodama*; in that event it would probably have been longer originally, but was melted down in the beadmaking process.

- *Collection*: Tokyo National Museum.
- *Date*: Tomb period.
- *Color*: Grayish blue.

15. LUMP OF UNWORKED GLASS ADHERING TO CLAY

Discovered in Tamatsukuri, Shimane Prefecture; from the shallow Tamatsukuri River.

- *Collection*: Tamatsukuriyu Shrine, Tamatsukuri, Yatsuka-gun, Shimane Prefecture.
- *Date*: Uncertain; possibly Tomb period.
- *Size*: Irregular, 6.7 × 7.6 cm.; T. 0.5 cm.
- *Color*: Black in appearance, but in sunlight one area shows amber yellow glints, and fragments broken away are light and dark amber color. Black, although not one of the most common colors, was used for Tomb period beads, and amber of honey-colored beads are known (Pl. 55).
- *Condition*: Surface has a dull film.
- *Remarks*: This is evidently a bit of glass batch still adhering to a fragment of a clay crucible.

16. TWO ADHERING LUMPS OF UNWORKED GLASS

Found on Tsukiyama, Tamatsukuri, Shimane Prefecture.

- *Collection*: Tamatsukuriyu Shrine, Tamatsukuri, Yatsuka-gun, Shimane Prefecture.
- *Date*: Uncertain; possibly Tomb period.
- *Size*: L. 6.15 cm.; T. 3.33 cm.
- *Color*: Intense blue; translucent—a common color in Tomb period glass.
- *Bubbles*: Full of circular bubbles, large and small.
- *Condition*: Good.
- *Remarks*: Other lumps from this area are omitted, as their glass is not characteristic of Tomb period beads.

17. TWO SMALL RODS OF SOLID GLASS

From a tomb in Kaminagai, Toyoka-mura, Katori-gun, Chiba Prefecture.

- *Collection*: Dr. Tei-ichi Asahina, Tokyo.
- *Date*: Tomb period.
- *Size*: L. 2.1 cm.
- *Condition*: Good.
- *Remarks*: Perhaps working materials, for use over a flame in the making of coiled *kodama*.

18. FRAGMENT OF THICK FLAT GLASS

Similar to that of Plate 48. Found in earth at the bottom of a tomb in the Fukumasawa-Hakozaki area, Yawata city, Fukuoka Prefecture. Associated articles included pavement pebbles and a gold ring.

- *Collection*: Archaeological Research Institute, Tokyo University.
- *Date*: Late 6th or early 7th century.
- *Size*: 4.9 × 5.7 cm.; T. 1.45 cm.
- *Color*: Dark green; translucent.
- *Composition*: Lead glass. Sp. Grav.: 4.828; Refr. Ind.: less than 1.543.[1]
- *Technique*: Cast in a shallow mold, as was the slab of Plate 48.
- *Condition*: Coated with areas of pale greenish, mosslike crystallization (also found on some pieces in the Shōsō-in) and areas of thin film of brilliant iridescence, violet and blue, over

the green glass. The surface, however, feels smooth and in parts suggests ivory.

Reference:
1. *Yoshito Harada, Tōa Kobunka no Kenkyū, Pl. 71.

19. TWO FRAGMENTS OF FLAT GLASS
Purportedly from Miyajidake Shrine (see Pl. 48).
- Collection: Mr. Toyo Motokuni, Hiroshima.
- Date: Late 6th or early 7th century.
   a. Size: L. 3.25 cm.; W. 2.175 cm.; T. 0.4 cm.
   - Color: Green; nearly transparent.
   - Technique: Cast in a shallow mold.
   - Condition: Creamy mat surface with gold and silver glints; where this has come off, the surface is brightly iridescent with reds, purples, greens, blues, gold, and silver, with several areas of smooth, glassy, creamy surface.
   b. Size: L. 7.45 cm.; W. 5.3 cm.; T. 0.45–1.0 cm.
   - Color: Bright darkish green, very glossy; transparent. IH.D.Refl.: Ch 12, 11-4-15.
   - Bubbles: Full of circular bubbles, various sizes.
   - Condition: Covered with iridescent film, some areas of whitish crystallization. Where the latter is chipped away, many broken bubbles and some exposed unbroken bubbles are visible.

20. MAGATAMA
From the same zenpō-kōen tomb as the ear pendants of Plate 65.[1]
- Collection: Archives and Mausolea Division, Imperial Household Agency (No. E 1-1/3).
- Date: Middle Tomb period.
- Size: L. 5.4 cm.; W. at center, 1.6 cm.; T. at center, 1.7 cm.
- Color: Green; translucent. IH.D.Refl.: Ch 13, 12– ca.3–4; IH.D.Trans.: 12–3 to 4–17.
- Bore: D. 0.25 cm.
- Bubbles: Generally minute and circular; some larger, of which a few are longitudinally oval. Some surface pits. At the main point of fracture, interior bubbles can be seen protruding

intact within a skin of glass, as though the break had followed around their peripheries.
- Composition: Inner devitrification has taken place. By microscopic examination of powder preserved from the break, "separately positioned crystals, some clustered in starlike formation, were observed. These were simple, square, needle-like crystals of wollastonite, a calcium silicate ($CaOSiO_2$), or of diopside ($CaOMgOSiO_2$). (The Shōsō-in bowl, Pl. 105, also contains these crystals.) The light dispersion angle was found to be 36–37°, within 5–6° of that of calcium silicate. The material being very limited, no accurate value for the refractive index was obtainable, but it was close to 1.66. Since that of diopside is 1.66–1.69 (while wollastonite is 1.616–1.631), it was concluded that magnesium was an ingredient of the raw material and therefore of the glass metal." Sp. Grav.: $2.49 < 1 < 2.54$; Refr. Ind.: ca. 1.66.[2]
- Technique: Mold cast, and incised.
- Condition: Broken; surface in good condition; all fractured surfaces carry a light iridescence.
- Remarks: In spite of breakage, this is a handsome specimen as regards color, form and execution, and suggests the Yayoi magatama, Plate 39, and the Tomb period magatama, Plate 49.

References:
1. Sampei Ueda, "Wakasa-no kuni Onyū-gun Onyū-mura Nishizuka" [The West Tomb at Uryū-mura, Onyū-gun, Wakasa Province], KKZ, VIII, 4, pp. 224–229.
2. *Asahina and Oda, "Shōsō-in Hagyoku. . . .," pp. 3, 4.

21. MAGATAMA WITH PLAIN HEAD
From the Juzen-no-Mori Tomb on the property of Mr. Y. Saitō, Fukui Prefecture. Found with bronze fragments; other glass magatama, two glass tombodama and various small glass beads.
- Date: Late(?) Tomb period.
- Size: L. 2.0 cm.; W. at center 0.825 cm.; T. at center 0.65 cm.
- Color: Colorless, with slight bluish tinge; semi-transparent.
- Bore: D. 0.125 cm. and 0.15 cm.; possibly drilled from one side.

- *Bubbles*: Very small, with one exception; surface pitting.
- *Technique*: Probably ground from glass metal.
- *Condition*: Surface rough, as though abraded, near the inner curve.
- *Remarks*: Another *magatama* found at this site is of the same colorless glass; both are unusual.

22. *MAGATAMA* WITH PLAIN HEAD AND FLATTENED SIDES.
Discovered shortly before 1919 in the Kadomae Tomb, Okayatanigawa, Ryūhō-maru, Yatsushiro-gun, Kumamoto Prefecture.
- *Collection*: Archives and Mausolea Division, Imperial Household Agency (No. 13 1-1/20).
- *Date*: Late Tomb period.
- *Size*: L. 2.0 cm.; W. at head, 0.9 cm.; T. at head, 0.5 cm.
- *Color*: Deep green; translucent. IH.D.Refl.: Ch 13, 12-*ca.* 4-14.
- *Bore*: D. 0.15 and 0.2 cm., apparently drilled from one end.
- *Composition*: Lead glass, with inner devitrification here and there.[1] Sp.Grav.: 4.86.[2] The glass is very similar in color and specific gravity to the glass slab found at Miyajidake Shrine (Pl. 48).
- *Technique*: Ground from a piece of glass. On each of the slightly flattened sides appear two softly rounded grooves, as though the *magatama* had been grasped with tongs while soft (perhaps during heating for fire polishing?). Plate 50 illustrates the process that produced the flattened sides.
- *Condition*: Good surface. Near the inner curve the surface is rough, as though abraded in the grinding process.

References:
1. *Asahina and Oda, "Shōsō-in Hagyoku. . . .," p. 4.
2. Calculated by Sadahiko Shimada and Kinzō Tazawa, quoted by *Yoshito Harada, *Tōa no Kobunka Kenkyū*, p. 423.

23. NINETEEN GLASS *KODAMA*
From Kasakayama, Oku-chō, Oku-gun, Okayama Prefecture. Burials in Oku-chō were excavated over a number of years by Mr. Kaoru Nagase. Associated objects include ceramics, carved stone items, stone beads, and a quantity of glass beads.
- *Collection*: The Corning Museum of Glass (No. 62.6.9).
- *Date*: Middle Tomb period.
- *Sizes*: D. *ca.* 0.2–0.45 cm.
- *Colors*: Four dark grayed blue; translucent. Fifteen of varying tones of turquoise blue; translucent.
- *Bores*: Of various diameters.
- *Composition*: Two independent spectrographic analyses, run at separate laboratories, are virtually identical and indicate soda-lime glass with a small lead content of about 0.03%. The bead analyzed is light blue, semiopaque. The analysis is virtually that of Plate 57. (R.H.Brill)
- *Technique*: Probably cut from tubes.

24. TWENTY *KODAMA*
From Yamada-no-Shōyama, Oku-chō, Oku-gun, Okayama Prefecture, excavated by Mr. Kaoru Nagase.
- *Collection*: The Corning Museum of Glass (No. 62.6.8).
- *Date*: Middle Tomb period.
- *Size*: H. 0.2–0.75 cm.; D. 0.3–0.5 cm.
- *Colors*: Varying tones of turquoise blue; slightly translucent. IH.D.Refl.: Ch 3 14-3-15, 14-4-18, 14-5-16.
- *Bores*: Varying diameters.
- *Composition*: Analysis virtually identical to that of Sup. N. 23 except for a copper content of approximately 1.0%.

25. TWENTY *KODAMA* FROM A SARAYAMA TOMB
From Tomb I, Nakamiya, Sarayama, Tsuyama city, Okayama Prefecture; a *zenpō-kōen* mound. Found with *haniwa* cylinders, *haji* and *iwaibe* pottery, *marudama* of black clay.[1]
- *Collection*: Tsuyama Kyōdokan, Tsuyama city, Okayama Prefecture
- *Date*: Middle or Late Tomb period.
- *Sizes*: H. 0.15–0.25 cm.; D. 0.3–0.5 cm.
- *Colors*: Dark, medium, and light blue, and brown; semitransparent.
- *Bores*: D. 0.15–0.25 cm.
- *Bubbles*: A few, and some pits on the surfaces.

- *Technique*: Tube cut, as evidenced by the longitudinal lines.
- *Condition*: Excellent.
  Reference:
  1. Yoshirō Kondō (compiler), *Sarayama Kofun-gun no Kenkyū* [Study of the Group of Old Tombs on Sarayama], I, Tsuyama, 1952.

26. THREE *MARUDAMA*
From a tomb in Kamo, Toyoda, Yoshimatsu-mura (new name, Ueki-machi), Kamoto-gun, Kumamoto Prefecture.
- *Collection*: Archives and Mausolea Division, Imperial Household Agency (Nos. C 2-1/3 [b]).
- *Date*: Late Tomb period.
- *Sizes*: H. *ca.* 0.5–0.8 cm.; D. 0.9–1.1 cm.
- *Color*: Deep green; translucent. IH.D.Refl.: nearest, Ch 12, 11-4-15; IH.D.Trans.: 11-5-16.
- *Bores*: D. *ca.* 0.35–0.4 cm.
- *Composition*: Lead glass; Sp.Grav.: 5.04.[1]
- *Remarks*: These beads present striking similarity to the glass material at Miyajidake Shrine (Pl. 48). Two other beads from this Kumamoto site, also preserved at the Imperial Household Agency (Nos. C 1-1/14 and C 1-1/15) are similar; they have no corrosion and show many tiny circular bubbles (some slightly oval). Their specific gravities differ somewhat, being 4.54– and 4.57.
  Reference:
  1. *Asahina and Oda, "Shōsō-in Hagyoku. . . . ," p. 3.

27. EIGHTY-SIX OPAQUE BROWNISH RED *KODAMA*
From an original four hundred or more excavated by Mr. Kaoru Nagase near Kasakayama in Oku-chō, Oku-gun, Okayama Prefecture. Many other *kodama* and *marudama*, in blues and greens, were also found here.
- *Collection*: The Corning Museum of Glass (No. 62.6.3). Presented to the author by the Oku-Kōkokan, Oku-chō, Okayama Prefecture.
- *Provenance*: Perhaps imported?
- *Date*: Middle Tomb period.
- *Sizes*: H. 0.1–0.375 cm.; D. 0.25–0.45 cm.

- *Color*: Dark brownish red; opaque. IH.D. Refl.: Ch 2, 1-7-13. The coloring agent is cuprous oxide. What seem to be longitudinal opaque dark stripes (see Pl. 59) is in reality transparent colorless glass (see page 57 and Appendix).
- *Bores*: D. 0.075–0.15 cm.
- *Composition*: Soda-lime glass. Sp. Grav.: 2.55; Refr. Ind.: 1.517.
  Basically a soda-lime glass with a rather high content of alumina oxide. The ratio of copper to tin (Cu_2O = approximately 1.7 and SnO_2 = approximately 0.25) indicates that the copper was introduced in some form of material derived from bronze; the Cu_2O should be 1.7%. A separate addition of lead was made, the lead content being approximately 2.5. This level of lead accounts for the fact that the refractive index and specific gravity of this glass are somewhat higher than the usual soda-lime glasses. The bead examined also contained about 0.17% antimony oxide (Sb_2O_3). (R.H.Brill)
- *Technique*: Cut from glass tubes, of which the stripes and body shapes are proof.
- *Condition*: Good.

28. *TOMBODAMA* WITH YELLOW INSERTS AT THE BORE ENDS
Found in 1955 near Oku-chō, Okayama Prefecture, by Mr. Kaoru Nagase in a small hillside chamber tomb lined with small stones. Associated objects were *iwaibe* pottery, a stone *magatama*, a stone *kudatama*, three crystal *kirikodama*, several stone and glass *marudama* and *kodama*.
- *Collection*: Oku-Kōkokan, Oku-chō, Oku-gun, Okayama Prefecture.
- *Provenance*: Possibly an import?
- *Date*: Tomb period.
- *Size*: H. *ca.* 0.925 cm.: D. 0.9 cm.
- *Colors*: Dark blue, slightly greenish glass predominates but is difficult to match. Yellow at the bore ends. IH.D.Refl.: Ch 9, 8-4-19. Both glasses are semitranslucent.
- *Bore*: D. *ca.* 0.1 cm.
- *Technique*: Uncertain whether the blue glass was coiled around a yellow base, or whether, as seems more likely, a yellow disc was imbedded at each end. In the latter case the bore

would have been drilled after the glass had solidified.

- *Condition*: Good, aside from a rough surface.
- *Remarks*: This is a curious bead, and in the author's experience unique in Japan. Four *tombodama* in Kyŏngju, Korea, however, have yellow at each bore end, which seem to be merely surface applications.

29. STRIPED *TOMBODAMA*

Excavated by Professor Takeshi Kagamiyama, Kyushu University, from the Zenigama Tomb, Kushima city, (formerly Fukushima-mura), Minami-Naka-gun, Miyazaki Prefecture.

- *Collection*: Museum of Miyazaki Shrine, Miyazaki city, Miyazaki Prefecture.
- *Date*: Late Tomb period.
- *Size*: H. 0.9 cm.; D. 1.15 cm.
- *Colors*: Stripes of colored opaque glass applied to an opaque white glass body; the order is red, white, turquoise, greenish blue, white, dark blue, white, red, which is repeated.
- *Bore*: D. 0.35 cm.
- *Technique*: Cut from a tube of glass that had been drawn out from a globule of opaque white glass with added spots of color; by twisting, the spots became spiraled stripes. The stripes penetrate the body for some distance but do not reach the bore; the cut ends of the bead reveal a curving-in of the stripes toward the bore.
- *Condition*: Fairly good, but the colors are dulled and there is a hole in the side of the bead.
- *Remarks*: In the Chōkokan of the Kōdai-jingū, Yamada-Ise, Mie Prefecture, there is a similar bead, but it is shorter and has a wider bore; its colors are red and green only on a cream-colored body, all being aged and mellowed.

30. SIX LARGE *KIRIKODAMA*

Recovered from Site 8, Okitsu-gū, Okinoshima, the unique island shrine in the Genkai Sea north of Kyushu, which belongs to Munakata Shrine on the mainland.[1] For discussion of this important shrine, its significance and other items found here, see Sup. N. 33. Site 8 is the latest site on the island.

- *Collection*: Munakata Shrine, Miya-tsukasa,

Tsuyazaki-machi, Munakata-gun, Fukuoka Prefecture.

- *Date*: 6th–7th century.
- *Size*: One example, H. 3.5 cm.; D. at center, 1.55 cm.
- *Color*: Dark green; transparent. IH.In.Trans.: Ch 11, 10-4-16. Some are of a lighter green.
- *Bores*: D. 0.3 cm. Ends, irregular and angular; interiors, whitish.
- *Bubbles*: Many closely adjacent surface pittings, possibly broken bubbles; at times a shallow honeycomb effect.
- *Composition*: Soda-lime glass with little, if any, lead content. Sp. Grav., one specimen: 2.539 or 2.536.[2] Refr. Ind.: $1.504 < n\ 1.509\ (19°C)$.[3]
- *Technique*: Three of these "*kirikodama*"[4] have curious, deep openings at one end, either from damage in cutting or, more likely, from inexperience or carelessness in making the basic form, as though the wrapped glass had not been pressed tightly enough for the ends to unite. The rather oval shape of the beads, and irregular bore openings, accentuate this theory. The octagonal aspect is elementary; this is also apparent in rock crystal *kirikodama* from this site.

References:
1. *Okinoshima.*
2. *Ibid.*, Appendix II, by Dr. Masao Mine, p. 2, Table Ib (1).
3. *Asahina and Oda, "Shōsō-in Hagyoku. . . . ," Table Ib (1).
4. *Okada, *Garasu*, Pl. 42, refers to these as *natsumedama.*

31. GLASS GLOBULES ATTACHED TO GILT-BRONZE HORSE TRAPPINGS

Excavated in 1954 at Shuku-no-shō, Toyokawa-mura, Mishima-gun, Osaka Prefecture, by Professor Yukio Kobayashi of Kyoto University. Associated objects: gilt-bronze horse ornaments; *iwaibe* pottery; several hundred glass beads of dark blue, green blue, opaque yellow and opaque orange red with inconspicuous "dark" lines.

- *Collection*: Archaeological Research Institute, Kyoto University.
- *Date*: Tomb period.
- *Sizes*: H. 0.25–0.45 cm.; D. 0.4–0.575 cm.
- *Color*: Dark blue; translucent. IH.D.Trans.:

Ch 5, 16-4-12, with highlights of 16-5-12, due perhaps to the light penetrating the hollow forms.

- *Technique*: Glossy, globular, hollow glass sets, slightly more than hemispherical in shape, flattened and occasionally slightly concave on the bottom. Often there is a tiny hole in this bottom face or, in some, two minute slots. A few of the globules have a slightly rounded excrescence at one side, near the bottom, suggesting a disengaging of a softened glass source at that point in the process of manufacture.
- *Condition*: Good, except that many have fallen from the bronze.
- *Remarks*: Corrosion of the bronze hinders inspection, but the glass seems to have been set into something added above the bronze surface.

32. GLASS IN THE TOMB OF THE EMPEROR NINTOKU

The tumulus that by tradition and literary allusion is that of Emperor Nintoku is the Daisan-ryō ("Great Mountain" Imperial Tomb) in Semboku-gun (formerly Otori-gun), Osaka Prefecture. It is a *zenkō-kōen* mound (Pl. 46) about 480 meters in length, with three encircling moats.

In 1872, as the result of storm damage, part of the tumulus slid away and ". . . the interior of the stone chamber, in which there was a stone coffin, became visible. At the front and back and left and right of the stone coffin many and various kinds of wares were installed, among which were glass vessels. One, which looked like a jar, was *ruri* colored [dark blue]; the other, which looked like a dish, was white."[1] We learn from an annotation on a picture of the exposed stone chamber sketched by one Masanori Kashiwagi, that here were "fragments of armor, glass vessels, swords, and metal fittings."[2] No drawings were made. The items were said to have been replaced in the chamber, but since a sword handle and mirror recognized as from the tomb later reposed in the Museum of Fine Arts, Boston, apparently those objects, at least, somehow got into the hands of a dealer. Could the glass also have remained outside?

According to modern revised chronology, it is considered that the tomb was constructed in the early fifth century. The Emperor Nintoku is recorded as reigning from 313 to 399. On the fifth of the tenth month in 379 he ". . . made a progress to the plain of Ishitsu in Kahachi, where he fixed upon a site for a *misasagi* [imperial tomb]." On the eighteenth day the work began. The emperor, according to the record, died in the spring of 399 and in the tenth month was interred "in the *misasagi* on Mosu Moor."[3] The glass interred with him must naturally antedate the time of burial, but we cannot know whether those pieces, like the vessels of Plates 1 and 105, showed characteristics of Iranian workmanship. The fact that the glass seemed to be a jar and a dish or plate suggests the two items from the Niizawa tomb (p. 61). Since the vessels from the Emperor Nintoku tomb cannot be studied today, the nineteenth century record of the glass is important.

References:
1. *Kurokawa, *Kurokawa Mayori Zenshū*, Pt. 3, p. 380.
2. *Fujisawa, "Ankan Tennō Ryō. . . .," p. 307.
3. Aston, *op. cit.* (see n. 1, p. 45), I, pp. 298–300.

33. TWO FRAGMENTS OF A GLASS BOWL WITH ROUNDELS IN RELIEF
National Treasure

From the ritual site No. 8 at Okitsu-gū of Munakata Shrine, on the island Okinoshima in the Genkai Sea, Fukuoka Prefecture.[1] Lying off the northern shore of Fukuoka Prefecture are two islands: a larger one, Ōshima; and farther away a smaller one, Okinoshima. Both belong to Munakata Shrine on the nearby Kyushu mainland, and on both islands are subsidiary small shrines. Okinoshima is a small rocky isle, which for centuries was uninhabited, although traces of both Jōmon and Yayoi dwelling sites have been found. The earliest of the Tomb period sites on Okinoshima thus far investigated date from the fourth and fifth centuries, when central control from Yamato was well established. The latest, Site 8, from which these glass fragments came, dates from the late sixth or the seventh century.

Okinoshima lay in an especially strategic position at the western entrance to the Inland Sea, that inner passageway leading to the heart of Japan in Yamato. It was natural that it became of especial importance in all international activities. "Munakata deities were highly revered at the Yamato Court . . . and the island was a place of importance . . . the rituals held on Okinoshima . . . appear to have been grand rites in which prayers were offered to the deities at times of nation-wide significance."[2] The *Nihon Shoki*, for the first day of the second month in the spring of 465, records that certain officials "were sent from Yamato to sacrifice to the Deity of Munagata."[3] The spirit enshrined at Munakata Shrine is traditionally described as a god of *magatama*, and it has been recorded that the *go-shintai* (the sacred symbol, or embodiment) of the deity is a "bead."[4]

The relics found on Okinoshima are therefore not burial offerings but ceremonial offerings to the gods. Many of the groups were found laid out on the ground in open crevasses formed by the out-jutting over the ground of huge, clifflike boulders. In ancient rituals, it is said, deities were invoked and invited down from heaven to trees, rocks, and other natural places, which were called *yori-shiro*. "The huge rocks here must have been suitable as *yori-shiro*."[5]

The island, through the centuries, has been holy ground and closed to lay visitors. During World War II this sacred isolation was broken when it became necessary to station a small defense force at this strategic spot. Since then, details of lighthouse keepers have been maintained on the island, and the shrine authorities, recognizing the growing need for protection and preservation of the offerings, finally permitted three archaeological projects in 1954, 1957, and 1958.[6]

It was at Site 8 that the glass included here was found. Associated objects were many miniature iron swords and knives; a decorated halberd sheath; bronze mirrors; gilt-bronze *gyoyo* (heart-shaped) and *uzu* (flaming-jewel shaped) ornaments for horse-trappings; *iwaibe* pottery;

many beads of various kinds, both stone and glass; the *kirikodama* of Sup. N. 30.

The two small glass fragments were found in separate investigations; one is very tiny but augments the other. They comprise a curved segment from a cut glass bowl and contain one complete roundel in relief and bits of the edges of two other nearby roundels. From the curvature of the body and these three raised parts it had been possible to draft the contour of the original bowl and relative positions of the roundels, as illustrated in the report,[7] but neither the height of the bowl nor the nature of its rim can be known. However, the bowl shown in Plate 67 suggests what the form probably was.

- *Collection*: Munkata Shrine, Miya-tsukasa, Tsuyazaki-machi, Munkata-gun, Fukuoka Prefecture.
- *Provenance*: Probably West Asia—more particularly, Iran.
- *Date*: 4th or 5th century, judging by similar examples of West Asian origin.
- *Size*: Body glass, T. 0.2 cm. Raised roundel, H. irregular, 0.3–0.6 cm.; D. *ca.* 2.6 cm.
- *Color*: Pale yellowish green; semitransparent. IH. matching difficult because of variations in thickness of the glass, but IH.In.Refl. was close to Ch 12, 11-2-18 and 11-3-18.
- *Bubbles*: Numerous, small, and circular.
- *Composition*: From the specific gravity and refractive index the inference has been drawn that the lead oxide content may be thought to be over 20%. Qualitative and quantitative analyses have not been made. Sp. Grav.: 2.773. Refr. Ind.: $1.540 < 1.548$ ($17°$ C).[8]
- *Technique*: Generally considered to have been mold cast, but the small size of the fragments makes this difficult to determine.
- *Condition*: Exterior surface pitted and slightly rough to the touch except in the hollow of the roundel, where it is somewhat smoother. The interior surface is also smoother. A thin iridescent film.
- *Remarks*: In The Corning Museum of Glass there is a complete bowl of this type (No. 61.1.11). As seen in Plate 67, one disc in relief forms the foot. On the body are two rows, the

upper one of eight discs and the lower one of six. The rim, which is about 0.5 cm. thick, slopes down at a sharp angle to the interior. In both the Okinoshima fragments and this bowl the upper surfaces of the discs are ever so slightly concave. Another intact bowl is said to have been discovered in Iran by Professor Shinji Fukai of Tokyo.

References:
1. *Okinoshima*, I, p. 222.
2. *Ibid.*, II, English summary, p. 28.
3. Aston, *op. cit.* (see n. 1, p. 45), p. 353.
4. *Chikushi Fudoki*, an eighth century gazeteer of Chikushi (Chikuzen) Province in present Fukuoka Prefecture.
5. *Okinoshima*, II, p. 28.
6. *Ibid.*, I and II.
7. *Ibid.*, I, Fig. 90.
8. Tei-ichi Asahina, and Sachiko Oda, as quoted by Dr. Masao Mine in *Okinoshima*, Appendix II, pp. 2–3.

Asuka and Hakuhō Periods

The artifacts of these periods available for cataloguing seem comparatively few, but one must remember that, whereas ancient sites are often excavated with relative freedom, the treasures of temples and shrines, a prime source after the Tomb period, are often so sacred that investigation is limited or even prohibited.

34. SMALL GLASS MATERIALS

From the *shari* installation under the foundation stone of the pagoda of Hōryū-ji. The date is controversial, but lies within the Asuka-Hakuhō period. All data are from the official investigation report.[1] The inclusion of these few glass accessories, with fragments of semi-precious stone, gold foil, and other items, is an indication of the growing importance of the glass craft in Japan.
- *Collection*: Reinstalled beneath the pagoda of Hōryū-ji.
- *Date*: Asuka or Hakuhō period.
- a. *Small tubular glass form, widening at one end.* Perhaps the remnant of a glass rod used in the making of coiled beads. At the wider end a globular form adheres.
  - *Size*: L. *ca*. 0.85 cm.; D. 0.25 cm., flaring to nearly 0.7 cm.

- *Color*: Green.
- b. *Two fragments of flat glass*
  - *Sizes*: T. *ca* 0.27 cm. and *ca*. 0.38 cm.
  - *Color*: Pale green; translucent. One is weathered and silvery on one face.
  - *Remarks*: There is no measurable curvature.

Reference:
1. *Hōryū-ji Gojū-no-tō*. . . . .

35. FRAGMENT OF A *MAGATAMA* WITH INCISED LINES ON THE HEAD

From the *shari* installation of Ango-in (only remaining part of Hōkō-ji, popularly known as Asuka-dera).
- *Collection*: Ango-in (Asuka-dera), Asuka-mura, Takaichi-gun, Nara Prefecture.
- *Date*: Installed in 593.
- *Size*: L. *ca*. 1.225 cm.; W. 0.75 cm.
- *Color*: Light aqua blue; translucent. IH.D. Trans.: nearest Ch 2, 13-4-16.
- *Bore*: D. 0.20 cm.
- *Bubbles*: Circular.
- *Composition*: Soda-lime glass.[1]
- *Technique*: Ground (?) and incised.
- *Condition*: Fragmentary; the surface rather rough.

Reference:
1. Kazuo Yamasaki, in *Asuka-dera*. . . . , p. 28, described this as lead glass; however, in his *"Garasu"* he corrects this to soda-lime glass, since the lead content is small.

36. GLASS BEADS

From the *shari* installation beneath the pagoda of Ango-in (Asuka-dera).
- *Collection*: Ango-in (Asuka-dera), Asuka-mura, Takaichi-gun, Nara Prefecture.
- *Date*: Installed in 593.
- a. *1,493 beads.*
  - *Sizes*: D. 0.5–1.0 cm.
  - *Color*: Dark blue; translucent.
  - *Bubbles*: Minute.
  - *Composition*: Soda-lime glass, colored by cobalt and copper; Sp. Grav.: 2.3–2.6.
- b. *251 beads.*
  - *Sizes*: D. 0.2–0.3 cm.
  - *Color*: Blue green; translucent. IH.D. Refl.: Ch 3, 14-4-15 to 4-17.
  - *Bubbles*: Minute.

- *Composition*: Soda-lime glass, colored by copper.
c. *234 beads*.
  - *Color*: Green; translucent and opaque. IH.D.Refl.: Ch 13, 12-2-15 or 16 and Ch 12, 11-4-17.
  - *Bubbles*: Some, and some surface pitting.
  - *Composition*: Soda-lime glass colored by copper.
d. *60 beads*.
  - *Sizes*: D. 0.3–0.4 cm.
  - *Color*: Brownish purple; translucent. Almost amber color with rosy tone.
e. *289 beads*.
  - *Color*: Yellow; opaque. IH.D.Refl.: Ch 9, 8-2-17, 3-18 and 4-19.
f. *Beads*.
  - *Color*: Black; opaque and mostly rough
  - surfaced.
  - *Composition*: Colored by iron.

37. *MARUDAMA* AND *KODAMA* OF HŌRYŪ-JI

From the *shari* installation beneath the five-storied pagoda of Hōryū-ji. The date is controversial, but within the Asuka-Hakuhō period. (For details of the installation, see Pl. 70. The following data were available from the official report.
- *Collection*: Reinstalled beneath the pagoda of Hōryū-ji.
- *Date*: Asuka or Hakuhō period.
a. *42 marudama*.
  - *Sizes*: H. 0.44–0.85 cm.; D. *ca.* 0.72–1.28 cm.
  - *Color*: Green.
b. *15 marudama*.
  - *Size*: H. 0.38–0.73 cm.; D. 0.63–0.9 cm.
  - *Color*: 13 are deep blue; 2 are green.
c. *115* kodama *of various shapes and sizes*.
  - *Color*: 76 blue and deep blue, sometimes intermingled, indicating incomplete fusion; 37 yellow green; 2 uncolored.

38. OPAQUE BROWNISH RED BEADS

From the *shari* installation beneath the pagoda of Ango-in (Asuka-dera).

- *Collection*: Ango-in (Asuka-dera), Asuka-mura, Takaichi-gun, Nara Prefecture.
- *Date*: Installed in 593, but there are some Tomb period aspects in the installation and in some other articles interred here.
- *Composition*: Soda-lime glass, colored by colloidal copper.
- *Remarks*: This is at present the only known instance of this bead type from a post-Tomb period site.

39. THREE *TOMBODAMA*

From the *shari* installation beneath the pagoda of Ango-in (Asuka-dera).
- *Collection*: Ango-in (Asuka-dera), Asuka-mura, Takaichi-gun, Nara Prefecture.
- *Date*: Installed in 593.
a. *Two* tombodama.
  - *Size*: H. 1.3–1.4 cm. D. 1.6 cm.
  - *Color*: Dark blue base, translucent, with four irregular spots of alternately yellow and medium green, both opaque. IH.D. Refl.: blue, close to Ch 6, 17-2-11 and Ch 7, 18-1-11; yellow, Ch 8, 7-3-19 and Ch 9, 2-4-18; green, Ch 12, 11-3-15.
  - *Bores*: D. 0.2 and 0.5 cm.
  - *Bubbles*: Pitted surface, especially in the yellow.
  - *Composition*: Soda-lime glass.
b. *One* tombodama.
  Similar to the above but with copper inlay instead of green and yellow glass.

40. 104 *TSUYUDAMA*

From the *shari* installation beneath the five-storied pagoda of Hōryū-ji.
- *Collection*: Reinstalled beneath the pagoda of Hōryū-ji.
- *Date*: Asuka-Hakuhō period.
- *Size*: H. 1.28 cm.; D. 1-1. 38 cm.
- *Color*: Green.
- *Bore*: Partial. Traces of a reddish brown color are perhaps an adhesive used to secure a wooden plug set in beside the end of the suspension wire.
- *Technique*: A small gather of glass twirled on the end of a clay-coated rod or pin until the

globular form solidified. The glass rises slightly at the end of the bore—a result of the twirling motion.
- Condition: Judging from the photograph in the official report, they seem to be excellently preserved.
- Remarks: This seems to be the earliest instance that can be presented of beads especially formed for suspension rather than for stringing.

41. SHARI-TSUBO OF THE HŌRIN-JI PAGODA SITE

From beneath the three-storied pagoda of Hōrin-ji at Mii, Tomisato-mura, Ikoma-gun, Nara Prefecture, in the neighborhood of Hōryū-ji. According to temple tradition, this pagoda was erected by Shōtoku Taishi in 622. The shari-tsubo was discovered in 1739, when the rotted pillar of the pagoda was removed. The shari installation was inspected, then re-interred and covered over. A horizontal scroll in the temple's treasures, the Busshari Engi,[1] records all this and includes sketches in color.

In 1944 the pagoda was struck by lightning and burned. The shari installation was then taken up and moved into the temple for safe-keeping. According to the scroll, the central pillar of the pagoda rested on a foundation stone about two meters square buried about three meters underground. In the center was a metal lid covering a hollowed out portion of the stone, where a metal jar (probably of gilt-bronze) had been installed, with incense piled around it. When this lid was lifted, "Fragrance filled the pagoda within and without." Within the jar was a square silver box, pictured in the scroll as secured with gold bands, housing a small round "jewel" of glass containing two shari, one red and a smaller one white. Associated objects included a rosary; some earthenware said to have been used by Shōtoku Taishi; and eleven clay figures of Shitennō (The Four Guardians). Among the treasures preserved at Hōrin-ji there are two shari, one red and one white, in a colorless glass or crystal reliquary mounted in a fine gilt-bronze pedestal form, which is a splendid example of metalwork of the Edo period. A dark metal jar (silver?) is actually more squat than the one shown in the scroll.

- Collection: Whereabouts now unknown; could it be within the Edo period bronze reliquary?
- Provenance: Judging from the details outlined in the scroll, this shari installation differs from that of Asuka-dera described on page 70, but in general is very like that of Hōryū-ji (Pl. 70). The shari-ki of the two differ, however; the tiny Hōrin-ji one resembles an even smaller one, of crystal, in the national museum at Puyo, Korea. It is impossible to say at this point whether the Hōrin-ji example was made in Japan or imported.
- Date: Perhaps early 7th century.
- Size (of the original shari-ki): H. ca. 3.64 cm.
- Color: According to the sketch in the Busshari Engi, the body is blue; the stopper is "white," but whether colorless glass or silver is intended is not known.
- Technique: The shape is that of blown glass.

Reference:
1. Full title, Sanjū no Hōtō Shinchū yori Shukken no Busshari Engi [Record of the Busshari Discovered in the Central Pillar of the Three-storied Sacred Pagoda]; a manuscript scroll. According to a colophon it was written in 1743 by Kisshoin Hōyu, and copied as the present scroll, in 1747 by Shonagon Sugawara Ason.

NARA PERIOD

THE SHŌSŌ-IN

42. KUDATAMA
- Former Location: Middle Section, in the "debris." No STM listing.
- Date: 8th century.
- Colors: Chiefly blues, ranging in intensity from pale to dark, but there are also some amber color and colorless.
- Technique: The special committee on Shōsō-in materials questioned whether they may not have been formed by cutting.[1]

Reference:
1. *SGZC, p. 79.

43. KODAMA
- Former Location: Middle Section, in the "debris". No STM listing.

- *Date*: 8th century.
- *Sizes*: D. 0.11–0.4 cm.
- *Colors*: Blues, greens, yellows; both translucent and opaque. Three very tiny ones are dark blue.
- *Technique*: Probably coiled.
- *Condition*: Excellent.

44. QUASI-*TSUYUDAMA* FORMS

There is in the Shōsō-in one special group of sixteen items that are not of true dewdrop form but suggest it. They have a rather coarsely bulbous body with a subsidiary swelling at the top, and in some there is a small protruberant collar at the mouth of the cavity. In the cavity are remains of metal wire, cloth, and a fragment of wood, so it seems that, like true *tsuyudama*, they were intended for suspension.[1] They differ from other beads in the Shōsō-in in their resemblance to glass paste.

- *Former Location*: Middle Section. No *STM* listing
- *Date*: 8th century.
- *Size*: Largest example, H. 4.225 cm.; D. 3.175 cm.
- *Colors*: Green: pale, medium, and dark; opaque. IH.D.Refl.: close to Ch 12, 11-4-14 and 15; Ch 13, 12-4-13.
- *Technique*: Probably formed as were the *tsuyudama* of Plate 85, center.
- *Condition*: Good.

Reference:

1. **SnG*, p. ix, suggests that "larger *tsuyudama*, some of which retain pieces of wood in their bores, appear to have been attached as weights to curtains and other such objects."

45. PRIEST'S CEREMONIAL FOOT-WEAR

Slippers of the oversize ceremonial type, fashioned of soft red leather lined with thin calfskin, the soles padded beneath a white twill lining. The seams are outlined with gold. On the upturned toe is a decoration of fan-shaped leather painted white. Applied floral motifs are of silver-gilt set with a central pearl surrounded by beads of amber and rock crystal and sets of blown glass in blue, green, and brown.

These are said to have been used by the Abdicant Emperor Shōmu when he wore the Buddhist *kesa* (a ritual shoulder mantle) over his ceremonial robes;[1] he may have worn them at the Eye Opening Ceremony.

- *Former location*: South Section. *STM* No. 687.
- *Date*: 8th century.
- *Size of shoes*: L. *ca.* 31.5 cm.; H. 12.5 cm.[2]
- *Technique*: The glass sets are of blown glass.[3]
- *Condition*: The glass is in excellent condition, but the slippers are very fragile.
- *Remarks*: For a color plate, see **Treasures of the Shōsō-in—The South Section*, Plate 92. Such footwear is seen in some Central Asian wall paintings of dignitaries in ceremonial dress.

References:

1. **STM* No. 687, p. 150.
2. **Treasures of the Shōsō-in—The North Section*, p. xiii.
3. **SGZC*, p. 80.

46. *JIKU-TAN* USED ON *KENMOTSUCHŌ*

Two of the Shōsō-in *Kenmotsuchō*, or "Deeds of Gift," have glass *jiku-tan*.

a. Glass *jiku-tan* of the *Kenmotsuchō* dedicating calligraphy by the great Chinese scholars Wang Hsi-chih and his son, Wang Hsien-chih. The scroll is mounted on blue hemp paper.

- *Former Location*: North Section. *STM* No. 4.
- *Date*: Dated the first day of the sixth month, 758; it would seem, therefore, that the glass *jikutan* are of approximately that date.[1]
- *Color*: Green; seen only through the case, the glass seemed almost opaque, and full of bubbles.
- *Remarks*: The quality seems finer than that of the unused *jiku-tan* of Sup. N. 47. Remains of a brown adhesive identified as soybean paste indicates the method of attaching the *jiku-tan* to the rod.[2]

b. Glass *jiku-tan* of the *Kenmotsuchō* of Prince Fujiwara's Autograph Screen.

The scroll is of white hemp paper. (Prince Fujiwara was the father of Empress Kōmyō.)

- *Former Location*: North Section. *STM* No. 5.

- *Date*: Dated the first day of the tenth month of 758;[1] the *jiku-tan* are presumably of about the same date.

References:
1. *ECTS, pp. 14, 15.
2. *SnG, p. 28.

47. UNUSED *JIKU* AND *JIKU-TAN*

These are *jiku* and *jiku-tan* never called upon for use. The rods are of wood; the ends, of various materials. Details given below refer, of course, only to the glass ends.

- *Former Location*: Middle Section. *STM* Nos. 380–381.
- *Date*: 8th century.
- *Colors*: Green, yellow, brown, dark blue, and opaque white.
- *Composition*: The dark blue examples have a specific gravity of about 2.7, calculated by dimensions and weight; they are of soda-lime glass colored by cobalt. The others are heavy and evidently of lead glass.
- *Technique*: Judging by clay coatings adhering to the insides of the *jiku-tan*, it is assumed that a clay-coated metal rod was thrust into molten glass and pressed into a mold. A few of the examples illustrated were neither cut down to size nor polished; they are about 4.0 cm. long.[1]

a. *220 unused* jiku.
  - *Sizes*: Overall L. 30 cm.[2] *Jiku-tan*, L. 2.0–2.07 cm.; outer D. *ca.* 1.0 cm., with flaring ends *ca.* 2.0 cm.; inner D. *ca.* 0.8 cm.
  - *Colors*: 104 dark and light yellow; 5 brown; 60 dark blue; 19 dark green; 32 of wood.

b. *Unused jiku-tan.*
  Fifty-seven pairs and 58 single items of agate, amethyst, rock crystal, wood, lacquered wood, wood painted in color, and glass. Thirteen are of glass, but colors and sizes cannot be given.
- *Remarks*: As these are inferior in both shape and color, they were considered as perhaps "unsatisfactory, rejected pieces" and therefore left unused.

References:
1. *SnG, pp. v-vi, 28.
2. *ECTS, pp. 14, 15, 82–83.

HEIAN PERIOD

48. FLAT TRIANGULAR GLASS FRAGMENT

From the coffin of Fujiwara no Motohira, installed in the Konjiki-dō of Chūson-ji. Found with glass beads.

- *Collection*: Chūson-ji, Hiraizumi, Nishi-Iwai-gun, Iwate Prefecture.
- *Date*: Fujiwara period, probably 12th century.
- *Size*: $1.9 \times 1.9 \times 2.89$ cm.; T. *ca.* 0.105–0.109 cm.[1]
- *Color*: Pale green.
- *Composition*: Sp. Grav.: by cubic volume, 3.13; by saturation, 3.75. Refr. Ind.: 1.576. On these bases, the lead oxide content was estimated at 33.5 to 49%. However, the cubic volume was only estimated; and the glass powder examined for the refractive index came from a weathered surface.
- *Condition*: Weathered white.
- *Remarks*: The nature and purpose of this fragment is not understood. It is an isosceles triangle with rounded base angles and a sharp peak. Possibly a bit of glass metal for beadmaking or for inlay, though it shows no signs of having been used as an inlay. It is too flat and too shaped to be a vessel fragment.

Reference:
1. *Asahina, Aida, and Oda, "Chūson-ji Garasu . . . . ," p. 4.

49. BEADS FROM THE MUMMY OF FUJIWARA NO MOTOHIRA

- *Collection*: Chūson-ji, Hiraizumi, Nishi-Iwai-gun, Iwate Prefecture.
- *Date*: 12th century

a. *Two blue beads.*
  - *Size*: H. 0.7 cm.; D. 1.0 cm.
  - *Color*: Rich bright blue; transparent. IH.: Ch 4, 15-4-19.
  - *Bore*: D. 0.425–0.475 cm.; rather large for the size of the bead.
  - *Bubbles*: Numerous, chiefly circular.
  - *Composition*: Sp. Grav.: 3.76; Refr. Ind.: 1.640. Lead content, 47.45%; coloring agent, copper. For full analysis, see the Appendix, Table VIII.

- *Technique*: Coiled, as evidenced by the tiny peaked collar.
- *Condition*: Surface rather dull, perhaps from weathering.
- *Remarks*: Said to have come from near the abdomen of the mummy, which seems to imply that they were inserted in the clothing as dedicatory and amuletic offerings.

b. *Ten yellowish brown beads.*
- *Size*: Slightly smaller than *a*.
- *Bores*: D. 0.425–0.475 cm.; comparatively large.
- *Composition*: Lead content, 47.81%, Sp. Grav.: 3.8; Refr. Ind.: 1.650. For full chemical analysis, see Appendix, Table VIII.
- *Technique*: Coiled, but not cut apart.
- *Condition*: Good.
- *Remarks*: Multiple unseparated beads of this sort were common in Korea.

c. *Other glass beads, some isolated and some in a* yōraku *fragment.*
- *Sizes*: Various.
- *Colors*: Pale blue, turquoise blue and a strong rich blue; dark yellow; colorless.
- *Composition*: Sp. Grav.: range from 2.35 to 4.40. Refr. Ind.: from 1.495 to 1.654.

Reference:
1. *Asahina, Aida, and Oda, "Chūson-ji Garasu . . . ," pp. 1–4. An elaborate method of checking the color of these beads included placing the bead in the light from a north window, with a blackboard as a background on which the scattered light from the transparent bead could be observed.

50. ONE OF A PAIR OF BUDDHIST ROSARIES

Important Cultural Property

Long rosaries of this sort seem to have been the mode in the Heian period, as they were in Nara times; they are seen in a number of painted portraits of famous Buddhist priests of the Heian period. Although the rosaries are attributed to the Heian period, an accompanying tag states that they were rearranged in 1720 or 1721.

The parent bead is a large and handsome *marudama* of rock crystal mounted with a sepallike cap and ring. Opposite in the string is another, but smaller, rock crystal bead. In addition, there are now twenty-four medium sized rock crystal beads, forty-four seeds of the sacred Bodhi tree (linden), four small crystal beads, and thirty-nine glass *tombodama*.

- *Collection*: Tokyo National Museum. Formerly owned by Hōryū-ji.
- *Provenance*: These *tombodama* seem strange for the Heian period and suggest imports from the West in the Edo period. Perhaps they are Venetian, added during the eighteenth century "rearrangement."
- *Date*: Heian period, but the *tombodama* may be much later.
- *Sizes*: Tombodama: H. 0.8 cm.; D. 1.0 cm.
- *Colors*: The ground of the *tombodama* is opaque black glass,[1] in which "eye" motifs are imbedded, some with red "pupils" on a white ground, others with red on a light blue or yellow ground, while still others are red on blue, or other combinations. There are also many monochrome spots in red, light blue, or yellow.
- *Bores*: D. *ca.* 0.2 cm. Areas around the bores do not display the glossiness of many Japanese beads of the Edo period.
- *Technique*: Coiled; the spots were added from the melting tips of glass rods, many of them imperfectly manipulated.
- *Condition*: Excellent.

Reference:
1. *Oda, "Nara Jidai no. . . . ," p. 23, refers to this as "a dark green ground that appears almost black."

51. SENJU KANNON (Thousand-Armed Kannon)

National Treasure

A hanging scroll painted in color on silk. Although the general elaborate detail is in true Fujiwara style, the unknown artist has retained something of the majesty of earlier Chinese-influenced painting. The "thousand" arms and the multiple heads are symbolic of the myriad ways in which this Bodhisattva extends mercy to mankind.

The many elaborate *yōraku*, in the crown and

on the body, are supplemented by strings of beads attached to the tips of the lotus petals of the pedestal. This latter innovation is indicative of a growing overelaboration in Fujiwara art.

The figure at the lower left carries a glass bowl of flowers.
- *Collection*: Tokyo National Museum.
- *Date*: Heian period.

52. BRONZE SUTRA CASE
Important Art Object
Discovered by the late Mr. Tomijirō Konomi in a sutra mound at Nishi-Aburayama, Fukuoka Prefecture. A large round stone container sheltered it.

The cylindrical body, with compound spreading base and lid, is 29.5 cm. high and 10.5 cm. in diameter. The lid is surmounted by a three-ringed finial with a *hōshu* terminal. From the topmost of the three rings, four *yōraku* extend to equidistant points on the circular lid; they are made of glass beads joined by characteristic long links of silver wire.
- *Collection*: Mrs. Tsumako Konomi, Fukuoka.
- *Date*: Late Heian period.
  BEADS:
- *Sizes*: H. 0.3 cm.; D. of larger beads, 0.5 cm.; of smaller beads, 0.34 cm.
- *Colors*: Pale green, medium green, dark blue, and some of a turquoise tone; translucent.
- *Technique*: Coiled.
- *Condition*: Good.
- *Remarks*: The bead stringing here is in a sequence from top to bottom of three, five, three, one, three, one—with two linked silver loops between each group. Two beads terminate each wire, beneath the eave of the lid; a very small one is threaded on a wire that then loops through the larger bead and runs back through the small one.

53. BRONZE *SHARI-TŌ* (Pagoda-Shaped *Shari* Receptacle)
Important Cultural Property
The pagoda is of gilt-bronze, 61 cm. high. In the main body, double doors were cut in each of the four directions, as in a real building. The

interior is hollow; its original contents are unknown, but one must suppose that some kind of sutra, or, since it is a *shari-tō*, some kind of *shari* container, with perhaps associated objects, was enshrined here.

Since no associated *shari-ki* is known, the chief interest in this is the elaborate *yōraku* suspended from beneath the eaves of the hip roof. The fringe hanging from the perforated metal bands on all four sides is made up of glass beads, of metal medallions with a glass bead wired onto the center, of single wire loops linked together, and of small leaf-shaped metal terminals. At each of the four corners there is an elaborate pendant of metal shapes, wire loops, and glass beads.
- *Collection*: Tokyo National Museum. Formerly owned by Hōryū-ji.
- *Date*: Inscribed on the bottom with a brush, Hōen 4 (1138).
- *Bead sizes*: Various sizes and shapes.
- *Technique*: Probably coiled; the larger, irregularly shaped beads (a new form) are definitely coiled.
- *Condition*: Generally good.
- *Remarks*: These beads were made with more skill than those of Plates 118 and 119, which confirms the opinion that the others were produced by less well-trained and supervised beadmakers, while these must have been the work of trained beadmakers nearer the capital, or by trained temple beadmakers. The new bead form already noted in Plate Note 119 is somewhat flat at one end, and narrower at the other end, giving it a jarlike appearance.

The manner of assembling the beads is more sophisticated than that shown by earlier work. For instance, some terminal beads have a very simple disc seat and are held in place by a loop of wire spread out to a near circle beneath the metal disc. This was also seen in fragments from the imperial crowns in the Shōsō-in. The attachment of a single bead to the front of a metal medallion seems new at this time. In place of the several sepal leaves that surmounted *tsuyudama* in the Shōsō-in, there is now a simplified or "short-cut" method in which a single piece of metal was folded around an ordinary *marudama* or *kodama* suspended sideways. This new mode of suspension is seen in many Heian *yōraku*.

54. DECORATED SWORD
National Treasure
The black lacquered sheath and silvered sharkskin hilt of this sword are decorated with applied gold-plated rosette forms. The hilt ornament (*menuki*) is more complex, having a cluster of glass *hankyūdama* set into a six-petaled gilded flower form enclosed within a collar.
- *Collection*: Kasuga-taisha, Nara.
- *Date*: Late Heian period.
Hankyūdama:
- *Sizes*: Center set, D. *ca*. 1.0 cm.; smaller sets, *ca*. 0.6 cm.
- *Colors*: Center set, red brown; smaller sets, probably green, but identification is difficult.
- *Condition*: The smaller sets are covered with film.

55. FRAGMENTS OF *SHARI-TSUBO* FROM THE NODAYAMA SUTRA MOUND
These fragments are parts of two, or even three, small *shari-tsubo* from a sutra mound at Hongō-machi, Toyoda-gun, Hiroshima Prefecture. Discovered in 1953, with numerous associated articles, including fifty-one small glass *marudama* (some with very wide bores) and bronze mirrors.
- *Collection*: Kyoto National Museum.
- *Date*: Late Heian period.
- *Size*: The complete jars are estimated by Mr. Haruki Kageyama, Kyoto National Museum, to have been about 3.0 cm. in diameter.
LARGEST LID FRAGMENT:
- *Color*: Green, as seen at one or two broken edges, but too minute to check on the color chart; seems to be a yellowish green.
- *Technique*: Blown. The applied knob is like a bead, flattened or sliced off on top. Two other lid fragments reveal *hōshu*-shaped knobs.
- *Condition*: Weathered chalky white, even on most of the fractured edges.
- *Remarks*: The lid form, with its broad and rather long, openmouthed neck, is similar to the lids

of Plate 122 and Sup. N. 56; it is rather a stopper than a lid.

56. FRAGMENTS OF A *SHARI-TSUBO* FROM KŌRYŪ-JI
Recovered from a sutra mound at Kōryū-ji, Uzumasa-mura, west of Kyoto. Associated with them were a bronze mirror and a few glass beads. The fragments are from lid, shoulder, and bottom. In the bottom fragment there is a slight kick.
- *Collection*: Archaeological Research Institute, Kyoto University.
- *Date*: Late Heian period.
LID FRAGMENT:
- *Size*: H. 2.8 cm.; D. at coiled edge, 2.1 cm.
- *Color*: Apparently light green, but obscured by patina.
- *Technique*: Free blown, with added coil. The neck is jagged where the blowpipe was broken away. The applied knob has the contour of a flattened bead.
- *Condition*: Weathered, with glossy brownish patina. The glass, because of deterioration, is now very thin.
- *Remarks*: The stopper-lid resembles that of the *shari-tsubo* from Nodayama (Sup. N. 55). Other fragments—part of the shoulder and a base—are related to the *shari-tsubo* of Denkō-ji (Pl. 122).

57. GLASS FRAGMENTS FROM THE SHAKA NYŌRAI IMAGE, SEIRYŌ-JI
National Treasure
Seiryō-ji (popularly known as Shaka-dō) is located in Saga-mura, Kyoto Prefecture. From the numerous glass fragments found within the Shaka image, two bottles can be reconstructed. A multitude of other fragments are too tiny to suggest any reconstruction.
- *Collection*: Seiryō-ji, Saga-mura, Kyoto Prefecture.
- *Provenance*: Chinese (?), or Persian (?). The shapes of the two bottles are quite non-Chinese. The applied mouth rim is suggestive of some Persian vessels. The reconstructed shapes and the nature of the glass show no resemblance to any contemporaneous glass of Japan.

• *Date*: The statue, as documented by records found within it, is Chinese; it was brought to Japan in 987. The substitute entrails found within the body are of Chinese silk brocade and are inferred to have been placed there before the image was brought to Japan.

a. Fragments of a high-necked bottle of at least two bulbous parts.

  • *Size*: D. at top of tubular neck, *ca.* 0.45 cm.; outside mouth, 1.45 cm.; greatest D. of upper bulbous section, 2.85 cm.

  • *Color*: Blue green, varying considerably in tone; semitransparent. IH.D.Refl.: Ch 2, 13-5-15 (neck) to Ch 3, 14-6-14 (body).

  • *Bubbles*: Many circular bubbles in the body; elongated ones in the neck, often with a tiny circular one adjacent at either left or right. In the mouth area they are both vertically and horizontally elongated. Pits on the mouth rim.

  • *Composition*: 55.8% lead glass.[1]

  • *Technique*: Blown. A complex coiling of glass threads forms the rim.

b. Fragments of an apparently more squat and simpler bottle than *a*, with a thicker, more columnar neck and more conventional coiling at the mouth.

  • *Size*: D. inside neck, 0.7 cm.; outside mouth, 1.5 cm. but irregular; T. 0.075–0.125 cm.

  • *Color*: Blue green, similar to the body of *a*; semitransparent. IH.D.Refl.: near Ch 2, 13-5-15 but slightly bluer.

  • *Bubbles*: Large and small, mostly circular; associated in the neck with several large oval ones; in the applied rim, small and circular with a few transversely oval ones.

  • *Technique*: Free blown, with a rough jagged edge where broken away from the blowing pipe. The mouth rim of coiled glass threads is more skillful than in *a*.

  • *Condition*: Broken. The glass has a glossy polished surface.

• *Remarks*: In addition to the above there are many small fragments, some of which are like sections of mouth rims, suggesting a third bottle. One of these fragments is light grayed green glass 0.025 cm. thick.

Reference:
1. Further reference may be made to *Yoshimizu, "Seiryō-ji Shaka. . . ."

58. CLOISONNÉ, BYŌDŌ-IN
National Treasure

Placed at the bottom of the two main doors of the Hōō-dō, Byōdō-in, Uji-machi, Uji-gun, Kyoto Prefecture, are mountings ornamented with cloisonné. Regrettably, the author can give no first-hand description or data, since she learned of them only on the eve of departure from Japan. According to Mr. Jō Okada they are cloisonné of about 1053. The design is in two colors, the flower motif in the center being red and the three-part motif in the outer range being blue green.[1]

This constitutes the only evidence to date of enamel work of the Heian period. Perhaps it should offer more support of literary references to *shippō* in Heian literature, some of which are mentioned on page 140. Certainly it is of importance as evidence of an early enamel tradition in Japan before the supposed introduction of the Western cloisonné technique. At present far too little is known about the evolution of early enamel work in East Asia.

Reference:
1. This has been reproduced in color in *Teshigawara, *et al*, Garasu, Pl. 19, and in Jō Okada, *Nihon no Kōgei*, III, Tokyo, Yomiuri Shinbunsha, 1968, p. 11.

KAMAKURA PERIOD

59. *YŌRAKU* OF A STATUETTE OF BYAKKŌ-SHIN (White and Shining Deity)
Important Cultural Property

A wood figure 59 cm. high. Both figure and lotus pedestal are painted white. The *yōraku* of the crown are thin and delicate, with tiny *kodama* of glass. Those of the body are heavier, with somewhat larger beads. Each petal tip of the pedestal bears a simple *yōraku* of one small glass bead from which hangs a long metal sepal within which is a single glass bead suspended sideways as was seen in Heian *yōraku*. The suspension wire is looped back through the pinched tip of the petal and secured by looping through another glass bead at the back of the petal.

- *Collection*: Kōzan-ji, Toganō, Kyoto Prefecture.
- *Date*: Kamakura period.

BEADS:

- *Sizes*: Vary, from very small *kodama* to larger *marudama*.
- *Colors*: Pale blue, lightish gray blue, rich green blue, deep yellow, and a deep red that may be amber; translucent.
- *Bores*: The bores of all beads are very small.
- *Condition*: In general, good; but accumulation of film precludes accurate assessment.

60. GILT-BRONZE *SHARI-TŌ* MOUNTED ON A TORTOISE FORM
National Treasure

This *shari-tō* ("pagoda for *shari*") was ordered by Priest Eison for the glass *shari-tsubo* of Plate 82 brought from China by the priest Ganjin. The columnar body is of perforated gilt-bronze, through which one may glimpse the strands of small varicolored *kodama* that hang in a circle from the top of the interior to "protect" the neck of the glass jar. A few glass beads are in the chains of the pagoda-shaped roof. The *shari-tsubo* rests upon a lotus seat of gilt-bronze, with erect prongs to hold the sacred treasure in place. The tortoise base symbolizes the reputed rescue of the *shari* at sea by a golden tortoise.

- *Collection*: Tōshōdai-ji, Nara.
- *Date*: 13th century.

61. GILT-BRONZE *SHARI-TŌ* RESEMBLING A HANGING LANTERN
National Treasure

From the point of view of proportions, elegance of balanced design, fine materials, and skilled workmanship, this seems the finest of the gilt-bronze reliquaries installed in Nara temples by Priest Eison. It is rumored that a glass *shari-tsubo* was originally preserved in the interior of this reliquary, but verification has not been possible. A *yōraku* of glass beads, now fragmentary, was hung in the open area at the top. There were also *yōraku* pendants of glass beads, bronze bells, and plaques suspended from the eavepoints of the lotus-form roof. As the glass beads have not been examined at close range, catalogue data are lacking.

- *Collection*: Saidai-ji, Fushimi-mura, Ikoma-gun, Nara Prefecture; often shown in the Nara National Museum.
- *Date*: Kamakura period.
- *Condition*: Good, but the *yōraku* are incomplete.

62. THE AMIDA TRINITY OF KŌDAI-IN, KŌYA-SAN
Important Cultural Property

The figures of this small trinity exude a spirit of calm poise typical of much Kamakura Buddhist art. The *yōraku* worn by the two attendant Bodhisattva have blue, honey-colored, and colorless glass beads. On each of the three lotus pedestals beneath the images rests a metal plate with projecting hooks from which are suspended *yōraku* with tiny glass *kodama*; this same device for suspension was cited under Plate 125 and occurs also in other sculpture of the time.

The upper octagonal platforms beneath the lotus pedestals still retain the upright metal pins, sixteen in each case, upon which some sort of ornaments were originally impaled. The author was once advised that ornaments of glass could be found in these pedestals; but they have now all disappeared. This type of embellishment was a common feature in Buddhist art, both Chinese and Japanese.[1]

The elaborate elongated halo of the Amida image had glass inset at the periphery. Although the halo itself is much damaged, some of the insets remain.

- *Collection*: Kōdai-in, Kōya-san, Kōya-machi, Ito-gun, Wakayama Prefecture.
- *Date*: Halo inscribed 1313.

GLASS INSETS:

- *Colors*: Green; translucent. There is also a grayer green. In the dark altar chamber it was impossible, with only a flashlight, to match the glass with the color chart.
- *Technique*: Mold cast.

- *Condition*: Only a few insets remain, but in general their condition is good.
Reference:
1. As seen, for example, in the pedestal of the Japanese image of Aizen Myō-ō, illus. in *Nihon Bunkashi Taikei* [Historical Survey of Japanese Culture], VI, Fig. 5, p. 70.

63. JIZŌ BOSATSU WITH A GLASS VESSEL

A painting in color on silk. The deity is shown on a cloud, carrying his jingling rings to advise the suffering spirits in the underworld of his merciful presence. He holds in the left hand a blue vessel, which has very much the look of a blue glass bowl of lobed shape. Curling upward from it is a wisp of incense smoke or vapor. The condition of the painting makes it practically impossible to describe the bowl in detail.
- *Collection*: Museum of Fine Arts, Boston (No. (11.6184).
- *Provenance*: Japanese.
- *Date*: Early 13th century.

MUROMACHI PERIOD

64. SCULPTURED IMAGE OF GOKEI MONJU BOSATSU (Mañjuśri)

Important Cultural Property

The wood figure, 43.6 cm. high, is by Shun-kakubo Shunkei, a Nara priest; painted by Hitachi Sadakyō of Nara.

Simple *yōraku* occur at the breast and on the petal tips of the pedestal, where they consist of a suspension wire carrying a few spaced glass beads and a flat, lobed, and perforated metal plaque from which depend three wire chains with a few more spaced glass beads.
- *Collection*: Hōju-in, Hōryū-ji, Ikoma-gun, Nara Prefecture.
- *Provenance of the beads*: Perhaps Chinese.
- *Date*: 1459.
- *Colors*: Pale blue; opaque. Colorless; translucent.
- *Technique*: Coiling of a crude sort, leaving the beads rough and corrugated, with exaggerated projecting points where the molten glass source was pulled away.

65. CANOPY OF A SHARI-TŌ, HŌRYŪ-JI

The *shari-tō* itself is kept in a closed shrine in the Shari-den of the Tō-in (East Precinct) at Hōryū-ji; it is said to be of crystal with a silver pedestal. The canopy, however, is hung nearby, outside the shrine. The design is complex and in its use of glass beads is an exception to what has been said previously about the scant use of beads in *yōraku* by this time. In the main it consists of a gilt-bronze circular roof piece, with a border of cut-out petal forms. Beneath, in a circular arrangement, are apsaras in relief flying about the orb of the sun. These are encircled by an openwork band formed of glass beads strung on wire. From this depend a number of bronze pieces. Enclosing this *yōraku* is a complex arrangement with a long circular fringe of strings of metal pieces and small glass *kodama*.
- *Collection*: Shari-den, Tō-in, Hōryū-ji, Nara Prefecture.
- *Provenance*: The opacity of numerous beads may be of significance in regard to their origin. This type was lacking in pre-Muromachi *yōraku*, where translucency and transparency were dominant. Possibly these were imports from China.
- *Date*: Teiji 4 (1365), according to temple authorities.
- *Sizes*: The larger beads are of irregular shapes and sizes.
- *Colors*: Beads of the inner openwork band; light blue, translucent; white, opaque; together with coral-colored wood. Small *kodama* of the outer fringe: lightish blue, blue, coral color, white, all opaque; blue, dark blue, amber, all translucent. Surfaces are very smooth.
- *Technique*: Coiling; in the larger beads this is very conspicuous.

66. YŌRAKU IN A SMALL SHARI, TOKUZEN-JI

An inscription on the base of the storage case of this small shrine dates it on the third day of the ninth month of Teiji 2 (1363) and gives the signature of Tettō Gikō, founder of Tokuzen-ji. The present abbot of Tokuzen-ji, Daiki Tachibana, commented that this may have indicated that Tettō Gikō had himself been the maker.

The open sides of the black lacquer framework of the shrine are filled in with black gauze stretched on gilded frames; each bears a gilded dragon. The roof is surmounted by a centrally placed *shari-tsubo* of crystal in *hōshu* shape surrounded by the usual bronze "flames."

Within the shrine is a miniature figure of the deity Dainichi Nyōrai, adorned with elaborate miniature *yōraku* containing tiny glass *kodama*. Tiny sepaled lotus forms of glass project outward from a lobed plate beneath the figure in the manner already seen in the Kamakura period (Pl. 125, Sup. N. 62). The angled platform of this small statuette bears small composite forms of two glass *kodama* mounted one above the other on silver bases, suggesting the previously mentioned impaling of beads on the platforms of sculptured figures.

From the ceiling of this shrine hangs a canopy of thin silver (or white metal?) with long pendant strings combining minute plaques of very thin metal, embossed with the Wheel of the Law motif (*hōrin*), interspersed with strings of glass *kodama*.

Some of the many small *shari* in the *shari-tsubo* are various kinds of stone, but a few seem to be of glass.

- *Collection*: Tokuzen-ji, Daitoku-ji, Murasakino, Kyoto.
- *Provenance*: At least some of the beads are perhaps Chinese.
- *Date*: 1363, according to the inscription.
- *Size*: Smallest *kodama*, D. 0.15 cm.
- *Colors*: The glass *shari* are of a yellowish honey color and of an intense sky blue tone, both translucent. Some *kodama* are of yellow or honey color, both translucent; others are of blue, dark blue, dull dark terracotta, black, and an unctious white, all of them opaque.
- *Technique*: Coiled, but crudely, showing only two or three turns of the rod for each bead. Possibly this aspect suggests Chinese export.
- *Remarks*: The elaborate *yōraku* of this miniature shrine seem to refute the theory of simplicity and paucity of glass beads in *yōraku* of the Muromachi period; this canopy and that of

Sup. N. 65 seem exceptional. The canopy is surprisingly like that larger one of Hōryū-ji. Is the fact that both date from the early Teiji era merely coincidental, or could both have been from the same workshop?

67. *MIKOSHI* OF KUMANO-HATAYAMA SHRINE
Important Cultural Property
This shrine is one of the Ryōbu-Shintō type. The *mikoshi* was dedicated by Ashikaga Yoshimitsu.[1] It is said to be of black lacquer with gilt-bronze mountings and *yōraku* with "gems," a not unusual way of referring to glass beads. The author has had no opportunity of inspecting it but includes it as a record of the continuing use of such *yōraku*.
- *Collection*: Kumano-Hayatama Shrine, Jingū-machi, Shingū city, Wakayama Prefecture.
- *Date*: Dedicated in 1390.
- *Reference*:
1. *Art Guide of Nippon*, Vol. I (Nara, Mie, and Wakayama Prefectures), Tokyo, Society of Friends of Eastern Art, 1943, p. 411.

68. BEADS IN A PAIR OF *GYOKU-HAI*
National Treasure
Gyoku-hai are groups of glass beads strung on thin gold wire connecting perforated units of gilt-bronze,[1] hanging from the sash to below the knees. They were worn by the emperor and courtiers.
- *Collection*: Kumano-Hayatama Shrine, Jingū-machi, Shingū city, Wakayama Prefecture.
- *Provenance*: Pink glass has not been observed before the Muromachi period and may indicate importation.
- *Date*: Muromachi period (?).
- *Size*: L. of the *gyoku-hai*, 57.0 cm.
- *Bead colors*: Light pink, blue, green, yellow, purple, and white.
- *Reference*:
1. Jō Okada, text accompanying Fig. 322, *Nihon Bunkashi Taikei*, VII, p. 205. Illustrated in *Okada, Garasu, Pl. 73.

69. LACQUER INKSTONE BOX WITH GLASS INLAY
The design on the cover of this inkstone and

stationery box is of young pine and plum-blossom sprays in gold and silver, beneath which are two rotund jars and long silken cords. The upper jar is of applied silver, but the other is a piece of glass cut to the shape of a jar. Since small silver characters inlaid in the lacquer refer to an incident in the *Umega-e* ("A Branch of Plum") volume of the *Genji Mono-gatari*, in which pine and plum branches were attached to glass jars, this design is considered to be in direct reference to that passage.[1]

- *Collection*: Mr. Sōgo, Yamada, Tokyo. This box is said to have belonged to the Shogun Ashikaga Yoshimasa (1443–72).
- *Date*: Muromachi period.

GLASS INLAY:

- *Color*: Colorless glass, but placed over a bluish green pigment; transparent.
- *Technique*: A fragment of glass, now cracked, cut to the shape of one of the two jars in the design and inlaid in the lacquer over pigment. Two lines of white painted on the shoulder accentuate the spherical body of the jar.
- *Condition*: Excellent except for a slight crack.

Reference:
1. Data regarding this box is from *Okada, "Ruri Kirihame. . . ."

EDO PERIOD

70. SILVERED GLASS GLOBE

An unusually large hollow globe, thickly silvered on the interior; the effect is extremely luminous and reflecting—enough perhaps to frighten away any unwanted insect in an unscreened room. The principle is the same as that of the long narrow slips of plain or twisted aluminum foil that twirl in the breezes above American and Japanese fields in our own time. As a number of the globes may have hung in a room, some of colored glass, some filled with bits of tinsel, or silvered like this one, the result must have been very gay, especially as light summer breezes sweeping through the open Japanese house twirled and swung them about.

- *Collection*: Mr. Shirō Tonomura, Nagasaki.
- *Date*: Early 19th century. Tradition in the

owner's family has it that this was used in the Bunka-Bunsei eras (1804–29).
- *Size*: D. 38.1–46.0 cm.
- *Color*: Faintly green; transparent.
- *Technique*: Blown glass, with silvery coating inside.
- *Condition*: Excellent.

71. LARGE *TOMBODAMA*

- *Collection*: The Corning Museum of Glass (No. 63.6.73).
- *Date*: Edo period.
- *Size*: H. 1.6 cm.; D. 1.8 cm.
- *Colors*: Body, yellow, but cannot match. On the shoulders, bands of white with thin spiraled lines of red and pale blue; on the body proper, four scroll-like insets of pale green, rose, and white.
- *Bore*: D. 0.25 cm.
- *Technique*: Coiled, with decoration added; very glassy surface.
- *Condition*: Some cracked areas, and chipping at the bore ends.

72. EIGHT-LOBED *TOMBODAMA* WITH HORIZONTAL STRIPES

- *Collection*: The Corning Museum of Glass (No. 63.6.86).
- *Date*: Edo period.
- *Size*: H. 1.2 cm.; D. 1.25 cm.
- *Colors*: Body, pale yellow orange (IH.D.Refl.: *ca*. Ch 7, 6-4-18); opaque. Horizontal stripes, yellowish red (IH.D.Refl.: *ca*. Ch 3, 2-8-16); transparent.
- *Bore*: D. *ca*. 0.25 cm.
- *Technique*: Coiled; threads added, then the whole irregularly lobed with some implement, or in a pincer mold.
- *Condition*: Good.

73. *KŌGAI*

A flattened rod with body and head in oar shape; at the upper end a tiny bird form is affixed.
- *Collection*: The Corning Museum of Glass (No. 61.6.18).
- *Date*: Probably 19th century.
- *Size*: L. 10.3 cm.; W. 0.4 cm.; T. 0.2 cm.

• *Color*: Oar, colorless; transparent. Bird form, bright medium blue; translucent.
• *Composition*: Lead glass (ultraviolet fluorescense).
• *Technique*: Lampwork.
• *Condition*: Excellent.

74. *KŌGAI*

This *kōgai* has a very small earspoon head with a hollow sphere below it partially filled with water, and is therefore known as a *mizudama* ("water bead").
• *Collection*: The Corning Museum of Glass (No. 61.6.22).
• *Date*: Probably 19th century.
• *Size*: L. 11.0 cm.; D. 0.4 cm.; D. of sphere, 0.8 cm.
• *Color*: Colorless; transparent.
• *Technique*: Lampwork.
• *Condition*: Excellent.

75. MINIATURE POCKET SUNDIAL AND COMPASS

An example of the delicate craftsmanship sought after in the Edo period. This very small pocket case of black lacquer with the Tokugawa crest in the gold design comes from the burial of the sixth shogun, Tokugawa Ienobu. Perhaps both sundial and compass originally had glass covers, but only that of the compass remains. Possibly this was ground down from a glass fragment, or possibly it was a watch glass.
• *Date*: Ca. 1711.
• *Glass color*: Colorless; transparent.
• *Condition*: Slightly corroded.

76. MINIATURE MEDICINE VIAL

In a small brocaded pocket case are five small silver (pewter?) boxes incised with flower, animal, and bird motifs. These either contain pellets or are now empty, except for one that holds a very delicate, minute glass vial.
• *Collection*: Tokyo National Museum.
• *Date*: Edo period.
• *Size*: L. 1.45 cm.; greatest D. 0.65 cm.; neck D. 0.25 cm.; T. of glass at mouth, 0.05–0.075 cm.

• *Color*: Colorless; transparent.
• *Technique*: Blown.
• *Condition*: Good.
• *Remarks*: For another small pocket accessory, see Sup. N. 75.

77. *KOZUKA* HANDLE BY HIRATA NARI-SUKE

Decorated in relief with a scene of Mount Fuji and a pine grove. The *kozuka* is a small knife whose blade fitted into a pocket in the scabbard of the samurai sword. Together with the sword-guard and other sword fittings, it offered opportunity for expressing the skill of metal workers, and in this case of a cloisonné craftsman as well.
• *Collection*: The Toledo Museum of Art (No. 12.985).
• *Provenance*: Edo.
• *Date*: Edo period, *ca.* 1800. Signed: Hirata Narisuke, one of the Hirata family founded by Dōnin (see page 247). Narisuke died in 1816.
• *Size*: L. 9.85 cm.
• *Colors*: Green, red, brown, and white enamels.
• *Condition*: Excellent.

78. BLANK OF A CUP FOR CUTTING, RED OVERLAY

To make an article in colored cut glass, it was necessary to start with a basic uncolored form cased in glass of the desired color. The outer casing was then cut away in a pattern, which left areas of color projecting in relief from the colorless background. This cup seems to be an early, still uncut, example, before experience had perfected the distribution of the red color evenly in the casing.
• *Collection*: Kagoshima Municipal Art Museum, Kagoshima city.
• *Date*: Ca. 1855 (?). An early experimental piece.
• *Size*: H. 8.85 cm.; D. 9.7 cm.; T. at rim, 0.5 cm.
• *Color*: Dark red; splotchy, with areas appearing almost like sea moss, or as though painted in with a brush; somewhat translucent. This cup and a bottle, also of red-overlaid Satsuma cut glass, owned by Mr. Seikichi Makino of the

Nanshūdō, Tokyo, are the only two examples known to the author that display this uneven color distribution.
- *Composition*: Not analyzed, but the coloring agent is copper.
- *Technique*: Blown and cased.
- *Condition*: Excellent.

79. BLANK OF A BOWL FOR CUTTING, RED OVERLAY

This, like Sup. N. 78, demonstrates the first step in producing the "red *biidoro*" of Satsuma. But this specimen shows greater skill in the distribution of the color. A slight slip at the rim reveals the underlying body of colorless transparent glass, which is otherwise concealed by the red casing.
- *Collection*: Shūseikan, Iso-kōen, Kagoshima city (No. 1464/112-1).
- *Date*: 1856–59.
- *Size*: H. *ca.* 4.1 cm.; D. at rim, 19.7 cm.; T. at rim, 0.09 cm.
- *Color*: Dark red: somewhat translucent.
- *Bubbles*: Some small ones.
- *Composition*: Not analyzed, but the coloring agent is copper.
- *Technique*: Free blown and cased; pontil mark not removed.
- *Condition*: Excellent.
- *Remarks*: Comparison with the following bowls shows what might have been the result had this bowl been completed.

80. SMALL CUT GLASS BOWL WITH RED OVERLAY

The preceding bowl is the blank that was the starting point for a bowl of Satsuma red cut glass. With the red portions cut away where clear uncolored glass was desired, and the remaining red portions cross-hatched as motifs in relief, very interesting effects were obtained. The design on the exterior base consists of radiating grooves. Full data are wanting.
- *Collection*: Shūseikan, Iso-kōen, Kagoshima city.
- *Date*: 1856–58.
- *Color*: Colorless; transparent. Dark red; translucent.

- *Technique*: Free blown, cased, and cut. Highly polished.

81. SHALLOW CUT GLASS BOWL WITH RED OVERLAY

Similar to the above, except that this has an edging of alternating pointed and round scallops, and the base design is an eight-pointed star, common characteristics of Satsuma cut glass.
- *Collection*: Kagoshima Municipal Art Museum, Kagoshima city.
- *Date*: 1857–58.
- *Size*: H. *ca.* 3.9 cm.
- *Technique*: Free blown, cased, and cut.
- *Condition*: Excellent.

82. CUT GLASS BOTTLE WITH RED OVERLAY

An excellent example; similar to Plate 25 and Sup. N. 83, but differing in the cut design, which consists of adjacent triangular areas.
- *Collection*: Mr. Seikichi Makino of the Nanshū-dō, Tokyo.
- *Date*: 1856–58; earlier than in Sup. N. 83 and 84.
- *Color*: Red overlay, varying in thickness according to the cutting; translucent. The colorless ground, transparent. The red color, as in Sup. N. 78, is uneven and "mossy," indicating early experimental work.
- *Composition*: Not analyzed, but the coloring agent is copper.
- *Technique*: Free blown, cased, and cut. Highly polished.
- *Condition*: Excellent.
- *Remarks*: On the bottom the pontil mark was ground away, exposing a small circular area of uncolored glass. This was customary although usually, as in Plate 25 and Sup. N. 83, this area was enlarged.

83. CUT GLASS BRUSH HOLDER WITH RED OVERLAY

A rich, handsome piece of intricate cutting in hollows and short grooves. Subtle color variations, due to varying depths of the cutting and consequent interplay of reflected and transmitted light, give a brilliance that is enhanced by high polishing. The bottom exterior shows a somewhat irregular circular area where the pontil mark and some of the red overlay were ground away; this seems typical of all examples of this type.

- *Collection*: Shūseikan, Iso-kōen, Kagoshima city (No. 1352/2).
- *Date*: 1856–58.
- *Size*: H. 12.7 cm.; D. at mouth, *ca.* 6.7 cm.
- *Color*: Varying tones of red, from the very deep tone of the bottom rim to a carmine red; varying degrees of translucence. IH.D.Refl.: cannot match accurately because of reflections in the glass, but nearest Ch 2, 1-4-11 to 1-4-14. The colorless areas are transparent.
- *Bubbles*: Noticeable only with transmitted light. Some tiny circular ones; a few larger ones are oval horizontally and spirally. There is some slight pitting (from polishing?).
- *Composition*: Not analyzed, but the coloring agent is copper.
- *Technique*: Free blown, cased, and cut. Highly polished.
- *Condition*: Seemingly excellent, but there are many minute nicks and scratches (from difficulty in polishing the minutely cut areas?).

84. HEAVY TEABOWL
A thick and heavy ceremonial teabowl of glass, of such a curious nature as to suggest that it was thrown on a potter's wheel. The very thick wall and the clumsy spiraled mass accumulated at the bottom clearly suggest an attempted potting technique applied to an unmanageable medium, which solidified before the shape could be completed. The handling of glass metal on such potter's wheel even with heated tongs or paddles of wood, would be a formidable project, but the upper part of the bowl actually has the appearance of a receptacle formed while being rotated. The irregularly round disc foot was added subsequently.

- *Collection*: Shūseikan, Iso-kōen, Kagoshima city. Displayed with ceramic teabowls potted by Shimazu Nariakira.
- *Date*: Probably about 1856 or 1857.

- *Size*: H. 9.7–9.85 cm.; D. at lip, 10.6–11.4 cm.; T. at lip, 0.3–0.5 cm.
- *Color*: Gray in a mixed effect with some black flecks; translucent. Dr. Masao Mine of Kyushu University considered the glass metal to have derived its gray and black tones from added soot.
- *Bubbles*: Numerous, from minute circular ones to spirally elongated ones of some size and irregular shape, with some large bubblelike areas 0.7 to 3.25 cm. long. There are also spiraled striations.
- *Technique*: An attempt by Shimazu Nariakira at "potting" glass on a wheel.
- *Condition*: Good.

85. CUT GLASS SAKÉ CUP
The cutting is high and sharp near the rim, but decreases toward the bottom. The bottom, and a narrow area at the top, are uncut. A comparatively high foot flares outward at the bottom, which is slightly distorted.

- *Collection*: Yamaguchi Museum, Yamaguchi city. In 1954 the cup was given to this museum by the Omura family, through Mr. Nobura Uchida.
- *Provenance*: The storage box bears the legend: "Stonelike glass wine cup made in the medical institute of Hagi Castle, summer of Bunkyū 2 [1862]. Day of departure for Edo." (Masujirō Omura, to whom the cup was given, was later to become the first Minister of War in the Meiji government. The "Day of Departure for Edo" in 1862 may have referred to his leaving Hagi, in attendance upon his lord, for the *sankin kōtai*.)
- *Date*: 1862.
- *Size*: H. 4.9 cm.; D. at rim, 9.2 cm.
- *Color*: Colorless; transparent.
- *Bubbles*: One large one in the foot.
- *Technique*: Blown, cut and polished; foot attached.
- *Condition*: Cracked at the bottom.

86. HEAVY, FOOTED BOWL
- *Collection*: Mr. Masami Kawanabe, Kagoshima city.
- *Date*: Probably late Meiji, or even Taishō, era.

The form and combined colors place it in a later era rather than in the Satsuma period, to which it is traditionally assigned.

- *Size*: H. 15.2 cm.; D. 27.95–30.5 cm.
- *Color*: Bowl, amber color; transparent. Hollow foot, lightish green; transparent.
- *Technique*: Free blown; exterior of the bowl cut with wide, rounded facets. Twelve Satsuma crests lightly incised on the interior in a circle around the center.
- *Condition*: Excellent.

87. HEAVY CYLINDRICAL VASE OF FIVE RING-SHAPED UNITS

- *Collection*: Mr. Masami Kawanabe, Kagoshima city.
- *Date*: Meiji or Taishō eras.
- *Size*: H. 20.0 cm.; the circular units increase regularly in their heights, from top to bottom.
- *Color*: Rich dark blue; translucent.
- *Technique*: Cast in a mold; on the upper surface of the next to the bottom unit, eight Satsuma crests are lightly incised; for discussion of this see pages 245.
- *Condition*: Excellent.

88. CUT GLASS BOWL

- *Collection*: The Corning Museum of Glass (No. 61.6.35)
- *Date*: Meiji era. The slightly grayish tone of this bowl places it in the early Meiji era, but whether it originated in Tokyo or Osaka is not known.
- *Size*: H. 11.1 cm.; D. at rim, 24.5 cm.
- *Color*: Colorless, but with a slightly gray tone.
- *Bubbles*: Near the rim a number of very small circular ones; a few stones.
- *Composition*: Lead glass (ultraviolet fluorescence).
- *Technique*: Free blown and cut.
- *Condition*: Excellent.

89. GLASS PAPERWEIGHT WITH INNER SPIRALS

Within the rod are two intertwined spirals, one broad and one slender. Neither emerges on the end surfaces, stopping just short. The ends are well finished, with narrow bevels. The un-even spirals and bumpy surface suggest the work of an experimenter.

- *Collection*: The Corning Museum of Glass (No. 61.6.24).
- *Provenance*: Although there has been no previous assignation for this, it seems that it may be a product of the Shinagawa factory, which was interested in attempting spiral decoration.
- *Date*: Meiji era.
- *Size*: L. 19.3 cm.; D. 1.2–1.3 cm.
- *Color*: Colorless; transparent. Threads, purplish blue; opaque.
- *Composition*: Transparent ground, lead glass (ultraviolet fluorescence).
- *Technique*: Drawn from a small gather of glass to which two dabs of blue glass, one larger than the other, had been applied, then twisted.
- *Condition*: Excellent.

90. DOUBLE-WALLED TUMBLER

A tumbler of "hario" glass designed to keep cold drinks cold and hot drinks hot.

- *Date*: 1963.
- *Color*: Colorless; transparent.
- *Composition*: Heat-resistant glass.
- *Technique*: Blown with a *tomosao*. Patented double walls enclosing "dry air of pressure."
- *Remarks*: As an experimental forerunner of this the author, in 1960, was offered hot tea in a lighter-weight, double-walled cup with a delicate floral spray in enamels on the exterior.

91. VARIEGATED SAKÉ CUP

Identified by Mr. Nakashima as his work previous to 1939, when the Fukuoka Art Glass Company was organized.

- *Collection*: The Toledo Museum of Art (No. 55.65).
- *Date*: Shōwa era, before 1939.
- *Size*: H. 2.9 cm.; D. at rim, 5.15–5.30 cm.; T. of wall at lip, 0.1 cm.
- *Color*: The body, at first glance, seems chiefly opaque green and browns, but when held against the light the basic color is seen to be transparent red in which green and browns show up as swirls spiraling up to the rim from an off-center point in the base. The base ring is an opaque darkish green.

- *Bubbles*: In the red glass, many, chiefly circular but some oval; in the green and yellow brown, they are like minute bumps on the opaque surface both inside and outside the cup.
- *Technique*: Free blown with foot-rim added.

92. VASE

Vase of thick body tapering to the rim; spiraling stripes of color.
- *Collection*: The Corning Museum of Glass (No. 61.6.42); Gift of the Fukuoka Art Glass Company.
- *Date*: 1960.
- *Size*: H. 22.8 cm.; D. at rim, 7.7 cm.
- *Color*: Ground, greenish honey color; transparent. Stripes, deep purple; IH. difficult to match.
- *Bubbles*: Several, elongated, adjoining the stripes.
- *Technique*: Free blown with dots of color applied to the gather. Bottom slightly hollowed with narrow border ground flat.

APPENDIX–CHEMICAL CONSIDERATIONS

ROBERT H. BRILL

THE USUAL reasons for undertaking chemical studies of early glasses are to classify them according to possible places and periods of manufacture or to make comparisons among objects in order to establish whether or not they have a common origin. The first objective requires large numbers of analyses in order that inferences drawn from the findings have statistical significance, while the other requires the framing beforehand of some very specific questions involving particular objects.

Although some two thousand or more reliable chemical analyses have been made of early glasses in general, all of the analyses of East Asian glasses combined, representing a wide range of date and provenance, probably number fewer than one hundred. Therefore, the analysis of early East Asian glasses is still in an exploratory stage, and it is difficult at present to make generalizations concerning the compositions of these glasses beyond noting the frequent use of lead, the high barium content of certain Chinese glasses, and an apparently earlier use of potash (K_2O) than occurred in the West. This is not to say, of course, that these analyses are not useful. On the contrary, they show promise that systematic analyses of further examples of East Asian glasses may reveal compositional patterns that could prove very useful. One notes, for example, the variations in concentrations of minor elements such as titanium and aluminum, in trace elements, and in relative proportions of sodium and potassium. The prospects are all the more attractive because of the possibilities of relating glass compositions to what is known from literary sources concerning other facets of early technology and science in East Asia.

Because of the observations above, the aim of this appendix has been limited to the simple assembling of some of those analyses of Japanese glasses. No attempt will be made to modify or add to the interpretations of the original investigations.

The routine chemical analyses applied to early glasses are of two types: quantitative wet-chemical analyses, requiring the sacrifice of substantial samples of glass, and spectrographic analyses, which, although they consume only very small samples, yield only semiquantative or qualitative results. Most of the analyses included here are of one or the other of these types. Other techniques now being used for glass analysis provide accurate information on smaller samples and do so more conveniently and quickly,[1] particularly, neutron-activation analysis and two types of X-ray fluorescense analysis. It should be noted, however, that there is no one method of analysis that is always the best. Different problems may best be solved by different methods of analysis. In connection with the question of lead it is well to note that, where it is of special interest, lead contents of glasses can be estimated by specific gravity determinations, which can for most objects be done completely nondestructively. Lead contents can also be estimated by refractive index measurements, and the presence or absence of lead can be determined by examination under ultraviolet light, chemical spot-tests, or by radiography.

Another area deserving attention is the identification of opacifiers (or colorant opacifiers), especially in the yellow and white opaque glasses. Such identifications can be done by X-ray diffraction, which is an important ancillary technique to chemical analysis, or in certain cases by nondestructive X-ray fluorescence analysis. Colorant opacifiers have already been thoroughly studied in early Western glasses and in a few specimens of East Asian glasses.[2] A more comprehensive study of East Asian glasses would certainly be worthwhile.

One of the most interesting facets of glass is color. Among the Japanese glasses catalogued here, and those described in the analyses, are but a few that are truly colorless. Perhaps the most common colors are the transparent blues: a dark blue produced by cobalt, and lighter blues from copper. When copper is present in an alkali-lime-silica glass, under oxidizing conditions, it goes into solution, producing the familiar blue color. If the glass contains a substantial portion of lead, as do many of the glasses of concern here, copper confers a green transparent color instead. Several examples are apparent in the following analyses. If a copper-containing glass is subjected in the molten state to strongly reducing conditions, the copper is reduced to cuprous oxide (Cu_2O), which may precipitate from the glass in the form of minute bright red crystals. These confer a bright red opaque color to the glass, or under slightly different conditions, an orange or brownish color. (This precipitation can take place in the alkali-lime-silica glasses, but it does so more readily where lead is present). The chemistry of these processes and the place such glasses played in ancient glasses from the West is beginning to be understood, but it would be very interesting to know the history of these red opaque glasses in East Asia. Because cuprous oxide is so sensitive to reoxidation in hot glass, even a few seconds of exposure to air may take it back into solution, producing local regions of transparent greenish glass. These appear as dark striations in finished objects, for example the beads of Plate 59 and Supplementary Note 27.

Some of the green transparent glasses mentioned in the analyses owe their color to iron, which is always present to some extent as an impurity in early glasses. In examples of stronger colors, iron was probably added as an intentional colorant. Under reducing conditions, with the presence of sulfur, the iron can produce a transparent amber color in glasses. These so-called carbon ambers were made in very early times in the West and have been in nearly continuous use up to the present day. Some examples are found among the analyses that follow.

A special word of caution should be raised concerning analyses of beads. Beads are ubiquitous, and literally millions of beads were made in early periods. They were made in different regions and traveled widely. This is at once the most appealing reason for analysing beads but at the same time the most compelling reason for applying restraint in the interpretation of the results of small numbers of such analyses. It is all too easy to be misled into conclusions that may not hold up as larger numbers of analyses are carried out. Here, as much as in any scientific research, one must state very precisely just what the samples and analyses represent, and limit one's conclusions accordingly. Among the complicating factors are the reuse of glass salvaged from earlier uses, and inhomogeneity, for the glasses employed for the making of the most ordinary beads did not have to be of particularly high quality. Both of these factors are expected to make the variability among the compositions of beads produced by any one workshop somewhat greater than the corresponding variability among vessels made of glass.

The frequent occurrence of lead in Japanese glasses, particularly in such abundant quantities, also suggests the application of another type of scientific investigation. It has been shown recently that the determination of isotope ratios of the lead contained in archaeological objects can be used to trace possible geographic sources of the lead.[3] This technique is applicable to metallic leads, alloys, pigments, glazes, and lead-containing glasses. Even though specific mining regions may not be uniquely identified by such determination, it is still possible to gain useful information by classifying objects according to similarities and differences.

In summary, the prospects for learning worthwhile information about Japanese and other East Asian glasses by various types of scientific studies look most promising. The pressing need is for well-dated and well-authenticated specimens of glasses that can be investigated. Curators and collectors should therefore feel encouraged to contact those analysts and laboratories that are conducting such analyses.

References:
1. For a general review of analytical methods and other techniques, see R. H. Brill, "The Scientific Investigation of Early Glasses," *Proceedings of the Eighth International Congress on Glass, 1968*, Sheffield, 1969, pp. 47–68.
2. A. E. Werner and M. Bimson, *Advances in Glass Technology*, Part 2, Plenum Press, 1963, pp. 303–305.
3. R. H. Brill and J. M. Wampler, "Isotope Studies of Ancient Lead," *American Journal of Archaeology*, 71, No. 1, January, 1967, pp. 63–77.

———, "Isotope Ratios in Archaeological Objects of Lead," *Application of Science in Examination of Works of Art*, Boston Museum of Fine Arts, 1965, pp. 155–166.

R. H. Brill, "Lead Isotopes in Ancient Glass," *Annales du 4ᵐᵉ Congrès des Journées Internationales du Verre*, Liège, 1969, pp. 255–61.

TABLE I

Object: *Kodama* from ancient tombs. A: from Nishi-tsubara, Koya-gun, Ōita Prefecture; light blue. B: from Mt. Mino, Teki-gun, Kyoto Prefecture; blue green. C: from Futago-zuka, Teki-gun, Kyoto Prefecture; dark purplish blue.
Date: Tomb period.

	Bead A	Bead B	Bead C
SiO_2	60.50	64.17	66.22
Al_2O_3	7.87	11.23	2.97
Fe_2O_3	2.03	1.63	1.30
CaO	3.30	3.40	7.33
MgO	0.70	0.57	3.27
MnO	0.77	0.33	0.50
Na_2O	15.42	13.41	14.36
K_2O	3.43	4.99	2.98
PbO	—	—	—
CuO	1.05	0.87	—
CoO	—	—	0.47
	95.07%	100.60%	99.40%
Sp. Grav.:	<2.5	<2.34	<2.48

References: Dr. Manzō Nakao, quoted by *Asahina, "Kodai Garasu. . . . ," p. 67.
*Yamasaki, Miwa, Ohashi, "Kofun Shutsudo Garasu. . . . ," p. 29.

TABLE II

Object: *Kodama*: greenish blue; transparent. IH.D.Refl.: Ch 3, 14-6-17.
Provenance: Ishiyama Tomb, Inako-mura, Naga-gun, Mie Prefecture; excavated by Dr. Yukio Kobayashi, Archaeological Research Institute, Kyoto University. In The Corning Museum of Glass there are fragments from this group (No. 63.6.116). Gift of Dr. Yukio Kobayashi.
Date: ca. 400 A.D.

SiO_2	74.80
Al_2O_3	3.26
Fe_2O_3	n.d.
CaO	—
Na_2O	1.41
K_2O	14.85
PbO	1.46
CuO	1.35
	97.13%
Ignition Loss	2.76
Sp. Grav.:	2.3471
Refr. Ind.:	1.494

Analysis by M. T. Watson, Jr., through Paul W. Close, General Research Division, Owens-Illinois Glass Company, Toledo, Ohio.

TABLE III

Object: Two *kodama*. A: light green; opaque. B: strong blue; transparent.
Provenance: Hakusanyabu Tomb, Donomae, Ajima, Kita-ku, Nagoya; excavated by Dr. Eiji Nakayama, Nanzan University, Nagoya.
Date: 4th century A.D.

	Bead A	Bead B
SiO_2	60.47	65.60
Al_2O_3	12.04	4.01
Fe_2O_3	0.18	0.24
TiO_2	0.34	0.09
MnO	0.56	0.004
CaO	6.68	7.18
MgO	0.42	2.43
Na_2O	14.91	15.63
K_2O	3.67	3.47
PbO	0.27	0.07
CuO	0.42	0.24
CoO	—	0.003
SO_3	0.17	0.44
	100.13%	100.24%
Sp. Grav.:	2.40	2.49
Refr. Ind.:	1.502[†]	1.505[†]

[†]Immersion Method

Reference: *Yamasaki, Miwa, Ohashi, "Kofun Shutsudo Garasu. . . ," p. 29.

TABLE IV

Object: *Magatama*, pale greenish blue.
Provenance: A tomb in Tohaku-gun, Tottori Prefecture.
Date: Tomb period.

SiO_2	55.7
Al_2O_3	12.7
Fe_2O_3	0.7
CaO	11.7
MgO	0.97
Na_2O	16.9
K_2O	2.2
CuO	—
CoO	—
PbO	—
BaO	—
Sp. Grav. (apparent):	2.5

Reference: *Yamasaki, "Namari Garasu to Sōda Garasu," p. 21, Table II(5).

TABLE V

Objects: Beads and bead fragments. From Site 8: No. 6, fragment, yellow, opaque; No. 7, fragment, blue, transparent; No. 8, bead, dark blue, transparent. From Site 7: No. 9, bead, green, opaque; No. 10, bead, green, opaque; No. 11, fragment, blue, transparent; No. 12, bead, orange, opaque.

Provenance: Ritual sites of Okitsu-gū, the island shrine of Munakata Shrine, Munakata-gun, Fukuoka Prefecture.

Date: Tomb period.

	No. 6.	No. 7.	No. 8.	No. 9.	No. 10.	No. 11.	No. 12.
Al_2O_3	5.52	5.40	4.28	5.84	5.12	5.42	5.32
Fe_2O_3	2.04	1.35	1.66	2.59	2.26	1.52	1.69
TiO_2	1.0	1.0	0.5>	0.7	0.7	0.5>	1.0
CaO	0.96	—	2.99	—	2.15	—	—
MgO	1.23	—	1.15	—	1.01	—	—
K_2O	1.12	2.77	1.97	1.42	1.79	2.97	3.0
Na_2O	20.9	22.7	20.5	15.8	16.2	23.1	14.1

Note: The lead content, by weight, was estimated as 10>; trace elements found include Cd, Cu, Mn, Ni, Sn, and V.

Reference: *Mine and Senba, "Chikuzen Okinoshima Shutsudo. . . ." This includes much detail regarding methods used and the trace elements, as well as reproductions of spectrographs.

TABLE VI

Object: Fragment of flat glass: green; translucent. See Plate 48; also the beads of Plate 58 fabricated from the same glass.

Provenance: Precincts of Miyajidake Shrine, Fukuoka Prefecture.

Date: Tomb period.

SiO_2	23.09
PbO	75.43
Al_2O_3	0.70
Fe_2O_3	0.07
CaO	0.05
MgO	0.14
Na_2O	trace
K_2O	0.79
CuO	0.42
CoO	—
BaO	—

Reference: *Yamasaki, "Namari Garasu to Sōda Garasu," p. 20, Table II(4). See also *Oda, "Miyajidake-jinja . . . ," p. 20, where X-ray fluorescence analysis is given for this.

TABLE VII

Object: Cinerary urn: dark green; transparent. See Plate 3.
Provenance: Burial in the precincts of Miyajidake Shrine, Tsuyazaki-machi, Munakata-gun, Fukuoka Prefecture.
Date: Uncertain; probably 7th century.

SiO_2	(not mentioned)
PbO	35.38†
Al_2O_3	10.07
Fe_2O_3	1.01
CaO	2.15
MgO	0.06
CuO	9.44‡
Refr. Ind.:	1.577

† The sample presented for testing was weathered-glass dust, which probably accounts for the low lead level, since a later sample, from the unweathered bottom of the urn, indicated, by X-ray fluorescence, a specific gravity of 5.

‡ The excessively high copper content is due to an admixture of copper dust from the outer bronze container (*Yamasaki, "Garasu," p. 399).

Reference: *Umehara, "Nihon Kodai no Garasu," p. 26, quoting Dr. Kazuo Yamasaki. See also *Oda, "Miyaji-dake-jinja. . . . ," p. 20.

TABLE VIII

Objects: Beads. A: light blue. B: yellowish brown. See Supplementary Note 49.
Provenance: Mummy of Fujiwara no Motohira in the Konjiki-dō of Chūson-ji, Hiraizumi, Iwate Prefecture.
Date: 12th century.

	Bead A	Bead B
SiO_2	39.32	34.58
Al_2O_3	0.05	1.69
Fe_2O_3	0.16	2.89
CaO	0.48	trace
MgO	—	trace
Na_2O	3.38	2.31
K_2O	7.89	10.26
PbO	47.45	47.81
CuO	0.49	—
SO_3	0.29	0.21
	99.48%	99.62%
Sp. Grav.:	3.76	3.80
Refr. Ind.:	1.640	1.650

Reference: *Asahina, "Kodai Garasu no Kenkyū," p. 68.

TABLE IX

Object: Tumbler-shaped wine cup: green; transparent. Others of this set are in The Toledo Museum of Art (Nos. 54.69 A-I). See Plate 152.
Date: Edo period

SiO_2	41.48
Al_2O_3	0.55
Fe_2O_3	0.041
CaO	2.98
MgO	0.44
Na_2O	2.00
K_2O	10.76
PbO	40.12
CuO	0.95
Ignition Loss	0.40
	99.72%
Sp. Grav.:	3.00
Refr. Ind.:	1.634

Analysis by M. T. Watson, Jr., through Paul W. Close, General Research Division, Owens-Illinois Glass Company, Toledo, Ohio.

TABLE X

Object: Fluted cup: colorless; transparent. Two other cups of this set are in The Toledo Museum of Art (No. 53.154 A and B). See Plate 153.
Date: Edo period.

SiO_2	43.02
Al_2O_3	0.12
Fe_2O_3	0.15
CaO	0.36
MgO	0.17
Na_2O	1.13
K_2O	9.17
PbO	45.28
Ignition Loss	0.10
	100.30%
Sp. Grav.:	3.00
Refr. Ind.:	1.624

Analysis by M. T. Watson, Jr., through Paul W. Close, General Research Division, Owens-Illinois Glass Company, Toledo, Ohio.

TABLE XI

Object: Covered bowl: colorless with slight greenish tone; transparent. Two other bowls of this set are in The Toledo Museum of Art (No. 53.155 A and B). See Plate 156.
Date: Edo period.

SiO$_2$	41.48
Al$_2$O$_3$	0.07
Fe$_2$O$_3$	0.12
CaO	0.12
MgO	0.09
Na$_2$O	0.08
K$_2$O	8.42
PbO	49.60
Ignition Loss	0.20
	100.18%
Sp. Grav.:	3.00
Refr. Ind. ND:	1.645

Analysis by M. T. Watson, Jr., through Paul W. Close, General Research Division, Owens-Illinois Glass Company, Toledo, Ohio.

TABLE XII

Objects: Parts of the glass ornaments of the *kasaboko* of Imauo-machi, Nagasaki (Pl. 157). Fragments are in The Corning Museum of Glass. No. 63.6.64, fish basket cord, dark blue; No. 63.6.18–19, reeds, green; No. 63.6.23I, fish basket, yellow; No. 63.6.21, fish scales, colorless; No. 63.6.22, bamboo pole, blue green.
Date: Edo period; mid 19th century(?).

No.	63.6.64	63.6.18–19	63.6.23I	63.6.21	63.6.22
PbO	64.00	63.00	70.00	69.00	51.00
SiO$_2$	32.00	33.00	28.00	31.00	36.09
Al$_2$O$_3$	0.10	0.15	0.09	0.18	0.03
CuO	0.02	0.60	—	—	1.58
Fe$_2$O$_3$					0.26
CaO					0.41
MgO					0.03
Na$_2$O					0.13
K$_2$O					8.47

References: *Yamasaki, "Nagasaki Suwa-jinja Matsuri. . . . ," p. 39. Spectrographic analyses with possible errors of ± 6%.
For No. 63.6.22: *Yamasaki, "Garasu," p. 404, Chart 6.

TABLE XIII

Object: Engraved covered bowl: colorless; transparent. In The Toledo Museum of Art there is a companion bowl (No. 54.67). See Plate 215.
Date: Early Meiji era.

SiO_2	70.86
Al_2O_3	3.31
Fe_2O_3	0.095
CaO	8.75
MgO	0.13
Na_2O	15.46
K_2O	1.58
PbO	—
Ignition Loss	N.D.
	100.185%
Sp. Grav.:	2.4905
Refr. Ind. ND:	1.518

Analysis by M. T. Watson, Jr., through Paul W. Close, General Research Division, Owens-Illinois Glass Company, Toledo, Ohio.

Edo Period Japanese Provinces

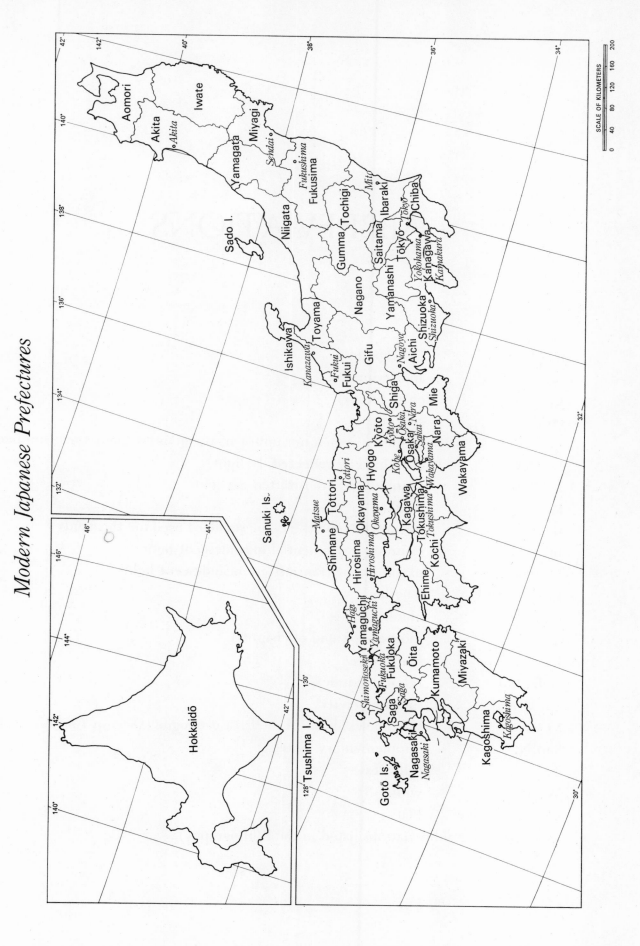

Modern Japanese Prefectures

Aomori
Akita
Akita
Iwate
Yamagata
Miyagi
Sendai
Fukushima
Fukusima
Sado I.
Niigata
Gumma
Tochigi
Mito
Ibaraki
Saitama
Tōkyō
Tōkyō
Chiba
Kamakura
Nagano
Yamanashi
Kanagawa
Yokohama
Shizuoka
Shizuoka
Toyama
Ishikawa
Kanazawa
Gifu
Aichi
Nagoya
Fukui
Fukui
Shiga
Kyōto
Kyōto
Osaka
Ōsaka
Mie
Nara
Sakai
Nara
Tottori
Tottori
Hyōgo
Kōbe
Wakayama
Wakayama
Sanuki Is.
Matsue
Shimane
Okayama
Okayama
Kagawa
Tokushima
Tokushima
Hiroshima
Hiroshima
Kōchi
Ehime
Hagi
Yamaguchi
Yamaguchi
Shimonoseki
Fukuoka
Fukuoka
Ōita
Miyazaki
Saga
Saga
Kumamoto
Nagasaki
Nagasaki
Gotō Is.
Kagoshima
Kagoshima
Kagoshima
Tsushima I.
Hokkaidō

SCALE OF KILOMETERS
0 40 80 120 160 200

ABBREVIATIONS

C.	Centigrade
ca.	approximately
Ch	chart (color)
cm.	centimeter
D.	diameter; when not uniform, the greatest diameter is implied
D. Refl.	examined by reflected daylight
D. Trans.	examined by transmitted daylight
H.	height
IH.	Iro no Hyōjun; the color standard used for this study
In. Refl.	examined by reflected incandescent light
In. Trans.	examined by transmitted incandescent light
L.	length
m.	meter
n.	footnote (at end of chapter)
PL. N.	Plate Note
Refr. Ind.	refractive index
Sp. Grav.	specific gravity
STM	the official Shōsō-in shelf list catalogue (*Shōsō-in Tanawake Mokuroku*)
Sup.N.	Supplementary Note
T.	thickness
W.	width
Pl.	Plate

(See also other abbreviations listed in the Bibliography)

BIBLIOGRAPHY

The Bibliography includes only those titles dealing specifically with Japanese glass, or containing extended or significant passages relating thereto. In the footnotes such references are cited only by the surname of the author, an abbreviated title, and the page reference; in each case an asterisk precedes the name. Other, more general, references cited only in footnotes are there given in full.

A few publications that recur frequently have been given abbreviated initials.

Many titles are in the library of The Corning Museum of Glass, either complete or as photostatic excerpts.

ABBREVIATIONS

DNK   *Dai Nippon Komonjo* [Ancient Documents of Japan]

ECTS   Jirō Harada, *English Catalogue of Treasures in the Imperial Repository Shōsō-in*

KK   *Kobunkazai no Kagaku* (English title: *Scientific Papers on Japanese Antiques and Art Crafts*)

KKZ   *Kōkogakuzasshi* [Journal of Archaeology]

KTDKH   *Kyōto Teikoku Daigaku Bungaku-bu Kōkogaku Kenkyū-shitsu Hōkoku* [Report of the Archaeological Research Institute. Faculty of Letters, Kyoto Imperial University]

NKYS   *Nihon Kinsei Yōgyōshi* [History of the Modern Ceramic Industry of Japan], IV—*Garasu Kōgyō* [The Glass Industry]

SGZ   *Shōsō-in Gyobutsu Zuroku* [Illustrated Catalogue of Imperial Treasures in the Shōsō-in]

SGZC   *Shōsō-in Gyobutsu Zaishitsu Chōsa* [Investigation of the Materials of the Imperial Treasures of the Shōsō-in]

SnG   *Shōsō-in no Garasu* [Glass Objects of the Shōsō-in]

STM   *Shōsō-in Tanawake Mokuroku* [Catalogue of the Shōsō-in According to Shelf Locations]

TASJ   Transactions of The Asiatic Society of Japan

Aida, Hironobu. "Shōsō-in Gyobutsu (Ōgon Ruri Den-hai Jū-ni-kyoku-kyō ni tsuite)" [Imperial Treasure of the Shōsō-in—A Twelve-lobed Mirror with Back Decorated with Gold and Glass], *Geppō*, 1951, pp. 1–4, illus.

Aizawa, Masahiko. "Sennan Garasu-kōgyōshi" [History of the Glass Industry in Sennan (in modern Osaka Prefecture)]. *Keizaishi Kenkyū* [Studies in Economic History], pp. 441–449. Tokyo: Nihon Hyōronsha, 1941.

Asahina, Tei-ichi. "Kodai Garasu no Kenkyū" [Study of Ancient Glass]. *Tōgyō Kyōkai Shi*, LXI, 685 (July 1953), pp. 66–71, illus.

Asahina, Tei-ichi; Aida, Gundayu; and Oda, Sachiko. "Chūson-ji Garasu no Kenkyū to Nihon no Kodai Garasu ni tsuite" English title: "Antique Glass from Chūson-ji Temple and a General Consideration of Ancient Japanese Glass." *KK*, No. 5 (March 1953), pp. 1–6, illus.

Asahina, Tei-ichi, and Oda, Sachiko. "Nihon Kodai Garasudama no Sekkei ni tsuite" [Shaping of Ancient Japanese Glass Beads]. *KK*, No. 7 (March 1954), pp. 10–13.

———. "Shōsō-in Hagyoku oyobi Kunaicho Shoryō-bu Hokan no Kofun Shutsudo Garasudama ni tsuite" (English title: "Studies on Some Fragments of Beads among the Glass Antiques Kept at the Shōsō-in Treasury and On Glass Beads Excavated from Ancient Tombs and Kept at the Archives and

Mausolea Division, Imperial Household Agency"). No. 9 (December 1954), pp. 1–10, illus.

Asahina, Tei-ichi; Yamazaki, Fumio; Ōtsuka, Iwao; Hamada, Tatsuji; Saitō, Kiyohiro; and Oda, Sachiko. "Tōshōdai-ji Haku-ruri Shari-bin narabini Denkō-ji Heki-ruri Shari-tsubo ni tsuite" (English title: "On the Ancient Glass of Śarīra Colourless Glass Bottle from Tōshōdai-ji Temple, and Śarīra Blue Glass Bowl from Denkō-ji Temple"). *KK*, No. 6 (September 1953), pp. 14–18, illus.

Asahina, Tei-ichi; Yamazaki, Fumio; and Yamasaki, Kazuo. "Investigation of Antique Relics by Means of Beta-ray Back Scattering." In *United Nations Educational, Scientific and Cultural Organization, International Conference on Radio-Isotopes in Scientific Research* (Unesco /NS / RIG/64), pp. 2–4, illus.

Asakura, Fumio. "Kako no Garasu Geijutsu" [The Art of Old Glass], *Chawan*, VII, 8 (No. 78; December 1937), pp. 2–8, illus.

Ashikaga, Otomaru. "Garasu Setsu" [Explanation of Glass], *Kōko Sōshi*, II (January 31, 1892), Sect. 7, pp. 1–5, illus.

Asuka-dera Hakkutsu Chōsa Hōkoku [Report of the Investigation and Excavation at the Temple Asuka-dera]. Nara National Institute of Cultural Properties. Kyoto, Shinyōsha, 1958.

Awashima, Masakichi. "Garasu-ki Zakkai" [Sundry Explanations of Glass Vessels]. *Mizue*, No. 612 (July 1956), pp. 59–72, illus. From an Exhibition of Chien-lung, Satsuma, and European glass.

Baba, Sajurō, trans. *Biidoro Seihō Shusetsu* [Glassmaking Methods Explained]. Edo: 1810.

Biidoroya Uhei Den [Biography of Biidoroya Uhei]. *Fukuoka*, No. 53, Fukuoka, 1931.

Blair, Dorothy. "East Asiatic Glass, Part III, Japan." *The Glass Industry*, XXXII, 9 (1951), pp. 459–462.

———. "Letter to the Editor." *Journal of Glass Studies*, V (1963), pp. 156–160. Concerning the dating of the cloisonné backed mirror of the Shōsō-in.

———. "The Cloisonné Backed Mirror in the Shōsō-in." *Journal of Glass Studies*, II (1960), pp. 82–93, illus.

——— (unsigned). *Exhibition of East Asiatic Glass*. Toledo: The Toledo Museum of Art, 1948.

Bowes, James L. *Japanese Enamels*. London: B. Quaritch, 1886 (also privately printed, 1884).

———. *Notes on Shippō, A Sequel to "Japanese Enamels."* London: Kegan Paul, Trench, Trubner & Co., Ltd., 1895.

Chait, Ralph M. "Letter to the Editor." *Journal of Glass Studies*, V (1963), pp. 155–156. Concerning the cloisonné backed mirror in the Shōsō-in.

———. "Some Comments on the Dating of Early Chinese Cloisonné." *Oriental Art*, First Series. III, No. 2 (1950), pp. 67–78, illus.

Dai Nihon Komonjo [Ancient Documents of Japan]. Tokyo: Tokyo Daigaku Shiryō Hensansho (Historiographical Institute of Tokyo University), 1901.

Dei, Akeari (?). "Giyaman, Biidoro Sadan" [Notes on *Giyaman* and *Biidoro*]. *Nihon Bijutsu Kōgei*, No. 250 (July 1959), pp. 19–28, illus.

Fujino, Katsuya. "Shōsō-in Zonzō Ryoku-hari Jū-ni-kyoku Chōhai no Shokumoyō" [The Plant Design of the Twelve-lobed Long Green Glass Cup Preserved in the Shōsō-in]. *Kodaigaku Kenkyū*, No. 10 (1954), pp. 29–30, illus.

Fujisawa, Kazuo. "Ankan Tennō Ryō Hakken no Haku-ruri Wan" [The White Glass Bowl Discovered at the Tomb of Emperor Ankan]. *Shiseki to Bijutsu*, No. 207 (November 1, 1950), pp. 303–309, illus.

———. "Ruri-wan no Kyōi—Ankan Teiryō Shutsu-do" [A Sensational Glass Bowl Relic from the Imperial Tomb of Ankan]. *Ashikabi* No. 1 (April 1, 1951), pp. 15–19, illus.

Fukai, Shinji. "A Persian Treasure in the Shōsō-in Repository." *Japan Quarterly*, VIII, 2, (April–June, 1960), pp. 169–175, illus.

———. "Giran-shū Shutsudo no Nijū Enkei Kiriko-sei Kazari Ruri-wan ni Kansuru Ikkōsetsu—Kyoto Kamigamo Shutsudo no Ruri-wan Hahen ni Taisuru Shiken" [On a Glass Bowl with Decoration of Doubled Circular Facets Excavated in Gilan—In Relation to a Fragment of Glass Bowl found at Kamigamo, Kyoto]. *The Memoirs of the Institute of Oriental Culture*, No. 45. Tokyo: March 1968, pp. 309–327, illus. English summary.

———. "Shōsō-in Hōmotsu Hakururi-wan Kō—Giran-shū Shutsudo no Ruri-wan ni Taisuru Miken" [Study of the White Glass Bowl among the Treasures of the Shōsō-in—My Views Contrasting it with the Glass Bowls Discovered in Gilan Province], *Kokka*, LXVIII, 11 (No. 812; 1959), pp. 401–413, illus.

———. *Study of Iranian Art and Archaeology—Glassware and Metalwork*. Tokyo; Yoshikawa Kobunkan, 1968, illus. English summary.

Fukuyama, Toshio. Remarks on the glass relics, in *Hōryū-ji Gojū-no-tō Hihō no Chōsa*, q.v., p. 23.

Furuya, Kiyoshi. "Hompō Jōdai Garasu ni Kansuru Shin-Kenkyū" [New Studies on Ancient Glass in Japan]. *KK* Pt. 1, II, 7 (March 1912), pp. 404–411; Pt. 2, II, 8 (April 1912), pp. 487–495; Pt. 3, II, 12 (August 1912), pp. 748–753; Pt. 4, III, 3 (November 1912), pp. 147–152; Pt. 5, III, 4 (December 1912), pp. 203–208; Pt. 6, III, 12 (August 1913), pp. 703–713.

Garasu no Sekaishi [International Glass History]. Tokyo National Museum, Cultural Series, No. 5.

Garner, Sir Harry. *Chinese and Japanese Cloisonné Enamels*. The Arts of the East, edited by Basil Gray. London: Faber and Faber, 1962.

Goodman, Grant K. "A Translation of Ōtsuki Gentaku's *Ransetsu Benwaku*." Occasional Papers, Center for Japanese Studies, University of Michigan, No. 3. Ann Arbor: University of Michigan Press, 1952, pp. 71–99.

Gotō, Shuichi (Morikazu). "Waga Jōko Jidai ni okeru Garasu" [Glass in Remote Antiquity in Japan]. *KKZ*, XVII, No. 12 (December 1927), pp. 761–790, illus.

Gotō, Toshihiko. "Shōsō-in Gyobutsu Kinkō-hin no Chokinteki Chōsa" [Investigation of the Chasing Technique of Metalwares in the Shōsō-in]. *Shoryō-bu Kiyō*, No. 5 (March 1955), illus. The cloisonné backed mirror discussed on pp. 70–73.

Hamada, Kōsaku, and Umehara, Sueji. *Keishū Kinkan-tsuka to Sono Ihō* (English title: *A Royal Tomb "Kinkantsuka" or the Gold Crown Tomb at Keishū and Its Treasures*). Government General of Chōsen [Korea], Special Research Report of Antique Remains, III. Kyoto: Shigyokudō, 1924, illus. English summary.

Harada, Dairoku. *Nihon Kofun Bunka* [The Culture of Ancient Japanese Tombs]. Tokyo: Tokyo University Press, 1954.

———. "Nihon Saikō no Garasu" [The Most Ancient Glass in Japan], *Shiko Bunrin*, February 1954, pp. 4–9.

Harada, Jirō. *English Catalogue of Treasures in the Imperial Repository Shōsō-in*, Tokyo: Imperial Household Museum, 1932.

Harada, Yoshito. "Ancient Glass in the History of Cultural Exchange between East and West." *Acta Asiatica*, III (1962), pp. 57–69.

———. "Hakubutsukan no Shinshu-hin—Kiriko no Garasu-hin—Ankan Tennō Ryō Shutsudo" [Newly Acquired Items in the Museum—A Cut-glass Vessel—Relic from the Tomb of Emperor Ankan]. *Museum*, No. 5 (August 1951), pp. 29–30, illus.

———. *Kodai Garasu* [Ancient Glass]. Bijutsu Nyūmon Sōsho [Guide to the Fine Arts]. Tokyo: Koyama Shōten, 1948.

———. "Nihon Kofun Shutsudo no Itagarasu-hen ni tsuite" [Study of Sheet Glass Fragments Discovered in an Ancient Japanese Tomb]. *Jinruigakuzasshi*, XLIV, 6 (June 1929), pp. 327–331, illus.

———. "Shōsō-in Garasu wo Megutte" [Returning to the Shōsō-in Glass]. *Museum*, No. 154 (January 1964), pp. 2–6, illus.

———. *Shōsō-in Garasu-yōki no Kenkyū* [Study of Glass Vessels in the Shōsō-in]. Tokyo: Zaūho Kankōkai, 1948.

———. *Tōa Kobunka no Kenkyū* [Studies of Ancient East Asian Cultures]. 2d ed., rev. Tokyo: Zaūho Kankōkai, 1941.

Hayashi, Genkichi. "Biidoro Saiku to Nagasaki" [Glassmaking and Nagasaki]. *Nagasaki Dansō*, No. 13 (1933), pp. 78–83, illus.

———. "Nagasaki no Biidoro to Giyaman" [*Biidoro* and *Giyaman* of Nagasaki]. *Chawan*, VII, 8 (No. 78; August 1937), pp. 24–33, illus.

Higuchi Kiyoyuki. "Sekki Jidai Ibutsu to Hanshutsuseru Garasu-sei Magatama" [Glass Magatama Found with Stone Age Remains]. *Shizen*, VI, 2 (1934).

Higuchi, Takayasu; Nishitani, Shinji; and Onoyama, Setsu. *Ōtani Kofun* (English title: *Ōtani—Report of the Excavation of the Ancient Burial Mound*). Archaeolgical Research Institute, Kyoto University. Kyoto: Benridō, 1959.

Horie, Yasuzō. "Nakashima Jihei to Yamaguchi-ken no Yōshiki Kōgyō" [Nakashima Jihei and the Foreign-type Industries of Yamaguchi Prefecture]. *Keizai Ronsō*, XL, 5 (May 1935), pp. 134–141.

Hōryū-ji Gojū-no-tō Hihō no Chōsa [Investigation of the Secret Treasure of the Five-storied Pagoda of Hōryū-ji]. Published by Hōryū-ji. Kyoto: Benridō, 1954. Compiled by Hōryū-ji Kokuhō Hoson Iinkai (Commission for the Protection of National Treasures of Hōryū-ji); preface by Dr. Tōru Haneda; articles by various scholars; illus.

Hosomi, Ryō (Kokōan). "Momoyama Jidai no Shitsumai Sōshoku Kanagu" [Momoyama Period Metal Fittings for Interior Decoration]. *Nihon Bijutsu Kōgei*, Pt. 1, No. 288 (September 1962), pp. 21–25; Pt. II, No. 289 (October 1962), pp. 14–18, illus.

———. "Momoyama Jidai Shippō Kanagu ni tsuite" [Cloisonné Mountings of the Momoyama Period]. *Nihon Bijutsu Kōgei*, No. 290 (November 1962), pp. 45–46, illus.

Ikenaga, Takeshi (unsigned). *Hōsai-bunka Daihōkan* [Catalogue of an Exotic Culture]. Osaka, 1933, illus. Includes glass in the Ikenaga Collection, now in the Kobe Municipal Art Museum.

Inaba, Shineimon. *Sōken Kishō* [Sword Ornaments and (Other) Fine Items]. VII, pp. 18–26. Osaka: Shinsuikan, 1781.

Ishida, Mosaku. Remarks on the glass *shari-yōki* of Hōryū-ji, in *Hōryū-ji Gojū-no-tō Hihō no Chōsa*, *q.v.*, pp. 33–34, illus.

———. "Sairin-ji Kyuzō no Hakururi Wan ni tsuite" [The White Glass Bowl Formerly Preserved at Sairin-ji]. *Yamato Bunka*, No. 5 (January 1952), pp. 53–55, illus.

———. "Shiryō Shōkai—Sairin-ji Hakururi Wan" [Historical Material Introduced—The White Glass Bowl of Sairin-ji]. *KKZ*, XXXVI, 4 (November 1950), pp. 52–57, illus.

———. "Sūfuku-ji no Tō Shinao Nochi-hin" [Things Interred in the Central Foundation of the Pagoda of Sūfuku-ji], *Museum*, No. 24 (March 1953), pp. 14–16, illus.

———. *The Use and Variety of "Tama" in the Nara Period*, Cultural Nippon Pamphlet Series, XXX, Tokyo: Nippon Bunka Chūō Renmei, 1941. Tr. from the Japanese in *KKZ*, XXX, No. 5 (May 1940), pp. 323–343, illus.

Ishida, Mosaku, and Wada, Gun-ichi. *Shōsō-in—The Shōsō-in, an Eighth Century Treasure-house*. Tokyo: Mainichi Shinbunsha, 1954, English resumé by Jirō Harada.

Ishida, Mosaku, ed. *Garasu no Sekaishi* [World History of Glass]. Tokyo National Museum, Cultural Series No. 5, Tokyo; 1953, illus.

Itō, Michio. "Shinagawa Garasu Seizō Nempyō" [Chronology of the Shinagawa Glassworks]. *Kaihō*, (*Shinagawa-kushi Kenkyū-kai*), No. 9 (December 1961), pp. 4–9.

Iwata, Tōshichi. "Fukigarasu e no Michi" [The Road to Blown Glass]. *Chawan*, VII, 8 (No. 78; December 1937), pp. 34–41, illus.

———. *Garasu no Geijutsu—Iwata Tōshichi Sakuhinshū* [The Art of Glass—Collected Works of Tōshichi Iwata]. Tokyo: Kodansha, 1972.

Kagami, Kōzō. *Garasu no Seichō* [The Development of Glass]. Rev. ed. Tokyo: Shichijō Shoin, 1943.

———. *Hompō no Garasu Kōgei* [The Japanese Glass Industry]. Teikoku Kōgei, V, 3.

———. "Kodai Garasu no Kakō" [Ancient Techniques of Glass]. *Museum*, No. 154 (January 1964), pp. 15–18, illus.

Katō, Koji. *Edoki no Garasu* [Glasswares of the Edo Period]. Tokyo: Tokuma Shoten, 1972. Japanese and English.

Katori, Hidemasa. *Kinkōshi* [History of the Metal Industry]. *Kōkogaku Kōza*, XVIII, September 1929. See pp. 113–120 for section "Sangatsu-dō Honzon Hōkan" [The Crown of the Principal Image in the Sangatsu-dō].

Kisha, Honshi. "Kagami Kurisutaru Seisaku-sho Hōmon Ki" [Report on a Visit to the Kagami Crystal Glassworks]. *Chawan*, VIII, 8, (No. 78; August 1937), pp. 42–54, illus.

Kishi, Kumakichi. "Taishō no Jū-go-nen no Hōryū-ji Yōki Chōsa Ki" [Record of the Investigation of the Vessels found at Hōryū-ji in 1926]. *Shiseki to Bijutsu*, No. 200 (1950), pp. 10–15.

Kiuchi, Takeo. "Shari Shōgongu ni tsuite" (English title: "Śarīra Caskets and Related Burial Offerings"). *Museum*, No. 127 (October 1961), pp. 6–10, illus.

Kondō, Ichitarō. "Biidoro wo Fuku Onna" [Woman Blowing a Biidoro]. *Yūbin*, VI, 12 (December 1954), pp. 2–3, illus.

Koshinaka, Tetsuya. "Garasu-kō (Josetsu)—Chūtoshite Nagasaki Garasu yori [Glass (Introduction)—Chiefly Glass of Nagasaki]. Bulletin of the Nagasaki Municipal Museum, No. 5 (1964), pp. 1–24.

———. "A Five-Colored *Biidoro* Bowl." *Better Life*, No. 5 (1967).

Kunii, Kitarō. "Iwata Tōshichi no Garasu-ki Kōba wo Tazune [Visit to the Glassware Factory of Tōshichi Iwata]. *Bijutsu Kōgei*, No. 2, illus.

Kurata, Osamu. "Hakururi-wan no Saikai—Shōsō-in Ten Yori" (English title: The Meeting of the Two White Glass Bowls—in the Exhibition from the Shōsō-in). *Museum*, No. 140 (November 1962), pp. 12–13, illus.

———. "Ruri Tōrō—Kasuga-taisha Zō" [Glass Lantern Preserved at Kasuga-taisha], *Hakubutsukan Nyūsu* (Tokyo National Museum), No. 137 (October 1, 1958), p. 1, illus.

Kurokawa, Masamichi, ed. *Kurokawa Mayori Zenshū* [Complete Works of Kurokawa Mayori]. Tokyo: Hayakawa Junsaburo, 1910. Dealing with glass: pp. 21–22, 108–110, 372–375, 376–381, 450–458.

Kurokawa, Mayori. *Kōgei Shiryō* [Historical Materials in the Field of Crafts]. 2d. ed. Tokyo: Ministry of the Imperial Household, 1888.

Masaki, Naohiko. "Kodai Bunna no Garasu" [Ancient Glass of Bunna (in Osaka Prefecture)]. *Osaka no Kōgei*, VI, 59.

Masuda, Sei-ichi. "Iran Aruboruzo no Garasu-ki" [Glass Vessels from the Elburz Mountains, Iran]. *Museum*, No. 108 (March 1960), pp. 25–28, illus.

———. "Kandai no Garasu-yōki" [Glass Vessels of the Han Dynasty]. *Museum*, No. 154 (January 1964), pp. 21–22.

Matsumoto, Bunsaburō. "Ruri Kō" [Concerning Glass]. *Geibun*, XIV, 5, pp. 1–27.

Matsumoto, Eiichi. "Biidoro wo Fuku Musume" [Young Woman Blowing a *Biidoro*]. *Museum*, No. 88 (July 1958), pp. 12–13, illus.

Meiji Bunkashi [Cultural History of the Meiji Era]. Tokyo: 1956. Glass: Vol. VIII, pp. 279–290.

Meiji Hattatsushi [History of Progress in the Meiji Era]. Tokyo: Hakuaikan, 1911. Glass: pp. 1011–1019.

Miki, Fumio. "Haku-ruri Wan" [White Glass Bowl]. *Museum*, No. 154 (January 1964), pp. 10, 11.

Mine, Masao, and Senba, Kimio. "Chikuzen Okino-shima Shutsudo Kodai Garasu ni tsuite" [Ancient Glass Recovered from Okinoshima, Chikuzen Province]. Appendix II of *Okinoshima—Munakata Jinja Okitsu-gū Saishi Iseki* (q.v.), I, 1958, pp. 2–7. Report, with tables, on scientific examination and spectrograph.

Misumi, Teikichi. "Biidoro-e Kō" [Paintings on Glass]. *Nihon Bijutsu Kōgei*, No. 250 (July 1959), pp. 10–18. illus.

Miyake, Yarai. *Bankin Sugiwai Bukuro* [literally, Occupations of Ten Thousand Pieces of Gold, or Lucrative Occupations]. *Seiho Taisei*. Part III. Osaka: Kunkyokudō, 1732. Glass, Pt. 3, pp. 15–117.

Miyazaki, Ryūjō, trans. *Hyakkō Seisaku Shinsho* [Manufacturing Methods of Various Crafts, Revised Edition]. Tokyo: Hakubunkan, 1st ed. 1877, revised ed., 1894, 3 vols. Translated from foreign books. Glass, Vol. III, pp. 36–46.

Mizuno, Sei-ichi, and Kobayashi, Yukio. *Zukai Kōkogaku-jiten* [Illustrated Archaeological Dictionary]. Tokyo: Sōgensha, 1959.

Mody, N. H. N. *A Collection of Nagasaki Colour Prints and Paintings, Showing the Influence of Chinese and European Art on That of Japan.* London: Kegan Paul, Trench, Trubner & Co., Ltd., and Kobe: J. L. Thompson & Co. (Retail), Ltd., 1939.

Mōri, Hisashi. "Shari-yōki ni tsuite" [*Shari* Reliquar-ies]. *Shiseki to Bijutsu*, No. 220 (February 1950), pp. 16–22.

Mori, Kōichi. "Garasu-ki wo Shutsudo-shita Kofun—Yamato Niizawa Senzuka no Chushin to shite" [An Ancient Tomb from which Glass Vessels Have Been Excavated—With Emphasis on the Senzuka Tombs at Niizawa, Yamato]. *Museum*, No. 154 (January 1964), pp. 12–14, illus.

———. *Nihon Genshi Bijutsu* [Primitive Japanese Art], vol. 6. Tokyo: Kodansha, 1968, p. 163, Pl. 140, and Color Plate XX.

Morihira, Sōichi. *Matsunami Garasu Seizō-jo Enkakushi* [History of the Matsunami Glass Factory]. Tokyo: 1940.

Nagasaki Kokon Shūran Meishō Zue [Illustrations of Famous Ancient and Present-day Scenes in Nagasaki]. Nagasaki: dated 1841. Manuscript set of volumes with illustrations, in part at least, by Ishizaki Yushi or Uchihashi Chiki-un; The "Picture of the Making of *Biidoro* Wares" is a rare depiction of methods of the time. Owned by the Nagasaki Municipal Museum.

Nakao, Manzō. *Shōsō-in Gokō no Kanyaku to Garasu narabini Tōki* [Drugs, Glass and Ceramics in the Shōsō-in Repository]. Shanghai: Y.M.C.A., pp. 1–39. Notes of a lecture given there in August 1931. Glass, pp. 24–38.

———. "Tōyō Kodai no Garasu to Uwagusuri" [Glass and Glaze in Ancient East Asia]. *KKZ*. Pt. I, XXI, 4 (April 1931), pp. 245–268; Pt. II, XXI, 5 (May 1931), pp. 337–354; Pt. III, unpublished.

Nakashima, Jihei. *Tamanoura Akunoura Seitetsu-jo Mitorizukai Seikoku Shoshu Kōsho Seihō-kyoku Sōko* [Sketches and Explanation of the Iron Foundries at Tamanoura (Nagasaki) and Akunoura (Sasebo) and Lecture Notes Taken at the Bureau for Technicians Concerning Various Western Craft Manufacturing Methods]. Manuscript only, owned by Keichi Nakashima, Hagi.

Nakayama, Heijirō. "Jigo Saishūseru Suku-Okamoto no Yōkan Ibutsu" [Additional Remains from a Clay Coffin at Suku-Okamoto]. *KKZ*, XVIII, 6 (June 1928), pp. 307–332, illus.

———. "Suku-Okamoto Hakken no Garasu-sei Kodama" [Glass *Kodama* Discovered at Suku-Okamoto]. *KKZ*, XI, 4 (April 1920).

———. "Suku-Okamoto Shin-hakken no Garasu-sei Magatama" [Glass Magatama Newly Discovered at Suku-Okamoto]. *Rekishi to Chiri*, XXIII, 2 (1929), pp. 125–147.

Nihon Kinsei Yōgyōshi, IV—Garasu Kōgyōshi [History of

the Modern Ceramic Industry of Japan, IV—History of the Glass Industry]. Compiled by the Dai Nippon Yōgyō Kyōkai (Japan Ceramics Association). Tokyo: 1917.

Noma, Seiroku. "Shippō Zuishō" [Reflections on Cloisonné]. *Chawan Ran Tokusetsu, Kobijutsu*, December 1946, pp. 40–41.

Nozu, Samanosuke. "Izumo Tamatsukuri ni okeru Kodai Garasu-seizō Kō" [Ancient Glass Manufacture in Tamatsukuri, Izumo Province]. *Shimanekenshi*, IV, pp. 416–502. Tokyo: 1925.

———. "Izumo Tamatsukuri ni okeru Kodai Garasu-seizō Kō" [Ancient Glass Manufacture in Tamatsukuri, Izumo Province]. *KKZ*, Pt. 1, XV, 9 (September 1925), pp. 570–581; Pt. 2, XVI, 5 (May 1926), pp. 287–296.

Oda, Sachiko. "Kodai Garasu no Fūka" [Weathering of Ancient Glass]. *Kagaku Goho*, IV, 12 (December 1956), pp. 58-59, illus.

———. "Miyajidake-jinja Keidai Shutsudo no Ryokushoku Garasu-sei Kotsu-tsubo" [Green Glass Cinerary Urn Excavated from the Miyajidake Shrine Precincts]. *Bunkazai*, No. 53 (February 1968), pp. 17–21, illus.

Oga, Ichirō, *et alii*. "Shōsō-in Gyobutsu Zaishitsu Chōsa" [Investigation of the Materials of the Treasures of the Shōsō-in]. *Shoryō-bu Kiyō*, 8 (March 1957), pp. 57–89.

Okada, Jō (Yuzuru). *Garasu* [Glass]. Nihon no Bijutsu, V, No. 37. Tokyo: Shibundō, 1969.

———. "Garasu no Rekishi" [History of Glass]. *Chawan*, XIX, 8, No. 208 (August 1949), pp. 23–27, illus.

———. *Garasu no Sekai* [The World of Glass]. Asahi Shashin Bukku [Asahi Photographic Books], No. 4. Tokyo: Asahi Shinbunsha, July 1954, illus.

———. *Japanese Handicrafts*, Tourist Library, XXI. Tokyo: Japan Tourist Bureau, March 1956. Glass, pp. 47–51, 91–99, 188.

———. "Koten Kaiga ni Miru Garasu-ki" [Glass Vessels Seen in Old Paintings]. *Museum*, No. 154 (January 1964), pp. 7–8, illus.

———. "Ruri Kirihame no Makie Suzuribako" [An Inkstone Box of Gold Lacquer Inlaid with Glass]. *Museum*, No. 58 (January 1956), pp. 10–12, illus.

———. "Shōsō-in Garasu-ki no Gihō" [Techniques of the Glass Vessels in the Shōsō-in]. *Museum*, No. 8 (November 1951), pp. 21–23, illus.

———. "Shōsō-in no Garasu-ki" [Glass Vessels in the Shōsō-in]. *Hakubutsukan Nyūsu*, No. 151, Tokyo National Museum, 1960.

Okinoshima—Munakata Jinja Okitsu-gū Saishi Iseki [Okinoshima—The Religious Sites of Okitsu-gū of Munakata Shrine]. Tokyo: Society for the Restoration of Munakata Shrine, Vol. I, 1958; Vol. II, 1961. English summaries.

Okamura, Chibiki. "Nihon Garasu Kō" [Study of Japanese Glass]. *Chawan*, VII, 8, (No. 78; August 1937), pp. 15–23, illus.

Ōno, Benkichi (Nakamura, Benkichi; art name, Itō). "Itō Shikyuroku—Seiyaku Jō—Ōno—Kakujūken" [Itō's Own Record—Manufacture of Pharmaceuticals, Pt. 1—Ōno——?], followed by a *kakihan* seal and "Kaoru." Manuscript, owned by Mr. Saichi Otomo, Kanazawa.

Ōno, Tadashige. *Doro-e to Garasu-e* [Clay Pictures and Painting on Glass]. Nihon no Minga [Japanese Folk Painting]. Tokyo: Asoka Shōbō, 1954.

Osaka no Garasu Kōgyō [Glass Industry of Osaka]. Compiled by the Industrial Department, Osaka City Hall. Osaka: Sanshodō, 1926.

Ōtsuki, Gentaku (Bansui). *Ransetsu Benwaku* [Classification of Perplexities Regarding Dutch Matters]. Completed 1788, first published 1798, illus. Included in *Bansui Zonkyō*. In many reprints the illustrations are omitted. For English translation, see Goodman, Grant K. *A Translation of Otsuki Gentaku's Ransetsu Benwaku*.

Sakuma, Shōsan, or Zōzan (Shuri). *Zōzan Zenshū* [Complete Works of Zōzan]. Nagano: Shinano Kyōikukai, 1913, 2 vols; Nagano: Shinano Mainichi Shinbunsha, enlarged ed., 1934–35.

Sasaki, Hideichi (Genzō). *Garasu ya Musashi Katari* [Glass and Tales of Olden Times]. Tokyo: Sasaki Garasu K.K., privately printed, 1935, illus.

Satō, Junshirō. *Garasu Hanashi* [The Story of Glass]. Tokyo(?): n.d., illus. Pamphlet for children.

———. "Nihon no Garasu-ki [Japanese Glassware]. *Kōgei Niyūsu*, XIX, 3 (August 1951), pp. 6–7, 9.

———. "Nihon no Garasu no Shuju Sō" [Various Aspects of Japanese Glass]. *Kōgei Gakkai Shi*, XXV (August 1951), p. 19.

———. "Yakō-hai Zatsudan" [Talk about Luminous Cups]. *Kobijutsu*, XVIII, 2 (February 1948), pp. 8–16, illus.

Satsuma Garasu no Enkaku [History of Satsuma Glass]. Compiled by Shimazu-ke Henshujo (Compilation Bureau of the Shimazu Family), Kagoshima: privately printed, n.d.

Sekai Garasu Kōgei Ten [Exhibition of Glass Crafts of the World]. Tokyo: Tōyoko Department Store, May 1959.

Sekai no Garasu Meihin Ten [Exhibition of Glass Masterpieces of the World]. Tokyo: Shirokiya Department Store, August 1962.

Shibui, Kiyoshi. "The Story of Glass in Japan." *This is Japan, 1963*, No. 10. Tokyo: Asahi Shinbunsha, 1963, pp. 114–123, illus.

Shimazu-ke no Meihō to Satsuma Katto-Garasu Ten [Exhibition of Rare Treasures of the Shimazu Family and of Satsuma Cut Glass]. Tokyo, Mitsukoshi Department Store, July 1960.

Shiota, Rikizō. "Garasu" [Glass]. Meiji Kōgyōshi [History of Industry in the Meiji Era]. *Kagaku Kōgyō Hen* [Volume on Chemical Industry], Sect. 2, Chap. 2 (Individual Industries), Tokyo: 1925, pp. 397–453.

"Shōsō-in Gyobutsu Zaishitsu Chōsa" [Report of the Investigation of the Materials of the Imperial Treasures of the Shōsō-in]. *Shoryō-bu Kiyo*, No. 8 (March 1957). Glass: pp. 75–81.

Shōsō-in Gyobutsu Zuroku [Illustrated Catalogue of the Imperial Treasures of the Shōsō-in], Tokyo, Imperial Household Museum, Vols. I-XVIII 1926–1955, illus. English notes by Jirō Harada.

Shōsō-in Hōmotsu (see *Treasures of the Shōsō-in*).

Shōsō-in no Garasu (English title: *Glass Objects in the Shōsō-in*). Written by Harada, Yoshito; Okada, Jō; Yamasaki, Kazuo; and Kagami, Kōzō, published by the Imperial Household Agency. Tokyo; Nihon Keizai Shinbunsha, 1965.

Shōsō-in Tanawake Mokuroku [Catalogue of the Shōsō-in According to Shelf Locations]. Imperial Household Agency, Division of Archives and Mausolea, Kyoto: Benridō, 1951, 1955.

Sugie, Jusei. *Biidoro* [Glass]. Kyoto: Kōchō Shorin, 1942.

———. *Garasu* [Glass]. Kyoto: Kyōritsusha, 1933, 1934, 1937, and 1940.

———. *Garasu no Kenkyū* [Study of Glass]. Tokyo: Kobunsha, 1949.

———. *Garasu to Seikatsu* [Glass and Living]. Tokyo, Kawada Shōbō, 1941.

———. *Nihon Garasu Kōgyōshi* [History of the Japanese Glass Industry]. Tokyo: Nihon Garasu Kōgyōshi Henshūiinkai, 1950.

———. "Nihon Kodai no Garasu" [Ancient Japanese Glass]. *Shizen*, No. 4 (1949), pp. 32–37.

Sugiyama, Sueo. *Ainu Tama* [Beads of the Ainu]. Sapporo: Imai Sapporo Shiten, 1936.

Tachibana, Minkō. *Shokunin Burui* [Various Types of Artisans]. Original ed., 1774; 2nd ed. 1784; reprint, Tokyo, Keiundō, 1916, as *Saiga Shokunin Burui*, incorporating text and illustrations of the first ed. and prefaces from both eds. 2 Vols; glass-blowing in Vol. I.

Takigawa, Masajirō. "Imono-no-tsukasa Garasu-seizō Kō" [Essay on Glass Manufacture at the Casting Bureau]. *Yamato Bunka*, V (January 1952), pp. 1–13.

Tamura, Yochinaga. "Hōryū-ji Gojū-no-tō shita no Kūdō to Hōrin-ji Shozō Sanjū-no-tō yori Shukken no 'Busshari no Ki' ni tsuite" [The Hollow under the Five-storied Pagoda of Hōryū-ji. In Relation to the *Record of Shari from the Three-storied Pagoda at Hōrin-ji*]. *KKZ*, XXI, 7 (July 1931), pp. 531–534.

Tanahashi, Junji. "Kinsei Nihon ni okeru Garasu Seizō-hō no Hatten to Sono Genkai" [Development of Glassmaking Methods in Modern Japan]. *Memoirs of Shōin Women's University*, Nos. 8–10; Pt. I (December 1966), pp. 215–260; Pt. II (December 1967), pp. 237–304; Pt. III (December 1968), pp. 23–174.

Terashima, Ryōan. *Wakan Sanzai Zue* [The Three Great Powers (Heaven, Earth and Man) of Japan and China, with Illustrations]. Osaka: Kyōrindō, 1713; undated reprint, 1958. The first Japanese encyclopedia; glass references, pp. 350, 373, 650, 651.

Teshigawara, Sōfu; Kunimitsu, Shirō; and Okada, Jō. *Garasu* [Glass]. Nihon no Kōgei (Japanese Crafts), No. 6. Kyoto: Tankōshinsha, 1966.

Tōyei Shukō [Illustrated Catalogue of Treasure of East Asia (in the Shōsō-in)]. Ed. Omura Seigai. Tokyo: Kunaishō Shuppan, Vols. I-VI, 1st ed. 1908–1909, illus.

Treasures of the Shōsō-in (Japanese title: *Shōsō-in Hōmotsu*). Compiled by the Shōsō-in Office, represented by Gun-ichi Wada; 3 vols., published by the Imperial Household Agency. Tokyo: Asahi Shinbunsha, 1960 (The Middle Section), 1961 (The South Section) and 1962 (The North Section). Text in both Japanese and English.

Uchida, Rokurō. *Garasu-e* [Painting on Glass]. Tokyo: Sorinsha, 1942.

Udagawa, Yōan, trans. *Seimi Kaiso* [Source Book of Chemistry]. Edo: 1805, 7 vols. Tr. from European texts; glass is outlined briefly in Vol. III.

Umehara, Sueji. "Ankan Ryō Shutsudo no Hari-wan ni tsuite" [The Glass Bowl Excavated from Ankan's Tomb]. *Shiseki to Bijutsu*, No. 209 (1951).

————. "Arata ni Shirareta Furui Hakururi Hyōkei Tsubo" [A Newly Known Ancient White Glass Gourd-shaped Jar]. *Museum*, No. 142 (January 1963), pp. 7–10, illus.

————. "Arata ni Shirareta Kodai no Jakkan no Hari-yōki" [A Few Ancient Glass Vessels Recently Brought to Light]. *Museum*, No. 192 (March 1967), pp. 29–33, illus.

————. "Chūgoku Shutsudo no Hari-yu (Shippō) no Ihin" [Cloisonné Relics Excavated in China]. *Museum*, No. 185 (August 1966), pp. 21–24, illus.

————. "Hari no Magatama" [Glass *Magatama*]. *Kobijutsu*, No. 20 (December 30, 1967), pp. 77–84, illus.

————. "Nihon Jōko no Hari" [Ancient Japanese Glass]. *Shirin*, XLIII, 1 (January 1960), pp. 1–18.

————. "Nihon Kodai no Garasu" [Ancient Japanese Glass]. *Museum*, No. 68 (November 1956), pp. 23–28.

————. "Ōmi Shiga-no-sato Sūfuku-ji Tōchi" [The Pagoda Site of Sūfuku-ji at Shiga-no-sato in Ōmi Province]. *Hōun*, Nos. 33 and 34.

————. Remarks on glass relics, in *Hōryū-ji Gojū-no-tō Hihō no Chōsa* (q.v.), pp. 23, 24–27, 31, 33–37.

————. *Settsu Abu-san Kobo Chōsa Hōkoku* [Report on the Investigation of an Old Grave on Abu-san, Settsu Province]. *Osaka-fū Shiseki Meisho Tennen Kinenbutsu Chōsa Hōkoku* [Reports of Investigations of Historic Spots and Famous Natural Relics in Osaka-*fū*], No. 7, Osaka: Osaka Municipal Office, 1936, Chap. 3, illus.

————. "Shinshutsudo Hari-ki no Rui" [Glassware Types Newly Excavated]. *Yamato Bunka Kenkyū*, X, 3 (March 1965), pp. 1–10, illus.

————. "Shippō no Butsuzō Daiza-hen" [Fragmentary Enameled Gilt-Bronze Pedestal for a Buddhist Image]. *Shiseki to Bijutsu*, No. 256 (October 1955), pp. 290–294, illus.

————. "Shōsō-in no Gyobutsu-kyō ni tsuite" [Mirrors among the Imperial Treasures of the Shōsō-in]. *Shoryō-bu Kiyō*, No. 7 (June 1956), illus; discussion of the cloisonné backed mirror, pp. 27–28.

————. "Sūfuku-ji no Mondai to Sono Keii" [Details of the Problem of Sūfuku-ji]. *Shiseki to Bijutsu*, No. 173.

————. "Tōdai-ji Sangatsu-dō Honzon Suika no Magatama ni tsuite" [*Magatama* Suspended in the Crown of the Principal Image of the Sangatsu-dō of Tōdai-ji]. *Shiseki to Bijutsu*, No. 200 (1950), pp. 2–9, illus.

Wada, Gun-ichi. *Shōsō-in*, Tokyo: Sōdensha, 1955.

Watanabe, Seiki. "Fukuoka-shi Yanagabaru Hakken Garasu-sei Magatama no I-gata" [A Mold for Glass *Magatama*, Discovered at Yanagabaru, Fukuoka.], *Kyōiku Fukuoka*, Fukuoka: Kyōiku Iinkai, No. 127 (July 1960).

Watanabe, Sōshu. *Heian Jidai no Kokumin Kōgei no Kenkyū* [Study of the National Crafts of the Heian Period]. Tokyo: Tōkyōdō, 1943.

Yajima, Kyōsuke. "Kōfuku-ji Kondō Shutsudo no Chindangu" [*Chindangu* Excavated from the Kondō of Kōfuku-ji]. *Museum*, No. 116 (November 1960), pp. 19–22.

————. "Tokyo-tō Yanaka no Gojū-no-tō Hakken no Kyoto narabini Shari-yōki" [Sutra Case and a Shari Reliquary Discovered at Yanaka, Tokyo]. *KKZ*, XLIII, 1 (October 1957), pp. 31–45.

————. "Tokyo-tō Yanaka no Gojū-no-tō Soseki Hakken no Konshi Konji-kyō to Busshari" [The Konji Sutra on Dark Blue Paper and the Buddhist *Shari* Excavated from the Foundation-stone of the Five-storied Pagoda of Yanaka, Tokyo]. *Museum*, No. 81 (December 1957), pp. 2–6, illus.

Yamada, Fujizō. *Nihon Garasu Sangyō no Seika* [The Flowering of the Japanese Glass Industry]. Osaka: Teikoku Garasu Shinpōsha, 1915 and 1928.

Yamasaki, Kazuo. "Garasu" [Glass]. *Nihon no Kokogaku, Rekishi Jidai* [Japanese Archaeology, Historical Periods], I, pp. 396–410. Tokyo: Kawada Shōbō, 1967.

————. "Hōō-dō Honzon Tainai Osameru Iremono-ju no Garasu Hahen ni tsuite" [Glass Fragments from the Reliquary Installed in the Principal Statue of the Phoenix Hall]. Appendix II of Fukuyama, Toshio, "Byōdō-in Hōō-dō Honzon Tainai Osame-oku Amida Daisho Ju Getsurin no Chōsa" [Investigation of the "Moon Disk" with Large and Small *Dharani* of Amida, which were placed as Offerings within the Principal Image of the Hōō-dō of Byōdō-in]. *Kenkyū Bijutsu*, No. 182 (July 1955), illus.

————. "Introductory Notes on the Ancient Glass of Japan," *Journal of Glass Studies*, I (1959), pp. 86–88, illus.

————. "Nagasaki Suwa-jinja no Kasaboko ni tsuite iru Garasu Saiku" [Glass Decorations Attached to a Kasaboko of Suwa Shrine, Nagasaki]. *KK*, No. 12 (February 1956), pp. 37–41, illus.

————. "Namari Garasu to Sōda Garasu" [Lead Glass and Soda Glass]. *Museum*, No. 154 (January 1964), pp. 19–21, illus.

————. "Technical Studies on the Ancient Art Objects of Japan, with Special Reference to the Treasures Preserved in the Shōsō-in," (Part of "The Application of Science in the Examination of Works of Art"). *Proceedings of the Seminar, September 7–16, 1965. Conducted by the Research Laboratory, Museum of Fine Arts, Boston*, 1967, pp. 114–126, illus.

Yamasaki, Kazuo; Miwa, Fusako; and Ohashi, Naoko. "Kofun Shutsudo Garasu Kodama no Kagaku Seibun ni tsuite" (English title: Chemical Composition of Glass Beads Found in an Ancient Tomb in Aichi Prefecture). *KK*, No. 3 (January 1952), pp. 28–30.

Yamasaki, Kazuo, and Saitō, Yoshihiko. "Investigation of Corroded Ancient Glasses by X-Ray Diffraction," *Proceedings of the Japan Academy*, XXXVI, 8, 1960, pp. 503–505.

Yokoi, Tokifuyu. *Kōgei Kagami* [History of Industrial Arts]. Tokyo: Rokugokan, 1894; reprint, 1927.

————. *Nihon Kōgyōshi* [History of Japanese Industry]. Tokyo: Yoshikawa Hanshichi, 1898.

————. "Waga no Kuni ni okeru Shippō no Hattatsu" [The Development of Cloisonné in Japan]. *Kokka*, No. 152, pp. 148–151; No. 153, pp. 167–170, illus.

Yōrō Shokuin Ryō [Personnel Regulations of the Yōrō Era], 718. Based on the now extinct *Taihō-Ritsu-Ryō* [civil and criminal Code of the Taihō Era] promulgated in 701–702; contains official regulations for the *Imono-no-tsukasa* (Casting Bureau) where, among other things, glass was made. This work appears, in modern Japanese, in various compilations.

Yoshimizu, Tsuneo. "Seiryō-ji Shaka Nyōrai Ritsuzo no Tainai Nōnyūbutsu no Garasu ni tsuite" [Glass Contained in the Body of the Standing Figure of Shaka Nyōrai in the Temple Seiryō-ji]. *Bijutsushi Kenkyū*, No. 4 (March 1966), pp. 53–72, illus.

————. "Shōsō-in no Konruri Tsubo ni tsuite" [The Dark Blue Glass Jar of the Shōsō-in]. *Bijutsushi*, XVII, 2–3 (December 1967), pp. 95–108, illus. English summary.

Yoshimura, Gen-o(?). *Shippō* [Cloisonné]. Kyoto: Maria Shobō, 1966.

Zōbutsu-sho Sakumotsuchō [Record of Things Made in the Office of Buddhist Construction]. Manuscript fragment of 734, preserved in the Shōsō-in.

LITERARY SOURCES

The following have kindly permitted use of verbatim quotations. Details appear in pertinent footnotes.

George Allen & Unwin, Ltd., London (Waley, *The Tale of Genji*).

Asiatic Society of Japan, Tokyo (various articles, as cited).

Harper & Row, New York (Rutherford, *The Capital of the Tycoon*).

Dr. Eijirō Honjō, the former Nihon Keizaishi Kenkyūjo, and Osaka Keizai Daigaku (Honjō, *The Social and Economic History of Japan*).

The Japan Society, London, *Proceedings* (Ponsonby-Fane, *Misasagi*: The Imperial Mausolea of Japan).

Rehabilitation Committee, Munakata Shrine (*Okinoshima*).

Stanford University Press, Stanford (Sansom, *History of Japan up to 1334*).

Tokyo National Museum, and Jirō Harada (Harada, *English Catalogue of Treasures in the Imperial Repository Shōsō-in*).

INDEX-GLOSSARY

Daiba Bon Kyō, 346, 347

Daibutsu ("Great Buddha"), Tōdai-ji, 90, 92, 101, 127, 340, 377, 391

Daigo-ji temple, 137

Dai Nihon Komonjo, 94

Dainishi, 127

dako (spitoon), 348–349

Date clan, 176, 179, 233, 251, 252

Deshima, 180, 191, 197, 252, 199

Dutch, 173–180, 187, 189–193, 196–199, 201, 207, 210, 234, 236–240, 242, 245, 251, 254, 255, 260, 283, 284, 403

Dutch East India Company, 177, 179, 195, 234

Edo, 174, 176, 195, 201, 202, 204, 206, 210, 234–247, 248, 249, 255, 259, 287, 351, 408

Egypt, 187, 336, 349, 391, 422

Eiga Monogatari, 141

Eijirō (or Eigorō), 207, 212

Enatsu, Jūrō, 249, 251

Engishiki, 51, 130, 132

Enkaku-ji temple, 155

Feith, Captain Arend Willem, 179

flint glass, 188

Frois, Father Luis, 159, 179

Fujimura Shōten, 286

Fujiwara clan, 69, 126–128, 132, 135, 141, 143, 148, 346, 366, 434

Fujiwara era, 126, 127, 133, 134–136, 145, 346, 347, 394, 435, 436

Fujiyama, Tanehirō, 255, 286, 289

Fukai Glass Factory, 283, 401

fukidama (吹玉): "Blown bead." "Blown" may referred originally to blowing up the fire for greater heat, and therefore connoted glass production. Today the term means simply "glass bead." 131

Fukuoka Art Glass Company, 293, 299–300, 446

Fukuoka fief, 248, 255, 256, 413

Fukusaku Sukehachi, 251

Fukutani, Keikichi, 255, 286, 289

Fumi no Nemaro, 71, 329

futago-dama, 95

game pieces, 103, 104, 137

gangidama, 205, 403

Gangō-ji temple, 96, 376

Ganjin (Chien-chen), Priest, 98, 378, 439

Ganzan Zakki, 198

garasu (硝子): "Glass." The pronunciation, since late in the Edo period, from the Dutch *gras* or the English "glass." Previously the common word for glass had been *biidoro* (*q. v.*). In writings of the Edo period sometimes other characters were used phonetically for the three syllables *ga-ra-su*. 191

garasu-e, 199

Geien Nisho, 198

Genji clan, see Minamoto

Genji Monogatari, (*The Tale of Genji*), 128, 139, 442

Gennōjo, 241

giyaman: Japanese transliteration of the Dutch word *diamant* ("diamond"). In contrast to *biidoro* (*q. v.*), it refers to the heavier lead glass introduced by the Dutch. *Giyaman kiriko* referred specifically to cut glass, for which the thick *giyaman* was peculiarly suited. There is, however, some confusion regarding the two terms, *giyaman* and *biidoro*, and it has been said that *giyaman*, whether engraved, cut, or plain, could even refer to high quality *biidoro*. 191, 200, 201, 202, 204, 210, 233, 235–237, 239–244, 246, 247, 287, 292

Go-Daigo, Emperor, 143, 144, 149, 379

Go-Saga, Emperor, 144, 148, 382

Go-Shirakawa, Emperor, 143

Go-Toba, Emperor, 132, 143

Goto, Rishun, 191

-gun (郡): Corresponds more or less to "county." Subdivision of a prefecture.

gyoku-chin, 69, 365–366

gyoku-hai, 153, 441

Hagi fief, 248, 256–260, 413–414, 445

Haikai Azuma Miyage, 182

hair ornaments, 198, 212, 245, 246

haji ware (土師土器): A pottery first produced in the Yayoi period. Characterized by a well-potted, reddish buff body, often thin.

Hamada, Yahei, 193, 194

Han dynasty, 52, 327, 335, 336

haniwa (埴輪): Hollow columns of *haji* ware, often used as reinforcements about a burial mound. Often they are surmounted by sculp-

suggests a peeled tangerine. Known in the West as a melon bead. 52, 59

mikoshi (御輿): The shrine palanquin in which the spirit of a Shintō deity is transported to his place of temporary abode at festival time. The term applies equally to an imperial palanquin. 130, 136, 146, 153, 197, 396–398, 441

Mikumo-Okamoto Site, 43–44

millefiori, 362–363, 404

Minagawa, Bunjirō, 244

Minagawa, Kyūbei II, 245

Minamoto clan (Genji), 128, 129

Minamoto no Yoritomo, 129, 143, 149, 150, 396

Minamoto no Yoshitsune, 149

Minato-mura, 202, 203

Mine, Dr. Masao, 323, 405, 445

Ming dynasty, 150, 152, 155, 398, 400

mirrors, 52, 71, 98, 102, 106–107, 134, 155, 180, 194, 202, 203, 243, 250, 284, 331, 339–346, 360, 361, 363, 364, 367, 374, 377, 419–420, 428, 429, 437

Miyajidake Shrine, 49–51, 65, 67, 71, 328–330, 336, 358, 362, 368, 374, 424–426

Miyamoto, Hideo, 293, 353

Miyazaki, Takejirō, 289

mizudama, 443

Mizuno, Chōbei, 413

Mizuno, Hambei, 413

Mizuo site, 60

Momoyama period, 140, 156–159, 174, 247, 344, 398–399

Mōri clan, 248, 254, 257

Mōri, Takachika (Keishin), Lord, 257, 260

Moriya, Jihei, 243

Mostafavi, Dr. M. T., 334

multi-glass, 299, 417

Murai, Mishinosuke, 288

Muramasu, Hikoshichi, 295

Murano, Italy, 157, 159

musen shippō, 296, 300

Nabeshima clan, 248

Nabeshima, Kansō, Lord, 254, 255

Nagasaki, 151, 157, 173, 175–177, 180–183, 187, 189–201, 206, 210, 233, 234, 236, 241, 245, 246, 251, 252, 254–258, 260, 281, 283, 290, 400–402

Nagasaki Glass Factory, 283

Nagasaki Kokon Shūran Meishō Zue, 185, 193, 197, 409

Nagasaki Yawasō, 195

Nagashimaya, Hanbei, 241

Nagoya, 210, 212, 284, 285, 296, 300, 301

Naigū Chōryaku Sōkan-fu Dajōkan-fu, 132

Nakahara, Yusuke, 249

Nakamichi, Tokichi, 293

Nakamura (Ōno), Benkichi, 189

Nakao, Shoso, 284

Nakashima, Hirokichi (Shōsei), 294, 299

Nakashima, Jihei, 257, 258, 414

Nakashima, Keichi, 260

Nakashima, Nobuyuki, 300, 417

Nakashima, Saburōemon, 257, 258

Nakasu Suzume, 241

namban-jin (南蛮): "Southern barbarians." Used for the early Portuguese and Spanish who arrived in Japan in the mid sixteenth century from ports to the south. 190, 195

Nambutetsu shippō, 301

Namikawa, Sōsuke, 295, 296

Namikawa, Yasuyuki, 212, 295

nankindama, 205, 405

Nansō-Gyōbutsu Mokuroku, 101

Naraharayama site, 134

Narcisco site, Philippines, 58

natsumedama (棗玉): "Jujube bead." A bead of greater length than width and slightly grooved, resembling the fruit of the jujube tree. 52, 59, 95, 132

nejiredama (捩玉): "Twisted bead" This appeared in the seventh century and was popular in the Nara period. Fashioned with flanges and subsequently twisted, it was perhaps in imitation of sacred seeds popular for rosaries but not available in Japan. 67, 68, 96–97, 103, 333

Ne-no-hi no Hōki ("Brooms for the Day of the Rat"), 104, 376, 381–382

netsuke, 204, 206, 246, 408

Nihon Glassworks, 291

Nihon Shoki (Nihongi), 41, 45–47, 49, 51, 61, 63, 68–70, 369, 387, 429

Niirō Hisamochi Fu, 251

Nijō Jinya, 178, 207

Nintoku, Emperor, 47, 61, 201, 428

Nishi-Miyayama site, 55

distance; into it was inserted the end of a suspension wire, with added bits of wood and cloth, and sometimes an adhesive, to hold it in place. 68, 97, 103, 104, 334, 380, 381 385, 394, 396, 431, 433, 436

Uemon, 255, 256
Umeda family, 260
Umeda Glass Factory, 283
Umeda, Nobufusa, 260
Umehara, Dr. Sueji, 43, 44, 54, 57, 344, 357, 361, 365, 366–368, 420
ungen: A system of coloration employing parallel or concentric prismatic bands of color gradations from light to dark. Popular in the Nara period. The idea is commonly considered to have derived from the color gradations of the rainbow. 381, 384, 385
Unosawa, Tatsumi, 294
Unosawa, Tatsuo, 294
Uryū-mura site, 60, 364
Ushuku, Hikouemon, 249
Utamaro, see Kitagawa, Utamaro.
Utsushima (Uchishima?), Shōbei, 285
   uzu, 135, 394, 429

Valignano, Father Alexander, 156, 157, 179
van Meedervoort, Dr. C. Pompé, 252, 258, 296, 412
V. Hoytema & C., 179
von Siebold, Dr. Philipp Franz, 177, 181

Wagner, Dr. Gottfried, 288, 295, 296
Wakan Sanzai Zue, 181, 201, 208, 383
Walton, Thomas, 288
Watanabe, Kihei, 201, 202
Watanabe, Yojirō, 212
Wei dynasty, North,

Xavier, Francisco, Father, 151, 176, 257

Yakushi-ji temple, 71
Yamada-dera temple, 71
Yamasaki, Dr. Kazuo, 44, 54, 323, 356, 422
Yamato, 46, 63, 64, 69, 91, 93, 367, 428
Yanagisawa, Kien, 406
Yōgakusho, 175
Yoneda Wakamatsu Shōten, 294, 415
yōraku (瓔珞): "Necklace." Term applied to any decorative use of strung beads, with or without the addition of pearls and small metal units. Often *yōraku* were suspended ornaments woven as a network of beads. 68–69, 95, 96, 97, 104, 132, 133, 134, 135, 145, 146, 152, 153, 383, 392–394, 396, 397, 435–437, 439–441
Yōrō Ritsuryō, 65
Yōrō Shokuinryō, 65–66, 94, 131
Yorozuya, Shōzaburō, 201
Yoshimatsu-mura site, 50
Yotsumoto, Kametarō, 249
Yüan dynasty, 147, 152, 155
yusen shippō, 300

za, 145
zakkō, 92–93
zenpō-kōen (前方後円): Ancient tomb with "square front and rounded back." The term "keyhole tomb" is applied by some scholars. 47, 48, 360, 366, 424, 425, 428
Zenigama Tomb, 427
Zennō-ji (Shippō-ji) temple, 141, 179
Zōbutsu-shō, 92, 131, 371
Zōbutsu-sho Sakumotsuchō, 94, 95, 103, 332, 344, 371–373, 384
zōgan shippō, 300
Zōji-no-tsukasa, 92
Zuigan-ji temple, 176

THE AUTHOR:
Dorothy Blair was born in Missouri in 1890 and graduated from Mount Holyoke College in 1914. Her post-
graduate work in the Japanese language was completed
at the University of Michigan. Her first trip to Japan was
in 1927 as a special student of Kyoto Imperial University
in the field of art and archaeology. From 1928 until
1950 she was assistant curator of Oriental art at The
Toledo Museum of Art. From 1952–56 and again from
1958–61, Miss Blair traveled in the Orient, researching
the field of East Asian glass, the last two years as a research fellow of The Corning Museum of Glass. From
1961 to the present, Miss Blair has resided in Corning,
New York, and has devoted her time entirely to the
preparation of this volume. Her numerous newspaper
and magazine articles, lectures, and museum catalogs,
have made Miss Blair known as the foremost Western
authority on Japanese glass.